KILLING HITLER'S REICH

THE BATTLE FOR HUNGARY, 1945

WILLIAM ALAN WEBB

Last Brigade Books

Bibliography for William Alan Webb

Non-Fiction

Killing Hitler's Reich
The Battle for Velikiye Luki, 1942-1943
The Battle for Hungary, 1945
The Battle for Austria, 1945

Second World War History
The Last Attack
The Combat History of SS–Kampfgruppe Division Böhmen und Mähren (planned for 2026)

American Civil War
Fight to the Finish: Essays on the American Civil War

Writing
Titans Rising, Publishing in the 21st Century (editor with Chris Kennedy)
Have Keyboard, Will Type; Hard Lessons, Learned Hard
Brief Lessons in Writing (editor with Chris Kennedy)

Fiction

The Last Brigade Universe
The Core Books
Standing At The Start, The Origin of Operation Overtime
Standing The Final Watch
Standing In The Storm
Standing At The Edge

Standing Before Hell's Gate
Standing With Righteous Rage
Standing Among The Tombstones
Standing When Others Fall
Standing Awash In Tears (May, 2025)

Task Force Zombie
The Nameless
Out For Blood
Not Enough Bullets
Third Squad
Chaos Road
War In Europe (December, 2024)

The Collapse (with John Babb)
Sowing Chaos
Unleashing Chaos
Trafficking Chaos
Salvaging Chaos

Freedom Rising (with John Babb)
Hell's Hip Pocket
A Reservation in Hell

Ghost Cavalry Battalion (with J. L. Salter)
Operation Snakebite
Operation Bushwhack
Operation Tombstone

Anthologies
Standing Fast
Standing Defiant
Standing Free
Standing Against All Odds (Winner of the Imadjinn Award)
Standing Free On Foreign Shores

Standing Defiant On Foreign Shores

Fantastic Stories in the Last Brigade Universe
The Hairy Man (Winner of the Imadjinn Award)
The River of Walking Spirits
The Ghost of Voodoo Village

Other
The Last Brigade Universe, The Definitive Guide

Hit World
The Trashman, The Web of Shadows Book 1
A Bullet for the Shooter, The Web of Shadows Book 2 (with Larry Hoy)
The Spider, The Web of Shadows Book 3 (with Marisa Wolf)
Demon's Kiss, Kisses and Chaos Book 1 (with Larry Hoy)
Skinwalker, Kisses and Chaos Book 2 (with Larry Hoy)
You Pay, We Slay (editor with Larry Hoy)

Four Horsemen Universe
High Mountain Hunters
Betrayals, Stories in the Four Horsemen Universe

Sharp Steel & High Adventure
Sharp Steel (Winner of the Darrell Award)
The Demon in the Jewel
Island of Bones
Beyond the Dead River (2025)
The Dragons of Anthar (2026)

Delta Private Investigations (with Kevin Steverson)

The Jazzman's Requiem and Blues, Booze, and Bullets
Crescent City Killers
The Lady in Red
Back Alleys and Side Streets

Time Wars
Jurassic Jail
Tail Gunner Joe
Cretaceous Kill (2025)
Dark Time (2026)

Jerry Pournelle's War World
Road Warriors

Five-Fold Universe
Mercia's Hammer

The Core (with Kayla Frederick)
Runners

Caine Riordan Universe (Murphy's Lawless, with Charles E. Gannon, Jr.)
Shadows
Watch the Skies (with Charles E. Gannon, Jr., Kacey Ezell and Kevin Ikenberry).

Judgment Day
Hell's Judgment, The Hand of God Book 1 (with April Kelley Jones)
Heaven's Judgment, The Hand of God Book 2 (with April Kelley Jones)
Final Judgment, The Hand of God Book 3 (with April Kelley Jones)
The Hand of God (Collected Stories) (with April Kelley Jones)

Born in Darkness, The Quest of God Book 1 (with Kristi Bradley)

Daughter of Darkness, The Quest of God Book 2 (with Kristi Bradley)

Redeeming Darkness, The Quest of God Book 3 with Kristi Bradley)

The Quest of God (Collected Stories) (with April Kelley Jones)

Salvage Title Universe
Through an Unknown Gate

The Unbroken Lion
The Sting of Fate

Other Anthologies
Shattering History's Mirror (Contributor and Editor)

Miscellaneous
Moles Need Women
Drumsticks Along the Mohawk
The Granite Man (Cthulhu Universe)
Hitler a la Mode
Grinning Soul

Author's Preface

Eighteen years after the writing of this book began, it was finished. *Killing Hitler's Reich, The Battle for Austria, 1945,* and its prequel, this book, *Killing Hitler's Reich, The Battle for Hungary, 1945,* began as one volume. For continuity's sake, some aspects of this narrative will include information that will not become needed until after this book ends and the next one begins. *25. Panzer Division,* for example, ended the war fighting as part of *Heeresgruppe Süd,* thus the relevance here.

The bulk of this narrative occurs between 1 January and 31 March, 1945. On 1 April, Second and Third Ukrainian Fronts crossed the Austrian border and the fight for Hungary more or less came to an end. For those interested in reading about the epic subsequent fight for Austria, check out the most comprehensive history of that campaign ever written in English, *Killing Hitler's Reich, The Battle for Austria, 1945,* also by this author.

By 1945, the distances between the Western, Eastern and Southern Fronts had shrunk from thousands of kilometers, to less than one thousand in flight distance. Events on one front directly affected conditions on another. For example, air attacks on German forces fighting in the Balkans and Hungary came from the Royal Air Force and American Army Air Force to the south in Italy, and the Red Air Force to the east. Because of this relative synchronicity, where appropriate each chapter will begin with a War Situation Report.

The dying Third *Reich* had too little of everything needed to fight a modern war. It's difficult to pin down the exact moment when Germany had its last realistic chance to avoid defeat, which is a very different thing from achieving victory. Bringing up such a topic among historians and history buffs inevitably leads to disagreements, with many moments of the war being

1

viable points of discussion. Some would say that losing *6. Armee* at Stalingrad left the *Reich* on the path to certain defeat, while others might put the date as 22 June, 1941, claiming that the moment Hitler turned on Stalin, Germany's fate was sealed.

July of 1943 is certainly a month that most people could agree was fatal for the *Wehrmacht*. Not only had *Panzerarmee Afrika* surrendered in May, with the loss of more than 250,000 Axis troops[1], but *Unternehmen Zitadelle*[2] cost the Germans virtually all of their remaining striking power in terms of *panzers*, aircraft and men. Worse, when the Allies invaded Sicily on 10 July, it precipitated Italy's withdrawal from the war.

Why *this* book?

I refer to myself as an interpretative historian. Facts are *not* malleable, but determining *truth* is, depending on who writes it. The modern world is seeing that happen even as these words are being typed. This author's style is to emphasize underlying currents that help explain the facts.

Anyone who has reads my work knows that I do not write dry accounts of factual events, and only repeat earlier research where necessary to move the narrative forward. My style is to dig out unknown parts of a given battle to augment what is already known. The epilogue to *Killing Hitler's Reich, The Battle for Velikiye Luki 1942-1943* is one example of what I mean. By researching the salvaging of a *Sturmgeschutz III* that fought in the battle, I was able to verify and illustrate the precise conditions under which the last spasms of the relief effort were fought.

Work on this book began in 2006, after a visit to Vienna, Austria with friends. I commented that in

---

[1] Exact number vary wildly depending on the source. The most reliable sources generally put the number between 250,000-275,000. Equipment losses were also catastrophic.

[2] Known in the West as the Battle of Kursk.

preparation for the vacation I had sought out a history of the fighting there in 1945, and much to my astonishment, found none. Later I found a few specialized books that covered some of those battles, but not all of them, and the best were in German. My friend declared that if no such book existed, then it must mean that I had to write it.

Now, 18 years later, here we are.

The original intent had been to compile a one-volume history detailing the combat that took place in Austria during 1945. I quickly realized that the fight for Austria could not easily be severed from the Russian conquest of Western Hungary, which also included the death of *Heeresgruppe Süd* in 1945. So I set to work writing that book, which I anticipated might take a year.

As I said, 18 years later here we are.

My research library grew to more than 800 volumes and periodicals, including records in various archives around the world, and at least 200 websites hosting information on every imaginable subject as it relates to the war in Austria and Hungary. In 2016 the text of the book had grown beyond 250,000 words with no end in sight, and then something funny happened on the way to the publisher... my first novel was a smash hit. The publisher wanted another one, and it, too, sold well, so then there was a third, and fourth, and now I have more than 75 fiction titles on the market in various lengths.

Notes on Sources

My novels exist because I am a storyteller. I want to entertain my audience to the best of my ability, and that desire influences all of my writing, the non-fiction as well as the fiction. Thus, I am more flexible in my choice of sources, although incorruptibility of the source remains paramount.

History was and is my first love, and I was determined to finish that book. So I decided to be rational, and split the narrative into two parts. *Killing Hitler's Reich, The Battle for Austria, 1945*, came out in 2019 at nearly 300,000 words. The research was immense, because virtually no official records survived the war, and I am immensely proud of how it turned out. It would have been a much easier task if microfiche records existed of German records, but they do not. A few reviewers criticized that book for not using official records, to which I can only answer that I would have done so, if I could.

Anyway, that left the months of January-March, 1945, yet to finish. Some terrific research has been done during the interim, vastly improving the high level view of events, but those familiar with my work know that I want to know the ground level view of the war too, the one experienced by the average soldier. When dealing with two totalitarian regimes such as the Third *Reich* and the Soviet Union, however, it is difficult to find unfiltered accounts.

One source that no longer exists except in fragments are the transcriptions of Hitler's Daily Conferences. Late in this narrative we have something which is close to a primary source: the diary of Joseph Goebbels. Much will be made of this due to its direct focus on the fighting in Hungary, and how it reflects on occurrences there. We cannot know (with a few precious exceptions) what Hitler had to say about the events in this book, but Goebbels is the next best thing.

Men and officers of the *Wehrmacht*, by and large, were allowed to write more or less what they wanted. That resulted in some excellent unit histories, provided the units in question had enough survivors to compile such a book. For purposes of this book, an example of the latter is *6. Panzer Division*, which has no such legacy written by its members, despite having been in nearly continuous combat from the beginning of the war in Russia until the end.

German officers had even more opportunity to write their version of events, which inevitably cast them

4

in the most favorable light possible. Some are quite excellent, some less so. Hermann Balck's self-serving *Order in Chaos* is perhaps the most egregious example of the latter type, being not only vague, but also deflecting blame for any misjudgments to others. Nothing was ever Hermann Balck's fault, which means that someone using his memoirs as a historical source must question everything against other evidence. Having no easily accessible counterpoint to Balck's book, readers consequently lapped up his version of events. Balck was, to be sure, a superb *panzer* officer; whatever his personality faults or disingenuous memories, nothing should obscure his brilliance for improvisation. But having said that, his ego and intolerance certainly had a negative effect on the performance of his army in Hungary.

The United States Army launched a series of interviews with German generals that resulted in some quite excellent histories in the postwar period, but even these must be approached with caution. In many cases, the Germans told their captors what they wanted to hear, which holds especially true for Germans in captivity other than American.

Anything coming out of the Soviet Union of the period must be viewed not only with skepticism, but open doubt. Particularly during the Stalinist period there was no such thing as 'truth.' Everything was malleable. In recent years, however, the opening of records (pre-Putin era) allowed for at least some transparency. What we still do not have in abundance are reliable personal accounts of the lowest ranks of the Red Army, the cannon fodder who charged the MG-42s through a forest of exploding mortar shells. They are used in my work when appropriate, and with the proper caveats.

Which brings us to the *Waffen-SS*. This researcher owes a huge debt to Georg Maier, Deputy IA of *6. SS–Panzerarmee*[3] for his monumental history of that formation during 1945. It is an amazing accomplishment, even if necessarily flawed by the lack of available documentation at the time. But it is an operational level viewpoint, not a ground level one. Where the *Waffen–SS* is concerned that leads us to the German equivalents of Soviet accounts, which means crimes are either glossed over or laid at the feet of someone else, or ignored completely. Apology is the name of the game, leaving the researcher to carefully sift the evidence for any underlying truth.

The Allied decision to declare the *Waffen–SS* a criminal organization *in toto* left the rank and file veterans of Himmler's Black Order little choice except to keep their mouths shut so as not to attract attention. This led to openly apologetic publications such as *Der Landser* and *Siegrunen*. Most historians reject these out of hand because of their dubious nature, and yet this researcher thinks that is a mistake. In essence they are no different than Soviet era accounts. With due diligence it is possible to glean nuggets of detail concerning troop movements or battles without the accompanying propaganda. I have rejected using *Der Landser* because it changes names and give no unit details, and as of this writing have no references included in this narrative from that source, and yet John Toland has done precisely the same thing in his works. *The Last 100 Days* was first published by Random House, now by Modern Library, both being major publishers. The book was long ago accepted by the historical community, yet with exactly the same problem of changed names for some of its sources.

As will be detailed later in this narrative, the *Waffen–SS panzer* leader 'Fritz Hagen' does not appear on the rolls of any unit, so do we dismiss Toland's attributions to this individual as being false, since they cannot be verified? Because in essence the quotes

---

[3] Only in April did it officially have the 'SS' attached to its name, but since most books refer to it through its history as *6. SS-Panzerarmee*, that is also how it appears here.

attributed to that German officer are no different than the stories of other *Waffen–SS* veterans who appear in *Siegrunen* and similar publications. That *Siegrunen* is an apologetic publication for the *Waffen–SS* is acknowledged in the same way that Soviet era accounts are for the Red Army. For this researcher the answer is that I use the latter where appropriate but with all due caution, which is substantively no different than using Soviet-era Russian sources. If they add some otherwise lacking point of view to the narrative without disputing better sources, then I may use them. As with everything in this book it's a judgment call.

Prologue

Why did Germany keep fighting long after defeat became inevitable?

The answer to that question is deceptively simple: because Adolf Hitler willed it so. The logical follow-up question is *why* did Hitler command the Third *Reich* to go down fighting? To that there can never be a definitive answer.

To understand the events in this book, however, it is only necessary to know that Hitler's adamantly refused to negotiate any termination of the war without doing so from a position of strength. (And the coalition arrayed against Germany would only accept Unconditional Surrender, ipso facto, in Hitler's mind the was outcome was win or die.) To achieve Hitler's condition for opening negotiations meant that Germany had to keep fighting regardless of losses. That was not enough, though. No matter how large of a defensive victory might be achieved, and no matter how severe the casualties that Russia or the Allies might suffer, Germany was being systematically destroyed from the air. So standing on the defensive might delay the inevitable, but ultimately was nothing more than an alternate path to defeat.

That only left one strategy: to attack whenever and wherever possible.

There is also a strong component to Germany's long and destructive path toward final surrender that involves the Nazi leadership's narcissism. Twelve years of relentless propaganda had attempted to make Adolf Hitler the living embodiment of Germany; that is, he was Germany incarnate. In the official state narrative, if Hitler fell, so would the Fatherland. German could not exist without Hitler.

Just as in the Soviet Union, where millions wept at the death of the greatest mass-murderer in recorded history, Josef Stalin, a large percentage of the German population believed the messianic myth created by Joseph Goebbels around the *Führer*. Of course millions did not, but in a totalitarian state so rigidly controlled as the Third *Reich* they dared not openly dissent from the official line.

Aggravating the situation was the shockingly out of touch vacuum in which many of the nation's leaders lived. *Generalfeldmarschall* Erich von Manstein, one of Germany's most brilliant officers, believed in his heart that if the situation became bad enough Hitler would step down. Other generals agreed with him. They clearly either misunderstood the nature of the man they had sworn to serve, or compartmentalized the evidence of their own experiences. Let us not forget that such generals became rich under the Nazis; Hitler routinely bribed them with lavish bonuses.

Either way, by the last year of the war, any influence that officers of the *Heer* might have held over their *Führer* was gone. Even von Manstein, possibly Germany's greatest field commander and one of the few officers that Hitler liked and respected, spent the last year or so of the war in retirement because he dared confront the *Führer* with unpleasant realities. Hitler said that once the *Heer* had been rebuilt he would bring von Manstein out of retirement to command it, because nobody was better when leading full strength divisions, and few performed worse when the units were under-strength. Although grossly unfair to von Manstein this decision allowed him to ride out the end of the war in safety.

Early in the war the General Staff had credibility with the *Führer*. Only in isolated cases did Hitler listen to anyone anymore, though, much less the *Heer*. Any residual *gravitas* given to the opinions of his *Heer* advisors largely evaporated in the wake of the 20 July, 1944, assassination attempt.

Therefore, by the turn of 1945 Heinrich Himmler was arguably the second most powerful man in Germany, because the organizations he had shaped and built, the *SS* and all of its branches, and specifically the various police departments such as the *Sicherheitsdienst, Geheimestaatspolizei (Gestapo),* and the *Kriminalpolizei (Kripo),* all of which projected power backed by real force. *Reichsmarschall* Hermann Göring, although head of the *Luftwaffe,* had by that point lost favor through mismanagement of his department and a consumptive lifestyle of which Hitler disapproved. In particular, his drug use made him the butt of derogatory comments, and even the *Führer* himself sometimes poked fun at the morbidly obese Göring. Worse, it was Göring's *Luftwaffe* that proved unable to prevent the flattening of Germany's cities under a rain of Allied bombs. Compared to the *Waffen–SS* and its checklist of security branches, Göring commanded no real combat power should push come to shove in a post-Hitler German civil war.

On paper that assertion could be challenged, though.

Reichsmarschall Hermann Göring had long walked a line between a clear-eyed view of the war situation, and a fantasy outlook that denied the mess he'd made of the *Luftwaffe,* including the wasteful manpower drain created by the *Luftwaffe* field divisions. His influence at Hitler's headquarters had largely evaporated by 1945, with a long string of broken promises and failed projects sapping his credibility. Nor did the Allied Strategic Bombing Campaign do anything to enhance his reputation, with the ruins of Germany's cities being a constant reminder of how vulnerable were the skies over the *Reich.*

Even so, Göring continued telling Hitler what the *Führer* wanted to hear, and Hitler would at least hear him out. It must also be noted that when *Generaloberst* Gotthard Heinrici tried to explain that the Oder Front could not hold out more than a few days, Göring instantly promised 100,000 men from the *Luftwaffe* to man the trenches east of Berlin. This begs the question of why those men hadn't been shifted into a ground force in time to be properly trained, and illustrates the wasteful nature of Himmler giving precious weapons to non-Germans who did not want to fight to preserve the *Reich*, when they could have been given to Germans. This topic will be explored later in the narrative.

In terms of sheer combat power, the *Luftwaffe* possessed countless *flak* units, including whole divisions, but while some were mobile most were not. And while counting the tubes of *Luftwaffe flak* batteries would yield an impressive number, the vast majority were static and could only be moved with great difficulty. Nor was *Luftwaffe* air power the war-winning component it had once been. On 1 January, 1945, the best estimates for *Luftwaffe* serviceable aircraft were about 1,500 machines of all types and in all theaters. After *Unternehmen Bodenplatte* the attack squadrons were ruined.

Worse, precious fuel stockpiles had been wasted and could not be replaced. Pilots could not be trained because there was neither time nor fuel. If Göring's influence had not already been irreparably damaged before *Bodenplatte*, it certainly was after.

Although large in numbers and generally about as well equipped as German units were in 1945, *Luftwaffe* ground forces had very little offensive power. Where those divisions excelled was in the defensive role, particularly the *Fallschirmjägers*. Theoretically Göring commanded a *Fallschirmpanzerkorps* too, and even *1 Fallschirmarmee*, but *no* planners ever built a major offensive action around *Luftwaffe* ground units.

The only other two senior Nazis who counted when it came to influencing Hitler were Joseph Goebbels and Martin Bormann. In his own way each man wielded great power, with Goebbels ending up as Hitler's chief confidant and Bormann being head of the NSDAP, the Nazi Party itself, along with his post as Hitler's secretary. Yet neither of those men commanded actual troops, aside from *Volkssturm*. As for the *Sturmabteilung*, the once feared *SA*, it had long since ceased to matter in terms of influence.

Himmler personally seems to have known that he was a dead man if Germany lost the war, yet chose to fool himself that maintaining order in the conquered *Reich* would somehow require the Allies to keep him in power. Whether he was truly as delusional as it seems cannot now be answered, although in the war's final weeks he negotiated with the Allies through Swedish Count Bernadotte, even going so far as to release several thousand Jews who were marked for liquidation, as if that would absolve him of his crimes. Weak and indecisive when dealing with higher level matters, Himmer was also ruthless toward subordinates, and those unable to defend themselves.

Himmler was temperamentally unsuited for was challenging Hitler in any meaningful way. By 1945 he was only nominally the head of the *Waffen-SS*, which plays a huge part in the events of this book. In a power vacuum following Hitler's death, and allowing that the *Waffen–SS* units were not fighting for survival against rampaging Russians, then Himmler might have been able to wield his creation for his own purposes.

Barring such a happenstance, however, *Waffen–SS* units fell under the authority of the local *Heeresgruppe* commander. Himmler's role remained organizational and, most importantly, to represent the best interests of the *SS* combat units at Hitler's court, something at which Himmler abjectly failed once Hitler became involved. The infamous Cuff Band Order will provide a spectacular example of this cowardice later in this narrative. Worse for Germany's efforts in the war, Himmler's penchant for creating new divisions from unreliable manpower will also play out, with the equipping of such units eating up huge quantities of supplies and weapons that were diverted from German units. (In fairness, Himmler's experiment using volunteers from Axis allies and volunteers from conquered countries did have its share of successes.)

Perhaps the correct answer to why Germany kept fighting was that the men in power wanted to preserve their own lives for as long as possible, and didn't care how many people died to accomplish that. Whether they truly believed themselves to be the living embodiment of Germany is both unanswerable and irrelevant to those who suffered because of their decisions.

Heeresgruppe Süd Command

Otto Wöhler

Wöhler was both a perfect and a terrible choice to command *Heeresgruppe Süd*. By all accounts he was an excellent staff officer, but only gained a combat command out of dire necessity. In November of 1942 he was Chief of Staff for *Generalfeldmarschall Günther von Kluge* at *Heeresgruppe Mitte*. When the Russians launched Operation Mars and its auxiliary operation to capture the critical rail junction at Velikiye Luki, Wöhler was ordered to take command of an ad hoc *kampfgruppe* to relieve that town's surrounded garrison. That he failed was not his fault. The then *Generalmajor* did nothing to distinguish himself in the attack, yet neither did he make any major mistakes. He was competent.

If any one word summed up Wöhler's career, that was it; competent.

Born to a respectable family by German standards of the day, in February, 1913 Wöhler did what was expected of so many educated young men; he enlisted in the Army. Commissioned as a *Leutnant* in *Infanterie-Regiment 167* in May of 1914, during the First World War Wöhler proved himself to be a brave soldier by winning both classes of the Iron Cross. This and his professional competence caused him to be retained by the *Reich*swehr during the interwar period, once again serving mostly in staff positions. Once Hitler came to power in 1933 and began expanding the armed forces, promotions followed. By June of 1935 he had risen to the rank of *Oberstleutnant*.

Promoted to *Oberst* on New Years day 1938, Wöhler was named Ia at *Gruppenkommando 5* at the beginning of April and was still holding this post when this unit was redesignated *14. Armee* when war broke out in September 1939. Having won the clasps to both classes of Iron Cross during the campaign in Poland, he served as Chief of Staff at *XVII Armeekorps* from the beginning of December until the beginning of October 1940 when he became Chief of Staff at the brand new *11. Armee*, a formation created for *Unternehmen Barbarossa* the coming summer.

Although promoted to *Generalmajor* on New Years Day 1942, the new rank was backdated to April for 1941 for seniority purposes. Even so, this put nearly two years between promotions during wartime, when attrition and expansion meant rapid advancement for many others. Future *Generalfeldmarschall* von Manstein, the commander of *11. Armee*, gave Wöhler very high marks for his staff work, which resulted in Wöhler being awarded the Knight's Cross.

April,1942 saw Wöhler elevated to Chief of Staff for *Heeresgruppe Mitte*, with a concurrent promotion to *Generalleutnant* soon to follow in October. An officer who made the exalted rank of *Generalleutnant*, equivalent to the Allied rank of Lieutenant Colonel, while being solely a staff officer for his entire career, had truly impressed his superiors. Finally, in November of 1942, a full three years after the war began, Otto Wöhler finally got his first combat command.

The Russians launched *three* offensives in November of 1942, all of which were part of a larger grand strategy aimed at destroying the entire German Army in Russia. The first stage of this was Operation Uranus, aimed to threaten the German *6. Armee* then attempting to capture Stalingrad. But although involving a major commitment of men and materiél, Operation Uranus was in actuality a diversion to draw off German reserves from the true offensive hammer meant to crush the *Wehrmacht*, Operation Mars. This aimed at a bulge in the line near Moscow, known as the Rzhev Salient. Under the command of Georgi Zhukov, Operation Mars involved nearly two million men. On the offensive's northern flank was an attack to capture the fortified city of Velikiye Luki.[4]

Nearly unique on the Eastern Front, Velikiye Luki had been fortified against a siege, so when Russian forces surrounded the garrison there was every reason to hope they could yet be rescued. A scratched corps-sized *gruppe* was hastily assembled from whatever units could be found, but there were no officers of suitable rank or experience to lead it. So, with Velikiye Luki surrounded, Otto Wöhler had the mission of relieving the city dumped into his lap.

Ultimately the forces available were not strong enough for the task. Wöhler did a commendable job in trying to punch through the Russian lines against terrible odds and in worse weather. The attack actually got close enough to allow at least some of the defenders to escape. After this, Wöhler returned to *Heeresgruppe Mitte* HQ until the beginning of April when he stood in for Phillip Kleffel as commander of *I Armeekorps*, as part of *Heeresgruppe Süd*. He held this command until mid-August, when, having been promoted to *General der Infanterie* in June, Wöhler was named as *General der Panzertruppe* Werner Kempf's replacement as commander of *8. Armee* the day after being awarded the Knights Cross on 14 August, 1943.

8. Armee suffered badly in the fighting of summer, 1943, but managed to retreat to the Dnieper River by late September relatively unscathed, mainly by using *3. SS–Panzer Division Totenkopf* and *Panzergrenadier Division Grossdeutschland* to launch short, savage counterattacks against Soviet spearheads whilst the slower units pulled back, and fought off the only major Soviet airborne operation. The partial collapse of both *4. Panzerarmee* to the north and *1. Panzerarmee* to the south threatened the entire *8. Armee* with encirclement. As the Soviets smashed across the last major defense line in Russia south of

---

[4] For an in-depth examination of this operation, see the author's *Killing Hitler's Reich, The Battle for Velikiye Luki, 1942-1943.*

Kiev and at Kremenchug, *XI and LII Armeekorps* were cut off west of Cherkassy around the small town of Korsun in January 1944.

Forced to fall back by increasing pressure on his flanks, Wöhler's command was pulled back to the south-east, once again using *3. Panzer Division Totenkopf* to blunt Soviet attempts to follow up their retreat. This positioned Wöhler's command nearly into Rumania.

Faced with such a crisis Hitler fell back on his standards command methods... he sacked various commanders. Assigned to *Heeresgruppe Süd-Ukraine*, Wöhler showed skill in keeping *8. Armee* intact when Rumania defected to the Soviet cause. Shortly after adding the Oak Leaves to his Knights Cross in late November, Wöhler replaced Johannes Freissner as commander of what had become *Heeresgruppe Süd*, turning over command of *8. Armee* to *General der Gebirgstruppe* Hans Kreysing.

Hans Kreysing

Defense of the northern flank of *Heeresgruppe Süd* fell to Wöhler's old command, *8. Armee*. Like Wöhler, its new commander, Hans Kreysing served in the First World War and managed to stay in the *Reichswehr* between the wars. He took over command of *3. Gebirgs Division* in October, 1940, and still commanded it during the Battle for Velikiye Luki, where the mountain troops shared the brunt of the fighting with *83. Infanterie-Division*. There is no record of he and Wöhler interacting during that period, and yet as one of the main commanders on the spot they must have coordinated their activities.

Autumn 1943 saw him take over command of *XVII Armeekorps*. By 1945 Kreysing had won the Knights Cross with Oak Leaves, and by all accounts was a brave and reliable officer. The formations that formed *8. Armee* were no different than the rest of the *Wehrmacht*, being worn out, depleted, and badly

18

supplied. Nevertheless, in the maelstrom of the war's final months, Otto Wöhler would rely on Kreysing to maximize his army's combat power, and Kreysing would come through.

Maximilian de Angelis

General der Artillerie de Angelis led what was arguably the weakest of the three armies that Wöhler commanded, *2. Panzerarmee.* His reputation within the *Heer* was excellent, as he was noted for being both relentless on offense and tenacious on defense. Also like Wöhler he'd already won the Knight's Cross with Oak Leaves.

But the most notable feature of *2. Panzerarmee* was that it had no *panzer* formations, and very few AFVs of any type. On his right flank, de Angelis had *Heeresgruppe E* in Italy, with *Heeresgruppe F* strung out to the southeast in the Balkans.

Hermann Black

Perhaps Wöhler's most talented army commander was also his most problematic. *General der Panzertruppe* Hermann Black had a long family tradition of military service, graduated from the Hanoverian War Academy, and fought on every major front during the First World War. Without question he was a talented officer, whose medals for bravery were well earned.

Only 4,000 officers served in the *Reichswehr* after the War ended, and Balck was one of them. His exploits during the Second World War only built on his reputation from the first. Balck specialized in *panzer* tactics and mobile warfare, achieving near miracles in some engagements. Starting the war as a regimental officers, Balck became only one of 27 officers in the entire war to win the Knight's Cross with Oak Leaves, Swords and Diamonds. By September, 1944, Balck's career peaked with his promotion to command

Heeresgruppe G in Alsace, France. His mission was to defeat George Patton and the United States Third Army.

Balck proved no more able to achieve the impossible than anyone else, so three months later Balck was removed from command and sent to the officer reserve. However, *Generaloberst* Heinz Guderian, *Generalstabschef des Oberkommando des Heeres,* (*OKH*), convinced Hitler to give Balck another command. In response, the failed army group commander was given a formation known as *Armeegruppe Balck.* Built around the rebuilt *6. Armee,* with two weak and dispirited Hungarian armies, on paper it looked like a powerful force, Like all German units of the period, though, the divisions were burned out shells.

By 1945 Hermann Balck seems to have lost the fire of earlier years. His memoir, *Order in Chaos,* is short on details of this period. Worse for Otto Wöhler, Balck utterly despised the *Waffen-SS.* In particular he hated *SS–Obergruppenführer und General der Waffen–SS* Otto Gille, the commander of *IV SS-Panzerkorps,* who shortly would be under Balck's command. Without question this animosity played a part in the campaign to come.

Judging from his book the bitterness Balck felt during this period of the war comes through loud and clear. At a time when the German war effort required maximum coordination and cooperation, Balck's hatred of the *Waffen–SS* stands as a glaring example of the disfunction that plagued the *Wehrmacht* during the last months of the war.

Of all the shortages Germany faced in 1945, however, none was more urgent than the manpower shortage; what the Germans needed most was more Germans. Warm bodies that could hold a rifle, if a rifle was available, were at a premium, and neither the Replacement Army nor the Personnel Office of the *Waffen–SS* was picky about where those bodies came from, or ultimately even their country of origin. Like manpower-starved formations throughout the *Reich*, *Heeresgruppe Süd* was no exception and, despite the influx of German units during the first months of 1945, *Heeresgruppe Süd* remained heavily dependent on the fighting ability of its Hungarian units to maintain a cohesive front. The quality of those units, therefore, was of major concern, not only from their level of equipment and armaments, but also from the standpoint of morale.

Like their German counterparts the Hungarian formations were under-strength and under-equipped, but while they were not necessarily enthusiastic allies, what is remarkable is that they stood and fought at all. When the Hungarian regent, Admiral Horthy, had signed an armistice with the Russians the previous autumn, only the quick reaction of the Germans kept Hungary in the Axis fold. After a lightning operation headed by the legendary Otto Skorzeny[5], the venerated Horthy was replaced by the head of the Arrow Cross party, Ferenc Szalasi, who an unpopular choice; Szalasi was not supported by either the Hungarian people or the Honved[6] and was rightly seen as a German puppet. Otto Wöhler and Hermann Balck both thought Szalasi unreliable, although Balck thought he understood operations well enough, but the judgment of Hungarian *Oberst* General Ruszkay was much harsher: "Power mad, a fanaticist with outsize ideas which he thoughtlessly expressed without regard to their practicality...totally undependable."[7] In consequence the Germans fully expected a collapse of Hungarian support, and while few Hungarian leaders supported Szalasi and some defected to the Russians and called on members of the military to do the same,

[5] *Unternehmen Panzerfaust.*
[6] The Royal Hungarian Army.
[7] Maier, *Drama Between Budapest and Vienna*, p. 10.

21

the number was surprisingly small. When forced to choose between Russian captivity or fighting with the Germans, most Hungarian formations chose the Germans. This was crucial to the German position at the southern end of the Eastern Front, for without the active support of those Honved formations *Heeresgruppe Süd* would have been crippled. Despite everything, many Hungarians fought to the bitter end.

At approximately 9 am on New Year's Day, 1945, an express train from Poland pulled into Raab (Gyor) station in Hungary, just south of the east-west leg of the Danube River, before it veers south again near Gran (Esztergom). Dismounting from the long journey were the headquarters personnel of the *5. SS–Panzer Division Wiking Division*, with orders to assemble the division as quickly as possible in the area west of Tata and prepare to attack the Red Army units to the east in concert with the remaining elements of *IV. SS–Panzerkorps* , as part of Army Balck, known officially as *6. Armee*[8]. Commanded by *SS–Oberfuhrer* Karl Ullrich, *5. SS Panzer Division Wiking* had left the Modlin area near Warsaw on Christmas Day, 1944, headed south through Slovakia by train to the Tata area. The rail cars were unheated, the men inside them cold and tired. According to Pierik they had been forced to bring along their own supplies of food and ammunition.[9] If so, this was likely because of one of two reasons: there were no supply dumps awaiting them in Hungary and

---

[8] As with so many accounts from this period, there is a disagreement on exactly what Wiking did and when they did it. In his history of *5. SS–Panzer Division Wiking* Tank Regiment, Ewald Klapdor seems to have Wiking spending New Year's Eve celebrating in Komorn, then moving into attack position the next day after a morning musical concert in the Komorn marketplace. His timeline is not completely clear, but the weight of evidence is overwhelming that Konrad I began on January 1.

[9] Pierik, p. 151.

they would be going straight into battle without time to stock up on supplies.

The advance elements of *Wiking* that arrived on New Year's Day were just that, advance elements. The entire division would not arrive for nearly a week but there was no time to wait, the attack would start as soon as possible with whatever components were on hand. *Wiking* was being transported on 87 trains, but as of 1 January only 28 had arrived, although they did carry most of the combat elements. German transport had become so slow and unreliable that none of the major formations leading the assault had fully arrived near the battlefield; on New Year's Day only 3 percent of *Wiking* was on hand, 43 percent of *96. Infanterie Division* and 66 percent of *Totenkopf*.[10] Already badly under-strength, those divisions would have to attack with whatever part of their combat power was present. It would not be until 8 January that all of the transport would be completed and the divisions would be present in their entirety.

Tata was a small town almost due east of Raab (Györ in Hungarian), astride the main highway from Vienna to Budapest. Conceived and ordered by Hitler himself, this attack by *IV. SS–Panzerkorps* , code-named *Konrad* but known to history as *Konrad I*, was an attempt to relieve the beleaguered German and Hungarian units surrounded and fighting for their lives in Budapest. Exactly like Stalingrad, Velikiye Luki and many other encircled cities and pockets defended by the Germans, the units trapped inside the Budapest perimeter had been ordered to stand fast and die rather than try to break out.

5. SS Panzer Division Wiking had been intended to serve as a model for future *Waffen-SS*, being composed of volunteers from at least 8 different nations, among them occupied countries such as the Netherlands, Denmark and Norway, as well as Sweden, Switzerland, the Baltic States and Finland. The officers

---

[10] Maier, *Drama Between Budapest and Vienna*, p. 17.

were mostly German and the command language was German, but if there was ever a Pan-European sub-current to the German war effort it was exemplified by *Wiking*. By and large these volunteers were anti-communists who bought the German recruiting slogans about protecting Europe from Bolshevist influences, although finding a dominant reason for their decision to fight for Germany is nearly impossible; "These motives usually boiled down to adventure seeking, material gain, or hopes for political advantage and status in the homeland."[11] By 1945, however, less than 5 percent of the division was composed of volunteers from Northern or Western Europe.[12] Most of the SS divisions had a patron who took a personal interest in their welfare, and for *Wiking* it was Felix Steiner, one of the most influential of the SS generals. According to Pierik, during its operational life through the end of December, 1944, the division had suffered 11,098 casualties of all types, more than half of its authorized strength.[13].

As of this New Year's Day, *Wiking* was also reinforced with another pan-European formation, the II Battalion of *SS–Regiment Ney*; the I Battalion was attached to *3. SS–Panzer Division Totenkopf*. This regiment was a Hungarian SS formation commanded by Dr. Karoli Ney von Pilis, a dedicated Arrow Cross member, and was organized from former Hungarian soldiers who were veterans of the Eastern Front. This formation originated from a Hungarian organization that brought together veterans of the Don River Army,

---

[11] Estes, Kenneth, *A European Anabasis: Western Volunteers in the German Army and SS, 1940-45* (London: Helion, 2019), via http://www.gutenberg-e.org/esk01/frames/fesk06.html (Accessed 5 May, 2014).

[12] Michaelis, *Panzer Divisions of the Waffen–SS*, p. 203.

[13] Pierik also reports that from the opening day of Operation Barbarossa, *3. SS Panzer Division Totenkopf* had suffered the unbelievable total of 53,794 casualties, meaning it had been completely destroyed almost three times. Such astronomical casualty rates are an indication of how important the SS divisions were to the Wehrmacht, being the *schwerpunkt* in attacks and the fire brigades on defense, but also show why Army officers often criticized *Waffen–SS* tactics, claiming they were reckless and led to unnecessary casualties.

called 'The Comradeship Federation of the Eastern Front', abbreviated as (KABSZ) in Hungarian. The group wore a black armband with a skull to denote membership.

Ney then added anti-communist volunteers until his regiment actually surpassed regimental strength, adding a 3rd Battalion (and later even a 4th battalion!) and topping out at more than 5,000 men, including supply troops.This actually made *SS–Regiment Ney* stronger than several divisions, at least in manpower, and it was eventually upgraded to a brigade. On New Year's Day, however, its strength was less than 2,000 men. The original intent had been for this formation to act as a replacement battalion for *22. SS-Kavallerie Division Maria Theresa*, but when that unit was surrounded in Budapest and Ney's formation continued to grow, it was given independent status within the *Waffen-SS*[14]. Nor was the regiment just another allied *SS* formation that sucked up resources without adding to the German war effort. With *IV. SS–Panzerkorps* in desperate need of infantry, especially veteran infantry, the regiment would prove itself for what it was: an assemblage of motivated veterans of the eastern front who were determined to keep the communists from overrunning their country.

The value of formations such as *SS–Regiment Ney* cannot be overstated. By 1945 the years of heavy casualties had taken their toll on every fighting formation in the Wehrmacht Order of Battle, whether it was *Waffen–SS* or not, and *5. SS–Panzer Division Wiking* was no exception. The manpower shortage mentioned previously was especially hard on *Wiking*, formed as it was around a core of pan-European volunteers, after many of its most fertile recruiting grounds were in Allied hands. As *Wiking* headed for Hungary relatively few men in its ranks were non-Germans champing at the bit to grapple with

---

[14] Ney's unit fought so well it was given the rare honor of having its own cuff band, authorized by Hitler, that read *SS–Regiment Ney*.

communism; there just were not enough volunteers to fill the void left by nearly four years of fighting in Hell. Only days before being transferred south for *Konrad I* the division had incorporated large numbers of replacements supplied by the *Luftwaffe*, surplus German manpower no longer needed by the decimated air units, who were involuntarily transferred to the *Waffen-SS*. The men were good physical examples, for the most part, but not trained to fight as infantry; it is unlikely they were thrilled by the idea of tramping through the snow to kill Russians at close range. On paper they might have brought the division close to authorized strength[15], but aircraft mechanics, flight controllers, armorers and fuel truck drivers were not able replacements for veteran combat infantry; fitting a man with an *SS* uniform[16] and handing him a Mauser K-98 did not make him a *panzergrenadier*. Thus were the veterans of *SS–Regiment Ney* a welcome addition to both *Totenkopf* and *Wiking*.

Wiking's sister unit in *IV. SS–Panzerkorps* had begun arriving on 28 December and so was in better shape for the coming attack. *3. SS–Panzer Division Totenkopf* was one of the most notorious of the now famous (and infamous) *SS* units. Once commanded by Theodore Eicke, first commandant of Dachau and later a key figure in setting up the concentration camp system, *Totenkopf's* record of atrocities was long, but its record of military achievements was even longer. It had been a brutal and brutally effective fighting force. Like every major German unit, by 1945 its best combat power was spent, with thousands of dead on fields across Eastern Europe and the Russian steppe.

To even the most casual observer of German tactics and tendencies up until that point in the war,

---

[15] Strength returns for German units of this period are relative. For example, Wiking's manpower total for December, 1944, was approximately 14,800. But in June of 1941 it had been more than 19,300.

[16] When SS uniforms were available. As Pierik points out later, *Kriegsmarine* replacements in *711. Infanterie-Division* went into battle wearing navy uniforms.

some sort of relief attack on Budapest should have been not only obvious, but expected. By this New Year's Day, 1945, Germany and the USSR had been at war for three and a half years, and the patterns of fighting were well established; aside from the introduction of new weapons there should have been few surprises left for either side. The Red Army had their way of fighting and the Wehrmacht had theirs and during the course of the war when German troops had been surrounded, especially when defending a city, they had been ordered to hold out while a relief attack was mounted from outside, often with supplies airlifted or dropped by parachute to the trapped formations.

The pattern had begun in early 1942 during the Soviet counterattacks around Moscow, when German troops were pocketed at both Demyansk and Cholm. Both times German generals urged relief attacks combined with breakouts by the encircled troops, both times Hitler ordered the ground held and the troops supplied by air, with relief attacks into the pockets. And both times the tactics worked. German losses were very heavy but the pockets were relieved, most of the ground was held and Hitler=s stubborn inflexibility became entrenched in his mind as evidence of his own superior military judgment. Standing fast became the *Führer*=s default answer to all situations where German troops were trapped. In truth, however, the successes stemmed mostly from the superiority of the German *soldat* of 1941 and his commanding officers over their early-war Soviet counterparts, and their ability to perform nearly miraculous feats in the face of a numerically superior enemy. Demyansk and Cholm should have served as a warning instead of a model. Future events were all too easy to predict.

The encirclement of the German 6. *Armee* at Stalingrad in November of 1942 is merely the best known example of this trend in the fighting that culminated with *IX. SS-Waffen-Gebirgs-Armeekorps der SS* surrounded in Budapest[17]. At Stalingrad, the Soviets attacked weak formations on either side of the city, poured west where the resistance was lightest and only tightened their grip once the pocket was closed. This became the Soviet attack template when faced with a defended city. That same November of 1942 saw the garrison surrounded at Velikiye Luki to the north and a relief attack that actually broke through to the city but was not strong enough to hold open a corridor, with the subsequent result that the city fell and the garrison was lost. It was Stalingrad on a smaller scale, complete with a failed re-supply plan from the air.

It may be noted in passing that on one of the few occasions when a city was not defended to the last man, at Kharkov in 1943, and when a brilliant German general was given freedom of action (even if by events) Erich von Manstein authored one of the most famous counterattacks in the modern history of warfare, the Soviets were crushed and the city re-taken. That this should have been the German template for flexible defense was obvious to all except the only man that mattered, Hitler. As happened all too often during the last years of the war, when the *Reich* was fighting for its life, many of Germany's best generals, such as Erich von Manstein, languished on the retired list[18].

After Stalingrad and Velikiye Luki came almost too many pockets to count: the Korsun-Cherkassy Pocket, the Courland Pocket, the Falaise Pocket (because of extreme tenacity on the part of the Germans, and extreme ineptitude on the part of the Allies, the Falaise Pocket was never quite closed), even the units then attacking at the Battle of the Bulge would almost be pocketed. That *IX. SS-Waffen-Gebirgs-Armeekorps der SS* had been surrounded in Budapest

---

[17] In a grand irony, IX SS Mountain Corps contained no significant mountain units, but did contain both SS cavalry divisions.

[18] Von Manstein had been sacked for disagreeing with Hitler, the story of many German generals.

and ordered to hold out indefinitely should have been no surprise to anyone. Nor should the inevitable relief attack.

In one respect, however, ordering Budapest held might actually have been the best course of action, at least in the beginning. None of the major formations trapped there would have been of much value in open country. The major German units trapped there were *8. SS–Freiwillige–Kavallerie Division Florian Geyer, 22. SS Freiwillige-Kavallerie Division Maria Theresa*[19], the battered and badly under-strength *13. Panzer Division,* a kampfgruppe of the *271. Infanterie Division,* the even smaller *kampfgruppe* of *Panzer Division Felldherrnhalle* and the assorted smaller units. On paper these forces should have totaled a minimum of 70,000 men, but in fact they numbered less than 33,000[20]. What is more, while the two *SS* Cavalry Divisions were useful for reconnaissance and exploiting breakthroughs, they were very weak in actual combat power because of small artillery detachments, few armored vehicles and the lighter weapons issued to Cavalry units.[21] Both were commanded by seasoned combat veterans, with *Florian Geyer* headed by *SS–Brigadeführer* Rumohr and *Maria Theresa* by *SS–Brigadeführer* Zehender, ensuring they would fight hard, but without the proper weapons they were severely handicapped. But both divisions were true cavalry divisions, that is, horse mounted. Fighting as dismounted infantry in an urban battlefield they were far more effective defensively than in the open.

Likewise, the *Panzer* units would have been of limited use in the open field, since they were nearly bereft of tanks, and fuel was low anyway, making

[19] The two SS cavalry divisions were considered sister units, with men often having served in both units.

[20] At least one source puts the German personnel total much lower, at 25,000.

[21] By this point in other armies, the term 'cavalry' was evolving to mean units armed with fast armored vehicles, but both 8th and 22nd SS divisions still rode horses into battle in great numbers.

29

maneuvering tricky. Had any of the trapped units been given defensive responsibilities in the open field it's hard to see how they could have successfully defended much ground given their depleted condition. In the attack, it was to be seen soon enough that cavalry divisions, even full strength ones, simply did not have the firepower to assault an entrenched enemy[22]. In a huge city like Budapest, however, those disadvantages were largely offset by the natural cover; urban environments were defensive force multipliers. Soviet firepower that could rip huge holes in a front line in open country would have something of the opposite effect in a city. In other words, it is hard to imagine that the German forces trapped in Budapest could have been more usefully employed elsewhere, except, perhaps, as reserves. As it was they tied down enormous Soviet forces for almost two months and blocked the best highways leading over the Danube to Western Hungary.

Trapped with the German forces were approximately 37,000 Hungarian troops under the command of *Oberst* General Ivan von Kinshind Hindy. Officially titled I Hungarian Corps, the core of this motley collection were the 10th and 12th Hungarian Infantry Divisions, as well as a large collection of what might be termed auxiliaries, students and civilians who backed the German-allied Arrow Cross government against the communists. Pierik (1998) lists some of these as, "*Sturmart.Gruppe* Billnitzer (*Generalmajor* Erno Billnitzer), *Oberst* Janza's *Flak-Rgt. 12* Budapest, Feldwebel Sipeki-Balazs' university assault battalion, the life guard battalion from the castle in Buda and the Arrow Cross and Gendarmerie units of General Kalandy." [23] It is highly debatable whether any of these units would have had much combat value in the open field, especially the university students, although in many cases they fought bravely and effectively amid

[22] This refers to *I Kavallerie Korps* attacking on the right flank of *Unternehmen Frühlingserwachen*, which occurs later in the narrative.
[23] Pierik, p. 136.

the flaming ruins of Budapest. It should be noted that the Germans developed weapons like the *panzerfaust* specifically for use by such untrained people in close quarters combat, making Budapest the ideal environment to maximize their effectiveness.

Regardless of whether or not this particular 'stand fast' order was good or bad strategy, however, the task confronting *Heeresgruppe Süd* that bitterly cold New Year's Day was a hard one indeed. For *IV. SS– Panzerkorps* , the job at hand would not have been easy under the best of circumstances, but being rapidly transported south over a rail network that was on the verge of collapse, then asked to de-train and march straight into the attack without all of your forces on hand, could not be interpreted as the best of circumstances, although they could arguably be the worst.

A *panzer* division could not be transported by rail in a train or two. It generally took dozens. Nor would just any train do. Hundreds of vehicles, and especially tanks and tank destroyers, required special rolling stock, the troops had to have some modicum of comfort and protection if they were to arrive in shape to fight (or at least food and water and some sanitation, if nothing else to prevent disease), the specialized equipment that tank divisions need could not simply be shoved into a cattle car. It all had to be organized and loaded correctly so that it could then be unloaded quickly and the division formed back into a fighting unit without delay. Tanks and armored personnel carriers were formidable fighting weapons, but in some respects they were also quite fragile. Maintenance was crucial; care had to be taken with spare parts. And during transport there was always a certain amount of stress on the machines. Lug-nuts could work themselves loose, cables could become unattached, wires break, the list was endless. To expect those complex machines to roll from a train car and go straight into battle was expecting a lot.

As existing units sped toward the Hungarian battlefield, the High Commands of both the German Army and the *Waffen–SS* were scrambling to create new units out of the human flotsam reeling back from the shattered borders, or the pool of surplus bodies fleshing out the Kriegsmarine and *Luftwaffe*. Even as *8. SS-Kavallerie Division Florian Geyer* and *22. SS–Kavallerie Division Maria Theresa* were being systematically destroyed in Budapest, their support units outside the city were rounded up with a view to amalgamation into an entirely new division. Those elements not in Budapest had been sent to a collection point at Marchfeld on the Hungarian-Slovak border, ostensibly to wait being reunited with their parent divisions. These were the medical, veterinary, supply and replacement formations within the *8. SS-Kavallerie Division Florian Geyer* and *22. SS–Kavallerie Division Maria Theresa*, as well as men who had been on leave when the two were surrounded in Budapest. There were even a few officers and men wounded in Budapest who were evacuated by air and had recovered sufficiently to return to combat. Perhaps the most surprising thing is that even in those dark days of defeat after defeat, the Wehrmacht and *Waffen–SS* still found a way to send men on leave.

Early in January these assembled fragments were moved to Greater Schuett Island in the Danube, near Pressburg (Bratislava) where the collection station for both the *8. SS-Kavallerie Division Florian Geyer* and the *22. SS–Kavallerie Division Maria Theresa* was established in the town of Senz. These were mainly just the specialist units that would be very hard to replace but had little potential combat value beyond supporting roles. Doctors and nurses, veterinarians and quartermasters, were all vital to keeping a military unit functioning, but were of little use in defending against tanks or assaulting bunkers. The commander of this refugee assortment was *SS–Oberfuhrer* Waldemar Fegelein, younger brother of Himmler's *SS* liaison officer at Hitler's headquarters, *SS–Grüppenführer* and Knight's Cross winner Hermann Fegelein.

Otto Wöhler was not a happy man that New Year's Day. Having replaced *Generaloberst* Friessner only on 22 December, the commander of *Heeresgruppe Süd* had been on the job for less than two weeks when he was given the unenviable task of breaking through Soviet lines to relieve the Budapest garrison[24]. Using a thrown-together attack plan based on units that had not even fully arrived on the battlefield and would have no time to organize once they did, over terrain that was unsuitable for tank warfare, in bitter winter weather, using an Army whose commander was even newer to his command than Wöhler was[25], he was expected to crack the Soviet defenses and rescue *IX. SS-Waffen-Gebirgs-Armeekorps der SS*. Plans for the attack were so chaotic they were only finalized on 31 December, the day before the attack was to commence. And if that were not bad enough the Germans were outnumbered; *Heeresgruppe Süd* could muster about 494 AFVs that New Year's Day, with another 554 under repair, while the Russians deployed some 1066 total operational AFVs.[26] *General der Panzertruppe* Hermann Balck, commander of *Armeegruppe Balck*, essentially the *6. Armee* and Third Hungarian Army, the man directly responsible for the attack's success, listed the disparity in forces as follows: "On the German side there were 7 Armored Divisions, 2 Cavalry Divisions and 4 Infantry

---

[24] Wöhler had previously commanded *8. Armee*, the northernmost Army under the command of *Heeresgruppe Süd*, and so was not totally unfamiliar with the situation.

[25] *General der Panzertruppe* Hermann Balck became commander of *6. Armee* on December 23rd.

[26] Ungvary, Krisztián, *The Siege of* Budapest (New Haven: Yale University Press, 2005), p. 325.

Divisions along with Hungarian troops, which were normally not to be included as a serious component...On the Russian side there were 54 Infantry Divisions, 5 Mechanized Corps, 3 Tank Corps, 2 Cavalry Corps, 4 Anti-Aircraft Divisions, 4 Anti-Tank Brigades [and] 3 Mortar Brigades."[27] And while none of the units on either side were close to authorized strength, the ratios clearly favored the defending Russians.

With the German penchant for organization, there is a difference between the terms '*armeegruppe*' and '*heeresgruppe*', even though both translate into English as 'army group.' '*Armeegruppe*' denotes two or more armies operating under one overall commander, but without some of the attached subordinate formations often found with '*heeresgruppe*', such as nebelwerfer battalions. This lead to situations like this, where Army Group Balck was subordinated to *Heeresgruppe Süd*.

As desperate as all of this might seem, though, it was old hat to Wöhler; he was a veteran at trying to break through to trapped garrisons and so he knew just how bad the situation was. As early as December of 1942 he had commanded a Corps sized group that tried to break through the encircling Russians at Velikiye Luki, coming close enough that a few of the trapped garrison were able to make it out; in early 1944 when Wöhler was commanding general of *8. Armee* he tried to rescue *XI* and *LII Armeekorps* trapped near Korsun. The rest of 1944 trying he spent trying not only to hold back the Russians but also to keep his command from being encircled. Unfortunately for the Germans the chief unit charged with carrying out a successful attack in Hungary was *6. Armee*, commanded by the aforementioned and recently demoted former commander of *Heeresgruppe G*, Hermann Balck.

[27] Maier, *Drama Between Budapest and Vienna*, p. 16.

On the face of it Balck seemed like an inspired choice for the mission. He was a brilliant *panzer* commander whose career had peaked the previous year when he was given command of the army group trying to hold back Patton in France. His demotion had not been based on his abilities but rather on his inability to work miracles; he was a very talented army commander and some of his exploits border on the heroic. However, *6. Armee*'s chief attack group was the newly arrived *IV. SS–Panzerkorps* and Balck was a questionable choice to command an *SS Panzer* Corps. He detested the *Waffen–SS* and frequently belittled the martial qualities of its formations, usually heaping derision on its officers although not its rank and file. He considered the soldiers brave to the point of being foolhardy but poorly trained and led.

Balck was a talented, experienced *panzer* commander, sometimes ranked as one of Germany's best tank generals. But the fact that he intensely disliked the *Waffen–SS* was a major problem for Wöhler, because his best unit was Gille's newly arrived Corps and its two veteran divisions. For his part, Gille was a battle-hardened commander with numerous admirers within the Army who considered him an excellent officer; unfortunately for all involved, Balck was not one of them. Nor did Balck's chief of staff, *Generalmajor* Heinz Gaedecke, help matters. Gaedecke knew Gille from the previous year when both men were trapped in the Cherkassy Pocket and came to despise each other. Balck trusted his chief of staff implicitly, they had previously served together in *1. Kavallerie Division*, so he accepted Gaedecke's evaluation of his new corps commander enough that, as Pierik quotes him saying, "when I met Gille my worries were confirmed."[28] Despite the need for close coordination, relations between Balck and Gille were stormy from the

[28] Pierik, p. 160.

start[29] and they would only grow worse as the weeks went by; once 6. *SS–Panzerarmee* showed up in Hungary Balck's antipathy for the *Waffen–SS* made close coordination between the two services extremely difficult.

Pierik goes on to make the point that while Wöhler's two subordinate commanders might not like each, they were both aggressive and improvisational in a fight, talents that a thrown-together offensive such as Konrad required to have any chance of success. Both men were convinced of their own competence and expected others to recognize their talents. Gille had won the Knight's Cross with Oak Leaves, Swords and Diamonds, a rare award.[30] Despite what Balck and Gaedecke might have believed he was very well thought of by many of his peers, especially after his actions in the Cherkassy and Kowel Pockets. Gille had fought his way into the Cherkassy Pocket in early 1944 and saved two army corps, then flew into the Kowel Pocket and took command, holding out until a relief force finally broke in to save them. His reputation was that of a general who could work miracles for surrounded troops and just his name brought hope to hopeless situations. So, despite their personal animosity, Balck and Gille's considerable talents might have overcome the obstacle of their poisoned relationship if they had given them the chance.

---

[29] One positive by-product of this rivalry was provoked by Balck writing his memoirs, *Ordnung im chaos*. The passages covering Balck's command of 6. *Armee*, and his opinions of Sepp Dietrich and 6. *SS–Panzerarmee* in particular, were so critical of the *Waffen–SS* that it provoked the Deputy Ia of Dietrich's command to write his own book on the subject, *Between Budapest and Vienna: The Final Battles of 6th SS–Panzer Army*, by Georg Maier, directly refuting Balck's allegations to the point that it sometimes detracts from the narrative, a flaw that is more than offset by the book's detailed narrative of the fighting. Had Balck not been so caustic we might not have Maier's work.

[30] The Knight's Cross was a highly coveted award in itself, with the higher grades being with Oak Leaves, Swords and Diamonds, and, in one case only, Golden Oak Leaves. Often these rare honors were presented by Hitler himself. Only 27 men won the Oak Leaves, Swords and Diamonds, and only Hans Ulrich-Rudel won the Golden Oak Leaves.

The operation that became known as *Konrad I* was a hastily organized attempt to relieve Budapest, as well as regaining the west bank of the Danube. But there were differing opinions on how best to accomplish that. The first plan, known as the Northern Plan and officially named Konrad, called for a direct attack along the southern line of the Danube that would clear that bank of the river before turning southeast for Budapest, with other columns moving directly for the city cross-country. The terrain for this attack was hilly, being separated into the Geresce and the Pilis Heights that topped out at more than 2,300 feet, but it offered the fastest route to the Budapest perimeter in the most weakly held sector of the front. A competing plan, known as the Southern Plan and bearing the title *Unternehmen Paula*, started out from the Margarethe line between Lakes Balaton and Velence and was loosely based on *Unternehmen Spätlese* (Late Harvest), yet another planned attack covering essentially the same territory. Eventually *Paula* was bypassed because, while the terrain was flat and much more favorable for armored movement, the distance to Budapest was greater and the flanks of the attack longer, requiring more screening forces. It also would have delayed the start of the offensive for up to five days, time that was crucial to the Budapest garrison. Worse, the longer route to Budapest and additional pre-attack maneuvering would have used at least 900 more cubic meters of fuel.[31] Nevertheless, Hitler dithered with indecision before finally settling on 'Konrad' although he would later conveniently forget that it was his decision to endorse the northern route.

Aside from the hurried nature of the operation, none of the assault units was anywhere close to authorized strength. *5. SS Panzer Division Wiking* was a good example of how under-strength they were. One source puts *Wiking's* authorized armored strength at

[31] Isayev, Aleksei & Kolomiets, Maksim, translated and edited by Britton, Stuart, *Tomb of the Panzerwaffe, The Defeat of 6. SS–Panzerarmee in Hungary 1945*, (Solihull: Helion, 2019), p. 16.

152, but on 1. January only 36 were combat ready,[32] about 25 percent of full strength.[33] (Truck transport was also depleted, having 658 of 921 authorized vehicles, while mechanized transport was even worse, with only 442 of 1,011 on hand, although 162 *SPWs*[34] of all types were ready for action. Mobility was listed at only 46 percent.

The division's total manpower was roughly 14,800 men, down from its original complement of nearly 19,400 in 1941, and its roster of 17,200 in June of 1944.[35] This graphically illustrates the uneven quality and strength of German divisions at this late date, even *Waffen–SS* divisions. Maier states that when the attack was launched it was numerically at half-strength; in other words, the already depleted divisions had only half of their remaining combat power available, or one-quarter of their authorized strength.[36]

In some ways *Totenkopf* was in much better shape, but there were still troubling shortages. Isaev and Kolomiets give the division a strength of 97 AFVs of all types, including *Sturmgeschütze* and *Jagdpanzers*, without adding 11 of the division's organic *Tiger* company that were operational. No truck totals are available for *Totenkopf*, but while the division was quite strong in some areas, it lacked other basic combat equipment that hampered its fighting strength, such as having less than 50 percent of the machine guns authorized and a paltry total of 69 ready *SPWs*.

---

[32], Klapdor, Ewald, *Viking Panzers* (Mechanicsburg: Stackpole, 2011). p. 387. The inventory for 1 January lists the combat ready AFVs at 10 Mark IVs, 4 Sturmgeschutz and 22 Panthers; all in all, about a weak battalion, or two line companies. Klapdor agrees with these totals for tanks, but does not list the 4 sturmgeschutz. He puts total tank strength at 20% of authorized.

[33] http://*Wiking*-ruf.com/*Wiking*'timetable.html#1945 (Accessed 17 February, 2012).

[34] *Schutzenpanzerwagen*, shorted to *SPW*. Literally 'armored protection car.' The Allied equivalent was the American M3 half-track.

[35] Even in Wiking's manpower strength sources vary widely, from the number listed here, up to a whopping 17,425 seen in other sources such as Isaev and Kolomiets' 'Tomb of the Panzerwaffe'.

[36] Maier, *Drama Between Budapest and Vienna*, p. 17.

Manpower is confusing, with Isaev and Kolomiets claiming an identical total for *Totenkopf* as for *Wiking*, 17,425, but without any mention of where these numbers come from. Do they include the attached battalions of *I./SS–Freiwillige–Panzergrenadier Regiment 23 Norge* (*Wiking*), *I./SS–Panzergrenadier Regiment 24 Westland* (*Totenkopf*) and the respective battalions of *SS–Regiment Ney*. If not, that would put both division's total manpower at close to 20,000, a staggering number. Given that mobility for *Totenkopf* was listed at 80 percent, the division would have to have nearly a full complement of trucks to achieve such a rating. However, if the 17,425 figure includes all attached units, with a divisional strength of around 15,000, then the mobility rating seems quite plausible.

At 17:00 hours on January 1, 1945, the headquarters of *5. SS–Panzer Division Wiking* had all units on the telephone and ready to attack on schedule at 1930 hours. The night was misty and cold with a temperature falling through the low 20s Fahrenheit as snow flurries swirled to a landscape already covered by deep snow. The roads were frozen solid making armored operations treacherous but feasible.

The units scheduled to participate in the attack had their northern flank hinged on the Danube River west of Gran (Eztergom), fanning back in an arc toward the southwest and west. On the north bank of the Danube, the LVII *Panzerkorps* was charged with protecting the Gran front. That corps had its own headquarters directly west of Esztergom and the Hungarian St. Lazlo Division facing the Danube directly south of the corps headquarters; then the *96. Infanterie Division* echeloned behind and west of the St. Lazlo Division, poised to cross the river when the attack began. South of the Danube came *3. SS–Panzer Division Totenkopf*, with I/*SS–Regiment Ney* attached ; *5. SS–Panzer Division Wiking* Viking, reinforced the previous November by the addition of the *I./SS– Freiwillige–Panzergrenadier Regiment 23 Norge*, commanded by Knight's Cross Winner *SS–*

Hauptsturmführer Fritz Vogt[37], as well as the *I./SS–Panzergrenadier Regiment 24 Danmark*[38] and *II/SS–Regiment Ney*; Kampfgruppe Bieber, named for Major General Martin Bieber, the commander of *271. Volksgrenadier Division* and formed from bits and pieces of that unit along with two Hungarian *SS* infantry battalions (which ones?); *Kampfgruppe Pape*, which comprised remnants from some army armored regiments, including the staff of *Panzer Division Felldherrnhalle*, the reconnaissance battalion from *1. Panzer Division*, the first elements of *711. Infanterie Division* would enter the theater the next day and would be attached to the *kampfgruppe*, with the whole commanded by former *Feldherrnhalle* officer Gunther Pape[39]; and, finally, *Kampfgruppe Philipp*, which was *Panzer Regiment 1* from *1. Panzer Division* reinforced by the orphan *I./Panzer Regiment 24* and *I./Artillery Regiment 73*; *1. Panzer Division* was the oldest *panzer* formation in the Wehrmacht[40]. Taken all together, the assault group for *Konrad I* was theoretically quite a powerful force. The primary Russian formation opposing *Konrad I* was 4th Guards Army, with other

[37] This veteran unit had initially been comprised large of Norwegians, thus the Regiment's honorific title Norge, and had been intended as one of the two regiments for 11th SS *Panzergrenadier* Division Nordland. The I. battalion had become separated from its parent unit, however; ruinous losses on more than one occasion meant the battalion had been rebuilt the previous year with an infusion of some 600 Austrians, Volga-Deutsche and Romanian Volks-Deutsch. There were also a few Norwegians still in the battalion, although fewer than 40 by this point.

[38] According to Richard Landwehr in Siegrunen #77, p. 21-22, the two battalions were virtual twins, with strengths in November, 1944, of 600 men each. Fighting in the trenches near Warsaw cost them a few casualties, but also exposed the green troops to battle.

[39] As with almost every facet of the fighting in Hungary and Austria during 1945, sources vary as to the composition of this kampfgruppe. Isaev and Kolomiets do not list Kampfgruppe Bieber at all, and assign the bulk of 271st Volksgrenadier Division to Kampfgruppe Pape, along with all elements of Panzer Grenadier Division Felldherrnhalle outside of Budapest, as well as 208th Panzer Battalion (p. 23).

[40] In his history of Wiking, Strassner has this lineup essentially the same, but with Kamfgruppe Pape sandwiched between two other kampfgruppen, Bieber and Philipp.

armies close by acting as de facto reserves. The *Luftwaffe* gave what support that it could but was badly outnumbered by the Red Air Force; 4th Guards Army had 953 aircraft devoted solely for its use.[41]

The attack was designed for mutual support between the assault divisions. *96. Infanterie Division* would cross the Danube in assault boats and land behind the Russian positions around Dunaalmas, outflanking them and clearing the river road for 3d *SS Panzer* Division *Totenkopf*, which would drive east from the area around Komarom. *96. Infanterie Division* would then drive due east to threaten Gran (Esztergom). Once *Totenkopf* had reached Bajot it would turn south and drive on Many, with *5. SS Panzer Division Wiking* moving more to the southeast in the direction of the important road junction of Bicske, where the main highway connecting Vienna and Budapest intersected other highways moving east-west. Capturing Many and Bicske would be a lynch-pin on which to anchor further advances, with the axis of attack then turning due east toward Budapest. At their back, Pierik says the crucial city of Komarom and its oil refineries were screened by some 'Gneisenau' fortress battalions and *Panzer Bataillon 208*, a veteran unit with 31 *Panzer* IVs and 17 *Jagdpanzers* IV/70As, making it a significant force[42].

As shown by *5. SS–Panzer Division Wiking* being ordered to immediately assemble for an attack as soon as it detrained in Hungary, the various new formations ordered to relieve Budapest were not showing up on schedule or with any regularity. The rail transport system was no longer up to the task of such massive simultaneous deployments and the fuel situation ruled out long road marches. Yet, with time of the essence, the assault units would have to begin their attack before they were fully assembled; later arriving components would be fed into the fighting piecemeal,

---

[41] Maier, *Drama Between Budapest and Vienna*, p. 17.
[42] Isaev and Kolomiets have *Panzer Battalion 208* attached to *Kampfgruppe Pape*.

nearly a guarantee of failure for German forces that were attacking a superior enemy in the first place.

Therefore, to have any chance whatsoever of breaking through, a diversionary attack in the direction of Osi, a small town about 10 miles west of Stuhlweissenburg, was ordered to proceed even before all of the units assigned were in the vicinity. One poorly thought out attack was to be preceded by another. Regaining the strip of land between Lakes Balaton and Velence would give the southern flank protection, and Stuhlweissenburg was the key to that objective, so the attack on Osi could have had tangible benefits beyond mere diversionary value if the forces committed were strong enough for such a mission. Regardless of their strength or weakness, however, Balck really had no other choice except to try a ruse de guerre to draw Russian reserves away from the schwerpunkt of *Konrad I*; his attacking formations were too under-strength to batter their way through.

Until all of his units arrived on the battlefield the main attack would not have enough weight to break through to Budapest, but because rail transport had become so iffy a commander could not count on a given unit being available until it actually arrived. Time was passing and Balck had to do something. Led by *1. Panzer Division* of *III. Panzerkorps*, which had just received *panzer* reinforcements, the attack recaptured the little village of Osi, but when the tanks withdrew the village could not be held and it was lost again. Nevertheless, the feint had the desired effect and 4th Guards Army expected an attack on its left wing, not its right.

Hitler's choice of a northerly attack route for *Konrad I*, endorsed by Balck, led partly through the Vértes and Pilis Mountains and was problematic given that the most powerful units were *Panzer* divisions; the gamble was that Balck's *panzers* could use the mountain roads to seize strongpoints before the Soviets could set up an adequate defense. Speed was the key to success. Otherwise, those *panzers* would be forced to advance over a landscape dominated by steep, thickly forested slopes cut by frequent deep ravines, where even footpaths were hard to find. Aside from being very slow going for heavy vehicles, where movement was even possible, a cross-country advance would leave them vulnerable to all manner of anti-tank traps and gun emplacements. *Kampfgruppe Pape* would drive on the southern (or right) flank, with *5. SS Panzer Division Wiking* on its left flank driving straight through the mountains. *3. SS–Panzer Division Totenkopf* was on *Wiking's* left flank and would initially follow the valley of the Danube before turning south before reaching Gran and driving behind the units facing *Wiking*. After crossing the river in assault boats the *96. Infanterie Division* would also drive east along the southern bank of the Danube, but when *Totenkopf* veered south the *96. Infanterie Division* would continue east. Screening the Russian occupied city of Esztergom due east of *96. Infanterie Division* was the Hungarian St. Lazlo Division of *LVII Panzerkorps*.

Aside from the feint at Osi, Balck was hoping for the same element of surprise that made the 1940 attack on France through the Ardennes successful, in other words, that the Soviets would never expect an offensive through country that was so disadvantageous for tanks. The Germans also had Soviet over-confidence on their side. As Strassner says, "this was at a time when the Commanders-in-Chief of both Ukrainian Fronts believed that *Heeresgruppe Süd* was no longer capable of mounting offensive operations following the blows it had suffered in December."[43] Marshals Tolbukhin and Malinovsky both knew that *IV. SS–Panzerkorps* had moved south, but not where, and did not view it as a threat to attack; by Russian Front standards one under-strength *panzerkorps* was not a major threat[44]. Complacency took the place of caution,

[43] Strassner, Peter, *European Volunteers: The 5. SS Panzer Division Wiking* (Winnipeg: J.J. Fedorowicz, 2006), p. 311.
[44] At least one source indicates that Russian intelligence knew Wiking had moved into Hungary, but not *Totenkopf*.

to the point where Isaev & Kolomietz report anti-tank mines were stacked beside the road instead of being emplaced.[45]

Indeed, along the front of 4th Guards Army some divisions only went over to the defensive on December 30th and did not even have a continuous trench system dug when the attack came. Making matters worse for the Russians, 4th Guards Army believed that if a German attack came, it would be on the Army's left flank near Stuhlweissenburg, not on the right, and deployed its forces accordingly; Balck's feint merely reinforced this belief.

Russians

For 1945, STAVKA focused on overrunning Hungary, as much of Austria as possible, and the former Czechoslovakia before the Western Allies could get there. Whatever agreements Stalin had made with Churchill and Roosevelt, he would only keep his words when dealing from a position of strength. Consequently, the war in Hungary and the Balkans was at the tail end of the Russian western front priority list.

Although many of their units were at half strength or less, the Russians held several powerful units were as reserves, partially offsetting 4th Guards Army's dangerously weak right flank. On 1 January, the 18th Tank Corp listed 110 T-34s, 18 SU-122 and 15 SU-85 self-propelled guns on its rolls. Part of the Corps was still in the line near Dunaalmasi along the Danube, while the rest was in reserve and could be used either against breakouts from Budapest, or any relief attacks. Also available was the full-strength 1st Guards Mechanized Corps, released from STAVKA reserve and newly arrived on Christmas Eve in

[45] Isayev & Kolomiets, *Defeat of 6. SS–Panzerarmee*, p. 30.

Hungary. Unfortunately for the Russians, the Corps had trained on T-34s but were issued Lend-Lease American Shermans and had no time to re-train on the foreign tank. Three self-propelled artillery regiments equipped with brand new SU-100s were attached; despite its lack of training, the Corps was a powerful force.

46th Army was involved in the fighting at Budapest, but three of its divisions were west of the capital, either as reserves or to block a breakout attempt. 86th Guards Rifle Division was south of Gran (Eztergom), then the battered 2nd Guards Mechanized Corps[46] and finally 49th Guards Rifle Division was west of Budapest clearing the forests there. None of those three divisions was in reserve against a German attack from outside the capital, but likewise none were engaged in combat and so could be easily redeployed.

Despite the disparity in ground forces the German commanders on the spot were confident. Not only did they believe in their own competence and the fighting prowess of their commands, but the situation in the air was better than might be expected. The *Luftwaffe* Air Fleet operating in Hungary, *Luftflotte 4*, had 588 combat aircraft of all types[47], including 49 transports, with almost half the total ground attack aircraft. Among those were the JU-87G Stuka tank busters of *Schlachtgeschwader 2*, commanded by the legendary Hans Ulrich Rudel[48]. This total is somewhat misleading, however, since all of the transport aircraft and most of the level bombers, mainly *Heinkel HE-111s*, would be dedicated to supplying the Budapest garrison. Not only would they not be available to

---

[46] In Russian military terminology, a Corps was the equivalent of a German Division, or even a regiment. Thus, a depleted 2nd Guards Mechanized Corps was the size of a German battalion, with 31 tanks and 17 self-propelled guns.

[47] This figure is for 10 January.

[48] Two of Rudel's three Gruppen would be transferred north before long, including him.

support ground operations, but their losses over Budapest would be ruinous.

The air component of 3rd Ukrainian Front, 17th Air Army, had the anemic total of 865 operational planes of all types, with nearly half of those IL-2 Ilyushin Sturmovik ground attack aircraft. Added to these were the 642 operational planes of 5th Air Fleet, attached to 2nd Ukrainian Front.[49] The Germans were therefore outnumbered in the air about 2.3-1, but plane for plane and pilot for pilot, the *Luftwaffe* retained its qualitative advantage over the Red Air Force, which made this a very favorable ratio compared to anywhere else on the Eastern Front. The *Luftwaffe* could no longer control the air but it could still contest it.

Wöhler went to *IV. SS–Panzerkorps* headquarters at Acs, some 8 kilometers southwest of Komárom, and met with the command staffs of *Totenkopf*, *Wiking* and *96. Infanterie Division*, all of whom believed they could achieve their mission; Balck was not at the meeting. *5. SS Panzer Division Wiking* had an initial target of Agostyan, some 4 kilometers east of Tata; the division was then supposed to speed to Biscke and seize the high ground before the Russians could react, thus seizing access to the highway leading straight into Budapest. *SS–Panzergrenadier Regiment 9 Germania* would deploy its 1st and 3rd battalions on either side of the road leading southeast for the initial attack. *I./SS–Panzergrenadier Regiment 23 Norge* would advance on the division's southern flank, starting in the area near the village of Boldogaszonypuszta.

The weather was bitterly cold with deep snow covering the land, but initially Balck's plan worked. In open country the snow reflected light from the full moon and made movement easier for the attackers,

[49] Isayev & Kolomiets, *Defeat of 6. SS–Panzerarmee*, p. 25.

although the primitive mountain roads were icy and dangerous. The attack of *IV. SS–Panzerkorps* began at 1930 hours from the area around Nazsaly-Tata without an artillery barrage which caught the Soviets completely by surprise. Hitler had ordered the strictest security for the move of *IV. SS–Panzerkorps* to the south, and while the Soviets had noted the Corps entrance into the theater, they did not find the well-concealed assembly areas and did not see the attack coming; even at this very late date, then, the German flair for organization allowed the transfer of an entire *Panzerkorps* from one section of the front to another in haste and in secret, after which they could hit the Red Army with a nasty tactical surprise attack.

Contact was made on *Wiking's* southern flank by the Fritz Vogt's orphaned battalion from Norge near Boldogaszonypuszta before midnight. Initial gains were encouraging to the Germans, although there was a short delay getting through the initial defenses because of a heavy minefield; it was after midnight before the road was cleared. The front of 80th Guards Rifle Division was broken and the Germans began moving toward the division's headquarters at Agostyan, while *Totenkopf* began moving east along the river.

Meanwhile, on *Wiking's* left flank, things could not have gone better. Even as *Wiking* was beginning its drive on Tarjan and Bicske, the combat elements of *96. Infanterie Division* that had arrived moved a short distance along the north bank of the Danube, crossed the river using more than 100 assault boats and established two bridgeheads on the south bank in the rear of the XXXI Guards Rifle Corps near Dunaalmas, in the area of 4th Guards Rifle Division. The river in that area was some 600-800 yards wide and the southern bank was dotted with industrial sites, with ridges up to 750 feet coming close to the water; a narrow strip of flat ground, perhaps a mile wide, quickly gave way to cliffs. Within that small area were a road and railroad that paralleled the river. The nighttime crossing was impressive but not without problems; strong currents and floating ice prevented some boats from crossing on time. The elements of *Grenadier-Regiment 287* that made it across hunkered down near Nyergesujfalu and waited for the rest of their comrades to make it across. A ferry system was rigged to bring more troops across, a perilous undertaking without resistance, but soon enough Russian artillery shells started hitting all around the bridgehead and the crossing point. Nevertheless, before long the rest of the and most of the *Grenadier-Regiment 283* Grenadier Regiments were over the river and attacking the nearby villages. After a short but vicious firefight the *Grenadier-Regiment 283* took Sutto while the *Grenadier Regiment 287* liberated Nyergesujfalu, and before long the ferry had been strengthened enough to bring heavy weapons across. Just in time the 75 mm PAKs from *Panzerjäger Abteilung 196* wear brought to bear as Russian counterattacks threatened to retake both villages[50]. Soon after *I./Artillerie Regiment 196* was also in the bridgehead.

Totenkopf's mission was to drive east and southeast, in a fanning pattern. With most of its armor still on trains to the north, the division had to rely on the *panzergrenadiers* on hand, although the *9. Kompanie* of *SS–Panzer Regiment 3* moved straight down the river road toward Dunallmas. There it was stopped cold by dug-in Russians and called for help.

The local Hungarians rejoiced as the Germans marched back into their towns and told grisly stories of Russian abuses, with women and girls repeatedly raped and every moment filled with terror of sudden death.

Once established, *96. Infanterie Division* threatened either an attack toward Eztergom or to turn

---

[50] This was probably the 170th Tank Brigade of 18th Tank Corps

southeast with the bend of the Danube to attack the rear of the Soviet 46th and 4th Guards Armies, but only if the ridges overlooking the road could be secured. If they could achieve this, more or less following as the Danube turned south toward Budapest, it would threaten all Soviet forces north of Lake Balaton with being cut off. *3. SS–Panzer Division Totenkopf* drove east and shortly engaged the Russian forces blocking the river road, pinning them in place as *96. Infanterie Division* moved in behind them. On *Wiking's* right flank, *III. Panzerkorps* launched its attack at 2030 hours and moved down the Felsogalla gap and retook Banhida, near Tatabanya, although elements of the corps were delayed by extensive minefields. All along the line tactical surprise was achieved.

Since 5 December, 1944, *Schwere–Panzer Abteilung 509* had been receiving new *Panzer Mk. VII 'Tiger IIs'* straight from the factory. On New Year's Day the battalion received the last of 45 machines and began preparing for battle. The battalion was protected from air attack by eight *Flakpanzer IVs*, the rarely seen but much-coveted *'Wirblewind'* (Whirlwind) mounting 4 20 mm anti-aircraft cannon in an open turret, on a *Panzer Mk. IV* chassis. Fast enough to keep up with any *panzer*, the guns could provide a devastating volume of fire against low-flying aircraft or ground targets.

The combat value of this unit cannot be overstated. The *Tiger II* was the penultimate representation of German firepower on the battlefield. When facing the enemy the *Tiger II* was virtually invulnerable to Russian tank-mounted and antitank weapons. No Russian vehicle was safe from the fearsome *88mm Kampfwagenkanone (KwK) 43*, with a caliber length of 71 that generated kinetic energy capable of penetrating anything it faced.

Being a battalion meant that *Schwere–Panzer Abteilung 509* had no organic infantry or artillery support. However, when attached to a properly equipped support regiment or division, at its full strength of 45 machines *Schwere–Panzer Abteilung 509* instantly transformed that unit into one of the most powerful in the German Order of Battle.

Assuming they had enough fuel to operate.

The War Situation on 1 January, 1945

The War Situation in the West

To understand the context of the operations of *Heeresgruppe Süd*, it is helpful to see them as part of the European War as a whole. And so the occasional foray into events that impacted the decisions made concerning that army group might be useful. Throughout the narrative they will be displayed at the beginning of the Chapter.

Following up the Ardennes Offensive, *Unternehmen Bodenplatte* was launched against Allied Airfields in Western Europe. Simultaneously, *Unternehmen Nordwind* kicked off as *Generaloberst* Johannes von Blaskowitz's *Heeresgruppe G* attacked the US Seventh Army in Alsace and Lorraine, forming the so-called Colmar Pocket. The Americans retreated, although General Dwight D. Eisenhower, commander-in-chief of Allied forces in Europe, ordered Strasbourg to be held after the leader of the Free French, General Charles de Gaulle, expressed concern that the loss of the city would affect French morale. The fighting was bitter. It cost the US 15,600 casualties, and the Germans, 25,000, but in the end it accomplished nothing.

Likewise, *Unternehmen Bodenplatte* backfired. Launched as a surprise *Luftwaffe* attack to temporarily cripple the Allied air forces, instead it led to substantial German losses that could not be replaced. Not in aircraft; the Germans actually had plenty of fighter aircraft. What they did *not* have in anything like sufficient quantities were fuel and trained pilots. The attack certainly took the Allies by surprise, and inflicted upwards of 250 aircraft destroyed, but the cost bankrupted the *Luftwaffe*. More than 150 pilots never returned, a devastating blow to an air force already short on aircrew and unable to properly train new ones because of the fuel crisis. The consequences of this failure rippled across the *Reich* as more and more of

51

the dwindling fighter units had to be committed to defend the remaining industrial areas, thereby giving Russian and Allied aircraft free reign over the German front lines. Only occasionally did the outnumbered *Luftwaffe* rise to defend the troops below.

The War Situation in the East

To the north of the Hungarian battlefields the Red Army launched attacks against *Heeresgruppe Mitte* in Czechoslovakia. The German-held area contained the last foreign industrial resources under the control of the Third *Reich*, which made them vital for continuing the war in any meaningful way. The Soviet Fronts between them had 853,000 men, 9986 guns, 590 tanks, and 1400 combat aircraft. German forces totaled 550,000 men, 5000 guns, and 700 combat aircraft. Given the Soviet indifference to casualties, and despite German fortifications and resistance, the Red Army made good progress.

An entry in the War Diary of *Heeresgruppe Süd* for 1 January, 1945: "In the sector between Lake Balaton and the Danube the enemy pushed forward his attack to open the Mor defile with concentrated forces and was again repelled with heavy losses. On the other fronts north and south of the Danube, the enemy continued to regroup and concentrate for an attack...Renewed massed attacks against Budapest focused against the Eastern side. They were again repelled by the garrison in heavy fighting lasting the entire day. Local enemy penetrations were sealed off."[51] These attacks were launched by elements of 4th Guards Army and were not part of a general offensive, but were meant to pinch off a German salient around Mor that could potentially threaten Russian rear areas either to the north or south.

[51] Maier, *Between Budapest and Vienna*, pp 16.

As fuel supplies dwindled, transport by rail and water grew in importance. In summer of 1944, the British launched Operation Gardener to interrupt river traffic on the Danube by sowing mines dropped from heavy bombers. The danger to the Germans became so acute that on November 23, 1944, *Minensuchstaffel 3* from *Minensuch Gruppe 2*, or 'Mine Search Group,' began operating out of Tulln/Langenlebarn Airfield west of Vienna. The aircraft were standard *Junkers JU-52 3M* trimotor transports, equipped with a magnetic ring underneath. Flying low over water containing magnetic mines, the field projected by the ring would detonate the mines.

By 1945 the myth of unlimited Russian manpower reserves was being exposed as fantasy. Fourth Guards Army was well under its authorized strength. According to Isaev and Kolomiets, "the average numerical strength of a rifle division of the 4th Guards Army was 5,386 men. Of the 4th Guards Army's 14 rifle divisions, 11 had a numerical strength of between 5,000 and 6,000 men, which was barely half of their table strength."[52] Russian divisions had a much smaller percentage of their personnel in support services, such as supply or administration, yet even so the majority of the front-line units in 2nd and 3rd Ukrainian Fronts were under-strength, in some cases worse than their German counterparts. The advantage, however, was that the Russians had a lot more divisions, so even in their depleted state they outnumbered their enemy.

Lend Lease

No discussion of the war on the Eastern Front in 1945 would be complete without mentioning the Lend Lease given to the Soviet Union. STAVKA prioritized the capture of Berlin and Czechoslovakia and directed their

---

[52] Isaev, Alexei and Kolomiets, Maksim, *Tomb of the Panzerwaffe, The Defeat of the 6. SS–Panzerarmee in Hungary 1945* (Havertown: Casemate, 2018), pp 23.

best forces to those fronts. Malinovsky's 2nd Ukrainian Front benefitted from this more than did Tolbukhin's 3rd Ukrainian Front, but neither had the ranks of their armored and mechanized units filled out with such a high percentage of the latest Russian tanks or aircraft. Thus, much Lend Lease equipment wound up in Slovakia, Hungary, and the Balkans.

The numbers are staggering.

Armored Fighting Vehicles (AFVs) Sent and Received

Country	Model	Sent	Received
British	Matilda IIA*	084	918
British	Valentine II/III/IV/V/IX/X	782	3,332
British	Valentine Bridgelayer	25	24
British	Churchill III/IV	301	
British	Cromwell	6	6
British	Tetrarch	20	19
British	Universal Carrier	2,560	2,560
American	M3A1 Stuart	1,676	1,233[A]
American	M5A1 Stuart	5	5
American	M24 Chaffee	2	2
American	M2A1 (medium tank)	few	Few
American	M3A3/M3A5 Lee/Grant	1,386	1,386[B]
American	M4A2 Sherman (75mm)	2,007	2,007[1]
American	M4A2 Sherman (76mm)	2,095	2,095[1]
American	M10 Wolverine	52	52
American	M18 Hellcat	5	5
American	M26 Pershing	1	1
American	M31 ARV	115	115
American	M15A1 MGMC	100	100
American	M17 MGMC	1,000	1,000

Country	Model	Sent	Received
American	T48 (Soviet name SU-57)	650	650
American	M2 halftrack	342	342
American	M3 halftrack	2	2
American	M5 halftrack	421	421
American	M9 halftrack	413	413
American	T16	96	96
American	M3A1 Scout	3,340	3,340
American	LVT	5	5

Note:

During transit, the following were lost to German interdiction or accidents:

- 417 M3 & M4 tanks
- 443 Stuarts
- 54 halftracks
- 228 Scouts
- 320 Valentines
- 43 Churchills
- 252 Matildas
- 224 Universal Carriers

The War Situation in Hungary and Slovakia

"By order of the *Führer*, the city of Budapest is to be defended to the last house."[53]

On Christmas Eve, 1944, units from the Russian 18th Tank Corps and the 6th Guards Tank Army met near the city of Esztergom, Gran in German, at the confluence of the Gran and the Danube Rivers, thus closing the ring around a surrounded Budapest, the political, social and emotional heart of Hungary. Trapped in the city were some 70,000 or so German and Hungarian soldiers from numerous shattered units who became its defenders, with the core of the defense

[53] Maier, *Between Budapest and Vienna*, pp 14.

built around *IX. SS-Waffen-Gebirgs-Armeekorps der SS.* In a strange quirk of history, *IX. SS-Waffen-Gebirgs-Armeekorps der SS* did not command any mountain troops, even though it had been established as a command formation for the two Croatian *SS* Mountain Divisions, *13. Waffen-Gebirgs Division of the SS Handschar* and *23. Waffen-Gebirgs Division Kama,*[54] nor did it command any Croatians, but it did have two *Waffen–SS* cavalry divisions, *8. SS Kavallerie-Division Florian Geyer* and *22. SS Freiwillige-Kavallerie Division Maria Theresa*[55]. As quoted above, Hitler ordered the city defended to the last bullet and man; no breakout would be allowed.

As the New Year began the Russians held only a loose grip on the approaches to Budapest from the west. Fighting within the city's eastern outskirts was heavy, but costly for both sides. The trapped Axis forces knew they could expect no mercy from the Russians and fought with vicious determination.

For his part Stalin's patience, never long, had begun to wear thin as 1945 dawned. He want Budapest in Russian hands and he wanted it *now*. Thus, the pressure on Marshal Malinovsky to capture the city was immense.

Since the Soviet counter-offensive near Moscow in December, 1941, Hitler had routinely forbade his forces from retreating, especially when great cities were involved, Stalingrad being the best known example. Aside from this rigid and counter-productive stubbornness, however, were there other factors that made holding Budapest at all costs worthwhile?

The disparity in forces made it clear that holding the city would be very difficult, if not impossible.

---

[54] Both *13.* and *23. Waffen-Gebirgs Divisions* had German officers but primarily Muslim soldiers. They were considered to be problematic and unreliable for front line duty, but lack of manpower forced the Germans to commit them for missions unsuited to their composition or leadership.

[55] Unlike the modern vernacular of the word 'cavalry', the two SS Cavalry Divisions were still formed around large numbers of horsemen.

T-34/85

LINE DRAWINGS OF THE T-34/85

The T-34/85 was the culmination of perhaps the most influential tank design in history. The 85mm main gun could rip through most German *panzers* at a considerable distance, and the upgraded armor kept the T-34/85 fighting after damage that would have destroyed its predecessors. It was fast and agile, but many of the defects remained, including a balky transmission and no radios in most of the units. This gave a command and control advantage to the Germans until the final days of the war. Even so, the T-34/85 represented the Russian way of war better than any other machine, namely, to overwhelm your opponent with firepower and sheer numbers. High casualties could be tolerate for victory.

Perhaps Buda, on the west bank of the Danube, could be held, but Pest on the eastern bank could not. Eliminating the Soviet bridgehead over the Danube south of Budapest made sound military sense, but trying to hold all of Budapest did not. Then why

commit Germany's dwindling resources to a mission
that seemed doomed from the start?

Map 1

The war situation for *Heeresgruppe Süd* at the time of *Konrad I.*

The *Führer* intended that Budapest would become like a rock in a flood, an island of resistance that the Red Army might flow around. Until the city was either relieved or captured it would continue to threaten the rear of any further Soviet advances and tie down large numbers of Russian and Rumanian troops. Moreover, action elsewhere on the Eastern Front was relatively light during that December, and while German intelligence identified numerous danger points along the line where the Red Army was clearly building for offensives, Hitler did what Hitler had been doing for at least several years: ignore reality and insist that his insights were correct, while citing that only he had all of the facts to make a strategic decision such as holding Budapest. And this is what he did. Whatever his real intentions were, and there will be more discussion of that later in this narrative, it was impossible for anyone to argue that holding the Hungarian oil fields was mandatory if Germany was to continue fighting.

The reader would do well to remember that every decision the German leadership made in 1945 centered around the availability of fuel. Not only had the Allied strategic bombing campaign devastated Germany's synthetic fuel industry, but attrition to the logistics system, railroads in particular, further complicated the distribution of what fuel was available. Making the situation worse, as 1945 approached the loss of the Ploesti oil fields meant that Germany's major source of natural oil was gone.

Whether or not Germany should not continue fighting, while obvious to all but the most fanatical Nazis, was a topic of conversation that would get a person shot very quickly if heard by the wrong ears. Some officers *did* bring this up to Hitler, usually with negative consequences for their careers, and sometimes for their health. Hitler dismissed all of it.

Another point to keep in the forefront was Hitler's complete disregard for any concerns other than victory. Whatever agony the garrison and population of

Budapest endured was of little interest to him, and therefore to sycophantic advisors such as Bormann or Goebbels. Budapest mattered because it would be the lynchpin of a German line established on the Danube and "it was clear to the Germans that by sacrificing Budapest they were protecting Vienna." Thus, Hitler's supreme representative in Hungary, Edwin Veesenmayer, declared that it mattered not to him if 'the city was destroyed ten times over if Vienna could be defended.'"[56] Austria had to be held for economic reasons, at the least, where oil refineries and armaments plants were critical to the staggering German war effort.

Thus was the stage set for a campaign which most readers in the west have never read about, or heard of in more than a passing reference. That Hitler ordered the bulk of Germany's *panzer* forces to fight in *Heeresgruppe Süd*, whose mission was at least partly to protect the capital of Hitler's homeland, Austria, likely has ulterior motives we will never fully understand.

What the Germans called a *Heeresgruppe* the Russians labeled a 'Front.' As the Russians pushed west toward Austria, two Fronts carried the fighting into Western Hungary, 2nd Ukrainian Front commanded by Marshal of the Soviet Union Rodion Yakovlevich Malinovsky, and 3rd Ukrainian Front under the command of Marshal of the Soviet Union Fyodor Ivanovich Tolbukhin. Both men were considered extremely talented officers and had worked well together for quite some time. As the fighting moved west over the course of January, February and March, both Fronts bent to the northwest as the Balkans narrowed leading to the base of the Italian peninsula. This had the effect of pushing the advancing Russians northwest, toward Vienna. Surrounding Budapest,

[56] Guillemot, p. 32

however, required some of Tolbukhin's forces to turn due north after crossing the Danube, thereby confusing boundaries between the two fronts. This overlapping would never be entirely straightened out.

The strengths of both Fronts was their armor. Russian operational strength totals broke down this way:

- ➤ XVIII Tank Corps - 120 T-34s, 19 JS-2s and 11 SU-85s.
- ➤ I Guards Mechanized Corps - 62 SU-100s and 184 M4A2 Shermans.
- ➤ II Guards Mechanized Corps – 55 T-34s, 9 JS-2s and 11 SU-85s.
- ➤ VII Mechanized Corps – 66 JS-2s, 12 SU-76s, 14 SU-85s and 10 SU-100s.
- ➤ V Guards Cavalry Corps – 2 T-34s and 12 SU-76s.
- ➤ XXIII Tank Corps – 174 JS-2s and 39 ISU-152s.

These totals show what the Germans were up against during January. Most of the Russian armor was committed to combat in Budapest, where they suffered heavy losses. The assault guns/tank destroyers proved both very effective in urban combat, and very vulnerable.

1 January, Monday

By the first day of 1945, Budapest was a smoke-choked maze of rubble where desperate soldiers of both sides fought for clumps of broken masonry and burned out cars, anything that might provide cover from enemy fire. Danger lurked everywhere in a city where daily life had become a clawing fight to stay alive amid crumbling ruins, raging fires and rampaging soldiers who shot first and only later worried about *who* they'd shot. Death came in many forms as shrapnel and rock splinters filled the air from exploding mortar and artillery shells, bullets of all calibers whizzed about, strafing Red Air Force fighter-bombers aimed bombs and bullets at anything that moved, masonry crumbled, jagged bits of metal rained down from anti-aircraft bursts, mines and booby-traps took their toll on the curious and desperate alike, not to mention starvation and hypothermia and illness. Budapest was Hell and Hell was everything Dante had imagined it to be.

The topography dictated much of the fighting to come. Pest was on the flat eastern shore while Buda had many large, craggy hills that made excellent defensive positions. On that 1 January the Red Army was slogging forward in Pest; during daylight the Russians captured the Eastern railway station, paying for each small advance in blood. Heavy artillery fire accompanied every attack and despite fierce resistance the noose around the city inexorably tightened. Buda, with its hills and fortifications, was a tougher nut to crack.

Exactly what German and Hungarian forces were trapped inside doomed Budapest? Within the besieged city, *IX SS Waffen-Gebirgskorps* counted a number of impressive sounding formations in its order of battle for the New Year. The Hungarian 10th, 12th and 23rd Infantry Divisions and the Hungarian 1st Armored Division, as well as the German *271. Volksgrenadier Division*; what remained of Major General

Schmidthuber's veteran *13. Panzer Division*; the remnant of Lt. *Oberst* Wolff's *Panzergrenadier Division Felldherrnhalle*;[57] and both *Waffen–SS* Cavalry Divisions, *8. Kavallerie Division Florian Geyer* and *22. Freiwillige-Kavallerie Division der SS Maria Theresa* , complete with their horses.[58] On paper it comprised nine divisions total, with various smaller formations too, such as *SS Polizei Regiment 6*. The combined manpower of the German units alone should have approached at least 70,000. The reality was otherwise. After the brutal fighting east of the Danube the German and Hungarian units had little strength left, with the actual total of German inside Budapest numbering a paltry 33,000 men, with few heavy weapons or AFVs. Pierik puts the number of AFVs of all types at around 70,[59] and the total garrison including the Hungarians was only about 70,000.

Guillemot is more specific, giving the strength breakdown as follows: *Panzer Division Felldherrnhalle*, with a strength of 7,255 men with 24 *Panzers* of mixed types Mark IV and *Mark V* Panthers; *13. Panzer Division* with 4,983 men and 17 tanks; *8. SS-Kavallerie Division Florian Geyer* with 8,000 men and 29 tanks; *22. SS-Kavallerie Division Maria Theresa* with 11,345 men and 17 tanks. He lists two battalions as answering directly to fortress headquarters, a *kampfgruppe* from *271. Volksgrenadier-Division* numbering 800 men and a police battalion of 700 men. For the Hungarian units he gives the following order of battle and strength: answering to I Hungarian Corps were the 10th Infantry Division with 7,500 men; 1st Hussars[60] with no

---

[57] Much confusion exists around this unit, with some sources listing is as a Panzer Division. The plan was to combine the division with *Panzer Brigade 109* in Hungary, but fighting in Eastern Hungary prevented that from happening before the division was committed to battle. Complicating things further, *13. Panzer Division* also had the honorific title *Felldherrnhalle'*.

[58] The horses would quickly become a significant source of food for the troops, since fodder was not available in meaningful quantities and the animals were going to die anyway.

[59] Pierik, p. 136

[60] This was a cavalry formation.

Map 2

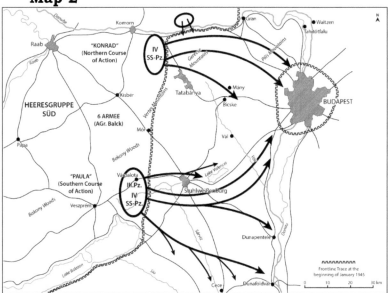

The two options for *Unternehmen Konrad I.* In the end, the norther option could be launched days sooner than the southern option, so that was the choice.

strength given; 1st Armored Division with 5,000 men and 7 tanks, mixed between Turans[61] and Mark IVs; an unnamed reserve division with 4,000 men, with a number of independent battalions answering directly to I Hungarian Infantry Corps Headquarters, including 600 parachutists, 1,000 Hungarian Air Force personnel, 1,500 gendarmes and 1,000 university students organized into two battalions.[62] Guillemot does not mention the Hungarian 12th[63] or 23rd Infantry Divisions, or any smaller units, nor does he give specifics for German tank types except for *Felldherrnhalle*, but it can be assumed that this means AFVs of all types, including *Jagdpanzers* and *Stürmgeschütze*. Pierik, in turn, does not mention the 1st Hussars. Guillemot's total for German and Hungarian AFVs is 94 instead of Pierik's 70. Neither source lists any Tiger II's. Guillemot also claims only

---

[61] A Hungarian made tank that was obsolete and outmatched by Soviet armor, but had some value against infantry.

[62] Guillemot, p. 34

[63] He does mention this unit later, however, in passing.

20,600 Hungarian troops, for a total Axis garrison of roughly 52,000[64].

Jagdpanzer IV/70

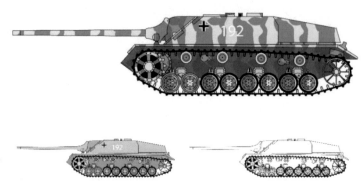

Jagdpanzer IV (SdKfz. 162/1)

Jagdpanzer IV/70

The standard German *Jagdpanzer* of the late war period, it was essentially a *Panzer Mark IV* without the turret. Out of necessity the Germans treated it like it had a turret, considering it a *panzer* for all practical purposes. Armed with the 7.5 cm *KwK L/70* gun and protected with 100 mm frontal and 40 to 50 mm of side armor. Guderian hated the project. Approximately 940 were built.

Artillery was in short supply, with a few precious *Hetzers* and *Hummels*, and some anti-aircraft batteries, both heavy and light. The 20 mm and 37 mm batteries that were grouped on Castle Hill in Buda proved very effective against low-flying Soviet bombers, while the flak detachment for *Maria Theresa* was stationed on the eastern side of the Danube in Pest and therefore wound up being used primarily against infantry and armor; the precious few 88 mm guns were mostly centered on the Adlerberg, Sas-hegy in Hungarian,[65] under the

[64] How, then to reconcile the varying figures for the garrison's strength? Guillemot has the later research, but most historians come closer to agreeing with Pierik.

[65] The prominent hill in south Buda got its name, Eagle Mountain, in 1686 when, after Christian forces had driven the Ottoman Turks from Buda Castle they held a parade on the mountain and were greeted by eagles flying overhead.

command of *Kampfgruppe Portugall* (more info in Landwehr's book on Budapest). Ammunition supplies were limited. There were approximately 800,000 civilians trapped in the city.

Supplies were already running low by New Year's Day, but this was largely the fault of *IX. SS-Waffen-Gebirgskorps* itself. According to Guillemot on December 26, 1944, a supply dump with "300,000 rations and 450 tonnes of ammunition" was captured by the Red Army through a combination of negligence on the part of the Corps command, and a Hungarian officer who was actually a resistance member.[66] Spare parts were in short supply, equipment was breaking down and specialists such as those of *Florian Geyer's SS-Nachtrichten-Abteilung 8* and *SS-Artillerie-Regiment 8* were being used as infantry.[67]

The defenders of Budapest were in a fatal position. But Budapest had been declared a Fortress by Hitler, and the garrison's commander, *SS-SS–Obergruppenführer* Pfeffer-Wildenbruch, had clear cut instructions on his mission. As Pierik puts it, he "had to make sure that the Red Army was forced to fight a fierce battle in every street of Budapest. In this way the Red Army had to concentrate on Budapest so fewer troops were available for the offensives on the oil wells."[68] Pfeffer-Wildenbruch was a veteran who had led *4. SS–Division Polizei* and lost both sons in combat, but despite this he was considered less of a combat commander and more of a political appointee. According to Guillemot, Pfeffer-Wildenbruch was more bureaucrat than combat commander and never left his headquarters bunker during the entire siege.[69] His loyalty to Hitler was absolute, however, especially with his family's well-being dependent on his performance.[70] And while there might be positives to having an

[66] Guillemot, p. 35
[67] Michaelis, p. 106.
[68] Pierik, p. 133.
[69] Guillemot, p. 36
[70]

67

autocratic bureaucrat in charge of a besieged garrison with limited supplies, Pfeffer-Wildenbruch's officious nature did not lend itself well to cooperation with his Hungarian allies. Throughout the siege the top ranking Hungarian commander, General Hindy, would find himself isolated and ignored in the decision making process and would, in turn, fail to pass on information to his German allies. A fractured German high command in Berlin passed on orders to a fractured German command in Budapest, which makes the resistance put up by the Budapest garrison all the more remarkable. Whatever his personal faults, Pfeffer-Wildenbruch's command fought well to the very end. Nor in did he have to be a brilliant tactician or an inspiring leader, they only had to stand and fight for as long as possible. His and his garrison's mission was to buy time for *Heeresgruppe Süd* to organize a defense of the Hungarian oil fields, and while it would be regrettable if they were lost, they were expendable.

But they were not forgotten. Demanding that Budapest be defended to the last man, Hitler was keeping his word that relief attacks were coming. Just as he had done at Stalingrad, at Velikiye Luki, at Cholm and during numerous other sieges, Hitler ordered attacks to break in and relieve the surrounded troops. Whether it made sound military sense or not, the relief attacks would be made.

For some weeks now, from every corner of the shrinking *Reich* military units had been pouring into Hungary aboard some of the relatively few working trains still available to Germany, with more to follow. From Galicia came the *96. Infanterie-Division*; while from Holland the *711. Infanterie Division* was in transit. Although a veteran of the Normandy landings, the *711. Infanterie Division* was never a first-class division, and had been bled white by the fighting in 1944. *3. SS–*

Panzer Division Totenkopf was already there, having begun arriving on December 28, followed shortly by *5. SS Panzer Division Wiking* and the rest of *IV SS-Panzerkorps*, pulled out of the line near Warsaw and sent to the rescue of their trapped *SS* comrades. This particular order had shocked not only the commanders of *Heeresgruppen A* and *Mitte*, who felt that the central front that was the shortest route into German territory should have received the highest priority, but also the *SS* veterans on the front lines. Transfer to Hungary instead of defending the *Reich*? It made no sense. As Pierik says, "The *IV. SS–Panzerkorps* which fell under the command of *SS-SS–Obergruppenführer* Herbert Otto Gille was astonished to receive such an order...but no one of course disputed orders from higher up. Hitler simply initiated his Hungarian Offensive and his soldiers were expected to support him whether there was logic to the reasoning or not."[71]

Even more astounded than Gille, however, was the man who had so carefully nurtured *IV. SS–Panzerkorps* along the road to recovery after the bitter fighting of the previous months: Heinz Guderian. Little by little, Guderian had cobbled together a small reserve for the most crucial sector of front held by *Heeresgruppe Mitte* and now the Chief of the General Staff was apoplectic that the only major mobile reserve behind the Warsaw front was being transferred to what he considered a secondary theater; even before Christmas he had railed against what he considered nearly suicidal stupidity, but his previous protests were no more successful than those he made on New Year's Night. The fantasy world in which Hitler lived made him believe what he wanted to believe, not what Guderian's intelligence chief, Reinhard Gehlen, gleaned from intelligence reports.

Hitler refused to believe that Stalin disposed of an enormity of power so great that he could launch major offensives in more than one area, and for Hitler

[71] Pierik, p. 151

the crucial spot was in the south. The overwhelming evidence presented by Gehlen was dismissed as the ravings of a lunatic.[72] Despite Guderian and Gehlen's passionate and prolonged efforts, Hitler's decision had stood; *IV. SS–Panzerkorps* would move to Hungary and go on the offensive.

That it was in no way, shape or form ready to attack made no difference. Despite Guderian's best efforts to rebuild Gille's command, the Corps was still badly under-strength, even in the most basic combat equipment, but that did not matter either. Whether they liked it or not, when Hitler ordered, his subordinates either obeyed or faced potentially fatal consequences; anything else would have constituted open rebellion, and after the previous year's assassination attempt any officers willing to do that has either been purged, or silenced. The relief of Budapest and defense had captured the *Führer*'s attention and he would not be distracted from his obsession with Hungary; indeed, his determination to win a decisive victory in the south overrode nearly all other considerations. Thorwald puts it this way, referring to Hitler's mental state by this stage of the war: "His imagination, to be sure, had left him. In its stead there remained a strange rigidity-he seemed unable to think, to judge, or to plan in any terms but those of his greatest days in power. But behind this rigidity still lay maniacal strength."[73] For the rest of the war, the scale of the fighting in Hungary was solely at Hitler's discretion and direction.

[72] Thorwald, p. 22
[73] Thorwald, p. 24

Hetzer

Jagdpanzer 38(t) (SdKfz. 138/2)

Hetzer

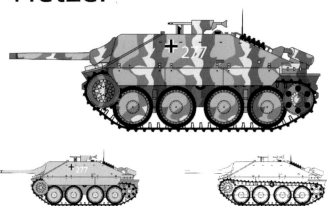

Ubiquitous among German units was the light *Jagdpanzer* nicknamed the *Hetzer*. The design was more or less an emergency stop-gap that could be built cheaply and in huge numbers. It had very little armor protection, but a reasonably good 75mm gun, and was dangerous when laying in ambush.

Underscoring all German activities anywhere in the *Reich* were questions of supply, primarily ammunition and fuel, and it was no different for *Heeresgruppe Süd*; even the most minor German operation was dependent on scrounging up sufficient supplies from wherever they could be found. No matter how many tanks might be in combat ready condition, or the number of artillery tubes available in a given sector, if fuel and shells were not available they remained static hunks of intricate, sculpted metal that could do no harm. Indeed, every tank that was added to the German rolls drank fuel that further limited mobility. Given the extra-ordinarily high number of motorized divisions in *Heeresgruppe Süd*'s Order of Battle for 1945, therefore, fuel topped the list of commodities most needed for combat operations, and as Deputy Ia[74] of *6. SS–Panzerarmee*, Georg Maier dealt with fuel shortages every day and gives a first-hand account of how crippling the situation was. "...The lack of fuel was an unyielding, pressing concern for all operations and movements and a severe operational and strategic obstacle on all fronts. Remarkably, the orders from Supreme Headquarters often stood in crass disregard of this situation, another indication of the increasing delusional state in the *Führer's* Headquarters."[75] That a veteran *Waffen–SS* officer would make such a statement about his *Führer* shows just how disillusioned even the most loyal German soldiers had become by early 1945. Yet even so they fought on.

The issues of supply were constantly on the mind of every German or Hungarian who fought in *Heeresgruppe Süd* in 1945, from the lowliest conscript to the man who was ultimately responsible for carrying out Hitler's unrealistic orders: *General der Infanterie* Otto Wöhler.

---

[74] The Ia was the Chief of Operations, which made him responsible for a variety of duties, from the command and tactical control of the unit, to leadership recommendations, training, transport, housing, air-raid protection, evaluation, presentation of combat options to the commander, and also stood in as the commander when the commander himself was not available. As Deputy Ia, Maier was in charge of making the orders of the Ia become reality. He was, therefore, at the center of army operations 24 hours a day.

[75] Maier, p. 5.

2 January, Tuesday

The War Situation

On the Western Front... In the Ardennes, US 3rd Army troops took Bonnerue, Hubertmont and Remagne in their counterattacks against the Germans in the Battle of the Bulge. In Alsace, the German pressure during *Unternehmen Nordwind* forced the US 7th Army withdrawals to continue. Hitler turned down requests from Model and Manteuffel for withdrawals from the area west of Houffalize, as the *Führer* clung to the fantasy of still taking Antwerp and dealing a decisive blow on the Western Front.

From Britain... Admiral Sir Bertram Ramsay, Naval Commander in Chief Allied Expeditionary Force, and organizer of the Dunkirk evacuation, is killed in an airplane accident while traveling from Paris to Belgium.

Konrad I

The biggest tactical drawback facing *Unternehmen Konrad I* was also it's largest tactical advantage: the haphazard nature of its planning. The various assault units simply attacked at the first opportunity and in the most expeditious manner possible. This produced both a disjointed effort and one that caught the Russian defenders totally off guard.

Weather across the Hungarian battlefield found temperatures in the low to mid 20's under partly cloudy skies; the roads and fields remained frozen. For the vast majority of the men on both sides there was no escape from wet clothes, numb fingers and toes and ice on every surface.

Dawn of the first full day of *Unternehmen Konrad I* found the Soviets still largely unaware of the offensive and Otto Wöhler urging his men to greater speed before the enemy realized what they were facing. The Russian 31st Corps, the main Soviet formation in the path of the rolling *panzers*, was too weak to hold for long and was soon penetrated in several places. It was only at noon that the headquarters of 46th Army and 4th Guards Army discovered their danger, with the German *96. Infanterie Division* threatening to drive southeast from the Gran region into their rear. The *96. Infanterie Division* was a veteran division that was well thought of in the Army. Pierik quotes Gaedecke, the Chief of Staff of *6. Armee*, as saying: "...we had excellent units, like for instance the 96. I.D."[76] The crossing of an ice-choked Danube the night before had been an impressive feat of engineering and tactical coordination that harkened back to the early days of the war, when German assault units seemed capable of battlefield miracles. Pierik goes on to report that the capture of the Hungarian wine growing region near the Danube led to men of both sides plundering wine cellars and getting drunk, with besotted Russians singing through the night.

For the most part Red Army reactions to defensive battles were consistent by this time, centering whenever possible in villages, towns and other built-up areas. Thomas Jentz quotes an after action report from *I./Panzer-Regiment 24*[77] to show the standard Russian pattern of defending urban battlefields. "The Russians understand defense of towns by the clever use of anti-tank guns and tanks. The enemy toughly and bitterly awaits his chance and lets the opponent advance to close range in order to possibly shoot him up from the flank. The Russian infantry is of little value and quickly leaves the battlefield as soon as our *panzers* appear."[78] To counter that on the Danube Road, the *96. Infanterie-Division's* epic river crossing had out-flanked the Russian defense

---

[76] Pierik, p. 161.

[77] This battalion was not part of Konrad I but entered combat in Hungary during Konrad III.

[78] Jentz, *Panzertruppen 2*, p. 224.

positions from the rear, while *3. SS–Panzer Division Totenkopf* attacked them from the front.

Totenkopf's 9. Panzer-Kompanie had been halted the previous night by Russian defenses around Dunallmas. *SS Panzer Grenadier Regiment 6 'Theodor Eicke'* had been on the *panzer* company's right flank to move southeast, but with the river road blocked the battalion shifted its axis of attack to the northeast and drove to the eastern edge of Dunallmas, dislodging the Russians from their defenses and getting the attack moving again.

Starting west of Nezmely, *Totenkopf* then fought through elements of the 170th Tank Brigade and 1438th Independent Artillery Regiment on the western fringe of that village, in the process encircling part of 80th Guards Rifle Division and 27 tanks of 170th Tank Brigade that had not moved fast enough to avoid being outflanked. With part of the attacking force left behind to pin the trapped Russians, the remainder drove the short distance to Sutto, where *Grenadier Regiment 283* from *96. Infanterie Division* was holding that village against Russian attacks. After joining their Army comrades the *SS* men sped through Piszke, then Labatlan, before there was more hard fighting on the road just west of Nyergessujfalu. The Russian 11th Guards Rifle Regiment was dug in protecting the road; supported by 16 tanks[79] and with one flank protected by the Danube it was an excellent defensive position and *Totenkopf* took casualties trying to overrun it, but having the *96. Infanterie Division* in the Russian's rear was the deciding factor: before long the *SS* men had linked with the *96. Infanterie Division's* bridgehead at Nyergesujfalu and the Russian defenses were so much wreckage. However, with much of its combat strength yet to detrain, *Totenkopf* could not exploit this success as it otherwise might have.

---

[79] Presumably these were also from 170th Tank Brigade that had not been encircled earlier in the day.

Russian counterattacks from south and southwest of the town were repulsed. The *panzers* then turned south on the road to Bajot to capture the crossroads just south of Nyergesujfalu, while the rest of the force continued east along the river road. This area was held by 86th Guards Rifle Division.

Although taken by surprise, the Russians quickly got over their shock. There was another violent battle involving both *96. Infanterie Division* and *Totenkopf* but once again, in what was to become a pattern, the Germans fought their way through after losing time and casualties. Progress in both directions was slowed by fierce resistance. A factory 4 miles east of Nyergesujfalu was heavily defended by the Russians and *Totenkopf*'s reinforced reconnaissance battalion attacked tenaciously to keep the drive moving forward, while the bulk of the division was ordered to attack Tokod and cut the railway passing through the town. Tokod lay in a narrow floodplain surrounded by hills and mountains and it was imperative that *Totenkopf* seize the town quickly, before further Russian reinforcements could arrive to fortify the high ground. Once Tokod was secured the division could then move to take Dorog, two miles to the east, and from there a narrow valley lead southeast between the Gerecse and Pilis Mountains toward Pilisvorosvar, a key town whose capture could unhinge the entire Russian position north of Lake Velence. Everything depended on speed.

On *Totenkopf*'s right flank, when the attack units of *5. SS Panzer Division Wiking* took their first objective, the small village of Agostyan, it happened just as the report from *I./Panzer-Regiment 24* said. Surprise was complete and many Russians fled from the *panzers*, but there were casualties and heavy fighting in places. The area was held by elements of General Gorba's 80th Guards Rifle Division. Two of that divisions' three rifle regiments were north of Agostyan, the 217th and 230th Rifle Regiments, while the third, 232nd Rifle Regiment, was southwest of the town; divisional headquarters were in Agostyan itself. *SS–Panzergrenadier Regiment 9*

Germania moved toward Agostyan, with *Wiking's Panzer* Regiment on its right. The *Panzers* ran into 232nd Guards Rifle Regiment southwest of Agostyan and had a fierce firefight, but *Germania* slipped through on the left and took the town, where the Russian local headquarters were disrupted and fled. Immediate counterattacks were thrown back and 232nd Guards was outflanked, while 217th and 230th Rifle Regiments were in danger of being surrounded. *Germania's* first battalion then swung southeast and made for Tardos.

Agostyan was a medieval town that had been abandoned in the 1600's after several centuries of existence that had been made possible by supplying nearby Tata Castle with various necessities, but Bavarian immigrants brought it back to life in 1733 and it had strongly identified with its German heritage ever since. The attackers freed 1,000 German and Hungarian prisoners being held there. Other prisoners, escapees from Budapest, were found dead in ditches, killed by the Russians, which enraged the *SS* men. Most likely these men had been interrogated at the headquarters in Agostyan before being executed.

The terrain was as much of an obstacle to a rapidly developed German attack as were the Russian defenses. The Gerecse and Pilis Heights were not towering mountains, but they were treacherous, ambushes were easy in the dense woods, the roads were narrow and winding and the sharp slopes were icy and snow swept.

As *Wiking* widened the breach in the early hours of 2 January the division continued pushing forward. Holding the Agostyan area was General Gorba's 80th Guards Rifle Division. Southeast of Agostyan the road to Tarjan was mined and Pak traps were set up, waiting for targets; some emplacements reportedly had up to 20 anti-tank guns. Such positions often had to be outflanked by infantry because the country was too rough and wooded for tanks, and artillery was largely ineffective because of the many hills. Infantry losses in the dense woods would gradually wear down the attackers as they fanned out to dislodge defenders and clear the roads for the armor. Meanwhile, the Germans endured strong flank attacks as they pushed down the frozen roads, with the initially fast pace of the attack slowing to a crawl. Russian infantry could attack from the heavy forests on either side of the road but armor could not pursue or effectively fight back because of the terrain, leaving the infantry to defend the flanks as well as assault fixed defenses. Combat engineers had to clear mines, often while under fire. The initially rapid pace of advance could not be maintained. "The forces laboriously fought their way forward, 100 meters at a time."[80] Nevertheless, *Wiking* was ordered to take Biscke via the roads through Tarjan; taking Biscke was the key to further advances toward Budapest. Despite the Russian resistance, Tardos was taken by 0900 hours by *Germania*'s first battalion and Baj fell to the divisional Pioneer battalion, which repulsed counterattacks by the desperately fighting 232nd Guards Rifle Regiment. Adding manpower to that sector of the front was the Russian 34th Guards Rifle Division in position near Vérteszollos.

But the Russians were awakening to the danger and, once aware of the offensive, Russian reactions were swift. Reserves began to pour into the area, while the Germans had no reserves, only the portions of the assault units that had not yet arrived in theater. Russian defenses fought stubbornly as German intentions became clear, and by the end of the day *Wiking's* spearheads were only halfway down the road to Vértestolna, a mere two miles southeast of Tardos; *Konrad I* was already behind schedule.

Both Marshals Tolbukhin and Malinovsky had put the units that had done most of the fighting in late December into reserve, a large force with some 500-600 tanks, both to rest and replenish them and with an eye toward defeating German relief attempts on Budapest.

[80] Strassner, p. 312.

Soon enough these forces were on the move to block Gille's progress; the 19th Rifle Division moved 190 km. from the south shore of Lake Balaton to the Adony area in less than two days.[81]

IV. SS–Panzerkorps would soon be badly outnumbered; combined with the ferocious winter weather, limited supplies and rugged terrain, Gille's men would soon find themselves fighting for every yard, while being bombed and strafed almost at will by ground attack and fighter aircraft. The Luftwaffe flew 260 sorties on the 2nd, an impressive total for so late in the war, but it was not enough to smash the stout Russian entrenchments holding up the offensive. Nor did it did help matters that IV. SS–Panzerkorps had to actually attack through the lines of III. Panzerkorps, jumbling troops and making command and control even more difficult. It was already obvious that the offensive did not have the weight to drive all the way to Budapest; reinforcements had to be found.

Otto Wöhler decided to take a risk. 8. Armee was defending the line of the Gran north of the Danube and needed every man and panzer to succeed, but Konrad I needed more firepower and there was nowhere else to find it than to weaken 8th Army. Consequently, Wöhler ordered 6. Panzer Division to move south of the Danube to reinforce IV. SS–Panzerkorps. 211. Volksgrenadier Division had to extend its front to take over 6. Panzer Division's positions, but this left the line dangerously thin; a Russian attack north of the Danube that threatened the vital river crossings at Komarom could become a disaster for Heeresgruppe Süd, threatening the rear of all units participating in Konrad I. It was a risk Wöhler felt he had to take.

On Wiking's right flank Kampfgruppe Pape was stalled west of Tatabanya in a belt of anti-tank guns

[81] Ungvary, The Siege of Budapest, p. 162.

and mines, where 4th Guards Rifle Division held Tatabanya, Banhida and Alsogalla. Taking the town would mean forming a new attack from the area of Tarjan, east of Tatabanya, thereby outflanking the Russian defenses. But first Tarjan would need to be captured. *Wiking* was ordered to capture the town and drive through the night to seize Biscke. With no reserves to follow *Wiking*, however, flank protection became problematic. *Kampfgruppe Pape* was therefore ordered to withdraw through Tata and follow *Wiking* into Tarjan, where it could drive into the Russian defenses around Tatabanya from the rear. The first parts of *711. Infanterie Division* arrived on the 2nd, about 14 percent of the total division, and were assigned to *Kampfgruppe Pape* until their own headquarters was set up and running. They were assigned the mission of clearing up pockets of resistance in forested areas that had been bypassed and held remnants of shattered Russian units, a huge area for so small a force, no more than 2,000 men.

Looking beyond *Konrad I*, and anticipating a successful result, *Heeresgruppe Süd* issued three critical orders for the continuation of the fighting. First, the Margarethe position between Lakes Balaton and Velence was to be retaken; this was essentially *Unternehmen Paula*, the southern option for relieving Budapest that would become *Konrad III*. The second order was to prepare plans for wiping out the Russian bridgehead over the Gran north of the Danube, what became *Unternehmen Südwind* in February. Lastly, and most ominously for the Budapest garrison, a breakout was only permitted in extreme circumstances, with no explanation for what that meant. In any event, no breakout was permitted without permission of *OKH*; i.e. Hitler.

For the men of *IX. SS-Waffen-Gebirgs-Armeekorps der SS* the order preventing a breakout did not matter, because the word had spread throughout Budapest: Gille was coming! The *SS* General had the reputation of being a miracle worker who would fight through to the city and save them all; had not he done it before? Morale spiked and resistance stiffened as desperate men clutched at anything that gave hope. If flesh and blood could do it, Budapest would hold out. But to fight men needed food, ammunition and courage; the first two were in short supply, but not the latter.

Otto Gille's name was virtually synonymous with miraculous deliverance, at least within the *Waffen-SS*, after his leadership in saving the men trapped in the Cherkassy Pocket the previous year. He was known as an innovative tactician who kept his cool even in the most dire circumstances.

By that last January of the war the Germans had a lot of experience dealing with trapped garrisons and surrounded troops, and the Siege of Budapest would mirror the earlier battles at Stalingrad, Velikiye Luki and numerous other places throughout the Eastern theater. The template was in place. There would be a relief effort to break in and rescue the garrison, but no breakout to meet the relief force would be allowed. In previous battles there had been successes and failures, but most of the failures had been when the Germans were trying to relieve a city and most of the successes while they were in open country. Supplies would be airlifted to the trapped men at great cost to the *Luftwaffe*, while specialists and the wounded were flown out, but usually the quantity of supplies was insufficient to give the trapped defenders a ^{chance} of holding on. Stern orders would be issued to fight to the last man, with draconian punishments meted out to those who did not follow orders.

The *Luftwaffe* had an array of specialized equipment for supplying trapped troops, including supply bombs dropped by dive and level bombers.

All of this had been done many times before and it had rarely worked.[82] Nevertheless, the airlift of supplies began early on in the siege.

The plan was to parachute a quarter of the supplies into the city with the remainder being delivered by transport aircraft. It was a dangerous mission, since the *Luftwaffe* transport department still relied heavily on its dwindling fleet of JU-52s, the lumbering tri-motor airplane that had begun life as an airliner and was obsolete by 1945, along with a motley collection of whatever aircraft were available that could carry a payload, usually *Heinkel HE-111* bombers. Running the gauntlet of Russian fighters and anti-aircraft in lumbering, heavily-laden aircraft took great courage and determination. According to Pierik, upwards of 100 daily sorties were flown at the beginning of the airlift, but this number quickly diminished as fuel ran low and losses ran high. He states that according to documents found at *Führer* headquarters, Hitler personally oversaw the operation, making sure that mail from home was delivered to the garrison along with ammunition, food and fuel, because morale among the defenders was vital to their ability to sustain prolonged resistance. When the final airfields were lost later in the month, *Reichsmarshall* Herman Göring suggested using gliders to land supplies and Hitler immediately latched onto the idea. In addition to gliders, Fiesler Storch reconnaissance aircraft were used because they were designed to land in very small areas, although their payload was miniscule compared to the need. Hitler supposedly even considered using seaplanes, presumably to land on the Danube, as well as experimental helicopters.[83] Considerable effort was put into the air supply of

---

[82] At Velikiye Luki in early 1943, an armored column actually did break in to relieve the garrison, but it was too weak to hold open a corridor and in the end the city fell with the loss of the entire defending force. Coincidentally, one of the units trying to lift the siege at Velikiye Luki had been 8th Panzer Division, which was deployed just north of the Danube during the Konrad operation.

[83] Pierik, pp. 142-143.

Budapest, as it had been during earlier sieges, but as before the supplies delivered were too inconsistent and in too little quantity to save the situation. Even with a vast majority of those supplies that did get through devoted to ammunition, it was not long before guns fell silent for lack of shells and bullets. The resupply effort did not succeed but the failure was not from lack of trying.

To understand how futile this effort was it helpful to view the effort in some detail. There is an example from German newsreel footage[84] showing the *Luftwaffe* performing a supply mission for the beleaguered city, with the small scale of the enterprise downplayed in favor of a more heroic tone. The newsreel shows the loading of gliders and their subsequent flights into the perimeter and the complete inadequacy of the effort can be seen in the grainy footage. The gliders were stuffed with food and ammunition, and metal cases holding *panzerfäuste*, but they were small, fragile craft, and the loaded supplies hardly seem adequate for a company, let alone an entire army; a glider loaded with supplies was little more than a thimble where a bucket was needed.

The Germans put every plane they had left into the air to supply their trapped countrymen and it was never close to enough. Guillemot tells us that 80 tons were the daily requirement for the airlift to be effective, but averaged only 47 tons.[85] This obviously helped, although the long-term goal of keeping the garrison fighting until relief could arrive could not be achieved without a huge upswing in deliverance of supplies. *Luftflotte 4* used what aircraft were left, but after the last airfield inside of the Budapest perimeter was lost on 30 December, 1944, they were forced to land on pasture land and makeshift airfields, such as the racetrack in Pest, some 17 in all. One piece of pasture was supposedly picked out by Hitler personally.[86]

[84] *Die Deutsche Wochenschau Nummer 751*, 10 Februar, 1945.
[85] Guillemot, p. 35.
[86] Pierik, p. 143.

Inevitably the best landing spots were discovered by the Russians and were brought under artillery fire, or were swarmed by the Red Air Force. Budapest's many hills were ideal for anti-aircraft batteries and artillery observers and as the Red Army captured them one by one, supply flights to the shrinking defensive ring inside the city became ever more hazardous. When it became impractical to land with supplies they were para-dropped, with a high percentage missing their German targets and winding up in Russian territory. Losses among the dwindling *Luftwaffe* transport command were heavy. Aircrews began to call Budapest the Blood-Land because of the scattered wreckage of *Luftwaffe* aircraft, with only 43 of 73 *Deutsche Forschungsanstalt für Segelflug DFS-230*[87] gliders dispatched with supplies actually making it to German territory.[88] This old design had been a *Luftwaffe* workhorse throughout the war, it had been used by airborne troops for the assault on the Belgian fortress of Eben-Emael in 1940 and the rescue of Benito Mussolini in 1943, but its payload was far too small for the mission at hand. At full capacity it could hold perhaps 2600 lbs, under ideal flying conditions. To properly supply the garrison for just one day would have required at least 73 gliders, the total used during the entire siege, and the effort seems more worthwhile as a morale booster than an actual avenue of supply. Towing a glider to Budapest was an arduous, fuel-expensive mission that must have hardly seemed worth the risk, with Red Air Force fighters on the prowl for such tempting targets and anti-aircraft batteries ringing the perimeter, since such a glider could only

[87] German Research Institute for Sail Plane Research, i.e. gliders. Slight improvements during the glider's developmental life allowed a heavier payload to be transported, but not enough more to make it a viable choice for transporting supplies into a surrounded city. The Germans simply had no other choice. It was probably not a mission too many pilots volunteered to fly.
[88] Guillemot gives a figure of 41 gliders successfully landing in German territory instead of Pierik's 43.

carry slightly more than one ton of supplies, a mere drop in the ocean for what was needed.

As one example of the effort, the *Kriegstagebuch* (War Diary) of *Heeresgruppe Süd* makes note of the resupply effort on 1 January by listing 61 HE-111s and 18 JU-52s being used to fly in supplies, opposed by strong Soviet fighter and anti-aircraft defenses; gliders are not mentioned in this entry. In theory this quantity of aircraft could deliver enough supplies to keep the garrison fighting, but the resupply effort was an increasingly desperate effort as losses mounted and airfields were lost. The effort during the night of 1-2 January brought a respectable 73 tons into the city and 268 wounded were evacuated, but successes like this became less and less common. Flying during the day became increasingly suicidal. Moreover, such a paltry total of bombers that could be mustered by an entire *Heeresgruppe* betrays the bankrupt state of the German war effort. Put into perspective, the Allies routinely sent 1,000 and more heavy bombers into Germany as part of the strategic bombing campaign, both night and day, and still blotted out German skies with thousands of medium bombers and fighter-bombers.

There was even an effort to float supplies into the city via the Danube, but that quickly broke down. In January the river was frozen and largely un-navigable, not to mention lined on both banks with Russian artillery. A solitary ship loaded with 400 tons of desperately needed supplies tried to sneak into the city but become stuck on a sandbar off Szentendre Island near Tahitotfalu, no more than 10 miles upriver from Budapest; although the ship was eventually refloated, the idea was given up as impractical. The supplies, however, did mostly make it to Budapest by small craft sneaking upstream over the course of several nights to offload the larger boat. This remarkable feat was accomplished by *Jagdverbande Donau*, an amalgamated group comprised of men from the *Waffen-SS*, *Kriegsmarine* and the Vlasov Army, captured

Russians fighting for the Germans, a group led by the by-then notorious *Oberstürmbannführer* Otto Skorzeny. Courage and daring aside, the operation was only made possible because while the Russians controlled both banks of the river, that particular area was considered of secondary importance and there were few Russian troops or artillery in the area. Once the boat was spotted, however, measures were taken to prevent the Germans trying it again.

Inside the doomed city the flak detachment for *22. SS-Kavallerie Division Maria Theresa* was deployed in Pest for ground fighting, with the 6 2 cm. guns of its light flak battery dug in at the eastern railroad station; they were "used almost exclusively against enemy infantry attacks."[89] The detachment numbered approximately 500 officers and men. In one example of the back and forth nature of the combat in Budapest the battery's positions were lost and retaken several times within a few hours.

Devoting anti-aircraft units to ground combat roles came with a cost: Russian aircraft bombed and strafed continuously. Combined with the almost constant artillery barrages it made life miserable for the defending Germans; brick, concrete and shell splinters were a constant danger. Heavy fighting raged all day and was particularly bad in the XVI District at Sashalom and the XIX District at Kis-Pest along the southern edge of the city and at the northern perimeter at Rakospalota. Positions were lost and retaken by counterattacks and then lost again, but by the end of the day the German line still held its ground, albeit at great cost in killed and wounded. Permission to launch a breakout was denied by Hitler, but some were confident that a breakout would not be necessary.

[89] Landwehr, *Siegrunen 38*, p. 26.

For the men pushing forward as part of *Konrad I* the day had seen hard fighting against dug-in enemy defenses. With artillery of limited value in the mountains and the *Luftwaffe* unable to muster more than moderate strength, the only way to destroy Russian defenses was to outflank and then assault them with infantry, a time-consuming and costly tactic. This *IV. SS–Panzerkorps* did, but not fast enough for its *Heer* and *Heeresgruppe* commanders. Around 2200 hours Wöhler and Balck discussed the days' events, with Hermann Balck criticizing the progress made because the attack was made on too narrow of a front; he had ordered the attack to be made on a broader front and if his orders had been followed then success would have been greater. This second-guessing is an example of Balck's extreme antipathy for the *Waffen–SS* in general, and Gaedecke, Balck's chief-of-staff's, hatred for Gille in particular. Gaedecke met his counterpart from *Heeresgruppe Süd* and his feelings on the day's action were recorded as follows: "The general impression is that nothing occurred to the commander and their subordinates after reading their first objectives. In contrast to the better trained leaders of 1941 and 1942, they lacked the initiative to exploit successes on their own and drive relentlessly ahead." The actual plan had called for *3. SS–Panzer Division Totenkopf* to attack down the Danube road, with parts of the division dividing off in echelon and driving southeast; attacking on a broad front would have defeated this aim. Parts of *96. Infanterie Division* had not crossed the Danube with the assault units so it was not whole and had its hands full continuing east down the Danube road. As for *5. SS–Panzer Division Wiking Division*, it was far too weak to attack on a wider front than it did.[90]

---

[90] Maier, p. 20.

To give *Konrad I* the combat power necessary to break through, *OKH* wanted to withdraw both *6. Panzer Division* and *8. Panzer Division* from the Gran Front and send them behind *Wiking* and *Totenkopf*, but *Heeresgruppe Süd* fought the move. Neither division was particularly strong, but if the Russians launched an attack against *8. Armee* north of the Danube they would be crucial to holding Komárom and preventing *6. Armee's* left flank being turned,[91] and with the imminent arrival of more combat elements of *Wiking* it was hoped that the two extra divisions would not be needed. With the approach of midnight the issue had not yet been settled.

The Red Air Force could not bomb or strafe effectively at night so under cover of darkness *IV. SS–Panzerkorps* renewed its attack and before the night ended progress had been made. Vértestolna was the next village standing in the way of the advance on Bicske and before midnight the fight began. Situated in a valley of low, rolling hills surrounded by wooded ridges, in freezing weather and icy roads under a dark night sky, the battle for Vértestolna was bitter house-to-house combat. It took *Wiking* hours to finally clear the village and regroup enough to press on through a narrow valley leading southeast, well past midnight into the early hours of 3. January.

Elsewhere, *Totenkopf* broke through at Bajot and was making good progress, driving on Bajna, while *96. Infanterie Division* not only captured Tokod but had its *284. Infanterie-Regiment*, along with the rest of *196 Artillerie-Regiment*, move through Komárom to join their comrades. Under cover of darkness Gille's men plowed toward their trapped comrades, and as the clock turned over to a new day there was cause for hope.

[91] Prescient caution, as it turned out.

3 January, Wednesday

The War Situation in the West

In the Ardennes the Germans attacked on the narrow corridor leading to Bastogne, which succeed in disrupting the timetable of the planned American counterattacks but failed to achieve any advances. Forces of the US 3rd Army and US 1st Army then attacked toward Houffalize from the south and the north, respectively. In Alsace, the German attacks and the American retreat continued. The US 6th Corps (part of US 7th Army) was being pressed particularly hard in the area around Bitche. Farther south, the newest German offensive, *Unternehmen Nordwind*, momentarily made Eisenhower consider abandoning Strasbourg.

The forces involved in France would have virtually ensured the success of *Konrad I.* But the Western Allies were nearing German's critical industrial zone, further underscoring the futility of continuing the war for any achievable national purpose.

Western Hungary had been both a homeland and a battlefield for millennia. Rome once considered it barbarian territory but bloody wars added it to the empire and for centuries it supplied soldiers for the legions as the Roman province of Pannonia. The area south of the Danube became the home territory for peoples fleeing waves of invaders from both north and east, until the invaders themselves arrived and settled down. Attila's two decade reign of terror against the dying Roman Empire was based in the area around Lakes Balaton and Velence, probably stretching eastward to the Danube near Budapest. In the savage fighting that would mark the next three months every shell impact, every rifle pit or earthworks thrown up around a *paknest,* every tracked vehicle chewing up farm fields, had the chance of destroying rare Hun artifacts that had survived fifteen centuries of weather and war. Not only was the tide of battle sweeping south from the Danube wiping out thousands of the men doing the fighting, it was wiping out history as well.

The weather remained bitterly cold, with a high of 27 degrees Fahrenheit, meaning the roads and fields were still frozen, making mechanized movements possible. Ominously for the Germans, however, the skies were clear and the Red Air Force was overhead in strength, thereby making daylight movement dangerous in the extreme.

Fighting in the Budapest pocket had become ferocious. Guillemot reports that within Budapest losses among the garrison were already grave, with the Hungarian 12th Reserve Division reporting battalion strengths of between 10 and 25 men. He also puts the combined remaining strength of *Panzer Division Felldherrnhalle, 13. Panzer Division,* the *kampfgruppe* of *271. Volksgrenadier Division , 22. SS-Kavallerie Division Maria Theresa* and the Hungarian 10th and 12th Infantry Divisions as an anemic combined total of 3,600 men.[92] There is no breakdown of killed, wounded or missing, and presumably a number of these men had fled underground to await the end of the fighting, or, in the case of the Hungarians, possibly changed sides. This total seems low, however, and no mention is made of how it was arrived at, since the only other major formations within Budapest were *8. SS Kavallerie-Division Florian Geyer* and the Hungarian 1st Hussars. When the breakout finally came on February 12th there were some 17,000 men involved, and while walking wounded are included in that total, it seems highly unlikely that as early as 3. January the

[92] Guillemot, p. 37.

garrison's rifle strength was in the range of 10,000, as Guillemot's figure implies. Even so, the point seems well made that Budapest's defenders had suffered heavy casualties and were gradually being ground into dust.

On the northwest flank of the Budapest perimeter, Matyas-hegy hill was the scene of vicious back-and-forth fighting, changing hands up to seven times as the defenders tried to hold onto the vital position at all costs. It was also in the general direction from which the rescuers participating in *Konrad I* would come, and the closer to them the perimeter could be held, the more likely that a breakthrough might be achieved. In peacetime a popular caving spot, the Hill was an important point in the defensive perimeter and could not be allowed to fall, but the Russians knew that its capture would put the defenders in a precarious position. At the end of the day, the defenders still held the heights, with both sides having suffered enormous losses. The Red Army had also pushed as far as the race course, one of the *Luftwaffe*'s make-shift airfields, denying its use to the garrison and leaving the field on Csepel as the only one still useable. On top of everything else, with the gas and electricity already off throughout the city, on the 3rd the water system failed as well. In the dead of winter the defenders had no heat, power or water.

Resupply efforts continued at a feverish pace. In addition to 59 *Heinkel HE-111s* and 34 *Junkers JU-52s* committed to the aerial effort, a second ship was being readied to float supplies down the river. Despite Russian air superiority, river ice and heavy losses, the Germans were determined to keep the Budapest garrison alive and fighting for as long as it took for the rescue operation to succeed.

As planned, after moving east on the Danube Road *3. SS–Panzer Division Totenkopf* had separated in echelon into multiple columns heading south toward differing objectives, fanning out to gobble up as much territory as possible before the Russians could react. Two battalions moved on Bajna, *III/SS Panzergrenadier Regiment 6 Theodor Eicke* from the northwest and *III/SS Panzergrenadier Regiment 5 Thule* from the north, capturing the town. The Russians immediately counter-attacked with 26 tanks from 110th Tank Brigade, supported by 363rd Heavy Self-Propelled Artillery Regiment and 32nd Guards Motorized Rifle Brigade, fighting their way back into the southern part of Bajna before a German counterattack drove them out. The fighting cost 11 Russian tanks destroyed, six reportedly with *panzerfäuste*, showing how close the combat became. The remaining Soviet forces moved onto the ridges to the southeast, determined to stop *Totenkopf* before it could move further south. A German thrust toward Epöl was thrown back.

As hard as the day's fighting would be for *Wiking* and *Totenkopf*, matters were even worse for the two flank attack units slogging forward against even stiffer resistance. Thus the two *panzer* divisions began to pull out in front, exposing their flanks and forcing them to take forces away from the spearheads to protect those flanks. This meant that the further they moved ahead, the weaker they became[93]. The same thing would happen during *Unternehmen Frühlingserwachen*.

96. Infanterie Division was fighting to clear the bank of the Danube near Nyergesufalu against a superior enemy force, eventually plowing two miles east of the town where the Russians still held a sugar factory. The Russian positions northwest of Sarisap were held by the newly arrived 86th Guards Rifle Division and the defenses continued to hold out against attacks by *96. Infanterie Division's Infanterie Regiment*

---

[93] This identical problem would drain strength from the schwerpunkt of *Unternehmen Frühlingserwachen* in March.

287, while the critical road junction of Tokod was still in Soviet hands. The fight for the sugar factory was bitter, although the Germans finally took it late in the day.

Nagysap had fallen to *Totenkopf*'s *III/Thule* and other elements, before that battalion moved on Bajna. *Totenkopf*'s reconnaissance battalion captured an important crossroads southeast of the village of Szarkas[94], threatening Sarisap which was within sight to the east. All in all, then, *Totenkopf* and *96. Infanterie Division* were making progress against stubborn resistance, but the pace was too slow; what was needed was not progress but a breakthrough.

On *Totenkopf*'s right flank, in the seam between that division and *Wiking*, the Russians continued to pour reinforcements into the area near Bajna. Nor was German intelligence on top of the situation. *6. Armee*'s nightly report noted the probable arrival in the area of XXXI Rifle Corps of II Guards Mechanized Corps and the definite transfer of 86th Rifle Division from the attack on Budapest to the battles near Biscke and Bajna[95], even though *Totenkopf* and *96. Infanterie Division* had been fighting 86th Rifle Division for two days.

The essential flaw with *Konrad I* was that the Germans were simply not strong enough to push back the increasing number of Russian units in their path. Once upon a time a full strength *IV. SS–Panzerkorps* was a fearsome steamroller that would have crushed the Russian defenses around Budapest. As has been seen, however, despite Guderian's best efforts to rebuild the shattered divisions, *IV. SS–Panzerkorps* was badly depleted when it left Poland. Then, after the long train journey and with no time to rest or get organized,

[94] This tiny settlement was just east of Bajot.
[95] Maier, p. 22.

IV. SS–Panzerkorps arrived and was committed to battle piecemeal; there was never enough weight behind the attack for it to break through and by the 3 January, with 48 hours of fighting behind them, the *SS* men were running out of steam. Casualties were high, the men were exhausted and the conditions in which they were fighting were terrible. But *5. SS Panzer Division Wiking* was still arriving in the theater, according to Maier 23 trainloads arrived on 3. January 3 loaded with combat elements which became available as they detrained, effectively acting as reinforcements.[96] Even with these new additions the assault forces were inadequate to the mission.

On a map the German forces appeared stronger than they really were and Hitler was pressing for progress. *OKH* was pressing to transfer *6. Panzer Division* and *8. Panzer Division* south of the Danube, but that risked *8. Armee's* front being ruptured by a Russian attack; regardless of the risk, *6. Panzer Division* was ordered south to be available on 4. January 4 to support *Konrad I,* even if Hitler and his advisors could not understand why that was necessary. For the *Führer,* however, relieving Budapest overrode all other concerns and he wanted answers on what was holding up the attack.

Under such pressure from above and trying to find out what the problem was, Otto Wöhler showed up with Hermann Balck at the headquarters of both *IV. SS–Panzerkorps* and *96. Infanterie Division*[97]. According to witnesses he was not impressed with what he saw, writing in the *Heeresgruppe Süd* War Diary, "I have the impression that the officers do not possess the qualities they had at the beginning of the war." This was almost verbatim what General Gaedecke had said to General von Grolman the previous evening, which

---

[96] Maier, pp. 22-23.

[97] The headquarters of *5. SS–Panzer Division Wiking* Panzer Division Wiking also housed the command for IV SS Panzer Corps, combining the two in one locations. The headquarters for *96. Infanterie Division* was still north of the Danube at Bucs.

seems like a suspicious coincidence. Given the poor opinion of the *6. Armee* commander and his chief of staff toward their *SS* subordinates, this echo of Gaedecke's opinion reflects the influence of their biases upon the *Heeresgruppe* Commander, Wöhler. To the men who were trying to force their way forward, however, the reasons for their difficulties were obvious: increasing Soviet resistance, very poor terrain, too few troops and a lack of firepower, not to mention the ice and cold.

Regardless of their previous views, Pierek says that *SS–Oberstürmführer* Gunther Jahnke (of *Wiking*) noted that both Wöhler and Balck seemed to have a better appreciation for the difficulties of the terrain over which *Wiking* was attacking when they left the corps (and division) headquarters.[98] Strassner agrees with this conclusion, that Wöhler and Balck seemed satisfied when they left *Wiking*.[99] Maier records that an entry to that effect was put into the *Heeresgruppe Süd* War Diary, wherein Wöhler stated that the lack of progress the previous day had not been the fault of *IV. SS–Panzerkorps*, but instead was due to forces beyond its control.[100] If that is true, if Wöhler and Balck did appreciate the difficulties *Wiking* was facing, it did not last long.

Disappointed though the *Heeresgruppe* Commander may have been with the progress of the operation, and leaving no doubt that speed was of the essence, the fact was that *Konrad I* had made progress in the first two days of operations. *5. SS Panzer Division Wiking* had enjoyed some initial success, but the further the division advanced beyond Agostyan the more difficult the fighting became. The Russian XXXI Guards Rifle Corps had been mauled and pushed back all along the attack front, but the Russians had gotten over their initial surprise and were reacting to the danger. If the strength of *Konrad I* would prove too

[98] Pierik, p. 168.
[99] Strassner, p. 312.
[100] Maier, p. 22.

weak to break through, it was because Marshal Tolbukhin withdrew substantial forces from the siege of Budapest and shifted them west into the path of the oncoming German rescue forces. Guillemot lists these Russian formations as "2nd GMC (Guards Mechanized Corps), 86th Rifle Division and 49th Guards Rifle Division."[101] Although the German kill-ratio remained heavily in their favor, with German units so weak it was proving not to be enough; the Russians kept throwing new units in front of them and the Germans simply could not kill them fast enough. Thus, since there were no reserves to speak of, *OKH* wanted to risk weakening *8. Armee* to reinforce *IV. SS–Panzerkorps* .

The ground was also a problem, as the Gersece and Pilis Mountains were rugged, with countless caves and other ideal spots for the ubiquitous Russian anti-tank guns. Snow and ice not only made footing treacherous but exhausted the men and used huge quantities of extra fuel in the machines. Between the weather, the terrain and the increasing Russian resistance, the elements of *5. SS–Panzer Division Wiking* moving from Agostyan to the Tarjan area found the going very hard.

During the night of 2-3 January, *Wiking's panzer* regiment had started moving again and before midnight the spearheads were in Tertestolna, some three and a half miles southeast of Agostyan. Moving straight through that village *Wiking* had only gone a kilometer or so toward the outskirts of Tarjan when it ran into yet another *paknest* just beyond Vértestolna, at a point where the road ran over a ridge with heavy woods on

[101] Guillemot, p. 312. Strassner says the Soviet reinforcements were even larger, being V Guards Cavalry Corps, VII Mechanized Corps, XVIII Tank Corps and II Guards Mechanized Corps (p. 313). It should be kept in mind that a Soviet 'Corps' was the equivalent of a strong German division; the Soviet equivalent of a German Corps was an Army.

either side, an excellent defensive position; the Russians were dug-in and waiting for them on the approaches to Tarjan. According to Klapdor, "an armored patrol determined that there was a strong Soviet anti-tank belt 1 kilometer southeast of Vértestolna...it did not appear possible to break-through the anti-tank defenses."[102] This *paknest* had their anti-tank guns registered on the road and their position heavily fortified, with densely wooded slopes on either side of the road.

The defenses were overcome with an attack on the *paknest's* rear that moved through Hereg and then came at Tarjan on the flat plain to the village's northeast; the Russians' eastern flank was largely open ground except for a narrow strip of trees along the road. The western flank, on the other hand, was thick woods; since this was the least likely direction of attack the Russians probably did not have guns positioned to defend that avenue. The difficulty of moving tanks through wooded slopes was immense but from existing sources this seems likely to have been the direction from which the attack came. Somehow the *panzers* managed to move off the road and down the wood line, which allowed the Germans to attack the *paknest* from two directions and wipe out the position without loss; some 17 Russian guns and a few tanks were destroyed[103].

As a side note, whenever possible the Germans repurposed the Russian 76mm anti-tank guns. They had captured so many during the war that rechambering them to use ammunition for their own 75mm *PAK 40* gun became common; many early *Marder jagdpanzer* vehicles used such a main gun. More often, however, they simply turned the gun around and used it against the Russians. It seems

---

[102] Klapdor, p. 388.

[103] Darges reportedly lead *Wiking's* Panzer Regiment cross-country through the woods to Tatabanya, but it seems likely that before moving on that town the panzers first carried out this flank attack on the paknest holding up the rest of the division.

likely that the units involved in the *Konrad* operations went into battle with some of these guns already in their possession, so the capture of such a *paknest* would be a good source for not only gaining new guns, but also replenishing ammunition.

Destroying the *paknest* near Tarjan did not mean the Germans had broken through; just outside of that town a hidden Russian assault gun knocked out a platoon leader's *panzer*, before it was destroyed in turn. The road leading southeast was flanked by high ground on both sides, funneling *Wiking's* spearheads into what seemed like a shooting gallery. Russian tanks were poised at spots along the road, but there was no choice; the terrain dictated the tactics, especially when time was of the essence. Making the German situation worse, the high ground on either side, up to 400 meters on the west side of the advance, meant that without follow-on units *Wiking* would have to peel off units and provide for its own flank security. This continually weakened the weight of the attack, although *Kampfgruppe Pape* was finally catching up to the spearheads. By 1500 hours a large part of the Kampfgruppe, some 20 *panzers* with mounted infantry, had arrived in the Tarjan area. This relatively powerful force and *Wiking's* own newly arrived combat elements provided enough replacement firepower to keep the advancing slugging forward, despite losses. *Kampfgruppe Pape* was designed to move toward Alsogalla, approaching its original objective from the east instead of the west.

On *Wiking's* left flank, north-northeast of Tarjan, the village of Hereg was taken quickly by troops of *Germania*, at least giving *Wiking's* left flank some protection.

The fighting then moved to Tarjan itself, where the 93rd Rifle Division was holding the village. A high ridge dominated the road on the west, which the Germans seized early on. During summer Tarjan was an idyllic and isolated retreat, lush with thick grass and red flowers; in January of 1945, it was muddy and blackened by explosions and fire. In fierce combat *Wiking* fought its way into Tarjan by 1500 hours, using a concentric attack to divide the enemy fire with *Germania*'s men doing most of the fighting. The Russians resisted fiercely and the fighting was merciless; it took almost until dark to before the village was completely in German hands. The combat had left the small settlement wrecked and burning. Despite capturing many prisoners and either destroying or capturing a large number of guns, and despite the joy of the residents at being liberated from the Russians, they stood at the roadside cheering the Germans, the victory was too slow in coming: it had taken nearly 24 hours to capture Tarjan, a timetable that was not fast enough to break through to Budapest before Russian reserves stopped the offensive. Speed was the watchword, however, so there was no pause after seizing Tarjan.

The division commander, *SS–Oberfuhrer* Ullrich, was with the lead elements urging them to speed and *Wiking's* headquarters moved into Tarjan even before fighting had ended; Ullrich knew how vital his mission was and wanted his headquarters well forward. He was also being urged to greater efforts by all of his superior officers, Gille, Balck and Wöhler.

Exhausted after 2 days of fighting day and night, but spurred on by higher commands, *Wiking* lost little time resting in Tarjan; the need for speed was obvious, the urge to push on infectious. But the pressing question was: where to go next? Drive straight on, as they had been doing? Biscke was the objective and there were only so many ways to get there, so what choice did they have, especially given the poor terrain and weather? Csabdi was the last significant town before Biscke and lay just across the highway, virtually a suburb of Tarjan. The most direct path to Csabdi lay south-southeast through a valley between wooded hills, but there were no roads leading directly to either Csabdi or Biscke so sticking to roads meant that the choice of route march would be circuitous at best. Taking the most direct path, south-southeast of Tarjan, the tree line on either side of the road receded substantially, opening up the *panzers* to flanking fire of the deadliest sort. This was dangerous in the extreme and could lead to heavy and unnecessary casualties, but it was also the shortest route. The division seemingly had no choice but to fight their way through, but the commander of 5. *SS–Panzer Division Wiking* Regiment, *SS–OberSS–Sturmbannführer* Fritz Darges, had seen this dilemma before. "Darges...decided to avoid a repetition of the 'running of the gauntlet' such as the tankers had experienced at Malgobek[104] more than two years previously. If they proceeded along the original route of advance, they would have to cross that section with exposed flanks, as a result of the friendly forces to either flank not being able to keep up with the '*Wiking* tankers."[105] Unfortunately for the *panzer* crews, even at their slow pace of advance they had outrun their infantry support.

And yet, despite flanks that were up in the air, a dense gauntlet of Russian defenses and the heavy losses already sustained, the offensive was moving forward, albeit slowly, and taking Tarjan was a substantial accomplishment. By 1630 hours *Wiking's* advance elements were more than three miles southeast of the town; at 1900 hours 6. *Armee* reported the division as five kilometers south of Tarjan and moving. But as resistance in the mountainous area increased, the Germans found themselves plowing forward against ever more dug-in anti-tanks guns and infantry in an escalating fury of combat that was little more than a head-on frontal attack. Maneuvering in the rugged terrain in icy winter weather was hard for infantry and almost impossible for vehicles. Progress

---

[104] The battles for and around Malgobek in fall of 1942 had cost Wiking thousands of casualties. Darges had been a company commander at the time and would have seen the situation facing him at Tarjan as very similar to that which Wiking had faced in 1942, when the panzers were forced to charge through a valley while being attacked from both flanks.

[105] Klapdor, p. 389.

was being made and more was hoped for during the night, but Bicske was still a long way away.

Kampfgruppe Pape's inability to take Tatabanya on the first day was stalling the offensive, as the plan had called for a multi-directional attack on Biscke from west and north. As the offensive had developed *IV. SS–Panzerkorps* was essentially launching frontal attacks from one direction only: north. Not only was this far more costly but unless the Russians' flank could be turned the offensive would fail. Weighing all choices, none of which were good, *SS–OberSS–Sturmbannführer* Darges decided to try the seemingly impossible: he would turn his *panzers* off the road and head across the ridges on his right, that is, to the west, moving cross-country to seize Tatabanya. That town lay across the main highway leading to Biscke and its southern outskirts were almost due south of his position; its capture would protect *Wiking's* right flank and make movement to Biscke easier. But it was a risk. With the Germans as outnumbered as they were their margin of error was thin. Night fell early in January but with speed of utmost importance Darges ordered his regiment to head west over the hills immediately, in the dark, regardless of consequences. Klapdor goes on to relate that as the tanks struggled up the slopes in the dark, the tankers joked that they would receive the Alpine badge for the feat. Later, the men of Fritz Vogt's *I./SS–Panzergrenadier Regiment 23 Norge* climbed onto the tanks, having caught up to the spearheads. As soon as the regiment arrived at Tatabanya it went into the attack.

Overhead the Red Air Force launched heavy attacks, although the heavy forest canopy mitigated their effectiveness somewhat and the Germans claimed to have taken a heavy toll with 35 Russian aircraft shot down, including those downed over Budapest. As for the *Luftwaffe*, *Luftflotte 4* was putting forth a maximum effort in both ground support and transport missions; 29 Russian tanks were claimed as destroyed and some 190 night bombing sorties made. The air fleet was also bolstered by the Stuka wing commanded by the most famous dive-bomber pilot of all time, Hans Ulrich Rudel, which might account for the high number of Russian tanks claimed as destroyed. Unfortunately for the Germans Rudel might also have influenced the outcome in another way.

In his memoirs Rudel relates a conference with Hitler at about this time[106], when he was summoned to Berlin to be given the unique award of the Golden Oak Leaves for his Knight's Cross, in which he describes the many flaws in *panzer* tactics he had witnessed in Hungary. Hitler is said to have used Rudel's testimony as evidence that his generals were lying to him and later events seem to bear this out. Strassner quotes Rudel's passage in his history of *5. SS Panzer Division Wiking* as evidence of poor generalship, probably directing this at both Wöhler and Balck, who had designed the attack, since those two Army officers never stopped attacking their *SS* brethren, even after the war. But there are two potential problems with Rudel's account.

After describing the conference in question, he goes on to say "He (Hitler) asks me what I think would be the most favorable terrain for the armored units to attack. I give my opinion. Later this operation is successful, and the assault group reaches the outposts of the defenders of Budapest who are able to break out."[107] This does not match up with the historical results of the *Konrad* offensives. As will be seen, the German spearheads came tantalizingly close to the

---

[106] It is generally recorded as having occurred on 1 January; this seems unlikely, however, since Rudel criticized the topography of the battlefield and its unsuitability for tanks, but Konrad I had not yet started. In all likelihood Rudel flew sorties in support of Konrad I and wondered why armored units were being used in such poor tank country.

[107] Rudel, *Stuka Pilot*, p. 188.

Budapest perimeter on two occasions but never reached it, although the vagueness of the word 'outposts' could mean almost anything.

The breakout part is more problematic. Hitler refused to allow a breakout until the city was lost and all ammunition had been fired off, and only a few men ever reached German lines; 99 percent of the garrison was lost. Rudel's advice may well have been taken, later events support his statement that Hitler believed his comments, but he was wrong that it helped save the defenders of Budapest[108]. Worse, while *IV. SS–Panzerkorps* might have agreed with Rudel's opinion of where the attack should take place before the fighting started, as shall be seen it might have led directly to the loss of the Budapest garrison when *Konrad II* was on the verge of a breakthrough. Regardless, in the end it seems probable that Rudel's comments backed up Hitler's own beliefs and directly lead to *Konrad III*. The second problem is that if Rudel's meeting took place on 1 January, as he states, then this was before *Konrad I* started. He could not then have discussed the terrain over which the attack was taking place, or the alternative route that should be taken.

The likely truth is somewhere in the middle. Like so many other German memoirs of the war, however, the flaws in Rudel's account likely stemmed from lack of access to records, missing records, faulty memory, and a desire to perhaps show the author in the best light possible. For a historian attempting to reconcile disparate accounts of the same action, it presents a difficult challenge.

---

[108] Rudel may well have told Hitler the best ground for an attack, and this may have been the route followed during Konrad III, but so few defenders of Budapest survived that Rudel's statement that the defenders of Budapest were able to break out can only be considered a gross exaggeration, at best, and outright incorrect at worst.

Two newly arrived battalions from *711. Infanterie Division* moved out from the Szomod area to join the rest of the division that was already clearing the wooded areas east and southeast of that town. Near the Danube the village of Dunaszentmiklos was still doggedly holding out against heavy attacks from the parts of *711. Infanterie Division* that had already arrived. This small town was less than five miles from the Danube Road that supplied *3. SS–Panzer Division Totenkopf's* attack to the east, and was virtually in the rear of *Wiking* and *Kampfgruppe Pape's* drive to the south. Combined with the Russian forces being engaged by *96. Infanterie Division* this meant that *Totenkopf's* supply lines would not be secure until all enemy troops were wiped out near the river and, until the two infantry divisions could catch up, the *SS* divisions would be forced to protect their own flanks. Situated in the seam between *Totenkopf* and *Wiking*, north of Agostyan and in the rear of both *panzer* divisions, the survivors of 170th Tank Brigade and 1438th Independent Artillery Brigade held Dunaszentmiklos throughout most of the day, but they were badly outnumbered and finally withdrew cross country to avoid being trapped. The terrain was terrible and the going slow, and by the end of 3 January the two brigades were still northwest of Tardos, but they had successfully disengaged from combat. Although they were on *Totenkopf's* unprotected right flank and *Wiking's* unprotected left flank, there was no way they could launch an attack. Strung out in bad country, with no clearings to assemble for an attack and with the fresh *soldaten* of the *711. Infanterie Division* hot on their heels, it was all the Russians could do to escape to fight another day.

As 3 January waned there was no clear cut verdict whether *Konrad I* was succeeding or failing.

According to Maier significant combat elements of both *Totenkopf* and *Wiking* only unloaded from their trains late on the 3rd. He blamed Wöhler and Balck for starting *Konrad I* too early and then faulting the *SS* divisions for their lack of progress. Given Gaedecke's hatred of Gille, and his influence on both Balck and the staff at *Heeresgruppe Süd*, it is hard not to see some measure of truth in this, although as an *SS* officer Maier was not a disinterested party.

Regardless of his complaints to Wöhler about the *SS* divisions, however, Balck was pleased with the results for 3 January and gave *Heeresgruppe Süd* his plans for the next day: as outlined by Balck these included *96. Infanterie Division* taking responsibility for protecting *Totenkopf*'s left flank but also advancing east past Tokod, while *Totenkopf* itself continued to attack south; *Wiking* driving on Bicske during the night, with *Kampfgruppe Pape* moving to attack Russian buildups near Alsogalla (Tatbanya) and *6. Panzer Division* joining the effort on *Wiking's* right flank once it arrived[109]. *4. Kavallerie-Brigade* would be pulled out of the line in the Vértes Mountains area to add weight to the attack and the elements of *711. Infanterie Division* that had arrived would be used for various mop-up duties.

The obvious hope was that 4. January would find *Wiking* taking Bicske with Tatbanya and Alsogalla cleared to protect its right flank, with *Totenkopf* pinning the Russian forces in front of it so that *Wiking* might turn due east and drive behind them toward Budapest. With any luck the attack might simultaneously relieve Budapest and trap all Russian forces north of the highway from Budapest to Bicske, thus annihilating a number of major Russian formations.

---

[109] The entirety of *6. Panzer Division* did not move south, only the heavy forces. Part of the division remained under 8th Army command as Kampfgruppe Bieber.

4 January, Thursday

The temperature across the battlefield remained in the low 20's Fahrenheit, with heavy icing in the mountains that made movement on roads treacherous even for tracked vehicles, and nearly impossible for trucks and other wheeled vehicles; flat areas were somewhat better. Existing newsreel footage shows German vehicles having to move slowly and carefully down an icy mountain road. Cloud conditions varied from clear to overcast, leading to a game of hide and seek between the German ground forces and prowling Russian attack aircraft. Around Lake Balaton, on *6. Armee*'s far right flank, where the Germans held the North bank and the Russians held the South, ice grew thick enough to support riflemen, but not AFVs, so a tank-supported thrust over the ice was unlikely.

Within Budapest Soviet attacks continued around the clock, especially on the eastern bank at Pest. The continual fighting caused supplies to be used up faster than expected and ammunition shortages became acute. Making things worse, the last airfield within the perimeter was lost. although *22. SS-Freiwillige-Kavallerie Division Maria Theresa* was ordered to recapture it; barring that the only way for supplies to get through to the beleaguered garrison was through airdrops and gliders.

Without asking permission, two railroad bridges were blown up to deprive their use by the Russians; Guderian countermanded the order too late. Because of this , in the future permission to destroy bridges could only come from *OKH*. Even as the garrison was under continuous attack and the situation was fluid the German High Command wanted to micro-manage the defense from Berlin.

After dark, however, the *Grenadier-Regiment 287* took Öröktarna-banya and Tokod station. The attack on Oroktarna began at 1400 hours with artillery and assault gun support. The western edge of that village just northeast of Tokod had strong *paknest*s and the fighting raged for hours, but the Germans finally prevailed; 2 assault guns were lost but a huge quantity of badly needed war materials were captured. On the right flank of *Grenadier-Regiment 287* was its sister regiment, the *Grenadier-Regiment 283*, as well as *Fusilier-Bataillon 96*. During the night those two units repulsed several counterattacks.

Standing just east of Nyergesujfalu, near the wrecked sugar factory seized the day before, the acting commander of *96. Infanterie Division,* Knight's Cross winner *Oberst* Hermann Harrendorf, deployed his 3 infantry regiments in line abreast with the *Grenadier-Regiment 287* on his left (facing south), then *Grenadier-Regiment 283* and *Grenadier-Regiment 284* on the right. In front of them were elements of 86th Rifle Division, supported by 37th Tank Brigade and 30th Guards Heavy Tank Regiment near Dorog. Moving off the Germans met resistance almost immediately, although *Grenadier-Regiment 284* took Annavolgy-banya and headed south toward Sarisap. On the left progress was torturous, with *Grenadier-Regiment 287* only gaining 1 kilometer or so in heavy fighting early in the day. The situation was so unsatisfactory that General Wöhler visited the division headquarters to find out what was the problem, probably at Hitler's instigation. The *Führer* could not understand what was taking so long, although the troops doing the fighting could; they desperately wanted to rescue their comrades in Budapest but the Russians were too strong. They were doing their best but it was not enough. On the far left of *Konrad I, 96. Infanterie Division* had the mission of threatening the Russian flank and drawing attention away from the *SS* spearheads, and so far it was not working.

As the day progressed, though, one source reports that the division managed to fight past the sugar factory near Nyergesufalu and push some 3 miles to the west of Kesztolc, a substantial advance.[110] And in the marshy lowlands beside the Danube, the Germans were trudging toward Gran.

The Russians contested every town, road and hill, and try as they might the men of *3. SS–Panzer Division Totenkopf* could only batter at one entrenched defensive position after another without breaking through. As opposition grew and losses mounted the situation grew ever more desperate, for without a breakthrough the Budapest garrison could not be saved. It was increasingly obvious that something must be done, but what? For the time being all the men of *Totenkopf* could do was keep attacking and hope for an end to the Russian reserves that kept showing up in their path of advance.

Fighting was particularly fierce west and south of Bajna, where the Russians still held a tongue of land between Hereg and Bajna that tied down forces from both *Totenkopf* and *Wiking*. This area was held by 181st Tank Brigade, and was also the route of retreat of 170th Tank Brigade and 1438th Self-Propelled Artillery Brigade, which came into the rear of the German attack from the northwest and reinforced the Russian defenses. Fighting in and around Bajna and Epöl was heavy, with both sides attacking and being

[110] Maier, *Between Budapest and Vienna,* p. 23. Maier reports this advance as "to a point 5 kilometers west of Korteles." However, Korteles is on the eastern side of the Danube and this would have meant an advance by the 96th Division all the way to Szentendre Island, nearly 20 miles. Clearly, this is not what happened and is another case of mis-identification by Maier, probably an error that occurred in his source materials. The only similar Hungarian town that fits the situation is Kesztolc.

repulsed. The villages were destroyed but late in the day the Germans broke through on the road to Szomor, threatening the right flank of 181st Tank Brigade, which immediately moved to block the *SS* men from taking Gyermely. From this position *Totenkopf*'s route south from Bajna and Szomor to the Zsambek-Tök area was in danger from Russian tanks, a threat that had to be eliminated before any further advance was possible. But more Russian reinforcements were moving to the front, in the form of 49th Guards Cavalry Division from the area just north of Tök.

On *Totenkopf*'s left flank, however, the reconnaissance battalion finally took Sarisap, threatening the road that lead southeast toward Tinnye[111]. An advance of several kilometers was considered a major success.

Marshal Tolbukhin and his staff had finally realized the extent of the German attack, as well as its main axis of advance: through Tarjan and Tatabanya to Bicske, then straight down the eastern highway to Budapest. They recognized *5. SS Panzer Division Wiking* as the primary attack force and threw every available unit into its path, so that by nightfall the division was opposed by "three rifle divisions, a mechanized brigade, a heavy tank regiment, four assault gun regiments, and six battalions of combat engineers...the artillery density reportedly amounted to about 40 guns and mortars per kilometer of front line."[112]

Moving from the vicinity of Many, the 1289th Self-Propelled Artillery Regiment, the 78th Guards Heavy Tank Regiment and 16th Guards Rifle Division intercepted *Wiking's* spearheads moving down the

[111] Maier has previously mis-identified this town as Szarkas in his narrative of the fighting on 3 January, and as Sarisan in the text for 4 January. (See note for 3 January)

[112] Maier, *Between Budapest and Vienna*, p. 23.

Szent Lazlo Canal around Vasztely. Even allowing for the badly depleted status of many Russian units this was a formidable force, but while *SS–Standartenführer* Ullrich was under intense pressure to keep moving forward despite the firestorm of Russian shelling and bombing, the rank and file *SS* men needed no prodding to try and break through to their surrounded comrades in Budapest. *Wiking's* advance on Csabdi stalled outside of Vasztely in heavy fighting.

As *5. SS–Panzer Division Wiking* regimental commander *SS–OberSS–Sturmbannführer* Fritz Darges pushed his men forward on their improbable march through the wooded ridges east and southeast of Tatabanya, an incident happened that illustrated one of the fundamental differences between the Germans and their Soviet enemies. Klapdor says that as the *panzer* column approached the city: "Kerchoff's[113] tank was hit by a Soviet anti-tank gun round in the running gear...The maintenance company, which was following the combat elements, was later able to provide Kerchoff with a repaired tank, with which he then rejoined his company north of Bicske."[114]

According to Maier, during the day those elements of *Wiking* took Tatabanya after eliminating the Soviet rear-guards, but were unable to clear Alsogalla, just south of Tatabanya. After head-on attacks from the north and northwest had failed to seize that key position in the previous days, it was hoped that a thrust from the east could come in behind the defenses and dislodge the Russians, but those attacks also failed. In fact, parts of Tatabanya were re-captured but much of the city remained in Russian hands. This was probably done by those elements of *Kampfgruppe Pape* that had been attached to *Wiking* and, while clearing Alsogalla would expedite movement through the area, it was not vital to the success of *Konrad I.* Darges, meanwhile, attacked further south and captured the a

---

[113] An *SS* platoon leader.
[114] Klapdor, p. 390

railroad crossing less than three miles southwest of Felsogalla, taking Kisnemetegyhaz and then Nagynemetegyhaz, and pushing to the outskirts of Ujtelep, which threatened 34th Guards Cavalry Division holding Tatabanya with encirclement; Soviet defenses and a wrecked bridge prevented *5. SS–Panzer Division Wiking* Regiment from tightening the noose further.

The Germans were frequently able to return damaged tanks to service, sometimes very quickly, due to well-trained mechanics and dedicated tank-recovery vehicles. In this case the maintenance company was following the tanks over rough country in bad weather. Hermann Balck himself commented after the war: "Also of great importance is good tank repair to turn around broken or damaged tanks as quickly as possible and get them back into battle—and you need this tank repair very near the front."[115] The Red Army had no equivalent service and damaged tanks were usually abandoned instead of being repaired, meaning that, for the most part, German tanks might need to be hit repeatedly to ultimately be destroyed, while Soviet tanks rarely came back into service after being damaged.

Once the Tatabanya area was at least neutralized, Darges turned back to the southeast with the next objective being Csabdi, about 9 miles away. Taking Csabdi would put *Wiking* less than a mile from Bicske and would cut the highway to Budapest,

---

[115] *Translation of Taped Conversation with German Hermann Balck, 13 April, 1979,* Performed Under Contract No. DAAK40-78-C-0004 (Battelle Columbus Tactical Technology Center, July, 1979), p. 52. Balck had further comments on how this repair was accomplished. "At the regimental level we had a maintenance unit for normal day-to-day care of the tanks. At the division level we had a full workshop that could do all kinds of repairs, change motors, etc.. For tanks that were too badly shot and too badly damaged to be repaired at the division, we simply sent them back to depots in the Homeland. We almost never had depots at levels between the division and the Homeland. As far as being able to recover tanks from the battlefield, we had special companies for doing this but we never provided enough capacity in this area. If we had had adequate capacity we would have been able to also recover lots of Russian tanks (p. 56).

making the Soviet position difficult. Nor was terrain an obstacle any longer, as the ground between Tatabanya and Csabdi was mostly flat with a good road linking the two towns. Combined with the frozen ground it made for ideal tank country. Nevertheless, as *Waffen–SS Panzergrenadier Regiment 9 Germania* in company with *5. SS–Panzer Division Wiking* pushed forward 5 kilometers on the 4 January, they were subjected to swarms of Red Army ground attack aircraft strafing and bombing them almost at will, and even the poor shooting Russian pilots could not miss every time. Bicske grew closer but the cost was high.

On *Wiking's* right flank its reconnaissance battalion closed within four miles of Bicske to the west, while the bulk of the division ran up against a *pakfront* just outside of Many, virtually within Bicske's northeastern city limits. The objective was literally within sight.

In Pest, by 4 January the supply situation had become so critical that one of the guns from the light flak battery of *SS–Flak–Abteilung* 22 was destroyed by its crew because the ammunition was all gone. The heavy infantry attacks near the Eastern Railroad Station had used up ammunition at a prodigious rate and the trickle of supplies being brought in by air was completely inadequate. The crew of the demolished gun then picked up small arms and fought as infantry.

Just as Otto Wöhler had feared, the Russians were paying close attention to the weakness of *8. Armee* north of the Danube. The days when Russian reaction to a German attack was sluggish were long gone by 1945; even as the assault units of *Konrad I* hammered toward Budapest, STAVKAsaw an opportunity to counterattack along a broad front, seize Komárom (Komarom) and drive into the rear of the *Konrad* attack, potentially pocketing *IV. SS–Panzerkorps* . Accordingly, at 0240 orders came from Moscow for 2nd and 3rd Ukrainian Fronts to prepare to go over to the offensive. North of the Danube 2nd Ukrainian Front was to use at least two corps from *Generaloberst* Shumilov's 7th Guards and General Kravschenko's 6th Guards Tank Armies to drive west from Sturovo[116] and capture Komárom (Komarom), while 3rd Ukrainian Front was to use forces from 5th Guards Cavalry Corps, 4th Guards Army, 18th Tank Corps and 1st Mechanized Corps to drive north-northwest from the Bicske area to Nezmely on the Danube; in other words, straight through *Wiking* and *Kampfgruppe Pape*. All available air forces were to support the attack. The date was set for January 6th.

German reconnaissance was quick to spot the movement of the forces gathering for the attack, particularly 6th Guards Tank Army, although where exactly the moving Russians were going was not yet known. Intelligence estimates decided they might be gathering for an attack on the extreme left flank of Konrad, that is, against *96. Infanterie Division*, or against Komárom out of the bridgehead west of the Gran, their true mission. Nevertheless, even as the storm gathered, the German withdrawal of *6. Panzer Division* from the very area targeted by the Russians proceeded apace. With the *Führer* breathing down his neck to relieve Budapest, Otto Wöhler had no choice except to gamble that *8. Armee* could hold even if attacked. Furthermore, while *8. Armee's* front was already weak enough to draw the attention of STAVKA, it was being contemplated to withdraw two more *panzer* divisions from the front lines, *3. Panzer Division* and *8. Panzer Division*. The loss of the veteran *6. Panzer Division* would by itself increase the danger to the German front north of the Danube, but losing both

---

[116] Sturovo is a small city on the north bank of the Danube opposite Esztergom on the south bank.

Panzer formations risked a complete frontal collapse. By a fortunate circumstance *6. Panzer Division* was to be committed in the very sector threatened by the southern part of the Soviet offensive, although the Germans did not know this at the time; attack, counterattack and counter-counterattack was the order of the day in Western Hungary.

As 4 January waned, the Hungarian battlefield was a roiling mass of trudging men, sliding tanks and crowded roads as units of both sides moved behind, up to and back from the front, and in the confusion Hermann Balck was on the verge of losing control of the battle. Units and parts of units had become intermingled, minor tactical objectives had been pursued in place of the larger operational ones and there was general confusion about not only what was happening, but about what should happen the next day. Regardless of *6. Armee*'s situation, Balck's orders to break through to Budapest had not changed, nor had the relentless pressure from his superiors slackened, so to accomplish his mission more firepower had to be brought to bear against the increasing Russian strength.

Despite ominous aerial reconnaissance photos predicting that a Soviet attack north of the Danube was a distinct possibility, *8. Armee* was further weakened as *3. Panzer Division* was ordered to cross to the south bank for attachment to *Kampfgruppe Breith*, aka *III. Panzerkorps*,[117] while *8. Panzer Division* was ordered to pull back into reserve.[118] *211. Volksgrenadier Division*

[117] *General der Panzertruppe* Herman Breith won the Knight's Cross with Oak Leaves and Swords. He was a very well respected commander.

[118] Although a veteran division with a long history of service on the Eastern Front, *8. Panzer Division* was considered an unlucky division. The author interviewed a former member of the division who claimed that regardless of circumstance, the division always seemed to be five minutes too early or too late.

and the Hungarian Svent Laszlo Divisions were ordered into the line to replace the departed *panzer* divisions. The Russian 6th Guards Tank Army was one of the units identified as moving east of the Gran and heavy artillery interdiction was ordered to try and disrupt its movements. Of course, using ammunition for interdiction missions fired off the limited stocks quickly.

Balck was glad for the reinforcements, but instead of using the new divisions to reinforce the assault units that were already engaged with the enemy, *6. Armee* issued a lengthy list of orders for future operations that widened both the scope of the offensive and its goals. As always, Hermann Balck thought he knew best and did not hesitate to exceed his orders.

Some of his new plans were realistic, some were not, but for any of them to become reality the Germans would have to overcome increasingly stiff resistance. Unfortunately for them the formations leading the attack were rapidly wearing down and Balck's decision not to reinforce them meant lessening pressure at the *schwerpunkt* against growing resistance. It is very hard not to see Balck's starving *IV. SS–Panzerkorps* of reinforcements as nothing less than a petty personal squabble ahead of operational needs. Nor was the confused command and supply situation helping matters.

After mopping up behind the attack, *711. Infanterie Division* was attached to *IV. SS–Panzerkorps* and ordered to take Esztergom to protect *96. Infanterie Division*'s flank, while *96. Infanterie Division* was to continue driving south from the Dorog-Csolnok area to Pilisvorosvar, a key position virtually within the borders of Budapest itself. The attack of *3. SS–Panzer Division Totenkopf* was to aim for southwest Budapest in the Erd-Tarnok area, with a main objective to capture the airfield at Budaörs so that supplies for the Budapest garrison would be immediately available. *5. SS–Panzer Division Wiking*, on *Totenkopf*'s right flank, now facing the heaviest resistance of the entire offensive, was ordered to first capture Biscke, then to push on to the southeast Martonvasar. This would cut the highway from Budapest to Stuhlweissenburg (Szekesfehersvar) and threaten the Soviet positions near that city. In *III. Panzerkorps*' sector, *6. Panzer Division* was first ordered to capture the heavily defended Felsogalla Gap, on the southern outskirts of Tatabanya, by an attack to the south-southwest, then together with *Kampfgruppe Pape* to force a passage all the way to Kapolnasnyek at the northeastern tip of Lake Velence, a distance of almost 25 miles[119].

No attack was to be made on Stuhlweissenburg itself, but *4. Kavallerie Brigade*, along with the armored elements of *1. Panzer Division* and *23. Panzer Division Division*, were to drive to the western tip of Lake Velence. The idea was to block the Russian retreat to the south while *Wiking* and *Kampfgruppe Pape* moved in to the east, thus cutting off and pocketing all Russian forces north of the lake and south of the Danube. Once *3. Panzer Division* arrived from the *8. Armee* sector it was intended as reinforcements for this attack, and *OKH* ordered the *3. Kavallerie Brigade* to Veszprem as further reinforcements from this effort. Balck reported that in total he was adding some 100 tanks to the effort.[120]

Had these efforts worked as planned the Germans would have won a major victory. 3rd Ukrainian Front would have been mangled, a blow from which it would take months to recover, Budapest would have been relieved and the vital defense line of the

---

[119] 25 miles might not seem like a long way, but there was only one road the Germans could use and Russian resistance was very determined. Considering that even with the advantage of tactical surprise Konrad had not yet captured anywhere near that amount of territory it is hard to think that an experienced commander like Hermann Balck believed his forces capable of such a feat. And yet, after the stinging rebuke of having been demoted from an Army Group Commander to a mere Army commander, it would be entirely understandable if Balck tried to pull off a miraculous victory to regain an Army Group Command, and with it perhaps a Marshal's baton.

[120] Maier, *Between Budapest and Vienna*, pp. 23-24.

Danube would have allowed the Germans to hold the front with fewer forces and, most crucially, with fewer armored formations. Those irreplaceable units could then have been used to blunt Russian offensives further to the north. Otto Wöhler and Hermann Balck were aiming high; relieving Budapest was no longer enough. Instead of concentrating all available firepower and trying to punch a hole in the Russian front that could open a corridor to Budapest, the two veteran German generals were looking for a signal victory, one that would change everything. Like the Ardennes Offensive before it and *Unternehmen Frühlingserwachen* (*Unternehmen Frühlingserwachen*) after, the mission's objective was nothing less than changing the face of the entire war, with unpredictable consequences of what might happen next.

At such a distance in time after the events it is impossible to know how possible the two generals considered their plans. However, there has long been speculation about why Hitler sent *all* of Germany's last offensive firepower to Hungary in 1945 to launch the terribly ill-conceived *Unternehmen Frühlingserwachen*, with his explanation of protecting the Hungarian oil reserves seeming like a thin excuse for the offensive as planned. Is it possible that Wöhler and Balck built on a formerly considered offensive that Hitler had been known to favor in late 1944.[121] The idea was essentially what later became *Konrad III* and, later, *Unternehmen Frühlingserwachen*. It certainly seems possible; once Hitler had an idea, he rarely gave up on it.

Planning and speculation inevitably gave way to reality, and it was all too much; *6. Armee* was simply not capable of achieving such monumental goals. Relieving Budapest had given way to larger ambitions

[121] Although never formalized into plans, the code name for this offensive has never been officially nailed down.

which, if the forces at hand had been organized, reinforced, rested and supplied properly, might have been possible. As things stood they were not. Aside from shortages of food, fuel and ammunition, exhaustion of the assault forces and the overall depleted state of the various units, even worse was the constant shuffling of forces for short-term tactical considerations. This policy was becoming entrenched in the attack planning as Wöhler and Balck responded to the constant pressure from *OKH* by promoting whatever idea seemed best at the moment. Divisions became intermingled and close coordination became more difficult; divisional components were split up to serve an immediate need, welded into a kampfgruppe and then divided again as needed. Orders of battle quickly became hopelessly confused.

Nor did on-the-spot decisions by commanders in the field help maintain cohesion, such as Fritz Darges' decision to move cross-country from Tarjan to Tatabanya, however much it might have been justified by the local tactical situation. According to Maier, by the end of 4 January this self-defeating policy of seeking the short-term tactical gain was becoming a regular feature of the conduct of the battle, much to the Germans' detriment[122]. "As a result of this continuous regrouping for the formation of *kampfgruppen*, the divisional formations lost their unit integrity...the cohesiveness of the units, the soldier's 'home'-the place the soldier clung to and which offered him moral support-was destroyed again and again by this emphasis on tactical considerations. This was a mistake in psychology and in combat leadership...Heeresgruppe Süd saw itself forced to remind *Armeegruppe Balck* [*6. Armee*] nonetheless of the necessity of 'restoring the integrity of the armored

---

[122] While Maier may well be correct in his interpretation of events, it must be remembered that just as Balck's memoirs of the battle served as a platform to attack the Waffen-SS, so did Maier's account allow him to attack Balck in defense of the Waffen-SS.

divisions in the course of the regrouping'."[123] The weakness of the units was compounded by their fragmentation and dispersal of effort.

As 4 January ended, no German from Hitler down the chain of command could reckon *Konrad* as having yet been successful. A note in the *Heeresgruppe Süd* war diary for 6 January noted that during the period 1–4 January, *IV. SS–Panzerkorps* had destroyed "79 tanks, 106 guns and 107 anti-tank guns."[124] This was a significant infliction of damage on the Russians, but even at a tactical level it would have been hard to be satisfied with the results of the attack to date. And in achieving what they had, the Germans themselves had suffered heavy losses that could not be made good. In particular, losses among the infantry were especially damaging. The need for more men was so acute that there was even a plan to order the shattered 1st Hungarian Hussar (Cavalry) Division back into combat. This veteran division had seen very heavy fighting in 1944 and had come close to being destroyed during Operation Bagration the previous summer; it fought so bravely that it was mentioned in dispatches and was even spoken highly of by General Guderian. But the toll had been terrible and the Hussars were withdrawn to reorganize on 31 December, with some elements of the division trapped with the Budapest garrison. The idea of re-committing it to combat was so devastating to the divisional operations officer, General Staff Major Laszlo Simon, that he killed himself in despair.

Entering the fifth day of *Konrad I* it was true that some ground had been recaptured, but none of it was strategic, or even particularly important. The overall objective of relieving Budapest remained distant. Unless something could be achieved quickly other measures would be required.

---

[123] Maier, *Drama Between Budapest and Vienna*, p. 24.
[124] Maier, *Drama Between Budapest and Vienna*, p. 98.

5 January, Friday

Weather in western Hungary remained gloomy and bitter, with highs staying in the low 20s and skies thickly overcast, hampering air operations for both sides. Strangely enough, however, elements of *8. Armee* reported being attacked by seven *JU-87 Stukas*. With no *Luftwaffe* aircraft flying in the area it was presumed the *Stukas* were flown by pilots of Germany's former ally, Rumania. No damage was noted.

By 5 January, however, the toll taken by the wet, seeping cold had begun to sap the strength of men who were entering their fifth consecutive day of combat. Nor could they expect help. With levels of infantry low throughout *Heeresgruppe Süd* there was no relief in sight. Exhausted men could only put their heads down and fight.

6. Armee spent much of 5 January reorganizing its forces, re-assessing objectives and redrawing boundary lines in recognition that the fractured command structure in the field was hampering the *Konrad* attacks. The intense struggle left some units close to combat ineffective. For days there had been confusion between *IV. SS–Panzerkorps* and *III. Panzerkorps*, aka *Kampfgruppe Breith*, about areas of responsibility; the boundary line between the two corps overlapped in a number of places, leading to *IV. SS–Panzerkorps* attacking through *III. Panzerkorps'* area of responsibility and a consequent fragmentation of effort. Logistics were a mess. On 5 January the boundary line was redrawn to stop this, a long overdue correction. Despite this tacit admission, however, Hermann Balck continued using his forces in a piecemeal fashion for the duration of the war.

On the plus side for *IV. SS–Panzerkorps* , the last trains containing elements of both *3. SS–Panzer*

Division Totenkopf and *5. SS Panzer Division Wiking* finally arrived in the theater. According to Maier, the intention had been for these fresh troops to take over the attack from the exhausted spearheads to keep up the pressure, however, losses had been so heavy that instead the new men were needed as reinforcements to keep the units already engaged fighting, with no chance to rest those troops who were entering the fourth day of the offensive.

Meanwhile, a shift of focus to the southern flank also picked up speed, as reinforcements continued to be sent to back the push toward Lake Velence at the expense of *IV. SS–Panzerkorps*. Instead, when the Germans opened an offensive on the south bank of the Danube, the Soviets countered with one of their own on the north bank, aimed at taking the vital bridge at Komárom.

To hold Komárom and keep the two *SS* divisions supplied in their offensive, the Germans had to commit the Army's *20. Panzer Division* out of the reserve. This unit had been nearly destroyed during the Soviet summer offensive, and by August its remnants were in East Prussia for re-fitting and re-training. Smaller armored units were absorbed, replacements and new equipment assigned, and by winter the division was considered fit for combat. It was not assigned to the Ardennes offensive, however, but instead went to Hungary to defend Komárom.

3. Panzer Division was assigned to the forces aimed in the direction of Stuhlweissenburg and assembled near Mor. Hitler supported this change of emphasis, even wanting to move the newly arriving *20. Panzer Division* to *6. Armee*'s far right flank. Guderian opposed this, sensing the danger threatening *8. Armee* as *Heeresgruppe Süd* feared a Russian attack north of the Danube. As things turned out, in this case the Russians attacked before Hitler had a chance to tell Guderian he was wrong.

During Roman Imperial times the Danube River marked the northern boundary of the Empire. There were occasional military forays beyond the river to keep this or that 'barbarian' tribe in check; Trajan's Dacian Wars in Bulgaria are one example of a war for the Danube, while Marcus Aurelius spent years campaigning in what is now Hungary and Slovakia to suppress the ever-increasing threat the Germanic peoples posed to Roman territory there. Violence could happen at any moment and fortified towns, known as 'castrum', were common for times when the Germanic tribes raided south of the Danube and the local populace needed a refuge. In twenty centuries very little had changed. The ruins of one such castrum were in the small city of Tokod, an important commercial crossroads for nearly two thousand years, where *96. Infanterie Division* was struggling to fight through Russian defenses, capturing a mill and small factory in the early hours of 5 January. On the western side of the attack the *Grenadier-Regiment 284* Grenadier Regiment made progress, but on the eastern flank the *Grenadier Regiment 287* lost its *II Bataillon* commander when he was wounded attacking Dorog, the regiment being thrown back with heavy losses. The Russians had dug in Stalin tanks from the 30th Guards Heavy Tank Regiment, a tactic used to great effect at Kursk, and the Germans were unable to dig them out without tanks of their own. Once again the firepower to blast a way through the defenses was lacking.

711. Infanterie Division began collecting its scattered parts in the area north of Tokod with the mission of moving off to the east and southeast, in the direction of Kesztolic and Csev through a relatively flat valley on the western edge of the Pilis Mountains. This would outflank the Russians still stubbornly defending Csolnok and Dorog. Other elements were also heading down the banks of the Danube toward Gran, a routine movement that would change everything.

On *96. Infanterie Division*'s right flank, *3. SS–Panzer Division Totenkopf* was also clawing its way forward, fighting for every yard. *SS–Panzergrenadier Regiment 6 Theodor Eicke* drove forward on both sides of the Bajna-Szomor Road, finally getting into the northern suburbs of that town despite heavy Russian defenses. Defending the Szomor area were 5th Guards Motorized Rifle Brigade on the Russian's right flank and 49th Guards Cavalry Division on the left. Supporting both were 110th and 170th Tank Brigades, 1438th Independent Self-Propelled Artillery Regiment and 363rd Heavy Self-Propelled Regiment. Taking Szomor was important to secure the left flank of *5. SS–Panzer Division Wiking Division*; less than a mile to the west was the small village of Gyermely, from where the Russians threatened *Wiking's* flank. The *Totenkopf* men were able to capture the northern part of Szomor but the Russians were there in great strength. "Forty-five tanks and numerous anti-tanks guns were confirmed at the northern entrance and in the northwest section of the village; 18 tanks and an anti-tank gun belt were on the high ground to the southwest."[125] The Russians to the southwest were a dual threat both to *Totenkopf* and to *Wiking*, but they were also in a precarious position, being nearly sandwiched between the two divisions. In a classic envelopment attack, *panzergrenadiers* from both of *Totenkopf's* regiments took Szomor in heavy house-to-house fighting, while elements of *5. SS–Panzer Division Wiking's Grenadier Regiment Thule* moved through the village and linked up with men from the *II./Westland* southwest of

[125] Maier, *Drame Between Budapest and Vienna*, pp. 24-25.

Szomor, near Vasztely. Thus, *Totenkopf* and *Wiking* were in contact and presenting a more or less unified front to the enemy. A counterattack on *Thule's* left flank by 5th Guards Motorized Rifle Brigade was repulsed.

Meanwhile, on orders from *IV. SS–Panzerkorps* to get both *Totenkopf* and *Wiking* moving again, the *III./Theodor Eicke* veered sharply northeast from the area just southeast of Epöl, cutting across the road leading from Sarisap to the southeast. *SS–Aufklärung Abteilung 3* had captured most of Sarisap the previous day but was unable to drive on the nearby village of Dag because of strong Russian defenses northwest of that village, where 86th Guards Rifle Division was dug-in and supported by 4th Guards Mechanized Brigade. The *panzergrenadiers* attacked south of the village and some ground was taken in the direction of Uny, but without Dag itself it did not help the situation much. The heights around Dag commanded the road south, so even though Sarisap was in German hands the road south was not safe, and until Dag was captured any traffic on that road would be under fire.

The fact that it was *Totenkopf's Aufklärung Abteilung* (reconnaissance battalion) attacking Dag exemplifies the slow and savage nature of the fighting; a reconnaissance battalion was built to scout and exploit the penetration of enemy defenses and to spread havoc in his rear, not to launch assaults on fixed positions. Reconnaissance battalions were equipped with fast, highly maneuverable armored cars and *SPWs*, but even the most heavily armed of those were no match for Russian tanks and bunkers. For example, while late war designs of the final German wheeled reconnaissance vehicle, the *Sd.Kfz. 234, Sonderkraftfahrzeug 234*[126] family of armored cars all featured large calibers guns compared to previous models, less than 500 were built during the war's final two years.

---

[126] Special purpose vehicle 234.

Puma

Schwerer Panzerspähwagen (SdKfz. 234/2)

Puma

The *Puma* series of heavy armored cars proved to be a superb design, being fast
at a top speed of 90 km/h and with an off-road range of 600 kilometers. The
Puma came with a variety of main guns, including 20mm, 50mm and 75mm.
Like so many other advanced German designs, the biggest drawback was its low
production numbers.

Instead, attacks by reconnaissance units
depended on speed and flanking maneuvers; blasting a
hole in a *pakfront* was not the intended mission for a
reconnaissance battalion. *SS–Aufklärung Abteilung 3*
had been looking for a hole in the Russian front but
could not find one.

The use of *III./Theodor Eicke* also conflicted with
the spirit of an order from *6. Armee* to broaden the *SS*
division's fronts as the army shifted the main
schwerpunkt of the offensive further south, from *IV.
SS–Panzerkorps* to *III. Panzerkorps*. This new emphasis
did not sit well with the *SS* leadership; instead of yet
another under-strength attack on a new objective, Otto
Gille wanted to use a *kampfgruppe* from *Wiking* to do
what *III./Theodor Eicke* had done, swing northeast and
drive behind the Russian forces holding up *Totenkopf*
at Szomor. This would not only have secured *Wiking's*
left flank but simultaneously opened a road south for
Totenkopf. Hermann Balck, however, refused the

request, despite what appeared to be a tactically sound move.

In the southern outskirts of Tatabanya, 34th Guards Cavalry Division still held Felsogalla and an attack from that area captured the high ground some 2 miles to the northeast. This incursion posed a serious threat to the far right flank of *IV. SS–Panzerkorps* but the Germans did what the Germans always did: they counterattacked immediately and recaptured the high ground. Moreover, they were able to hold it and so, with the threat eliminated, the attack south could continue. Another attack toward Tarjan was repulsed at Baglyas-hegy by the *II./Panzergrenadier Regiment 4*, of *6. Panzer Division*.

Elements of *Wiking* had been pushing forward throughout the night from the Tarjan area heading for Csabdi; meanwhile, Fritz Darges' *panzer* regiment took advantage of darkness to rejoin the division northeast of Csabdi in the area of Tükrös. The move had been hard, with prime movers necessary to drag some of the *panzers* up steep inclines while working in the blackness of night, but ultimately it was successful. Around dawn, the advance elements found the road to Bicske, less than two miles from that city[127]. This area was held by 16th Motorized Rifle Brigade but Darges' command slipped around the right flank and the Russians were caught completely off-guard; a supply convoy was utterly destroyed, including four 122mm guns, four 76mm antitank guns, 12 trucks and dozens

---

[127] Maier says that *5. SS–Panzer Division Wiking* Tank Regiment joined with elements of Germania 3 miles northwest of Many before turning southwest toward Csabdi. Was this incident the one that led to the capture of Regis Castle on Hegykastely? Maier does not say either way. The presence of both Westland and Germania would argue against it, since they were not trapped at Regis Castle. But the addition of I/Norge argues for it, as does the mention of the supply convoy. If this is not the convoy destroyed in Darges' attack on Hegykastely then there must have been two such destroyed.

of other vehicles. Using both of its *panzergrenadier* regiments, *Germania* and *Westland*, and backed by the heaviest possible artillery support, *Wiking* clawed its way as far as Vasztely and the northern outskirts of Csabdi on 5 January.

Russian counterattacks came in from all directions, and the *II./Westland* drove off a large counterattack from the direction of Gyermely on the eastern flank, although once *Totenkopf* captured Szomor the Russians at Gyermely were faced with destruction from their rear. Confusion threatened to descend into chaos all along the front, yet despite the ferocious opposition Bicske was within the German grasp. Unfortunately for them, with every advance the impetus of the attack was slowing as both divisions grew progressively weaker, even as the rescuers got within 23 miles of Budapest.

(The division's reconnaissance battalion had become trapped in the fighting less than 2 miles northwest of Csabdi, but was rescued from encirclement by elements of the newly arrived *6. Panzer Division*. Along with *Kampfgruppe Pape*, *6. Panzer Division* had been subordinated to *IV. SS–Panzerkorps* [128]. The combined forces then resumed their attack to the southeast.

Konrad had not quite bogged down, with forward progress still being made, but it was not being made fast enough to suit an ever-more-impatient *Fuhrer*. Hitler needed and expected a quick and decisive victory, not a drawn-out slugfest, since *IV. SS–Panzerkorps* might have to be transferred to a critical hotspot elsewhere along the Eastern Front at a moment's notice.

---

[128] Minus Kampfgruppe Beiber, the division's lighter elements, that were left behind to support 271st Volksgrenadier Division on the Gran Front.

So, as the operation began to sputter out short of Budapest, Heinz Guderian travelled to Hungary aboard a special command train to find out for himself exactly what was going wrong so that he could report back to Hitler, with recommendations of what to do next. With him traveled *Chef der Operationsabteilung des Generalstabs des Heeres* (Chief of the Operations Section of the Army General Staff), *Oberst* von Bonin[129]. In his memoirs, Guderian says "during the period 5–January-8th I visited General Wöhler...General Balck and the *SS* General Gille; I discussed with them the future prosecution of operations in Hungary and found out why the attack to relieve Budapest had failed. The principal reason seemed to be that the initial success won during the night attack of January 1st had not been exploited with sufficient boldness to constitute a breakthrough on the following night. We had neither the commanders nor troops of the 1940 quality anymore[130]; otherwise this attack might well have been successful, troops might then have been available for transfer elsewhere, and the Danube front might have been stabilized for a time."[131]

Guderian's mention of the quality of the men and officers echoes what Wöhler wrote in the *Heeresgruppe Süd* War Diary entry for 3 January, giving the impression that Wöhler and Guderian must have discussed this point, and Guderian either agreed with the assessment or adopted it as his own[132]. Regardless of what Guderian wrote later, he and Wöhler must have

[129] Within two weeks von Bonin would be arrested by the Gestapo for giving Army Group A permission to retreat in Poland, thereby contradicting a Führer Order.

[130] Yet again we hear echoes of Gaedecke's condemnation of the SS that had made its way into the *Heeresgruppe Süd* War Diary, a recurring theme that would continue for the rest of the war.

[131] Guderian, *Panzer Leader*, p. 386.

[132] It seems unlikely that Guderian would have formed this opinion from his own observations, since he was not on the scene at the time in question. Nor would he have given Gille's opinion much weight. In all likelihood we see Balck influencing first Wöhler and then Guderian to blame those actually doing the fighting for poor combat skills, i.e., the *Waffen–SS*.

realized that a large part of the problem with *Konrad I* was not the talent or experience of his commanders and their troops, the real problem was that they just were not strong enough to penetrate the Russian defenses. Aside from the fact that *Wiking's panzer* regiment was only at percent strength, it was unreasonable to expect troops who had ridden a train for more than a week to detrain and march virtually straight into offensive operations with little rest, less air support, missing key components of their formations, in icy winter weather and with no chance to properly reconnoiter the ground over which they would attack, and then to continue the attack for four days virtually without pause. Even in their heyday this would have been asking for a miracle, but German troops were not miracle workers any longer, over-achieving on the battlefield through sheer professionalism, so unless more weight could be added to the attack it was doomed to failure.

Pierik concurs, reporting that Wöhler knew more forces had to be found to reinforce the faltering spearheads of *IV. SS–Panzerkorps* , and reluctantly looked to the Gran Front for additional units as the *OKH* had been urging him to do. Both *Kampfgruppe Pape* and the heavy elements of *6. Panzer Division* had already joined the battle south of the Danube but Wöhler knew that would not be enough. Even so, the German defense along the Gran River was shaky and Wöhler had no choice but to leave *8. Panzer, 211. Volksgrenadier Division* and the Hungarian St. Lazlo Division in place to hold that front, but he pulled out *3. Panzer Division* to reinforce the main effort at relieving Budapest. He was gambling that the Gran front could hold long enough for the additional forces to break through to Budapest, a gamble that would nearly fail.

But instead of sending the reinforcements to *IV. SS–Panzerkorps* , as previously discussed, the new schwerpunkt was moved south to *III. Panzerkorps*; thus, *3. Panzer Division* was attached to that corps in the area near Mör for the attack on Stuhlweissenburg.

Wöhler also wanted *Kampfgruppe Pape* to get moving again, with both *III. Panzerkorps* and *I Kavallerie Korps* supporting it by attacking near Zámoly.

IV. SS–Panzerkorps was to receive some help, however. At Neuhammer, the *Waffen–SS* training grounds in Thuringia, the ski battalions from the two still-forming Hungarians divisions *Hungaria* and *Hunyadi* were entrained and sent to Hungary to reinforce the efforts to break through to Budapest. Neither battalion was fully battle-worthy being deficient in arms and equipment of all types, and with their training incomplete. Still, warm bodies were warm bodies.

And the attacks *were* relieving pressure on the garrison of Budapest. According to Pierik, while on New Year's Day the defenders of Buda had faced nine Soviet divisions and were under heavy pressure, by 5 January that number was down to four divisions as units were shifted and withdrawn to fight Operation *Konrad I*.[133] Unfortunately for the Germans, breathing space wasn't what the defenders of Budapest needed, salvation was, and that remained nothing more than a flickering hope.

[133] Pierik, p. 141.

6 January, Saturday

"Although January was indeed unfavorable for flying – there were a total of 7 days suitable for flying and 13 days suitable for limited flying – the German Command sent out masses of flights. The 101/I-II Fighter Battalions participated in 136 flight deployments, won 49 air combats (6 of them without witnesses), and also lost 6 men killed."[134]

Given the overall lack of surviving records it is no surprise that air battles over the Hungarian battlefield in 1945 are so poorly documented. The above quote gives some indication of how hard the Germans pushed their limited resources to try and partially compensate for inadequate numbers.

Periodic snow and overcast conditions once again prevailed over most of the battlefield as *Konrad I* entered its fifth full day of combat, with temperatures still hovering in the mid 20's F. and air operations hampered by low-hanging clouds. Men of both sides suffered, with no chance to dry wet uniforms and boots; risking a fire was courting death. Shivering expended energy and sapped strength, and the more sleep-deprived the men were, the more food they needed to energize their exhausted bodies. Yet not only was food in short supply, but opportunities to rest and eat were also infrequent. Misery was the watchword of the day.

Despite the sky conditions the Red Air Force flew through the snow squalls and cloud cover and

---

[134] Miklós, Szabó *Establishment of the Hungarian Air Force and the Activity of the Hungarian Royal "Honvéd" Air Force in World War II Respectively, N.° 110 - 3* (The Institute of National Defense: Primavera, 2005), p. 208.

continued with relentless ground attacks on anything that moved. Chunks of ice clogged both the Danube and Lake Balaton, while road conditions remained slippery and dangerous. Fields stayed frozen so that cross-country mobile operations were not only feasible, but often better than on the road network. Yet fields covered in deep snow could hide natural tank-traps, such as ditches or stream-beds, and a broken axle was just as effective as a 76 mm anti-tank gun at putting an *SPW* out of action.

In low-lying Pest, German losses were not only mounting rapidly; they were becoming so heavy that Pfeffer-Wildenbruch was running out of men to hold the front; large gaps appeared in the defense. Pierik says that by 6 January, casualties for *IX. SS-Waffen-Gebirgs-Armeekorps der SS* had reached 5,621.[135] This is from a report by *IX. SS-Waffen-Gebirgs-Armeekorps der SS* sent on the 7 January giving an overall view of the situation. Ammunition was also being used up much faster than originally predicted and it began to appear that Budapest might fall long before the Germans had thought. Worse, on 6 January the Soviets captured the last factory in Pest that was still manufacturing spare parts, while simultaneously being utilized as a vehicle repair depot.

With the situation in Pest growing worse by the hour, the remaining guns of *SS–Flak–Abteilung 22* were withdrawn over the Danube to Buda. Food supplies were rapidly being used up. Virtually the entire food ration for *22. SS-Kavallerie Division Maria Theresa* came from the 16 horses each regiment of the division was slaughtering daily.[136]

---

[135] Pierik, p. 141. No breakdown of this number is given and it is assumed this represents killed, wounded and missing.

[136] Landwehr, Richard, *Siegrunen #38*, p. 26.

A landing field was re-established on Csepel Island, however, allowing 38 tons of supplies to be flown in; 23 out of 36 JU-52s managed to land and take off again, carrying 228 wounded out with them. Another 40 tons worth of supplies were air-dropped by 9 JU-52s and 49 HE-111s, and while this was a significant resupply effort accomplished only by extreme effort and courage by the *Luftwaffe* crews running the gauntlet of Russian air defenses, in the long run it was not nearly enough. Once known to the Russians they quickly brought the landing field under fire and it became too dangerous to use, leaving the garrison once again dependent solely on air-drops, while the food and ammunition stocks were virtually gone; artillery ammunition was especially low and at least 3,000 wounded needed to be evacuated. What had been a flash of hope quickly vanished.[137]

Meanwhile, at 0300 hours just to the northwest, Soviet spearheads from 2nd Ukrainian Front crossed the Gran River and slammed into the Svent László Hungarian Parachute Division and *Kampfgruppe Bieber*,[138] the forward elements of *LVII Panzerkorps*. The offensive was designed not only to penetrate further into Slovakia but also to threaten turning the flank of *Heeresgruppe Süd*, particularly *IV. SS–Panzerkorps* in the Pilis and Gerecse Mountains, by seizing Komárom, with its oil refineries and standing bridge over the Danube. The two ready reserve divisions, *8. Panzer Division* and *211. Volksgrenadier Division*, were immediately committed to battle but were unable to stop the assault; Wöhler's gamble to pull *3. Panzer Division* out of its defensive positions

[137] Maier, *Drama Between Budapest and Vienna*, pp. 26-27.
[138] The elements of *6. Panzer Division* still on the Gran Front, stripped of their heavy weapons.

along the Gran to reinforce the attack on Budapest had backfired.

The two Russian Guards Armies[139] used in the offensive, 6th Guards Tank Army, commanded by Gen. Kravschenko, and 7th Guards Army, commanded by *Generaloberst* Schumilov, launched a powerful attack that stunned then penetrated the Svent László Parachute Division, brushed aside *211. Volksgrenadier Division* and the veteran *8. Panzer Division* as they tried to plug the gap, and began the drive on Komárom. The Germans fought hard along the Gran and took a heavy toll of the attackers; the Russians lost 23 tanks achieving their breakthrough, but by the end of the day the 53rd Rifle Division (commanded by Colonel D.V. Vasilevsky) had fought its way down the road paralleling the north bank of the Danube to seize Kravany nad Dunajom, a small town about a third of the way to Komárom. 5th Guards Tank Corps (Major General M.I. Saveliev) cut through a determined defense to capture Batorove Kosihy, about 7 miles north-northeast of Kravany nad Dunajom, and further north 9th Guards Mechanized Corps (Lt. General M.L. Volkov) and 375th Rifle Division also had to fight through a vicious defense to take Gbelce, lagging somewhat behind the southern flank of the attack. On the northern flank the advance was less menacing, as 6th Guards (*Oberst* G.V. Ivanov) and 409th Rifle (Major General G.P. Grechany) Divisions could only penetrate some 3 miles, but the northern flank was not the crucial sector. Komárom was the key to the entire German position in Western Hungary and Komárom was under a direct threat.

The sledgehammer was the elite 6th Guards Tank Army, with over 250 tanks, which was mostly responsible for ripping the ten-mile-wide gap through the German and Hungarian defenses. Over the following three days, the force advanced 80 kilometers

---

[139] Two Armies would be the equivalent of two German Corps, or one German Army, still a very powerful force.

toward Komárom, a crucial rail hub supplying much of the Axis effort in Hungary. By 8 January, the offensive had lost momentum on the outskirts of Komárom, similar to how Gille's panzer corps was held up at the Bicske road junction. This created a striking parallel, with the Germans pushing east on the southern bank of the Danube while an equally powerful Soviet force advanced west on the northern bank.

But on 6 January the Russian spearheads had penetrated nearly 18 kilometers in places.[140] Numerous German kampfgruppen had been surrounded and were fighting for their lives. Once word of this advance and the threat to Komárom became known it spread panic up the German chain of command, all the way to Hitler. The small city on the Danube was important not only for its oil refineries, but also because it had the only remaining permanent bridge over the Danube connecting Slovakia and Hungary. A patchwork defense was thrown together from whatever units could be found. The *panzerjäger* battalion from *13. Panzer Division* had not been trapped in Budapest with the rest of the division and was used in the defense, along with the 12 tanks of *Panzer Bataillon 208*,[141] *Flak Bataillon 286* and an army machine gun battalion. None of these formations was impressive when compared to the Russian equivalent of a German *Panzer* Army, but reinforcements were on the way in the form of *20. Panzer Division*. Commanded by *Generalmajor* Herman von Oppeln-Browikowski it moved quickly south to join the defense,[142] a decision made because Guderian happened to be on the scene of the unfolding disaster and changed *20. Panzer*

[140] One source said 25 miles but most claim 16 kilometers.
[141] 12 tanks would not even make one complete company, much less a battalion.
[142] *Generalmajor* von Oppeln-Browikowski was an interesting character. He was considered a superb *panzer* commander who held a noticeable contempt for his superiors. He also drank heavily, yet this never affected his combat leadership. On 6 June, 1944, he led a *panzer* counterattack that actually broke through to the coast, but without support had to retreat before the few *panzers* could disrupt the landings.

Division's destination on the spot. Instead of moving to Altsohl (Zvolen), under command of *Heeresgruppe Mitte*, it was detoured to Neuhäusel, (Nove Zamky) and given to *Heeresgruppe Süd*. Combined with the reorganizing *8. Panzer Division* and *211. Volksgrenadier Division*, and what was left of the mauled St. Lazlo Division, it was hoped that this force could stop the Soviet drive and save Komárom. It did... barely. But *8. Panzer Division* had always been considered something of a black sheep division, never quite living up to expectations, and its sluggish response to the Soviet attack cost its commander his job. Promoted to *Generalmajor* on the spot, Heinrich-Georg Hax happened to be available and was given command of *8. Panzer Division*, as well as defense of Komárom. Aside from being a long Eastern Front veteran and holder of the Knight's Cross, Hax was the son of fabled German Olympian Georg Hax.

By nightfall on 6 January a continuous defensive front had not yet been established, the Russians retained freedom of movement and there was no clear cut way to stop them. Pierik puts their end of day advance positions as on a line "Kobolkut-Libad-Kam-Darmotsky-Kemend."[143] This salient west of the Gran constituted a direct threat to Balck's *6. Armee* and jeopardized future German operations, notably *Unternehmen Frühlingserwachen*, which was already forming itself in Hitler's mind. The Russian bulge was dangerous and would have to first be stopped, then eliminated.

96. Infanterie Division continued struggling south on three axes centered on its three infantry regiments, toward Csolnok and Dorog, and although slight progress was made the attack bogged down just north of Körteles. The Russian 37th Tank Brigade defended

[143] Pierik, p. 176.

Dorog's northern flank while 30th Heavy Tank Regiment still had its Stalins dug in on the south, and the firepower of these stationary tanks was too much to overcome without more support. *96. Infanterie Division* headquarters moved into the newly captured cloth mill in Tokod with the various support services strung out in small villages along the Danube Road. In Csolnok there were only minor gains.

The IS-1 Heavy Tank was first in a series of heavy tanks named for Joseph Stalin, the 'IS' being his initials in the Russian language. Purpose-built in response to the *Panzer Mark V Tiger I*, the Stalin series of tanks were formidable opponents. With heavy armor and heavier guns, the platform remained a basic design in Soviet tank production for many years.

Severe losses in all sectors crippled operations but attacks from the Red Air Force were particularly heavy, making almost any movement perilous.

Despite jokes about the accuracy of Russian pilots, air operations were a major impediment to German attacks, as well as inflicting losses on an almost continual basis. Attrition was high and it was becoming obvious that nowhere were the Germans strong enough to break through.

Heinz Guderian was in the second day of his visit to the Hungarian front to assess the progress of *Konrad I* and prod the commanders on the spot to greater efforts, emphasizing the urgency in relieving Budapest for both military and political reasons. Guderian knew that the fall of Budapest would essentially mean the fall of Hungary; at the least it would further demoralize the Hungarian formations still fighting beside the Germans. Their combat value was already low; the shortage of German units meant that *Heeresgruppe*

Süd had no choice but to rely on depleted Hungarian formations to hold the line and further diminution of their morale could only make things worse; there was the very real possibility they might simply melt away at further contact with the enemy.

The IS-II heavy tank went through a number of modifications during its production run, with the early variants having significant design problems. In particular, limited ammunition storage space meant frequent replenishment during the heat of battle, something which often led to disaster. Once all the kinks had been smoothed out, however, the IS-II proved a vicious weapon against which only a *Tiger II* might stand. The 122mm main gun was bigger than anything the Germans mounted on a tank.[144]

Guderian first visited the headquarters of *IV. SS–Panzerkorps* but quickly left because of the perceived danger of air attack. Once back at *6. Armee* headquarters he quickly adopted Gaedecke and Balck's view of things, namely that the right wing of *IV. SS–Panzerkorps* , comprising *Kampfgruppe Pape, 6. Panzer Division, 5. SS Panzer Division Wiking* and *3. SS–Panzer Division Totenkopf,* had been almost stopped by superior Russian forces[145].

[144] Technically, the *Panzerkampfwagen VII Maus* had a bigger gun with the 128mm main battery, but except for when the prototype fought in defense of its factory the type never saw action, or even moved into production.

[145] Balck and Gaedecke had seemingly already convinced Guderian that the SS divisions did not move fast enough in Konrad's first day to seize the initiative before Russian reinforcements could stop them.

Map 3

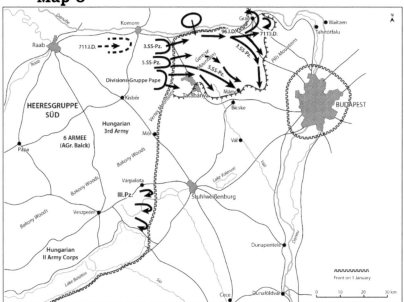

The high water mark for *Untermehmen Konrad III*

The Russian defenses were explained as being a line of strong *pakfront s* and strongpoints that followed the line Alsögalla-Felsögalla-Ujbarok-Csabdi-Bicske-Many-Zsambek-Kirva-Csolnok-Körteles, with mobile forces attacking or counter-attacking through the gaps. Moreover, as part of the Russian offensive to capture Komárom, 46th Army was attacking *Kampfgruppe Pape, 6. Panzer Division* and *5. SS Panzer Division Wiking* with an eye to breaking through to the Danube.

As Maier puts it: "The 6th of January brought the turning point. The Russians had long since recovered from their initial surprise and continuously committed into the battle new formations from their substantial reserves. Eight rifle divisions and three motorized units were moved in to repel the attacking German assault formations."[146]. The German assault forces simply were

---

[146] Maier, *Drama Between Budapest and* Vienna, pp. 26-27. While Maier was a high-ranking officer in the *Waffen–SS* whose invaluable work on the fighting is quoted here, and who is a frequent defender of the SS formations

not strong enough to break through, but, knowing that Hitler would never accept such a harsh reality, excuses needed to be made and alternatives agreed upon. In the dying Third *Reich* finding a scapegoat was never a bad idea so the army generals blamed the *SS*, the *SS* blamed the army and acrimony hampered operations. As outlined above, the real reason for Konrad breaking down was easily found, had the atmosphere been less paranoid.

But saving Budapest was still the mission so that a way had to be found. If Bicske could not be taken other lines of attack would have to be opened. Therefore, the southern option centered on *III. Panzerkorps* had to be reinforced while a way had to be found for *IV. SS–Panzerkorps* to keep up the pressure. Things looked bleak.

And yet progress *was* being made by the most unlikely unit in the German Order of Battle. When reinforcements had arrived in the form of the veteran *711. Infanterie Division*, having come all the way from Holland, Otto Wöhler could not have expected much from the division. The first elements to arrive had been given the necessary but unheralded job of clearing bypassed areas on the flanks of *Totenkopf* and *Wiking*, an important task but one that a second-rate division could perform while leaving the better units to attack the Russian main line of defense.

The *711. Infanterie Division* had been one of the first units to oppose the Normandy landings the previous summer, and while it was experienced, the *711. Infanterie Division* had never been a first class division, although at that point any cohesive infantry division must have seemed like a God-send to the commander of *Heeresgruppe Süd*. Disappointing Hitler was never a good idea and so far, in its first five days, *Konrad I* had disappointed him greatly. Progress had been made, but not enough progress, and not fast

---

during the fighting in Hungary and Austria, his point here is nevertheless well made.

142

enough. When *Konrad I* started it was felt the *711. Infanterie Division* could only marginally help the situation, due to its low quality. Taking severe losses during the fighting in Normandy, the division barely escaped total destruction in the Falaise Pocket and was subsequently rebuilt, although it had never had much offensive strength[147]. Manpower was found anywhere and everywhere it could be found, including the other service branches, with men shipped to the unit unprepared and untrained and, in many cases, improperly clothed. Pierik describes the *711. Infanterie Division* as "a motley collection of soldiers dressed in different uniforms." He goes on to say that some still wore Kriegsmarine uniforms, and it is not clear whether or not they had winter uniforms or even greatcoats. This situation would be repeated countless times in countless units throughout the remaining months of the war, as the replacement system sputtered into chaos and men wound up in unlikely places with unlikely jobs. Even worse, not only was the *711. Infanterie Division* a mass of mismatched and largely untrained men, many of those men arrived sick. A large number of them had eaten their emergency rations, amounting to some four pounds of Dutch biscuits, and drunk their schnapps rations, during the train-trip to Hungary. This caused a mini-epidemic of diarrhea, which on a crowded troop train could only have been miserable. Heading for the Russian front they had simply panicked and thought they were about to die. Once in Hungary the *711. Infanterie Division* was attached to *IV. SS–Panzerkorps* . The unit had arrived with bicycles which, despite the snow and ice of a Hungarian winter, gave them more mobility than foot-bound infantry. The first elements of the division to arrive had been assigned to *Kampfgruppe Pape* for mop-up duties in the forests bypassed by *Wiking* and

---

[147] Why it was rebuilt instead of being dissolved and its personnel assigned to other units is probably because it was not a high caliber unit; its personnel would not have added much value to whatever division they were assigned to, or so it was thought.

143

Totenkopf, but eventually the entire division had arrived in the theater and was reassembled into a whole.

Then, almost immediately after it was intact again as a division, this ramshackle unit filled with sick and untrained men marched east along the Danube and captured the key river city of Gran, Esztergom in Hungarian, much to the shock of the German command. The division had not only fought through the defenses screening the city at Zsidodipatak, just north of Dorog, but then pushed on without stopping to grab Gran before the Russians could react.

Generalleutnant Josef *Reichert* had commanded the division for nearly two years by that point, throughout the ordeal at Normandy, and knew his men better than anyone. Although never elevated to Corps command, and generally unknown today, *Reichert* clearly made an excellent commanding officer for such a second-rate unit.

Gran was an ancient city known for its famed Basilica, the Primatial Basilica of the Blessed Virgin Mary Assumed Into Heaven and St. Adalbert, with the altar-piece painted by Grigolctto. The Basilica's dome dominated the city skyline but the Marie Valerie Bridge spanning the Danube had been destroyed when the Germans evacuated the city, leaving the bridge at Komárom as the only permanent bridge over the river. Nevertheless, seizing Gran gave the Germans not only a cornerstone for their defense in the Danube bend, and a jumping off point for operations to rescue Budapest, but an assault river crossing to Sturovo on the north bank would threaten the Russian armies participating in the counter-offensive against Komárom. Whether or not the threat of an assault crossing was real, the Russians had to remember *96. Infanterie Division* doing that very thing a mere five nights before and wonder if history might not repeat itself.

As if capturing Gran was not enough, however, the *711. Infanterie Division* deployed all available forces south of the city and began a push to the Pilis Mountains. The division's energetic actions would shortly change the entire focus of *IV. SS–Panzerkorps'* effort to relieve Budapest.

Re-capturing Gran might have been encouraging, but if Budapest was going to be saved the real effort had to come from the two *SS panzer* divisions, *Totenkopf* and *Wiking*, and both were bashing themselves out of existence against fierce resistance. Losses had been heavy so a *kampfgruppe* of three infantry battalions from the 23rd Hungarian Infantry Division was attached to *IV. SS–Panzerkorps* , but this weak reinforcement was "only a 'drop of water on a hot stone.'"[148]

On *Totenkopf's* right flank the high ground west-northwest of Zsambek was taken, but a thick *pakfront* blocked both sides of the Szomor-Zsambek road, effectively halting the advance on the right, while attacks on the left to finally take Dag from the Sarisap area proved futile; the Russians even retained the eastern edge of Sarisap itself. 86th Guards Rifle Division and 4th Guards Mechanized Brigade were dug in and frontal attacks were not going to dig them out. *III./ SS–Panzergrenadier Regiment 5 Thule* followed up a small advance toward Uny with an attack that captured Mariahalom on 6 January, but neither penetration was deep enough to threaten the Russian flank at Dag. After capturing Szomor the day before, *SS–Panzergrenadier Regiment 6 Theodor Eicke* attacked on both sides of the road leading to Zsambek, into the teeth of the defenses set up by the 4th Russian armored units defending there: 1438th Self-Propelled Artillery Regiment, 170th Tank Brigade, 110th Tank Brigade and 363rd Heavy Self-propelled Artillery Regiment. On the eastern side of the road progress was good, but along

[148] Maier, *Drama Between Budapest and Vienna*, p. 26.

the road itself and on the western side attacks were pinned down, then driven back. A slight bulge had been driven in the direction of Zsambek and some progress had been made during the day, but not enough.

Meanwhile, *Wiking* was desperately trying to seize Biscke. On the division's left flank a thrust toward Many made good progress, driving within sight of the town. 41st Guards Rifle Division found itself in an increasingly precarious position as *Totenkopf* drove to its east and *Wiking* the west, with the result that the Guards found themselves squeezed into a tongue of land between the two German divisions. Reinforcements were at their back, however, as 181st Tank Brigade and 32 Guards Motorized Rifle Brigade moved into the line around Many. The attack was stopped and further advances were going to be hard going.

Because of this, during the night of the 5th-6th an episode began that is difficult to sort out even today. The commander of *5. SS–Panzer Division Wiking* Regiment, Fritz Darges, was determined to find a way through the lines of the 41st Guards Rifle Division near Csabdi. *Wiking* was being attacked from several directions and stout Russian defenses blocked seemingly every line of advance, yet the incessant pressure to break through did not let up. At full authorized strength the division might have battered its way through, but in its weakened condition other means would have to be found: the *SS* men needed to find a chink in the defense and exploit immediately.

Since the first day of the attack, Biscke had been considered the key objective to success or failure. Darges was a veteran commander and had once been Hitler's personal adjutant. His men were tired, his regiment was not even as strong as a weak battalion and the machines were badly in need of servicing, but Darges knew that time was against them and so he pushed his remaining *panzer* crews hard, probing, moving forward at every chance, and just after dawn he

146

finally found a weak spot in the Russian defenses east of Csabdi. Along with the *I./SS–Panzergrenadier Regiment 23 Norge*, commanded by Fritz Vogt, Darges broke through and drove forward until they seized the 19th century Castle on Hegykastely, on the Hegyiks Estate, situated on the side of a small promontory in southern Csabdi overlooking Biscke.[149] Most commonly known as Mountain Castle, it was less of a castle in the traditional sense than a large manor house surrounded by a stone wall, making it less defensible of a structure as a traditional castle might have been, but it was more than they had often had on the steppes of Russia. A prominent family had built an observatory in Biscke and the Castle had been meant as the residence for the astronomers. Taking the position would be important if the Germans could reinforce his success, but Darges had moved too far ahead of the rest of the division; attacks on both flanks failed and before he knew it, Darges and his regiment were surrounded. The story of the fighting during the next few days at Mountain Castle is confused and often contradictory[150].

As has been seen and would continue, pressure had been mounting to keep moving forward at all costs. Beginning with *OKH*[151] urging Wöhler to keep moving, then Guderian personally showing up to urge everyone

---

[149] Hegykastely means either Mountain Palace or Mountain Castle. Like so much of this period, the date of the exact date of this attack is in question. Many sources put the date of Darges and Vogt's attack on the Castle Regis as 4 January, while the best sources put it as the 6 January. It is unlikely in the extreme that *Wiking* made enough progress for this to have occurred on the 4 January.

[150] Like so many other events surrounding *Heeresgruppe Süd* in 1945, the exact day that *5. SS–Panzer Division Wiking* Panzer Regiment seized Regis Castle is in dispute. Some sources say it occurred on January 4th, others the 5th, but Strassner says that it happened just after dawn on the 6th. Maier is mostly quiet on the subject, except for the comment that "an armored group was still surrounded by the enemy 2.5 km east of Bicske" (p. 26). This is probably not a reference to the panzer regiment, as Regis Castle is on the northern periphery of Bicske. A lesser source even puts the date that the castle was seized as the 7th! In this instance Strassner's narrative holds up as the mostly likely.

[151] Hence Guderian's visit to the front.

to greater speed led to Wöhler prodding Balck at *6. Armee* and Balck berating Gille's *IV. SS–Panzerkorps* for

its slow pace, so by the time the pressure reached Ullrich at *5. SS Panzer Division Wiking* it had become a veritable avalanche. As early as 3 January the War Diary for *Heeresgruppe Süd* recorded Wöhler as saying that "the assault groups were ordered to reach the key points of Biscke…with at least their lead elements by tonight, [the 3rd] if at all possible."[152] There would be finger-pointing after the fact concerning Darges' attack, but what is clear is that for nearly a week every commander in *IV. SS–Panzerkorps* had heard nothing except 'advance at all costs', which is precisely what Darges did.

Like all *panzer* divisions *Wiking* had several significant combat units, such as the reconnaissance battalion and the two *panzergrenadier* regiments (*Westland* and *Germania*), but the most powerful of them all was Darges' *Panzer* Regiment. What seems quite likely is that Darges simply did exactly what he had been told to do, move toward Biscke by whatever means possible, as rapidly as possible.

[152] Maier, *Drama Between Budapest and Vienna*, p. 22.

At first glance this small breakthrough seemed like a victory. During the attack a Red Army convoy had been wiped out, with four 122mm and four 76 mm anti-tank guns destroyed, as well as a number of trucks and supply vehicles[153]. It appeared that a hole had been ripped in the front[154]. However, the main highway to Budapest ran between Csabdi and Biscke, and Soviet reinforcements poured into the area; it was not long before the Germans themselves were surrounded and fighting for their lives. The loss of *Wiking's panzer* regiment would have been devastating for the division and the Soviets knew it, not to mention Vogt's battalion of infantry.

With the castle situated on a small slope, Darges put his infantry and tanks behind the stone wall, with observation points and automatic weapons on the outside. His command post was set up inside the castle itself. Almost immediately, the Soviets began shelling and bombing the German positions, intent on wiping them out. A probing attack toward Many was repulsed.

According to some sources, Fritz Vogt was said to care more about adding the Oak Leaves to his Knight's Cross than his own men, sending them out on a night attack to try and take Biscke, a decision that resulted in *1. Kompanie* losing more than 100 men and being reduced to some 25 exhausted survivors. The other three companies also suffered heavy losses, but Vogt sent them back into the attack anyway. At the end of the siege his battalion was reduced to 40 or so men.[155] Even if these attacks took place, however, and there is debate even on that point, they were entirely in keeping

---

[153] Whether or not this is the same convoy reported destroyed the day before is impossible now to determine, but all sources seem to agree that at least one convoy was wiped out.

[154] The exact contents of the convoy that was destroyed vary among the extant accounts. Pierik gives the toll as a dozen trucks, six pieces of artillery and some wagons.

[155] If this means that 40 men were still combat effective, this may well be true. After a lengthy period of re-organization the battalion was only able to field 3 weak companies, probably around 200 men, many of whom were undoubtedly wounded returned to service.

with the orders to advance regardless of losses then ringing in the ears of every commander in *IV. SS–Panzerkorps* , as well as the general attitude of the *Waffen–SS* to always be aggressive. Bicske was the objective they had been fighting toward for six days and this was the only attack that reportedly took place on the town; if the attacks did occur Vogt should have been commended for doing precisely as he had been ordered.

An observer on the scene mentions nothing of these attacks, though, and instead has Vogt and his battalion resolutely defending the castle and its perimeter. A war correspondent from *SS–Standarte Kurt Eggers*, a battalion of *Waffen–SS* writers who were attached to combat units for the purpose of recording their exploits, is quoted in full by Strassner and emphasized how close Vogt was to the wall where the defenses had been established. He mentions a number of forays by Russians probing the perimeter with both tanks and infantry, with all such incursions repulsed. Klapdor backs up this version, stating that "the Norwegian battalion defended with extraordinary bravery and was able to seal off and clear every penetration."[156] The reality may lie somewhere between the two accounts. Perhaps Vogt sent out probing attacks, such as the one toward Many, reconnaissance patrols, or local counterattacks to retake some critical spot, as would be expected when defending a fixed position, and these were confused with attacks on Biscke itself. Or perhaps he *did* launch attacks on Bicske in accordance with his orders, settling down to defense only when they failed, although this seems unlikely[157].

[156] Strassner, p. 391.

[157] The SS war correspondent surely would have written about attacks on what was the main objective of the whole offensive, Bicske, even if they failed. Whether they were successful or not, or wise or foolish, they would have been seen as totally in keeping with the mission objectives. That an eye witness whose job it was to record such things makes no mention of them has to weight the evidence against their having taken place.

Ammunition, fuel and food began to run low as day faded into night and Darges, as the overall commander of the trapped men, had to decide whether to fight it out on the spot or retreat. Without re-supply they would eventually be overrun. The Soviets kept pounding their positions with artillery and tried to break in, but were still being driven off. Darges was said to have decided that no matter how low they were on supplies, they would stay and fight rather than withdraw, the idea being that Bicske was an important jumping off point to relieve Budapest and the castle was a key to taking Bicske. Eventually, a supply convoy would fight its way into the castle compound and the trapped men would be re-supplied, but that was still days away.

Yet another account is given by Pierik, who says that as the Russian noose began to tighten, the German commanders were "drunk and desperate". He goes on to report that Vogt's whole attack was poorly thought out, the castle was destroyed and that Balck was aggravated by the whole matter.[158] He cites no sources for this point of view, however, and seems to dismiss the accounts of the SS men themselves as reported in *Die Schwarze Korps* and in postwar accounts; that is, accounts like the one from the *SS–tandarte Kurt Eggers* correspondent. He credits the attack to Darges having been punished by Hitler and trying to get back in the *Führer*'s good graces by doing something spectacular[159], and ranks Vogt's supporting attack with his Norwegian battalion as reckless. Thus, two different sources credit the attack to *Waffen–SS* commanders looking for personal aggrandizement,

[158] Pierik, p. 170.
[159] Darges told the story of how on July 19, 1944, the day before von Stauffenberg's bomb nearly killed Hitler, he was at a briefing at the Wolf's Lair when a fly annoyed Hitler. Hitler told Darges to kill it, but the SS man joked that since it was aerial in nature it should be the job of the Luftwaffe liason man, Colonel Nicholas von Below, to take care of it. Hitler became enraged and ordered him to report to his regiment for front-line service. Oddly enough that reprimand might have saved his life.

although with Pierik giving no sources for his version the story could simply be circular.[160] As may be seen later in this narrative, it is quite possible that one source has been used for multiple later accounts. Regardless, this whole line of reasoning essentially lays out the complaints that Army commanders had had about the *Waffen–SS* since its debut in combat, namely, that the men were individually brave but were poorly led by officers with little understanding of tactics who were interested mostly in covering themselves with glory.

That does not make the accusations true, however. The enmity some Army officers felt for their *Waffen–SS* counterparts not only makes it difficult for the modern researcher to determine the truth, but adversely affected operations during 1945; the *Waffen–SS* counter-argument was that their army counterparts were too timid and wanted only to cover themselves with excuses should an operation fail. Given the enmity between the Army and *SS* commanders on the ground in Hungary in 1945, ferreting truth from slander is nearly impossible at this remove in time. Such ill-will made harmony of purpose difficult, if not impossible. And that is the larger point at work here, one that shows how understanding this internal conflict is essential to seeing its ramifications in battle, especially after Dietrich's *6. SS–Panzerarmee* arrived in Hungary, and later in considering its influence on the infamous Cuff Band Order. Because while the Germans in Hungary and Austria were heavily outnumbered by the Red Army in all categories, nevertheless, the inability of officers from the two services to get along with each other seriously eroded German command and control, and adversely affected operations.

Fighting at Mountain Castle on Hegykastely was prolonged and bloody, often hand-to-hand, while the castle grounds were continually being pummeled by air

---

[160] Neither source was a primary one, however, and both could have used the same original source for the stories.

raids and artillery. And as if its *panzer* regiment being surrounded were not bad enough, *Wiking* as a whole was being attacked on all sides and the divisional staff was worried about the flanks, as adjacent units were lagging behind; in particular, *Totenkopf*'s inability to clear the Szomor-Zsambek road was worrisome. All reserves were already committed so that a Russian breakthrough could not be sealed. As midnight passed the situation for the Germans looked grim.

   I Kavallerie Korps, commanded by *General der Kavallerie* Gustav Harteneck, was readying an attack that it was hoped would drive behind the Russian defenses around Bicske and outflank them on the south, forcing the Red Army units to either retreat or risk being cut off. From the area northwest of Stuhlweissenburg, the *4. Kavallerie-Brigade, 3. Panzer Division* and *23. Panzer Division* were to drive northeast with the objective of capturing Csakvar, about 13 miles southwest of Bicske, and then pushing on to Val. Once past Csakvar the ground became relatively flat, giving hope for fast results. The attack group could deploy more than 100 armored vehicles of all types but, as always, fuel was a problem.
   The first objective would be the ancient town of Zámoly, within 10 kilometers east of the assault units. Zámoly dated back at least until 1046, or 20 years before the Battle of Hastings delivered England into the hands of the Normans. The town had strategic significance because it sits in a basin between the Vértes and Bakony Mountains and had historically been astride multiple highways using the low ground for their roadbeds. Abundant water and fertile fields made cattle farming and vineyards the town's main industries; Zámoly is in the heart of the famous wine-growing region of Mór, with a unique flavor and bouquet that makes the grapes ideal for sweet dessert

wines. Zámoly's population was only around 2,000 but it's area was more than 18 square miles, with spaces between houses largely taken up with family farms, making for excellent fields of fire for the defenders. The lands around Zámoly were excellent tank country, but just to their east were the Vértes mountains.

Further reinforcement of either *I Kavallerie Korps* or *III. Panzerkorps* was being contemplated. Otto Gille knew that his right flank and center were stopped and unlikely to get going again, and therefore wanted to shift emphasis to his left flank, where *711. Infanterie Division* had made some progress. Reinforcing that limited success might open the way to Budapest. The best options for moving a unit to that flank quickly were either *6. Panzer Division* or *Wiking*. The leadership of *6. Armee* and *Heeresgruppe Süd*, however, believed *6. Panzer Division* should be sent south to the far right flank of *6. Armee*, so yet another dispute broke out between the *IV. SS–Panzerkorps* commander and his *6. Armee* and *Heeresgruppe Süd* superiors.

But the squabble fragmented into disagreement between even the Army staffs of *6. Armee* and *Heeresgruppe Süd* over the timing of such a move, and its effect on *IV. SS–Panzerkorps*, with von Grolman wanting to move the division immediately and Gaedecke wanting to await the effects of the attack north of Stuhlweissenburg, scheduled for the next day. If that attack succeeded then both *6. Panzer Division* and *Wiking* might see the Russians in front of them retreat, leading to a potentially rapid movement down the Bicske-Budapest highway. Being the simplest choice, it was decided to wait before deciding.

Yet even this wait and see attitude was not the full story. Indecision had haunted *Konrad* from the outset and Maier points out a revealing passage in the war diary of *Heeresgruppe Süd* that shows just how scattered Hermann Balck's thoughts were on what to do next: "the Commander-in-Chief of *Armeegruppe Balck* [*6. Armee*] was also considering an attack by the *6. Panzer Division* out of the area south of Gran

154

through the Pilis Mountains to Budapest, if the garrison at Budapest got into too critical a situation."[161]

This remarkable entry starkly displays the utter confusion in both *6. Armee* and *Heeresgruppe Süd* over even the most fundamental concepts of the *Konrad I* attack. Indeed, if planning for 7 January could not even identify the proposed *schwerpunkt* for the offensive as a whole, then a successful outcome was almost impossible. *6. Panzer Division* was being considered for moves to the far right flank of the Army Group, or south to support *I Kavallerie Korps*, or to stay where it was and await developments, or, apparently, to the far left flank of *IV. SS–Panzerkorps* . Any movement at all would have been required a major effort by the division, but preparing for three different moves could not have been done efficiently in so short a time.

Even more telling than this damning confusion, however, is the final caveat of the entry, "if the garrison at Budapest got into too critical a situation." Hermann Balck was being daily bombarded with desperate pleas from the Budapest garrison, which was, after all, under the direct command of *6. Armee*. The trapped men were *his* men. Where was the sense of urgency? He was being harangued by superior officers from Otto Wöhler to Adolf Hitler himself to move faster because the situation at Budapest was nearly catastrophic. Heinz Guderian had even made a special trip to Hungary just to speed things up, yet Balck still did not consider the garrison's plight as critical? With the advantage of historical hindsight it is easy to judge Hermann Balck's decision-making and leadership during this campaign as not simply erratic, but incompetent; certainly an army commander with four *SS* divisions under his command could have done more to foster cooperation

---

[161] Maier, *Drama Between Budapest and Vienna*, p. 28. Even taking account for Maier's antipathy toward Balck this is a remarkable statement, and makes clear that Balck had no real idea of how to go about breaking through to Budapest.

between the Army and the *Waffen–SS*. Yet it is also impossible at such an historical remove to recreate the conditions under which such decisions were made, so to be fair to Balck one must ultimately assume there were factors unknown now that, in his mind, mitigated the plight of the Budapest garrison during those early days of the *Konrad* offensives[162].

[162] If the Siege of Budapest dates to Christmas Eve, 1944, then 6 January was day 13 since the garrison had been surrounded, not yet a fortnight.

156

7 January, Sunday

The situation in Hungary was critical; with results from *Konrad I* so far unsatisfactory, and much of *Wiking* surrounded, 7 January was the day to decide how best to relieve Budapest in the face of the fierce Russian resistance. Heinz Guderian was still on hand pressuring for the attack to get moving. Balck and Guderian had known each other for a long time; when Guderian's *Panzerkorps* broke through the French line near Sedan in 1940, it was Balck's motorized infantry regiment that led the way and Balck himself who greeted Guderian on the far bank. That sunny day in May was nearly five years in the past and Balck knew that all Guderian cared about were results, not reasons for failure, regardless of how legitimate those reasons might be. Therefore somewhere, somehow, someone had to find a weak spot and break through, but whom, how and where? As we have seen already, Balck appears to have had no clear insight into what to do next; there were many possibilities and none of them were promising.

On the southern flank, would the heralded attack of *Korpsgruppe Breith* drive into the rear of those Russian forces facing *IV. SS–Panzerkorps*, thus either forcing the Russians to retreat or be trapped? Should *6. Panzer Division* be moved further south to support Breith's attack? Or would the unlikely attack on *IV. SS–Panzerkorps*' left flank through the Pilis Mountains achieve a miraculous breakthrough? Should an armored division be withdrawn from the Bicske front to reinforce *711. Infanterie Division* in the vicinity of Pilisszentkerest, and if so, which one? Should units be sent north of the Danube into the rear of the Russians attacking there, or to reinforce the hard-pressed *8. Armee*? There were multiple crises and more questions than troops.

As Otto Wöhler, Hermann Balck and Otto Gille argued and debated what to do next, and as Hitler demanded results, the weather turned worse over

Western Hungary. Thick cloud cover and heavy snows gave some respite from the incessant Red Air Force attacks but also hampered movement, especially on the mountain roads where deep snow drifts covered black ice. Temperatures remained in the 20s Fahrenheit. Conditions for the riflemen of both sides were horrendous. The *landser* trudging forward through deep snow were hungry, exhausted and soaked; exhaled breath froze on stubbled beards and mustaches. And while the Russians were more acclimated to winter weather than the Germans, they were not impervious to cold and hunger. As the fighting escalated into some of the most vicious of the war the men of both sides were miserable amidst the danger.

North of the Danube *8. Armee* was struggling to contain the Russian attacks, with enemy spearheads on the southern flank having broken through and heading for Komárom. Yet the surprise of the day before was gone and German resistance stiffened. Nevertheless, 5th Guard Tank Corps fought to the eastern outskirts of Komárom before being stopped by a determined defense centered on a belt of anti-tank guns some nine miles from the city. 9th Guards Mechanized Corps followed a road northwest before being stopped at the village of Pribeta, a gain of nearly 11 miles from Gbelce. The German defense fought tenaciously but were too badly outgunned and outnumbered, while the Russian salient driven into *8. Armee's* front was fast becoming a crisis. Counterattacks proved futile, as *8. Armee* could only deploy forces that were weak and inadequate and did nothing to stop the Russians.

Otto Wöhler and his subordinate generals faced the increasingly difficult mission of trying to shift their inferior available forces to whatever point needed them most, whether for attack or defense, against an enemy with greater resources. Hermann Balck, in particular, had to make fast decisions with far-reaching consequences, which makes his seeming indecision all the worse.

The Russian threat north of the Danube was particularly dangerous and there now appeared to be only three possible responses. First, continue the defense with available forces until *20. Panzer Division* had arrived and was committed to battle; second, shift forces involved in the *Konrad* operation north of the river; and lastly, have some *Konrad* forces do an about-face and attack across the Danube from South to North to take the Russians in the rear; only the capture of Gran had made choice three a valid option.

Of course, Wöhler and Balck's task was nearly impossible, to accomplish divergent aims with insufficient forces and with Hitler questioning every move. The decision finally came to choose the option one, i.e. for *8. Armee* to hold with available forces until *20. Panzer Division* arrived, although that division had been delayed by partisan attacks on its railroad route.[163] This decision risked the loss of Komárom but any other choice would have left *Konrad* with no chance of breaking through to Budapest and the relief of Budapest was paramount in Hitler's mind.

This choice was simply picking one's poison, however: for German units fighting south of the Danube, *96. Infanterie Division* in particular, were suddenly in the unnerving position of having the Russians pouring into the space that division had

---

[163] Throughout the last year of the war the German railway transport network was devastated by strategic and tactical bomber attacks in the west and partisan attacks in the east. The diminishing rolling stock, lack of spare parts and rails and fuel shortages, including coal, which was not always available when and where it was needed, made delays for redeployed units the norm, not the exception.

vacated mere days before, directly in its rear, separated only by the ice-choked river from the division's non-combat support units. Indeed, by the end of the day on 7 January, the northern bank in the rear of *IV. SS–Panzerkorps* was entirely in Russian hands, with the main supply road on the southern bank well within artillery range. A Russian counter-crossing from north to south could have been disastrous for the Germans, and while for the moment such a crossing seemed highly unlikely, the same could have been said six days previous when *96. Infanterie Division* accomplished a similar feat. Nothing could be taken for granted. So as Gille's men drove southeast their rear was under fire and protected only by the Danube.

As for Balck, much hope was pinned on that day's attack by *Korpsgruppe Breith* on *6. Armee*'s southern flank,[164] and *I Kavallerie Korps* in particular, breaking through and relieving the pressure in front of *IV. SS–Panzerkorps* . For the moment Balck subjugated all other concerns to giving this attack the best chance to crack the Russian lines, even if it meant gambling on his own defense north of the Danube being able to hang on with the forces at hand. But *20. Panzer Division* could not arrive fast enough.

Within Budapest, the burden on the garrison of caring for the mounting casualties had become overwhelming; the total casualty count given on the previous day of 5,621 escalated rapidly. Medicines and even bandages were almost gone. Worse, as conditions within the city deteriorated, *IX. SS-Waffen-Gebirgs-Armeekorps der SS* reported that Hungarian civilians

---

[164] *Korpsgruppe Breith* was another name for *III. Panzerkorps*, and is sometimes referred to as *Panzergruppe Breith* or *Panzer-Gruppe Breith.* Named for the commander of *III. Panzerkorps, General der Panzertruppe* Herman Breith, a recipient of the Knight's Cross with Oak Leaves and Swords, Breith was one of Germany's most experienced *panzer* leaders.

were "starting to become hostile toward the German forces."[165] Desperation had set in among the citizens of Budapest.

As with every siege throughout history, the devastation of the city steadily increased as bombs, shells and bullets swept the streets and laced the air with shrapnel; food was scarce, and lack of power and fresh water meant that sanitary conditions worsened to the point of failing completely. The winter air was heavy with fog and smoke as a pall hung low over the shattered buildings. Terror stalked the streets as gangs of Arrow Cross militiamen looked for 'traitors', and as the people weakened, so did their fear of both the Germans and the Russians. Many felt that if the city were doomed to seizure by the Red Army anyway then further destruction was pointless.

Having only been brought into operation the previous day, on 7 January the last workable airfield on Csepel Island came under artillery fire, cratering the landing strip and making it useless for further landings. Holding the island itself was fast becoming untenable as the Russians advanced in both Buda and Pest. In response came a frantic counterattack to try and regain the racetrack, an attack that was repulsed with heavy losses to the garrison. With no airfields left, or even flat spaces free from artillery fire, from then on air supply meant gliders and parachute drops.

The fighting itself grew even more intense, especially in Pest. The attack had become a contest of grinding attrition that the Russians knew they would win, as long as the relief attacks did not break through to the city. The Germans had few heavy weapons or anti-aircraft guns and ammunition for the ones they did have was running low, while Russian aircraft and artillery pounded their positions relentlessly. Around the East Railway Station and to its south several Russian breakthroughs were sealed off with immediate counterattacks; regardless of how well the garrison

[165] Pierik, p. 143.

fought, however, little by little the city and its defenders were being lost.

Hermann Balck had determined that to save anything from the Budapest debacle the defenders had to withdraw from the increasingly untenable eastern bridgehead, that is, from Pest, to reinforce the western garrison, who would then attack in the direction of *96. Infanterie Division* and *711. Infanterie Division* in the Pilis Mountains. Gille had been promoting just such a solution for days, including reinforcing the relief force by shifting a *panzer* division from *IV. SS–Panzerkorps'* right flank to its left, and apparently Balck was coming to that conclusion also. Unbeknownst to both men, however, Balck's chief-of-staff, General Gaedecke, found the plan foolish.

For their part, the Russians were discovering that using non-Russian formations wasn't the great idea it seemed at first glance. More than 36,000 Rumanians led the assault into Pest, but after only three weeks in combat they had to be withdrawn for rest and reorganization. Suffering more than 11,000 casualties, they had no combat value left. The Hungarian defenders loathed their former Romanian allies, and stood to fight them when against Russians they might have withdrawn.

It wasn't only the Romanians who encountered nasty surprises, though; Russian armor casualties skyrocketed as the *panzerfaust* took a fearsome toll. Garrison tactics honed over the course of the fighting led them to first drive the infantry accompanying the tanks back to cover, and then getting close enough to disable the vehicles with *panzerfäuste*.

Konrad I had run out of steam; on the 7th day of the offensive that was obvious. Instead of the rapid thrust through surprised Russian defenses envisioned by its planners, the offensive had become a 'creeping...relief force."[166] Like so many such efforts before it, *Konrad I* turned into a battle of attrition that the Germans could not win.

Losses totaled at least 39 AFVs of all types in *IV. SS–Panzerkorps*, a huge percentage of the number it took into battle. The operation had made solid gains, especially considering the relative weakness of *IV. SS–Panzerkorps* against superior Russian forces, advancing the front lines some 28 miles from their starting point. But regaining some rural Hungarian territory was not strategically significant, only rescuing the Budapest garrison mattered, and, despite extreme bravery and heavy losses, the Germans simply were not strong enough to break through as the Russians kept throwing new units in their way. Even as the attack of *Korpsgruppe Breith* got underway the question at hand was: if that did not work, what to do next? Somehow, someway, *Heeresgruppe Süd* had to save Budapest.

In the meantime, there was nothing left except to keep fighting. *96. Infanterie Division* kept slugging away trying to force a passage through the rolling hills on the western edge of the Pilis Mountains. *Grenadier-Regiment 284* was engaged in heavy fighting southeast of Sarisap and seemed to be making headway, but still could not capture Dag, where 6th Guards Motorized Infantry Brigade and 86th Guards Artillery Division held firm. The Russians counter-attacked toward Sarisap on the 7 January and were thrown back, but it was an ominous signal that *Totenkopf*'s left flank was vulnerable.

On the eastern flank Dorog proved impregnable. The dug-in Russian 37th Tank Brigade and 30th Guards Heavy Self-Propelled Artillery Regiment simply had too much firepower to overcome. Unable to take Dorog, *Fusilier Bataillon 96* attacked the town of Csolnok, while *Grenadier-Regiment 283* was re-directed against Dorog on the south side of the road leading from Tokod, and the *Grenadier-Regiment 287* attacked on

---

[166] Maier, *Drama Between Budapest and Vienna*, p. 31.

the north side. See-saw fighting in Dorog lasted much of the day. After the Germans had taken most of the town a Russian counterattack backed by armor retook the southern part. Despite vicious fighting neither side could completely capture the ruined town. More importantly, once again the Germans had been stopped while suffering ruinous casualties; *96. Infanterie Division* was fast losing its combat power.

To *96. Infanterie Division*'s left, however, on the northern edge of the offensive, *711. Infanterie Division* was still surpassing expectations; no one had expected a second-rate unit with limited mobility to accomplish much of anything, but apparently neither had the Russians. After its surprise capture of Gran, the division first moved east to secure the critical heights overlooking the town, then turned south and advanced into the gap between Gran and Dorog, with its first objective being the town of Pilisszentlelek; once that was captured, the next objective was the nearby town of Pilissezenrkereszt, less than five miles to the southeast. Then, with Pilisszentkerest in German hands, it was a mere eight miles down the road to Pomaz, virtually inside Budapest itself. There was an airfield at Pomaz that could be used to fly in supplies and evacuate the wounded. Against all odds and expectations, *Konrad I* might work after all.

The plan would depend on *711. Infanterie Division* finding another weak spot in the Russian defenses, and this is exactly what happened. When *711. Infanterie Division* moved out of Gran, *II./Grenadier-Regiment 284* Infantry took over its defense. Given the Russian presence across the Danube, holding the newly recaptured town was paramount.

One reason for the surprise success of *711. Infanterie Division* is clear. Since *96. Infanterie Division* was fighting close by it had drawn in most of the Russian forces in the region, temporarily denuding the area under attack by *711. Infanterie Division* of major forces; it was a moment of opportunity, and for once

164

the Germans were in the right place at the right time. With the Russians throwing all of their reserves in the path of *Totenkopf* and *Wiking*, the *711. Infanterie Division* had found a weak point in the Soviet front and was able to move quickly and take immediate advantage, so that by 2300 hours on 7 January the division had taken its first objective, Piliszentlelek and pushed more than a mile down the road leading southeast. The division was now only 12 miles from Pomaz and, while this movement to the southeast meant that the *711. Infanterie Division* would not be crossing the Danube into the rear of the Russian forces attacking *8. Armee,* it gave Otto Wöhler and Hermann Balck hope that *Konrad* might yet break through; with an impatient Hitler wanting results, the two men finally looked for a way to reinforce success, just as Otto Gille had been urging.

The terrain on *711. Infanterie Division* Division's route to the southeast was rolling and forested, and with the deep snow it made for challenging attack conditions. Nevertheless, it was not overly rugged and the towns themselves were small enough so as not to offer the defenders the advantages inherent in larger urban areas. The ground did present some problems, however, and only one road led southeast through the mountains. Enveloping attacks were difficult in such broken country but that did not stop yet another diffusion of effort being ordered. As the main body of *711. Infanterie Division* pushed down the road toward the southeast, it was ordered to send a kampfgruppe west through the mountains to outflank the Russian positions at Kosztölc that were holding up *96. Infanterie Division.* The three quarreling commanders, Wöhler, Balck and Gille, could all see the opportunity that *711. Infanterie Division*'s surprise success had given them and were determined to take advantage, yet in trying to broaden the gap in the Russian defenses they diluted the very effort that could bring a breakthrough; still, the three commanders had high hopes for the attack. They also agreed that reinforcement of *711. Infanterie Division* by a *panzer* division might yet achieve the breakthrough.

The terrain was much worse for vehicles than for infantry. Sending armor through difficult mountain terrain in winter went against accepted logic; indeed, Balck had already used this very argument on Guderian. And yet he advocated doing just that in the Pilis Mountains. Nor was there no basis for thinking it could be done, that mountainous terrain prohibited breakthrough tank warfare. Hermann Balck had broken through the British and Greek lines in 1941 by doing that very thing as commander of *Panzer Regiment 3*, even earning accolades from the British for his feat. The differences in situations was obvious: the weather was dreadful in Hungary instead of spring weather in Greece; the pre-Barbarossa *panzer* units were staffed with young, motivated and energetic men, contrasting with the exhausted and physically drained crews of 1945; and the tanks themselves were vastly different, with those of 1941 being smaller, lighter and more maneuverable. The *Panzer III* was the main battle tank in 1941, and while the late war variant of the *Panzer IV* was not much heavier, the Panther weighed nearly twice as much. Asking any of the *panzer* divisions under consideration for moving to support *711. Infanterie Division* Infantry, either *6. Panzer Division* of *5. SS–Panzer Division Wiking Division*, to attack down a single road in rough country was asking a lot. Hermann Balck, however, had confidence it could be done.

But not Balck's acerbic chief-of-staff, Gaedecke. Demonstrating the differing opinions and agendas that plagued *Heeresgruppe Süd* throughout the duration of the war, Gaedecke sourly dismissed any hope that a breakthrough could be achieved in the Pilis Mountains due to the rough terrain, and therefore opposed transferring a *panzer* division to the area. "According to intelligence reports, the enemy has moved 3 divisions from the area north of the Danube into the Pilis Mountains. The attempt to advance through the Pilis

Mountains to Budapest with an armored formation offered no chance of success."[167]

Looking ahead, it is hard not to see the second *Konrad* attack as being undermined before it ever began. *711. Infanterie Division* was not an armored formation, but discussions between *6. Armee* and *Heeresgruppe Süd* to send a *panzer* division to reinforce *711. Infanterie Division* had been going on for some time. The timing is difficult to synchronize and it is difficult to know exactly what Russian formations Gaedecke was referring to, or if they existed at all, but he seems to have declared the forthcoming attempt to break through via Pilisszentkereszt using *5. SS Panzer Division Wiking* as a failure days before the attack even began.[168] Given the very short window of time that *Unternehmen Konrad II* would have to succeed, and the cancellation of that attack just at the moment it appeared likely to break through, it is impossible not to trace that decision back, at least in part, to Gaedecke's negative influence. Combined with Hans Ulrich-Rudel's earlier described condemnation of the tank attacks being launched in unfavorable terrain, Gaedecke may well have reinforced Hitler's determination to call off the forthcoming *Konrad II* just as it verged on success.

The key objective to success for what became *Konrad II* was some 13 miles from Bicske, where *IV. SS–Panzerkorps* remained engaged in battle. If Pilisszentkereszt could be seized it was less than seven miles to Pomaz, which could open a rescue corridor to the Budapest garrison. There was only one road leading

---

[167] Maier, *Drama Between Budapest and Vienna*, p. 30. With his own commanding officer urging that very solution, Gaedecke's hatred for Gille appears to have once again influenced the decision making. What is clear is that the two top officers in *6. Armee* could not agree on how to proceed at a critical moment in the battle.

[168] The timeline is not helped by Gaedecke's (or the translators) use of differing tenses.

south through Piliszentkereszt, however, and the country around Piliszentkereszt favored defense, especially with the landscape clotted with ice and snow. The town itself was in a valley but the surrounding terrain had steep ravines and thick forests. The progress made by *711. Infanterie Division* encouraged Balck and Gille to shift their focus, since there appeared to be no chance of *IV. SS–Panzerkorps* breaking through at Bicske, and while the attack of *Korpsgruppe Breith* was just then getting underway and it was believed that the combination of *III. Panzerkorps* and *I Kavallerie Korps* was strong enough to break through on the southern flank, reinforcing the far left flank of the offensive would threaten the Russian forces west of the Danube with a classic pincer attack. Confusion was rife as Balck seemed to want to attack everywhere and was cheerfully optimistic that every move would be successful, while Gille wanted to focus on his own left flank and seize Pilisszentkerest.

Meanwhile, *5. SS Panzer Division Wiking* was still trying to fight down the main highway leading to the Hungarian capital, but two things had become painfully obvious: first, that unless Biscke could be taken they could not break through, and second, that Bicske could not be taken by direct assault. The highway from Budapest led straight to Bicske and made it easy for Russian reinforcements to move into their path. In some respects it was similar to the situation facing *6. SS–Panzerarmee* at Bastogne the month before: seize the road junction quickly and unhinge the enemy position, or be willing to shift focus elsewhere if that did not happen. In the Ardennes Offensive Hitler insisted that the Germans keep battering away at Bastogne long after its value was lost, and to his credit Hermann Balck did not want to repeat that mistake. To Wöhler and Balck that moment had not yet come for Bicske, yet at what moment was an objective's value negated?

Regardless of the answer to that question there was one problem Balck could not overcome: simply put, there just were not enough Germans to do the job, or enough firepower behind the Germans who were there. Fuel and ammunition shortages limited options. Fire support missions could only use a fraction of the ammunition needed to be effective, and all movement required first ensuring that fuel stocks could be found.

The same stubbornness that had launched attacks on the Bastogne perimeter long after its strategic value was gone, however, also influenced the higher officers of *Heeresgruppe Süd*. Not wanting to give up quite yet on capturing Bicske, especially with *Wiking's panzer* regiment surrounded near the town, the commander of *IV. SS–Panzerkorps*, SS–SS–*Obergruppenführer* Gille, wrote an Order of the Day recapping the purpose of Heinz Guderian's visit to the Corps headquarters, re-stating the importance of the Corps mission in relieving Budapest and calling on each man to do his utmost. "This operation..." he wrote, "could bring about a change to the fighting in the area of Hungary and possibly influence decisively the conduct of the war on the entire Eastern Front."[169] So even as he was preparing to shift the focus of his attack, Gille wanted one more push to try and break the Russian resistance around Bicske.

The Soviets were having none of it. Resistance grew stiffer as they threw more units into the Germans' path and it became obvious that more weight of attack was needed, more firepower, firepower that could only come from artillery or armored vehicles, both of which were in short supply.

Totenkopf renewed its push with an attack toward the small village of Anyacsa but progress was stopped at the outskirts. How strong the Russians had become by pulling units away from the attack on Budapest is exemplified by the massive buildup in the

[169] Strassner, p. 315.

area of Perbal, Tök and Zsambek. Between Perbal and Tök a *pakfront* had been built, supported by 141st, 144th and 149th Guards Infantry Regiments, 110th and 170th Tank Brigades, 1438th Independent Self-Propelled Artillery Regiment and 382nd Guards Independent Self-Propelled Artillery Regiment. A frontal attack into this assemblage was driven back, as was a late attack toward the village of Felsoörputszta.

At Mountain Castle in Csabdi, *5. SS–Panzer Regiment* and *I./SS–Panzergrenadier Regiment 23 Norge* endured incessant artillery and air attacks, with ground attacks by infantry and armor constantly probing the perimeter. The first battalion commander, *SS–Hauptsturmführer* Hein, was badly wounded by a grenade and was replaced by *SS–ObersturmFührer* Bauer. Casualties mounted quickly, but it seems that morale remained high. Klapdor cites the story of an *SS–Oberscharführer* who, having already lost an arm, went back to the front lines and was shot in the mouth. "Since he could not speak, he wrote on the door of the room where the wounded were being treated: 'Am I going to die?' Dr. Kalbsdorf calmed his patient: 'If you keep your mouth shut, perhaps not!'"[170] The German headquarters had originally been set up on the second floor but Soviet artillery striking the building soon forced them into the basement.

The fighting was vicious and relentless, but after dark on 7 January a supply convoy broke through to the trapped regiment so supplies could be brought in and the wounded evacuated under cover of night. Despite this minor success the situation was still critical and the *panzers* could not disengage. The regiment's right flank was up in the air; friendly forces were nowhere to be found. Heavy snow hampered all movement. Russian infiltration attacks during the

[170] Klapdor, p. 391.

night broke into the compound and there was close quarters combat in the dark, with only muzzle flashes and flames for light. Being unable to break contact amid such ceaseless attacks, the regiment would defend the castle estate until 12 January, thus missing participation in *Konrad II*. Whether or not the few serviceable *panzers* would have made a difference on the claustrophobic battlegrounds near Pilisszentkerest is doubtful.

The rest of the division attacked all along its front. Most of Csabdi was finally captured and Russian counterattacks were repulsed, but they were still short of Darges. On *Wiking's* right flank, the forward elements of *6. Panzer Division* was consolidating for an attack on 8 January.

Even as *5. SS Panzer Division Wiking* was still fighting at Bicske the decision was made that it would shortly be ordered to disengage and to swing north to join the two infantry divisions in trying to seize Pilisszentkerezst, and then on to the airport at Pomaz, thus enabling supplies to be flown in. As battles so often do, the fight for Pilisszentkerezst would take on a life of its own as both sides poured troops into the area, with Wöhler, Balck and Gille desperately trying to find a place to break through and the Russians shifting troops to block them. The suspension of *Konrad I* and relocation of the Schwerpunkt north has gone down in history as *Konrad II* and it would come close to saving the garrison. In reality, however, *Konrad II* was not a separate operation but was simply a continuation of *Konrad I*, with a shift of focus that revolved around *Wiking* being moved to a new point of attack.

Wiking's Westland regiment was the first component committed there[171] and the Russians fought hard to keep the town; when Westland arrived in the general vicinity of Pilisszentkereszt it was still assembling when it came under mortar fire, a harbinger of things to come. All of *Wiking* would not be

---

[171] Presumably including the attached *SS–Regiment Ney*.

shifted, however, since *5. SS–Panzer Division Wiking* Regiment was still fighting for its life around the Mountain Castle at Csabdi.

Unlike Bicske, which was astride the main highway linking Budapest to Vienna, there were no major highways leading from Pilisszentkereszt to Budapest. The country was rough and wooded, and was treacherous with a layer of snow hiding holes and ravines. Although usually referred to as the Pilis Mountains, the Transdanubian region where the fighting took place was really more in the Visegrad Mountains instead of the Pilis, with the dividing line between the two running along the tectonic plate between Pomaz and Pilisszentkereszt. This was important because the Pilis range was not as craggy or steep as the Visegrad due to differing volcanic processes in the ancient past. Once Pilisszentkereszt was captured by the Germans, the Russians would have been defending smaller mountains with wider valleys, with one valley running directly to Budapest, making for much faster armored movement. Once that valley was reached, the Budapest perimeter was literally a half hour's drive away, if there was no opposition. In the icy conditions of early January this could have given the attackers a major advantage by providing better traction and speeding up the attack, as well as giving clearer fields of fire for artillery. Of course, it would also have made *Wiking's* vehicles clearer targets for prowling Red Air Force ground attack aircraft.

After a full week of fighting, *IV. SS–Panzerkorps* had suffered severe losses from its already depleted combat units. More than 400 men of all ranks were reported killed, 2200 wounded and 320 missing, nearly 4000 men in total. Losses among the commissioned and non-commissioned officers were particularly high. Having arrived in theater with only weak armored forces, the total loss of 14 *Panzer Mark V Panthers*, 10 *Panzer Mark IVs*, two *Jagdpanzer IVs*, three *Jagdpanzer 38s* and nine *Sturmhaubitzen* assault guns was crippling. Damaged vehicles under short and long-term repair further drained the Corps' armored strength, and so the repair of those vehicles was vital to future operations. As they had been throughout the war, the Germans fought on a shoestring, with too little of everything.

"The Germans experienced very few instances where it was not considered worthwhile to recover a disabled tank. The guiding principle was that no tank would be abandoned unless it was blown to bits or completely burnt out. In every other case recovery was mandatory, even though cannibalization was often the only possible use to which the recovered vehicle could be put."[172]

The crews of *panzers* awaiting repairs stayed with their machine until it the mechanics either restored it to combat readiness, or wrote it off as a loss. This usually occurred in a rear area, and by this late stage of the war this waiting period offered the chance to rest and relax away from the front, and it was no coincidence that some tanks came in for repair more often than others. The crews were expected to help in fixing their tank, but working on their machine was far preferable to being shot at, shelled and strafed. Further extending the period needed to service a broken-down *panzer* was the general lack of spare parts that had plagued the Wehrmacht for years, which was exacerbated by the poor transport situation.

As fragmented, indecisive and disjointed as the German attacks were becoming by 7 January, perhaps none was more pointless than a thrust along the line of the Danube by a small unit under the command of *Oberstleutnant* Ernst Phillipp, known officially as

[172] Mueller-Hillebrand, *Generalmajor* Burkhart H., *Department of the Army Pamphlet 20-202, German Tank Maintenance During World War Two*, (Washington D.C.: Department of the Army, 1954), p. 36.

Kampfgruppe Philipp, with its objective being Budapest itself. Even the *kampfgruppe's* experienced and highly decorated commander found this a preposterous mission, given that his unit was little more than a battalion. *Kampfgruppe Philipp* had: "five tanks, six SPWs, II 'FHH [II./Felldnerrnhalle]'and I./Art.Rgt.3". What is even more incredible, *Kampfgruppe Philipp* was actually mentioned in the *Heeresgruppe Süd* war diary.[173] The idea for this small force and its wild expectations for success probably came from Hermann Balck himself, as an effort to exploit the weak Russian defense east and southeast of Gran on the road to Budapest had been in Balck's mind for days. This, at least, is the conclusion by Maier, based on the entry in the war diary of *Heeresgruppe Süd* which quoted General Grolman on the issue; there is even speculation that the order came from Hitler directly, but now, so far after the fact it is impossible to determine exactly who dreamed up the scheme. And while Otto Gille had been advocating a shift of *schwerpunkt* to the far left flank for days, such a small *kampfgruppe* was more an illustration of Hermann Balck's optimistic tendency to attack in multiple places than a serious attempt to rescue Budapest.

Presumably, the *kampfgruppe* had its own flag on the maps of the higher commands and may have seemed like more of a force than it actually was. Philipp was a veteran officer and must have known an impossible order when he saw one, but like it or not *Kampfgruppe Philipp* was the northwestern flank of *Konrad II* and his tiny force had to move forward as ordered. In the end it was quickly stopped and accomplished nothing, while the motorized battalion from *Feldherrnhalle* was badly needed at any number of other places.

[173] Pierik, p. 178.

Further south, in the area of *III. Panzerkorps* and *I Kavallerie Korps*, the attack which had been invested with so much hope began before dawn. The effort came under the command of *Korpsgruppe Breith*, an army-sized battle group that did not have all of the supporting forces necessary to be classified as an army,[174] just as *Armeegruppe Balck*[175] was an army-group sized unit that did not have all of the necessary auxiliary forces to be a full *Heeresgruppe*. The long-time Commanding Officer of *III. Panzerkorps*, *General der Panzertruppe* Hermann Breith, was in charge of the *Korpsgruppe*. Breith was a veteran commander and winner of the Knight's Cross with Oak Leaves and Swords, a man who had seen it all and was not easily put off his mission.

Korpsgruppe Breith consisted of Breith's permanent command, *III. Panzerkorps*, as well as *I Kavallerie Korps*, and the order of battle for the attack sounded impressive: *1. Panzer Division, 3. Panzer Division* and *23. Panzer Divisions 4. Kavallerie-Brigade* and *Schwere Panzer Bataillon Felldherrnhalle*, (renamed on 21 December, previously *Schwere Panzer Bataillon 503*). In reality, however, those formations were skeletons, only fielding a total of 116 AFVs and 116 guns between them,[176] with a rifle strength of about 5700 *landser*. *3. Panzer Division* possessed a mere 5 functioning tanks, or one platoon. Opposing them, the

---

[174] Even today much confusion attends the exact composition of this formation; indeed, it is often referred to as Kampfgruppe Breith or Gruppe Breith. The *Heeresgruppe Süd* War Diary refers to is as 'Korpsgruppe Breith', literally a grouping of Corps', so that is the term used here.

[175] Also commonly referred to as *Armee Balck*.

[176] Maier, *Drama Between Budapest and Vienna*, (p. 26). Notes an entry in the *Heeresgruppe Süd* War Diary that the attack units would have more than 100 armored vehicles and that much was expected from it. However, 100 armored vehicles was not even the authorized strength for one 1944 panzer division, much less three, with a cavalry division and heavy panzer battalion attached. If one divides the total of 116 panzers, *jagdpanzers* and *sturmgeschützen* equally between the 4 armored units it gives an average strength of 29. For the panzer divisions this is approximately 20 percent of authorized strength, for the heavy panzer battalion about 50 percent. In other words, the units were burned out shells.

Soviets had only 70 tanks, but 260 guns and some 10,500 infantry.[177] Both sides had already been bled white. It is noteworthy, however, that the German commanders all found the total number of AFVs used in the attack as impressive. Given that this was less than the authorized strength of one 1944 *panzer* division[178], it shows how far German expectations had fallen.

Breith's attack went off on schedule early on 7 January but found the Russians waiting for him behind very strong defenses; the Germans were immediately engaged in vicious fighting. Indeed, Pierik quotes STAVKAas saying: "It is the heaviest fighting since Stalingrad."[179]. Regardless, the Germans were soon through the front and moving east. *3. Panzer Division's* reconnaissance battalion swept forward on the northern flank and made if halfway to the Tata-Zámoly Road; the Russians responded by moving 63rd Rifle Division into their path. On their right flank *II./Panzergrenadier Regiment 3* drove on western Zámoly but ran into a counterattack from 41st Guards Tank Brigade and was stopped. At Csakbereny, on the northern flank of the attack, the defense line was broken; *I Kavallerie Korps* reported the destruction of "30 enemy tanks, 45 anti-tank guns, 14 guns."[180] As late as 1010 that morning Balck thought this breakthrough would carry *I Kavallerie Korps* as far as Budaors, virtually within Budapest itself.

---

[177] Ungvary, *The Siege of Budapest*, p. 326.

[178] This should not imply unanimity of organization among Wehrmacht panzer and *panzergrenadier* divisions; if one thing is clear about German late-war divisional organization, it is that there was no uniformity among the various divisions. Patronage, vehicle availability, losses and a host of other factors make assigning authorized strength totals to any one unit virtually impossible. What should be noted is that 116 AFVs would not have been considered full strength for any of the divisions involved.

[179] Pierik, p. 177. Pierik does not give a source for this quote, merely "the Russian Stavka", but presumably it is found in a daily summary from either one of the armies engaged against *Konrad*, or possibly 2nd Ukrainian Front. The author was unable to independently verify it in the Russian records.

[180] Maier, *Drama Between Budapest and Vienna*, p. 29.

Other elements drove due east through the 11th Guards Rifle Regiment and by nightfall were in the southern outskirts of Zámoly, where they were stopped. Encouraging progress was being made everywhere; in particular, *Panzergrenadier Regiment 123* took western Sarkeresztes only a few miles north of Stuhlweissenburg, while the rest of the division closed in on Zámoly from three directions. South of Zámoly the spearheads shoved 63rd Guards Motorized Rifle Brigade back and cut the Zámoly-Stuhlweissenburg road, threatening to outflank the Russian defenses at Zámoly.

And yet even in the moment of triumph, defeat was imminent. Much was expected of this effort to outflank the Russian defenses around Bicske. Once again the Germans were putting forth a maximum effort, but the early optimism faded as it soon became apparent that *Korpsgruppe Breith* simply did not have the firepower to break through; the Russians had been expecting precisely such an attack and were prepared. Reinforcements were rushed to the threatened sector. Outnumbered and outgunned, the Germans once again found themselves battering against firm defenses instead of breaking through for enveloping attacks; only German professionalism allowed for any advance at all. Instead of threatening the rear of those Russian units facing *IV. SS–Panzerkorps* , and aside from inflicting (and suffering) heavy casualties on the defenders, all the first day of Breith's attack achieved was to carve a penetration of the Russian defenses 6 kilometers wide and 6 kilometers deep. The ever pessimistic Gaedecke wrote: "he had hoped for a greater success from today's attack by *Korpsgruppe Breith* with 137 friendly armored vehicles...it had been a mistake to advance on Zámoly today with the armored group from the west."[181] By nightfall the Russians were counter-attacking *Korpsgruppe Breith* from all directions. Dissipation of *Heeresgruppe Süd's* limited armored strength once again failed to achieve a decisive success.

As if Otto Wöhler did not have enough worries, the Hungarian Third Army felt compelled to issue an order threatening draconian penalties for deserters and their families after the 5th company of the 1st Infantry Regiment defected to the Russians en masse. What magnified the loss was that the company was newly refitted with scarce equipment that they took with them. The deserters were to be executed, their families thrown into labor camps and all of their possessions confiscated. Given that most of Hungary was under Russian control, however, it is doubtful if the threats were taken seriously.

As 7 January came to an end nothing was settled on the German side and the chokepoint in the Wehrmacht command structure that required every major decision go through Hitler once again crippled their combat performance. *OKH*, in other words Hitler and Guderian, had no faith in *Korpsgruppe Breith* breaking through and favored shifting the entire force north of the Danube to deal with the threat to *8. Armee.* Since Wöhler felt that Komárom could be held with the forces already on hand he opposed this move. Being on the scene, Guderian reluctantly delayed issuing such an order, but it was understood that Komárom could not be lost. Then Wöhler ordered Gille to reinforce *711. Infanterie Division* on *IV. SS–*

[181] Maier, *Drama Between Budapest and Vienna*, p. 31.

Panzerkorps' left flank and Guderian suggested that perhaps the Budapest garrison could launch its own attack to meet up with him, another suggestion that required Hitler's approval. There was also the question of how much longer Pest could hold out and whether the defenders could be withdrawn into Buda, yet another move that needed Hitler's assent. Guderian promised to get answers by the next day.

And so Day Seven of the first and second *Konrad* attacks ended in a swirl of confusion and questions. Guderian favored moving *I Kavallerie Korps* and *III. Panzerkorps* north of the Danube, while simultaneously expecting *IV. SS–Panzerkorps* to shift a division from its right flank to its left and, for that division to then cut its way into Budapest while the garrison both held its ground and attacked to meet Gille's men. If the Father of the Blitzkrieg truly believed these conflicting goals were all possible with the troops on hand, then it shows either how desperate he was or how deluded he had become by Hitler's fantasies of what was and was not possible.

Maier openly wonders whether Hitler and Guderian were being given all of the facts regarding the situation or if reports were being falsified to make the situation seem better than it really was. And while Maier was not yet on the spot to personally observe matters, his summation of the situation on 7 January is worth quoting at length. "With all this confusion, with all these half-hearted attempts, the question still arises as to why one did not follow Gille's repeated suggestion and concentrate forces to push through the Pilis Mountains along both sides of the Gran-Budapest Road."[182] He suggests that perhaps the real objective was not to rescue the Budapest garrison but to tie down Russian troops. Viewed from a distance of decades this seems highly unlikely, however, and is probably a product of the undercurrent of dislike and distrust that hampers both his work and Balck's

---

[182] Maier, *Drama Between Budapest and Vienna*, p. 33.

regarding the fighting in Hungary in 1945. In fact, Hermann Balck's career suggests that he was used to striking advancing Russian forces without warning, then moving quickly to strike again in a different location. With German forces of the early years this often resulted in tactical victories, but the worn-out Wehrmacht of 1945 could no longer successfully fight that way.

8 January, Monday

From the beginning of the first *Konrad* offensive, the only real hope of successfully breaking through to Budapest lay in concentrating as strong of an attack force as possible, and then attacking a weak sector in overwhelming strength. Given the disparity in men, vehicles, supplies, artillery and aircraft, in favor of the Russians, the need for speed and surprise became even more critical, and that is precisely what did not happen. Instead, German offensive power was scattered along a broad front in a vain hope to stretch the Red Army defenses until they broke, an unlikely outcome given Soviet interior lines of communication, superior logistics and a ready source of reinforcements in the Budapest assault armies. Nor was the situation helped by Hitler's obsessive need to control even the smallest details, which left Otto Wöhler and Hermann Balck little room for decision making, a management style that exacerbated Balck's tendency to dither to the point of indecision. Having just been demoted from command of an Army Group, it is not hard to see this as an attempt by Balck to ingratiate himself back into Hitler's good graces, since bad decisions were quickly punished but no decisions were less likely to be disciplined. Put another way, the situation called for commanders on the spot who were willing to dispute Hitler's commands if they were unrealistic or dangerous, and who would take chances on their own authority if they believed them to be in the best interest of their men and mission. Neither Wöhler nor Balck was such a man.

Inside the Budapest perimeter, attacks on Buda lessened throughout the day as Russian units executed an about-face to deal with the relentless German pressure. Across the Danube in Pest, however, there was no respite. Russian penetrations in Kis-Pest[183], and around the East Railway Station forced *22. SS-Freiwilligen-Kavallerie Division Maria Theresa* to pull back once again.

Along *8. Armee's* front north of the Danube the energy of the initial Russian assault had dissipated as exhaustion overcame both sides, although fighting went on throughout the day. Reinforcements flowed to the battlefield. The Germans brought *20. Panzer Division* and *46. Infanterie Division* to the area around Nove Zamky, about 25 miles north of Komárom, while *8. Panzer Division* and *211. Volksgrenadier Division* regrouped for a counterattack nearby to the east of that town. *153. Reserve Division*[184] went into the line near Hurbanovo, just south of Nove Zamky.

The Russians also brought up reserves, with 4th Guards Mechanized Corps (Lt. General V.I. Zhdanov) on the right wing and 72nd Guards Rifle Division to bolster the attack on Nove Zamky. 9th Guards Mechanized Corps renewed its attack on Nove Zamky which, if captured, would outflank the German defenders of Komárom. The attack was repulsed with the Russians reaching Dvory nad Zivatou on the eastern edge of Nove Zamky, but unable to advance further. 5th Guards Tank Corps once again stormed Komárom and once again was beaten back with heavy losses.

---

[183] Now the XIXth District of Budapest, but in 1945 not technically within the boundaries of Pest itself.

[184] Also known as the *153. Feld–Ausbildungs Division* and *153. Grenadier Division*.

Staring at the desolate Hungarian battlefield that freezing morning of 8 January, veteran German *Soldaten* must have felt a sense of déjà vu as they once again prepared to launch themselves against heavily fortified Russian positions; in many ways it was Kursk all over again. During that ill-fated offensive *3. Panzer Division, 6. Panzer Division, 8. Panzer Division* and *20. Panzer Division*, as well as *1. SS–Panzer Division Leibstandarte Adolf Hitler, 2. SS–Panzer Division Das Reich* and *3. SS–Panzer Division Totenkopf*, had all plowed forward into belt after belt of Russian defenses during *Unternehmen Zitadelle*, Operation Citadel, in July of 1943, a grinding bloodbath that saw them assaulting one Russian strongpoint after another in a vain attempt to break through fortified positions and surround Russian armies near Kursk. *Pakfront* after *pakfront* had slowed, bled and finally stopped the greatest armored assault that Germany ever launched. The Red Army had suffered greater casualties and at times it seemed like the German spearheads might actually succeed in breaking through, but in the end all that *Zitadelle* achieved was the destruction of Germany's strategic battlefield initiative. *Konrad I* was no different, although the veteran divisions were mere shadows of their former selves; few men remained from that hot summer offensive. (Regaining the strategic initiative, of course, was never a possibility). And, just like Kursk, a *Heeresgruppe* Level attack that began with multiple assault corps' would eventually devolve into sporadic advances first by divisions, then by regiments and finally battalions.

As 8 January progressed the decisions facing Wöhler, Balck and Gille became more acute. "Whether it [success] can still be attained, seems doubtful in the face of the developing situation."[185] Gille was still determined to break through to Budapest, but Wöhler and Balck doubted it could be done unless the garrison was allowed to attack and meet them, and only Hitler

[185] Maier, *Drama Between Budapest and Vienna*, p. 32.

could sign off on a breakout. If *Konrad* was called off then units would be available to stop the Russian attack north of the Danube, but discontinuing the relief effort would *also* require Hitler's authorization. The only thing either Wöhler or Balck could do without first asking Hitler was to keep attacking to relieve Budapest.

SS–SS–Obergruppenführer Gille had been requesting for several days that *6. Panzer Division* be withdrawn from the Felsogalla Gap to reinforce the drive through the Pilis Mountains. Reluctant to give up on *Konrad*, and probably influenced by his and Gaedecke's animosity toward Gille personally, Balck had dithered on the decision. Finally, he ordered *6. Panzer Division* to prepare to move into the Pilisszentlelek area, but not to begin moving until he (Balck) gave the order.

That was not the only option being explored, however, as Wöhler and Balck seemed unsure of exactly what objective was important. Their orders were to relieve Budapest at all costs, but as previously discussed, indecision at the highest levels crippled the effort. There was more discussion of sending *6. Panzer Division* to the right wing to strengthen *Korpsgruppe Breith*'s efforts to drive past Zámoly; to have *23. Panzer Division* or *4. Kavallerie-Brigade* straighten the line by attacking the bulge in the Vértes Mountains between Zámoly and Tatabanya; or even to send *3. Panzer Division* north of the Danube. None of these would save *XIX. SS-Waffen-Gebirgs-Armeekorps der SS*, their primary mission; ultimately, it was decided to try variations of all of them at once.

As night was falling, Gaedecke issued five directives for *Armeegruppe Balck* to continue operations the next day. These first included *Kampfgruppe Phillip* driving all the way to Pomaz, with *96. Infanterie Division* breaking through Russian defenses to allow this and *711. Infanterie Division* continuing to attack in the Pilis Mountains, supported by a strong kampfgruppe from *Wiking* instead of *6. Panzer Division*; second, *Korpsgruppe Breith* would maintain its attack to both draw in Russian reserves and prevent the enemy from shifting forces to block *Kampfgruppe Phillip*; third, a presumption was made that permission would be granted to give up the eastern Budapest bridgehead, that is, Pest, after which a breakout to the northwest would be authorized to link up with either *Kampfgruppe Phillip* or *711. Infanterie Division* and *Wiking*, after which the Budapest garrison would conduct a fighting retreat through the Pilis Mountains; fourth, to blunt the Red Army attack north of the Danube, *20. Panzer Division* would immediately attack with whatever components were on hand in the vicinity of Neuhäusel, while forces near Komárom launched fixing attacks to prevent redeployment of enemy units there; and, lastly, the Hungarian Cavalry and whatever German forces could be found would launch holding attacks in the Vértes Mountains, with *3. Kavallerie Brigade* to be committed there after it arrived from *2. Panzerarmee*.

Using Hungarian units was risky at best. Aside from their questionable morale and reliability, they were much weaker than their German allies. The Hungarian 2nd Armored Division was nothing more than a *kampfgruppe* by this point, and not a particularly strong one. It listed 27 *Mark IV* and two *Mark V Panthers* on its tank inventory, but only 16 of the *Mark IVs* were combat ready. Some Hungarian AFVs were also available, although numbers are unknown. The unit was weak in heavy weapons and low on supplies. Morale among all of the Hungarian units was fragile; some of the men were still willing to fight if there seemed like hope of victory, but were dubious of their chances.

More than anything else, these orders clearly indicate how confused the command of *Armeegruppe Balck* was in terms of both the nature of their mission and the reality of their situation. The whole focus of this plan's four missions south of the Danube was to free *Kampfgruppe Phillip* to drive on Pomaz, a distance of more than 25 miles. To that end was everything else subsumed, except arguably the attack of *711. Infanterie Division* reinforced by *Wiking*. Yet the plan was predicated on false hope that bordered on delusion. To begin with, expecting *96. Infanterie Division* to break through in a new sector immediately, when it could not do so in another area after days of fighting, was to believe in miracles: it could happen, but was not likely. Then, if that unlikely event did occur, the exploitation force, *Kampfgruppe Phillip*, was very weak, so that even if it took Pomaz the likelihood of holding it against severe Russian counterattacks was a very long shot. But perhaps the largest miscalculation was believing that Hitler would first allow the evacuation of Pest, when his 'stand fast or die' order was still in effect, and then, in the almost unbelievable circumstance that he would agree to said evacuation, that he would allow a breakout, when he had repeatedly denied such requests. And then, if he changed his mind in two characteristically unheard of ways, that he would allow the abandonment of Buda and the entire western shore of the Danube. None of this was likely, even if it proved feasible.

Neither *Heeresgruppe Süd*'s Chief of Staff, *General der Kavallerie* von Grolman, nor it's commander, Otto Wöhler, had any illusions concerning the possibility of Hitler granting permission to evacuate Pest. Indeed, both considered it so unlikely that Balck was explicitly commanded to send an order to *IX. SS-Waffen-Gebirgs-Armeekorps der SS* to: "hold the eastern bridgehead until it received a *Führer* order to the contrary. According to *Generaloberst* Guderian the *Führer*'s permission would not be granted."[186] Therefore, none of the supporting attacks could be justified unless Hitler first approved of three things which would have indicated a fundamental change of his mind, which nobody expected would happen. Yet as things would turn out, all of the supporting attacks would take place anyway, and one of them would

[186] Maier, *Drama Between Budapest and Vienna*, p. 34.

almost work, only to be called off at the moment of success.

On *IV. SS–Panzerkorps'* left flank the fighting died down on 8 January. *96. Infanterie Division* went over to the defensive, still outside of Dorog and Csolnok, its combat power exhausted for the moment. *Kampfgruppe Phillip* moved into Gran area but was not yet ready to move down the banks of the Danube, and the Russians reacted by bringing in fresh forces and blocking the Danube Road. In a bizarre twist, Balck's Chief of Staff, Gaedecke, was highly optimistic about the possibility of *Kampfgruppe Phillip* driving all the way to Pomaz, there to link up with a breakout attempt by *IX. SS-Waffen-Gebirgs-Armeekorps der SS*. The exact cause for such rosy thinking is hard to understand now, since the *Kampfgruppe* was essentially a motorized *panzergrenadier* battalion with modest tank and artillery support, probably no more than 1200 men or so. The distance to be covered was more than 25 miles, or about the same distance that all of *Armeegruppe Balck* had so far been able to recapture since the beginning of the offensive. *Kampfgruppe Phillip* was far too small to break through Russian defenses encountered after *96. Infanterie Division* initially punched a hole in the front lines, and even if it succeeded in its mission there were no follow-on forces to protect its flanks; in essence it would be surrounded almost immediately. Maier puts it this way: "it was difficult to understand what this raid along the road running along the Danube was supposed to accomplish. It could be taken under fire from the 'Russian' north bank for almost its entire length. In soldier jargon, this was a suicide mission, if ever there was one."[187] The 21st century observer can only wonder what might have been possible using *Kampfgruppe*

[187] Maier, *Drama Between Budapest and Vienna*, p. 34.

Phillip as a reinforcement for either *3. SS–Panzer Division Totenkopf* or *5. SS–Panzer Division Wiking Division*, instead of yet another new attack with too little strength to accomplish anything useful.

711. Infanterie Division was prepared to move off from Pilisszentlelek toward Pilisszentkerest, but was diverted west to Kesztölc to try and outflank the Russian defenses at Dorog. Little progress was made before Russian counterattacks from 99th Infantry Division blocked that move and drove them back to their start line. The *711. Infanterie Division*'s spearheads were briefly cut off when Russian forces cut the Gran-Pilisszentkerest Road after attacking from the area of Zsidodipatak. The road was cleared by two battalion's from *711. Infanterie Division* that had not yet moved from Gran.

Totenkopf's left flank was also quiet around Sarisap. Near Zsambek, however, one attack column drove to the outskirts of that town, virtually surrounding 170th Tank Brigade and 1438th Independent Self-Propelled Artillery Regiment to their west. When another attack captured Felsoörsputsza, those two units were shoved back with heavy losses. An adjacent attack on Many by *Wiking* failed, however, allowing the Russian armor to escape.

A final push from *Wiking* at Many on 8 January was also stopped, and it became obvious that *Konrad I* had failed. Yet another Soviet unit had also been committed, the 18th Tank Corps, with 3 anti-tank regiments numbering between 40 and 50 guns per regiment. Overcoming such firepower was simply beyond the division's grasp. What was left of *Wiking*'s battered *panzer* regiment was still fighting for its life at Mountain Castle. Attacks on Darges' command were coming from both Bicske and Many and were driven back, but the remainder of the division was a spent force. Only blood and determination had taken the *SS* men to the outskirts of their objective, but it was not enough. The offensive had pushed deep into Soviet lines, but a combination of poor terrain, bad weather, a willingness by Tolbukhin to strip units from the Budapest offensive and reserves to throw into the path of the German attack, and too little fuel, ammunition and firepower, all combined to doom the German effort.

On *Wiking's* right flank, *6. Panzer Division* launched a local attack that gained some ridges around Obarokputza, but 11th and 12th Guards Cavalry Divisions prevented any significant advance by counter-attacking from the Bicske area, supported by tanks. *6. Panzer Division* repulsed the attacks and held the high ground, but could not push forward. It had become obvious to all that further advances could only be made by bleeding *IV. SS–Panzerkorps* white.

Casualties on both sides were heavy, and in some cases approaching ruinous. "The attempt had cost the *IV. SS–Panzerkorps* (minus the *711. Infanterie Division*) the loss of 2,938 men from 1-7 January, 1945. In the period from 1-4 January 1945, the Corps destroyed, knocked out or captured 79 tanks, 160 guns and 107 anti-tank guns."[188] Strassner does not break down the German casualties into killed, wounded and missing, but Maier does and adds that the figure quoted by Strassner is only the total for enlisted men; adding in officers and non-commissioned officers runs the total near 4,000, or ten percent of the corps' total authorized manpower and a much higher percentage of its combat strength.[189] As mentioned above some 39 armored vehicles were total write-offs. Such disastrous casualties left Hermann Balck desperately looking for manpower anywhere he could find it, and while the Russians had suffered even higher casualties, they could afford it while the Germans could not.

---

[188] Strassner, p. 315.

[189] Given that the Corps was well under-strength when it arrived in Hungary, this meant that many of the units were very badly damaged even at this early point in the fighting. Most of the casualties were suffered before 5 January. In reality, *Konrad I* probably cost Gille 25 percent of his men or more.

Moving off from the region just south of Csakbereny, *3. Panzer Division's* various components moved northeast in the direction of Csakvar; some progress was made, but where the Germans needed breakthroughs they could only make modest penetrations. Minor Russian counterattacks were thrown back, but further advances were not possible. *23. Panzer Division* fought its way closer to the western outskirts of Zámoly, even capturing the southern suburbs, but 9th Guards Tank Corps moved into position to block further advances. South of Zámoly, 1st Guards Motorized Infantry Brigade moved into the line beside 93rd Infantry Division, blocking *23. Panzer Division's* spearheads attacking in the direction of Lovasbereny. On 7 January those spearheads had punched a narrow corridor into Russian territory, exposing the southern flank where the advance could not keep up. This danger was cleared up on the 8th, when other elements of *23. Panzer Division* swept through the positions of 64th Motorized Infantry Brigade and advanced the front past the Zámoly-Stuhlweissenburg highway. On the far right flank of the offensive, however, Sarkeresztes held out against attacks by *128. Panzergrenadier Regiment*, threatening the lengthening right flank.

To be clear, the effort that came to be known as *Konrad II* was not really a new plan; instead, it was a continuation of *Konrad I* with the emphasis on a new sector. Many histories separate it into something distinct, however. Certain *Heeresgruppe Süd* considered it as a different effort. Either way, as we have seen *SS–SS–Obergruppenführer und General der Waffen–SS* Gille had been arguing for days that the *schwerpunkt* should be moved from his right flank to his left, and with progress in the Bicske area stopped it was decided to give that a try. Nor did *Kampfgruppe Phillip* represent a realistic effort.

To that end, during the night of 8-9 January a strong *kampfgruppe*, with *SS–Panzergrenadier Bataillon Westland* as its core, was detached from *Wiking* and began disengaging before Bicske and moving along roads just behind the front to assembly areas in the Gran region. According to Maier (p. 100), the kampfgruppe also contained *5. SS–Panzer Division Wiking's Pioneer Bataillon*, two artillery battalions, an anti-tank battalion, one company from *5. SS–Panzer Division Wiking's Aufklärung Abteilung*, a nebelwerfer battalion and various other medical and supply units.

Nor was this all that would reinforce the attack that came to be known as *Konrad II*. In response to the manpower shortage, the two existing *Waffen–SS* ski battalions shipped from Neuhammer to Hungary were combined to form the *1. Ungarische SS-Sturm Regiment*, a *sondertruppe* (special unit) of the *Reichsführer SS* headquarters, in the area of Raab. The two battalions were supposed to have been part of the two Hungarian *Waffen–SS* divisions. Since these two divisions were not combat ready in early January their two ski battalions were combined for use in the relief attacks toward Budapest, a reinforcement that Hermann Balck was all too glad to receive, even if the regiment was only marginally combat-ready[190]. As the name implies the unit was trained in ski warfare. Its strength on forming was about 1,500 men, very strong for new units of this period. The commander was *SS–Sturmbannführer* Kelemen Rideph.

The hurried nature of this unit's creation was borne out in how it was equipped. Their uniforms were mostly those of *SS* mountain troops, not ski troops, while the arms and equipment were almost all captured French Army stores, obsolescent and unreliable. On the day of its formation, 8 January, the regiment was

---

[190] Although not fully trained, in comparison to *Kriegsmarine* and *Luftwaffe* men with no ground combat training whatsoever, the Hungarian *Waffen–SS* men must have seem like grizzled veterans.

attached to *IV. SS–Panzerkorps* and was ordered forward to the region south of the Danube in the area of Gran, (Esztergom), there to meet up with the advance elements of *Wiking*.

711. Infanterie Division and *96. Infanterie Divisions* were already in the vicinity but lacked the firepower to punch through Russian defenses near Pilissventkereszt and it was hoped that the surprise re-deployment of *Wiking* might break through before the Russians realized what was happening. The winter weather was foggy with snow showers, shielding the division's road march from the Red Air Force and enemy artillery spotters so that it could move during daylight, thus speeding up its approach to the assembly areas.

Just before midnight, *SS–Regiment Ney* was attached to *1. Panzer Division* for use during *Konrad II*. The unit was a significant boost in infantry for the depleted *panzer* division, not only in numbers but also in combat power. The Hungarians of Ney's regiment were motivated veterans, either avowed enemies of Communism, true believers in Fascism or its Hungarian equivalent, or both.

As 8 January 8, the Russian high command was not pleased with the situation in Hungary. Like the Western Allies before the Ardennes Offensive, STAVKAhad thought the Germans in the sector of 2nd and 3rd Ukrainian Fronts were finished. The deep penetration made by *Konrad I* came as a nasty surprise, as did the continuing fierce resistance in Budapest. Progress was expected and excuses would not be accepted.

Never shy about twisting the truth, or making up stories to support its propaganda, the Russians reported that Hitler was personally directing the Budapest relief effort from a secret lair in Hungary. Ludicrous as this was, even at the time, like all good propaganda there was a grain of truth: Guderian *was* in Hungary, on Hitler's personal order, to direct the offensive. So while the *Führer* was not personally on hand, his Chief of the General Staff was.

9 January, Tuesday

North of the Danube, General Weather came to the aid of the hard-pressed *8. Armee* when a sudden thaw turned the frozen ground into a muddy pudding that made large-scale mechanized movement impossible. The temperature hovered around freezing, but a heavy, wet snow made simply walking an exhausting effort. The Russians were as committed to seizing Komárom as they had been four days earlier, but their advantage in armor and firepower had been greatly reduced and supplies were about to become a serious problem. The Gran River was swollen and overflowed its banks which, in turn, washed away the temporary bridges over which 7th Guards and 6th Guards Tank Army's supplies were carried. Until those bridges could be repaired or replaced, the Russians west of the Gran were cut off.

Cross-country movement in the mountains was virtually impossible for vehicles. Even road travel was problematic, as snow and black ice glazed the few paved surfaces available. Infantry could struggle forward, but slowly.

In Pest, the Red Army launched an attack on the Rakosredenzo train station on the northeast corner of the defensive perimeter. With *Konrad II* kicking off across the Danube not far to the west, and the Germans making progress toward the city, the Russians redoubled their efforts to crush the defenders once and for all. Malinovsky had decided to try and cut the remaining salient in Pest in two and this attack was the first step. The fighting was savage.

As the Russians advanced along both banks of the Danube on the southern side of the perimeter, Csepel Island had finally become untenable and was evacuated.

When Soviet tanks captured the racetrack on 9 January, the Germans repurposed the Vérmező, an eight-hundred-yard-long park just below Castle Hill, into a final landing zone. This narrow strip of land, aptly named the *Blutwiese* (Bloody Meadow), was under constant fire as small aircraft, often gliders piloted by fearless teenage Hitler Youth from Germany's junior flying clubs, daringly landed under the cover of night. The "Blood Meadow" (also known as "Vérmező" in Hungarian) is a historical site in Budapest, Hungary, with a somber past. The name "Vérmező" translates to "Blood Field" or "Bloody Meadow," and it is located in the 1st district of Budapest, near the Buda Castle.

By 8 January even Hitler had come to realize that the Ardennes Offensive had failed. The battle did not end right away, of course, but the *Führer* must have known that any chance of German success had vanished. The only question remaining became what to do with *6. SS-Panzerarmee.*

In company with *Generalmajor* Reinhard Gehlen, the head of *Fremde Herre Ost,* Foreign Armies East, the German intelligence bureau for the Eastern Front, Heinz Guderian once more pleaded with Adolf Hitler to withdraw *6. SS–Panzerarmee* from the western front and to send it as desperately needed reinforcements for *Heeresgruppe A* in Poland, before the expected Russian offensive was launched. Guderian knew how weak the defenses were in Poland, and how non-existent the reserves to seal off breakthroughs, but all of his efforts were for naught.

The *Waffen–SS Panzer* divisions would not be going to Poland; as Hitler told Guderian, "the eastern front would 'have to make do with what it's got.'"[191] Unbeknownst to Guderian, Hitler did not intend for *6.*

[191] Kershaw, p. 170.

SS–Panzerarmee to stay in the west, either; it was heading to Hungary.

Unternehmen Konrad II

The timeline and exact movements of German and Hungarian units during Operation *Konrad II* are hard to pin down; different sources give different times and actions. Some are quite definite about their schedules of events, yet those definite times disagree depending on the author or source. The timeline to be followed here will be one gleaned from numerous sources and seems the most likely.

As *711. Infanterie Division* had moved out of Esztergom to attack through the Pilis Mountains, *Grenadier-Regiment 284* Grenadier Regiment of *96. Infanterie Division* was pulled out of the line and sent to defend that city against Russian counterattacks. This freed up all of *711. Infanterie Division* to try and punch through to Budapest, but correspondingly weakened *96. Infanterie Division*'s attempt to force through a parallel route west of *711. Infanterie Division*'s main axis of advance. Instead of three infantry regiments *96. Infanterie Division* now had only two, along with its Fusilier battalion, and each had to cover a portion of the front the *Grenadier-Regiment 284* Grenadiers had previously occupied. Not only that, but the division was also expected to break through the Russian defense on the Danube Road so that *Kampfgruppe Phillip* could drive all the way to Pomaz. Stretching the depleted regiments in this way effectively put *96. Infanterie Division* into a defensive mode, regardless of its attack mission southeast of Gran. Russian air attacks were so frequent that the *Grenadier-Regiment 284* Grenadiers could not make the short march to Gran, about 10 miles, until night had fallen; anything moving on the

197

roads was bombed and strafed by prowling ground attack aircraft.

The fighting slacked off in *IV. SS–Panzerkorps'* center as *Wiking* re-deployed much of its strength to the Piliszentkerest area. For the exhausted men of both sides the respite was a God-send. Many had not eaten much for days. Everything they wore was wet or frozen, and little piles of snow tended to filter into the bottom of their boots. Toes, fingers and even noses were numb, but mostly not yet frostbitten. All of the men huddling in muddy trenches wished they were inside, even if just a bunker.

The fighting near Zámoly swirled in attacks and counterattacks as the Russians moved quickly to block the latest German offensive. On *Korpsgruppe Breith's* northern flank, *3. Panzergrenadier Regiment* had pushed the front within sight of the Tatabanya-Zámoly road, but 5th Guards Rifle Division and *63. Kavallerie Division* both counter-attacked and drove the Germans back several kilometers from Felso Major, the high water mark of the German penetration. *3. Panzer Division* then launched its own counterattack and stopped the cavalry penetration, while just to the north *II./3. Panzergrenadier Regiment* held its ground and stopped 5th Guards. Compared to *IV. SS–Panzerkorps*, *Korpsgruppe Breith* was fighting a battle of movement, but in truth the distances covered were quite small.

At Zámoly, where *4. Kavallerie-Brigade* and *II./Panzergrenadier Regiment 126* had pushed into the town on the southern side, the German penetrations were promptly pushed backward half a kilometer and more by a large Russian armored attack. On the north side of the attack, 9th Guards Tank Corps and a battalion from 9th Guards Tank Division sliced through the positions of II/126. *Panzer Division* Grenadiers, with the rest of 9th Guards Tank Division moving into the area later in the day. 18th Guards Tank (??) and 1st Guards Motorized Infantry Brigade broke through the remainder of *II./Panzergrenadier Regiment 126*. Both prongs of the attack moved forward past Borbala Major and seemed poised to cause havoc in the German rear, but the Germans counter-attacked with their usual speed. *Schwere Panzer Bataillon Felldherrnhalle* split into two *kampfgruppe*, one attacking the lead Soviet elements around Also-putsza and inflicting heavy losses and sending the survivors reeling backwards. This force then moved half a kilometer south and smashed into the flanks of the lead Russian units in the second attack column, near Borbala-putsza, driving them backward as well. The second *kampfgruppe* from *Schwere Panzer Bataillon Felldherrnhalle* swept around the flank of the northern Russian column and re-captured Borbala Major, thus threatening to cut off the entire Russian attack. The battalion's Tiger IIs had once again proven their mastery of the battlefield, when used properly. Other German attacks along the line were turned back, so that by the end of 9 January the Germans had recovered much of the lost ground. Their foothold in Zámoly, however, was gone.

10 January, Wednesday

The farther the narrative moves into 1945, confusion with so many details of the fighting in Hungary, dates and times, increases, as sources are often contradictory. The period January 9-10 has large segments from the transcripts of the *Führer* conferences for those days, although there are numerous gaps in the record and it is sometimes impossible to know what is being referenced.

With fighting in the west dying down and the Russian offensive in Poland still in the future, discussion at the midday *Führer* conference centered largely on the situation in Hungary. Supplying Budapest had been a forlorn hope from the start, and *Luftwaffe Major* Herbert Büchs' report during the briefing at Hitler's Adlerhorst Headquarters indicates just how inadequate the effort was. "The delivery of supplies to Budapest was only possible with very limited forces, because of bad weather. Yesterday 39 aircraft were employed during the day; 22 of them reached the target, including 4 JU-52s that landed."[192]

Barely half of the small number of aircraft flying the dangerous route into Budapest even made it over the city. The inference is that aside from the four JU-52s that landed, and it was never fully confirmed that they had, in fact, landed, the other 18 aircraft that reached Budapest dropped supplies by parachute. Since it was virtually impossible not to drop a percentage of the parachutes inside Russian lines, not even the full complement of those supplies that actually reached the city made it into the hands of the garrison. Airfields were needed, but there were none left. Hitler spent time poring over a map looking for places to build emergency airfields, but to no avail. *Reichsmarshall* Hermann Göring suggested using gliders and Hitler latched onto the idea, spending more

[192] Heimer & Glantz, p. 605.

time selecting places for the gliders to land[193]. Ice conditions on the Danube were then discussed with an eye to possibly using more boats to float in supplies, or even to land aircraft on the ice itself, but neither idea proved feasible; with the Russians in possession of both banks north of the city, artillery and mortar fire could be brought to bear on anything moving on the river, and after the first attempt to ferry supplies on a boat the enemy was alert to the possibility. No matter what ideas were tried, however, instead of the steady flow of supplies needed to keep *IX. SS-Waffen-Gebirgs-Armeekorps der SS* fighting, it received only a trickle.

By 10 January, news from the Western Front was all bad; the Ardennes Offensive was an obvious failure, *Unternehmen Bodenplatte* had been a disaster that cost the *Luftwaffe*'s last reserves, the result of *Unternehmen Nordwind* seemed to be an obvious failure, and the *Führer* was faced with the decision of where to deploy Germany's most powerful remaining offensive asset, *6. SS–Panzerarmee*. Guderian had been lobbying for nearly two weeks for this army to move east as a reserve for *Heeresgruppe A*, although by 10 January he realized it would never arrive before the Russian offensive launched out of the Baranov bridgehead, an attack that was expected on 12 January. As damaged as *6. SS–Panzerarmee* had been during the Ardennes Offensive,[194] *AA–Oberstgruppenführer* Sepp Dietrich's army was nevertheless the most powerful force left in the German Order of Battle. Unknown to everyone but the *Führer*, however, Hitler already had in the back of his mind the outline for *Unternehmen Frühlingserwachen*, with *6. SS–Panzerarmee* as the main offensive force. He had never forgotten the canceled Operation *Spätlese* [195] the previous December and became fixated on regaining the Margarethe Line, setting the stage for both *Konrad*

---

[193] This effort has been detailed previously in the narrative.

[194] Known in the west as the Battle of the Bulge.

[195] Whether this was the proposed code name or not is debatable. Earlier in this narrative it was referred to as 'Paula.' Either or neither is possible.

III and *Unternehmen Frühlingserwachen*. But the plan needed Budapest to be firmly in German hands if the offensive was going to deliver the crushing, war-turning defeat of the Russians that Hitler had in mind.

711. Infanterie Division had been trying to do just that but its strength was waning. Having driven through the small town of Pilisszentlelek it had moved on to try and take Pilisszentkereszt, halfway between Gran and Budapest, but as the Russians kept pulling forces from the attack on Budapest to stop the German relief effort it became apparent that *711. Infanterie Division* was not strong enough to break through. *96. Infanterie Division* on its right flank was also stuck after one of its regiments took over defense of Gran (Esztergom), although a bridgehead south of the Danube had been carved out.

There were no reserves to throw in to help *711. Infanterie Division* force its way through the Pilis Mountains; *IV. SS–Panzerkorps* was also needed for that effort, so the pressure from *Führer* Headquarters was mounting for Gille to break through quickly and save Budapest.

So, even as bad as the overall war situation was, the effort that came to be known as *Konrad II* was making progress and had a realistic chance of breaking through to the Budapest perimeter, if only fresh forces could once and for all break the Russian defense. That task fell on *IV. SS–Panzerkorps* , so even before Gille could get his Corps attacking again after moving from the final positions it held during *Konrad I*, the pressure from *Führer* Headquarters was mounting for him to break through quickly and save Budapest. Unfortunately for Gille, his attack had not started that morning as scheduled. The attack had been scheduled to jump off at daybreak, but around 0100 hours it was postponed, allegedly by Hitler[196]. The SS men began to chaff; they were very close to Budapest and badly

---

[196] If Hitler did indeed postpone it, this would be totally in character. In moments of hard decisions Hitler often dithered.

wanted to break through and save the garrison. Whatever the reason for the delay, Gille knew that his time was running out and he fretted over every lost hour. Finally, the attack was re-scheduled for 2030 hours.

For the Germans doing the actual fighting, the delay was galling. They cared nothing of grand strategy or the movements of armies, they only knew that their comrades were surrounded and suffering and they were the only hope of relief. Balck tried to win some sort of realistic concession from Hitler that would allow *IX. SS-Waffen-Gebirgs-Armeekorps der SS* to at least try to meet him halfway, perhaps at Pomaz, drawing off Russian troops from in front of the Konrad forces; as with most such requests it never had a chance. Guderian had been skeptical that Hitler would grant the request and his pessimism was proven accurate: even though the new axis of attack had only just been reinforced that morning, Balck and Gille were given one more day to break through to Budapest or abandon the attempt.

IV. SS–Panzerkorps had suffered heavy losses during *Konrad I* but received welcome reinforcements. Having been formed two days earlier and assigned to *IV. SS–Panzerkorps* , the *1. Ungarische SS–Sturm Regiment* was subordinated on 10 January to *5. SS Panzer Division Wiking* in the area south of Esztergom near Pilisszentkereszt. The unit's strength was 1500 ski-trained troops, mostly equipped with old French Army materiel and wearing uniforms of the mountain troops, but that hardly mattered; the men were desperately needed and in the chaos of combat weapons could be scavenged from the dead and wounded of both sides.

Fighting around Pilisszentkereszt had been fierce and casualties high, but the progress made had been encouraging, which is what lead Hermann Balck to shift *IV. SS–Panzerkorps* from the attack at Bicske to exploit the gains made south of Gran by *711. Infanterie Division* and *96. Infanterie Division*s. Reinforcing success was a valid concept, but *IV. SS–Panzerkorps* had been fighting hard for more than a week by then, and had suffered heavy casualties; the addition of a full strength regiment was very welcome to the exhausted *SS* men, even if the reinforcements were green and their weaponry was second rate.

According to Strassner, once the attack was launched surprise was complete and the Germans moved against surprisingly light opposition, as most of the defenders simply ran away. The terrain continued to hamper the attacks, though.

From the extant evidence it is clear that *Konrad II* did not have the support of the German High Command, i.e. Hitler. During the *Führer* briefing very early in the morning on 10 January, conducted by Jodl's senior staff officer *Oberstleutnant* Waizenegger, discussion first centered on *Generalleutnant* Hermann Breith's *III. Panzerkorps* and the heavy fighting north of Stuhlweissenburg.[197] The Russians had shifted powerful reserves into the path of *Konrad I* and were making counterattacks in several places. Waizenegger and Hitler appear to be discussing *III. Panzerkorps* when the former refers to a formation as possessing 80 tanks and that he had ordered the concentration of 70 of those tanks near Zámoly,[198] apparently to oppose the Soviet breakthrough(?). Hitler seems dispirited when he replies: "that is the one corps that is theoretically supposed to have 150 [*panzers*]. But half of it is

---

[197] The details of this section come from the surviving fragments of Hitler's military conferences, which were dutifully recorded word for word by a team of stenographers from late 1942 onward. For a variety of reasons there are many gaps in the record and it is sometimes hard to know exactly what is being discussed in terms of the tactical situation, but the value of having Hitler's word for word thoughts where the record exists is invaluable.

[198] A gap in the narrative makes it hard to be completely certain, but Zámoly was in III Panzer Corp's zone of operation.

gone.[199]" In all likelihood this referred, at least in part, to *23. Panzer Division's 128. Panzergrenadier Regiment,* which launched a counterattack against 1st Guards Motorized Infantry Brigade that failed. After the attacks and counterattacks of the previous day, the line in Breith's sector had stabilized west of Zámoly.

Discussion then turned to operations south of Gran (Esztergom), where *Konrad II* was scheduled to begin shortly,[200] although 'begin' may not be the right word; the attacks by *96. Infanterie Division* and *711. Infanterie Division* never really stopped, they were simply reinforced by *5. SS–Panzer Division Wiking.* At any rate, neither Hitler nor Guderian had any faith that the new attack would succeed due to the difficult terrain of the Pilis Mountains, a heavily forested area with narrow, twisting roads under a blanket of very deep snow. Hitler was irritated that *IV. SS–Panzerkorps* would not immediately be in position to attack on its new axis even though *Wiking's* march behind the lines had been done with all due haste considering the Russian dominance of the skies. He was worried about the lack of infantry to support the attack also, since *panzers* and *SPWs* could not face the Russian anti-tank guns on the narrow mountain roads in the area without incurring ruinous losses. Hitler was blunt about his opinion on *Konrad II*'s prospects, telling Waizenegger "they will also fail; that is quite sure...I

[199] Heiber & Glantz, p. 594.

[200] According to the transcript of this conference as published by Heimer & Glantz, it began at 12:55 a.m. on 9 January. However, as is made clear by the order in which the conference notes were published in their book, this conference probably began at 12:55 a.m. on 10 January. The portion of the original transcript containing the date was lost, so the supposition that this represents a conference early on 10 January is based on the best evidence available. This is critical to understanding the sequence of events that influenced *Konrad II.* If the date of 10 January is correct, then the conference began at almost the exact moment the attack by IV SS Panzer Corps was due to begin, and while there is nothing in the existing transcript by way of an order to postpone the attack by *IV. SS–Panzerkorps,* the transcript is not whole. Based on Hitler's professed doubts about the validity of the operation, it seems probable that he ordered the attack postponed at the outset of the meeting, or perhaps just before it began.

consider the whole thing impossible."[201] Sixteen hours later at the midday conference Hitler was nearly apoplectic that no significant progress had been made "Three days have now been wasted here, while we go on hoping...-while the enemy is steadily adding reinforcements while we are not getting any stronger-that some miracle will allow us to advance."[202] This pre-formed opinion would become crucial in the coming days.

But even as the early conference continued around 0100, the first elements of *Wiking* began arriving in their assembly areas south of Gran, with 08the division's attack toward Pilisszentkereszt scheduled for daybreak. The plan was for *Germania* to be on the left and *Westland* the right; there was no armor support though, as *5. SS–Panzer Regiment* had been left behind, still trapped around Mountain Castle. However, at about 0100 hours on 10 January the attack was postponed, ostensibly on direct orders from Hitler.[203]

Meanwhile, a report was introduced during the same *Führer* conference, attributed to Otto Wöhler, that 1st Guards Mechanized Corps had suddenly shown up northwest of Budapest with 150 tanks;[204] the Corps had not been spotted by German intelligence since Romania the previous autumn.[205] With an exact timeline impossible now to recreate, this report of a fresh Russian armored corps directly in the path of *Konrad II* may have been what prompted Hitler to delay the attack.

---

[201] Heiber & Glantz, p. 594.

[202] Heiber & Glanz, pp. 605-606.

[203] Although portions of the transcribed military conference that could confirm this are missing, in the documents still extant Hitler is upset that the attack was not already under way. If Hitler did, indeed, postpone the attack, it would seem to contradict what he was saying during this same time period.

[204] In fact, the Corps was even stronger than that. Counting tanks and self-propelled guns of all types, 1st Guards Mechanized Corps fielded more than 200 AFVs and 20,000+ men, as well as an artillery contingent of more than 70 medium guns and enough trucks for the entire unit to be motorized.

[205] It had gone into STAVKAreserve.

1st Guards Mechanized Corps was entirely equipped with Lend-Lease American M4-A2 Sherman tanks, the upgraded model mounting the improved long-barrel 76 mm main battery instead of the short-barrel 75 mm version on the M4-A1[206], and while the Sherman's armor was still insufficient protection against German guns, in particular the high-velocity 75 mm 75L71mounted on the *Mark V Panther* and the ubiquitous 88mm gun in both its artillery/anti-aircraft configuration and as mounted on the *Tiger I* and *Tiger II* heavy tanks, Russians loved the Sherman for its reliability, electric versus manual turret-traverse, larger magazine, ease of maintenance and overall crew-friendly design.[207] Shermans were fast and there were a lot of them. Compared to the cranky transmissions and gear boxes of Russian tanks, the American machines seemed like luxurious rides.

Finally, discussion turned to the serious situation north of the Danube, where Russian attacks had penetrated dangerously close to Komárom and threatened the northern flank of *Heeresgruppe Süd* itself. The direct target had been Komárom and its bridges over the Danube, but separating *8. Armee* from the rest of *Heeresgruppe Süd* would have leveraged a huge hole in the front. Apparently the news had not yet reached *OKH* Headquarters that the Russian supply bridges over the Gran had been washed away. Waizenegger told Hitler that 51 enemy tanks had been destroyed the day before[208] and seven more that day in fighting throughout the territory north of Danube and west of the Gran River. He then reported that 30 of the 70 total trains moving *20. Panzer Division* into the area

---

[206] The penetration power of the 76.2/L55 American 76 mm gun compared very favorably with the Russian 85/L52 main battery that equipped the latest version of the T-34, the T-34/85.

[207] Soviet propaganda relentlessly derided the Sherman for being under-armored, but in fact it compared very favorably to or surpassed the T-34 is most areas.

[208] Since the conference seems to have begun just after midnight on the 10th, he probably meant the tanks had been knocked out on the 8th.

near Komárom had arrived at Nitra, site of the first Christian Church in what was to become Slovakia. The transportation difficulties facing the German railway system throughout the *Reich* were no better on the southern end of the front, however, as the division was arriving at Speed 8; that is, eight trains per day, a very slow pace. With 40 trains yet to arrive, this meant that it would be five more days before the entire division was ready for combat. Nevertheless, the gravity of the situation left no choice but for fighting elements of *20. Panzer Division* that had arrived to counterattack immediately, which it had done. One group from the division attacked south toward Ogyalla (Hurbanovo) and took the small towns of Imely and Nesvady while a second *kampfgruppe* drove toward Perpeto. Both *Panzer Abteilung 208* and *211. Volksgrenadier Division* were counterattacking the Russian incursions west of the Gran near Nove Zamky, and with the Russians cut off from supply by the bad weather, the worm had turned and suddenly it was them fighting for their lives.

Around 10 January, Hans Ulrich-Rudel found himself summoned to the headquarters of Hungarian leader Ferenc Szalasi, south of Sopron, to be awarded the Hungarian Medal for Bravery. He had already been awarded the Golden Oak Leaves for his Knight's Cross, an award created by Hitler specifically for him, and was already a legend in the *Luftwaffe*. He was accompanied to his meeting with Szalasi by the commander of the Hungarian Air Force, *General der Flieger* Kuno Heribert Fütterer.[209] Rudel was only the 8th man to receive the Hungarian Medal of Bravery and was the first non-

---

[209] Fütterer had been appointed by Göring as head of the *Luftwaffe* in Hungary, and with it came command of the Royal Honvéd Air Force. This appointment came after German occupation of the country in March, 1944, to prevent Hungary from switching sides.

Hungarian. He and his tank-busters flew endless sorties against the Soviet armored columns in both *Focke-Wulf FW-190s* and *Junkers JU-87Gs*, the slow, obsolete *Stukas* that were sitting ducks for Soviet fighters but made ideal gun platforms for the two 37 mm tank-killing cannon mounted under the wings. Regardless of how many T-34s and Stalins they shot up, though, there seemed to always be more to replace them. Aside from his achievements in the air, however, Rudel's stamp on operations in Hungary may be larger than has previously been assumed.

The history of the Third *Reich* is rife with mysterious unilateral decisions taken by Hitler that defy logic or circumstances and events in Hungary in 1945 provide their share of such occurrences. The story of *Konrad II* is one in a very long list of such episodes. Given Hitler's skepticism about *Konrad II*, the visit of his favorite *Luftwaffe* pilot and the events surrounding that visit around New Year's Day[210] may shed light on exactly why Hitler made the decision he later made concerning *Konrad II.*

Rudel had given Hitler his opinion of *panzer* tactics in Hungary, and told the *Führer* that the ground selected for the attack was poor.[211] And he was right, the ground was not ideal for mobile warfare, especially in the dead of winter; it was heavily forested with narrow roads and sharp slopes. He suggested more open terrain, almost surely that chosen for *Konrad III.* Hitler was a great admirer of Rudel's and no doubt gave his opinion great weight; indeed, it reinforced his own thinking about where to attack. The terrain for *Konrad I* had been very difficult and the operational results were not up to Hitler's expectations, backing up Rudel's assertions that the attack was made at the wrong place. Instead of moving the *schwehrpunkt* south to the open ground suggested by Rudel, however, Balck moved it northeast. *Konrad II* was more of the same; if

[210] See text for 3 January. Since Rudel didn't give specific dates for any of these events it is impossible now to pinpoint them with 100 percent accuracy.
[211] Konrad I

anything, the terrain was even more difficult. Hitler did not want the attack to take place there but allowed it to be made anyway, since *711. Infanterie Division* was making some progress and more weight of attack might break through; however, results had to be immediate. Balck had enough residual credibility to choose his point of attack and to reinforce a modest success, but not enough to give it time to succeed, and therein lies the potential damage done by Rudel's meddling in affairs that were not his concern: at it turned out, *Konrad II* was cancelled at the moment it might have on the verge of succeeding. How much Hitler was influenced by Rudel is impossible to say, but it would be well within his character to believe his favorite pilot instead of the generals he did not trust much at all, even the *SS* generals.

11 January, Thursday

Without supplies the 7th Guards and 6th Guards Tank Armies trying to seize Komárom north of the Danube were in serious trouble. Losses had been terrible among the attackers, 6th Guards Tank Army had 72 tanks left on the 11th, with mobility hindered by mud and the Germans fiercely counter-attacking, mostly using *6. Panzer Division, 8. Panzer Division* and *20. Panzer Division.* With both sides wallowing in the mud, under heavy counterattacks and short of fuel and ammunition, the Russians were driven back toward the Gran River.

Heeding the advice of STAVK, Marshal Rodion Malinovsky finally joined the two separate groups assaulting Budapest into a single entity, Group Budapest, under the headquarters staff of 18th Special Rifle Corps, commanded by General Afonyin. The idea was to better coordinate attacks against Buda and Pest.

SS–Regiment Ney, already blooded during *Konrad I* with its two battalions assigned one each to *Totenkopf* and *Wiking*, added a third combat-ready battalion on 11 January, bringing its total strength to well over 2000 men. As more refugee Hungarians who wanted to keep fighting needed a home, they were sent to join Ney.

Fighting continued to the north around Piliszentkerest, but with the coming of the new day the

Germans found themselves finally almost out of the Pilis Mountains and ready to enter a valley of low rolling hills that was much better tank country. Just ahead of them in the middle of the valley was the last town to capture before they could began driving for either Pomaz to the east, or turn southeast and make directly for the outskirts of Budapest: Pilisvorosvar, astride the main highway to Budapest. This was the next objective.

From the top of the spa at Dobogoko,[212] the tiny village inside of Pilisszentkereszt itself and, at almost 2200 feet, the highest point in the Pilis Mountains, through the haze of winter and despite the pall of smoke hanging over the burning city, forward elements could see the spires of Budapest's churches. The view was panoramic, with winter snow blanketing the wooded slopes on all sides, blackened and churned where war had passed. *IV. SS–Panzerkorps* was less than 17 miles from the Hungarian capital; the similarity to German spearheads sighting the spires of the Kremlin in 1941 must have been apparent to the men viewing Budapest on that cold winter's day.

For the third time in two days the *1. Ungarische SS–Sturm Regiment* found itself re-assigned to a new parent formation, this time to the *Westland* Regiment of *5. SS–Panzer Division Wiking.* Heavy casualties in both of *Wiking's panzer*grenadier regiments had left them depleted, so the infusion of the fresh Hungarians was a god-send. According to one source, the *1. Ungarische SS–Sturm Regiment* was immediately sent into action near Pilisvoeroersvar (Pilisvorosvar), site of the longest railroad tunnel in Hungary, the 779 meter tunnel connecting Pilisvorosvar and Piliscsaba. The regiment was spearheading the effort to push the Soviets down the last slopes of the Pilis Mountains and into the valley below, where the German armor could finally operate in the open.

---

[212] In Hungarian, the word 'Dobogoko' means 'pulsating stone'. The mountain is believed to be an intersection point for energy fields, in the same way as Stonehenge or Macchu Picchu.

In Roman times the Pilisvorosvar site had been a way station for legions moving through the valley and the town's crest featured a castle of red clay erected in the sixteenth century, for which the town was named. The town was almost exactly halfway between Gran (Esztergom) and Budapest and both sides knew its' importance; it was a key point on the road between the two cities. Taking the town would open the gateway to Pomaz, virtually within Budapest, and the Hungarians fought with desperation to get into the valley. Unknown to them, Hitler was closely watching the progress and was on the verge of cancelling the whole operation.

Meanwhile, Otto Gille knew that time was running out, not only for the Budapest garrison but also with the limits of Hitler's patience, and pushed his men to their utmost. Combat was ferocious; for example, losses showed just how fiercely the Hungarian *SS* men had fought. Casualties in the *1. Ungarische SS–Sturm Regiment* were enormous, with 2 officers and 127 other ranks killed, and 19 missing, almost 10% of the units' total strength. Such a loss rate was not sustainable if the regiment was to remain viable for combat, but it illustrates the scale of combat. The outside observer has to wonder if *Westland's* commander might not have given these attached troops the hardest mission in the attack, so as to preserve the men with whom he had lived and worked for years, or whether he was simply too short of infantry to worry about such details? Whether it happened in this case or not that was always a concern for small, independent units attached to larger units, a frequent occurrence in the last six months of the war.

As *Konrad II* came closer to breaking through, Pierik tells of a scheme proposed to Hitler sometime around 11 January by the commander of *Flak Regiment 12, Oberst* Ernst Jansa. Essentially, a parachute drop would be made at Budaors in conjunction with a further push by the forces involved in *Konrad II*. The chief problem was that the *fallschirmjägers* would be dropped behind enemy lines. The plan was deemed too complex and Hitler rejected it, commenting that he was also reluctant to add more forces to the Budapest garrison since they were already trapped; Pierik quotes the *Heeresgruppe Süd* diary as saying, "that Hitler 'did not want to fly in any more forces now that the situation with regard to Budapest had become so uncertain.'"[213] Where the transports necessary for this idea might have come from is another matter, although a small scale parachute operation *had* accompanied the Ardennes offensive. The failure of the operation to achieve anything significant might have affected Hitler's thinking vis-à-vis Jansa's suggestion.

On the southern tail of the front, *Korpsgruppe Breith* was not giving up its effort to drive into the Russian rear northeast of Stuhlweissenburg. *3. Panzer Division* recaptured the ground it had lost the day before, retaking the homestead known as Felso Major. At Zámoly, the *4. Kavallerie-Brigade* and *Panzergrenadier Regiment 126* drove into the town from the west, were repulsed, then slid left past the defenders and captured the northeast corner. Meanwhile, *Schwere Panzer Bataillon Felldherrnhalle* drove from three miles south of the town straight down the highway leading into eastern Zámoly, smashing into the flank of 9th Guards Tank Corps and forcing them to retreat. Russian counterattacks failed to stop the Germans so that by nightfall Zámoly was fully in German hands. On the far southern flank, the rest of *23. Panzer Division* stayed on the defensive.

Aside from the various shortages facing both sides, but affecting the Germans more, and putting aside the weather, the terrain around Zámoly made it a poor choice for any sort of large-scale offensive

[213] Pierik, p. 144.

operations. Unlike the objectives of *IV. SS–Panzerkorps*, those facing *Korpsgruppe Breith* had no good roads leading into them from the west, nor heading further east toward Budapest. Capturing the town would protect Stuhlweissenburg's northern flank, and thus allow the larger city to be used as a springboard for larger movements to the east, but even that would come at too high of a price. The very real danger was that even if the Germans captured their objectives, the Russians would simply recapture them shortly thereafter.

12 January, Friday

The re-capture of Gran had been a major victory for *Heeresgruppe Süd* but keeping control of the city was vital to the *Konrad* operations and both sides knew it; fighting would be fierce. *II./Grenadier-Regiment 284* occupied a peak of nearly 1000 feet on the right flank and was attached to the headquarters of *Panzerkorps Felldherrnhalle*. Commanded by *General der Panzertruppe* Ulrich Kleemann, *Panzerkorps Felldherrnhalle* was bereft of major subordinate commands: the two divisions organic to that corps, *Panzergrenadier Division Felldherrnhalle* and *13. Panzer Division*[214], were trapped in Budapest.

Map 4

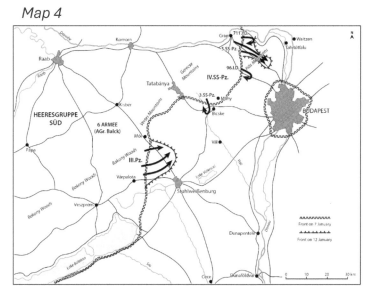

Unternehmen Konrad II. IV. SS–Panzerkorps came close to Budapest, but Hitler called off the attack at the moment it might have broken through.

[214] Although never actually under command of the corps headquarters, *13. Panzer Division* was intended to be part of Panzer Corps Felldherrnhalle and the reformed 13th Panzer Division would, indeed, be officially renamed as a Felldherrnhalle division and assigned to its namesake corps.

With the situation dire, casualties high, supplies low and nothing more to be gained from holding their defensive perimeter at Hegykastely, *SS–Panzer Regiment 5* and the attached *I./SS–Panzergrenadier Regiment Norge* finally fought their way out of their position at Mountain Castle. The regiment was in no condition to join the fighting near Pilisszentkerest, so instead it withdrew to Raab where it entrained for transport to Vezsprem in anticipation of *Konrad III*. The men and vehicles were completely worn down and needed rest and refit before they could fight again. Fritz Darges would be awarded the Knight's Cross and Vogt the Oak Leaves for his Knight's Cross for their leadership during this action[215].

Fritz Vogt's command, the *I./SS Panzergrenadier Regiment 23 Norge*, was so depleted that it was first ordered to gather at Tarjan, then withdrawn to Vesprem for four days of rebuilding and reorganization, but resources were scarce and it could only form three small companies. Nevertheless, the battalion would be back in action soon enough. Vogt was later to be given command of *Wiking's Aufklärung Abteilung*, while his former command stayed attached to *Wiking* for the duration of the war.

As *SS–Panzer Division Regiment 5* withdrew from a battlefield of craters, mud, blood, debris and shell casings, they left behind the burned out war machines that could not be salvaged or saved, massive tombstones to the hundreds of men of both sides who had died on the Hungarian hillside. The hulks of more than 30 Russian tanks also littered the battlefield.

Wiking, and its *panzer* regiment, would be heavily criticized by Hermann Balck and his Chief of Staff, Gaedecke, for their performance in *Konrad I*, criticisms that were absorbed by Heinz Guderian and which influenced his own opinion. Chief among the condemnations were the supposed lack of initiative in

---

[215] There is no doubt that Vogt won his Oak Leaves, but sources differ as to exactly when. Some say for the battle at Hegykastely, others for the battle at Pettend later in the month.

creating a breakthrough and then exploiting it, but in fact *Wiking* and *Totenkopf* were simply too weak in heavy weapons to achieve success. Comparing the fighting in Hungary to the legendary breakthrough in the Ardennes in 1940, Klapdor says: "…tank formations in 1940 never attacked with 20 percent of their authorized strength."[216] In previous years, a tank regiment reduced to 20 percent of its combat strength would have been considered *hors de combat* in all but the direst situations. If anything, the progress made toward Biscke by such weak formations shows just how dangerous the best German divisions still were; had they been anywhere close to authorized strength they would have broken through easily. Balck's criticisms, and Guderian's by extension, seem petty and self-serving when viewed through the lens of time.

South of the action around Bicske the Russians finally took Zámoly after heavy fighting over a period of days. The German attacks to relieve Budapest had met with bloody results and limited success, but so had Russian attempts to capture Komárom. Both sides had expended thousands of lives for no substantial territorial gains, but the Russians didn't need territory, they needed time to grind down the Budapest garrison. In that regard, the fighting so far tilted heavily in their favor.

Strassner records that the capture of Pilisszentkereszt, the crucial strongpoint that was the last way station before Pomaz and within the metropolitan area of Budapest, was relatively easy against light opposition. With the capture of the crucial town, the *SS* men established radio contact with *IX. SS-Waffen-Gebirgs-Armeekorps der SS* and it seemed they would soon break through. Excitement rippled through the ranks of the rescuers as all of the sacrifices seemed

[216] Klapdor, p. 392.

worthwhile; all of the suffering and fighting and losses would not be in vain when the trapped men were rescued. Preparations were made for evacuees from the trapped city, with food kitchens and hospitals readying themselves for an influx of hungry and wounded men.

And yet to the only man who mattered, progress toward Budapest was steady but too slow, and Hitler fretted. Pierik gives this description of Hitler's reaction to how the battle was proceeding, "...Hitler began to lose patience. On 10 January, during the *Führer* conference, he criticized the operation in the mountains as 'utterly pointless.'"[217] Hitler said this even as *Wiking's panzergrenadiers* moved through Piliszentlelek heading east on the frozen roads and into the fight at Pilisszentkereszt. He was already thinking of changing the attack route yet again for what would become *Konrad III.*

Having only been formed for four days, the decimated *1. Ungarische SS–Sturm Regiment* was ordered to regroup near Pomaz after suffering heavy losses fighting for Pilisvorosvar. This left them in the general area of operations of *Konrad II* on the left flank of the attack, while also allowing the unit to reorganize. The regiment had lost nearly ten percent of its strength the day before while attached to *5. SS–Panzer Division Wiking* Viking's Westland regiment, a testament to the Hungarians fighting spirit, even though much of their equipment and weaponry was old captured French material. Meanwhile, even without the *1. Ungarische SS–Sturm Regiment, Wiking* had taken the vital high ground at Pilisszentkereszt and was closing in on its target, Budapest. "Then the incomprehensible happened: At approximately 2000 hours, orders arrived to break off the attack."[218] Incredibly and inexplicably,

[217] Pierik, p. 178.
[218] Strassner, p. 316.

Hitler canceled *Konrad II*. The operation had been delayed on his orders on 10 January and only two days into the attack he had given up hope, just as a breakthrough seemed imminent. *IV. SS–Panzerkorps* was to move southwest to Vezprem in the Lake Balaton area[219].

Thiele describes Gille's reaction to this decision as disbelief, saying "'this is unbelievable,' he (*IV. SS–Panzerkorps* commander Gille) remarked to his chief of staff Schoenfelder. 'Two more valleys and tomorrow we would be in Budapest.'"[220] The dumb-founded *SS* commander immediately appealed to *Heeresgruppe Süd* to have the order rescinded. *IV. SS–Panzerkorps* was strung out, it was true, casualties had been heavy and the troops were exhausted, but the hardest part was over, they were almost out of the Pilis Mountains and the ground leading to Budapest was then relatively flat valley, and the men were anxious to break through and rescue their trapped comrades. Strassner puts it this way: "this measure was completely unintelligible to everyone, especially since the division (*Wiking*) was facing a weak and outgunned enemy...the enemy was still reeling from surprise. Could such an operation have started under more favorable auspices?"[221] But it was no use, the appeal was rejected; Hitler could not be budged. *IV. SS–Panzerkorps* would move to the Vezprem area as ordered. After one last look from Dobogeko at the spires and turrets of Budapest, the Corps prepared for a road march.

Why would Hitler cancel an attack just as it seemed on the verge of success? At least two reasons come to mind.

First, the episode with Hans Ulrich-Rudel may explain the decision. Hitler had not believed in the

---

[219] Sources differ on exactly when Hitler halted the attack, with Rolf Michaelis giving the date as the 13th and others reporting it as 'near midnight'. The time given here is 2000 hours but the safe assumption is somewhere late on the night of the 12th.

[220] Thiele, p. 317.

[221] Strassner, p. 317.

attack from the very beginning, preferring instead the better tank country in the vicinity of Lakes Balaton and Velence, south of Stuhlweissenburg, just as Rudel suggested. Delaying the start of *Konrad II* early on 10 January indicated how little faith he had in its success, although in the end he was talked into allowing the commander on the spot, Hermann Balck, to reinforce what seemed a potentially crucial success by *711. Infanterie Division.* Did Rudel put this doubt in Hitler's mind or did he merely reinforce what Hitler already believed? Was Rudel's opinion even taken seriously? Rudel certainly thought so. There is no way to now be certain, but it seems all too likely that Hitler saw Rudel's opinion as correct because it mirrored his own and reacted accordingly; it would fit with his disdain for the views of Army generals and increasing reliance on his own 'intuition.' Even before the assassination attempt in July of 1944 Hitler's lack of faith in Army generalship had grown to the point where he micro-managed every facet of the ground war, but after Stauffenberg's bomb exploded his skepticism had evolved into open contempt; if an Army general suggested a course of action Hitler's first reaction was suspicion and opposition; almost by default, if an Army general suggested something it must be wrong. The avenue of advance for *Konrad III* also repeated that of the proposed Operation *Spätlese* , which Hitler had favored, the rejected Southern Option for *Konrad I* and the future path for *Unternehmen Frühlingserwachen.*

But secondly, the poisoned atmosphere created by Balck and Gaedecke might also have played a part. There is no way now to know what communications might have taken place that were not recorded, perhaps between old comrades Guderian and Balck, that undermined confidence in Gille.

The furthest unit forward was *SS–Panzergrenadier Regiment 10 Westland,* which reached Pilisszentkereszt and the area near Pilisszanto, about halfway from Esztergom to Budapest, a point that was barely outside the Budapest city suburbs. Pilisvörösvar was less than five miles from Pilisszanto, and the valley in which both towns lay was a virtual highway directly to Budapest's Castle District. Not only were *Wiking's* forward units nearly within metropolitan Budapest but the Danube bend was almost within German hands once more, which would provide a strong defensive position and release troops needed elsewhere. None of that mattered. Hitler ordered the attack to stop and *Wiking* to pull back just as success seemed within reach. So, regardless of the results from *Konrad II*, the *Führer* wanted the *panzer* forces moved south and south they would move.

Joining them would be the newly rebuilt *Schwere Panzer Abteilung 509*, with its 45 brand new *Tiger IIs* and *Flakpanzer IVs*, who entrained for the trip to Hungary. Although the threatened front in Poland desperately needed such a powerful force, Hitler was determined to prove his point in Hungary; *Konrad III* would have as much firepower as he could send it, and the consequences be damned.

13 January, Saturday

Still trying to regroup after its bloody initiation to combat on 11 January, the *1. Ungarische SS–Sturm Regiment* was ordered from the vicinity of Tomaz back to Tata. Meanwhile, following the suspension of *Konrad II*, *SS–Regiment Ney* was removed from *IV. SS–Panzerkorps* in preparation for *Konrad III*.

In the general shift of focus and reorganization aimed at preparing for *Konrad III*, *I./SS–Panzergrenadier Regiment Danmark* was detached from *6. Panzer Division*, *I./Panzergrenadier Regiment 23 Norge* and *I./SS–Panzergrenadier Regiment Germania* were detached from *5. SS Panzer Division Wiking* and assigned to *1. Panzer Division* in the Stuhlweissenburg sector; Norge would soon be back with *Wiking*, however. Infantry was in short supply and the Germans were trying to find the right balance for what they had left. *Wiking*, meanwhile, began its 50 mile move to the area of Csajag, near the northeastern tip of Lake Balaton.

The remaining defenders of Pest were driven back to the banks of the Danube. Pest had always been harder to defend than Buda because of the relative flatness of the terrain, and as casualties mounted it was impossible to maintain a cohesive front line. The defense had long since become a series of strong points that were threatened with being surrounded, forcing the defenders into an ever smaller perimeter, until finally their backs were to the river. In addition, while the two Konrad operations had drained Soviet forces away from the attack on Buda, they had not had the same effect on the attackers of Pest. Being on the opposite side of the Danube, the Soviet formations attacking Buda literally had German forces driving into their rear, and so had to turn and fight. Not so in Pest, where the Hungarian countryside at their backs had been occupied and pacified. And as the defenders retreated the Red Air Force swarmed over the city like flocks of raptors hunting prey, attacking anything that moved and hampering all movement by day. Guillemot quotes a report from *IX. SS-Waffen-Gebirgs-Armeekorps der SS* as reporting "the Pest bridgehead is under constant attack supported by artillery, planes and tanks...we must be prepared to see Pest fall rapidly after the 15th."[222] Time was running out.

But at some point near this time, aircraft must still have been leaving the beleaguered city, because a German newsreel shows artillery, mortar and flak batteries in operation in Budapest, with Buda Castle in the background of some frames. In all likelihood, the guns are those of *Kampfgruppe Portugall*, stationed on the Adlerberg in Buda, although a large mortar is also filmed in action. And while the footage is grainy, palls of smoke can clearly be seen hanging over the ruined city. The newsreel also mentions *Konrad III*, although not by that name, and that relief forces were on the Danube just southwest of the city. Editing could have spliced together action from varying points of the battle and made it seem as though the Budapest footing was contemporary with the footage from *Konrad III*, when in fact the footage was shot over several weeks.

There is no way to know for certain. However, it does prove that at some point during the siege not only were the Propaganda Korps personnel in Budapest still supplied with film and doing their duty, but they were also able to deliver their combat footage to the outside world, and the only way to do that was by air)

[222] Guillemot, p. 37.

14 January, Sunday

After nearly a week of being cut off west of the Gran River, Russian engineers finally rebuilt the bridges that had been washed away on 8 January and supplies again flowed to 7th Guards and 6th Guards Tank Armies. Much of what had been won was lost, yet the Russians still held a sizeable bridgehead west of the Gran, a dangerous dagger aimed at the rear of all German forces operating south of the Danube. The front lines ran from Kravany nad Dunajom near the Danube, to Batorove-Strekov-Svodin-Bruty and finally to Bina. Although the threat to Komárom had been stopped for the moment, the bridgehead was a running sore where the topography gave no help to defenders, ideal tank country when conditions were dry with no significant geographical features to defend. Until and unless the bulge could be eliminated and the line of the Gran regained, *Heeresgruppe Süd* would be in imminent danger.

After only being in existence for six days, and having been moved all over northwestern Hungary and subordinated to various commands, then having a gory introduction to combat on 11 January, the *1. Ungarische SS–Sturm Regiment* was re-organized into a force of only 900 men, from an original complement of 1500, and was sent to the town of Csor, a small town just west of Stuhlweissenburg. Within one week 40 percent of the regiment was gone, dead, wounded or captured.

Within Budapest, *IX. SS-Waffen-Gebirgs-Armeekorps der SS* reported that it was out of artillery ammunition and fuel, and that small arms ammunition was running low. Consequently it had to destroy its remaining vehicles and artillery pieces to deprive the enemy of their use. As the airlift of supplies proved insufficient a boat had been loaded with 4,000 tons of ammunition and floated down the Danube. The scheme might have sounded good in the planning, but with the Danube in Soviet hands the mission was doomed. Few of the supplies filtered through to the garrison.

In Pest, the Soviets finally broke through to the Danube, cutting the pocket in two and marking the beginning of the end for the eastern garrison. The mission now was to hold out as long as possible, then withdraw to the west without allowing a bridge to fall into Soviet hands. The pace of the fighting did not slow, however, but raged on fiercely in an endless cycle of attack and counterattack.

As ordered, *5. SS Panzer Division Wiking* pulled out of the line near Pilisszentkereszt and road marched first to Komarom, then to Raab, on to Papa and finally to its assembly areas near Vesprem, just north of Lake Balaton. Along with *Totenkopf* and *Wiking*, *IV. SS–Panzerkorps* would be reinforced with *1. Panzer Division* and *3. Panzer Division* for *Konrad III*.

15 January, Monday

The War Situation in the West

Strength returns for *1. SS–Panzer Division Leibstandarte Adolf Hitler (LAH)* on 15 January show a once powerful division reduced to a skeleton of its former strength, but being given priority for replenishment. 31 *panzers* were ready for action, but only 11 were *Mark V Panthers* and 16 were *Mark IVs*. A mere three *flakpanzers* were operational, a critical shortage at that state of the war when air attack was a constant threat; they were a prime target for ground-attack aircraft and were in chronically short supply. There were 52 *panzer* reinforcements on the way, however, including 29 *Mark V Panthers* and 20 *Mark IVs*; the latter mounted the 75/L48 gun, which was good enough against American and British armor, but far less effective against the more heavily armored Russian tanks of the JS-1 and JS-2 series. The division had 11 *panzers* under repair, for a total of 94 *panzers* of all types, against an authorized strength of 180 or more. There were only 14 *jagdpanzers* ready, with 11 in repair. And the total of all armored vehicles available of all types was 118, with 64 more in repair and 69 reinforcements on the way. What this shows more than anything is the value of the priority given the *Waffen–SS* formations for new vehicles and men after the Ardennes Offensive.[223]

The rest of *6. SS–Panzerarmee* was in similar condition. Rebuilding the shattered divisions required a full effort from the German war economy, the last time it would be able to achieve such a feat. Beset by existential threats coming from both east and west, it was clear to every German privy to a full understanding of the war situation that the *Reich*'s last offensive asset had to be sent east, to stop the Russians in Poland

---

[223] http://www.panzerworld.net/oob-1sspzdiv (Accessed 23 April, 2013).

before they came within striking range of Berlin. The Allies would first have to cross the Rhine before entering the Ruhr industrial area, and that would take months yet. But the Russians... the Russians were closing in. And since using *6. SS-Panzerarmee* in Poland was the only logical use for Germany's final hope, Hitler naturally rejected it and sent Sepp Dietrich and his army to Hungary.

As predicted, however, the Russian offensive from the Baranov bridgehead in Poland ripped through the thin German front lines and sped west, exactly as Guderian had warned. Hans Ulrich-Rudel and his *Luftwaffe* veterans immediately left Hungary for Silesia, leaving behind only a single squadron to fight in the south. In the absence of ground forces Rudel's obsolescent *Stukas* were asked to hold back the Red Army flood. The problem was that the German front in Poland wasn't the only dam that had broken.

Leaving out the *Mark IIs* and *Mark IIIs*, which likely were used for special purposes and not combat, the total combat ready AFVs on 15 January was 454. Another 404 were in short or long term repair, and 214 more were in transit, including the powerful *Schwere–Panzer Abteilung 509*.

This sounds like an impressive total until it is realized this inventory includes any vehicles reported to still be in Budapest, and those in the three armies that made up *Heeresgruppe Süd: 8. Armee, Armeegruppe Balck,* and *2. Panzerarmee.* For example, *18. SS-Freiwilligen-Panzergrenadier Division Horst Wessel* had its own organic *panzer* battalion, which would have been included in the *panzerlage.* The actual number of vehicles available for *Konrad III* was much smaller.

On the eve of *Unternehmen Konrad III* the official *panzerlage* (*panzer* inventory) for *Heeresgruppe Süd* showed as follows:

Army group	Status	Pz Kpfw II	Pz Kpfw III	Pz Kpfw IV	Panther	Tiger	Assault guns
Eastern Front							
Heeresgruppe Kurland	Combat ready	-	13	26	31	22	361
	Undergoing maintenance	-	5	12	16	-	102
	In transit	-	-	-	-	-	85
Heeresgruppe Weichsel	Combat ready	1	6	63	45	51	241
	Undergoing maintenance	3	5	18	29	4	28
	In transit	-	-	33	-	1	66
Heeresgruppe Nord	Combat ready	10	20	56	93	66	504
	Undergoing maintenance	-	6	49	54	22	63
	In transit	-	-	124	-	-	91
Heeresgruppe Mitte	Combat ready	3	18	239	171	-	469
	Undergoing maintenance	-	2	48	25	-	73
	In transit	-	1	83	32	-	170
Heeresgruppe Süd	Combat ready	3	12	137	82	7	228
	Undergoing maintenance	5	10	88	161	27	128
	In transit	-	-	70	77	45	22 [224]

Just behind the German lines in the Margarethe position, a welcome reinforcement detrained at Veszprem, the *Schwere Panzer Abteilung 509* with its 45 *Tiger IIs*. Given the weak state of the *panzer* regiments of *6. Armee's panzer* divisions, these dominating machines added a serious punch to the coming offensive; indeed, wherever they appeared on the battlefield would give the Germans overwhelming firepower at the point of attack, or effective defense against a counter-attack. But their cross-country

---

[224] https://panzerworld.com/german-armor-inventory-army-groups-1945-01-15 (Accessed 1 January, 2024).

performance limited their range, especially in deep snows and on soft roads.

Schwere Panzer Abteilung 509 is often confused in sources with Schwere Panzer Abteilung 503, which had been in Hungary for some time and seen heavy fighting. That battalion also fielded Tiger IIs and had suffered terrible losses during late 1944.

16 January, Tuesday

Even as the *Konrad* offensives drained away Soviet pressure on Buda, the perimeter in Pest continued to shrink under relentless attacks. "...The eastern bridgehead had been reduced to the area Franz Joseph Bridge- Calvin Square – Elizabeth Ring – Baro Street to the Danube. Margaret Island formed its northern tip."[225] The Soviets concentrated on trying to split the remaining perimeter, and under the increasing pressure it became obvious that the time had come to withdraw what could be saved across the three standing bridges to Buda. The end came for the defenders of Pest when those who were able fled across the Danube to Buda, after which the Horthy Bridge was blown up.

By this point, nearly one million civilians in Budapest were sheltering in basements, ground-floor apartments, and tunnels scattered across the city. On Castle Hill, thousands were packed into miles of tunnels carved into the natural limestone formations. In this damp and foul environment, several German and Hungarian field hospitals were in operation. A German war correspondent vividly depicted these dire conditions:

> "At first the girls, women and men of Budapest worked on. They wore fur coats and built barricades under the orders of the SS. In the beginning, they cowered together when a round exploded nearby. For a while they tried to carry on. But at last they disappeared in the cellars and sat or lay down with their hunger. Like the people of Budapest — this city that crumbles more on all sides with each passing day — like these people sitting down there in the cellars, the women in fur coats and silk stockings sheer as breath, the girls who mechanically

---

[225] Michaleis, p. 197.

reached for their lipstick and compact now and then, as if they had to pretty themselves up in the usual big city manner for Death the Cavalier, the confused peasant girls in colorful headscarves and, in between, the children with long, lowered eyelashes, none of them had anything left to eat, yet nobody felt the hunger anymore.... Yes, it was not easy to bear the sight of it. Civilian corpses already lay in the streets."[226]

The three great offensives in the west, *Unternehmen Wacht am Rhein* (the Ardennes Offensive, aka, the Battle of the Bulge), *Unternehmen Bodenplatte* and *Unternehmen Nordwind*, had failed; even Adolf Hitler was finally forced to admit that reality. Nothing indicated that he realized this more than his return to Berlin on 16 January, abandoning his headquarters near the Western Front for the dreary ruin of the capital. All of the careful hoarding of resources, all the secrecy and planning, all of it had been for naught. The Ardennes Offensive had inflicted severe casualties on the enemy, it was true, but Germany had suffered even worse, and Germany could not make good her losses while the Allies could. *Unternehmen Bodenplatte* had been meant to win back the skies, at least in the short run, but instead had broken the *Luftwaffe* once and for all. *Unternehmen Nordwind* briefly caused Eisenhower to consider evacuating Strasburg, and put a fleeting strain on France's alliance with England and America, but the eight-division weight of the attack was too weak to threaten a critical rupture in the Allied lines. By mid-January, all Germany had to show for her attacks was a very long casualty list.

[226] E Howard, "World War II: Siege of Budapest," (Accessed /7/2024. https://www.historynet.com/world-war-ii-siege-of-budapest/).

As January, 1945 passed and Germany's enemies closed in for the kill, the only decision remaining to the German High Command was what to do with the two armies that had done most of the fighting in the Ardennes. Both *5. Panzerarmee* and *6. SS–Panzerarmee*[227] had spear-headed the attack that was aimed at splitting Allied forces in Belgium and re-capturing Antwerp, an overly ambitious plan that had failed miserably and, in so doing, had cost Germany enormously in both manpower and material [228]. Yet despite their heavy losses, those two armies remained vital to the final German defense of the *Reich*, especially *6. SS–Panzerarmee*. As damaged as the *Waffen–SS Panzer* divisions may have been, they had not been destroyed and their remaining framework meant they could be resurrected. When Hitler's private train pulled into Berlin for the last time on 16 January, the debate within the German High Command then became how best to use *6. SS–Panzerarmee*. Little did anyone know that Hitler had already decided.

The choices were limited. Leaving it where it was, or perhaps moving it somewhere else on the Western Front, might have been reasonable in other circumstances. The Allies were closing in on the Rhine and no matter how formidable that river barrier was,

[227] The issue of what this army was actually called is convoluted, to say the least. Until early April, 1945, the army was known in German communiqués and parlance as simply *6. Panzerarmee*. In his memoirs, the Chief of the General Staff *Generaloberst* Heinz Guderian consistently omits the '*SS*' title. At some point it began to be called *6. SS–Panzerarmee*, more or less simultaneous with Dr. Lothar Rendulic being named as Commander of *Heeresgruppe Ostmark* in April of 1945, although the name was never officially changed. Adding to the confusion, an addendum to the bottom of the *OKW* War Diary for 1 January, 1945, says "Effective January 1, 1945: 6. SS Panzer-Armee..." (Maier, p. 3). The vast majority of histories referring to *SS–Oberstgruppenfürher* Sepp Dietrich's command refer to it throughout its operational life with the added '*SS*' description, even during the Ardennes Offensive in December of 1944. Therefore, even though this was not its official title, to avoid confusion with the vast preponderance of existing works, it will be referred to here by its commonly accepted name of *6. SS–Panzerarmee*.

[228] Estimates of German losses in the Ardennes Offensive vary widely. (Give examples of this)

with the forces on hand it was doubtful that even the Rhine could be held, so strong mobile reserves would be needed to seal off any breakthroughs. But Germany's position was far too precarious for that; there were other places in far greater danger in the east. Transferring *6. SS–Panzerarmee* to the Berlin front seemed the logical choice; given the success of their offensive that had started on 12 January, the Russians at that moment seemed likely to jump the Oder River on the run and make a dash for Berlin before defenses could be erected. But while this seemed the most logical choice for re-deploying *6. SS–Panzerarmee* to many, if not most, German generals, there was another choice none of them had seriously considered: sending the army to *Heeresgruppe Süd* for operations in Hungary. Hitler had already decided to attack Tolbukhin's Second Ukrainian and Malinovsky's Third Ukrainian Fronts, thereby not only stopping their expected Vienna offensive but relieving the mounting threat to the Hungarian oil fields near the Austrian border. Once those missions were accomplished he would then, and only then, allow the transfer of *6. SS–Panzerarmee* to the Berlin sector. This was merely an upscaled *Unternehmen Spätlese* and *Konrad III*. As always, once Hitler convinced himself of a course of action, he could perhaps be put off, but not dissuaded.

Hitler's decision was controversial in 1945 and his motives for ordering the offensive that would become *Unternehmen Frühlingserwachen* are still not completely understood. Was the coming attack purely economic, to protect the Hungarian and Austrian oilfields? Was it, as he sometimes said, a foreign policy issue designed to keep Hungary in the war? Was there an underlying sentimentality that drew the *Führer* to protect his homeland instead of his life[229], as discussed below? Did Hitler feel that the time for defense was long since passed and Germany's only hope lay in the

---

[229] Although seemingly preposterous on its surface, there may be more to this possibility than previously thought; it is discussed in several places throughout the narrative.

attack[230]? Or was the decision some combination of all of these? There is no question of the value Hitler assigned to the Hungarian oilfield at Nagykanisza and the Austrian field at Zistersdorf; even on April 27th, as Russian artillery shells burst nearby and Russian tanks roamed the streets of Berlin's government district, Hitler came back to the value of those oil facilities. "We no longer have any oil areas. As long as we had them, anything could be done. The two oil areas in Austria provided us with a total of 120,000 tons. That could be increased to 180,000 tons."[231]

The fourth choice may well have been the underlying belief that led him to send *6. SS–Panzerarmee* South after he had attempted largely the same thing in the Ardennes Offensive. "I can't wait for a long time...I have to keep moving forward. Otherwise, whatever stops moving will be destroyed as well. "[232] Attack or die; even with the *Reich* itself being consumed from the air and overrun on the ground, Hitler could think of nothing more than striking his enemies.

But with the capital of the *Reich* squarely in the Russian cross-hairs the decision regarding *6. Panzerarmee* made no sense to many of his advisers, including one of the few German generals who dared to stand up to him. The debate fundamentally came down to a contest of wills between two men: Heinz Guderian and Adolf Hitler. Regardless of what the other Generals may have believed was the best choice they were not

[230] Postwar readers and historians know that Germany had no hope of avoiding defeat by 1945, regardless of what Hitler did or did not do.

[231] Heiber & Glantz, p. 733. The Austrian oilfields at Zistersdorf are almost always dismissed by historians as being insignificant, too small to be of any strategic value, yet here Hitler clearly states the opposite. The conclusion has been that Hitler was either delusional or using the fields to justify decisions based on ulterior motives. Yet finds made after the war clearly indicate that there was more oil at Zistersdorf than is usually acknowledged.

[232] Heiber & Glantz, p. 622. To be clear, Hitler was probably referring specifically to attacks in Hungary, not to a general philosophy, in the quote. However, in context it seems to betray an overall conviction that victory could only come through attack, not defense.

prepared to challenge the *Führer's* will past a certain point, and certainly not to the point of angering him; that was a potentially fatal mistake. As Chief of the General Staff, Guderian was not a man who was loved by many of his contemporaries in the Army, anyway. Despite his reputation as the Father of the Blitzkrieg, and his legendary successes in France and the early months of Operation Barbarossa, he had fallen out of Hitler's favor and only been restored to command in 1943 as Inspector General of *Panzer* Troops. He rose to the lofty position of Chief of the General Staff in the days following the 20 July 20, assassination attempt against Hitler[233], then condemned the plotters and sided with those who ordered them hunted down and executed. Most of them had been Guderian's brother Army officers and many within the Army never forgave him for this supposed betrayal. Guderian had no sympathy for them, however, viewing Operation Valkyrie as a heinous act in the face of impending national destruction. But while many in the Army despised him, Guderian was no Hitler toady, either, and often clashed with the *Führer,* being a man who was "almost aggressively frank."[234] Guderian possessed a flair for honesty and bluntness that did not endear him to Hitler.

Several versions of the debates concerning the fate of *6. SS–Panzerarmee* exist, including Guderian's memoir *Panzer General*[235] and the War Diary kept by *Chef des Wehrmachtführungsstab im Oberkommando der Wehrmacht* (Chief of the Operations Staff of the Armed Forces High Command) *Generaloberst* Alfred Jodl,[236] from which Former *Stellvertreter Chef des*

---

[233] *Unternehmen Walküre*, aka Operation Valkyrie.

[234] Thorwald, p. 13.

[235] Guderian's book has been criticized for being self-serving in places, but generally seems accurate regarding the question of 6th SS Panzer Army's deployment.

[236] Chief of the Armed Forces High Command Operations Staff meant that Jodl took part in planning, authorizing and directing all German military operations.

Wehrmachtführungsstab Oberkommando der Wehrmacht [237] *General der Artillerie* Walter Warlimont drew his research when writing his account of this debate in *Inside Hitler's Headquarters 1943-1945* (1990). Warlimont knew both Guderian and Jodl quite well and his account reconciles events surrounding this decision and rings true about those often-heated arguments.

Warlimont writes that on 16 January, "Hitler ordered that Sixth *SS Panzer* Army...'should be thrown into Hungary to protect the vital oil area.'"[238]Guderian's account more or less back this up, as he protested immediately and vehemently. "On hearing this I lost my self-control and expressed my disgust to Jodl in very plain terms...[239]" Guderian wanted *6. SS–Panzerarmee* transferred north to defend Berlin. The argument lasted much of the day and in Guderian's words the "disagreements were violent."[240] Warlimont backs up Guderian's assertion with the words of *Generalfeldmarschall* Wilhelm Keitel,[241] *Chef des Oberkommando der Wehrmacht*, whom Warlimont quotes as having said: "that Hitler 'considered the protection of Vienna and Austria as of vital importance' and that he [Hitler] would 'rather see Berlin fall than lose the Hungarian oil area and Austria.'"[242]

In essence, then, Guderian wanted the army used either east of Berlin as a mobile defense force, or

---

[237] Deputy Chief of Operations for the High Command of the Armed Forces. In essence, Jodl's number two.

[238] Warlimont, Gen. Walter, *Inside Hitler's Headquarters 1939-1945* (Novato: Presidio Press, 1990), p. 499.

[239] Guderian, *Panzer Leader*, p. 321.

[240] Ibid, p. 322.

[241] As chief of the Armed Forces High Command, *Generalfeldmarschall* Wilhelm Keitel was, in theory, Hitler's highest ranking military advisor. His main qualification for this position was his complete inability to disagree with Hitler about virtually anything. Behind his back he was nicknamed 'lakeitel', which in German means 'lackey.' In an ironic twist, his son was a member of the *Waffen–SS* and commanded a battle-group fighting in Hungary and Austria during the period in question, his unit (Kampfgruppe Keitel) being attached to *6. SS–Panzerarmee* on several occasions.

[242] Warlimont, *Inside Hitler's Headquarters*, p. 499.

241

as part of an attack against Zhukov's spearheads east of the Oder, and according to Michael Reynolds, Sepp Dietrich agreed with Guderian. Whether in a counterattack from Pomerania[243], or as an armored reserve for *Heeresgruppe Vistula*,[244] the two generals agreed that *6. SS–Panzerarmee* should move north. This would serve to stop Zhukov and buy time to build the defenses in front of Berlin. They argued their case passionately but to no avail since, according to Reynolds, "Hitler would have none of it."[245] As quoted above, Hitler believed that Germany could not win the war by either remaining on the defensive, or by small-scale attacks; she simply was not strong enough to hold out much longer.[246]. Winning the war, therefore, meant attacking in strength, trying to inflict so much damage that one or the other of her enemies might give up the fight. The Ardennes Offensive had failed to accomplish this against the Western Allies, so the time had come to strike the Soviets, and Hitler had decided to do that in the south. Never mind that Germany no longer had the strength to inflict fatal damage on her opponents, Hitler would attack anyway. And despite Guderian's protests, in Nazi Germany Hitler's orders were all that mattered. *6. SS–Panzerarmee* was ordered to move to Hungary and prepare for offensive action.

   6. SS–Panzerarmee was commanded by one of Hitler's oldest confidants, *SS–Oberstgruppenführer* Joseph 'Sepp' Dietrich. Dietrich was an early follower,

---

[243] Such an attack took place anyway, without either *I. SS–Panzerkorps* or *II. SS–Panzerkorps*. Known as Operation Solstice, it had little firepower but managed to scare the Russian Supreme Command into clearing Pomerania before advancing on Berlin.

[244] The Soviet winter offensive came to a halt on the Oder River in January of 1945, leaving them some 60 miles from Berlin. Defending the western bank of the Oder, between the Red Army and the capital, was Army Group Vistula.

[245] Reynolds, Michael, *Sons of the Reich: The History of II. SS–Panzerkorps*, (Havertown: Casemate, 2008), p. 247.

[246] The obvious conclusion here is that Germany could not win the war under any circumstances, but is it unlikely that any circumstance could have driven Hitler to sue for peace.

and led a firing squad during the purge of the *Sturmabteilung* in 1934, also known as The Night of the Long Knives. The core components of the army were *I. SS–Panzerkorps* and *II SS Panzerkorps*, containing four of the most powerful divisions in the German Wehrmacht.[247] *I. SS–Panzerkorps* had in its Order of Battle the only two German units allowed to use Hitler's name in their honorific title, *1. SS–Panzer Division Leibstandarte Adolf Hitler* (LAH) and *12. SS– Panzer Division Hitlerjugend (HJ).*[248] *II. SS–Panzerkorps* had *9. SS–Panzer Division Hohenstauffen* and *2. SS Panzer Division Das Reich (DR).*[249] While other units would be attached and released, these four *panzer* divisions were the army's permanent components.

In determining Hitler's motives for sending *6. SS– Panzerarmee* to Hungary, there is one more to consider, the one that seems the least likely; that Hitler valued protecting his Austrian homeland more than his own life. A curious historical footnote to the conversations and debates about Sepp Dietrich's command are the quoted words of Hitler that Keitel recorded in the War Diary of the *Chef des Oberkommando der Wehrmacht*: "Hitler considered the protection of Vienna and Austria as of vital importance...(he would) rather see Berlin fall than lose the Hungarian oil area and Austria."[250] Within those few words of Hitler resides a mystery that can probably never be solved. On its face it seems that there is nothing to dispute, Vienna and Austria were vital parts of the *Reich*, containing heavy industry and

---

[247] The term 'Wehrmacht' is often mis-interpreted as meaning the German Army, but in fact it means the entirety of the German Armed Forces, including both the Luftwaffe and the Kriegsmarine. The German word for army was 'Heer'.

[248] Liebstandarte translates as 'Life Guards', derived from the division's origins as Hitler's SS bodyguard company in the early days of the Nazi Party, while Hitlerjugend is 'Hitler Youth'. 12th SS was formed only in late 1943, with the rank and file mostly drawn from 17 and 18 year old Hitler Youth members.

[249] Hohenstauffen was the name of a prominent German family in the 11th-13th centuries, to which the legendary king Frederick Barbarossa was a member.

[250] Warlimont, *Inside Hitler's Headquarters*, p. 499.

oil refineries and other strategic assets, but in context the quote still seems strange. Vienna and Austria were very important, even vital, but more than the capital?

Guderian meant for *6. SS–Panzerarmee* to be used near Berlin, giving protection of the capital priority over every other potential target in the *Reich*, and it is hard to argue with this conclusion. Berlin and, more to the point, the person of Adolf Hitler, were the embodiment of German resistance; if Berlin fell, or Hitler died, the war was essentially over. Yet Hitler considered Vienna and Austria as even more in need of protection than either his capital or himself. Keitel makes this clear when he says that Hitler found Berlin less important than "the Hungarian oil area and Austria." Protecting Austria was more vital than protecting Berlin and, almost by default, Hitler himself? Hitler was the very embodiment of German resistance; without him no other leader could rally enough loyalty to continue the fight; as Ian Kershaw puts it, "total capitulation followed in just over a week from the final act of the drama in the bunker...Hitler was crucial to the last."[251] In other words, no Hitler, no war; Germany would, and did, surrender shortly after his death. Perhaps he truly believed that Berlin had become a secondary target, or deluded himself into believing it, but Helmut Heimer and David Glantz have no qualms about Hitler's sentimentality for his homeland being a deciding factor in why he chose to commit his best Army to the Austro-Hungarian region. "He [Hitler] would soon attempt to motivate the protection of the last remaining oil sources with exclusively foreign-policy arguments, although the primary reason lay more in the fact that Hitler felt closer to Vienna (despite the love-hate relationship) and his whole Austrian homeland than to the other German districts."[252]

The lack of oil was a crippling impediment to the German war machine in the final months of the war.

---

[251] Kershaw, p. 12.
[252] Heiber & Glantz, p. 1096.

With the synthetic oil industry virtually bombed out of existence Germany was facing the very real possibility of seeing its armies grind to a halt for lack of fuel. Protecting the Hungarian oil fields has long been recognized as an obsession of Hitler's at that stage of the war, so the quote in question merely shows how crucial he knew this economic to be. And the transportation of what little oil Germany still possessed was becoming more and more problematic as the *Reich*'s infrastructure and rail network were captured or destroyed, providing yet another reason to send *6. SS–Panzerarmee* to Hungary; that's where the oil was, and long distance transport was not necessary.

But the question still remains, what did Keitel mean about "and Austria." Did this mean that Hitler put the protection of Austria itself as of primary importance? The very strangeness of the idea that Vienna and Austria were more important to Hitler than Berlin almost requires further questions must be asked, as if there were any way to actually answer them. There is not. The only man who could have answered them shot himself in his bunker under the *Reich* Chancellery. But that does not mean they cannot at least be asked and considered as a possible explanation for so much of what was to come. *Generalleutnant* Kurt von Tippelskirch had this to say on the subject: "the liberation of the city [Budapest] and the control of the territory of Western Hungary had become an idée fixe for Hitler, to which he subordinated all other considerations, and which he supported sometimes by foreign policy considerations and sometimes by the necessity for protecting the last sources of oil in Hungary and Austria...he probably felt closer to this region and Vienna just beyond it than to the other German Districts."[253]

So was there something more to Hitler's decision to attach *6. SS–Panzerarmee* to *Heeresgruppe Süd* than simple economics? As an Austrian, was Hitler

---

[253] Maier, *Drama Between Budapest and Vienna*, p. 13.

protecting his homeland over his adopted land? Was this a manifestation of the sentimental streak he could occasionally show toward those close to him? The questions are now nothing more than interesting historical ponderings, and yet the ramifications of Hitler's sending the army south may be greater than have heretofore been recognized, ramifications that will be looked at in due course.

There will never be hard evidence to support such a conclusion that Hitler sent *6. SS–Panzerarmee* south because he was an Austrian and felt some kinship to his homeland, so Hitler's strange quote is noted in passing as an interesting anomaly in a decision that was, to Heinz Guderian, madness. *6. Panzer Division* Army was needed in the north, holding back Zhukov's First Belorussian Front, not in the south opposing Second and Third Ukrainian Fronts. None of Guderian's protests mattered in the long run, of course, because in Nazi Germany Hitler's orders were the only ones that counted.

As seen earlier, regardless of where *6. SS–Panzerarmee* was to be committed, if it was going to be even marginally effective it first had to be rebuilt. Referring to *1. SS–Panzer Division LAH*, Michael Reynolds put it this way: "once more the Leibstandarte had been shattered beyond recognition and once more it would be rebuilt."[254] The same held true for the other *SS* units of *6. SS–Panzerarmee*.

But Germany no longer had the resources it once did. Rebuilding the depleted units first required new manpower, wherever it could be found, and by this point in the war the original voluntary nature of the *Waffen–SS* and the once stringent acceptance standards had long since been forgotten, including the minimum height requirement. Nor was age an issue. As

---

[254] Reynolds, Michael, *The Devil's Adjutant*, p. 248.

the American handbook on the German military stated at the time concerning conscription of 16 year-olds , "in the past 2 years a large proportion of the youngest age class has been induced by various kinds of pressure to volunteer, largely for the *Waffen-SS*" [255]. Induced, in Nazi Germany, meant coerced, but forcing them to join or even drafting 16 year-olds could not, by itself, make good the losses. Germany scraped the bottom of the manpower barrel to bring *6. SS–Panzerarmee* back up to strength. Some of the reinforcements were veteran *SS* men who were returning from leave or recovered from wounds, but many were surplus *Luftwaffe* and *Kriegsmarine*[256] men with no infantry training. However physically fit they may have been, in battle such men were virtually useless[257]. Moreover, *6. SS–Panzerarmee* as a whole was critically short of both officers and NCOs, meaning that younger, less experienced men were promoted to fill positions for which they were not qualified, or that such positions of leadership went unfilled. But whoever the men were and whatever their qualifications might have been bringing the *SS* divisions back up to strength was the only thing that mattered, by whatever means were necessary.

But exactly how strong should an *SS Panzer* division of this period have been, and how strong were they? The *panzer* forces had undergone numerous re-organizations since 1943 in an effort to maximize the effectiveness of a force that was increasingly out-numbered, making it difficult to establish precisely what their authorized strength was in early 1945. It

---

[255] War Department Technical Manual TM-E30-451 Handbook on German Military Forces, 15 March, 1945, Washington: War Department, 1945; via website http://www.ibiblio.org/hyperwar/Germany/HB/HB-1.html, accessed 22 February, 2011, page I-57

[256] The German Air Force and Navy.

[257] As the postwar American historian S.L.A. Marshall discovered in Men Against Fire, training men to shoot to kill another man, even an enemy, was more of an art than a science. Training could, however, offset experience when it came to things like maintaining unit coherence in the face of enemy action. Without even the basics of such training, the value of men who often did not even know how to use their personal weapon was very limited.

might even be surmised that the armored strength of a *Waffen–SS Panzer* division was whatever the *Waffen–SS* wanted it to be. For example, in June of 1944, prior to the Normandy Invasion, *1. SS–Panzer Division LAH* boasted an AFV complement totaling 219 vehicles, and *12. SS–Panzer Division HJ* had another 153. This gave *I. SS–Panzerkorps* the impressive total of 372 *panzers*, *jagdpanzers* and assault guns, more than all of *6. SS–Panzerarmee* would have when *Unternehmen Frühlingserwachen* was launched. Given the myriad of problems facing the German replacement system in 1945, it might be more accurate to say of *Waffen–SS Panzer* Divisions in 1945 that their authorized strength was whatever they could beg, borrow or steal it to be, as tables of organization became more and more out of touch with reality. Most sources agree, however, that on paper the total number of *panzers, jagdpanzers* and assault guns, that were authorized for a late war *Waffen–SS Panzer* division, should have been somewhere near 200, far more than for an ordinary Army *panzer* division.[258] Earlier in the war a distinction was made between *panzers* (tanks), with a rotating turret, and vehicles with a fixed gun such as a tank destroyer or assault gun, but the days for such specificity were gone as the divisions grew progressively weaker. Vehicles with fixed guns were much cheaper and faster to make and often became a de facto substitute for the more complex *panzers*.

Continuing to use *1. SS–Panzer Division LAH* strength returns as a measuring reference for all of the *Waffen–SS Panzer* divisions, Reynolds lists slightly different totals than quoted previously. According to

[258] The final reorganization of the panzer forces in March, 1945, for example, limited such a division to a mere 40 tanks, roughly one quarter of what the authorized strength had once been. The SS divisions, however, did not fall under this reorganization plan, and few, if any, Army divisions were actually so changed. Not only that, some panzer divisions were special units with a different authorized order of battle, GrossDeutschland and the Herman Goring Division, for example. To confuse matters even more, by 1945 there was no practical difference in the authorized strength of a panzer division and a panzergrenadier division.

him the returns for 15 January, show a mere 49 AFVs ready for action, made up of 29 Panthers[259], 18 *Mark IVs* and two *Jagdpanzer IVs*, but like *Mark IVs* in most divisions those *Mark IVs* all mounted the 75/L48 main gun, which was an upgrade from older models but had nowhere near the penetrating power of the *Mark V Panther's* 75/L70 gun.[260] The *Mark IV* tank was almost obsolescent by that point anyway, having served in front-line duty since 1939, but was still dangerous in the hands of a good crew. Even the improved 75/L48 gun, however, was only marginally effective against the new Soviet heavy tanks of the JS-I and JS-II types; only a perfect hit could damage or disable the Soviet behemoths. Nevertheless, given the scarcity of *panzers* in general, the *Mark IV* was a welcome addition, and while reinforcements would shortly join *LAH*, even a cursory comparison to the number of AFVs from seven months previously shows just how badly the division had fared during the fighting in France and during the Ardennes Offensive. By 1 March, 1945, after participating in *Unternehmen Südwind*, LAH's total combat-ready AFV strength had fallen to a mere 74, barely a third of what it had been 9 months before[261].

II. SS–Panzerkorps was in similarly poor condition. Even after the Corps' two divisions had been reinforced, Reynolds asserts that when the time came for *Unternehmen Frühlingserwachen* the Corps could

<hr />

[259] The Panzer Mark V 'Panther' is considered by some the best overall tank of World War II. A medium tank with a high velocity 75mm main gun, the Panther incorporated much of the design of the Soviet T-34. It was feared by its enemies and was deadly in the hands of a veteran crew, but also had ongoing mechanical problems that were never wholly solved.

[260] Reynolds, Michael, *Men of Steel: The History of I SS-Panzerkorps*, (Havertown: Casemate, 2005), p. 157.

[261] Chris Bishop states that in early February the Leibstandarte's headquarters company for the 1st SS Panzer Regiment had 8 3.7 cm Flankpanzers (*Waffen–SS* Divisions 1939-45, p. 26).

field only "...185 tanks, *Jagdpanzers* and *Sturmgeschütze*, between them...50 percent below their authorized holdings."[262] Guillemot is more specific, giving the total number of AFVs for *2. SS–Panzer Division Das Reich* as 76 and for *9. SS–Panzer Division Hohenstauffen* as 77, for a total of 153. The discrepancy in Reynolds and Guillemot is hard to reconcile, unless Reynolds did not remove tanks that were in repair from his figures.

Sturmgeschütz IIIG

No vehicle is more representative of the late war German *panzer* and *panzergrenadier* formations than the *Sturmgeschütz IIIG*. The *StuG III G,* which was armed with a modified long-barrelled *75 mm Sturmkanone (StuK) 40 L/48* tank gun, had the same armor-penetrating power as the *Panzer IV H*. More than 8,000 were produced during the war.

Even among the vehicles that were ready to fight, though, a great number were surely vehicles repaired by the Corps maintenance personnel and were not newly manufactured. In *SPWs, Hohenstaufen* was well below strength with 167, while *Das Reich* had 258; *Das Reich's* artillery component was near full strength but *Hohenstaufen* was only at half strength.

[262] Reynolds, *Sons of the Reich*, p. 250.

In short, by robbing the other services and conscripting teenagers, *II. SS–Panzerkorps* had close to its full complement of men; in late winter of 1945 that was very unusual among German units. In terms of actual combat power, however, the Corps was nowhere near as strong as it should have been.

After fighting alongside the Germans in *Konrad I*, on 16 January the Hungarian 2nd Armored Division listed its strength as 27 *Panzer IVs*, five 40M Nimróds,[263] two half-tracks of an unspecified type, four motorized rifle battalions and two artillery batteries. In reality, the 'division' was nothing more than a regimental *kampfgruppe*.

SU-100

The Samokhodnaya Ustanovka 85 and its upgraded brother, the SU-100, were the direct Russian equivalents of the *Jagdpanzer* and *Jagdpanther*. Built on the chassis of a T-34 and mounting a 100mm main gun, the SU-100 could take on virtually any German tank and kill it from a distance. Meanwhile, its 125mm thick frontal armor and 55 degree slope made it impervious to German counter-fire at all but the closest ranges. Even a *Tiger I* had to get within a kilometer to hurt the SU-100. Thousands were built, although how many entered service before the end of the war is not known with any reliability..

---

[263] The Nimród was a license-built copy of the Swedish Landsverk L62 Anti I Self-Propelled Anti-Aircraft Guns. Mounting a 40mm Bofors gun, proved effective against aircraft, but wholly inadequate in its secondary role as a tank destroyer. Worse, its thin armor, measuring 6-13mm, made it vulnerable to anything larger than machine guns.

At Sared in Slovakia, east of Pressburg (Bratislava), the *357. Infanterie Division* absorbed the Spanish volunteers left over when the final incarnation of the Spanish volunteer formations was dissolved. Those were the Spanish Volunteer Battalions, the last remnant of the rather sizeable commitment the Spanish made to the war on Communism with the *250. Infanterie Division,* known as the Blue Division, earlier in the war. Around mid-January of 1945, the last two infantry companies were assigned to the *357 Infanterie Division,* with the Germans attaching two of their officers and 42 of their men as a cadre, and with six interpreters per company. Further recruitment of Spanish volunteers was stopped and 'useless' personnel were assigned to labor companies. Few of the Spanish were deemed fit for officer rank in either company. So ended the last trace of independent Spanish involvement in the war, with Franco's refusal to join the war on Germany's side having been ultimately justified by the course of events.

After four days of rest and reorganization, Fritz Vogt's *I./SS–Panzergrenadier Regiment 23 Norge* moved south to attack positions near the northeast tip of Lake Balaton, in preparation for *Konrad III.*

17 January, Wednesday

In Pest, the end had come. Chaos reigned as the eastern bridgehead was evacuated and Pest was completely occupied by the Red Army.[264] Guillemot describes the frantic dash across the Danube as the Russians were pressing forward: "according to eyewitness accounts, the withdrawal took place in an indescribable chaos of vehicles, soldiers of all units and civilians, whilst Soviet shells fell around them."[265] Crumbling masonry, shell splinters whizzing through the smoky air, jammed streets filled with cars and *SPWs* and *panzers* and motorcycles, men in a variety of uniforms and civilians of all ages and professions...the final rush to the illusory freedom of the western shore must have driven everyone involved to the brink of madness. The Russians were close behind and mercy would not be given those who fell into the hands of the Red Army.

At 0700, the Franz Joseph Bridge over the Danube was blown up by the garrison. The smaller the area held by the Germans, the more concentrated became the Russian bombardment. As more people crowded into less space, casualties soared.

Throughout *Heeresgruppe Süd*'s theater of operations, men milled around the rear areas in great numbers, and there was coming and going from one combatant army to the next that seemed almost continuous. For the most part, defectors were leaving the Axis side and going over to the Soviets, but not always.

---

[264] Pierik, p. 144. Pierik seems to disagree and gives the date for this as 15 January, not 17 January, and lists these as men of the 'Schmidthuber Group', remnants of *13. Panzer Division*.

[265] Guillemot, p. 27.

On 17 January a Romanian cavalry troop fighting with the Soviets entered German lines to join the Axis. Lead by Captain Ion Valeriu Emilian, they found refuge with the *Infanterie Regiment 91* of *4. Gebirgsjäger Division*, fighting in the Tatra Mountains of northern Slovakia. The small force had four officers, six NCOs and 109 other ranks. Emilian had fought alongside the Germans earlier in the war, before Romania switched sides. Sent to Vienna after a brief interrogation, Emilian was offered a spot in the Romanian government-in-exile, which would have been about as comfortable a post as a Romanian defector could ask for. Instead, he chose to return to the front by joining the *Waffen–SS* with the rank of *SS–Hauptsturmführer*.

By this time the *Waffen–Grenadier Regiment ser SS Rumänische* had been upgraded to nominal divisional status, and Emilian was attached to its Fusilier Battalion, whose mode of transport was to be bicycles due to the lack of motor transport. His men were also attached to the Fusilier Battalion. They had brought with them 43 horses and these were also attached. As time went on, though, efforts centering on the Romanians became focused on getting the *Waffen–Grenadier Regiment ser SS Rumänische* combat ready as soon as possible, leaving the rest of the division to muddle along. Most of the manpower for this unit came from the Romanian 4th Infantry Division. When Romania switched sides in August of 1944 and joined the Soviets in fighting the Germans, the 4th Infantry Division was in German-held territory refitting and wound up being captured. Some Iron Guard members filtered into German lines at various points and were funneled to the new *SS* unit. Once the *Waffen–Grenadier Regiment ser SS Rumänische* was combat ready, however, with three companies, it was shipped north where it would not encounter other Romanian units fighting with the Red Army. Some of the men, perhaps 70, joined *SS–Jagdverband Südost*.

The founder of this commando style unit was none other than 'the most dangerous man in Europe,' *SS–Obersturmbannführer* Otto Skorzeny. Whether Skorzeny's derring-do had significant military value or he was merely an excellent showman, there could be no doubting his courage. A brief unit history and table of organization is below:

The *SS-Jagdverband Südost* was formed from the *Brandenburg* unit *Streifkorps Karpaten*, which was incorporated into the *Waffen–SS* in September 1944. *Jagdkommando Donau* was subordinated to *SS-Jagdeinsatz Ungarn* and composed of members of the *Waffen–SS* and *Kriegsmarine*. It was used for several unsuccessful attempts to support the surrounded German troops in Budapest in December 1944. Some parts of the *SS-Jagdverband Südost* were stationed in Yugoslavia, where they fought the partisans, and then moved to Austria, where they fought the Red Army. Parts of the unit lived to see the end of the war at Bratislava. (These elements left ahead of Bratislava's capture.)

Commanders:
SS-Obersturmbannführer Benesch (?1944 - ?)
SS–Hauptsturmführer Alexander Auch (? - ? 1945)

Structure:
SS-Jagdeinsatz Rumänien
SS-Jagdeinsatz Serbien/Kroatien
SS-Jagdeinsatz Bulgarien
SS-Jagdeinsatz Ungarn
(*SS-Jagdkommando Donau: SS–Hauptsturmführer Primer*)
SS-Jagdeinsatz Griechenland
SS-Jagdeinsatz Slowakei: SS-Obersturmführer Dr.

All major armies used specialized units for secret or particularly dangerous missions, but the British and Germans put tremendous effort into what we now refer to as 'irregular warfare.' In the American navy, for example, extensive use was made of Underwater Demolition Teams to reconnoiter invasion beaches and destroy obstacles such as mines. This legacy eventually grew into today's SEALs.

On this day *Generalfeldmarschall* Keitel issued a strange order. In essence, and in order to foster better relations between the *Waffen–SS* and the Army, it was ordered that for purposes of military courtesy and for clarification of military rank superiority, the ranks of the two organizations would thence forth recognize the superiority of the ranks of the other. That is, *Waffen–SS* officers out-ranked all Army NCOs and lower ranks, and vice versa, and the same rule applied to NCOs. Army officers would salute *Waffen–SS* officers of higher rank, and the reverse. There had always been rivalry between the two organizations, friction that sometimes grew into outright hatred, but for the High Command to be concerned with something which in the larger picture seems so trivial, and so impossible to enforce, at such a late stage of the war, gives a clear indication of how out of touch with reality Hitler and his entourage had become. It also reflects on how bad the situation must have become in Hungary, because Keitel would never write such an order without Hitler's express permission. After all, his derogatory nickname wasn't *lakeitel* (lackey) for nothing.

[266] https://www.armedconflicts.com/SS-Jagdverband-Suedost-t43841, (Accessed 25 December, 2023).

Grueling as it was, *IV. SS–Panzerkorps* completed its road march behind the front lines in time for the launching of *Konrad III* on the next day. According to Ungvary, the Germans could scrape together some 300 AFVs for the offensive, and the Soviets opposed them with about 250.

SS–Panzer Regiment 5 moved up to its start lines near Veszprem as the sun set and twilight hid their movements. Reliable numbers for the regiment are impossible to determine, but in all likelihood there were less than 25 *panzers* in working order, despite the best efforts of the repair company over the previous days. What was left of the regiment lined up behind *SS–Panzergrenadier Regiment 9 Germania* on the left of *Wiking's* front.

18 January, Thursday

With Hitler's permission, on 17 January the increasingly desperate garrison of Budapest blew up the last standing bridges over the Danube, the Ketting and the Elisabeth bridges, severing connections with the eastern shore.[267] The bridges were reportedly crowded with refugees scrambling for the illusory safety of Buda when they crashed into the river. Pest was already lost the day before when a kampfgruppe of *13. Panzer Division* crossed to Buda, even though the defense of the western part seemed untenable. The city was aflame and command and control was nearly impossible. Some stories from those bloody days almost defy belief, though, as happened after the last bridges were blown up. "SS Armored Reconnaissance 8 occupied positions on the west bank of the Danube at the Margaret Bridge, where they found that the Hungarians had constructed barricades using stacks of flour!"[268] Food was in critically short supply but some Hungarians were using what little they had to stop bullets.

Reliable numbers from this period are almost impossible to compile. One source claims that 22,000 men of the garrison were either killed or captured in Pest, while another puts the remaining garrison at 34,000, with 11,000 wounded stuffed under the Var-Hegy in appalling conditions.[269] Official German records are either lost or incomplete. However, given the number of men who would eventually attempt a breakout, the higher figure seems more plausible.

With medicines gone there was little that could be done for the wounded; during the airlift, pilots who landed within the perimeter visited the injured men to let them know that the outside world had not forgotten

[267] Guillemot puts the downing of these two bridges as happening the day before.
[268] Michaelis, p. 106.
[269] Pierik, p. 144.

them, but this was a poor substitute for pain killers and clean sheets.

Vital supplies might have been nearing exhaustion but the *Propaganda Korps* was not yet out of film. Brian Davis includes a photograph that caught the Hungarian Minister of War, Karoly Beregfy, supposedly inspecting front line defenses inside the dying city accompanied by an unnamed *SS* officer. The two men's eyes are locked and Beregfy's expression seems to be asking where their promised rescuers were. Beregfy was an Arrow Cross loyalist, but with Pest already lost and Buda being ground into bloody powder, it is hard to imagine what Beregfy could have been inspecting that was worth a photograph.[270]

One major infusion of combat power came from the army. Sometime in January before the launch of *Konrad III*, the *I./Panzer Regiment 24* was transferred to *Heeresgruppe Süd* and attached to at least 4 different *panzer* divisions during the remainder of the war, mostly with *1. Panzer Division*.[271]

Evidence for this is contradictory, since the battalion's parent division fought in the far north near the Baltic coast. If true, however, it marked a huge upswing in *Heeresgruppe Süd's* armored punch, and the best sources verify its presence in Hungary.

The battalion was at full strength, reportedly with 60 *Mark V Panthers* in four companies, an unheard of total for that late in the war. If this figure is accurate, and the best evidence suggests that it is, the attachment of such a powerful tank force gave whatever division it was attached to a potent offensive punch.

Written by its commander, *Major* Gert-Axel Weidemann, the battalion's after-action report notes

---

[270] Davis, Brian L., *Waffen–SS* (London: landford Press, 1987), p. 170.

[271] Samuel Mitcham, Jr., has the *I./Panzer Regiment 24* attached to *1. Panzer Division* in July of 1944 onward and that it participated in the fierce tank battles in Hungary that summer. (*The Panzer Legions*, p. 176). Presumably, it then returned to German to be rearmed with new tanks. Jentz, however, states that the battalion was sent to the Eastern Front in January of 1945.

that during an attack on the 18 January in support of *Konrad III*, the tactical commander lost control of the situation and consequently tanks were scattered all over the area. Because of the confused Russian reaction to the offensive this confusion did not lead to any unnecessary German casualties, but it easily could have and was indicative of the lowered performance level of German command and control. Too many talented veterans were dead, wounded or captured and too many officers had been promoted past their level of competence.[272]

No mention is made of which unit the battalion had been attached to, or if it was a Corps directed formation. Regardless, 60 *Panthers* was a formidable force.

The launch day for *Konrad III* had come and the Russians were dug in and waiting. The Soviet defense line ran from Imremajor in the northwest to Gusztuspusztu, between Varpolota and Stuhlweissenburg, then to Szigetpusztu. From there it ran to Lake Balaton.

The plan called for an attack by *IV. SS–Panzerkorps* to the southeast and east to penetrate the Russian lines, followed by a drive east to the Danube, then a turn north toward Budapest, capturing Stuhlweissenburg in the process and potentially cutting off the Red Army units there. Aside from being a key strategic prize, Stuhlweissenburg was also the burial site for King Stephen, who aside from being the personification of the Hungarian nation was, in a very real sense, the nation's soul. He is credited with converting Hungary from a pagan nation to a Christian one during the 11th Century, and for being the first King of Hungary. The symbolism of the city was well known to both sides.

[272] Jentz, *Panzertruppen 2*, p. 224.

Unlike the previous two relief efforts aimed at Budapest, *Konrad III* would mostly take place on flat, frozen ground, ideal for tank warfare, and would prove that even in the final months of the war the Germans were still masters of the form of warfare they had pioneered, the sudden, violent attack of massed tanks. In favorable conditions, the German armored force was still dangerous. But no matter how much damage they could still inflict on the Red Army, their numbers and support were no longer enough for them to win decisive victories. There simply weren't enough Germans, aircraft or *panzers* left. But they would cause panic in the Soviet command structure and come very close to saving their trapped comrades.

All four of *IV. SS–Panzerkorps* assault divisions had infantry units attached to try and compensate for the dire shortage in their own organic infantry, but most of the men in those attached units were non-Germans. *6. Armee's* attack formation had *3. Panzer Division* on the right flank, that is, the furthest south, with *1. Ungarische SS–Sturm Regiment* attached. That newly formed regiment, resting for the past few days near Csor with 900 men, had already lost 40 percent of its original strength of 1,500 in just a few days' fighting. During its then ten day existence this was the unit's fourth parent formation and the second Corps command to which it reported.

5. SS–Panzer Division Wiking Division, with Fritz Vogt's *I./Norge* attached, came next; then *3. SS–Panzer Division Totenkopf*, with *I./Danmark* attached and finally *1. Panzer Division* on the left flank. *1. Panzer Division* was still reinforced by two battalions from *SS–Regiment Ney*, as well as three Hungarian battalions; the Ney Regiment's third battalion, commanded by *SS–SS–Hauptsturmführer*Paul Vadon, was held back for the second stage of the offensive on 20 January.[273] On *1. Panzer Division's* far left flank, that is, the far left of *IV. SS–Panzerkorps* , for command purposes the division

---

[273] Pencz, Rudolf, *Siegrunen Volume 76*, p. 15.

had split off various components to form a fairly strong force called *Kampfgruppe Huppert*. This *kampfgruppe* had two battalions from *Panzergrenadier Regiment 1*, the first two battalions from *SS–Regiment Ney*, and the three Hungarian battalions, two from the 24th Regiment and one from the 54th Regiment. Artillery was supplied by two detachments from *Panzer–Artillerie Regiment 73*.

The operational missions for *Konrad III* broke down as follows: on the far right of the offensive, *3. Panzer Division*, under the command of *Generalmajor* Soth, had initial objectives of Lepseny and Enying near the eastern tip of Lake Balaton, attacking in a southeast then southerly direction to anchor the offensive's right flank. Once those objectives were taken it would swing east-southeast to protect the southern flank. *Wiking* started near Csajag and was slated to move on an initial southeastern axis to Balatonfokajar, then turn almost due east, while *Totenkopf*'s jump-off line was near Berhida, to the north of *Wiking* and on that division's left flank. *Totenkopf*'s first objective was the Polgardi area, between Fule and Jeno, where they would also turn east for the Danube. Finally, *1. Panzer Division*, under the command of *Generalmajor* Eberhard Thunert, was given the hardest mission, to protect by attacking toward Stuhlweissenburg.

In a supporting role on *IV. SS–Panzerkorps*' left flank was *III. Panzerkorps*, with its chief contribution to the offensive being *23. Panzer Division* adjacent to *Kampfgruppe Huppert* (thus, *1. Panzer Division*), with the mission of driving east-southeast for Stuhlweissenburg.

At 0500[274], with only a short artillery barrage preceding it, *IV. SS–Panzerkorps* launched *Konrad III* from its positions west of Stuhlweissenburg. *Luftflotte 4* scraped together 135 aircraft to support the effort. The ground over which *1. Panzer Division* had to attack was swampy, which made for hard going. From the outset fighting in the Varpalota region was bitter, but

[274] Some sources say 0430.

eventually the Germans broke through in the Retipuszta area. During the day, patrols in front of *1. Panzer Division* on the Sàrviz Canal reported that the Soviet 21st Guards Rifle Corps had withdrawn east of the canal. During the night, therefore, the division launched *Kampfgruppe Phillip*,[275] consisting of the *panzer regiment*, a battalion from *Panzergrenadier Regiment 113* and supporting artillery, across the canal and in search of the enemy. The infantry was carried on the Panthers and this *kampfgruppe* was followed by *Kampfgruppe Weber*, essentially the other battalion of *Panzergrenadier Regiment 113* mounted in *SPWs*. This *II./Panzergrenadier Regiment 113*, defeated the Soviet defenses at Urhida and headed over the Sàrviz Canal, establishing a bridgehead. The Soviets were pushed back to Sarpentele, a suburb of Stuhlweissenburg.

5. SS Panzer Division Wiking moved off on time but ran into the usual Russian minefields and *paknests*, augmented with electrified barbed wire. The defense was ferocious; by afternoon the division was stopped cold and was forced to commit *Kampfgruppe Dorr* to overwhelm the defenders.[276] This additional firepower did the trick and by nightfall the division had taken Berhida and was approaching Nadesdladany on roads slick with snow.[277]

Konrad III was making progress despite the lack of surprise. Stuhlweissenburg (Szekesfehervar) was within reach. As *23. Panzer Division* and *SS-Regiment Ney* made for that city from the northwest, *1. Panzer Division's* Pioneers worked on the damaged bridge over the Sàrviz so that it could support the division's *Panther* tanks. Three miles to the south the regiment's *I. battalion* established a second bridgehead at Falubattyan.

---

[275] This is not the same *kampfgruppe* as earlier in the narrative, although the officer after which it is named is the same.

[276] This *kampfgruppe* was commanded by *SS–Obersturmbannführer Hans Dorr*, the commander of *SS–Panzergrenadier Regiment 9 Germania*.

[277] Klapdor, p. 394.

Further south, *Konrad III* did not have a promising start. "In fact, at the beginning, the attack made little progress at all. The enemy defended his main line of resistance desperately, which was not only heavily mined, but featured electrically charged detonators for the first time."[278] The Soviet main line of resistance was heavily fortified, but the real problem was that the Germans just weren't strong enough to break through. In *Wiking's* sector, Gille showed up at *SS-Oberführer* Karl Ullrich's headquarters with *Generalmajor* Gaedtke, Chief-of-Staff for *6. Armee*, in tow. The two men were upset that progress was slow and prodded *Wiking's* commander to commit the reserves he was holding back as an exploitation force once a breakthrough was forced. This was *Kampfgruppe Dorr*. Hans Dorr had already been wounded fifteen times during the war. Ullrich was reluctant to throw in his last unit, but in the end he had no choice.

The extra punch was enough and the Germans broke through the Russian line. Beyond the fortified front there was no defense-in-depth, only scattered Soviet units that were no hindrance to the advance. Despite night having fallen, the Germans seized their chance and moved east rapidly. They were finally in open ground and weren't about to stop.

Schwere–Panzer Abteilung 509 immediately found the going tough, immediately slamming into Russian armor in its attempt to break through in the center of the offensive. The first encounter with Russian resistance came as it conducted an attack on hills 197 and 188 south of Jenö, dead center between Lakes Balaton and Velence, and continued attacking with 18 *Tiger IIs* via Felsösomlyo to Alsosomlyö. The battalion crossed the Sárviz River south of Szabad-Battyan. The area was mostly flat with long sight lines, ideal for

[278] Strassner, p. 317.

armored combat. Twenty Soviet tanks were destroyed, as were 11 *Tiger IIs*. Only seven were total write-offs, yet that was a terrible loss rate for the first day of fighting. It is unknown what type of Russian tanks the Germans claimed to have destroyed, but most of the heaviest example were fighting at Budapest. At day's end *Schwere–Panzer Abteilung 509* had a total number of 38 Tiger IIs.

Although not directly a part of this narrative, a unit that would soon play an important role for *Heeresgruppe Süd* at war's end came into existence during this period. Following its participation in the Ardennes Offensive, the *Führer Grenadier Brigade* was ordered expanded to a full division. A week later, on 25 January, the formation of *Panzer Regiment 101* began with five *Mark IVs*, 18 *Mark V Panthers*, 13 *Jagdpanzer IV/70s* and four *Flakpanzer IVs* on hand. The regiment would be fleshed out on 15 February with 10 precious *Jagdpanthers* and on 17 February with an additional 16 *Mark V Panthers*, all from the *Heeres-Zeugamt*.[279] Given its status as a favored formation having Hitler himself as a patron, and with a young commander who was popular with the Nazi hierarchy, *Generalmajor* Erich von Hassenstein, the *Führer Grenadier Division* was that rarity in the Wehrmacht of 1945: a division that was not grossly understrength.

Whether it ever achieved full authorized strength is debated in the sources. Suffice to say the division would see extensive combat in March but would report for duty in the defense of Vienna in early April very strong for a German division of the late war period, being near full strength in men and at least half so in vehicles.

The longer the war lasted, the more Hitler developed a taste for creating new units instead of

[279] Army Depot.

bringing existing ones up to strength. The vehicles and men committed to expanding the *Führer Grenadier Brigade* to a division might have gone a long way toward refilling a veteran unit such as *1. Panzer Division.*

The spearhead of *1. Panzer Division,* *II./Panzergrenadier Regiment 113*, defeated the Soviet defenses at Urhida and headed over the Sàrviz Canal, widening their bridgehead. Seemingly against all odds, *Konrad III* was making progress despite the lack of surprise. The early progress must have given Hitler a sense of once again intuitively knowing the correct route of attack, despite the objections of his generals. That he was wrong far more often than he was right would not, of course, have come up.

Panzerjäger V Jagdpanther

Panzerjager V (SdKfz. 173)

Jagdpanther

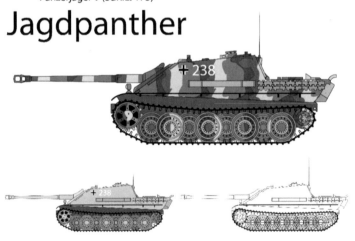

Germany's penultimate *Jagdpanzer* was the excellent *Jagdpanther*. Mounted on the reliable *Mark V Panther* chassis, the tank destroyer version had the same gun as the dangerous *Mark VI Tiger I*, the iconic 88mm *Pak 43*. With 80mm of armor protection sloped at a 55 degree angle, survivability in combat was excellent. The *Jagdpanther's* only serious drawback was its low production numbers; only about 400 were built.

Stuhlweissenburg (Szekesfehervar) was within reach. As *23. Panzer Division* and *SS–Regiment Ney* pushed ever closer from the northwest, *1. Panzer Division* moved over the Sarvis Canal in strength.

19 January, Friday

As discussed earlier in this narrative, the most feared Russian defense fortifications for German *panzer* crews was the *pakfront* [280], an innovation that had tormented the Germans throughout the Russian war and took full advantage of the ubiquitous and deadly Soviet anti-tank guns, especially the 76.2 mm gun. Jentz quotes a report from the *I./Panzer Regiment 24* during the period of *Konrad III* that perfectly illustrates the dangers from such defenses. "The meaning of '*Pakfront*' does not totally describe the actual situations experienced in combat by the *Abteilung* because the opponent employs this weapon more concentrated in so-called '*Paknest*' in an effect to achieve a long-range flanking effect. Sometimes the *Paknest* consist of 6 to 7 anti-tank guns in a circle of only 40-50 meters." A number of these *Paknest*s would then be grouped close enough to be mutually supporting, thus making up a Pakfront. Maximizing the terrain to full advantage for camouflage, including removing the wheels from the guns to lower their profile, the Russians would usually allow the leading *panzers* to pass by and then open fire on their flanks. The key to overcoming the *Paknest* lay in speed of response, long-range firepower and quick capture of the position through flanking attacks. "If the Russian anti-tank crews are spotted and taken under well-aimed fire, they quickly leave their weapon. However, they quickly reman the guns when not observed or when firing ceases and again take up the firefight". Attacking a *pakfront* head-on was tantamount to suicide. "The firing range is decisive for fighting with *Pakneste* that appear beside each other in a row as a *pakfront*. If a *panzer* formation is fired upon at surprisingly short range, all weapons need to be employed immediately." Engaged at medium or long-

---

[280] 'Pak' is an abbreviation for the German word 'Panzerabwehrkanone', or 'anti-tank gun.' Thus, a 'paknest' is a grouping of anti-tank guns and a '*pakfront* ' is a grouping of 'paknests.'

ranges, the *panzers* best tactic was to withdraw until other avenues of attack could be found.[281]

And yet, despite the Russian skill in erecting field fortifications, enough of the old German elan still remained so that by its second day *Konrad III* had ripped open the Soviet front south and southwest of Stuhlweissenburg to a breadth of 65 kilometers; behind the initial line of resistance there had been little to stop the German onslaught. The shifting of the German schwerpunkt from the Pilisszentkerezt area had caught Third Ukrainian Front unaware and there were few reserves readily available. The Germans drove forward relentlessly, while the Red Army scrambled to cobble together a defense that would hold. By 0300 *Kampfgruppe Dorr* reached the town of Kisland, south of Stuhlweissenburg and some 25 miles from the start line. For the first time in a very long while, the *panzers* were rolling forward against a surprised and disorganized enemy; unfortunately for the Germans the Red Army of 1945 was a far more formidable enemy than its 1941 counterpart.

Not even darkness could slow the German breakthrough, and a mere 24 hours after it began, the spearheads of *Konrad III* reached the Danube River south of Budapest, where *3. Panzer Division* attacked the industrial town of Dunaujvaros. This was a key position on the southern flank of the overall attack of *Konrad III.* The fighting lasted well into 20 January, and reached a level of ferocity rarely seen even on the Russian Front.

Illustrating this are the known German losses. Attached to *3. Panzer Division* was the shrunken *1. SS-Ungarishe-Sturm Regiment,* down to 900 men from its original 1,500. Like its first fight a week before, the Regiment once again suffered disastrous casualties,

[281] Jentz, *Panzertruppen 2,* pp. 223-224.

this time a staggering 160 killed and 70 wounded, a full third of its overall strength, effectively making it nothing more than an under-strength battalion. Late in the day the regiment was again re-assigned, this time back to the *5. SS–Panzer Division Wiking*, under whose command it had suffered so horribly the week before. The new objective was Stuhlweissenburg, some 30 miles to the north-northwest, where the Russian defense was intact and putting up very stiff resistance.

Once there, the Hungarians of *1. SS-Ungarishe-Sturm Regiment* found themselves fighting alongside their countrymen in *SS–Regiment Ney*, who were on the left flank of *1. Panzer Division*'s attack. *1. Panzer Division* was faced with having to cross the Sàrviz Canal a second time as it drove toward Stuhlweissenburg. Part of *Panzer Regiment 1*, along with *SS–Regiment Ney*, ran into a stonewall and fought for much of the day trying to break the stubborn Russian defense near the Sarszentmihaly train station, less than three miles southwest of the Stuhlweissenburg city limits. Here, the Russians were standing and fighting hard, but their left flank was up in the air; just to their south there was no cohesive defense whatsoever.

Elsewhere, faced with minimal opposition on *1. Panzer Division*'s right flank, *Kampfgruppe Bradel* drove forward rapidly. This force consisted of *Panzergrenadier Regiment 113, Panzerjäger Abteilung 37, Panzer-Pioneer Abteilung 37,* and three companies from *Panzer Regiment 1*.[282] *Kampfgruppe Bradel* made it as far as Lake Velence, with the objective of taking Dinyes; however, much of its force was left behind to protect the road from Stuhlweissenburg to Seregelyes, a vital supply link with the rest of *IV. SS–Panzerkorps* as it drove for the Danube. This was a wise precaution, as the Soviets reacted quickly and counterattacks were not long in coming.

---

[282] Pencz, *Siegrunen Volume 76*, p. 16.

Supporting *Kampfgruppe Bradel, Schwere–Panzer Abteilung 509* completely crossed the Sarvis River after engineers complete bridges that could bear the weight of the *Tigers IIs*. After dusk, the leading vehicles reached the Stuhlweissenburg-Sarkeresztur road and turned northeast.

5. SS Panzer Division Wiking moved out early with the two *panzer* companies on either flanks and *SPWs* between them. The terrain was good tank country, low rolling hills with clear fields of fire. When the snow tapered off visibility improved. Despite heavy Russian artillery fire and air strikes, *Wiking* punched through the last of the Russian defenses into the open, crossed the Sàrviz canal near at the village of Kaloz, due south of Stuhlweissenburg, and headed east toward the Sarodz area. With light opposition and frozen ground, the Germans were eating up ground quickly[283].

The Russians were less pleased with the progress of the German attack. Badly worried about *Konrad III*'s immediate success, and greatly over-estimating the strength of the German assault forces, Marshal Tolbukhin personally took over the defense of the threatened region from General Zakarov. Thinking the Germans were actually much stronger than they really were, and misjudging their intentions, he worried that both 57th Guards Army and the 1st Bulgarian Army would be caught between *6. Armee* and *2. Panzerarmee* and wiped out. Assuming the Germans even had enough strength to pull this off, and they did not, it would have meant turning the attack south to meet *2. Panzerarmee*, instead of north to relieve Budapest. In other words, he anticipated *Unternehmen Frühlingserwachen* by two full months. For the moment, however, Marshal Tolbukhin could not be

---

[283] Strassner says Wiking crossed the canal on the 20th.

sure of the German intentions, and had to assume the worst until he could be sure of exactly where his enemy was heading.

Fighting in *Konrad III* and for the next month, *I./Panzer Regiment 24* destroyed the remarkable total of 110 Russian tanks, 153 anti-tank guns and 13 artillery pieces of various calibers, and captured an amazing 74 anti-tank guns. While there is no record of what it did with those captured guns, it may be safely assumed that every operable tube was put back into service against its former owners. Along with the guns, another assumption is that a comparable amount of ammunition was also captured. This alone would upgrade the battalion's combat power by a significant amount.

20 January, Saturday

With most of Budapest and all of eastern Hungary in Soviet hands, the provisional Hungarian government installed by the Russians signed an armistice with the Allies and the USSR and declared war on Germany. The former Chief of Staff of the Hungarian Army, General Janos Vörös, who had first helped thwart Admiral Horthy's attempt to surrender to the Russians in October of 1944 and then defected to the Russians on November 1st, was appointed Minister of Defense in the new government. When he gave himself up to the Russians in November, he had been driven into Soviet lines in the staff car Heinz Guderian had given him as a present for his loyalty[284]. Thus did Hungary have two governments, one at war with the Allies, one at war with the Axis, and both at war with each other.

In the sector of *III. Panzerkorps*, the most direct highways to Budapest and to the northern front, where *Konrad II* had been fought, led north of Lake Velence through Stuhlweissenburg, and thus were directly in the path of *23. Panzer Division* and, attached to *1. Panzer Division, SS–Regiment Ney*. This meant that those units bore the brunt of the Soviet reaction to *Konrad III* in the form of violent counterattacks aimed at out-flanking *IV. SS–Panzerkorps* from the north. *SS–Regiment Ney* withdrew past Stuhlweissenburg during the night while being heavily attacked by Red Army formations. Losses for the regiment during this fighting were given as 171 dead, more than 300 wounded and 100 missing, a total of almost 30 percent of its ration

---

[284] Like most turncoats who trusted the Russians, Vörös came to regret his decision when he was arrested in 1949 and charged with being an American spy. He managed to survive 7 years in prison before being freed in the 1956 revolution.

strength at the time and a testament to just how severe the fighting had become. Along with *1. Ungarische–SS–Sturm Regiment* the Hungarians were paying dearly for trying to stop the Russians from overrunning the rest of their nation.

The Corps reported having destroyed 17 Soviet tanks during the same *SS–Regiment Ney's* III battalion joined the attack. After leaving its positions near Balatonkenese it was sent to join *1. Panzer Division's* attack on Stuhlweissenburg. This battalion numbered between 400 and 500 men and, being relatively fresh, pushed forward quickly. By nightfall the battalion, as part of the large *Kampfgruppe Huppert* that also included the rest of *SS–Regiment Ney* and the *Panzergrenadier Regiment 1*, had penetrated the Russian defenses at Edinapuszta and gotten over the Sàrviz Canal, while the Russian defense was pushed almost to the edge of Stuhlweissenburg itself.

Meanwhile, as the sky darkened and the Russians grimly held onto Stuhlweissenburg, a perfectly executed night attack by *I./ Panzer Regiment 24* seized the key village of Kapolnasnyek at the eastern tip of Lake Velence, threatening the vital highway that lead from Budapest to Stuhlweissenburg. Night attacks were difficult to pull off even for veteran troops and failure always meant very heavy losses, but in this case German expertise lead to victory.

> "On 20 January, during a night attack on Kapolnas-Nyok (sic), which was occupied by anti-tank guns and tanks that could not be made out in the darkness, the *Abteilung* with 20 *Panzers* fired a barrage of 15 rounds per *Panzer* at the edge of the village. The Russians fled from their positions and attempted to get away with tanks and anti-guns across the eastern tip of Velence Lake. At dawn, tanks that had broken through

the ice and were abandoned by their crews revealed the effectiveness of the weapons."[285]

This was a critical position to take. Now the Russians defending north of the lake had to fear being cut off and utterly destroyed. Worse, the Germans now had access to good all-weather roads leading directly to the capital, a mere 44 kilometers from Budapest.

On the maps of *Heeresgruppe Süd* and *OKH*, it suddenly seemed like 1942 again: *Konrad III* had torn a gaping hole in the Russian front lines and German motorized units were racing to exploit the success. When on the attack, the depleted German armored force showed that it was still a potent weapon despite a paucity of numbers and the overall lack of training and experience of its soldiers. *5. SS Panzer Division Wiking* was more than 20 miles from its start line and crossed the Sàrviz Canal on 20 January, headed for Sarodz, with *3. SS–Panzer Division Totenkopf* and *1. Panzer Division* somewhat behind. As *Wiking* headed east, however, all across the attack front Soviet counterattacks were increasing and hastily built defenses inflicted casualties the division could not afford. The terrain was rolling, good tank country; outside of Sarodz the division's *panzergrenadiers* captured a farmhouse on top of a ridge, only to be driven back by a Soviet counterattack using tanks. The Germans then sent in the *Mark V Panthers* of *5. Kompanie* to try and re-capture the burning farmstead, but the Russians outnumbered them so badly they retreated after losing a number of *panzers*, as well as both the *5. Kompanie* commander and his replacement.

Nevertheless, on the southern flank of *Konrad III*, where *3. Panzer Division* reached the Danube at Dunapentele (Dunaujvaros); in just under two days,

[285] Jentz, *Panzertruppen 2*, p. 225.

the offensive had smashed through Soviet positions and achieved its first goals. *3. Panzer Division* had raced some 70 miles to the east and started firing on Russian shipping in the river, interdicting supplies and causing serious worry in the Soviet command. Budapest was due north, and the southern thrust had reached its objective. With success so unexpected, Wöhler and Balck had to decide where to go next.

The rapid pace of the attack left Russian defenses south of Stuhlweissenburg in disarray. Supported by *Schwere–Panzer Abteilung 509*, the airport in that city's southern approaches fell to the advancing Germans. Nor did the momentum stop there, as 26 *Tiger IIs* kept moving toward Seregelyes, 15 kilometers to the southeast.

21 January, Sunday

On 21 January a new German unit readied either for transfer or for frontline action. Another of *Reichsführer–SS* Heinrich Himmler's efforts to turn Nazism into a Pan-European anti-Communist movement led to the creation of *14. Waffen–Grenadier Division der SS (1. Galizien)*. Originally filled with thousands of Ukrainians eager to fight the Russians, the division had been virtually destroyed the previous summer during the Battle of Brody. Efforts to refill it using new volunteers did not attract nearly as many men as previously, so the ranks were filled with various existing Ukrainian formations, some of whom had bloody reputations. Nor did the division's officers have any faith in its' combat value. But with the efforts to relieve Budapest growing ever more desperate, this large, fully equipped division could have expected to be thrown into the fighting, at least to hold the line and relieve a German division for offensive duty.

At least, with *Konrad III* moving east rapidly, *14. Waffen–Grenadier Division der SS (1. Galizien)* could have been an ideal follow-on force to hold a flank or take over front-line duty for a *panzer* division. The division's fighting quality for anything other than second-line duties was considered problematic, but with the uneven strength and quality of German divisions by this time, *1. Galizien* could have been of some use, in some capacity. Instead, it received orders to transfer to Styria, away from the fighting. The transfer was to be made on foot. Nor could it use the main Zilina-Bratislava-Vienna highway, as it was reserved for traffic flowing to and from the front.

During the last desperate weeks in April the division was the only unit that could attack and seal a large hole in the front. It did so over the protests of its own commanding general, *SS-Brigadeführer und*

Generalmajor der Waffen–SS Fritz Freitag, and performed well.[286]

SS–*Regiment Ney* and parts of *Panzergrenadier Regiment 1* kept pushing forward into the western suburbs of Stuhlweissenburg. With the progress made during the day, around 2000 hours the decision was made for *IV. SS–Panzerkorps* to make its capture a priority, without waiting for promised reinforcements.[287] So, around that same time the regiments *I./Panzergrenadier Regiment 1* and *II./Panzergrenadier Regiment 1* went into the attack from the west, and *III./Panzergrenadier Regiment 1* from the south. During confused and heavy fighting, one source notes that some of the regiment was nearly cut off when a Russian battalion of 400-500 men moved past their right flank in the direction of Sarpantele, forcing the regiment back into Stuhlweissenburg.[288]

Meanwhile *5. SS Panzer Division Wiking* took Sarosd, but Soviet counterattacks grew ever stronger and on 21 January they struck *Wiking* at Sarosd. "In the process, the division's spearhead was cut off and Sarosd temporarily occupied by the enemy."[289] A moment of crisis had come.

Gille and *Wiking's* commanding officer, *SS-Oberführer* Ullrich took immediate action without waiting for orders from Balck. *Wiking* immediately counterattacked, and by early afternoon Sarosd was back in German hands with *Wiking* was once again on

---

[286] Despite his division performing well at Brody, Freitag angered Himmler by suggesting it be disbanded.

[287] Pencz, *Siegrunen Volume 76*, p. 17.

[288] According to one source, on 21 January *SS–Regiment Ney* was attached to the *Holste Division Gruppe*, which consisted of elements from *6. Panzer Division*, 2nd Hungarian Armored Division, the 4th Hungarian Cavalry Brigade and one battalion from the Hungarian 20th Infantry Division.

[289] Strassner, p. 318.

the move. But the victory did not come without loss. During an officer's conference, an anti-tank round slammed into the headquarters vehicle of *SS–Panzergrenadier Regiment 9 Germania*, wounding the intrepid long-time commander, *SS–Obersturmbannführer* Hans Dorr, for the sixteenth time. It would be the last. Dorr was evacuated to Vienna and later transferred out of the path of the Red Army, but on 17 April he died from this wound; later that afternoon, once Sarosd was securely in German hands, *Wiking* turned northeast, heading for Adony on the Danube.[290]

Five miles to the northwest, Fritz Vogt's *I./SS–Panzergrenadier Regiment 23 Norge* managed to capture Seregelyes but Soviet counterattacks retook that town, too. "The Reds soon counter-attacked with a powerful infantry-supported tank force and the Norwegian battalion was not able to hold its positions". The Russian attack was so swift and violent that a German hospital was overrun, and reports are that both the staff and patients were burned alive in a nearby wine cellar, including the battalion's medical officer, *SS–Obersturmführer* Dr. Storm.[291] Further north on that vital road, parts of *Kampfgruppe Bradel* had been fighting Russian attacks since the day before.

On the eastern tip of Lake Velence the morning dawned with promise after *I./Panzer Regiment 24* captured the vital village of Kapolnasnyek during the night; the leading Germans were now 24 miles from beleaguered Budapest and no more than 5 miles from Pazmand, a key town close by to the north whose capture would have made the Russian position at

---

[290] There is a variant account of Dorr's wounding. According to that version, Dorr and *Germania's* command staff had gathered in a barn when an astute Russian gun commander saw them and fired.

[291] Landwehr, Richard, *Siegrunen Volume 77*, p. 25. This account is included here with a note of caution. Landwehr was an *SS* apologist, which permitted him to obtain interviews others could not, but also leaves his accounts of such atrocities in question. The story may be apocryphal, but it *was* the type of thing Russian troops did *en masse* as they moved into Western Europe.

Stuhlweissenburg untenable. Abandoning their positions near Stuhlweissenburg would have freed up German forces for the final drive to Budapest; suddenly rescue seemed imminent. The fourth day of *Konrad III* was shaping up to be the decisive day for the liberation of *IX. SS-Waffen-Gebirgs-Armeekorps der SS*.

Marshal Tolbukhin had plenty of problems of his own. Russian losses in the first phase of *Konrad III* had been very heavy, including 193 tanks, 229 artillery tubes, 257 anti-tank guns and at least 1,175 prisoners. Such massive casualties meant that:

"There were shortages of everything: Reinforcements...and ammunition..."[292] Part of those shortages resulted from his decision to blow up his own bridges over the Danube at Dunapentele and Dunafoldvar, which cut off supplies to his units that were still engaged. Tolbukhin was still undecided about ordering the evacuation of 57th Guards Army to the east bank of the Danube, and decided to wait and see which direction the German attack turned now that it had reached that river.

The Marshal's biggest problem wasn't the Germans, however, it was Stalin, who wanted to know what the hell was going on down in Hungary, and why Budapest was not yet in Russian hands.

---

[292] Strassner, p. 318.

22 January, Monday

Inside Budapest life grew increasingly miserable. For the troops and the general population, what food could be found consisted primarily of horseflesh and thin soup. Some of the cavalry horses escaped before the siege, but more than 17,000 remained in the city as a ready source of meat for the garrison. The poor creatures were a common sight, being confined anywhere and everywhere until either Russian shrapnel killed them, or their turn came to be slaughtered. Skeletal carcasses lay in yards, gardens and streets.

The wealthier residents living in lavish Buda villas had no such concerns. They were well-prepared for the siege with fully-stocked larders of food and alcohol. These villas became prized objectives for both the Soviets and Germans, resulting in intense battles. The Germans had a tactic of letting the Soviets seize a villa stocked with wine and spirits, then launching a counterattack in the early morning when the enemy was still groggy and drunk.

Unfortunately, not everyone in Budapest had access to such provisions. The poorer or displaced civilians often searched for scraps of food at night, risking their lives as they scoured the streets. However, even basic necessities like water were hard to come by as inhabitants risked their lives sneaking to the Danube to fill containers.

The bombing and shelling raged on, night and day, a relentless onslaught of death and destruction. Venturing outside was a game of life and death, with lives being lost in the scramble for water or a moment of reprieve in the courtyard. Inhabitants sought refuge in cellars, but even there they were not safe from the constant terror. Life became trying to stay alive until one side won and the fighting ceased, of enduring a living hell, cold, hungry, thirsty, filthy, scurrying about like rats in hiding. It was a miracle any buildings still stood, though shattered windows served as grim reminders of what could've been. Whole neighborhoods became unrecognizable, reduced to rubble by the merciless barrage of bursting bombs and artillery shells.

Taking Stuhlweissenburg was crucial to the success of *Konrad III* as an anchor for defending the northern flank of *IV. SS–Panzerkorps* , and the Germans' determination to re-capture the city was indicative of its importance. As fierce as the attack was, however, central coordination was lacking and some of the smaller units, such as *III./SS–Regiment Ney*, fought forward alone. *Kampfgruppe Huppert* ran into ferocious resistance in the western part of the city along the railroad line, while *III./SS–Regiment Ney* drove on the city from the southwest, through Sarpentele, until by nightfall it had reached the Market Place railroad station inside the city itself. Elsewhere in the southwest sector an armored battle broke out, involving elements of *Panzer Regiment 1* and *Panzerjäger Abteilung 37*. The fighting swept through Hero's Plaza, behind the Szekesfehervar Basilica[293], near the 15th Century St. Anna Chapel and the Citadel area. Every available German artillery battery was brought to bear, including *Panzer–Artillerie Regiment 73* and *Volksartillerie Korps 403*;[294] the fighting escalated until eventually the attackers inflicted terrible losses on the defending Soviets, essentially wiping them out, but at great loss themselves. (

By afternoon the fighting was over and the Germans had re-taken the city. The recapture of

[293] Reputed to keep as a Holy Relic part of the skull of St. Stephen

[294] Originally Heeres-Artillerie-Brigade 403, newly formed in October 1944 in the Bückeburg area under command of Knight's Cross winner *Oberst* Heinz Steinwachs. It was equipped with a large variety of guns, including Russian captured ones and the 210 mm *Mörser*. His unit was soon renamed into Volks-Artillerie-Korps 403,

Stuhlweissenburg was largely because of the determination of *SS–Regiment Ney*'s three battalions. For their bravery in battle, Hitler signed an order giving *SS–Regiment Ney* the right wear a cuff band with that inscription in silver. This was a high and singular honor, as *SS* formations were not automatically granted an honorific title or the right to wear a cuff band[295], and was a very special recognition.

During the daily military conference, the topic of re-deploying the *6. SS–Panzerarmee* came up yet again. Guderian stuck to his insistence that Germany's most powerful remaining force should be shipped to Poland, while Hitler continued to insist on an offensive to protect the Hungarian oil fields. "First the oil and then the Central Front,' said Hitler on January 22."[296] Hitler remained adamant that *6. SS–Panzerarmee* was heading for Hungary, and he kept giving the reason of protecting the oil fields; Guderian's protestations were futile.

Hitler did have a point, but it was a point without a solution; without oil, there was no way to continue the war. Yet the Hungarian oilfields, and larger Austrian field,[297] could not supply anything close to the quantity of oil needed by the German war machine. They were the only sources of natural oil left to the *Reich*, it was true, but their production was low compared to the needs of the *Wehrmacht*. Their value may have been artificially inflated since the Allied Strategic Bombing Campaign had crushed the German

[295] The *31. SS–Freiwilligen Grenadier Division*, for example, another partly Hungarian *SS* unit, was never given an honorific, despite a good track record in battle. It is sometimes erroneously given the honorific title 'Bohemia and Moravia', but this is inaccurate.

[296] Pierik, p. 132.

[297] The Austrian fields at Zistersdorf are often claimed to be small, virtually insignificant. This was not true. For a full discussion of this topic see the author's *Killing Hitler's Reich, The Battle for Austria, 1945*.

synthetic oil industry, but were the oilfields worth protecting with Germany's last offensive assets? And Guderian had a point, as well; to try to keep Berlin out of the hands of the Red Army, because once Berlin fell the war would be over. Germany could not fight long without oil, or without Hitler and Berlin. Both objectives needed *6. SS–Panzerarmee*. There were no good answers available, only opinions. In the end, the two opinions were not compatible, and Hitler's was the only one that ultimately mattered.

On the Vali River a bare 15 miles from Budapest, *IV. SS–Panzerkorps* reached the closest point it would reach to the desperate garrison during *Konrad III*. The appearance of both *SS panzer* divisions on the north bank of Lake Velence, however, finally told Marshal Tolbukhin the ultimate target of the German assault: relieving Budapest, not destroying his forces south of Lake Balaton. Once this was known, the Marshal threw in everything he could to keep the Germans from breaking into the city. Tolbukhin was determined to stop them.

As the pace of the fighting in Budapest became more and more severe, casualties skyrocketed. Lieutenant General Ivan Afonyin, Commanding Officer XVIII Guards Rifle Corps, was badly wounded by 18 pieces of shrapnel that knocked him out of action during extraordinarily heavy fighting; he was replaced by General I. M. Managorov, who commanded 53rd Army.

23 January, Tuesday

The badly depleted *1. Ungarische SS–Sturm Regiment* was split up on this day and its headquarters disbanded. One battalion was assigned to *III. Panzerkorps.* The nearly destroyed *II./1. Ungarische SS–Sturm Regiment* is reported to have later fought near Lake Balaton at Lepseny and Balatonvilagos in company with *5. SS Panzer Division Wiking*, although the timing for this seems wrong. Sub units were ordered back to Csor with plans to reform the regiment, although there was not much left to reform.

Thus ended the experiment of the partially trained Hungarian volunteer ski troops. In this instance Himmler's investment in equipping a foreign unit paid off, although the resulting combat unit did not long survive its baptism of fire.

The advance elements of *5. SS Panzer Division Wiking* reached the Danube at Adony, 28 miles downriver from Budapest. In five days the Germans had blasted an enormous hole in Third Ukrainian Front and cut the army group in half west of the Danube. But *Wiking* had been badly understrength when the attack started and after nearly a week of rapid advancement the division was strung out and needed to regroup before it could start the final push to relieve *IX. SS-Waffen-Gebirgs-Armeekorps der SS*; *I./SS–Panzergrenadier Regiment 23 Norge* was on the division's left flank to the west-northwest at Dinnyes, on the southern bank of Lake Velence, although by this point it was little more than a company in strength. But *3. SS–Panzer Division Totenkopf* also reached the Danube on 23 January and the relief of Budapest seemed imminent. The imminent success was illusory; heavy German losses had left the attacking divisions dangerously weak, with long stretches of their flanks open and unprotected.

Map 5

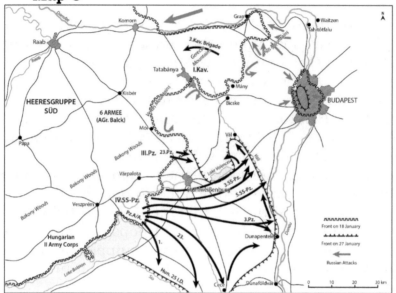

Unternehmen Konrad III. The Germans lost everything they had fought to gain.

With Stuhlweissenburg once again in German hands, those parts of *1. Panzer Division* that had been sucked into the urban fighting were withdrawn during the night of 22-23 January for further offensive operations elsewhere, primarily *Panzergrenadier Regiment 1. SS–Regiment Ney* was left behind to act as a garrison and to rest and reorganize after the brutal fight to capture the city, along with the 20th Hungarian Infantry Division and *Volksartillerie Korps 403*. *SS–Regiment Ney* also incorporated a company of Hungarian air force men into their ranks. Now The Hungarian infantry were deployed in the east and northeastern parts of the city, which were the front lines. "The Wine Garden at Oreghely[298] constituted no-man's land with the main front line running along Fiskalis Street to the outskirts of a munitions factory."[299] (This position would remain static until 22

---

[298] Oreghely is Hungarian for Old Hill.
[299] Pencz, *Siegrunen Volume 76*, p. 17.

March, although heavy fighting would occur at times as the Russians never ceased trying to retake the city.

24 January, Wednesday

North-northwest of Stuhlweissenburg, in the Vértes Mountains, the Hungarian 1st Hussar Division attacked as the northern pincer of *Konrad III*, with support from the Hungarian 2nd Armored Division and the German *4. Kavallerie Brigade.* The Hungarians then attacked Csakvar with 11 *Panzer Mark IVs* and 4 Nimrods. By itself this was not much force, but any pressure against the Russian defenses added to Malinovsky's dilemma about how best to slow the Germans. Unfortunately for the attackers, the ubiquitous Russian antitank guns took a heavy toll. Nine Hungarian and German tanks were knocked out by the Soviets in action around Csakvar.

At Stuhlweissenburg itself, the attack eastward down the highway that led directly to Budapest was stymied by the Russian defenses. However, as the mobile forces south of Lake Velence rushed first eastward, then turned to the north, they began to filter into the deep rear of the Soviet forces near Stuhlweissenburg. This would put the German spearheads in a position to either turn east for Budapest, or west to encircle the Red Army units at Stuhlweissenburg.

According to Strassner, on 24 January *Wiking* was concentrated enough to go back into the attack. *SS–Panzergrenadier Regiment 9 Germania* crossed the Danube and attacked north, while *SS–Panzergrenadier Regiment Westland* stayed on the west bank and moved toward Budapest. This was a remarkable feat, as ice filled the Danube and the depths of winter made it dangerous to simply be outdoors.

In terrible weather against stiffening Soviet resistance, progress was difficult. Undated German newsreel footage of *Konrad III* shows a unit crossing an ice-choked river that must surely be *Germania* crossing the Danube, with Red Air Force ground-attack aircraft trying to stop the crossing, but failing.

Elsewhere, overnight *Panzergrenadier Regiment 1* of *1. Panzer Division* was sucked into the fighting at Pettend, along with that divisions' mechanized pioneers, *Kampfgruppe Marcks* and the remnants of *I./SS–Panzergrenadier Regiment 23 Norge* on the left flank. "The fighting here was unbelievably bitter, since the grenadiers had been witness to the indescribable cruelty inflicted by the Russians on the German and Hungarian wounded."[300] Vogt's mixed battalion of Norwegians, Romanian-Germans and Germans found itself swamped with Russians and in desperate straits. They were "forced to adopt 'hedgehog' defensive positions that faced in all directions."[301] At the very moment when victory seemed possible, *Konrad III* began to lose momentum.

The tank battle at Pettend is one of the most poorly documented actions of the late war period, yet also one of the largest and fiercest. In a very real sense it was the graveyard of *Schwere Panzer Abteilung 509*, which left many of its factory fresh *Mark VI Tiger IIs* on the battlefield as burned-out shells.

[300] Strassner, p. 319.
[301] Landwehr, *Siegrunen Volume 77*, p. 25.

25 January, Thursday

The shell game of transferring units to the most threatened sector of the *Reich* continued. Reinforcements from Italy began to arriving in Hungary in the form of the *356. Infanterie Division*, which was deployed to Stuhlweissenburg on the 25th. Although most German divisions by this point in the war had been involved in serious fighting somewhere, the *356. Infanterie Division* had spent most of its life on the Italian Riviera, only being re-assigned from that duty in August, 1944. Once in Stuhlweissenburg it took up defensive positions in the eastern part of the city. *SS–Regiment Ney* was subordinated to *I./Reiter Regiment 41,* part of *4. Kavallerie Brigade*, and was therefore integrated into *Kampfgruppe Holste*.[302]

Even as the spearheads of *Konrad III* tried to keep pushing forward the combination of inexperienced junior officers and the relative scarcity of *panzers* was eroding any chance the attack had for success. The numbers of AFVs had been marginal in the first place; the *SS* divisions, in particular, were far below authorized strength, although the addition of *I./Panzer Regiment 24* had been a major boost to the overall attack. In the week since *Konrad III* had been launched the Germans had re-captured a huge swath of territory, but significant losses had further weakened the *panzer* units. Worse, with *panzers* in short supply, the very principle of concentration of power that the German form of combined arms warfare through concentration of force in a *schwerpunkt* had been based upon, was forgotten as commanders tried to achieve too many

---

[302] A different source says that the regiment was attached to *356. Infanterie Division*. If so, the reaction of the hard-bitten Hungarian veterans to a being under the command of a unit that had spent a year patrolling the warm, picturesque coast of northern Italy would have been interesting.

objectives with too few tanks. Not only were there too few officers overall, many officers had been promoted beyond their talent level and experience. Under the strain of combat inexperienced officers sometimes tried to accomplish too much with too little, and wound up failing. Fighting with *1. Panzer Division, I./Panzer Regiment 24* saw this command inexperience and dispersal of combat power first hand.

"The strained tactical situation in no way allows maintenance pauses so that the number of operational *panzers* is significantly reduced during an action. All of the available *panzers* must be concentrated to achieve a single combat task. Do not disperse! However, this mistake was repeatedly made. This resulted in three or four *panzers* being halted and knocked out by the first *paknest* that they encountered, sometimes by surprise, because of their numerically low strength."[303]

The village of Pettend is astride the road to Budapest between Kápolnásnyék, at the eastern tip of Lake Velence, and Baracska. The surrounding terrain is flat farmland, ideal for both tanks and antitank guns, with the result that the fight there in 1945 took on the nature of a heavyweight boxing match. Both sides hit each other hard and fast. Casualties were terrible on both sides, but for the Russians the trade was a necessary expenditure of men and machines to stop the German relief attacks. Stalin had denied Malinovsky's request to pull back east of the Danube, so the Marshal had no choice except to use every unit at his disposal west of the Danube. That effort coalesced at Pettend.

Some details of the combat can be ferreted out, though. Fritz Vogt won the Oakleaves to his recently awarded Knight's Cross at Pettend, and the citation notes his actions there.

[303] Jentz, *Panzertruppen 2*, p. 224.

After quickly orienting himself as to the terrain, SS-Hauptsturmführer Vogt made the decision to immediately strike the village in a surprise maneuver from the flank. To this end he did a magnificent job of swiftly bringing up his Bataillon, organizing them for an assault and then swiftly prosecuting the attack towards its intended end. From the ranks of the spearhead Kompanie he entered into the village in the face of a fearsome defense. House after house had to be taken in close combat. Nonetheless, following a ferocious three hour battle, the village was captured…17 tanks were destroyed in the process, and 120 prisoners as well as abundant quantities of weapons and equipment were captured.[304]

After savage fighting the day before, the Germans managed to capture the village of Pettend on 25 January. But in doing so they lost the capability to fight through to the capital.

[304] https://www.tracesofwar.com/persons/14051/Vogt-Fritz-Waffen-SS.htm (Accessed 10 May, 2024).

26 January, Friday

In the hilly vineyard section of Stuhlweissenburg, *SS–Regiment Ney* made local attacks to try and better its defensive lines, but were driven back with heavy losses. One of the main objectives was, and would remain, Hill 182, a promontory that gave its owner a tactical advantage in the hilly terrain.

"No longer was *Konrad III* rolling forward, but instead every movement, every lurch, had a price in blood. The old *elán* was not completely gone, but the skills and training that made the Germans masters of Europe were no longer in evidence. Too few men, too little equipment and too little training were combining with desperate Russian resistance to stop the Germans before they could rescue their starving brethren in Budapest. Another example of this happened when, during the night of 25-26 January, the *Panzers* of *I./Panzer Regiment 24* moved toward Pettend, but once again poor cooperation between the *Mark V Panthers* and the infantry cost the Germans dearly. "An exact orientation on the direction of attack and setting up the *Panzers* was rendered more difficult by the continuous pressure from the Grenadier commander. After the attack advanced 2 kilometers, a short halt to reorganize was interrupted by the Kampfgruppen commander. As a result the *Panzers* arrived at the first objective scattered and no longer under the control of the *Panzer* commander. Accomplishing the orders was made difficult by poor visibility. Buildup of a new *Schwerpunkt* was delayed."[305]

---

[305] Jentz, *Panzertruppen 2*, p. 230.

When success demanded the closest cooperation the German armor and infantry were often as cross-purposes.

As morning dawned on 26 January there was no choice but to recognize that, after a week, *Konrad III* had been stopped. On a map the results did (and still do) appear to be impressive. A huge chunk of territory had been captured, it was true, but the primary mission of saving Budapest remained distant. Heavy losses blunted the spearheads and left them unable to break through, especially losses among the infantry. Once again *I./Panzer Regiment 24* fills in the blanks of what the German situation was at the time. The regiment was in the area east of Lake Velence around Pettend and lost four *Panzers* because the lack of *Panzer*grenadiers left them vulnerable to attacks by infiltrating Russian infantry; all four of the *panzers* were total write-offs, a serious loss. The *panzers* had been standing guard in a field without infantry support, something fundamentally contrary to doctrine, but if there were no infantry to stand guard then the *panzers* had to do it. In the extreme circumstances of the time discipline began to break down. The combination of inexperienced commanders and troop shortages lead many veteran *panzer* officers to take matters into their own hands. "Many exorbitantly demanded tasks were consciously not carried out by the *Panzer* commanders, thereby preventing higher losses."[306] The disobedience was not widespread, but even isolated incidents were unusual. Such incidents would become more and more common, though, as the end of the war approached, and commanding officers refused to follow suicidal orders that would only result in the death of men they had grown to know and respect.

[306] Jentz, *Panzertruppen 2*, p. 311.

27 January, Saturday

Flying weather over the Hungarian region was good, with cloud cover around 3000 feet, although it was snowing on Budapest. Nevertheless, medals were dropped into Buda for the garrison officers, with Pfeffer-Wildenbruch being awarded the Knight's Cross. The commander of I Hungarian Army Corps, General Hindy, was promoted to *Generaloberst*. The days of dropping supplies to the garrison were fast coming to an end, however, as the Russians had reached the *Blutweise*, the chief aiming and collection point. German counterattacks tried to drive them back but failed.

The name originates from the executions that took place there following the failed Hungarian Revolution of 1848-1849. After the revolution, the Habsburg authorities conducted a series of public executions of Hungarian revolutionary leaders and soldiers at this site, staining the area with the memory of those events. Over time, the name "Blood Meadow" became a symbol of the sacrifice and struggle for Hungarian independence.

Hitler's midday situation report conference was a crowded affair and dealt extensively with *Heeresgruppe Süd* and the final stages of *Konrad III*. *Generaloberst* Heinz Guderian reported on what must have been the final attacks between Lake Velence and Vali toward the north on the previous night, 26 January, as the Germans tried to cut off Russian forces near Stuhlweissenburg to protect their left flank in the final drive to Budapest. When the advance units had rounded the eastern end of Lake Velence and turned north they were faced with three choices as to direction: west, to isolate Russian forces near Stuhlweissenburg; north to Biscke, where they could pocket a much larger Russian force, or east-northeast toward Budapest. Whatever choice was made meant exposed flanks. The route chosen, and probably the best one for success of the overall offensive, was to turn west toward Stuhlweissenburg. Destroying the Russian forces there would have freed up large German forces for the final relief attacks aimed at Budapest.

But while the German spearheads had made enormous gains, they were also dangerously extended, inviting the counterattacks that were aimed at cutting them off and destroying them. Heavy losses had eaten away at their core and the situation was deteriorating quickly. Even Hitler realized that the forces were not strong enough to break through; however, he insisted that, if the attacks had stalled, then the advance units had to dig in and fight on that line. He also wanted to know why the attacks had failed. At the critical moment when a choice of directions had to be made, orders directing a westerly advance route did not reach the spearheads promptly, allowing the Russians to reinforce the threatened sector. "According to General Wöhler and General Balck...the turning toward the west happened too slowly. Certain complications in the transmission of orders and in the reporting system have caused delays."[307]

Strength of the attacking divisions was a second factor, Russian reinforcements were a third. Guderian reported that the 18th Tank Corps had been reinforced by the 7th Guards Mechanized Corps and possibly the Pliev Cavalry-Mechanized Group. The entirety of this news made Hitler realize that *Konrad III* was not going to break the ring around Budapest, that the assault divisions were a spent force. "With the forces that are here now, we can't do it. That is clear...pushing through (toward Budapest) makes no sense anymore."[308] Russian counterattacks were coming from

[307] Heimer & Glantz, pp. 621-624.
[308] In fact, both Guderian and Hitler believed the Pliev Group had gone north of the Danube to either replace or reinforce 6th Guards Tank Army for an

all four directions on the forces furthest forward and some had broken through, and while heavy tank losses had been inflicted, not all of the breakthroughs had been sealed off. By that 9th day of *Konrad III*, the Germans had gone from having a slight numerical superiority in AFVs when the attack began, to being outnumbered by about 2 to 1.[309]

With the words "as far as I'm concerned, the Gille Corps [*IV. SS–Panzerkorps*] can change to defense," *Konrad III* was officially cancelled by Hitler; the German spearheads were simply not strong enough to break through without some sort of concurrent breakout from the garrison, and that was no longer possible.[310] Hitler and Guderian's focus shifted to countering the inevitable Russian counterattacks against the strung-out German formations now that the impetus of their own attacks had been stopped, but try as they might to shift their own understrength *panzer* divisions into better positions for defense, in the end there was no good solution without reinforcements.

Attention was paid to the estimated arrival date of *6. SS–Panzerarmee* in Hungary, with Hitler skeptical that it could be done in anything less than two weeks and probably much longer than that. *Unternehmen Frühlingserwachen* was already on the agenda and his impatience to get on with that attack was tempered only by the realities of transporting a major combat force from the western front to the east in the face of Allied air supremacy; marauding Allied fighter-bombers shot up anything that moved while strategic bombing wiped out railroad marshalling yards in cities throughout Germany. Locomotives and rolling stock were in short supply and were often delayed by air attacks or damaged tracks. Hitler showed during this conference that he knew these hard realities, although he ignored them when it suited his mood. He was

---

attack into the area just vacated by *20. Panzer Division* Division, but they were not positive.

[309] Ungvary, *the siege of Budapest*, p. 328, Table 21.
[310] Heimer & Glantz, p. 638.

clearly worried that both *I. SS–Panzerkorps* and *II. SS–Panzerkorps* would not only arrive slowly, but piecemeal, and would therefore require a long time to get organized, time that Germany did not have.

Later, an off-hand remark of Guderian's prompted a nasty retort from Hitler about the fuel supply; the *Führer* could not resist digging at Guderian yet again about the reasons for *Unternehmen Frühlingserwachen* and the transfer of *6. SS–Panzerarmee* to Hungary.

When Guderian said: "Our main problem is the fuel issue at the moment," Hitler's response was short on words but long on condescension. "That's why I'm concerned Guderian-if something happens down there [the Lake Balaton region], it's over. That's the most dangerous point. We can improvise everywhere else, but not there. I can't improvise with the fuel. Unfortunately, I can't hang a generator on a *panzer*."[311]

When the conversation shifted to matters north of the Danube the concern was that if the front should break there was nothing in reserve to seal it. The Russians had barely been held earlier in the month and further attacks in the direction of Komarom were expected, but if the defense were punctured both Pressburg (Bratislava) and Vienna were but a day's drive to the west. In response *46. Infanterie Division* was being pulled back to shorten the front. Together with the *44. Reichs Grenadier Division Hoch und Deutschmeister* and the *357. Infanterie Division* the front had to hold else Komarom would be lost, and together with it the railroad bridges over the Danube, meaning that German positions south of the Danube would be outflanked. Guderian suggested moving the *356. Infanterie Division* into the threatened sector and

[311] Heimer & Glantz, p. 651,

Hitler agreed[312], but the *Führer* also saw the Russian bridgehead west of the Gran as a threat that had to be eliminated, a situation that would evolve into the last successful German attack of the war: *Unternehmen Südwind*. He hoped not to use additional forces to eliminate the danger, forces that could only have come from *6. SS–Panzerarmee*, since he had other plans for them. "We have to do it, so we can stop this whole thing here without having to use the corps or the army here, which I want to deploy in the south. But one can see how dangerous it is. That must be cleared out."[313] As events would show, however, Hitler realized that if further attacks south of the Danube were going to be made then the Russian bridgehead north of the river had to be eliminated at any cost, even if it meant using the *SS* units of *6. SS–Panzerarmee*.

One of *8. SS–Freiwillige–Kavallerie Division Florian Geyer*'s most veteran soldiers became the only Slovak to win the Knight's Cross. Even as the Red Army inexorably closed in for the kill on the Budapest garrison, the few remaining healthy veterans made them pay a very high price for crawling through the wreckage. *SS–SS–Hauptscharführer* Gustav Wendrisky was a Slovak who reported himself as *Volksdeutsch* and had served with Florian Geyer since at least 1942. By the time he was trapped in Budapest, Wendrisky commanded an anti-tank platoon, and in a letter to his father before Budapest was surrounded he claimed to have destroyed 41 Russian tanks with his 75 mm anti-tank gun.[314]

---

[312] 31 trains carrying much of the *356. Infanterie Division*, and most of its combat elements, left Italy at Speed 8 heading for Hungary. Speed 8 was very slow.

[313] Heimer & Glantz, p. 623.

[314] It is not clear if by this he meant his own personal gun, or those of his platoon.

On 27 January, the following message was sent to the *Führer's* Headquarters by Florian Geyer's commander, *SS–Brigadeführer und Generalmajor der SS* Joachim Romohr: "*SS–Oberscharführer* Gustav Wendrisky in a confusing situation without infantry support and attacked by many tanks, did destroy with his anti-tank cannon 3 tanks of the enemy. Then, armed with a heavy machine-gun, he held off the oncoming enemy's infantry until his gun could be removed to another position. The situation evolved in such a way that he was cutoff. Nevertheless, dressed in Hungarian civilian clothes, he managed to destroy two more enemy tanks with *Panzerfäuste* and bring back a tractor (*zugmaschine*) previously captured by Russians, safely to our own lines."[315] Hitler ordered that Wendrisky immediately be awarded the Knight's Cross, and he was also promoted to *SS–Hauptscharführer*. Wendrisky would survive until the very end in Budapest, but would die along with thousands of others in the suicidal breakout attempt when Hitler finally allowed the emaciated survivors to try and escape.

After being repulsed the previous day, *SS–Regiment Ney* once again attacked to try and completely clear the Red Army from Stuhlweissenburg. The promontory called Hill 182, locally known as the Altberg, fell quickly and the Hungarians pushed on to the eastern limits of the urban area at the Nagyszombati Road. The terrain was hilly and draped with vineyards, difficult to advance across and with limited fields of fire. A battery of Hungarian 10.5 cm artillery from III/53rd Replacement Artillery Battalion supported them. Fighting was at close quarters, but Hill 182 was vital to both sides and the *SS* men were unable to hold their new positions for long against

[315] Volko, Vojteck, *Siegrunen Volume 76*, p. 13.

Soviet counterattacks. During the coming weeks the tussle over the area would continue with positions changing hands repeatedly.

In the bitter weather of late January, the fighting around Pettend was brutal. The Russian 23rd Tank Corps was mauled during the day, losing 45 T-34s destroyed and 13 more damaged, as well as 1 ISU-122 destroyed and 2 more damaged, although this was far fewer than the 122 tanks claimed as destroyed in the War Diary of *Heeresgruppe Süd*[316]. *Schwere–Panzer Abteilung 509* claimed 34 T-34s killed by its *Tiger IIs* at the cost of minor damage to one *panzer* from friendly fire. Whether exaggerated or not, the numbers illustrated the scale and ferocity of the combat around Pettend.

As badly as the Russians suffered, however, there was no denying that *Konrad III* had been stopped in its bloody tracks and, despite Hitler's direct orders to hold what had been gained, there was also no denying that once again he had ordered the impossible.

[316] German damage claims routinely overestimated Soviet losses.

28 January, Sunday

Even after Hitler cancelled *Konrad III* the attacks sporadically continued and made gains. *Kampfgruppe Philipp* of *1. Panzer Division* fought to a point within 10 miles of the perimeter in Budapest. Only then did orders come to stop the attack, ostensibly because they were no longer strong enough to force their way into the city, nor to hold open the corridor for long, and Hitler forbade the trapped garrison from breaking out.[317] Both were true; it was Velikiye Luki all over again. Maybe the relief forces could enter the city... *maybe...* but that wasn't enough. A corridor had to be strong enough to withstand Russian attacks to close it, something *Kampfgruppe Phillip* could never have done.

In the recently overrun areas south and east of Lake Velence, the retreat had to be well-handled lest disaster strike. Over-extended flanks once again threatened the forward German elements, with the only saving grace being the offensive had done so much damage to 3rd Ukrainian Front that Marshal Tolbukhin had no forces to take advantage of the tactical situation. Indeed, had Hitler ordered *Konrad III* to change its direction of attack from south to north once the leading units reached the Danube, it was momentarily possible they might have reached *2. Panzerarmee* on the Drava River and cut off the entire Russian force west of the Danube and south of the line Lake Balaton-Velence. That was the objective of *Unternehmen Frühlingserwachen* and it could have worked in January, but Hitler instead sent *III. Panzerkorps* and *IV SS-Panzerkorps* north toward Budapest. And it must be said that his opinion of the correct place to attack was correct, harkening back to the cancelled *Unternehmen Paula*. But of course, war is dynamic and there was no guarantee the Russians might not have been ready for such an axis of advance earlier in the year.

---

[317] Strassner puts this as occurring on the 26th.

Too late, the Germans tried to assemble a strike force to move south. Consisting of the remaining mobile elements of *Totenkopf*, it required time to gather them from across the battlefield, time the Germans did not have. *Despite* heavy losses from *Konrad III*, the Russians launched everything they had left to destroy *IV. SS–Panzerkorps* while it remained in such an exposed position. Their own armored losses had been severe, though, and by necessity the Russians had to use large masses of infantry supported by the few remaining tanks and assault guns. Foot soldiers struggling through snow-covered fields could not take advantage of gaps in the German lines fast enough, which resulted in the Germans either mowing them down in large numbers, or counterattacking penetrations before they could be consolidated. The net result was that all Russians attacks failed in severe fighting.

The bulk of *IV. SS–Panzerkorps* was strung out near the Danube, north of the Russian bridgehead at Dunaföldvar. The main direction of the Russian counterattack was northwest toward the village of Perkáta, a place best known for the majestic Gyóry Castle. For Gille and his command, the attack represented mortal danger, as it thrust into the rear area of *IV. SS–Panzerkorps*. The only reserves available to meet the Russian thrust were the elements of *Totenkopf* that had been assembled for the move south. *SS-Brigade Ney* was once again handed over to the command of *IV. SS–Panzerkorps* and assigned to support the *3. SS–Panzer Division Totenkopf*, although direct command of the formation would change the next day.

Casualties and slower-than-expected progress led the Russians to form the Budapest Group, a powerful formation designed to punch through the defense perimeter. This unified and coordinated attacks with the idea of maximizing damage to the defenders.

Russian fighters and fighter bombers swept low overhead, bombing and strafing anything that moved. Concentrating on the northern and northwestern, very heavy attack supported by tanks and ground support aircraft threatened breakthroughs all along the line. The last Hungarian reserves prevented that, but the Russians captured ground up to the western and southwestern corners of the *Blutweise.* Pushing the lines so far into the city forced a retreat during the night to prevent being outflanked. This Russian surge meant the *Blutweise* could now be swept by machine gun fire in addition to mortars and artillery, making it unsuitable for supply aircraft.

Margaret Island also saw intense fighting on the ground and in the air, both during the day and after dark. Russian landings on the east bank made some headway, but ultimately had to be withdrawn after the assault force was torn by very heavy casualties.

Luftflotte 4 flew more than 500 sorties over that 24 hour period, an absolute maximum effort that could not be sustained for long. Some 130 tons of supplies reached the garrison, if such a high figure can be believed. Night-bombing raids concentrated on troop concentration areas near Margaret Island, an attempt to prevent renewed attacks when morning came.

29 January, Monday

The *25. Waffen-Grenadier Division der SS* was officially given its honorific title, *Hungaria*. Unlike its sister Division, *26. Waffen–Grenadier Division der SS Hunyadi*, the majority of men in the *25. Waffen-Grenadier Division der SS* were not Hungarian army veterans but instead were civilian draftees and volunteers. In terms of numbers, the division was not inconsequential: as of 24 December, 1944, it listed a total strength of 8,100 men, but by early January its numbers had shot to 16,761 men of all ranks. Like so many other formations, German and non-German alike, the real problem was equipping the new unit with uniforms, boots, the usual military necessities and, most of all, weapons; there was just not enough of anything to go around. Estimates are that around this time some 10,000 men were still wearing civilian clothing, while those who did have a uniform may well have still been wearing their Hungarian uniform, with only about 20 percent of the division in standard *Waffen–SS* field gray. The two Hungarian Divisions would spend most of their war training at Neuhammer before fleeing west as the Red Army overran their training center, inflicting heavy losses. Eventually they would make their way into western Austria.

SS-Brigade Ney continued its odyssey of reassignments, being put under the direct control of the newly arrived *356. Infanterie Division*, along with their fellow Hungarians in the battered *1. SS–Ungarische–Sturm Regiment*. Together, they attacked Russian positions north-northeast of Stuhlweissenburg, but with little effect; the Russians were too strong now to allow major incursions against their defenses.

In Budapest, the headquarters of *IX. SS-Waffen-Gebirgs-Armeekorps der SS* reported that for the first time the wounded outnumbered the effectives. The defensive perimeter had shrunk to Gellert Hill and Castle Hill. More than 100 feet above the Danube, Castle Hill, with Budapest Castle on its top and Gellert Hill, 140 feet high, were strong-points difficult to take, despite continual bombing and shelling. Atop Gellert Hill is The Citadel, a fortress built in the early 1850's by the Hapsburgs as a way to control the city after the Hungarian War for Independence. During the Siege of Budapest it served the same purpose for the defenders. The city itself is built on a honeycomb of underground passageways and caves, which offered some protection for the wounded, even though there was little doctors could do for them. An account from one such wounded man, Helmut Schreiber, an artilleryman fighting as infantry in *8. SS–Freiwillige–Kavallerie Division Florian Geyer*, gives some sense of what it was like in the tunnels under Castle Hill. "The cellar vaults were filled with badly wounded men, lying on the floor without beds, covered with paper. Rations consisted of a slice of bread and a cup of tea...On 12 February the Russians fetched us out of the cellars. What happened then was hell. Those who could not walk were shot."[318]

Strassner says *Wiking* was supposed to kick off its final attack on Budapest at 0700, with intelligence reporting only the remnants of a Russian cavalry division in front of Westland, but fog delayed the attack first until 0800, then 0900, and then the Russians took the initiative away from the Germans. With clouds of Red Air Force ground attack aircraft hammering the

[318] Michaelis, p. 119.

German positions, a previously unknown tank corps 180 strong slammed into the German left flank on ground held by *I./Panzergrenadier Regiment 23 Norge*. The flank should have collapsed, but Norge's orphan battalion somehow managed to slow down the Russians; its Commander, *SS–SturmbannFührer* Vogt, reportedly destroyed 6 tanks by himself using *panzerfäuste*.[319]

> "Following the seizure of Pettend on the 25.01.1945 the *Bataillon* received the mission of defending the village, as it was believed that the enemy would use every means at their disposal to retake this important position. This conjecture was already realized on the night of the 26./27.01.1945. Throughout the entire night the enemy pounded the village with a fury that only seemed to increase. Friendly patrols were able to confirm that strong enemy tank and infantry forces were assembling in the area northeast of Pettend.
>
> At 06:30 the enemy attacking along the railroad line with about 20 tanks and 250 men. With this *SS-Hauptsturmführer* Vogt and his men became locked in a heroic battle for the village. After the Grenadiers had let the tanks overrun them they engaged the hostile infantry. Despite the great enemy superiority as well as the fact that the Bataillon lacked any armour piercing weapons (both of its Pak guns were overrun by enemy tanks at the outset of the engagement), the enemy proved unable to eject the Bataillon from the village. *SS-Hauptsturmführer* Vogt repeatedly launched lightning counterstrikes with just a few men each time, and these inflicted high losses on the foe. By the afternoon of the same day every single officer of the

---

[319] This is the engagement where Vogt won the Oak Leaves to his Knight's Cross.

Bataillon (excluding the commander) had fallen in battle.

Eventually enemy tanks made it to the *Bataillon* command post (located in the village centre), and due to heavy friendly losses the enemy was able to penetrate our lines all along the edge of the village. With this all contact towards the rear was lost, and so [SS] *Hauptsturmführer* Vogt decided to pull back the remnants of his Bataillon for a last stand defense of the village centre (namely the estate). The enemy surrounded this structure with their tanks and pounded it with unending fire.

To counter this *SS-Hauptsturmführer* Vogt assembled a small group together before assaulting the enemy tanks with close combat weapons. With a short time 8 enemy tanks were knocked out, 3 by the commander personally via Panzerfausts. After this it was possible to force the enemy out of the majority of the village, and so at 23:00 in the evening the Bataillon commander could report that the village was under friendly control. On this day a total of 53 enemy tanks were destroyed in the sector of the *Bataillon*, and a previously lost howitzer Batterie belonging to the Wehrmacht was recaptured.

On the following day the enemy renewed their attacks with powerful formations that had just arrived on the battlefield. Thus another bitter fight took place for the keystone position; the estate. 20-25 enemy tanks formed a firm ring around the 3 buildings, which were blasted by their continuous volleys of fire. However the commander and his Bataillon stood firm in the whirlwind of destruction, and the wreckage of the estate was held. During the afternoon hours he exhibited an unprecedented demonstration of readiness and dutifulness by ordering friendly artillery fire to come down on his own position in order to combat those opposing tanks that stood directly before him. After the last rounds of ammunition and last Panzerfausts had been expended, *SS-SS–HauptsturmführerVogt* ordered the remnants of his Bataillon to break out. He was the last to leave the village, and he led his men safely back to friendly lines."[320]

Vogt's story is well documented compared to that of the thousands of men on both sides who fought and died in Hungary. It serves as an example of what were likely many others, Russian, German, Hungarian and other ethnicities, whose stories were not recorded.

The situation was desperate enough to commit *Wiking's* last reserve, *5. SS–Panzer–Aufklärung Abteilung*, which had been held back as the final exploitation force to break into Budapest. With *Konrad III* officially cancelled the battalion was freed to act as a general reserve.

Fighting around Pettend continued to be severe, with another tank battle lasting several hours. Ungvary says that during all of the fighting around Pettend "although the Germans destroyed 122 Soviet tanks on the first day, they had to abandon many of the occupied territories, with the notable exception of Székesfehérvár [Stuhlweissenburg]. Near the village of Vereb alone, the wrecks of 70 tanks and 35 assault guns bore witness to the heavy fighting."[321] And while losses on both sides were very heavy, the Germans had lost so heavily during a month of fighting that they did not even have the strength to hold their ground, much less continue to offensive. During the night, they pulled back to the area around Baracska-Pettend.

---

[320] https://www.tracesofwar.com/persons/14051/Vogt-Fritz-Waffen-SS.htm (Accessed 6 June, 2024.)
[321] Ungvary, *The Siege of Budapest*, p. 170.

In less than two weeks Operation *Konrad III* had smashed through the Soviet front west and north of Lakes Balaton and Velence, poured through the holes and swept the Soviets back all the way to the Danube, like a tidal wave washing away flotsam. Stuhlweissenburg had been re-captured, German troops once again set foot on the east bank of the Danube, and for one brief moment the highway to Budapest had seemed open. In previous years the leadership of the Red Army might have panicked and the Germans might have penetrated all the way to Budapest, thus saving *IX. SS-Waffen-Gebirgs-Armeekorps der SS* and the Budapest garrison.

But the Soviets had learned their lessons, and despite some early apprehension Marshal Tolbukhin had not overreacted to the threat. Whether because Stalin forbade it, or Tolbukhin found it within himself to stand firm, the Russians held their ground. In much the same way that Patton saw a chance to turn the tables during the Ardennes Offensive and cut off the German spearheads, Tolbukhin saw a similar chance to force the Germans back by threatening their flanks. The offensive had come tantalizingly close to success, but the German formations were just too burned out to break through completely. And so, in the end, *Konrad III* had failed, and there were no units powerful enough left to mount a fourth attempt. Budapest was doomed, and the Germans were forced to retreat under very heavy pressure, fighting their way back to the Margarethe Position between Lakes Balaton and Velence. Casualties mounted rapidly.

30 January, Tuesday

Morale throughout the *Reich* was collapsing as doubt crept into the minds of even the most loyal of Hitler's paladins. The 12th Anniversary of Hitler's rise to power as Chancellor of Germany found *SS–Obergruppenführer* Karl Wolff giving his staff a pep talk. Wolff was the head of *SS* and Police in Italy and as loyal an *SS* officer as could be found. Although not particularly intelligent, the dire circumstances Germany found herself in were obvious even to him. As he tried to convince his subordinates that all was well and the war would still be won, Wolff decided to see Himmler in person and demand to know where the promised wonder weapons were. "And if Himmler couldn't answer the question, he would ask the *Führer*, and if put off again with evasions, he would insist upon an honorable peace."[322]

Wolff was a main cog in the machinery of the Third *Reich*, the sort of supremely loyal true believer without whom the *SS* could not have functioned. When doubts came even to men such as he, things were well and truly lost. But not to the one man whose opinion mattered most. In far-off Berlin, Hitler was holding one of his occasional political talks after the daily military conference. After explaining why he had launched *Unternehmen Wacht am Rhein*, the Battle of the Bulge, he went on to explain why he had sent *6. SS–Panzerarmee* to Hungary against the advice of most of his generals.

The reason, he said, went far beyond the military. First, Dietrich was about to launch a surprise attack that would not only save their last oil resources in Hungary but would regain the oil of Rumania. Second, and more important, he was buying time.[323] Once again the debate over exactly why Hitler sent the best remaining Germany army to his Austrian

[322] Toland, John, *The Last Hundred Days*, (New York:), p. 131).
[323] Ibid, p. 41.

317

homeland, instead of to the Oder Front east of Berlin, comes to mind. Was it simply to save the last oilfield, minor as it was? Did he actually believe that his armies could drive all the way back to Ploesti, in Rumania? Or was there another reason, a hidden reason? It is impossible today to say for certain what all of his motives were, but protecting the country of his birth does not seem preposterous as at least *a* motive, if not *the* motive.

Hitler believed that the Anglo-American alliance was tearing itself apart over the issue of allowing Stalin dominance in much of Europe. The longer the war lasted, he believed, the better the chance that the Allies would turn on their Soviet allies. The *Führer* worked himself up over what he believed was the imminent split with Stalin, when a combined German-American-English force would drive the eastern hordes back into their own land. The disconnection between Hitler and even his most loyal followers, like Wolff, is striking. The *Waffen–SS* was still doing its best to carry out orders regardless of how impossible they might prove, but the bonds linking them to their *Führer* were loosening.

Conspicuous for his gallantry and inspired leadership of *96. Infanterie Division*, Hermann Harrendorf was promoted to *Generalmajor* and made permanent commander of the division. It was a brief moment of good news in an otherwise bleak day.

Konrad III might have been over, but the fighting was not; the Soviets had every intention of reclaiming the ground they had lost, and the Germans were not strong enough to stop them. The Chief of Staff of *6. Armee*, *Generalmajor* Gaedecke, reported to the Chief-of-Staff of *Heeresgruppe Süd* that the combat ready AFV strength for *Totenkopf* was nine and for *Wiking* 14, a total of 23 AFVs in service. In other words, *IV. SS–Panzerkorps* could deploy perhaps two companies of armored fighting vehicles. These numbers graphically illustrate that the *SS panzer* divisions were shattered, their combat power was weak, and they were divisions in name only; in reality, both *Totenkopf* and *Wiking* were nothing more than large *kampfgruppen*. Nor would they ever be again.

31 January, Wednesday

After 10 days of preparation, the *14. Waffen–Grenadier Division der SS (1. Galizien)*finally set out across Austria for Styria. The closer it came to British and US air bases in Italy, the more it had to duck out of sight in daylight. Road marches were strictly limited to nighttime, which slowed it down. Nevertheless it still suffered casualties from air attacks, mostly from strafing. This was a huge division, with an even larger caravan of hangers-on, family members and refugees, an enormous target crawling slowly along secondary roads that was simply too big to hide completely.

The *Konrad* attacks had taken a terrible toll on *IV. SS–Panzerkorps* , a toll that left broken German bodies, guns and tanks scattered all over Western Hungary. By the end of the month, the combined casualty totals for *Totenkopf* and *Wiking* were almost 8,000, including some 200 officers, who had been in short supply even before offensive operations began. *Totenkopf* had suffered 4,350 total casualties, including 51 officers killed, while *Wiking's* losses were 3,079 and also 51 officers killed. Between the two divisions 152 officers were wounded. The *panzer* and *panzergrenadier* regiments were virtually non-existent and neither division would ever again come close to full combat strength, or regain its capability for offensive operations, and while replacement personnel scraped from every organization in the *Reich* would partly flesh out the *panzergrenadier* regiments with bodies, there would be no replacement vehicles to rebuild the *panzer* regiments, and no effort to even try. The ranks of the men would now be nothing more than cannon fodder, and the AFVs were gone forever. Whatever *panzers* they later had were either repaired casualties or cobbled together from shattered hulks.[324] A few sources list an effort to repurpose enemy tanks, *beutepanzers*, as had been done in the past, with unknown results.

Schwere–Panzers Abteilung 509 started *Konrad III* with 45 operational *Mark VI Tiger IIs*. On 29 January only five were operational, but with a total of 38 still on the rolls. Seven had therefore been written off, either completely destroyed or captured.

Casualties for *III. Panzerkorps* are not available in any reliable capacity.

As usual the Russians suffered even worse casualties than the Germans, and while Russian resources of men and equipment were also far greater, they were not inexhaustible. When the time came to counterattack they did not hesitate. Nothing changed in the overall scheme of how the Red Army conducted operations. Casualties continued to be relatively meaningless to Russian commanders but the day was coming when even the mighty Red Army would start to run out of replacements.

Following their recapture of Zimoly, north of Stuhlweissenburg, Red Army units kept moving into the northern outskirts of Stuhlweissenburg where the Soviet attack, accompanied by at least 14 tanks, slammed into the German defenses manned by *SS–Regiment Ney, Infanterie Regiment 871* and *356. Infanterie Division* Engineer Battalion from *356. Infanterie Division*. Elements of *3. SS–Panzer Division Totenkopf*, including *panzers*, were drawn into the battle and during the night the Russian attacks finally collapsed; all of the 14 Russian tanks were destroyed,[325]

[324] http://Wiking-ruf.com/Wikingtimetable.html#1945 (Accessed 22 March, 2010).
[325] Pencz, *Siegrunen Volume 76*, p. 19.

After being out of touch with higher authorities for 12 days following its flight from Poland, *26. Waffen–Grenadier Division der SS Hungaria*[326] finally made contact with both the *SS Hauptamt* (Main Office) in Berlin and the commander of the *Waffen–SS* training compound at Neuhammer; the German relief was palpable. The *SS* had invested a lot of scarce resources and manpower in the under-armed Hungarian division and were very concerned that it had been caught in the path of the Red Army steamroller with no way to defend itself. The upper echelon of the *SS* believed the Hungarians could be molded into a powerful and motivated corps, which might have proven true if it were used to fight in Hungary itself. But most of Hungary was already lost to the Russians and if the corps was ever going to go into combat to defend its homeland, it needed to hurry.

Near the end of January *9. SS–Panzer Division Hohenstaufen* had been rebuilt prior to its transfer to Hungary, reporting itself with a total strength of all ranks of 19,462, nearly 1,700 men over its authorized strength of 17,797. As impressive as this may seem, few of the new replacements had any training as infantry and the division was badly under-strength in both officers and non-commissioned officers. "This high level in personnel strength no longer had any effect on operational capability. Replenished with older age groups, *Volksdeutsche*, and foreigners of the *SS-Ausbildungs-und-Ersatzeinheiten* units, the formation's fighting power declined steadily, and this was not only

---

[326] The honorific 'Hungaria' is generally accepted for this division, although a few sources give the alternate title 'Gömbos', after Hungarian statesman and soldier Gyula Gömbös de Jákfa (December 26, 1886 until October 6, 1936), a one-time Minister of War who believed Hungary's future should be tied to Hitler's Germany.

due to the lack of ammunition, weapons, and supplies."[327] The division would have an extended period in Hungary before going into combat and training would be intensive, but training could only go so far to offset the limitations of men who were not fit for first line combat.

[327] Michaelis, Rolf, *Panzer Divisions of the Waffen–SS*, (Atglen: Schiffer Military Publishing, 2014), p. 236.

1 February, Thursday

Early in February the casualty figures for *8. SS Kavallerie-Division Florian Geyer* became available. According to Michaelis, there were four officers and 217 other ranks killed, seven officers and 1,079 other ranks wounded, with 32 missing. In other words, before the worst fighting began the division had suffered more than 1,300 casualties.[328] In addition, Michaleis lists more than 11,000 wounded for the garrison, a staggering number. He puts daily rations of half a slice of bread and 15 grams of legumes, but there were only two more days before that food ran out. That the garrison was starving seems beyond dispute, but exactly what rations they were getting at this point is not quite as clear. According to Guillemot, General Hindy wrote in a report that "the daily ration of a soldier was 5 grams of fat, a slice of bread, and horse meat when available," with no mention of legumes. The discrepancy might be explained if Michaelis were referring to German rations, and Hindy to Hungarian. But if that was the case it would seem more likely that it was the Germans eating horse meat, since the cavalry brought their horses with them.

Regardless of who ate what, nobody in the doomed city was eating much of anything. For days their chief sustenance had been the approach of *IV. SS–Panzerkorps* , as represented by the single word 'Gille'. Strassner quotes Dr. Hubner of *Panzer Division Felldherrnhalle* as writing that "new 'shithouse' rumors in the pocket concerning the approach of Gille circulated hourly.[329]" Using another source, he then says "The news of Gille filtered down to the last foxhole...he was like the anchor of our morale everywhere. For hours at a time people forgot the terrible privation and accommodated themselves to the

---

[328] Michaelis, *Cavalry Divisions*, p. 107.
[329] Strassner, p. 320.

repulsive conditions in the cellars. Our rescue was getting nearer!"[330]

By 1 February, however, the truth started to become apparent: Gille had been stopped. Rescue was not coming.

Morale sank.

It had certainly become clear to the men of *Wiking* that they had failed in their mission of rescuing the Budapest garrison. "It was clear down to the last man in the division that the relief of Budapest had failed, once and for all."[331] It might have been cold comfort but the failure was not their fault, as their casualty statistics clearly show. In addition to the figures mentioned earlier that *Wiking* and *Totenkopf* combined had lost almost 8,000 men[332], *SS–Panzer Regiment 5* was virtually wiped out. *Wiking's* armored fist listed a strength of combat-ready vehicles on 1 February as nine, down from the 14 General Gaedecke reported two days prior, from an authorized strength of 152; the composition was three *Mark IVs* and six *Mark V Panthers*. This meant that the mangled division could field only two *panzer* platoons. The two *panzergrenadier* regiments, *Germania* and *Westland*, had suffered equally appalling losses. All of this combined to have a devastating effect on the morale of the survivors. No matter how great their sacrifice, and no matter how much they realized that they had done everything humanly possible to break through to Budapest, "it changed little the fate of their surrounded comrades and less the general dejection of the soldiers, who perhaps had also begun to suspect that the war was

---

[330] Ibid, p. 321.

[331] Ibid, p. 320.

[332] Since the beginning of the war, *Totenkopf* had lost 55,000 men killed, wounded or missing, about 3 times its total enrollment.

coming to an unhappy end."[333] The division had become so weak in manpower, material and morale that it was ordered back from the Danube to a rest and recovery area to the west. This was easier said than done, however.

As fighting continued along Stuhlweissenburg's northern border, the elements of *356. Infanterie Division, 3. SS–Panzer Division Totenkopf* and *SS–Regiment Ney* that were holding the line there were further reinforced by additional troops from *Totenkopf*,[334] *1. Panzer Division* and the *Mark VI Tiger IIs* of *Schwere–Panzer Abteilung 509.* With *Konrad III* a failure, the attack units were moving back westward to take up defensive positions and reorganize, while the Russians continued attacking to both cut them off, and to retake lost ground in preparation for their own offensive. Both sides were worn down from the recent fighting and neither was anywhere close to peak fighting trim. The Germans, in particular, were feeling the effects of the inexperience of many in the rank and file. The after-action report from *I./Panzer Regiment 24*[335] emphasized the lack of training among *panzergrenadiers* and the losses that resulted. "During the advance of our own *panzers* on February 1 on the north side of Stuhlweissenburg, our own *Panzer*(s) suffered losses from hidden anti-tank guns on the flank that could have been spotted in time and fought if escorting Grenadiere had advanced with the *Panzers.*"[336]

However much the attacking Germans had lost, the Russian casualties were higher. As an example of

[333] Strassner, p. 321.

[334] Michaelis puts the arrival of *Totenkopf* in Stuhlweissenburg as 2 February (*Panzer Divisions of the Waffen SS*, p. 161).

[335] Probably attached to 1st Panzer Division.

[336] Jentz, *Panzertruppen 2*, p. 225.

how ferocious the fighting had been, a dispatch from *Wehrmachtbericht* gave figures for the casualties *Totenkopf* had inflicted since New Year's Day: captured or destroyed 387 tanks, 792 guns and 832 trucks."[337] Even allowing for these numbers being inflated it is obvious that a badly weakened *Totenkopf* had inflicted massive damage during the three *Konrad* offensives, but in the process that division was left emaciated and fit only for defense. It would never recover.

[337] Michaelis, *Panzer Divisions*, p. 161.

2 February, Friday

Weather across the battlefield warmed enough to cause sticky ground conditions, and large areas of fog. With all of his forces more or less back at their starting point, Hermann Balck finally had enough forces available to at least form a coherent main line of resistance (MLR). What *Armeegruppe Balck* needed more than anything was time to rest and reorganize. Fortunately for the Germans, their enemy did too.

Maintenance of machines required more attention in the harsh winter months than in warmer times. Vehicles needed filters changed, axles greased and hoses replaced, along with a thousand other checks. Guns needed cleaning, ammunition and fuel stocks near the front lines needed replenishing, and replacements needed integration into units.

As for the men, what they needed most was a hot meal and a good night's sleep out of the ice and snow. But not all of the men; the fighting paused in some place while continuing with undiminished ferocity in others. *5. SS Panzer Division Wiking* was attached to *III. Panzerkorps* as it fought its way westward after the failure of *Konrad III*. Taking a route south of Lake Velence that took it through Seregelyes, where one of the frequent Russian attacks broke through. Only an immediate counterattack by elements of both *Totenkopf* and *Wiking* prevented the Russians from cutting off *Wiking's* rear guard. The entire *IV. SS–Panzerkorps* would eventually wind up in and around Stuhlweissenburg, dogged by pursuing Soviets the entire way.

The next concern for the Germans was closing the gap in their lines north of Stuhlweissenburg and Zámoly, a distance of about six kilometers. Intended to stabilize the front and relieve pressure on Stuhlweissenburg, there were no new forces to use in an attack the next day. Consequently, *Totenkopf, 1. Panzer Division* and *4. Kavallerie Division* spent the

329

afternoon and evening of 2 February assembling near their jump-off positions.

Meanwhile, Russian attacks continued along the northern edge of Stuhlweissenburg, with the loss of eight tanks and no significant gains. The fighting took place in the vicinity of the brick works, while to the east *SS–Regiment Ney* stood firm against Soviet infantry attacks. In all likelihood the losses were inflicted by *I./Panzer Regiment 24*, which claimed five Shermans and three T-34s destroyed in the brick factory on the northern edge of the city. No source mentions *SS–Regiment Ney* and *I./Panzer Regiment 24* fighting side by side, but combining all sources verifies this must have been the case.[338]

What Balck had not yet done was order Gille's command to pull back in its entirety. On 2 February this led to Balck and Gille once again clashing when the Deputy Ia of *IV. SS–Panzerkorps*, the same position that Georg Maier held with *6. SS–Panzerarmee*, *SS–Sturmbannführer* Fritz Rentrop, was captured by a minor Russian incursion along the Seregélyes–Stuhlweissenburg road. No more than 60 men with two tanks pushed forward in a thick fog, probing German lines north of Seregélyes. Rentrop and a small group of others moved out of the corps headquarters to the new location at Stuhlweissenburg. Dense fog hung low to the landscape, and only one road connected the two towns. Balck had supposedly forbidden use of that road because the Russians were close, but there was no alternative except moving cross-country, an even more dangerous proposition. Moreover, Balck's claims of ordering the road closed were made after the war, not in the moment, and the War Diary of *Heeresgruppe Süd* makes no mention of such an order.

[338] Jentz, *Panzertruppen 2*, p. 225.

At the time, though, Balck was furious that Rentrop had been taken with important documents, potentially compromising the position of *Armeegruppe Balck*. Regardless of what actually happened, this incident further inflamed an already hostile situation between the army and the *Waffen–SS*. As for Rentrop, his body was found soon after, severely beaten. No doubt his captors had tortured him for whatever he could tell them about the tactical situation.

The poor weather proved catastrophic for air supply drops to the Budapest garrison, with a mere 2.5 tons making it into the city. In the end, to Hitler it only mattered how long the garrison could tie up significant enemy forces; with the failure of *Konrad III*, and his refusal to allow a breakout, the men in Budapest were doomed no matter how many supplies got through.

For the men still fighting inside Budapest, however, that reality was only beginning to sink in. One of the only ways for German units in the field to get news was from the official *Wehrmacht* daily report. For the past weeks the garrison's heroic fight in Budapest had been mentioned... but on 1 February it stopped. Nor did it resume the next day. That could only mean one thing: relief wasn't coming. They had been abandoned.[339]

For their parts, both Malinovsky and Tolbukhin felt it had already taken too long to capture the city. One of the heaviest bombardments yet ripped into the German and Hungarian positions south and west of the *Blutweise*, which continued to be the focus of Russian attacks. Along the south edge the garrison more or less held their ground, but in the west the pounding from artillery proved so devastating that the

---

[339] As we have read, the garrison *had* been abandoned; the outside forces simply weren't strong enough to break the Russian ring around Budapest. Except nobody bothered to tell the garrison.

Russians gained full kilometer in the direction of the final garrison positions along the Danube.

3 February, Saturday

Were the Soviets aware of the arrival of *6. SS–Panzerarmee* in Hungary before the Gran offensive? According to John Toland, Stalin reportedly said during the Yalta conference "the Nazis were stupid to leave eleven armored divisions around Budapest." (Whether Stalin meant other armored formations and not *6. SS–Panzerarmee,* or was exaggerating to emphasize the difference in the number of enemy units on each front, is not clear.) During this same meeting, FDR reportedly showed his Germanophobia by telling Stalin "I hope you again propose a toast to the execution of fifty thousand officers of the German Army."[340]

These feelings are very representative of Roosevelt's attitude regarding Germany in general; he saw no need for mercy to any German, nor any need for a trial of those fifty thousand officers before having them summarily executed. Such quotes went a long way toward stiffening German resistance, giving Goebbels' propaganda machine ammunition that it did not need to manufacture, just as FDR's unilateral call for unconditional surrender had done.

Although fighting occurred the previous day, for the most part the Russians spent 2 February resting and reorganizing. Not so on 3 February, when attacks began again. Units left depleted by combat were replaced by reinforcements, lending fresh energy to the Russian assaults. Heavy artillery bombardments shook the defenders, but if there was any good news to be found, the foggy weather limited Red Air Force missions.

The heaviest attacks once again struck around and to the south of Lake Velence, with tanks once

---

[340] Toland, *The Ladt Hundred Days*, p. 165.

again supporting infantry. The front lines here were thinly held by elements of *3. Panzer Division* and *5. SS–Panzer Division Wiking*. Numerous penetrations chopped the defenders into *kampfgruppen*, each of which had to be relieved by an immediate counterattack. Using all possible emergency reserves, the Germans restored a fragile line of resistance.

Balck considered withdrawing further, acknowledging that his forces were not adequate to holding their current positions. The rolling terrain prevented spotting Russian attack gathering points for interdiction by German artillery, and the fog that grounded the Red Air Force also blinded the Germans to incoming attacks. Having only sound for warning, the first hints of an assault often came when Russian infantry materialized out of the fog.

Unfortunately for the German command, friction between the *Waffen–SS* and Wöhler/Balck once again hampered operations. In its midday report, *Armeegruppe Balck* claimed that *3. SS–Panzer Division Totenkopf* had moved north of Stuhlweissenburg without orders, despite them having been sent there for the coming attack to plug the gap between Zámoly and Stuhlweissenburg. The previous day Balck had reported that "he had the impression that the Russians were at the end of their strength."[341] The newest attacks proved that to be untrue, meaning that Balck needed to distance himself from *Totenkopf's* movement in case it backfired.

As for the action in question along Stuhlweissenburg's northern boundary, the German counterattacks using *panzers* drove the Russians back in the area of the munitions factory, which they captured. The AFVs came from *I./Panzer Regiment 24* and *Totenkopf*, while another component of the attacking force was *SS–Regiment Ney*, which that day was at the center of a controversy so ludicrous that it almost defies belief.

[341] Maier, *Drama Between Budapest and Vienna*, p. 78.

As noted earlier, the ruler of Hungary at that moment was Ferenc Szalasi, head of the Arrow Cross movement whom the Germans installed to replace the deposed Admiral Horthy during the previous November, when Horthy tried to switch sides and have Hungary join the Soviets in fighting against their erstwhile allies, the Germans. Led by Otto Skorzeny, the Germans staged a coup to replace Horthy with someone more loyal to the Axis cause, and Szalasi was chosen. Hungary was largely overrun by this point, of course, and the only thing keeping Szalasi in power was Hitler's continued favor. Nevertheless, Szalasi seems to have been playing a game to try and curry favor with the Allies after the war was over, by not agreeing that Hungarian troops could be used against the Western Allies; that is, they could only fight against the Red Army[342].

On 3 February, Ney himself was handed, at his command post, an order carried by special courier from Szalasi, stating that his unit was fighting illegally, came under the command of the Hungarian Honved and that it should immediately detach itself from the fighting and report to Koszeg, there to await further orders. The order went on to say that if Ney did not obey the order, then he and his men would be stripped of their Hungarian citizenship. Ney pointed to the Hungarian-German Treaty as the basis for his not following the order. Needless to say, when Ney ignored the order both he and his men were deprived of their citizenship,[343] although this had no significant effect in

---

[342] This issue came up again very late in the war, when the two Hungarian SS divisions, the 25th and 26th, were ordered to fight against the advancing Americans, only to be led by their commanders to the lake region of Western Austria where they eventually surrendered after only skirmishes with the Americans.

[343] It would be interesting to know why the Germans allowed such an attitude from a puppet who ruled solely at their discretion. Granted, had they have moved against him it might have angered many of the Hungarians still fighting the Russians, but such benevolence toward allies was not something that typically happened. Perhaps since Ney ignored the order Hitler or the High Command saw no need for further action.

the short term. It *does* go to show the duplicity of even Germany's most loyal (supposedly) allies. A man like Szalasi only continued living through the protection of the Germans; without them he held absolutely no power.

As for Stuhlweissenburg, the fighting raged along its northern boundary by a Russian attack that nearly broke through into the city. A report from *I./Panzer Regiment 24* says that the battalion commander saw the danger but was ordered to attack the heights three kilometers north of the city to threaten the rear of the Soviet tank group, along with an unknown group of *Tigers*, which must surely have come from *Schwere Panzer Abteilung 509*. In any event they had to be *Tiger IIs*.

Despite his protests that conditions were too poor the *I./Panzer Regiment 24* was ordered once again to attack, which it did in mist and fog; visibility was less than 100 meters and the battalion had little idea of what it faced. Inevitably it stumbled into strong Russian defenses and was stopped after taking losses, while the *Tiger IIs* were frantically ordered back to Stuhlweissenburg's northern perimeter to stave off the Russian tank attack before it could completely shatter the German defense.[344]

There is no record now of who ordered the attack. The only thing that can be stated for sure are the result. Men died, irreplaceable *panzers* went up in flames and nothing was accomplished. The end result of the day's fighting was that the Russians north of Stuhlweissenburg were thrown onto the defense, at great cost to the Germans.

[344] Jentz, *Panzertruppen 2*, p. 224.

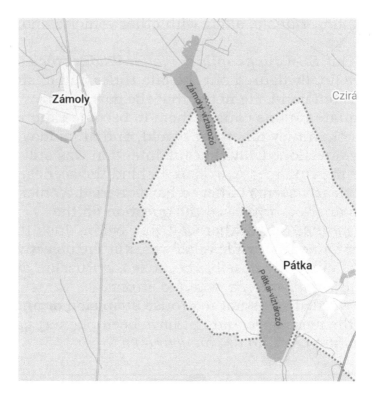

The intention was to renew the attack on 4 February, aiming for the village of Patka, which lay on the eastern edge of a reservoir. Close by on the north was another reservoir, this one of Zámoly, with only a narrow land bridge between the two bodies of water. This was a strong defensive position for an army with too few forces to properly man its front lines.

Events within Budapest ground toward their inevitable end.

The focus of Russian assaults remained to the south, southwest and west, along with the Palace District. A particularly severe thrust backed by tanks cut deep into the German defense along the western perimeter, splintering the defenders into isolated strongpoints. In the south, *IX SS–Gebirgs–Armee Korps* noted eight Russian tanks destroyed, mostly using

using *panzerfäuste*, along with other vehicles and guns.

But *SS–Gruppenführer Pfeffer-Wildenbruch* seems to have finally figured out the fate Hitler had in store for his command. He noted that the garrison's inadequate rations caused them to become exhausted sooner than they otherwise would, and at midday he openly questioned whether the intention was still to relieve the Budapest garrison. Behind the scenes, Balck clearly seems either to have queried Wöhler on how to answer, or passed the question on the *Heeresgruppe Süd*. Either way, just before dusk the answer came that while relief was still the objective, it was not currently possible because the Russian attacks on *IV. SS–Panzerkorps* were too strong.

Worded so as not to arouse suspicion or anger by *OKH*, the message could not have been plainer; *you've been written off and are on your own.*

4 February, Sunday

In a very real sense the Germans were in a race against time to establish a defensive line that could hold, before the fall of Budapest released all of those attack forces for use elsewhere. Having made progress the day before, and forced the Russians onto the defensive, *1. Panzer Division* and *3. SS–Panzer Division Totenkopf* again moved forward in the same area as previously, aiming for the village of Patka.

As before the fighting proved hard and the spearheads reached the Zámoly-Stuhlweissenburg Road. However, plans to keep moving east toward Patka gave way to realities of the moment; fighting to the south and west threatened to overwhelm *IV. SS–Panzerkorps*. Reports of renewed Russian attacks into the so-called Stuhlweissenburg Gap were written off by *Heeresgruppe Süd* intelligence as likely being deceptions.

Regardless, in the short term the Russian attack to retake Stuhlweissenburg from the north was finally crushed on the 4 February, driving the Soviets back to their original defensive lines with the loss of 47 tanks. *I./Panzer Regiment 24* reported catching the Russians in a pincer movement and claimed 26 tanks and 45 anti-tank guns destroyed. Such a devastating defeat relieved the pressure on the city and gave the Germans a brief period of respite from the weeks of nearly continuous combat; in the weeks to come those 47 Russian tanks might have made the difference between survival and destruction for *Heeresgruppe Süd*.

Balck had bigger worries, though. The danger to *IV. SS–Panzerkorps* near Lake Velence had the potential to turn catastrophic. Worse, while few aerial reconnaissance flights could penetrate the fog, those that did showed an estimated 800-1,000 Russian vehicles assembling for a counterattack north of Stuhlweissenberg. With no reserves, Balck requested permission to withdraw both *1. Panzer Division* and *3.*

Panzer Division to form a mobile reserve in case of an enemy breakthrough in either position.

A further benefit would be that since the Germans paid dearly for their victory between Zámoly and Stuhlweissenburg, the heavy price might be partially mitigated by allowing the maintenance crews of *1. Panzer Division* to restore the huge backlog of damaged and broken down *Mark V Panthers* back to service. In the meantime, though, the *panzer* divisions fielded an average of 10 serviceable *panzers*, while their *panzergrenadier* regiments had perhaps 200 men fit to fight.

The commander of *III–Panzerkorps*, *General der Panzertruppe* Breith, openly wondered whether such a move was even possible. The two divisions were under his command, and had suffered such terrible casualties they might not be able to disengage. Regardless, *Heeresgruppe Süd* sent the request through to Hitler, and waited for his reply.

Late in the day *SS–Obergruppenführer* Pfeffer-Wildenbruch sent a long and borderline insubordinate report from inside the shrinking Axis-controlled portion of Budapest. At this point the garrison might have had enough power to launch a breakout attempt to save some of them, but thousands of wounded would have to be left to the Russians; nobody had any illusions of what that meant. If they weren't shot out of hand, at best they could look forward to a life of slavery in Siberia.

Prefer-Wildenbruch started by describing the terrible fighting over the last few days, primarily from the south and the northwest. The Russian assaults came in great strength and using numerous tanks, and while the German MLR mostly held in place, there were two break-ins that needed to be sealed off. He also applauds the *Luftwaffe* for positively affecting the fighting by bombing and strafing the Russian concentrations, while also engaging the Red Air Force and preventing attacks on the garrison. *Luftflotte 4* record 460 ground-attack sorties on 4 February, a huge total for so late in the war. Aside from airplane numbers, that represented a major expenditure of fuel. Unfortunately, only a trickle of 6.9 tons of supplies were dropped into German lines.

It is worth quoting part of the transmission at length. First, he responds to a message received on 3 February to hold until relieved.

> "The overwhelming enemy superiority in men and materiel and the events of the war at home have had a very depressing effect on the men. A slice of bread and horsemeat is the only daily ration for the personnel. Every movement is hard because of physical weakness. Despite that, in spite of six weeks of promised relief, the men continue to fight hard and stubbornly and to obey... Typhus is increasing in the miserable holes and casemates, but no effective measures against it are possible..."

To be clear, Pfeffer-Wildenbruch was an *SS* Police General, the *Ordnungspolizei*, not the *Waffen–SS*. Having served on Himmler's staff, he was a true believer in Hitler and Nazism. For him to not-so-subtly reprimand the command staff, and indirectly Hitler himself, shows how far his spirits had fallen. Living amid constant warfare and observing the daily suffering of everyone involved, enemy and friend alike, not to mention civilians caught in the maelstrom, must have taken its toll on his resolve. On the morning of 4 February he sent the message that must have been forming itself in his thoughts for days.

> "On the basis of the message dated 1905 hours on 3 February – *Führer* order to fight until relieved – is not practicable as a consequence of

reasons already known. Request local command authority for any tactical measures."

Hermann Balck dutifully relayed the message to *OKH,* but cautioned that in the meantime nothing had changed. A full 12 hours later the response was that Hitler had not yet made up his mind about Budapest, because he (Hitler) had to concern himself with the Big Picture, his usual excuse for intransigence.[345]

Pfeffer-Wildenbruch might as well have asked for passage to the moon.

[345] Maier, *Drama Between Budapest and Vienna,* p. 80.

5 February, Monday

In Budapest, very strong Russian attacks crushed parts of the MLR on the west, either killing the defenders or forcing them to retreat toward the final positions. In particular, the Sashegy, aka Adler Hill, was finally taken by the Soviets and the various flak batteries there, the 88s of *Kampfgruppe Portugall* and the smaller 37 and 20 mm guns, all had to be withdrawn to the last lines of defense around the university and castle. Every withdrawal further concentrated the relentless Russian bombardment, which increased German casualties and precipitated more retreats.

Russian artillery fire could now hit nearly anywhere within the garrison's perimeter. In particular, the positions of the German artillery came under direct fire, which made them nearly indefensible. Yet they were the last land link between Buda Castle and the Citadel. Built in the 1850s atop Gellért Hill, the Citadel was a purpose-built fortress that, while not constructed to withstand modern artillery, nevertheless provided the best defensive position left in Buda. With Russian shells now raining down on their own artillery batteries, it became increasingly clear the final days had come.

The end drew near.

Prefer-Wildenbruch did not give up on saving those he could, however. Late in the day he radioed *Armeegruppe Balck* "Holding Budapest and the destruction of the pocket was a question of days. At that point the tying down of enemy forces would become moot."[346]

He went on to say that a good number of men could likely fight their way to German lines the next day, if orders were received in a timely fashion. This was probably both true, and probably the last such opportunity. The Russian advance on 5 February had

---

[346] Maier, *Drama Between Budapest and Vienna*, p. 80.

been so great they might not have had time to consolidate their gains yet. The odds of escape diminished with each passing hour, though.

Armeegruppe Balck passed the message up to *Heeresgruppe Süd*. *General der Infanterie* Wöhler sent Prefer-Wildenbruch's message, but added an addendum that the *Führerbefehl* concerning the garrison's mission, to hold out until relieved, was understood, the order was still being followed by *Heeresgruppe Süd*, and could not have been more clear. In order to stay on Hitler's good side, Wöhler and Balck once again thought nothing of placing the blame on the *SS*. The overall negative effect on morale was easy to predict.

However, in the early afternoon Balck did propose yet another relief effort, a *Konrad IV* or something similar. Balck claimed that such a force could succeed because to enemy was so weakened by earlier attacks as to make it possible. The axis would move through the northern Vértes Mountains straight to Budapest, then follow the Danube south to crush 3rd Ukrainian Front and protect the oil fields. The plan called for using forces already on the rolls of *Heeresgruppe Süd*.

On the surface of it the plan was preposterous. None of the divisions left in *Heeresgruppe Süd* had marginal offensive capabilities, much less enough firepower to break into Budapest. The question now is whether Balck actually believed this fantasy, or was pandering to Hitler at the expense of the *Waffen-SS*. At its core the attack was simply a repeat of *Konrad II*, the least successful of the three previous attempts.

There is no doubt that had the forces been available Balck could have been right. His record as a sterling *panzer* commander could not be questioned. Yet in the same message he stated the poor state of both *1. Panzer Division* and *3. Panzer Division*. With *every* division in the same condition, what 'fresh forces' did he propose using? And when?

344

There were no units in either *8. Armee* or *2. Panzerarmee* capable of offensive action. Indeed, *8. Armee* could not even eliminate the dangerous Russian bridgehead west of the Gran River. So why did Balck propose something he had to know was impossible?

At 0040 hours, Hitler permitted the withdrawal of *1. Panzer Division* and *3. Panzer Division* to their reserve position. As they did so the Russians did not immediately follow; the Germans were well-known for launching counterattacks under such circumstances, to catch their enemy off-balance and strung out while advancing.

That did not mean they ceased all attacks, though. Seregélyes remained the gateway to the Margarethe Position and the Russians had no intention of easing the pressure against *5. SS–Panzer Division Wiking.* Heavy tank-supported attacks penetrated in two places, and while breakthroughs were prevented by quick counterattacks, the lost ground could not be recovered.

Defeat of the Russian attacks along Stuhlweissenburg's northern limits allowed *SS–Regiment Ney,* by now a valued but battered and depleted formation, to be withdrawn from the front to reorganize, absorb replacements and rest at the small town of Sur, south of Kisber.[347] It was once again attached to *IV. SS–Panzerkorps* as a reserve. During the fight for Stuhlweissenburg, the Regiment had suffered extreme losses, with casualties of 171 men killed, 300 wounded and 49 missing. It had destroyed 17 tanks during the battle, nearly fifty percent of all Russian tank losses suffered in battle; in addition, 12 German tanks that had been taken by the Russians were

---

[347] Once source puts this withdrawal as 26 January, and another as 23 January, with the second source claiming that one battalion was left behind in Stuhlweissenburg.

recaptured and, after being repaired, were turned over the *6./Panzer Regiment 1.* Numerous awards were authorized, including the German Cross in gold to the Regiment's commander, Karoly Ney.[348]

Unlike the *1. Ungarische SS–Sturm Regiment,* which had suffered badly and then been disbanded to provide infantry for other formations, on the personal order of Adolf Hitler *SS–Regiment Ney* had been awarded an honorific cuff band for its prowess and courage and was kept intact. Because of its origin as a unit composed of Eastern Front Hungarian veterans, and also the political power of those who helped it organize, it was granted full status as an *SS* formation, unlike many Axis Allied formations that had a secondary status denoted by the designation of 'Waffen'; for example, *14. Waffen–Grenadier Division der SS 'Galicia',*[349] or the *25. Waffen–Grenadier Division der SS* and *26. Waffen–Grenadier Division der SS.*[350] Such units were considered part of the *Waffen–SS,* but of a lower order than a full *SS* unit, much like Roman Auxiliaries in the days of the Roman Republic and Empire. Upgrading *SS–Regiment Ney* meant that it was how considered the equal of German *SS* units.

As part of its reorganization, the unit was designated as a cavalry/reinforced mounted regiment. Replacements and new volunteers poured into the regiment, and it was ordered that the regiment expand into a brigade, officially titled *SS Cavalry Brigade Ney,* but almost always referred to simply as '*SS-Brigade Ney'.*[351] The new men were either *Volksdeutsche* or

---

[348] Pencz, *Siegrunen Volume 76,* p. 17.

[349] Later re-designated 'Ukraine'.

[350] One difference between the two types of SS units was that the two Hungarian divisions technically came under the command of the Hungarian Army, the Honved, while all other SS formations, including SS-Bridgade Ney, were commanded by the SS Main Office. On the surface of it this would not seem terribly important, but in practice this convoluted command structure may have kept the two Hungarian SS divisions out of serious combat with the Western Allies.

[351] An obvious question is why so many men wanted to join Ney's unit, with Germany's defeat so clearly in sight. Wouldn't Hungarian men have wanted

Germans who spoke Hungarian. A great number of them were specialists, such as translators, radiomen and other signals troops. As the unit continued to grow it even added a reconnaissance detachment. Unusually for the *Waffen-SS*, the new brigade had a chaplain, a Franciscan monk who held services and administered to the unit's many Catholics.[352]

---

to melt into the back country and hope to avoid notice? There are no records to officially indicate preferential supply treatment for *Waffen–SS* units, and yet the circumstantial evidence is compelling. Men in the *Waffen–SS* would be fed if it was humanly possible to do so.

[352] Pencz, *Siegrunen Volume 76*, p. 19-20.

6 February, Tuesday

A German press release announced that Joachim Peiper had been awarded the Swords for his Knight's Cross, given to him by Hitler personally on 4 February. After the turn of the New Year, Peiper mysteriously dropped out of the records of the *1. SS Panzer* Division LAH, with famed *Waffen–SS* historian Michael Reynolds speculating that, based on medical records which still exist, Peiper probably broke down under the strain of command during the Ardennes Offensive and had been on convalescent leave for the following month or so.[353] Peiper eventually returned to the division, where he saw heavy fighting in Hungary and Austria until the final surrender in May. *Kampfgruppe Peiper* would again terrorize the battlefield.

5. SS Panzer Division Wiking had tried to reform its defensive positions at the so-called Margarethe Line, between Selegelyes and Lake Velence. *Wiking* was worn-out and barely combat capable, on 6 February it was downgraded to a *kampfgruppe* because of its weakened condition. The Russians quickly learned of its depleted state and wasted no time in attacking. Despite standing their ground and not retreating, Red Army spearheads nevertheless penetrated the German positions and heavy fighting was the result.

Wiking reeled backward, with various sub-units being scattered ahead of advancing Russian armor. Some 20 or so tanks attacked north from a breakthrough at Seregélyes toward Stuhlweissenburg, and were only stopped with difficulty. The line finally held, but only with help from elements of *1. Panzer*

---

[353] Reynolds, Michael, *The Devil's Adjutant*, (Barnsley: Pen & Sword, 2009), pp. 247-248.

Division that had only recently been withdrawn from the front lines.

SS–Obergruppenführer und General der Waffen–SS Gille traveled to the headquarters of *III. Panzerkorps* to award the Knight's Cross to *Generalmajor* Eberhard Thunert, commander of *1. Panzer Division.* Despite the derision of his Army superiors, Gille had always been a beloved leader whose chief concern was the welfare of his men, and he looked far more like an academic than a warrior.[354] With a large nose, ready smile and ever-present glasses, the 47 year-old Gille appeared nothing like what he was: the most decorated man in the *Waffen-SS*, winner of the Knight's Cross with Oak Leaves, Swords and Diamonds. His men would, and did, march through Hell for him.

It should be noted that Balck and Wöhler both had the respect of their men, with both being personally brave and, better, highly respected as professionals. Wöhler's noted competence commanded respect from his fellow officers, since he'd been most impressive as a staff officer. Balck aggressive nature, coolness under fire and extreme competence as a division commander made those under his command believe that he could lead them to victory. Balck's failure as commander of a *Heeresgruppe* had little to do with him, being mostly owed to the Germans being outnumbered and outgunned. From the standpoint of the Germans, therefore, the rift the two men exacerbated with the *Waffen–SS* units under their command only tarnished their heretofore excellent records.

However, it *was* true that Wöhler wanted to recover the initiative in his area by renewing offensive operations, so perhaps Balck either convinced Wöhler

---

[354] After the war, Gille became a mail order bookseller, something that suited his appearance perfectly.

to do this, or vice versa. *IV. SS–Panzerkorps* would again be the attack force, supported by another (unnamed) division. Furthermore, *8. Armee* would eliminate the Gran Bridgehead, and *6. Panzer Division* would move south.

Once again this proposal had no bearing on reality. *IV. SS–Panzerkorps* was fought out, and its two divisions would never recover. Nor were any other armored formations more than burned-out formations. *OKH* did not reject these ideas, but did warn Wöhler not to count on any reinforcements. Hitler did allow moving *6. Panzer Division* into reserve, though, a minor victory for *Heeresgruppe Süd*. At least if needed further south it would not have to withdraw from the MLR.

The death knell officially sounded for the Budapest garrison at 0240 hours on 6 February, and seen from a distance of 80 years it could not have been more absurd.

> "... the *Führer* had turned down the request of the Commanding General of the *IX SS–Gebirgs–Armee–Korps*... He saw no further possibility for the garrison to break out intact. The few that could fight their way through in small groups did not compensate for the enemy forces that could be tied down by the garrison while it was still in one place."[355]

For weeks Hitler had forbade a breakout to tie down enemy forces. Now that the garrison was on the verge of being wiped out, he denied letting them break out because they were too weak.

It was Stalingrad all over again. Hitler had learned nothing in two years of war. The men dying in his name were mere numbers. Nor could there be any

[355] Maier, *Drama Between Budapest and Vienna*, p. 81.

reason for their sacrifice now, except to delay the inevitable, and the only advantage in that lay in prolonging the lives of those ordering the men to die.

Loss of the Adler Hill meant certain doom for the garrison, with fragmentation of the perimeter being only a matter of how long the survivors could hold out. Fighting continued around the next-to-last positions, the South Railway Station and the artillery positions. The torpor of the defenders from exhaustion and lack of food contributed materially to their diminishing capacity to resist, although considering the conditions it was incredible they still fought at all. No one wanted to fall into Russian hands, so the only alternative was to keep fighting and pray for deliverance. As a final note for the day, the garrison reported having 11,000 wounded in their lines, whose only rations were 15 grams of beans and a half slice of bread daily, roughly 100 calories.

7 February, Wednesday

Local combat had reached something of a lull, although combat continued in many locations. In the Margarethe Position between the Sarviz Canal and Lake Balaton, Russian attacks dislodged the Hungarian 25th Infantry Division. Possessing few heavy weapons, the Hungarians did not have the means of the morale to fight against heavy odds or raining artillery barrages. The possibility that the division might simply melt away left Wöhler and Balck struggling with how to close the gap given the paucity of forces on hand.

Complicating the situation, further east in the sector defended by *III. Panzerkorps*, a breakthrough by a strong Russian armored group, likely the same 20 tanks that attacked north from the breakthrough at Seregélyes on 6 February, was destroyed by the combined effort of *1. Panzer Division*, parts of *3. Panzer Division*, and *Wiking*. Eighteen Russian tanks were destroyed in the counterattack, but it required the efforts of three divisions to do it.

If there seemed a moment to take a deep breath and refocus, it was short-lived. Otto Wöhler was ordered to personally report to Hitler to discuss future operations in Hungary. Following this, *Heeresgruppe Süd* received an order for the conduct of defensive operations. It was transmitted by courier, not radio, an indication of how important *OKH* considered its contents.

The document showed a clear understanding of future Red Army attack plans aimed at capturing Stuhlweissenburg and the industrial regions to the west, which included bringing 6th Guards Tank Army to the front and reconstituting their mechanized forces in the Stuhlweissenburg Gap. It also predicted an attack out of the Gran Bridgehead by 7th Guards Tank Army along with the Pliyev Group, officially known as the 1st Guards Mechanized Cavalry Group. Formed by Hero of the Soviet Union Lieutenant General Issa Pliyev, the Pliyev Group was an Army-sized deep-exploitation force that had been extremely successful in the years since Stalingrad. Powerful and well-equipped, it was an excellent predictor of future Russian plans.

Heeresgruppe Süd was ordered to form a defense-in-depth according to *OKH* plans, showing once again how little commanders could influence events on their own fronts. But... Wöhler was being given *four panzer divisions* to "bolster the defense."[356] Sepp Dietrich was on his way with *6. SS–Panzerarmee*. The order went so far as to instruct Wöhler and Balck where to quarter this massive infusion of combat power, and to prepare the 'Klara' position for their arrival. This defensive position was more marks on a map than reality, since even the most rudimentary fortifications required constant maintenance to be useable when needed. Oddly, the *Aufklärungsabteilungen* from those four *SS Panzer Divisions* were all to be assembled in one command north of the Danube, near Komorn, to act as a ready reserve. This could only have been done to try and counter movements from the Pliyev Group.

Wöhler must have been simultaneously dubious and excited at receiving the most powerful armored formation left in the German Order of Battle. He likely wasn't aware of how weak the divisions were compared to their authorized Tables of Organization and Equipment, yet given the skeletal nature of his *Heeresgruppe* any reinforcements would have been welcome.

Hermann Balck, on the other hand, does not seem to have been overly impressed by the news. Otto Gille was an *SS–Obergruppenführer*, the equivalent to a *Generalleutnant* of the *Heer*. Other *Heer* specialized ranks, such as Hermann Balck as a *General der Panzertruppen* and Otto Wöhler as a *General der Infanterie*, were merely another version of a *Generalleutnant*. Therefore, *SS–Obergruppenführer* Gille was the same rank as Wöhler and Balck.

---

[356] Maier, *Drama Between Budapest and Vienna*, p. 419.

As an *SS–Oberstgruppenführer*, Sepp Dietrich theoretically outranked them all, with the rank equivalent to a *Generaloberst* in the *Heer*. This made him the same rank as Heinz Guderian. His army would not be under the command of Hermann Balck. No doubt Gille hoped to be put under Dietrich's command, but that would not happen.

No respite came for the defenders of Budapest. As expected, the intensity of the bombardment increased; the Russians had just as many artillery tubes, but a much smaller target area. Heavy attacks continued around the South Railway Station as the MLR continued to fragment. Surrounded groups could no longer be relieved, and had no choice save to fight their way back to friendly lines.

And yet despite poor weather conditions, the *Luftwaffe* managed to fly ground-support sorties in the area of the South Railway Station, and to drop 16 tons of supplies within the perimeter. Given the small area still controlled by the garrison, this was a difficult task. Sixteen tons would not sustain resistance for long, though.

8 February, Thursday

The Russian 297th Infantry Division, supported by units for 3rd Tank Brigade, 23rd Tank Corps, had virtually surrounded the South Railway Station after days of vicious fighting. Strategically speaking the position was critical as the last fortified strongpoint west of the *Blutweise*, which itself was considered by the Germans as the final position. Once taken, the Russians could cross the Bloody Meadow and assault the final redoubts on Castle Hill.

Rather than cut their way out to join the remnants of the garrison, the defenders were told to hang on until relieved. Held by starving and exhausted elements of *Florian Geyer*, the only relief force available was a single platoon of Hungarians, likely 20-30 men strong, from the 102nd Chemical Warfare Battalion. Crossing Bloody Meadow under heavy fire, the Hungarians suffered heavy casualties for little gain.

Simultaneously from the southwest, attacks by the fresh 25th Guards Rifle Division followed yet another heavy mortar and artillery bombardment and made significant progress. Elsewhere at Gellért Hill, fighting reached the lower slopes.

None of the Russian penetrations proved fatal to the defense, but it took stripping defenses along the Danube to maintain any sort of cohesive perimeter. Along the river, though, only outposts remained; a determined crossing from Pest would have met minimal resistance.

Using the last of their ammunition, the guns of *SS–Flak Abteilung 8*, the antiaircraft component of *8 Waffen–SS–Kavallerie Division Florian Geyer*, shot down their 75th aircraft over Budapest. The useless guns were finally left on the grounds of the university near Castle Hill, while their crews served as infantry.

The garrison was clearly in its death throes. Using maximum effort, *Luftflotte 4* managed to drop 4.5 tons of supplies. The garrison appreciated the effort but the actual effects no longer made sense versus the risk.

Nor were the Hungarian Honvéd units willing to die for Hitler any longer; desertions to the enemy increased dramatically. One day the Hungarians fought with the Germans to kill Russians, and the next day they fought with the Russians to kill Germans.

On 8 February the *SS–Führungshauptamt (SS-FHA)* authorized the formation of a third *SS* Cavalry Division, the *33. SS-Freiwilligen Kavallerie Division,* "from remnant elements of the 8th Cavalry Division destroyed in Budapest[357] and the 22nd *SS* Volunteer Cavalry Division plus ... Hungarian ethnic Germans and Hungarian volunteers."[358]

As with so many late war units there is considerable confusion surrounding the unit's formation. This division is often dismissed as never having been fully formed, or not seeing action. In fact, the core of the division were 6,000 ethnic German Hungarians who had been inducted the previous autumn but never assigned to a unit, along with the re-forming *SS–Reiter Regiment 17.* Other men came from the *SS Kavallerie Ausbildung und Ersatz Abteilung* in Beneschau, near Prague. Unlike the *8. SS–Freiwillige–Kavallerie Division Florian Geyer, 33. Waffen–SS–Freiwilligen–Kavallerie Division* was only to have two cavalry regiments of two battalions each, and an authorized strength of only 6,600 men. The numbering of other newly forming *SS* divisions forced a change in the division's number, however, and by February 19 the new *SS* cavalry division was being referred to as the *37. Waffen–SS Freiwilligen–Kavallerie Division.*

In the west, *II. SS–Panzerkorps* began loading for the harrowing train-ride east. While within range of

---

[357] It is significant that on February 8th , even as the desperate survivors of 8th SS were still fighting in Budapest, that the SS had already written the division off as destroyed.

[358] Michaelis, *Cavalry Division of the Waffen SS*, p. 126.

Allied fighter-bombers the trains would move by night and hide by day. Only the most senior officers knew their final destination, those of division command or higher, but as the men moved through Munich and then Salzburg, they correctly surmised their final destination as Hungary.

For most of *Heeresgruppe Süd* the relative quiet that settled over the area must have come as a welcome interlude. Not so for those who knew what the calm presaged; replenishment and refilling of depleted enemy formations, introduction of new equipment, training, return of wounded to their home units, and the stockpiling of supplies for future operations. As the fall of Budapest became imminent, German intelligence understood the flood of Russian forces that would be released for use elsewhere. Of particular concern was the heavy artillery that could by itself tear holes in the fragile front lines of *Armeegruppe Balck*.

As 8 February closed, word came from the *Führer* Headquarters once again denying the Budapest garrison's request to breakout, and for the same reasons as before; they were going to die either way, so they might as well die tying down Russian forces for as long as possible. To Hitler such ruthlessly pragmatic arithmetic made perfect sense, but not to the flesh and blood men the numbers represented. To them, any chance was better than no chance.

9 February, Friday

Berlin

Chef der Generalstabs Heinz Guderian, the father of the blitzkrieg and Germany's leading proponent of massed tank tactics before the war, went to the daily *Führer* conference at the *Reich* Chancellery with one thought in mind: a final showdown over the disposition of troops to stop Zhukov's drive on Berlin. Never a man given to thinking in terms of defense, Guderian wanted to launch an immediate counterattack on Zhukov's spearheads to cut them off and destroy them. The idea was sound, even Hitler liked the idea of the attack and would eventually order it carried out as *Unternehmen Solstice*. The troops to make it successful, however, were not available without the evacuation of the Kurland Peninsula, Königsberg, Italy, Norway and the transfer of *6. SS–Panzerarmee* to the north, not the south.

Hitler would not hear any of it. Those troops must hold where they were, Hitler insisted, acting as bridgeheads for when the inevitable counterattack took place, most likely in conjunction with American and British troops.

The *Generaloberst* appears to have been trying to play Hitler to get a concession. Guderian could not have been serious about including units from Norway, Italy or even Kurland. Such an attack would have needed to be launched quickly, before Zhukov could consolidate his gains, and the transport capacity to ship units from the outlying reaches of even the shrunken *Reich* would have been very hard to arrange. Most likely he included them knowing this, intending them as concessions in the argument that he must have known was coming from Hitler. But sending *6. SS–Panzerarmee* northeast to the Oder Front instead of Hungary was very much more possible and, indeed, seemed like the obvious move. *6. SS–Panzerarmee* was the most powerful combat Army left to Germany and at that moment it was earmarked for Hungary after a series of loud and violent arguments with Hitler. Guderian simply could not understand committing this last offensive asset anywhere but on the Berlin front. The problem of fueling all of those tanks and *SPWs* was for a later day.

The issue of what to do with *6. SS–Panzerarmee* had been debated within *Führer* Headquarter for more than three weeks at that point, but was finally coming to a head; as it turned out, Guderian lost his argument, but not without a fight. The bigger issue was that of finding reserves for the Berlin Front, and all of the formations listed above. He reportedly said "you must believe me when I say that it is not stubbornness that makes me keep insisting on the evacuation of Kurland. I can see no other way left to us of accumulating reserves, and without reserves we cannot hope to defend the capital."[359] This was all well and good and completely within Guderian's duties as *Chef der Generalstabs*; had he left it there he might even have won a concession or two on troop movements. Never the diplomat, though, the *Generaloberst* kept going with words that had precisely the opposite effect than he intended. "I assure you I am acting solely in Germany's interests," he said.

That roused a heretofore relatively calm *Führer* to fury. Self-restraint had never been a trait that Adolf Hitler was known for and as the war went against Germany he was less and less in control of his temper. With Berlin in ruins around him that day was no exception.

"How dare you speak to me like that?" he said, rising, his body trembling. "'Don't you think I am fighting for Germany? My whole life has been one long struggle for Germany!"[360]

Reichsmarschall Herman Göring led Guderian out of the conference room to calm down, before Hitler ordered him to be shot. But when Guderian returned to

---

[359] Toland, *The Last 100 Days*, p. 84.
[360] Ibid.

the conference the argument flared up again and Guderian was removed a second time. Finally, when both men had regained control of themselves, Hitler agreed to Guderian's attack plans, but only with forces already on hand. No units would be withdrawn from anywhere, and *6. SS–Panzerarmee* would go to Hungary.

In Hungary's dying capital, the defenders learned what *SS–Obergruppenführer* Pfeffer-Wildenbruch already knew; that *IX. SS-Waffen-Gebirgs-Armeekorps der SS*' request to be allowed to break out was turned down by Hitler yet again, primarily because it was too late and would throw away troops that were tying down large numbers of Russian troops. In effect, Hitler told them to die in place.

And dying they were. Except for horse meat, the meager rations would be gone the next day. Artillery ammunition was down to three or four days, even at the reduced usage rate. There was no real perimeter anymore, but more of a loosely connected pocket.

Heavy attacks once again struck the west and southwest sectors, and it became obvious that one thrust aimed at the Elizabeth Bridge, which would have the result of driving a wedge between the defenders. Nor could the Russians be wholly stopped anymore, or thrown back after penetrations. Much ground was lost around the South Railway Station. The fighting moved into multi-story buildings that acted as elevated observation and firing positions. The defenders became ever more compressed, leaving less and less room to retreat.

The smaller portion of Gellért Hill changed hands several times, until the Russians finally secured possession. Losing that hill was a blow. Nor did air supply raise the German spirits; heavy snow grounded the *Luftwaffe.*

For *Armeegruppe Balck* the brief interval of
relative quiet ended in renewed Russian attacks
between the Sarviz Canal and Stuhlweissenburg. As
feared, the Hungarian 25th Infantry Division broke up
under a heavy assault and scattered, allowing the
Russians to rip a 12 kilometer wide gap in the front.
Fortunately for the Germans, Balck had foreseen such
an eventuality and finagled having 6. *Panzer Division* in
place as a ready reserve. An immediate counterattack
not only threw the Russians back, but re-established
contact with *III. Panzerkorps*.

New attacks hit the same area as in previous
days between Lake Velence and Seregélyes. In some
places the Russians penetrated the defenses, such as
the village of Dinnyés, a critical position located directly
in the middle of a land bridge between flooded lowlands
on the west, and Lake Velence on the east. With little
terrain suitable for tanks, its loss would have been a
blow to the German defense of Stuhlweissenburg. For a
time the defenders were cut off and surrounded, before
counterattacks restored them to the German MLR. But
it was a close-run thing.

From that point forward the defenders could only
be supplied during periods that obscured the trucks
from Russian artillery spotters, that is, in dense fog or
at night. The prepared positions of the Margarethe Line
lay to the north, nearer Stuhlweissenburg, so the
decision to abandon Dinnyés was not an easy one. Yet
the village was no longer defensible, either. He could
not take even this relatively minor action on his own
initiative, though, so he sent a request up the chain of
command.

Everywhere else along the front of *Armeegruppe
Balck* things remained fairly quiet, except for patrolling
by both sides. The real problem now was what to do
with the Hungarian 25th Infantry Division. Under ideal

circumstances the division might have been stood down, or even broken up to provide replacements for better units. That was not an option for Hermann Balck or Otto Wöhler, who needed every man they could find to hold the front lines.

The Hungarians were forward of the Margarethe Line, and Balck feared that if they were allowed to retreat to those positions that would crack again, only with no fall back options. Once the Russians moved north of Lake Balaton, *Armeegruppe Balck* would be fatally outflanked. Yet he also could not trust the Hungarians not to flee a second time under Russian attacks.

Nor was the concern only for that single isolated infantry division. *Every* Hungarian unit was suspect, particularly the Hungarian 3rd Army in the north Vértes Mountains. Even the elite Svent László Division had cracked in the past, meaning the supposedly first-rate Hussar Division might do the same thing. *Heeresgruppe Süd* blamed Hungarian leadership for the failures, as those units could withstand heavy Russian attacks for short periods, but unlike most German formations they would dissolve under continued pressure.

To solve this problem, Wöhler proposed placing the divisions under German control. As an immediate measure, Balck ordered the escort companies of both *Waffen–SS Panzer Divisions* to Polgardi, behind the Hungarian 25th Infantry Division, as a 'security measure.' Whether that was a direct threat to any Hungarians who might choose to leave their positions, or simply a quick-reaction force is impossible to say now with any certainly. It may have been both. It is interesting, however, that when Balck needed troops who would do as ordered regardless of their personal feelings, he turned to the *Waffen–SS*.

One more concern weighed on Wöhler and Balck: ammunition supplies. Fuel had already been restricted as deliveries dwindled, and now it was time to restrict artillery ammunition in the quiet sectors of the front. Only direct fire missions would be allowed.

10 February, Saturday

After the lower Gellért Hill in Budapest was captured by the Soviets, that left only the citadel and castle remaining in German and Hungarian hands. Led by tanks and assault guns the Russians broke through to the banks of the Danube. Now, even if the *Luftwaffe* did drop supplies, the target areas were overrun.

Narrow corridors still connected the various pockets within the larger pocket. Direct assaults on the Citadel followed intense artillery bombardments and tank cannon fire. The defenders held out, but the final days had clearly come. The only question was how and when the fighting for Budapest would end.

Command of *2. SS–Panzer Division Das Reich* was handed over by temporary commander Karl Kreutz to Knight's Cross winner *SS–Gruppenführer* Werner Ostendorff, one of the youngest and brightest generals in the *Waffen-SS*. Ostendorff had previously commanded *17. SS–Panzergrenadier Division Götz von Berlichingen*, and was coming off a stint as *Chef der Stabs* for Heinrich Himmler's *Oberkommando Oberhein*. Paul Hausser thought very highly of Ostendorff, a charismatic general who led from the front lines and had already been badly wounded twice, and whose personal bravery could not be questioned. Command of *Das Reich* was one of the most prestigious appointments in the *Waffen–SS* and required a strong leader in the best of times, but with all of Hitler's hopes for staving off defeat riding on *Unternehmen Frühlingserwachen*, and with *Das Reich* a critical component of that offensive, the position was absolutely critical and required a commander of the highest caliber.

Almost unique among high-ranking *Waffen–SS* officers, Ostendorff remained a very religious man until his death in May of 1945. It is a measure of his worth as a combat officer that, given Himmler's pathologically anti-Christian attitude, Ostendorff gained as much influence and respect as he did.

According to Richard Landwehr, on 10 February, *I./SS–Panzergrenadier Regiment 23 Norge*, along with *I SS–Panzergrenadier Regiment Danmark*, were both ordered by the *SS Hauptamt* in Berlin to return to their parent formation, *11. SS–Freiwilligen Panzergrenadier Division Nordland*. Nordland had been evacuated from the Courland Pocket in January, having suffered very heavy casualties while fighting there; the division numbered only some 9,000 men. Attached to Felix Steiner's *11. SS–Panzerarmee*, it was scheduled to attack on 16 February as part of *Unternehmen Südwind*, the offensive aimed at defending Pomerania. Obviously, the *SS Hauptamt* wanted to reunite the two battalions to their respective regiments. However, as things turned out, neither battalion was ever detached from *Heeresgruppe Süd*, as Hermann Balck and the *OKH* overruled this, ordering both units to remain under the command of *5. SS–Panzer Division Wiking*. Their contribution to *Nordland's* combat power would have been minimal, anyway. The battalion from *Norge* had been virtually destroyed, with only 100 men left from its original strength of 600, including two company commanders and one platoon commander in just the previous week. The *Danmark* battalion was not quite as depleted and could still field some 300 *panzergrenadiers*. Both went into the trenches near Dennyes, on the southwestern tip of Lake Velence.[361]

As for *Wiking* itself, the division was reunited with its parent command on 10 February, being once more attached to *IV. SS–Panzerkorps* .

<hr />

[361] Pencz, *Siegrunen Volume 77*, p. 25.

The *Mark V Panthers* of *I./Panzer Regiment 24* attacked Russian positions south of Lepseny but poor communications with the local commander led to failure; the battalion's after-action report makes it clear that inexperience from the *kampfgruppe* commander caused the attack to fail, another consequence of the low state of training and experience throughout the Wehrmacht in 1945. This was at least the second time the battalion suffered because of an incompetent commander, the first coming at Stuhlweissenburg only a handful of days before.[362]

On the southern wing, a strong attack by *1. Panzer Division* and *6. Panzer Division* slammed into the Russian positions captured when the Hungarian 25th Infantry Division broke up. The two veteran division inflicted terrible casualties on the Russians, effectively destroying the forces that had broken through. It was a signal success, but the numbers involved were smaller than might be indicated by the use of two divisions. Both were burned-out skeletons of what they had once been. Aside from beating away a moderate Russian attack near Lake Velence, most of *Armeegruppe Balck's* front remained quiet.

Late in the day, Otto Wöhler returned from his meeting with Hitler. Details of his trip to Berlin are few. All that is known for certain is that when he returned, Wöhler had new orders from the *Führer* for yet another surprise offensive that would turn the tide in the east.

[362] Jentz, *Panzertruppen 2*, p. 231.

11 February, Sunday

The end was within sight in Budapest. *SS–Obergruppenführer* Pfeffer-Wildenbruch informed *OKW* by radio that the last defenders of Budapest were in danger of being overrun and further resistance could accomplish nothing. He had finally decided to order a break-out. As Pierik puts it, Pfeffer-Wildenbruch really had no choice, since he considered that there were now only "two possible outcomes: unconditional capitulation or certain massacre."[363] The pathetic survivors of *Festung* Budapest were divided into four groups for the purpose of escape. Most of the men would head in a north-westerly direction, with a smaller number trying to make it into the underground sewers. Those going underground were mainly from *Panzer Division Felldherrnhalle*, with a few men from the signals battalion of *8. SS–Freiwilligen–Kavallerie Division Florian Geyer*. The commander of the detachment, *SS–Hauptsturmführer* Harry Weckmann, died in the attempt to get out. On 14 February one man, *SS–Unterscharführer* Gronarth, was admitted to the reserve hospital at the Archduke Johann Hotel in Semmering, Austria; he was the only survivor of the detachment to make it back to German lines.

The remaining units were all hollow shells of what they had been when Budapest was surrounded. *SS–Flak–Abteilung* 22, for example, had lost 203 officers and men from a total of 500, a 40 percent loss rate; in material the unit had lost 18 guns and 38 trucks. During the breakout the survivors would try to fight their way out.

Despite the strictest secrecy, the Soviets got wind of the breakout and began shelling the Castle area where the groups were assembling around 20:00 hours. The Russians had learned about the breakout from turncoat Hungarians and German prisoners. Their guns were pre-registered, their automatic

---

[363] Pierik, p. 146.

weapons pre-positioned to sweep the escape routes of any and all escaping Germans and Hungarians. Marshal Malinovsky had no intentions of letting even a mouse get out of the flaming city alive.

More than 90 percent of the would-be escapees would be killed trying to get through the Russian lines and the rest would be taken prisoner. Pierik quotes *SS–Oberstumführer* Kurt Portugall, commander of the 88's that had caused so much trouble on Adler Hill, as estimating the number of men assembled for the breakout at 18,000, of whom 6,000 were walking wounded.[364] The survivors were in bad shape, weak from hunger, exhaustion and weight loss, dirty, sick and desperate. Looking at the ferocity of the battle it seems almost incredible that *IX. SS-Waffen-Gebirgs-Armeekorps der SS* still had 18,000 men fit for duty. Or at least, fit enough for a breakout. That number would not last long, though.

On 11 February *Heeresgruppe Mitte* was ordered to refurbish *25. Panzer Division* as a *kampfgruppe*. The division had seen heavy fighting during the previous six weeks and was almost destroyed; casualties by the end of February included 611 dead, 2318 wounded and the massive total of 6030 missing, for a total of 8959 casualties.[365] Refilling the emptied ranks proceeded quickly, given the circumstances; 21 *Mark IVs* were shipped to the division on 18 February from the *Heeres-Zeugamt*, 10 *Jagdpanzer IV/70s* on 19 February, plus 10 more *Mark IVs* and 10 *Mark V Panthers* on 3 March. This brought *25. Panzer Division* almost up to the greatly reduced authorized strength of the 1945 *Kampfgruppe Panzer Division*, but it would never again come close to full divisional strength.

[364] Pierik, p. 147.
[365] Micham, *The Panzer Legions*, p. 182.

Map 6

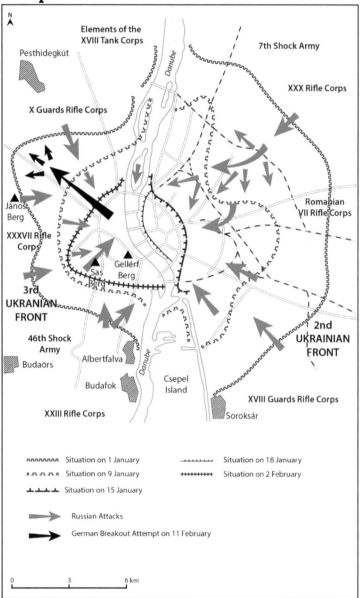

Elements of the
XVIII Tank Corps

Pesthidegkút

7th Shock Army

XXX Rifle Corps

X Guards Rifle Corps

Jáno
Berg

XXXVII Rifle
Corps

3rd
UKRANIAN
FRONT

46th Shock
Army

Budaörs

Albertfalva

Budafok

Csepel
Island

XXIII Rifle Corps

Soroksár

Romanian
VII Rifle Corps

2nd
UKRAINIAN
FRONT

XVIII Guards Rifle Corps

Gellérf
Sas Berg
Berg

Situation on 1 January

Situation on 9 January

Situation on 15 January

Situation on 18 January

Situation on 2 February

Russian Attacks

German Breakout Attempt on 11 February

0   3   6 km

Yard by yard, the Russians drove the garrison of Budapest into the Castle District of Buda, until Hitler finally allowed a breakout. By then it was far too late.

374

12 February, Monday

A whirlwind of steel hit those attempting to get out of Budapest. After surviving the slaughter as the breakout began, Knight's Cross winner *SS–Hauptscharführer* Gustav Wendrisky and his *panzerjäger* platoon almost made it back to German lines. They got as far as Csobanka, almost to Pilisszentkerest, when Wendrisky was killed by a shot to the head. Along with thousands of others he was buried in a mass grave near that village.

5. SS Panzer Division Wiking relieved *Totenkopf* in the area southwest of Stuhlweissenburg, stretching its line to cover up to that city's southern edge, with the division's headquarters in Sarpentele. The division was once again subordinated to *IV. SS–Panzerkorps.*

It is doubtful that the *SS* rank and file knew that Sepp Dietrich's army was on the way, but it was, and there was nothing anyone could say to change Hitler's mind. So as the formations of 6th *SS Panzerkorps* began to move toward Hungary and settle into the areas west of Raab, they were tasked not only with moving their men and equipment but also to incorporate large numbers of new soldiers into their ranks, most of whom had no training or experience in ground warfare. The strength return for *1. SS–Panzer Division Leibstandarte Adolf Hitler* dated 12 February reflects the preference that *Waffen–SS* units were given over other branches of the Wehrmacht during this period, especially *SS* divisions that had a sponsor: authorized manpower for a *Waffen–SS Panzer* Division of the time was 18,355 total men, but in fact *LAH* was over-strength by nearly 800 men with 19,055 of all ranks. On paper this looks impressive, but aside from the new men being little more than cannon fodder, the division was desperately short of both officers and non-commissioned officers. Authorized to carry 615 officers on its rolls, the division actually had 513, while the non-commissioned officers situation was worse, with 4,037 authorized but only 3165 on hand.

Compounding this was the inexperience of many of those officers and non-commissioned officers who had been promoted to fill vacancies caused by losses; they might have been combat veterans, but not at their new rank. Unlike most German divisions, *LAH* might have been robust in numbers but was desperately short of expertise.[366]

[366] Michaelis, *Panzer Divisions of the Waffen–SS*, p. 50.

13 February, Tuesday

Suddenly, it was over. Hissing rubble clogged streets that still echoed with the rumbling of the explosions that rent the Hungarian capital mere hours before. Here and there were cries from the wounded, both man and beast; most animals had long since either fled or been eaten, but the few that were recently killed or wounded were quickly butchered. Horses, dogs, rats, it did not matter; meat was meat. Blackened hulks of cars and trucks and armored vehicles littered the boulevards as the first brave souls poked their heads from the burrows they had crawled in during the last desperate days of fighting. Where once delicate spires rose from gingerbread buildings to reflect from the swift waters of the Danube in colorful chimeras, now there was only crumpled brick and shattered glass to darken waters choked with fallen bridges and bloated bodies; the regal, elegant and magical outline of fair Budapest was reduced to a burned-out maze of crumbling ruins that reeked of smoke and death, where the very air tasted of roasted flesh and ash.

Despite some disagreement over what constituted victory, 13 February was the official day selected by the Soviets for the fall of Budapest; it was certainly a day when the Red Army ran amok in the destroyed city. The ferocity of the fighting had been shocking; as bad as Stalingrad, according to some. Guillemot quotes Malinovsky's former chief-of-staff, Zakharov, as writing that, "Every building had been turned into a fortress. During the (first) twenty days of the offensive, our troops only took 114 blocks out of a total of 722."[367]

The battle had been long and hard and very costly for the Russians, and they were intent on having revenge on somebody and everybody. The Russian High Command may have been indifferent about losses, but the common soldier who had just seen his friends killed or mutilated was not. The bodies of dead German

[367] Guillemot, p. 36.

and Hungarian soldiers that lay in heaps where they had been slaughtered during the breakout were left to rot where they fell, or to be run over repeatedly until they became little more than a grotesque paste. Many of the German wounded were simply shot[368], as were Arrow Cross men, men with German sounding names and suspicious persons. As usual when the Red Army overran an Axis city, or any city, rape was rampant[369]. According to Pierik some 30,000 people were rounded up and deported.[370] Guillemot says the figure was 50,000 civilians, who were 'taken prisoner' because Malinovsky had been manipulating the figures and realized the numbers of real prisoners taken did not match what he had claimed. The civilians were sent into the Gulag system along with the true prisoners of war, and 13,000 never came back. The battle had been pitiless and it appeared the peace would be no different.

Members of the Swiss legation had stayed in Budapest throughout the battle and testified later what happened when the Soviets came. Looting on a mass scale started before the battle was over, with small knots of men with mine detectors roaming the city looking for hidden valuables such as gold rings or silver flatware, while others scrounged food from every building. Looting was general and profound, but not always systematic. It happened, for instance, that a man was deprived of all his trousers, but his jackets were left to him. And once the Russians had sated their lust for loot, the Russians allowed the working class to loot again, rustling for whatever was left. Thus every apartment, shop, bank, etc. was looted several times. Furniture and larger objects of art, etc. that could not be taken away were frequently simply destroyed. In many cases, after looting, the homes were also put on

[368] Pierik reports that one bunker under Castle Hill that was filled with wounded was flooded with gasoline and set ablaze (p. 148).

[369] And not always an Axis city, as some towns and cities in Poland were also subjected to the depredations of the Red Army.

[370] Pierik, p. 148.

fire, causing a vast total loss. Even the Swiss Legation itself was looted, four times, while the Swedish Legation had a huge safe hauled off in its entirety, with secret papers still locked inside.

Thousands of people were rounded up and put to work without even being able to tell their families where they were; they simply disappeared off the street for weeks or months, although most eventually returned home. Tens of thousands of others, however, wound up in a concentration camp near Godollo, where their only choice of survival was agreeing to go work in the Soviet Union. Anyone of Germanic origin, regardless of age, was deported without exception to Russia.

But as bad as the looting was, and as bad as the deportations and press-ganged labor was, the occupation of Budapest was quickly followed by the most infamous crime that followed the Red Army wherever it set foot in conquered territory: rape, mass rape, often quite brutal rape. Girls of 10 and great-grandmothers of 80 were equally at risk; gang rapes over a period of days were not uncommon. Suicides among victims was frequent and sexually transmitted disease became epidemic, as medicines were not available to anybody, including the Russians themselves. Even women in the Red Army were guilty of rape.

Damage to certain parts of the city was almost total, especially the Commercial District and the hills of Buda, with the Russians claiming the destruction as worse than Stalingrad.

"In the Fortress there is almost no house standing. The Royal Palace was burned down. The Coronation Church collapsed. The Parliament Building is severely damaged, but its skyline has remained intact. The hotels Ritz, Hungária, Carlton, Vadaszkurt, and Gellért are all in ruins. The Vaczi- utca has suffered very much. The house of Gerbeaud is damaged, but

379

still stands. A stable was set up during the siege in the great hall of the confectionery store. The Commercial Bank is more damaged than the Credit Bank. The buildings housing the other banks, Moktar, Adria, the National Casino, were burned down completely. The French legation was entirely destroyed by the Germans. The house of the Hubayfamily next to the French legation also suffered a lot during the siege."[371]

Along the waterfront the quays and berths on the Buda side were entirely destroyed, although a small portion of the Pest side could still handle shipping, and the two most famous bridges, the Chain Bridge and the Elizabeth Bridge, lay broken in the Danube. All of the other bridges were badly damaged but temporary repairs in the coming weeks would at least make foot traffic possible. Navigating the Danube itself was tricky and dangerous, as flotsam broke free randomly and could puncture the hull of a boat and wreckage just under the surface could tear out the bottom of even larger vessels.

Enhanced image of Ruined Budapest.

[371] (http://www.hungarianhistory.com/lib/montgo/montgo21.htm, (Accessed 4 May 4 2014).

For weeks there had been no reliable utilities, water, gas or electricity, and the final days of fighting had made the situation worse, particularly in Buda; repairs could not be started while street fighting swept back and forth and explosions created ever deeper piles of debris. The sanitary situation had deteriorated into a state of city-wide filth and degradation as garbage piled high, waste went uncollected and untreated, rotting corpses of man and beast attracted rats and other scavengers, including starving humans who ate whatever they could find and became ill from their desperation. (Before Summer typhus would stalk the ruined city.) Wholesome food was almost non-existent and prices on the black market were astronomical. Only cold weather had prevented the stench of death from making the air unbreathable.

For years afterward life in Budapest would be periodically disrupted by the discovery of unexploded ordnance. In May of 2013 alone a German 70 kilogram bomb was found near the Royal Palace, while a week later a Russian bomb was discovered lodged in the roof of City Hall, forcing the evacuation of more than 1,000 people. In July of that same year 80 residential blocks would be evacuated because an unexploded 50 kg bomb was discovered near Buda Castle; it was the 14th time since 2008 live ordnance had been found. How many citizens and tourists had strolled near or over those bombs since the city had been reconstructed? How many more bombs still lay dormant in the now-built-over rubble? The legacy of the Battle of Budapest lives on far after the last round was fired and the last fire extinguished.

With the greatest possible secrecy, the trains carrying *2. SS–Panzer Division Das Reich* from the bloody battlefields of Belgium to the as-yet undisturbed backwaters of Hungary began to arrive at their destinations in the area near and west of Kisber. All components of *6. SS–Panzerarmee* had been given code names during the transfer to hide the move, including the individual men having to remove their cuff bands so as not to tip off enemy spies or sympathizers of their presence.[372] Parts of the Army had been routed through Berlin, including Sepp Dietrich's headquarters, to fool Soviet intelligence into thinking that *6. SS–Panzerarmee* was being deployed on the Oder Front. Dietrich himself moved about the capital to give the impression that his army was following him. Groups and convoys were strictly forbidden once the divisions arrived at their destinations. All possible secrecy measures were taken.[373] So successful were the efforts to hide the arrival of the *6. SS–Panzerarmee* in Hungary that, according to Weidinger, *Das Reich's* new commanding officer, *SS–GruppenFührer* Werner Ostendorff, had trouble finding his command[374].

After the ferocity of the fighting during the Ardennes Offensive and the subsequent American counter-attack, the survivors of *6. SS–Panzerarmee* would cherish the relative peace and solitude of western Hungary as the *SS* divisions were infused with new recruits and rebuilt with new and repaired equipment. Those few days would be their last chance to rest and refit until the end of the war; from this period forward would be one long, ceaseless battle.

---

[372] This removal of cuff bands would be a bizarre footnote to the controversy of the 'Cuff-Band Order' in late March, when Hitler ordered the SS men to remove their cuff bands as a penalty for not achieving their objectives in *Unternehmen Frühlingserwachen*. In almost all cases the cuff bands had never been sewn back on after being removed during the transport of 6th SS Panzer Army to Hungary, making the Cuff Band Order not only insulting, but superfluous.

[373] The question of how effective those security measures had been would become moot once 1st SS Panzer Corps participated in the Gran Offensive, when it would be starkly obvious that 6th SS Panzer Army was in Hungary.

[374] Most sources state that Ostendorff took command on January 29th, but Weidinger explicitly states that he did not actually join Das *Reich* until after its arrival in Hungary. Given that Weidinger is the best source available this is the timeline used here.

Losses in all of the *SS* divisions had been very high during the month of fighting in the Ardennes area. The recuperation period in Hungary gave many of those men who had been wounded a chance to recover and return to the division, a critical factor given the acute overall shortage of leaders of all ranks. Likewise, after a few days of rest, the units were given a chance to refurbish and repair their equipment, mend clothing and take inventory of what was on hand, and request necessary items for future combat, however unlikely it might have been that such requests could be fulfilled.

On the Western Front, Germans had to constantly be on the alert for attacks from the dreaded '*Jabos*', the Allied Tactical Air Forces. Not only did swarms of deadly ground attack aircraft, such as the Hawker Tempest, North American P-51 Mustang or the Republic P-47 Thunderbolt, suddenly appear out of nowhere, strafing and unloading racks of rockets or bombs, but the Allied aircraft were crewed by skilled pilots and deadly marksmen. Attacks were also well coordinated between groups of aircraft; being on the receiving end of such an air raid meant a high likelihood of the target being splattered with ordnance. If you were the target, you were in trouble. Soviet air attacks, on the other hand, were nowhere near as coordinated or effective. The ground attack aircraft were first-rate, especially the heavily armored Ilyushin IL-2 Sturmovik, and the sheer numbers of Red Air Force aircraft were enormous, but the training, coordination, tactics and marksmanship were nowhere near as effective as the Allied Air Forces.

As commander of *SS–Panzergrenadier Regiment 4 Der Führer*, Otto Weidinger was present during the movement and gives a good feel for the transition that all of the *SS* divisions must have felt during the move to Hungary, from a feeling of omnipresent danger from air attack to one more akin to annoyance. "The first Russian bombers made their appearance over the Hungarian plain. Road intersections and railroad hubs were attacked with small bombs. The impacts were several hundred meters from their targets most of the time. Everyone gave a sigh of relief to finally have escaped from the constant threat of American *Jabos* in the west."[375] This was not to say that there was no danger from the Red Air Force, but that compared to the threat from the western air forces the danger seemed minimal to the veteran *SS* men. Still, vehicles caught on open roads in daylight were easy prey even for Russian pilots so caution in movement remained the watchword.

[375] Weidinger, Otto, *Division Das Reich V, The 2ⁿᵈ SS–Panzer Division "Das Reich", The History of the Original Division of the Waffen-SS*, (Winnipeg: J. J. Fedorowicz, 2012), p. 326.

14 February, Thursday

The first survivors of the breakout by the Budapest garrison began trickling in to the German front lines this day, mostly in the vicinity of Zsambek, roughly 17 miles west of Budapest. The small town was famous for its old Roman church built in the 1200's, which was ruined by a later earthquake, but Zsambek must have seemed like paradise to those of the 785 survivors who eventually came out of the winter mists to safety in the German lines. Only 100 or so were from *8. SS Kavallerie-Division Florian Geyer* and they were incorporated into the newly forming *37. SS–Freiwilligen–Kavallerie Division*, which had already been given the honorific title of *Lützow*. Although with a combat career lasting less than two months, it is doubtful that *any* German formation saw more combat-per-hour than did *Lützow*.

Plans for *Unternehmen Frühlingserwachen* may not have been finalized, but the launching of the offensive was set in stone, and the men would who fight it were beginning to suspect that it was coming. *II. SS–Panzerkorps* had given the two divisions under its command, *2. SS–Panzer Division Das Reich* and *9. SS–Panzer Division Hohenstaufen*, four weeks to rebuild themselves after the shattering losses suffered in the Ardennes Offensive and its aftermath. The specific timeframe told the division's old hands that a new mission had already been assigned to them. *Das Reich* had just detrained in Hungary the day before, but already just one day later replacements were being delivered to the division and the date they had to be ready for action was known. But as was common in the final months of the war, the men were almost completely untrained for ground warfare, so a frantic schedule of trying to bring the new recruits up to

Waffen–SS training standards was initiated. "It was planned for theoretical topics, target shooting and weapon and vehicle maintenance to be carried out during the day, while the night hours were used for field exercises. The companies were in the field from early evening to morning."[376]

Regardless of how important training might have been, fuel shortages meant that vehicles could only be used sporadically, and because of the need for secrecy they could only be driven at night even when fuel was available.

[376] Weidinger, *Das Reich V*, p. 327.

15 February, Friday

The Wehrmacht communiqué admitted the loss of Budapest but tried to put it in a positive light. "Following the complete encirclement of Budapest, the defenders have held the city almost 50 days against fierce enemy attacks by vastly superior Soviet forces. Its ammunition and food gone, as per orders, the courageous German and Hungarian garrison has broken through the siege ring. The first elements have already reached our front west of Budapest."[377] Technically this was all true, even while hiding the loss of 99 percent of the garrison. Regardless of how much it was intended to sound like part of a larger plan, it is hard to imagine all but the most fanatical party member or believer in Hitler seeing the loss of the Hungarian capital as anything except a disaster.

In the trenches near Dennyes, south of Lake Velence, during the afternoon "a massive Soviet tank force advanced to within 100 meters of the *I./SS–Panzergrenadier Regiment 24 Danmark* positions and opened up a deadly fire on the *Waffen–SS* trenches." The battalion could not bring their anti-tank weapons to bear and were forced to withdraw, losing the battalion commander, *SS–Sturmbannführer* Herman Im Masche, in the process. This left Vogt's *I./SS–Panzergrenadier Regiment 23 Norge* outflanked and they, too, were forced to withdraw, suffering many casualties as artillery and mortar fire followed them off the battlefield.[378]

[377] Michaelis, p. 108.
[378] Landwehr, *Siegrunen Volume 77*, p. 26.

3. SS–Panzergrenadier Regiment Deutschland did not long stay in western Hungary. Around the middle of February the regiment was sent to the area west of the Gran River, where it was intended to act as a reserve for *I. SS–Panzerkorps* during the upcoming offensive to clear out the Soviet bridgehead over the Gran. This bulge in the front meant that the German lines in northern Hungary into Slovakia had no natural defense barrier, a dangerous enough situation given the overall weakness of *Heeresgruppe Süd,* and Eighth Army in particular, but securing this northern flank was critical before *Unternehmen Frühlingserwachen* could be launched. The threat was obvious: should the Red Army have attacked and seized Komárom, then crossed the Danube, it would have outflanked most of *Heeresgruppe Süd* and potentially unhinged the entire German position in Western Hungary. Once *Unternehmen Frühlingserwachen* was underway, and the mobile forces engaged so that redeployment against a threat to their rear was almost impossible, the loss of Komárom would have been a catastrophe. Thus the need to use the precious *1. SS–Panzer Division Leibstandarte Adolf Hitler* and *12. SS–Panzer Division Hitlerjugend* to eliminate this threat, despite the inevitability of weakening them through even more losses in combat and probably losing the secrecy of their presence in Hungary, and thus also the further commitment of Deutschland to the effort as a reserve. The rest of *2. SS–Panzer Division Das Reich* stayed put in the area west of Kisber and continued getting ready for the final German offensive of the Second World War.

Sometime in mid-February Colonel Ilya Dmitrievich Andryukov took command of the Russian 180th Rifle Division from Major-General Anton Aleksandrovich Pavlovich. Pavlovich's fate is uncertain; he may well died, but from what cause is unclear. In the Red Army that could mean death from combat, from natural causes or he could have disappeared into the gulag system like Alexandr Solzhenitsyn.

The scale and ferocity of the tank battle at Pettend during *Konrad III* only became evident after the fact. Being mentioned in a report or dispatch was a noteworthy honor, and on 15 February *Schwere–Panzer Abteilung 509* was officially credited with destroying 203 Russian tanks, 143 guns of various sizes, and five aircraft, during the period 18 January-8 February, 1945. In return, 10 of the 45 *Tiger IIs* the battalion started the battle with were totally destroyed. Perhaps the numbers were inflated or incorrect, but it should be noted these were credited kills, not merely claims. Even in the face of Russia's new breed of heavy tanks, the JS-1 and JS-2, in the hands of a skilled crew the *Tiger II* ruled the battlefield.

16 February, Friday

The medieval town of Loeben in south-Central Austria, in the Steiermark, has long been known as The Gateway to the Styrian Iron Road, a center of the Austrian iron mining industry since the Middle Ages. Goss Abbey, the oldest convent in Styria, was founded in 1020 A.D. Next to the Abbey was a brewery and the city was filled with Baroque and Art-Nouveau architecture. The picturesque town could have been, and sometimes was, the subject of a tranquil postcard.

Into this undamaged oasis of beauty and serenity came the *1. Ungarische SS–Ski Abteilung*, which had until two days before been training at Neuhammer in Silesia before the Red Army flooded the area with tanks and armored infantry. Like *SS–Brigade Ney* and other Hungarian formations, the *1. Ungarische SS–Ski Abteilung* had been formed in October, 1944, after Admiral Horthy's government had been deposed and replaced by the Arrow Cross government of Ferenc Szalasi. Volunteers signed up for service with the German military for various reasons, either to defend Hungary, or to promote fascism, to stop communism or protect their families, or just to have steady access to food. Some were Volksdeutsch driven from their homes and were either conscripted or had no other means of survival; whatever their reasons, a large percentage of these men wound up in the *Waffen-SS*. At that point in the fall of 1944, the Germans were still able to arm such formations reasonably well, not only with lighter weapons such as the *StG 44 Sturmgewehr*, forerunner of most modern automatic and semi-automatic rifles, including the ubiquitous AK-47 and all its variants, but also with mortars and MG-42 machine guns. The *1. Ungarische SS–Ski Abteilung* was sent to Neuhammer for training, with the original purpose of it serving as a replacement battalion for both the *Waffen–SS* Hungarian Divisions.

Back in mid-January when the Russian offensive in Poland broke through and was closing in on the training grounds, the Battalion supplied a reinforced company for the rear-guard defense. In conjunction with *kampfgruppen* from both Hungarian *SS* Divisions, the Russian offensive was delayed long enough for the two divisions to safely withdraw to the west. The defense had been stubborn, given the overwhelming superiority of the attacking Russians, and the price paid was also overwhelming: the *1. Ungarische SS–Ski Abteilung's* reinforced company of 222 men lost 214 of them either killed, wounded or missing. Only eight men survived unscathed.

The *1. Ungarische SS–Ski Abteilung* , which in reality was at this point two battalions strong and would later grow to three, did not stop in Loeben but kept moving to the southeast, past Graz, until reaching the small town of Judenberg due south of Vienna. There it began intensive training at the nearby High Mountain Warfare School Troop Training Ground 'Seetaler Alp,' in the famous Seetaler Alps on the Styrian-Carinthian border. What exactly, the crumbling Wehrmacht needed with ski troops is not clear.

Unternehmen Südwind

The planning for *Unternehmen Südwind* was carried out by *General der Gebirgstruppe* Hans Kreysing's *8. Armee*, whose staff could call upon two *Panzerkorps* for the attack: these were General Ulrich Kleemann's *Panzerkorps Feldherrnhalle*, already present in the area and, as detailed above, did not possess the combat power of one division, much less two. The other formation came from *6. SS–Panzerarmee* in the form of *SS-Obergruppenführer und General der Waffen-SS* Hermann Priess's *I SS Panzerkorps*, diverted from the preparation for the upcoming *Unternehmen Frühlingserwachen*. These two formations' armored strength was high, totalling 282 *panzers* and *sturmgeschütze*. Included in the total were 44 *Mark IV Tiger IIs* from the two *Schwere– Panzer Abteilungen*.

The Soviets were defending the bridgehead with General Major Dmitri P. Onuprienko's XXIV Guards Corps and the XXV Corps of General Colonel Mikhail S. Shumilov's 7th Guards Army within Marshal Sovetskogo Soyuza Rodion Ya. Malinovsky's 2nd Ukrainian Front. The most powerful formation, General Colonel Andrei G. Kravchenko's 6th Guards Tank Army, had been withdrawn from the area to the eastern bank of the Garam river for rest and rehabilitation. German aerial reconnaissance revealed that the Soviets had established a deeply echeloned system of defenses, based on trenches supported by tank blocking positions. A relatively small number of Soviet tanks and self-propelled guns (totalling 26 and five machines respectively) was available in the bridgehead, but some armored reinforcements were to arrive later.

The German plan called for the infantry of the *Panzerkorps Feldherrnhalle* to attack from the north in the direction of Magyarszögyén and Bart. The divisions from the *I SS Panzerkorps* were then to take over, cross the Párizs Canal, and drive farther via Muzsla toward the final objective, which was Esztergom. Finally, bridgeheads were to be gained on the eastern bank of the Garam river.

Kreysing had under command the *I SS Panzerkorps* with *SS-Brigadeführer und Generalmajor der Waffen-SS* Otto Kumm's *1. SS–Panzer Division 'Leibstandarte Adolf Hitler'*, the *501. SS–Schwere Panzer Abteilung* and *SS-Brigadeführer und Generalmajor der Waffen-SS* Hugo Kraas's *12. SS Panzer Division 'Hitlerjugend'*; the *Panzerkorps Feldherrnhalle* with *Generalmajor* Erich Reuter's *46. Infanterie Division*, *Generalleutnant* Hans-Günther von Rost's *44. Reichs Grenadier Division Hoch- und Deutschmeister*, *Generalmajor* Johann-Heinrich Eckhardt's *211. Volksgrenadier Division*, *Oberstleutnant* Hans Schöneich's *Kampfgruppe Schöneich* with the *Schwere– Panzer Abteilung 'Feldherrnhalle* and the *208. Panzer*

Abteilung; and Oberst G. Anton Staubwasser's
Kampfgruppe Staubwasser with three battalions of
Generalleutnant Josef Rintelen's *357. Infanterie
Division.* Also available to the *8. Armee* were elements
of Hermann Balck's *6. Armee* in the form of units of *I.
Kavalleriekorps*, being essentially such as
Oberstleutnant Joachim-Friedrich Hupe's *Kampfgruppe
Hupe* of *Generalmajor* Hermann Harrendorf's *96.
Infanterie Division* and *Generalleutnant* Josef Reichert's
711 Infanterie Division. Both of the latter were near
Esztergom on the south bank of the Danube.

Colonel General Mikhail Shumilov commanded
units from his own 7th Guards Army, including Major
General Appolon Ya. Kruze's XXIV Guards Corps,
which comprised Major General Anatoli I. Losev's 72nd
Guards Division, Colonel M. A. Orlov's 81st Guards
Division, and Major General Major Mikhail N.
Smirnov's 6th Guards Parachute Division. Additionally,
he had Lieutenant General Z. V. Ivanovich's IV Guards
Mechanized Corps, which included Colonel N. A.
Nikitin's 14th Guards Mechanized Brigade and Colonel
P. S. Zhukov's 36th Guards Tank Brigade. Lieutenant
General Gani B. Safiulin's XXV Guards Corps also
supported the defense, featuring Major General Vasili
D. Karpukhin's 375th Division, Major General Yevstafi
P. Grechany's 409th Division, parts of Colonel David V.
Vasilevsky's 53rd Division, Colonel Nikolai M.
Brishinev's 27th Independent Guards Tank Brigade,
and Colonel P. M. Marol's 93rd Guards Division.

17 February, Saturday

The former commanding officer of *18. SS–Freiwilligen–Panzergrenadier Division Horst Wessel*, Knight's Cross winner *SS–Brigadeführer* August-Wilhelm Trabandt, took over command of the *SS–Panzer*grenadier School at Kienschlag, near Prague. Trabandt would shortly be called upon to organize the men of his school into a regiment that would be part of a new unit, *SS–Kampfgruppe Division Böhmen und Mähren*, the last *SS* division ever authorized for creation. Its component parts would be engaged in combat from the very start.

In Moscow, STAVKA issued Directive No. 11027 detailing a new offensive plan aimed at capturing Vienna[379]. There is circumstantial evidence that the Russian plans were far more ambitious than merely capturing the old capital of Austria, and that the ultimate objective was nothing less than Munich. That would place the Red Army well inside the Allied zones of occupation, but since when did treaties and agreements mean anything to Stalin?

Unternehmen Südwind

The preparations for *Unternehmen Frühlingserwachen* were proceeding apace, but all of the work was for naught unless the Russian bridgehead north of the Danube and west of the Gran was eliminated first. The almost 20 kilometer by 20 kilometer area threatened the flank of any German

---

[379] Domanski and Ledwoch say the directive was issued two days after the fall of Budapest, so this could be Feb. 14.

operations south of the Danube, as it could be used as a springboard for attack into the flank of 3rd Hungarian Army or *6. Armee*, or for a Russian drive west toward Vienna which could threaten a deep envelopment of all of *Heeresgruppe Süd*. So on the morning of 17 February the last successful major German attack of the Second World War struck Russian forces in the Gran Bridgehead.

To recap, the attack involved *Panzerkorps Felldherrnhalle* and *I. SS–Panzerkorps*; each corps had a heavy tank battalion operating with one of its divisions, with *SS–Schwere–Panzer Abteilung 501* still attached to *1. SS–Panzer Division Leibstandarte Adolf Hitler* and *Schwere Panzer Abteilung 503*[380] given to *44. Reichs Grenadier Division Hoch und Deutschmeister* for the attack. Neither battalion was anywhere close to full strength. On paper *SS–Schwere–Panzer Abteilung 501* had 36 Tiger IIs, but only 19 were combat ready, while *Schwere Panzer Abteilung 503* had 22 operational Tiger IIs.

46. Infanterie Division also fought hard during the offensive.[381] On 30 January 1945, the division was pulled out and moved to the south-west via Neutra-Neuhacusl on the Danube. On 5 February, it moved back into position in the Gran Bridgehead, east of Komorn, but on 13 February it was moved north-east

---

[380] *Schwere Panzer Abteilung 503* was an organic component of Panzer Corps Felldherrnhalle.

[381] The War Diary of *Heeresgruppe Süd* lists the strength of this division as Infantry: 3 average battalions; 2 average battalions; 1 strong field-replacement battalion; 1 average engineer battalion; Subordinated: 1 medium-strong battalion (from *13.Panzer-Division*); 1 average battalion (from *Panzer-Division \Feldherrnhalle*); 3 strong Hungarian battalions (in process of training). Total infantry combat strength: 1,800 German- and 1,200 Hungarian infantrymen, 400 troops in the field-replacement battalion, 200 engineers. *Panzers* and AT guns: 22 heavy AT guns
Subordinated: 3 heavy AT guns (from *13.Panzer-Division*). Artillery: 8 light- and 1 heavy batteries, Detached: 3 light batteries (to *Kampfgruppe Staubwasser*), Subordinated: 4 light batteries (from 23rd Infantry-Division). Degree of mobility: motorized: 50 percent; horse-drawn: 90 percent. Combat worth: German units – II; Hungarian units – need additional training. Ration strength was approximately 9,000 men.

again to the Farnad-Kolta area, in preparation for the attack

The morning started under a low, gray sky, the fog hanging thick over the snow-covered Slovakian fields. The air was cold, heavy with the tension of what was to come. At dawn, the stillness was broken by the deafening roar of German artillery, marking the beginning of *Unternehmen Südwind*.

At 5 am the attack began with *Panzerkorps Felldherrnhalle* smashing into Russian lines near Svodin and penetrating quickly, followed by *I. SS–Panzerkorps*. Carefully hoarded stores of artillery ammunition were unleashed in a coordinated artillery barrage aimed at Soviet positions near the villages of Kamenín and Štúrovo. The Soviets, part of the 7th Guards Army, had entrenched themselves on the western side of the Gran River, their positions fortified with trenches, bunkers, and anti-tank obstacles. The artillery fire was relentless, pounding Soviet positions with a mix of high-explosive and armor-piercing shells, designed to destroy defenses and shake the resolve of the defenders.

The initial bombardment lasted for more than an hour, creating a curtain of fire that obscured visibility and disoriented the Soviet defenders. The German artillery targeted Soviet strongholds, communications lines, and likely positions of artillery batteries. The noise was overwhelming, with the ground shaking under the continuous detonations. Soviet officers tried to rally their troops, but many soldiers huddled in their trenches and foxholes, unsure of when the shelling would stop.

Shortly after the artillery barrage, at approximately 0730, the German ground assault began. Surprise was almost total, but because of weather the attack centered around infantry, supported by tanks wherever possible. Despite the devastating artillery barrage, the Soviet defenders, many of them veterans of the brutal Eastern Front campaigns, were far from broken.

Facing the toughest opposition was *44. Reichs–Grenadier Division Hoch und Deutschmeister* on the northwestern fringe of the offensive, and *211. Infanterie Division* nearest the Gran River. Soviet commanders, although shocked by the timing of the attack, had anticipated the German offensive and had reinforced key positions along the river. As the German tanks and infantry approached, Soviet artillery and anti-tank guns opened fire, targeting the advancing *panzers*. The crack of Soviet 76 mm field guns echoed across the battlefield as shells arced toward the German armor, their impacts kicking up plumes of snow and dirt.

The first wave of *panzers* encountered fierce resistance near the village of Kamenín, where Soviet anti-tank guns and well-concealed T-34 tanks were lying in wait. The initial skirmishes were brutal, with German armor trading fire with Soviet defenders from positions barely visible through the fog. The terrain around the village was uneven, and this slowed the German advance, forcing the tanks to navigate carefully to avoid becoming bogged down in the snow or exposing their vulnerable sides to Soviet fire.

At several points, the *panzers* were able to break through the outer layers of Soviet defenses, only to be met with determined resistance from Soviet infantry armed with anti-tank rifles, Molotov cocktails, and grenades.[382] The fighting in and around Kamenín became chaotic, with German *panzers* and infantry pressing forward, while Soviet troops clung to every defensive position, counterattacking when the opportunity presented itself.

As the German forces continued to push into the Soviet positions, the battle descended into close-quarters combat. In the village streets, Soviet and German infantry exchanged fire at point-blank range, darting between buildings and barricades. Soviet machine guns, placed in buildings and hidden

---

[382] The PTRS family of antitank rifles was used by the Russians throughout the Second World War. Firing a 14.5mm armor-piercing shell, the rifle was most effective when firing at the hull plating behind the drive wheels.

emplacements, poured fire onto the advancing Germans. The Germans responded with grenades, flamethrowers, and submachine guns, trying to clear the Soviet defenders from their fortified positions.

The fighting in Kamenín was particularly intense. German assault teams, supported by the ever-present *Sturmgeschütze*, attempted to dislodge Soviet defenders from key positions in the village, moving from house to house in brutal street fighting. At one point, a German platoon managed to overrun a Soviet machine gun nest, but their success was short-lived as a Soviet counterattack forced them to retreat into the ruins of a nearby building. The narrow streets and rubble-strewn alleyways of the village made it impossible for the Germans to effectively deploy their tanks, leaving much of the fighting to the infantry.

In the surrounding countryside, the German advance was similarly contested. Soviet artillery, though shaken by the earlier bombardment, began to regroup, and Soviet commanders ordered their men to hold their ground. The German armor, which had initially made rapid gains, found themselves bogged down in the muddy, uneven terrain near the riverbanks. Soviet infantry took advantage of this, launching ambushes from wooded areas and using the cover of the fog to infiltrate German lines.

By midday, the battle had become a grinding stalemate, with neither side able to secure a decisive advantage. The German forces had made significant gains in some areas, capturing parts of Kamenín and pushing the Soviet defenders back toward the river, but at a heavy cost. Soviet artillery and anti-tank fire had destroyed a number of *panzers*, and the advancing infantry had suffered high casualties as they fought their way through the Soviet defenses.

Soviet losses were equally severe. Many of their defensive positions had been overrun, and large sections of the front were in danger of collapsing under the weight of the German assault. However, the Soviet commanders, aware of the importance of holding the bridgehead, committed reserves to the fight. Reinforcements from nearby units were rushed into the

Map 7

OPERATION SOUTHWIND
17–24 FEBRUARY, 1945

Phase 1 17–21 Feb. 1945
Phase 2 22–24 Feb. 1945

fray, bolstering the beleaguered Soviet defenders and slowing the German advance.

By late afternoon, the fog had begun to lift, exposing both sides to each other's artillery fire. The open terrain near the Gran River became a killing field, with both German and Soviet artillery raining shells down on infantry and armor alike. The German advance had ground to a halt in several places, and Soviet forces were desperately attempting to consolidate their remaining positions.

As darkness began to fall, the fighting slowed but did not cease entirely. Skirmishes continued throughout the evening, with both sides launching probing attacks in an attempt to find weak points in the other's lines. The Germans, though exhausted from the day's heavy fighting, dug in and prepared for a renewed assault the following day. The Soviets, though battered, were still holding key positions along the river and had not yet been dislodged from the bridgehead.

The day ended in something of a bloody stalemate. The Germans had made some gains but had failed to achieve their primary objective of breaking through the Soviet lines and destroying the bridgehead. Both sides had suffered heavy casualties, and the battlefield was littered with the wreckage of destroyed tanks, artillery, and the bodies of fallen soldiers. The day's fighting had set the tone for the rest of *Unternehmen Südwind*, with neither side willing to give an inch without a brutal fight.

The big problem for the Russian was that, while they only gave ground after severe resistance, the battle area was relatively small. Giving *any* ground brought defeat closer.

18 February, Sunday

At Mauthausen prison during the night, when temperatures dipped well below freezing, hero of the Soviet Union Lt. General Dmitriy Karbyshev and some 500 other prisoners were drenched with water and made to stand outside, where they all died of exposure. Karbyshev had been captured in August, 1941, when he was wounded while trying to escape encirclement near the Dnepr River. He spent the next three and one half years in various German camps, resisting intense pressure to turn against Stalin. A memorial to him now stands at the camp, a giant white stone with the image of a man buried in the rock.

But the officer who oversaw Karbyshev's death, and that of thousands more besides him, never faced justice for his crimes. More than 60 years after the fall of Austria and the liberation of Mauthausen, dim echoes of the war still reverberated. Aribert Heim was known as the Butcher of Mauthausen. In the mold of Joseph Mengele, Aribert was known for conducting medical experiments on inmates in the Austrian death camp. Among his more gruesome activities was removing human organs without anesthetic just to see how long what he called his 'patients,' but which we would call his victims, would live without their organ. After the war he served two years in jail before returning to his practice as a gynecologist.

But not for long.

In 1962 he was alerted to his imminent arrest by the German government and fled for parts unknown, never to be seen again. Like so many wanted Nazis there were sightings all over the world, from Egypt to Chile. The Simon Wiesenthal Centre moved him up to second on its most wanted list and in July of 2007 Austria offered a reward of nearly $70,000 for information leading to his capture. Nearly 80 years after the fall of Mauthausen its Butcher was still being hunted.

A claim was made in the early 2000s, however, that Heim was killed in 1982 by a Jewish Search and Destroy organization named 'The Owl.' The story is that Heim was caught on an island off the California coast, shot, burned and dumped into the Pacific. True or false, even right decades later the flotsam of war was still drifting through the world.

Unternehmen Südwind

Weather north of the Danube had warmed slightly, from high 20s Fahrenheit at night, to 43 degrees during daytime.

Using the advantage gained by both the surprise of the day before, and the weight of the attack, *8. Armee* continued *Unternehmen Südwind* beginning in the pre-dawn hours, even while its left flank came under heavy Russian attack. *Kampfgruppe Staubwasser* joined the attack from directly west. This unit consisted of reconstituted portions of the shattered *357. Infanterie Division,* and had three battalions. The exact composition is difficult to ascertain, but given its record in combat during the last three months of the war it may have had a high percentage of veterans.

All throughout the battle area Russian resistance proved stubborn and resilient, forcing the Germans to fight for every foot of ground. Despite this, so far the Russian high command had not poured fresh troops into the fighting, seeming to prefer the continued reconstitution of units mauled taking Budapest. And for once the Germans had enough firepower to blast their way forward.

Air battles overhead mirrored the ferocity of the fighting below. Both sides hit enemy positions and troop concentrations with ground attack aircraft, bombing and strafing anything that moved, but

German fighters proved decisive in protecting their own bombers. *Luftflotte 4* suffered heavy losses, as did the Red Air Force.

What had already become clear after only two days was that infantry alone wasn't going to advance far without massive artillery and/or air support. Instead, the formations that ripped apart the Russian defenses were the two *SS-Panzer Divisions* of *IV. SS–Panzerkorps.*

In response to *Unternehmen Südwind* fresh attacks hit the area now held by *IV. SS–Panzerkorps.* Permission had not yet been granted for the defender sto give up the village of Dinnyés, but the Russians rendered the question irrelevant by capturing the town and driving the Germans back with heavy losses. The usual counterattacks failed, but Otto Wöhler made it clear that under no circumstance was contact to be lost with Lake Velence.

This was the only major point of combat other than in the sector of *8. Armee,* however. Marshal Malinovsky spent the day hurrying reinforcements toward the Gran Bridgehead, while Marshal Tolbukhin gathered strike forces for attack to relieve the pressure in the north.

19 February, Monday

A stray bomb from a bombing raid hit the zoo at Schönbrunn Palace, killing all beasts of prey. The Germans had allegedly sited a high military office in the Hapsburg summer palace, making it a legitimate target. Some 1200 exotic birds were killed or escaped and the government asked anyone finding them to bring them back.[383]

Reichsführer SS Heinrich Himmler on this day signed the order officially creating the *37. SS–Freiwilligen–Kavallerie Division*, soon to be given the honorific title *Lützow*. It's initial composition was the grouping of units from the two *SS* cavalry divisions that were not trapped in Budapest but were then assembled at the collection city of Senz, on Schuett Island in the Danube. Unlike the original plans for the division's first incarnation as *33. SS–Kavallerie Division*, it was intended that the new division should have three regiments of two battalions each;[384] as it happened only two regiments were ever formed and neither one achieved its authorized strength, although both saw extensive combat as *Kampfgruppen Ameiser* and *Keitel*.

At first the division had no real combat strength, as it was composed mostly of the medical, veterinary, supply and replacement components of those two lost divisions. The combat regiments would be built around soldiers of the *8. SS–Kavallerie Division Florian Geyer* and *22. SS–Freiwilligen–Kavallerie Division Maria Teresa,* who had been on leave and not trapped in Budapest, or recovered wounded who had been

---

[383] Weyr, Thomas, *The Setting of the Pearl, Vienna Under Hitler*, pp. 257-258.

[384] As originally envisaged, 33rd SS Volunteer Cavalry Division would have only been authorized for 2 regiments of 2 battalions each, and a strength of 6,600 men.

evacuated by air, and the few who had somehow survived the siege and the breakout and made their way to German lines.

It's hard to understand exactly why, at this very late stage of the war, the *SS Hauptamt*, and Himmler in particular, saw any value to creating a brand new Cavalry Division, as in horse cavalry, just as it was hard to understand why *I. SS–Ski Abteilung* was training in mountain warfare in Austria. The specialized support units were in place for a cavalry division, it is true, but such specialists were also needed in ordinary infantry divisions where horse-drawn transport was predominant even before the fuel shortages of the late war. On the open steppes of Russia there was a use for such a cavalry division in the reconnaissance role, or perhaps as a break-through exploitation force. But the German's role in 1945 was primarily defensive, even allowing for knowledge of the upcoming *Unternehmen Südwind* and *Unternehmen Frühlingserwachen* Offensives, and the last thing horse cavalry was good for was holding ground. The only thing that makes sense is that all of the support forces were in place for at least one cavalry division, there was at least a sprinkling of veterans to flesh out its combat elements, the heavy weapons necessary for an infantry division were in short supply, so the new division might as well be cavalry as infantry. Or perhaps Himmler just liked the romance of a cavalry division.

I./SS–Panzergrenadier Regiment 23 Norge was finally withdrawn from the front lines on 19 February. *SS–Hauptsturmführer* Fritz Vogt's command had been in the thick of some of the heaviest fighting in January, from its ordeal at Hegykastely with *5. SS–Panzer Division Wiking* Regiment to facing the brunt of the Soviet counterattacks at Pettend, and its latest nightmare in the trenches near Dennyes. As it withdrew westward to the small village of Vrkut west of Veszprem, the battalion numbered somewhere around 65 men, about 10 percent of its original strength of 600.[385] Sent to rest and reorganize, the battalion filled out somewhat with the return of some wounded and an infusion of men from the *Luftwaffe* and *Kriegsmarine*. These they hastily trained as infantry and formed into three weak companies that were short of everything from officers to heavy weapons. *I./SS–Panzergrenadier Regiment Danmark* was similarly reorganized but was somewhat stronger, having had more survivors to build around.

Unternehmen Südwind

On 19 February 1945, *Unternehmen Südwind* entered a critical phase as German forces sought to eliminate the Soviet presence in the Gran Bridgehead near Szolnok. This relatively small yet fiercely contested area held great strategic importance for both the Axis and Soviet forces, although as events would unfold, the significance of the Gran River as a defensive barrier was highly exaggerated. Nevertheless, Hitler and *OKH* viewed the Gran Bridgehead as a threat so dire as to justify the heavy losses already suffered by *I. SS–Panzerkorps*.

The fighting on 19 February saw heavy involvement for all of the key German units, including the *211. Volksgrenadier Division, 1. SS–Panzer Division, 12. SS–Panzer Division, Panzer Division Feldherrnhalle, Kampfgruppe Staubwasser*, and the *46. Infantry Division*. These units spearheaded the German counteroffensive, engaging in intense combat against well-entrenched Soviet forces.

The *211. Volksgrenadier Division*, commanded by *Generalmajor* Franz Sensfuss, hammered away at

---

[385] This would make the battalion about the strength of a weak company.

Soviet positions near the village of Kéménd, once again without much success. Their opponent here was the 81st Guards Infantry Division. The German division was made up of a mix of veteran soldiers and hastily conscripted personnel, which was nearly the definition of a *Volksgrenadier* division.

At dawn on 19 February, the division commenced its assault with yet another artillery barrage aimed at Soviet positions entrenched along a series of ridgelines overlooking the Gran River. The Russians, already well entrenched, expected the attack to begin when it did. , As the Germans advanced, they encountered fierce resistance from Soviet machine guns and artillery, which slowed their progress across the open ground.

The *Volksgrenadiers* pressed forward, and without sufficient antitank guns relied on their *panzerfäuste* to neutralize Russian tanks and self-propelled guns supporting the infantry. By midday, Sensfuss's division had managed to secure several key positions along the ridgelines but could not break through the Soviet defenses entirely. At relatively close quarters the fighting turned into a brutal, grinding battle of attrition, with both sides suffering significant casualties.

Positioned adjacent to the *Volksgrenadiers* to the west, the *1. SS–Panzer Division LAH* blasted its way meter by meter through the 72nd Guards Infantry Division, however, difficult terrain and heavy Soviet artillery fire hindered their advance. The *panzergrenadiers*, even when supported by *sturmgeschütze*, faced intense resistance from the usual Soviet anti-tank guns and entrenched infantry.

In the afternoon, a group of *Tiger IIs* and *panzergrenadiers* launched an assault near Szob. Despite facing heavy artillery and air attacks, the *1. SS–Panzer Division* managed to push the Soviets back several kilometers. However, they were unable to encircle the Soviet defenders, and the fighting ground to a halt without a decisive breakthrough. The 72nd

Guards Infantry Division had been shoved around and suffered many casualties, but had not yet broken.

Beside the *LAH* to its right, that is to the west, *46. Infanterie Division* ran into the same problem as the other infantry divisions, namely, insufficient combat power to break through the Russian defenses. In this case, the division struck the seam in the defense between 72nd Guards Infantry Division, and the 6th Guards Parachute Division. The infantry benefitted as the *panzer divisions* on either flank advanced, forcing Russians back all along the front. Nor were the infantry necessarily tasked with tearing holes in the front; tying down troops that could not be shifted against the *panzers* fulfilled their mission.

Continuing to move counter-clockwise, or to the west-southwest, the *12. SS–Panzer Division Hitlerjugend*, commanded by *SS-Brigadeführer* Hugo Kraas, struck the 6th Guards Parachute Division. Composed mainly of young recruits from the Hitler Youth, the *12. SS–Panzer Division* had distinguished itself in earlier campaigns, particularly in Normandy. Despite the relative inexperience of many of its soldiers, the division was known for its fanaticism and determination in battle.

On 19 February, the *12. SS–Panzer Division* was tasked with launching a flanking maneuver against Soviet positions near Muzsla. The division's *Mark V Panthers* spearheaded the attack, moving swiftly across the muddy plains to outflank the Soviet defenders. However, the difficult terrain took its toll on the armored vehicles, with several *Panthers* becoming bogged down and vulnerable to Soviet anti-tank teams.

Despite the setbacks, the *Hitlerjugend Panzergrenadiers* engaged Soviet forces in brutal close-quarters combat. The Soviets, having lost their well-prepared front line fortifications, were now entrenched in makeshift defensive positions. They fought back as fiercely as ever, but the Germans were able to push through and secure several key points by the evening. However, like their counterparts in the *1. SS–Panzer*

Division, the *12. SS–Panzer Division* was unable to achieve the breakthrough that the German high command had hoped for, and the battle remained deadlocked.

On *Hitlerjugend's* right flank, however, *44. Reichs–Grenadier Division Hoch und Deutschmeister* struck between the left flank of the 6th Guards Parachute Division, and the 409th Infantry Division, and gained ground.

Panzerkorps Feldherrnhalle, a unit formed from the remnants of earlier German formations, also played a vital role in the fighting on 19 February. Equipped with a mixture of *Mark IVs* and *Sturmgeschütze III* assault guns, the division was tasked with taking advantage of any breakthrough created by the infantry on either side. It should be remembered that *Felldherrnhalle* possessed nothing like the combat power of a true *panzerkorps*.

Throughout the day, *Panzerkorps Feldherrnhalle* fought in heavy combat near the village of Párkány. Soviet anti-tank guns and artillery, positioned on the far side of the Gran River, made it difficult for the German tanks to advance without sustaining significant losses. The division's *Sturmgeschütze IIIs* proved instrumental in providing close support to the infantry, destroying Soviet bunkers and machine-gun nests with their 75mm cannons.[386]

While the division made steady progress, securing several Soviet positions by the end of the day, the overall pace of the advance was slower than anticipated. *Panzer Division Feldherrnhalle*, like the other units involved in the attack, struggled to achieve a decisive breakthrough, and by nightfall, the Soviets still held critical ground that the Germans had to capture or fail.

Kampfgruppe Staubwasser, an ad hoc battle group formed from various German units, was tasked

---

[386] Caution is suggested in the assumption that all 'assault guns' as noted in the sources were, in actuality, *Sturmgeschütze*. There is the very real possibility that some were instead *Hetzers*.

with holding the western flank of the German offensive. Composed mainly of infantry and supported by a handful of AFVs and artillery pieces, the *kampfgruppe* engaged in heavy fighting near the town of Bátorkeszi.

The *kampfgruppe's* mission was to pin the 357th Infantry Division along the bridgehead's western edge, thereby preventing the Russians from falling back as the *panzers* drove into their rear from the north. Soviet forces launched repeated counterattacks throughout the day, attempting to break through the German lines in order to disrupt the *kampfgruppe*. The fighting was intense, with both sides suffering heavy losses. Despite being heavily outnumbered, *Kampfgruppe Staubwasser* managed to hold its positions, using a combination of mobile defense tactics and well-placed artillery to repel the Soviet attacks. By the end of the day, *Kampfgruppe Staubwasser* had successfully prevented the Soviets from reinforcing their positions, though the cost in terms of men and materiel was high.

By the end of 19 February 1945, the German offensive had made limited progress, but the overall situation remained fluid. While the *211. Volksgrenadier Division, 1. SS–Panzer Division, 12. SS–Panzer Division,* and *Panzer Division Feldherrnhalle* had managed to gain ground, the Soviet forces held their key positions, and the fighting showed no sign of letting up.

20 February, Tuesday

Unternehmen Südwind

Weather over the area warmed into the mid-40s Fahrenheit, with scattered clouds in mostly sunny skies. In other words, terrible weather for the Germans. Mechanized formations had to stay on major roads, as secondary and cross-country routes more resembled pudding than paths for travel. The Red Army also flew unhindered by overcast or fog; *Luftflotte 4* put forth another maximum effort in support of the offensive, 220 sorties, but the number kept shrinking day by day. German losses could not be made good. Each day of fighting saw *Luftflotte 4* grow weaker. It wasn't machines the Germans lacked, it was pilots and fuel.

On the fourth day of the offensive, the assault formations paused to rest and restock, to the degree that the supply situation allowed. Night attacks managed to gain some ground. At the coming of dawn, however, the assault divisions came under incessant attack from Russian aircraft, as well as enduring a rain of artillery and mortar fire from the east bank of the Gran River.

Some gains were made here and there, and in places ground was lost. The city of Esztergom, (Gran in German), came under very heavy artillery fire, and both *711. Infanterie Division and 96. Infanterie Division* had to reposition in the face of enemy action. *Kampfgruppe Hupe* and part of *Hitlerjugend* had been cut off, a situation that was relieved through an attack by *44. Reichs–Grenadier Division Hoch und Deutschmeister* that broke through the light Russian cordon.

German reconnaissance flights found long columns of Russian vehicles moving north from the Budapest area, 3,600 and more clogged all useable roads. The Germans now faced an uncertain situation, as they were unsure if the Soviets would manage to hold onto the remnants of their bridgehead or attempt to reinforce it. What were the intentions of the Soviet

415

forces and the specific role of the 6th Guards Tank Army, which had already been partially identified within the bridgehead? The question German intelligence couldn't answer was where they were going... into the bridgehead, further north, or some other purpose. Estimates of Russian losses in the Gran Bridgehead so far claimed multiple divisions destroyed or so badly damaged as to make them *hors de combat.* What could be said without question was that large numbers of anti-aircraft guns *had* been moved west of the Gran River, a sure indication that the Russians had no intention of evacuating the area.

Movements for renewing the offensive on 21 February were carried out the night of 20-21 February to shield the AFVs from Russia air attack. *Heeresgruppe Süd* estimated that *Unternehmen Südwind* should be wrapped up within a few days, and had already begun planning what would come next.

21 February, Wednesday

The damage caused by the one bomb that struck the Schönbrunn Tiergarten Zoo on 19 February was minor compared to the dozens of bombs that struck it on 21 February. Birds were killed when bombs also hit the small pheasant gardens section. The much beloved bull rhino >Toni=, who let the zookeeper ride on his back to the delight of zoo visitors, was killed.

The blow to Vienna's morale was severe. The zoo had introduced the practice of breeding endangered animals and was much loved by the populace of Vienna. After the First World War some 85 percent of its animals had been lost but with the help of both public and private donations, and under the direction of Otto Antonius, it was rebuilt and had become a vital part of the city's life. After the bombs fell on 21February it was a cratered graveyard.

Schönbrunn Palace itself was also badly damaged. Of the 269 bombs that hit the Palace, gardens and zoo, one remained stuck in the ceiling of the middle Palace building on the second floor gallery, where the paintings of Gregorio Gugliemis were hung. Why these were not evacuated like most of the Third *Reich*'s other artwork remains a mystery, but dilettantism by the *Gauleiter* of Vienna, Baldur von Schirach, would seem a likely explanation. Fortunately, the bomb was a dud, but the damage it caused to the ceiling was ironic: it ruined the allegorical (fresco) painting representing the military power of Austria. After the war restoration took more than two years and the painting was not restored until 1948. Damage was spread all over the Palace grounds, from the Gloriette (smashed virtually flat on the east side), to the garden near the Main Gate, the Eastern Cavalier Quarters, the Desert House and the Palm House.

On 21 February Ernst Andreas, a twenty-two year old *gefreiter* assigned as a clerk to a Pioneer Battalion office in the Hofburg, sat in the palace cellar forty feet below street level during a massive bombing raid that damaged the university, ripped the roof off city hall and tore open streets all the way to Schwarzenbergplatz. A B-17 crashed behind the Burgtheater.[387] Vienna had seen bombing attacks many times before, yet the severity increased exponentially in 1945, and the worst was yet to come.

SdKfz. 251 Ausf. D

Hanomag

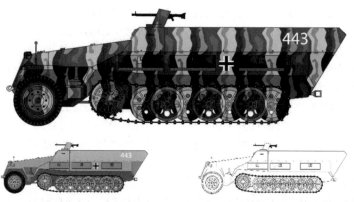

The standard German half-track, shown here with a machine gun.

In Slovakia, the *232. Panzer Division* was formed by the simple expedient of renaming *Panzer Feld-Ausbildungs Division Tatra*. Commanded by *Generalmajor* Hans-Ulrich Back it was soon attached to *Heeresgruppe Süd*.

During the Slovak uprising of the previous summer, *Tatra* had been an emergency *kampfgruppe* created from a variety of miscellaneous fragments.

[387] Weyr, *Setting of the Pearl*, p. 258.

Despite being hastily formed in late August 1944, *Panzer Division Tatra* was similar in size and firepower to a *Panzergrenadier Division*. It was cobbled together from various training, reserve, and militia units, all under the command of the *178. Panzer Division's staff,* and quickly thrust into battle.

The division included a mix of well-equipped *SS Sturmgrenadiers,* Landesschützen, replacement troops, *Schupo,*[388] and local *Volkssturm*. Its armor was diverse, featuring everything from the common *Sturmgeschütz*

---

[388] The *Schupo*, short for *Schutzpolizei*, were a branch of the German police during World War II. The term *Schutzpolizei* translates to "Protection Police" in English. The *Schupo* were responsible for maintaining public order and general policing duties in German cities, towns, and other localities.

Here are some key points about the Schupo during WWII:

1. Structure and Role: The Schupo were part of the *Ordnungspolizei (Orpo)*, which was the uniformed police force of Nazi Germany. They were mainly tasked with standard police duties such as traffic control, crime prevention, and maintaining public order. However, as the war progressed, their role expanded significantly.

2. Paramilitary Functions: During the war, the *Schupo* were increasingly militarized and often took on roles that blurred the lines between civil policing and military operations. They were involved in anti-partisan operations, especially in occupied territories in Eastern Europe, where they participated in actions against resistance movements and were complicit in war crimes, including atrocities against civilian populations and Jews.

3. Composition and Recruitment: The *Schutzpolizei* comprised both professional police officers and recruits drafted into service, often from other police agencies or auxiliary organizations. As the war continued and German manpower needs grew, the Schupo also absorbed personnel from other groups, including veterans, older men, and those considered less fit for frontline military service.

4. Integration with the *SS*: The *Schupo* were under the authority of Heinrich Himmler, who was not only the head of the *SS* but also the Chief of German Police. This integration placed the *Schutzpolizei* within the broader framework of Nazi control and ideology, aligning their activities more closely with the objectives of the *SS* and the regime's policies, including those related to occupation policies.

5. Uniforms and Equipment: The *Schupo* wore distinct green-grey uniforms and were equipped with a range of weapons typical of a paramilitary force. Their uniforms often included the police eagle and swastika insignia on their sleeves, distinguishing them from the military and *SS* units.

In summary, the *Schupo* were a critical component of the Nazi regime's internal security apparatus, playing a versatile role that extended far beyond traditional policing, contributing significantly to the enforcement of Nazi policies and the conduct of the war, particularly in occupied territories.

III G and *Mark IV Panzer H* to older *Panzer III, Panzer 38(t)*, and a few *Tiger Is*. The division also had *Hetzer, Jagdpanzer IV*, and *Marder III jagdpanzers*. Most of the artillery was made up of Czech guns.

Despite a shortage of anti-aircraft capabilities, *Panzer Division Tatra* was a surprisingly well-rounded mechanized *kampfgruppe*, bolstered by its infantry strength and air support. Total size was estimated at between 9,000-12,000 men, although the combat value of those troops varied wildly.

More staff came from a training facility at Malacky and other personnel were scraped together from everywhere and anywhere. One *panzer* battalion was formed around the hodge-podge of vehicles, 28 *Mark IIIs* which were wholly obsolete by that point, and various models of *Mark IVs*. It still had three *Tiger Is*. With the conversion from training to a combat formation, the infantry components were named *Panzergrenadier Regiments 101. And 102.*

Despite its hasty origins and glued-together pieces, *Tatra* fought well and helped crush the Slovak rebels and even recaptured the capital city of Pressburg (Bratislava). After the rebellion had been put down the division was kept intact and was converted to a training formation, but the armored vehicles were distributed elsewhere. Personnel were shuffled. The veterans from *1. Panzer Division* transferred out and other components were transferred in: the staff of *XVII Panzer* Corps, some *panzergrenadiers* from that command, and surplus men from various military districts.

Once Tatra became the *232. Panzer Division,* no *panzer* battalion was authorized and the division wound up with only two AFVs, although a *Panzerjäger* battalion was promised but never materialized. Like *2. Panzerarmee* it had 'Panzer' in its title but no *panzers* on hand with which to fight.[389] Exactly why it was formed as a combat formation in the first place is

---

[389] Actually it had 2.

unknown now, as is an exact ration strength. Equally mysterious is precisely what it was expected to do.

Unternehmen Südwind

Weather remained in the low 40s Fahrenheit, with light frost at night. Clear skies prevailed, but the days of dry weather had improved driving conditions all across the Grand Bridgehead. For the Russians, this proved ominous.

A Kampfgruppe from the *1. SS–Panzer Division Leibstandarte Adolf Hitler* advanced from the south toward Köhidgyarmat, Kam in German, while another group from the *46. Infanterie Division* attacked from the west. Being the last village before the Gran River itself, the village was strongly defended, with dense minefields. German losses were terrible. It was not until around 21:00, after nightfall, that they managed to capture the town. The remaining Soviet bridgehead, now defended by the 81st Guards Division, 72nd Guards Division, 6th Guards Airborne Division, and 93rd Guards Division, measured about 10 kilometers in width and four kilometers in depth.

Meanwhile, *Kampfgruppe 'Schöneich'* and other elements of the *46. Infanterie Division* launched an offensive north of the Párizs Canal in the direction of Kéménd, north of Köhidgyarmat. Those assaults failed due to the strong resistance of the XXIV Guards Corps, along with heavy artillery and air support. Nevertheless, at this point the Germans had nearly accomplished their objective of clearing the west bank of the Gran.

Despite fierce Russian resistance, and having to endure sometimes overwhelming air and artillery bombardments, the German offensive was on the verge of success. So close, in fact, that *General der Infanterie* Wöhler began to make plans for the coming offensive that Hitler had briefed him about during Wöhler's trip to see the *Führer*, namely, *Unternehmen Frühlingserwachen*.

To that end was the clock ticking. Only a few days remained before *I. SS–Panzerkorps* would have to entrain for the south to begin attack preparations. If *Unternehmen Südwind* had not been successfully concluded by then, it would be too late. One bit of good news seemed to be that both 6thGuards Tank Army and the Pliyev Group would remain east of the Gran River, a reserve force in case the Germans tried to cross. The area on the west bank that remained in Russian hands was now small, too small for the movement of large armored formations.

22 February, Thursday

Kampfgruppe 5. SS Panzer Division Wiking had enjoyed nearly two weeks of relative peace to rest and regroup, when on 22 February it was transferred to the front on both sides of Stuhlweissenburg. New recruits were coming in to flesh out its ranks, mostly from the *Kriegsmarine* and *Luftwaffe*, but their lack of training made them little more than targets.

Unternehmen Südwind

On 22 February, nighttime frost once again gave way to daytime temperatures reaching 43 degrees Fahrenheit, with alternating sun, clouds, and light rain, allowing the roads to continue drying. Despite these conditions, Soviet forces fiercely defended the portion of the bridgehead they still controlled. The *1. SS–Panzer Division Leibstandarte Adolf Hitler* and portions of the *46. Infanterie Division* continued their efforts to completely clear Köhidgyarmat and its surrounding areas. A *Waffen–SS Kampfgruppe* secured the road junction between Kéménd and Köhidgyarmat along the bank of the Párizs Canal. Meanwhile, the *46. Infanterie Division*, reinforced by *Kampfgruppe Schöneich*, captured Bibit-Puszta and advanced another kilometer beyond. However, by evening, the Soviets counterattacked and regained the territory.

At 0445, the *12. SS–Panzer Division Hitlerjugend* launched an assault on Bart, with both *SS–Panzergrenadier* regiments moving forward side by side, supported by *Panzers*, in a classic advance. The fighting was intense, but a rapid advance by the SPW-mounted *panzergrenadiers*, some armed with single- or triple-barrel 20-mm cannons, enabled the grenadiers to enter the town. A few T-34s resisted but withdrew toward Bény once they were abandoned by their supporting infantry. The Soviets managed to mount several counterattacks, but these were successfully repulsed. Elements of the *211. Volksgrenadier Division* approached Bart from the south, and by midday, the village was fully cleared. During the day, *6. SS–Panzerarmee* requested permission to withdraw its armored units from the bridgehead, but this request was denied by *Heeresgruppe Süd.*

23 February, Friday

Unternehmen Südwind

Conditions on 23 February kept to the familiar pattern; a night frost followed by a temperature of 43 degrees Fahrenheit during the day, cloud clearing at about 1200, but no further improvement in road conditions. The Germans used the whole day for regrouping and preparing for the final blow, and for the latter a night attack seemed to offer the best chance of success. The attack was set for 0200 on 24 February.

During overcast periods, the Germans were able to reorganize and resupply the various forward units. Artillery duels continued, with both sides using prodigious quantities of ammunition. Unusually, *Luftflotte 4* flew 85 night bombing missions against Russian supply columns.

Intelligence evidence mounted that one reason the Russians had not poured massive reinforcements into the bridgehead west of the Gran, was because they believed the Germans definitely planned to keep going and to cross that river. The Pliyev Group and 6th Guards Tank Army would then counterattack before the German offensive could become established on the east bank, and smash the attackers once and for all. After such a decisive blow, regaining the bridgehead area would be simple.

24 February, Saturday

When *Generalmajor* Gerhard Schmidhuber died on 11 February during the breakout from Budapest, command of the *13. Panzer Division* fell to Wilhelm Schoening, *Oberstleutnant der Reserves*. Somehow, Schoening survived the Russian trap and made it back to German lines, along with some 300-500 men of the *13. Panzer Division*. Using them as a nucleus, a new *Panzer* Division was activated on 24 February. Unofficially known as *13. Panzer Division*, its official name was *Panzer Division Felldherrnhalle 2*, a grand sounding title for a small formation of worn-out men. This unit is the perfect example of the late war German policy of creating new units instead of using the available men to replenish the existing ones. Nor can the excuse be used that transport to the needy units was too difficult, since there were plenty of under-strength *panzer* divisions in the southern area that could have used an infusion of veterans.

Unternehmen Südwind

The weather on the following day brought frost overnight, once more rising low 40s during the day, by the sunshine was gone. Instead, thick clouds brought sporadic rain. Combined with the sudden thaw, unpaved roads and open terrain became mud pits, making movement nearly impossible, even for tracked vehicles. Around Kémend, Soviet forces had established a deep defensive system, including a *pakfront* of 37 heavy anti-tank guns, the omnipresent 76mm cannon.

Kémend was the key remaining position. Located directly on the banks of the Gran River, its capture would signal the end of the bridgehead, making the remaSupported by a *kampfgruppe* from the *44. Reichs–Grenadier Division 'Hoch- und Deutschmeister*, the *1.*

SS–Panzer Division LAH managed to break through the *pakfront* after intense fighting, eventually forcing their way into the town. Attacking such a position required heavy air and artillery support. Without that, and with armored formations hampered by the muddy conditions, it fell on the *panzers* to provide direct fire support as the infantry struggled forward. The battle then turned into a drawn-out house-to-house struggle, which lasted until late in the afternoon when the Germans finally secured Kéménd. In an effort to prevent the Germans from advancing further, the Soviets demolished the bridge at Kéménd. The remaining Soviet troops crossed the Garam River, using the ice and fording points. Throughout the day, Soviet artillery, firing from the eastern bank of the river, heavily shelled Kéménd and Bény, disregarding their own retreating soldiers to hinder the German forces' attempts to cross.

What remained of the Russian defense began to crumble. The *SS–Panzergrenadier Regiment 26* of the *12. SS Panzer Division Hitlerjugend,* with armor support, carried out a swift attack on Bény. By 0830, they had secured most of the town, and by noon, Bény was entirely under German control. As the *Waffen–SS Panzergrenadiers* approached, the Soviets destroyed the bridge at Bény to delay further German advances, but stranding any Russians still on the west bank. Building on the success at Bény, the *211. Volksgrenadier Division* moved to capture Leand-Puszta later that morning.

At 1720, the *8. Armee* reported to *Heeresgruppe Süd* that the Soviet bridgehead had been fully eliminated, a message that was relayed to the *Oberkommando des Heeres* at 1745. *Unternehmen 'Südwind* had officially ended, marking the last successful army-level German offensive of the Second World War, as it completely eradicated the Soviet bridgehead and the threat it posed.

According to Soviet accounts, the 7th Guards Army suffered losses of 8,194 personnel, 54 tanks and

428

self-propelled guns, and 459 pieces of artillery. German casualties were also high, largely due to the Panzergrenadier units bearing most of the fighting. The Germans lost 6,471 men, including 969 killed, 4,601 wounded, and 901 missing. Their equipment losses totaled around 130 *panzers* and *sturmgeschütze*, though many were recoverable. For example, out of the 44 Tiger IIs available at the start on 17 February, only 13 remained operational on 20 February, and just seven by the end of the offensive. However, of the 37 Tiger IIs lost, only one was a complete write-off, while only two had to be sent back to Germany for extensive repairs. This ability to repair damaged tanks was far more advanced than the Russians, which was critical to Germany's ability to continue fighting even when production of armored vehicles plummeted.

The commander of 7th Guards Army. Its commander, Colonel General Shumilov, was heavily criticized for failure during the battle and 2nd Ukrainian Front's commander, Marshal Malinovsky, was also censured for failing to recognize the importance of the Gran Bridgehead. Some of this may be written off to politics within the Soviet High Command, but some of it stuck, too. And was warranted; the Russians would pay heavily in blood when they recrossed the Gran River heading west.

The complete success of the attack even took the Germans by surprise. During the evening situation report in Berlin, *Oberstleutnant* von Humboldt of the *OKH* staff reported that "the bridgehead on the Gran has been cleaned out." Such unequivocal success took Hitler by surprise.

"Really?"

"Yes, it has been cleared out completely-it's in order. The two *SS* divisions are already pulling out."

"Wonderful!"

After a short discussion of what division to leave in the sector for defense, Hitler once more had to make certain that he understood correctly.

"So that's completely cleared out?"

"Yes, it's completely cleared out."

"That went well," Hitler said.[390]

After months of failed German attacks and catastrophic enemy offensives, Hitler was finally reminded of what it was like for German troops to win a battle. With the exception of the liberation of Lauban in March, however, it would be the very last time the *panzer* divisions would roll forward to victory.

But while *Unternehmen Südwind* was an unqualified tactical success, it was a strategic disaster. Stalin's words at Yalta notwithstanding, German deceptions measures had worked perfectly and the Russians had not been sure of exactly where *6. SS–Panzerarmee* was, with the assumption being that it was deployed in reserve near Berlin. *I. SS–Panzerkorps* was that army's most powerful unit, however, and when it participated in *Südwind* the Russian intelligence service finally knew without a doubt where Sepp Dietrich's army had gone. Once that knowledge became known it was child's play to deduce that it was in Hungary to attack and the point of that attack was equally easy to figure out, as the only terrain that made sense was the same as had been covered in *Konrad III*. With why and where known the only question became when, but knowing that it would take time for *I. SS–Panzerkorps* to deploy to the Lake Balaton area the Russians began bulking up their defenses in the area; their plans began to evolve then, spawning the idea of bleeding the attacking German forces white then launching a flank attack at the precise moment when Dietrich's men were exhausted and over-stretched. And that is exactly what they did.

Despite its success, the operation had an unintended consequence: it revealed the presence of the *I. SS–Panzerkorps* in Hungary to the Soviets, and by

[390] Heimer & Glantz, pp. 667-668.

extension *6. SS–Panzerarmee*, thereby allowing them to adjust their strategies in response to the upcoming *Unternehmen Frühlingserwachen.* The question in retrospect is whether or not *Unternehmen Südwind* was worth the cost.

As always, it has to be recognized that Germany could do nothing to avoid its upcoming defeat. Even in 1945 that was true to most of the men doing the fighting, at least in the officer ranks. They fought on for a variety of reasons, but none moreso than adherence to their oath of allegiance, which reflected on their personal sense of honor. So the bigger question becomes what might have happened had *Südwind* not be launched.

Keeping the presence of the four most famous *Waffen–SS panzer* divisions secret for the 10 day span between the end of *Südwind* and the start of *Frühlingserwachen* seems highly improbable. At best the time given for the Russians to prepare might have been lessened. Given the conditions under which *Frühlingserwachen* was launched, however, it is doubtful this would have made much difference to the outcome.

On the other hand, allowing the bridgehead west of the Gran River to serve as a launching area for the sure-to-come offensive by 2nd Ukrainian Front aimed at Bratislava and further west, would have been disastrous. As it was, the *8. Armee* front broke but did not shatter. Thus it is difficult to judge that *Unternehmen Südwind* was not a well-conceived and necessary offensive. The Germans showed that, when given any chance of success through proper supplies of fuel and ammunition, they could still fight the Russians and win.

Unfortunately for them, it would never happen again.

25 February, Sunday

Knight's Cross winner *SS–Sturmbannführer* Ameiser was ordered to form a kampfgruppe centered on *SS–Reiter Regiment 92*, the unit he already commanded. In addition, *Kampfgruppe Ameiser* would have one battery from *SS–Artillerie Regiment 37* and other of the division's elements that were combat ready, including some *Pioneers*, a *Nachrichten* (Signals) platoon and Supply personnel. In total, the *kampfgruppe* was some 1,400 strong. It was attached to *Armeegruppe Balck*, *6. Armee*, for *Unternehmen Frühlingserwachen*, specifically the *96. Infanterie Division*, Hungarian VIII Army Corps.

According to Michael Reynolds, by 25 February the *1. SS–Panzer Division LAH* had suffered terrible *panzer* losses during *Unternehmen Südwind*, leaving the regiment with "four Tigers, eleven Panthers and twelve Mark IV tanks."[391] The *Tigers* were undoubtedly part of *Schwere Panzer Abteilung 501*, which had begun the fight with 19 operational *panzers*. As heavy as losses were, Michaelis gives a pre-offensive manpower total of 19,055 and a total afterward of 18,871, a difference of only 284 of all ranks.[392] Further, he goes on to give *12. SS–Panzer Division Hitlerjugend* a strength of 17,423 after the offensive.[393]

In southern Germany, at a testing ground in the military training area Heuberg in the vicinity of Stetten am kalten Markt, a full-scale test flight of Erich

[391] Reynolds, *The Devil's Adjutant*, p. 249.
[392] Michaelis, *Panzer Divisions of the Waffen–SS*, p. 50.
[393] Ibid, p. 305.

Bachem's revolutionary vertical takeoff aircraft, the *Natter*, successfully proved that the design was sound. Using a dummy instead of a live pilot, the flight was a huge success and the aircraft operated exactly as planned, although the re-useable parts of the fuselage exploded when they hit the ground from residual fuel. Nevertheless, the flight was considered a milestone. The Natter in its final configuration would have a nose filled with 72 rockets that would be fired in a salvo at American bombers, making it a potentially lethal antidote to the Strategic Bombing Campaign. Even with the desperation of the moment, however, the *Natter* had to first be successfully flown with a pilot and time was running out.

26 February, Monday

On 26 February Maria Czedik wrote in her diary that most mornings the city of Vienna resembled an ant hill. "Masses of humanity push and shove each other to get into the public cellars. The *Wiedner Hauptstrasse* (a main thoroughfare in the fourth district) is a mass migration flowing out of the tenth district."[394]

All involved on both sides knew that the ultimate prize of the fighting in Hungary was never Budapest, it was Vienna, the city where in 1913 Hitler, Lenin, Trotsky, Freud, Tito and Stalin all lived at the same time. Indeed, they all frequented the same coffeehouses, including Hitler's favorite, the Cáfe Sperl.

Sometime around 26 February, *SS Reiter Regiment 92*, the second combat regiment for the newly authorized *37. SS–Freiwilligen–Kavallerie Division Lützow*, began forming in the region of Gaenserdorf-Leopoldsdorf-Orth-on-the-Danube. The Regiment was commanded by the son of *Generalfeldmarschall* Wilhelm Keitel, *SS–Sturmbannführer* K.H. Keitel. He had been a regimental commander with the *22. SS–Freiwilligen–Kavallerie Division Maria Theresa*, was trapped and wounded in Budapest and evacuated by air. The division's *SS* Artillery Detachment also began forming about this time. The first battery was shipped quickly to Grossenzersdorf, east of Vienna. The process of collecting and forming these units went on into early March.

[394] Weyr, *The Setting of the Pearl*, pp. 258-259.

27 February, Tuesday

This day's was the first entry found in the final chapters from Joseph Goebbels' diary. Goebbels often related military facts that must have come directly from the *Führer* conference, and while they are usually fairly factual as such, the excuses and reasons for the long litany of setbacks is instructive as an indication of what was being said around and to Hitler.

"We must be as Frederick the Great was and act as he did. The *Führer* agrees with me entirely when I say to him that it should be our ambition to ensure that...our grandchildren should look back on us as a heroic example of steadfastness."[395]

In Berlin, Hitler spent much of the early evening of 26 February closeted with Goebbels discussing shortcomings in the leadership of the Nazi Party, specifically Göring, as the Byzantine intrigues of the Third *Reich* continued even as the war situation deteriorated. Göring and Goebbels had been political rivals for years and the Propaganda Minister never lost a chance to denigrate the *Reichsmarshall*. *Grossadmiral* Dönitz was praised as a fine National Socialist, probably because he had no political ambitions.

Goebbels reports that 80 US bombers flying from Italy peeled off from an attack on Augsburg and bombed Salzburg. The attacking unit was the 469th Bomb Group (H), which aimed for the railroad marshalling yards but wound up also hitting a residential district.

In recognition of his leadership in combat, the commander of SS-Brigade Ney, Dr. Karoly Ney, was

[395] Trevor-Roper, Professor Hugh, Translator and Editor, *Final Entries 1945 The Diaries of Joseph Goebbels* (New York: Avon, 1978), p. 1.

promoted to *SS–Sturmbannführer,* and a number of awards were handed out to the men of the brigade.

Elsewhere, having been brought back to strength by a massive infusion of nearly worthless untrained recruits, *Wiking* was once again designated as a *panzer* division. This was misleading, however, as its *panzer* regiment was almost non-existent and its transport was only slightly better. It was fit only for defensive operations and would not participate in the upcoming *Unternehmen Frühlingserwachen.*[396] Indeed, within another month the *panzer* regiment would be disbanded altogether, and the highly trained and veteran crews sent to fight as ordinary infantry.

[396] Michaelis, *Panzer Divisions of the Waffen–SS,* p. 202.

28 February, Wednesday

The German manpower shortage had become so critical that Goebbels confided to his diary it might be time for extreme measures. In the second *Volkssturm* levy, he floated the idea that it might be time to form women's battalions, presumably combat formations, and even battalions of criminals from the concentration camps, strictly supervised, of course. Goebbels seems to have been tossing the ideas back and forth in his mind, as if by writing it down it helped him think about the issue.

The morale of the front line troops was also a problem well known in the highest circles in Berlin. Goebbels proposed increasing circulation of a newspaper for the front-line troops titled *Front und Heimat* (Front and Home) from once a week to three times a week. Paper shortages made this impractical but he commented to his diary Re-establishment of our troops' morale and will to resist is now of decisive importance."[397]

[397] Trevor-Roper, *Final Entries*, p. 13.

1 March, Thursday

Sometime in early March *SS–Standartenführer* Karl Gesle took over command of the still forming *37. SS–Freiwilligen–Kavallerie Division Lützow*. Gesle was the former First Staff Officer of *8. SS–Kavallerie Division Florian Geyer*.

In his diary entry for 2 March, Goebbels mentions that on this day, meaning on 1 March, he spoke with the commander of *6. SS–Panzerarmee*, Sepp Dietrich, about the upcoming operation in Hungary, *Unternehmen Frühlingserwachen*. Dietrich gave as estimate some 10-12 days for the operations' completion and "if all goes well we can anticipate enormous success." He goes on to say that Dietrich thinks he will be available for operations in Eastern Germany in 14 days, and major offensive operations in eastern Germany, or the Oder Front, would be possible by late March.

Dietrich may not have been the Wehrmacht's most capable commander, but neither was he a fool. It's not hard to be to believe that he told Goebbels what he wanted to hear, but it's very hard to believe that Dietrich actually thought his army would be ready for transport to fight in front of Berlin within two weeks of *Unternehmen Frühlingserwachen* beginning. However, Goebbels mentions that so far the deception measures had kept *6. SS–Panzerarmee* from becoming known to the enemy, which was untrue. Stalin may have known about the transfer for weeks and the Gran Offensive had certainly made it quite clear that the cream of the *Waffen–SS* was in Hungary. Perhaps the High Command was deluded, or perhaps they were afraid to bear bad tidings to Hitler, but they convinced Goebbels, and Hitler, that the appearance of the *Waffen–SS panzer* divisions would come as a huge surprise. In fact, the Red Army was waiting for them.

One crucial paragraph of Goebbels' entry for 1 March relates very clearly how Dietrich felt about the nation's leadership and how that leadership viewed its subordinates. The mess of Germany's command structure is encapsulated by the words of its second or third most powerful man, Josef Goebbels: "Dietrich quite openly criticized measures taken by the *Führer*. He complains that the *Führer* does not give his military staff a sufficiently free hand and that this tendency has now become so pronounced that the *Führer* even lays down the employment of individual companies. But Dietrich is in no position to judge. The *Führer* cannot rely on his military advisers. They have so often deceived him and thrown dust in his eyes that he now has to attend to every detail. Thank God he does attend to them, for if he did not matters would be even worse than they are anyway."

This is an extraordinarily candid portrait of Hitler and his entourage on the cusp of the final disasters. Like any decent commander, Dietrich complains that he is being told how to do his job and that Hitler does not trust him to do it. The implication is that if hc is not good enough to fight his own battles, why does he have his command? But, more amazing, we have a picture of Hitler giving one of his oldest comrades, and presumably one of those he still trusted, detailed instruction on how to use companies that could not have numbered more than 80 or 100 men. The *Führer* of the *Reich* worrying about the deployment of a rifle company hundreds of miles away! This was bizarre enough, but then we have the spectacle of the *Reich* Minister of Propaganda and Enlightenment (*Reichsministerium für Volksaufklärung und Propaganda*; RMVP) defending this micro-management as being necessary for the survival of the state, and chastising the commander on the spot for not understanding why this had to be done.

Dietrich had commanded Hitler's personal bodyguard. There was a time when he spent days and weeks on end with Hitler. He was a pivotal player during the Night of the Long Knives. If Hitler should have had faith in anyone, it was Dietrich.[398]

A bombing raid staged on Moosbierbaum near Vienna by B-24 Liberators ended for one bomber when it was shot down over Hungary, crashing near Acteszer, but not before eight crewmen bailed out. The eight downed US airmen were captured by members of *SS–Brigade Ney* near Sur. Five of the prisoners were later to be tortured, tried as spies and then executed by the *SS* men, while three were sent on to the Germans for internment. In 1946 six men of the unit were tried in Salzburg and convicted of the murders, including the Regiment's founder and commander, Karoly Ney. Sentenced to death, his and another man's sentence were commuted to life in prison[399], two others received life in prison, while two of the *SS* men were executed.

The *panzer* strength of *5. SS Panzer Division Wiking* was little better than it had been a month before, with 14 AFVs from an authorized strength of 152. The division had three *Mark IVs*, two *Sturmgeschütze* and *Mark V Panthers*, although others were in long-term repair. In contrast, *2. SS–Panzer Division Das Reich* reported a manpower strength on 1 March of 19,542 men of all ranks, well over its authorized strength. This gave *Das Reich* a fighting strength of roughly 10,000 men.

[398] Trevor-Roper, *Final Entries*, pp. 27-28.
[399] Ney would later be released to work for the Americans during the early stages of the Cold War.

Like *Das Reich, Totenkopf* had been infused with new blood and had recovered remarkably in a month, according to Michaelis. On a daily average the division only suffered three men killed during February, most of those probably to artillery and mortar fire, so that by the end of the month it was also over-strength with a total of all ranks of 19,353. Although still badly deficient in officers, a weakness that plagued all German formations in 1945, *Totenkopf* was also over-strength in non-commissioned officers. This was probably a result of promotions to fill gaps combined with wounded that had recovered and returned to the division. Although under-strength, its *panzer* regiment was considerably stronger than *Wiking's*. On hand there were (only) 16 *Mark IVs, eight Mark V Panthers,* seven *Tigers*[400] and 17 Sturmgeschütze, for a total of 48 combat-ready AFVs of all types, or the strength of an average battalion. Nevertheless, at this point in the war that made the division stronger than many. Five light and five heavy batteries of artillery were left for fire support and the division reported itself 80 percent.[401]

The discrepancy between the three divisions cannot be accounted to *Wiking's* position as a nominally pan-European formation; by this point in the war the vast number of its men were either native or ethnic Germans, as most of the occupied countries had already been liberated. Instead, this discrepancy is further evidence of the patronage system that had always been a hallmark of the *Waffen-SS*. Curiously, on 1 March the Hungarian 2nd Armored Division had an operational strength of 17 *Mark IVs* and one *Mark V Panther,* with 7 *Mark IVs* and two *Mark V Panthers* in repair. Thus, even a remnant Hungarian division had

---

[400] Exactly which model *Tiger* is hard to say, because *Totenkopf* was the rare German formation with an organic *Tiger* company. *9./SS–Panzer Regiment 3* still had operable machines in March, 1945, and these are likely the ones mentioned. In that case they would be *Mark VI Tiger Is. SS–Schwere–Panzer Abteilung 501,* known to be near *Totenkopf,* operated with *Tiger IIs.*

[401] Michaelis, *Panzer Divisions,* p. 162.

more combat ready armor than *Wiking,* one of the elite formations of the *Waffen-SS.*

The commander of *I./SS–Panzergrenadier Regiment 23 Norge,* Fritz Vogt, was promoted to command the reconnaissance battalion of *5. SS–Panzer Division Wiking Division,* and was replaced by *SS–Sturmbannführer* Barth.[402] Holding the line against massive Soviet attacks during *Konrad III* was an impressive achievement. Whether Vogt had been an intrepid and courageous warrior while commanding the battalion, as his defenders claim, or a glory-hound advancing his career on a carpet of his own dead men, the correct eulogy according to his critics, there is no question that the battalion both suffered and inflicted enormous casualties under his leadership.

After an extraordinarily successful unmanned test flight, the first manned flight of Erich Bachem's brainchild vertical takeoff aircraft, the *Natter Ba 349A M2,* was a disaster. Test pilot *Leutnant* Lothar Sieber squeezed into the cramped cockpit and lay flat, legs extended skyward, and was then strapped into the machine by several technicians. Weather conditions were not optimal, fog enveloped the test area at Heuberg, but desperate times called for desperate measures, and the Third *Reich* was frantic to find any successful weapon to defend its skies against Allied bombers, so the test flight was ordered to proceed.

Like all test pilots Sieber was a daredevil, but he was not suicidal. Even as his country was being

---

[402] Who, exactly, this new commander was is still being debated. The most likely candidate seem to be Fritz Barth, who was killed in action on March 20, 1945, the same day I/Norge had yet another commander.

destroyed around him Sieber was optimistic enough to become engaged, and the night before his final doomed flight he told friends: ""I hope it will not be worse than my previous mission – I know I can do the most crazy things without putting myself in jeopardy."[403]

Bachem BA-349 Natter

Shortly after takeoff the aircraft veered off course, looped over, the cockpit canopy flew off and the Natter crashed in a mushroom of flame. Later calculations determined that the Natter achieved a powered upward speed of 750 kilometers per hour. Sieber was buried two days later with full military honors, but the Natter program did not follow him into the grave quite yet. Nevertheless, despite the Third *Reich*'s desperate need for some new weapon to hold back the invaders and stop the incessant bombing of German cities, the Natter program had to find the problem before it could try again. And time was running out.

[403]

http://www.opsjournal.org/assets/SecureDocumentLibrary/DocumentLibraryMan ager/documents/SpaceOpsNews-Lothar%20Sieber.pdf, accessed 12/2/2014).

For some time the Germans had been putting a great deal of scarce resources and effort into the formation, training and equipping of the *XVII SS Armeekorps* and it's first two divisions, *25. SS–Grenadier Division Hunyadi (Ungarische No. 1)* and *26. SS–Grenadier Division Hungaria (Ungarische No. 2)*. The Inspector General of this formation was a First World War veteran who had just been appointed to the rank of *SS–SS–Obergruppenführer* by Himmler, Jeno Ruszkay. He was a man that the leader of the Hungarian government, Ferenc Szalasi, thought was too pro-German and opposed to oversee the Hungarian *SSArmeekorps*, to the point that Szalasi stripped him of his citizenship. On 1 March, Ruszkay set up his headquarters in a castle at Baden, south of Vienna; while there he did essentially nothing. Meanwhile, the next day the command headquarters of *XVII SS–Armeekorps* was established across Austria and just inside Germany at Burghausen.

As *Unternehmen Frühlingserwachen* approached, the 20th Hungarian Assault Battalion fielded 23 operational Hetzers with 13 more under repair. Although considered a light tank destroyer, as opposed to the heavier *Jagdpanzer IVs* and *Jagdpanzer Vs*, at this point the Germans no longer differentiated between AFVs with a turret and those with fixed guns of limited traverse, instead putting all such AFVs into the '*panzer*' category. Thus, the 20th Hungarian Assault Battalion had more operational armor than did *Wiking*, and German-built armor at that. The battalion would shortly be assigned to *I. Kavallerie Korps* to support the attack near Lake Balaton.

2 March, Friday

The closer the Soviets came, the greater grew resistance to the Germans. This was true in all of the occupied countries, and even in Austria. A general accounting of the Austrian resistance is outside the scope of this narrative, but does come into play during April, 1945, when the narrative of this book's companion volume moves into Austria.

Weyr covers the resistance generally, with special concentration on an organization known as *O–5*.[404] "On 2 March he (Schoner) still had little faith or hope in any Austrian resistance. 'Fear of the *Gestapo, SD* and *SS* is too great. People are less actively opposed to the regime than they are tired and resigned...everybody sees the end coming but keeps muddling through.'"[405]

By this point in early March, Vienna had become a bomb-damaged, burnt, hungry city with irregular power and gas, very little running water, streets filled with garbage and rubble and a population who simply wanted things over with. Corpses were buried in mass graves in the Central cemetery.

Propaganda Minister Goebbel's entry for 2 March, 1945, contains a wealth of information concerning the mood of the country as the enemy closed in on the *Reich*, what the people were concerned with and the troubles of those in command. In his regular diary entry for the day, Goebbels admits that morale among the troops and people was beginning to crack. Given that this was his area of responsibility, he was the chief moral officer of the *Reich*, in a manner of

---

[404] The code name *O–5* or *O5*, came from the abbreviation for *Österreich*, the German word for Austria, where "O" indicates the first letter of the abbreviation (OE), and the "5" indicated the fifth letter of the German alphabet (E).

[405] Weyr, *The Setting of the Pearl*, p. 271.

speaking, this candid admission is startling and may well have understated the situation. But Goebbels made it his business to know and he can be believed in this.

"...In general the people remain comparatively solid. There is too much grumbling about the officers however... (Here he means in the *Wehrmacht*, not the general population) It is too facile to ascribe the defeats of the last two years to sabotage by officers. Things are not as simple as that."[406]

This is likely a reaction to the previous summer's assassination attempt on Hitler and the backlash of blame directed at the Army officer class, flames directed at the *Heer* by Goebbel's own propaganda machine. Now, as the *Reich* was fighting for its life, the soldiers didn't trust their officers, which meant they might not follow orders. As the narrative of battle came closer and closer to Vienna this backdrop of unease and mistrust should be remembered, as it will manifest itself later in the people's extraordinary shows of rebellion as that city was invaded.

But Goebbels also contradicts himself to some extent in the same entry.

"The scandal of desertions has increased dramatically. It is suspected that there are tens of thousands of soldiers in the major German cities who are supposedly stragglers but in practice are evading service at the front."[407]

It's hard now to ascertain whether this is Goebbels making excuses or whether the problem really existed to the extent he claims, but it's not hard to see in this statement the rationale for the flying courts-martial that were such a feature behind the German lines. Any man suspected of desertion was shot, hung, stabbed, and/or made into an example of

[406] Trevor-Roper, *Final Entries*, p. 30.
[407] Trevor-Roper, *Final Entries*, p. 31.

cowardice, usually with a placard proclaiming his 'crime.' Whether or not this was Goebbels echoing what he heard elsewhere is hard to say. In the end, though, it does not matter. Mass paranoia was the order of the day behind German lines, making re-supply difficult, harassing messengers passing between units and interrupting reconnaissance duties. Numerous instances of men on legitimate errands and with the proper papers being shot anyway by rear-echelon goons.

As the situation at the front crumbled and the home front came ever closer to being the war front, Goebbels went on to say, "in the letters I receive there is much criticism of our war leadership in general and it is now also directed at the *Führer* personally."[408]

Surely there were few people in the Third *Reich* insane enough to write Joseph Goebbels letters criticizing Hitler; that was a guaranteed ticket to being the main event at a firing squad. More likely, Goebbels here refers to intelligence summaries gleaned from letters intercepted by postal censors that reflect the mood of the country. But whichever is true it shows the unease and dread that gripped the *Reich*, because by this late date its citizens could be left in no doubt what fate awaited those who dwelt on such 'defeatism.' In the same paragraph he goes on to worry about food riots as the breadbasket areas of Eastern Germany were lost and transport problems made it impossible to get food into the big cities. "We must anticipate the most dangerous problems here." Once again, the citizenry surely knew of the draconian penalties for even the smallest crimes, yet Goebbels is openly worrying about food riots.[409]

When discussing the movements of troops to the south, and in particular in the buildup to *Unternehmen Frühlingserwachen*, transport difficulties are mentioned often, both the sporadic functioning of the railways and

---

[408] Ibid, p. 32.
[409] Ibid, p. 32.

the lack of gasoline. And yet both are hard concepts to quantify. How late was a given unit reaching the battlefield because the railways were damaged, what movements did a *panzer* division not make because it did not have the fuel? If, say, a *Sturmgeschütz* was blown up by its crew because it was out of gas and the Russians were 100 yards away, that is a simple enough image. But if a company of *Mark V Panthers* needed to move 15 kilometers into a blocking position but did not because the fuel was low, that is not quite as easy to picture. And so the time Goebbels spends discussing the transport difficulties all over the country, and the time that Armaments Minister Albert Speer spent trying to overcome those problems, has great relevance to the picture of war in Hungary and Austria. It also shows, perhaps more clearly than any other single source, exactly why Hitler committed so many armored units so far to the south. Put quite simply, the *panzer* units were deployed in the south because that was where the fuel and refineries were, and little transport was needed to get it to the fighting troops.

> "Speer is now at work re-establishing the transport network. He has put 80,000 men on to repair of marshaling yards, primarily in the west. If we can once succeed in clearing the marshaling yards, traffic will run smoothly again and the numerous stranded trains can get on the move once more. This is the nub of the problem as far as our run-down transport system is concerned. Numerous stranded trains can get on the move once more."[410]

It is obvious that all over Germany trains were moving fitfully, if at all, with no schedules possible and no reliability to deliveries. And while *Heeresgruppe Süd* may have been closer to the fuel sources and oil refineries than units to the north, it was also much

[410] Trevor-Roper, *Final Entries*, p. 33.

further away from the few functioning armaments factories to the north and west.

Goebbels goes on to write that 350 US bombers flying out of Italy bombed Linz, with a few scattered bombs falling on Graz and Villach. In comparison, the *Luftwaffe* had grown so feeble that Hitler was told that fighter-bombers flying southeast of Budapest destroyed two locomotives and that six fighters shot down three Russian aircraft while losing four of their own; the *Führer* was now concerning himself with the day-to-day activities of handfuls of aircraft.

As if Otto Wöhler didn't have his hands full planning *Unternehmen* Frühlingserwachen, along his norther flank Russian attacks in the area of Altsohl (Zvolen) continued. The Slovakian city lay astride the Gran River and constituted a key position in the area. The bridgehead further south may have been wiped out, but by no means had the Russians accepted defeat.

The *357. Infanterie Division*, with its two companies of Spanish volunteers, had been serving along the Gran front as part of *8. Armee* since mid-January. The two companies were the last remnants of a once large Spanish commitment to stopping communism without actually going to war. By Spring of 1945, however, Franco knew that Germany had lost and wanted no part of her defeat. The *357. Infanterie Division* was ordered back through the Lower Carpathians to a point some 25 miles north of Bratislava (Pressburg). Sometime in early April the division gave up its Spaniards, who were attached to *SS–Division Nordland* on the Vistula Front. A few of them wound up fighting the last-ditch battle for the *Reichsklanzie* on 1 May, strangely enough alongside French *SS* troopers.

2. SS–Panzer Division Das Reich was alerted for imminent action on 2 March, having completed barely two weeks training for the new recruits. The division was in such poor condition that two battalions, *I./SS–Panzergrenadier Regiment 3 Der Fuhrer* and *II./SS–Panzergrenadier Regiment 4 Deutschland* were unfit for combat, both from the soldiers' state of training being so low and from a lack of vehicles. Without these men "both *panzer*grenadier regiments marched into their assembly areas with only two-thirds of their infantry strength."[411] The manpower shortage was already a critical weakness for *Heeresgruppe Süd* as a whole and *6. SS–Panzerarmee* in particular, but in the coming battle when weather would make the use of armored vehicles nearly impossible and would place the burden for attack chiefly on the infantry, every last man would be needed.

The commanding general of *Heeresgruppe E*, *Generaloberst* Löhr, was present during the midday situation report at the *Führer* Headquarters; in support of *Unternehmen Frühlingserwachen, Heeresgruppe E* was ordered to seize two bridges over the Drava River before driving on Kaposvar, far to the south. Löhr was on hand to ensure that he understood his mission clearly. The two bridges in question were both pre-war structures, strong and sturdy, built from stone and steel. The *11. Luftwaffe Feld Division* was given the mission of capturing the bridge at Valpovo, while *194. Jäger Division* and *297. Infantry Division* were tasked with taking the bridge at Donji Miholjac, with *Generalleutnant* later *SS–Gruppenführer*) Helmuth von Pannwitz's *XV SS–Kosaken–Kavallerie–Korps* on hand

[411] Weidinger, *Das Reich V*, p. 329.

as an exploitation force to pour through any gap torn in the Russian lines.[412]

The Cossacks were volunteers who loved and admired their commander, because von Pannwitz returned their respect and did not look upon Slavs and Russians as inferiors. Starting in February *XV SS–Kosaken–Kavallerie–Korps* had been put under *Waffen–SS* control for purposes of supplies and replacements, but it was not actually part of the *Waffen–SS* proper until March.

Despite his disdain for non-Germans Hitler felt a certain affinity toward the Cossacks, seeing them as warriors who fought with a flair and ferocity that set them apart from others; he especially admired their uniforms, which appealed to his fascination with pageantry and symbolism.

Von Pannwitz's force was fast and highly mobile but lightly armed with little artillery support, and while it could rapidly encircle a Russian force it could not hold the line against determined armored attacks. Speed and firepower were the order of the day; Pannwitz's Corps had speed but not firepower.

What was needed was armor[413] artillery and high morale, three things *Heeresgruppe E* simply did not have, but Hitler made no allowances for the weakness of the forces. Löhr was made to understand that regardless of his Army Group's deficiencies, somehow the Germans would have to cross the Drava, penetrate the Russian defense zones and head for the unprotected area around Kaposvar to meet up with 6. *SS–Panzerarmee* driving south from the Lake Balaton region.

This would cut off Russian forces facing 2. *Panzerarmee* in the Nagykanizsa area and secure the precious oilfield, destroying one threat and protecting the southern flank of *Unternehmen Frühlingserwachen*

---

[412] This Corps was not initially part of the *Waffen–SS*. Von Pannwitz was strong-armed into transferring the Cossacks into *SS* control and eventually relented.

[413] And dry enough weather for armor to be used effectively.

as other forces drove for the Danube. On paper it was a brilliant plan, in reality it was absurd.

3 March, Saturday

Commenting once again on the dire transport situation in the *Reich*, Joseph Goebbels mused once again on increasing distribution of his political paper *'Front und Heimat'* to three times a week. "In one respect it is easier to get this newspaper into the hands of the troops but in another it is harder. It is easier since distances to the front have now become shorter, harder because routing has now become extraordinarily complicated owing to the destruction of transport communications."[414]

For his outstanding leadership of *1. Panzerarmee* and First Hungarian Army, Gotthard Heinrici was awarded the Swords to the Oak Leaves of the Knight's Cross. For a general as experienced as Heinrici, a man who had held back the Russians time and again in seemingly hopeless situations, this award seemed late in coming. But Hitler did not like Heinrici at all. The son of a protestant minister, Heinrici read a bible tract daily and never stopped attending church, despite ominous warnings that Hitler was none too pleased about his activities. Nor would he carry out the more draconian measures ordered by either his superiors, or by Hitler himself, for punishing stragglers and deserters.

Heinrici had been sidelined for months at a retirement home in Karlsbad, Czechoslovakia, more or less shoved aside and out of sight. When he was finally brought back to try and stabilize the crumbling front in Hungary and Slovakia, his direct superior was *Generaloberst* Ferdinand Schörner, an ardent Nazi and a Hitler favorite. Schörner issued a directive that "any soldier found behind the front without orders was to be

[414] Trevor-Roper, *Final Entries*, p. 40.

executed immediately and his body exhibited as a warning." Heinrici flatly refused. "Such methods have never been used under my command, and never will be."[415]

Very few generals could have gotten away with this in the post-Valkyrie atmosphere of paranoia gripping Hitler and his command circle. That makes Heinrici's Swords award all that more impressive, although it was completely within character for the *Führer*, who had a long history of bribing his generals with huge cash or land grants, promotions and medals.

The day of attack was fast approaching when *II. SS–Panzerkorps* was ordered to its forward assembly areas, and some of the unit commanders began reconnoitering their jumping-off positions. What was readily apparent was the terrible weather.

Which brings up a controversial anecdote that has still not been resolved. John Toland, in *The Last 100 Days,* relates the story of an *SS–Obersturmbannführer* he calls Fritz Hagen, a pseudonym, who supposedly commanded a *kampfgruppe* scheduled as a leading attack unit for *Unternehmen Frühlingserwachen.* Scouting his launching off point on 3 March in a driving rain, this Hagen, said to be one of the most aggressive *panzer* commanders in the *Waffen SS,* pointed east at the endless mud and said "Gentlemen, we are now at the jumping-off point." Making his way back to Veszprem, just down the road from Das *Reich's* assembly area near Varpalota, he phoned Corps headquarters and reportedly said "I have tanks, not submarines! You can kiss my ass but I won't do it!"

This story has the feel of the apocryphal to it, especially without knowing Hagen's true identity. The

[415] Ryan, Cornelius, *The Last Battle,* (New York: Simon & Schuster, 1966), p. 63.

SS–Panzer regiments had some extremely aggressive commanders in their ranks, so that is no clue to the man's identity to verify the story. Previously in his narrative Toland wrote that *6. SS–Panzerarmee* was involved in the relief attempts of Budapest, which was obviously untrue. He had confused Hermann Balck's *6. Armee* with Dietrich's *6. SS–Panzerarmee,* the same glaring mistake that Goebbels made so often.[416]

Later, he states that *Unternehmen Frühlingserwachen* had three assault divisions with sixteen follow-on divisions, neither of which is accurate; perhaps he meant three assault corps, although it actually had four. In any event, such inaccuracies make the story of this *SS–Obersturmbannführer* Hagen suspect, and without this officer's real name and unit it is impossible to verify. However, even if Hagen's tale is nothing more than an apocryphal story it accurately relates the appalling weather conditions in the days preceding *Unternehmen Frühlingserwachen,* as well as the fatalistic complacency at *Heeresgruppe Süd.*

Continuing with Hagen's story, he was reportedly told by Corps Headquarters[417] that the Army Group[418] was aware of the conditions and that Hitler was being asked for a postponement. In the meantime Hagen should move his *kampfgruppe* to the front and prepare for the attack.

Meanwhile just to Hagen's left, that is, to the north-northeast, two Soviet officers had just surrendered to *Leutnant* Erich Kernmayr, of a unit unnamed by Toland. Kernmayr's identity can probably be guessed at, however. This Erich Kernmayr might well have later become the journalist Erich Kern, who was on the staff of *IV. SS–Panzerkorps* during the fight

---

[416] Toland, *The Last 100 Days*, pp. 205-207.

[417] Based on the later part of the story, the Corps could have been *IV. SS–Panzerkorps*, although it more likely been either *I. SS–Panzerkorps* or *II. SS–Panzerkorps*. Kernmayr's part, however, is definitely related to *IV. SS–Panzerkorps*.

[418] This would probably have been *Heeresgruppe Süd*

for Hungary and Austria, and that Corps was on the far left flank of the offensive north of *III. Panzerkorps*. Kern was a well-traveled veteran who had served in numerous *Waffen–SS* units, including both *Das Reich* and *Wiking*. According to Toland the two Russian officers told Kernmayer that just to the east some 3,000 armored vehicles were massed for an attack. The number 3,000 comes up throughout the battle but as total vehicles, not as 3,000 armored vehicles. As a veteran, Kernmayr must have been a good judge of credibility and he believed the two men. If the attack went forward, the assault units would be driving south while their eastern flank was threatened by a flood of Russian armor that could break at any moment against *Heeresgruppe Süd*'s fragile defensive front north of Stuhlweissenburg; the further that the assault units of *Unternehmen Frühlingserwachen* drove to the south, the greater their peril. All the Soviets had to do was wait until the weather cleared and the German drive lost momentum and was heavily engaged, then attack due west into the thinly held flank. The key would be Stuhlweissenburg, the ancient city just north of Lake Velence. Once that city was taken there was no natural barrier to defend before reaching the northeastern tip of Lake Balaton, the moment when any German unit south of the line between lakes Balaton and Velence would be cut off and doomed. If the Russians timed things correctly that would mean most of both *6. Armee* and *6. SS–Panzerarmee*. That is, most of *Heeresgruppe Süd*.

Kernmayr understood the threat and personally escorted the two Russians to *Heeresgruppe Süd* Headquarters, where complacency was the order of the day.[419] *Oberstleutnant* Graf von Rittberg, Intelligence Officer for *Heeresgruppe Süd*, was not impressed with Kernmayr's prisoners or their intelligence about a

---

[419] Although Toland says they went to Army Group headquarters, the story makes far more sense if instead they headed for *Armeegruppe Balck* headquarters and not *Heeresgruppe Süd*, since *IV. SS–Panzerkorps* was still under Balck's command.

coming Soviet offensive. He did promise to "tell the general over lunch," although which general isn't mentioned. Hours passed as Kernmayr waited while Rittberg rode his horse, played chess, and attended a birthday celebration. It was almost dark when he reappeared.

"The General was most interested in that story of yours," he said cheerfully. "Really most interested. Give my regards to General Gille." When he saw Kernmayr's look of consternation, he said, "Was there anything else?"

"But what's going to be done about it? What am I to report? After all, this is an extremely dangerous threat to our flank."

"Oh, my dear fellow," said the Count, "don't worry. You've got the 25th Hungarian Hussars...[420]"

Kernmayr reminded him that the Hungarians only had two machine guns to a company.

"Everything's under control, my dear fellow. Army Group will do all that's necessary."[421]

Whether or not this incident was ever used in an intelligence summary, it is highly doubtful that it would have made a difference in changing Hitler's mind about the timing of the offensive. By 3 March reports were increasing that the Soviets were preparing their own offensive aimed at Vienna, but Hitler was far beyond tolerating bad news, preferring to shoot the messenger.

Moreover, if headquarters of *Armeegruppe Balck* or *Heeresgruppe Süd* were truly so complacent about the value of Hungarian formations, then they were probably ignoring the evidence of their own surroundings. Otto Weidinger, commander of *SS–Panzergrenadier Regiment Der Führer*, made his own observations about Honved units when he arrived in

---

[420] He must mean the 25th Hungarian Infantry Division, a depleted formation with few heavy weapons. In reality it was nowhere near divisional strength, and was nothing more than a large *kampfgruppe*. Or, perhaps he meant the 1st Hungarian Hussar Division, the veteran but burned out cavalry division.

[421] Toland, *The Last 100 Days*, pp. 205-206.

Hungary in mid-February. "At that time, it was noted that many Hungarian troops, mostly in company strength and without weapons, but with smoking field kitchens and some trains vehicles, appeared to be marching aimlessly, without destination, through the land. It was apparent that the Hungarian Army leadership intended to prevent the units from being employed, by constantly transferring them to other places."[422] If this observation is true, and Weidinger has to get the benefit of the doubt since he was actually there, then this shows not only how demoralized Germany's Hungarian allies were, but also represented an enormous drain on the logistics of *Heeresgruppe Süd* by feeding and supplying Hungarian units that had little or no combat value, and even less desire to die fighting the Russians.

If Toland's story of the two captured Russian officers is true, then it illustrates perfectly just how badly more than five years of war had eroded the professionalism of the German Army. For the Intelligence Officer of *Heeresgruppe Süd* not to have known of this situation, or to have blithely ignored it, shows how incompetent, demoralized, arrogant or deluded the Army Group's leadership had become by this point.

Moreover, the passage "The General was most interested in that story of yours," he said cheerfully. "Really most interested. Give my regards to General Gille..." as related above, smacks of the condescension Herman Balck and his staff felt toward the commander of *IV. SS–Panzerkorps*. Was this yet another example of Balck's arrogance getting in the way of operations? As much as may now be told from a distance of eight decades, it certainly seems possible.

[422] Weidinger, *Das Reich V*, p. 327.

As the hour of attack grew closer it was becoming increasingly obvious that, aside from the entrenched Soviet defenses, the greatest enemy of *Unternehmen Frühlingserwachen* was the weather. An early thaw combined with incessant rain left the rural Hungarian countryside little more than a lake of mud. The *razputitza* was the well-known weather phenomenon that happened twice a year, in spring with the melting of the winter snows, and in fall during the rainy season before the temperatures dropped below freezing, where dirt roads became impassable rivers of mud. It was a disaster for anything attempting to move over the sodden unpaved roads in the hinterland, be those roads in Russia or Hungary.

As rain and snow fell over Western Hungary, the various sub-units of *2. SS–Panzer Division Das Reich* set off in the early morning to the divisional assembly area near Varpalota, while those of *9. SS–Panzer Division Hohenstaufen* made for the vicinity of Mor. Road conditions were terrible, with the non-paved routes nothing more than muddy swamps; progress was very slow and used up a lot of precious fuel. It was only at nightfall that most of the division completed the short move, but *Das Reich* was not close to being ready for an attack.

Hohenstaufen reported an armored strength of 19 *Panzer Mark IVs*, 24 *Mark V Panthers*, 16 *Sturmgeschütz*, 17 *Jagdpanzer IVs* and 10 *Jagdpanzer Vs*, for a total of 83 AFVs of all types, about half strength.[423] It also had four *Flakpanzer IVs* and 15

---

[423] The *Jagdpanzer IV* was basically a casemate mounted onto the chassis of a *Panzer Mark IV* and mounting a 75mm gun. By this point in the war they were probably the better Pak 42 L/70, the same gun used on the *Mark V Panther*. This later variant was officially referred to as the *Jagdpanzer IV/70*. The *Jagdpanzer V* was the far more deadly *Jagdpanther*. Built on the chassis of a *Panzer Mark V*, the *Jagdpanther* mounted the same 88mm gun as the *Tiger II*, in a turretless casemate similar to the *Jagdpanzer IV/70/*

75mm anti-tank guns. So despite being over-strength in men, the division's combat power was drastically diminished.

Five of the eight B-24 crewmen captured by *SS-Brigade Ney* on 1 March were charged with being spies, along with four Hungarian civilians who sought to aid them. The ominous nature of the charges must surely have been apparent to the American airmen.

4 March, Sunday

Throughout the *Reich* the Allied air forces ranged freely to bomb and strafe at will. P47's, P-51's, B-26's, Typhoons, Spitfires, medium and heavy bombers of many types, all flew almost with impudence over Germany. Only occasionally did the *Luftwaffe* put up fighters to contest the carnage. By early March, however, the sight of hundreds and thousands of B-17s, B-24s and Lancasters dropping loads of bombs on German cities had become so much a part of daily life that Goebbels commented on the phenomenon.

"Unfortunately there have been very heavy air raids on Germany in the last 24 hours. They can no longer be recorded in detail. The Americans overfly German territory almost unresisted and are destroying one town after another; the damage done to our armaments potential is quite beyond repair."

And there, writing on 4March, Goebbels all but admits that the war is lost. The strategic bombing campaign is so pervasive, with so many cities being bombed on a daily basis, that there is no point in discussing them further, at least not in detail. The German ability to produce weapons has been wrecked beyond salvage. He does not here say >all is lost,= but that seems to follow, as later on he states Athe only hope for a successful end to the war is that the split in the enemy camp becomes irreparable before we are flat on the floor.@ In other words, militarily there is no hope. Finally, in a summation almost dripping with despair, he writes Athe general mood in the *Reich* Chancellory is pretty dismal. I would rather not go there again because the atmosphere is infectious. The generals hang their heads and the *Führer* alone holds his head high.@ The reader may be forgiven if he were to snidely remark that this was because the generals were pragmatists who understood the situation clearly, while Hitler was slipping into fantasy.

On this day Goebbels also gives us a look at how the war situation was affecting Hitler. Given that *Unternehmen Frühlingserwachen* was, at this point, little more than 24 hours from kicking off, it is illustrative to note that Goebbels found that "in contrast to the last time I found him somewhat depressed- understandable in the light of the military developments. Physically too he is somewhat hampered; I noticed with dismay that the nervous twitch of his left hand had greatly increased."

Goebbels goes into some detail about the impressions and hopes for *Unternehmen Frühlingserwachen* in Hitler's command circle, and so it is worth exploring this diary entry in some detail. Surprisingly, given his later reactions, Hitler is waiting for *Unternehmen Frühlingserwachen* with mixed feelings. Clearly, some part of Hitler's mind could still register reality and was not completely lost to delusions. It is also interesting that, given the size of the forces involved, Goebbels does not put more emphasis on this coming attack, he does not overreact with hope, as often seems the case. Nor do we get a picture of Adolf Hitler having any particular hopes for this offensive. "Our blow in Hungary is due to fall on 6 March, in other words this coming Tuesday. The *Führer* is afraid that the enemy already knows all about our concentration in this area and has made the necessary preparations." Which was, indeed, the case. The use of *I. SS–Panzerkorps* in *Unternehmen Südwind* had dispelled all notions of keeping *6. SS–Panzerarmee's* presence in Hungary a secret. The truly important revelations here are that Hitler was well aware that Dietrich and his men were running into an enemy that was prepared and waiting. Given his later reactions to the lack of progress, and the cuff band order especially, this illustrates perfectly the dual nature of his psychology at this point, the rational being overruled by the irrational.

But the seeds of the outlandish expectations were already present. "Nevertheless he (Hitler) hopes that our measures will lead to complete victory. We have assembled first-class troops under command of Sepp Dietrich for our offensive here." In a sense this was true: the battered formations of *6. SS–Panzerarmee* had not been first class formations for some time, but by the standards of the Wehrmacht in early 1945, they were absolutely the best available.

"The General Staff now sees the necessity for our offensive in Hungary." The student of history wishes Goebbels had named names here, because in the accounts of those who survived there is nowhere anything but resignation about *Unternehmen Frühlingserwachen.* If the generals did sign off on the offensive, it was probably because the alternative was dangerous. Keitel may have agreed with Hitler, and perhaps other sycophants, but the fighting generals such as Guderian all disagreed, at least that's what they stated after the fact. "Previously it had fought tooth and nail to prevent priority being given to this area. Now it realizes that the petrol supply question is overriding and that we must in all circumstances hold in Hungary if motorized warfare is not to come to a complete standstill...Had we lost the Hungarian and Viennese oil (here he must surely mean the Viennese oil refineries, or perhaps the Zistersdorf oil fields) we should have been totally incapable of conducting a counter-offensive, as we are planning to do in the east." The somewhat offhand remark that the General Staff fought "tooth and nail" against *Unternehmen Frühlingserwachen* backs up Guderian's claims that he did his best to divert the *6. SS–Panzerarmee* to the Oder Front, because Goebbels does not often remark on the General Staff disagreeing with Hitler openly, and the acquiescence he mentions seems more like resignation than agreement.

If Goebbels entries for 4 March make anything clear it is the fantasy world surrounding Hitler conflicting with the reality of the situation. Goebbels sees things fairly clearly when he is on his own, but after discussions with Hitler he becomes optimistic beyond reason. For *Heeresgruppe Süd* the truth would quite soon become dangerous to report to a man who expected nothing less than a miracle.[424]

Even as the launch of *Unternehmen Frühlingserwachen* approached, and the various assault divisions were in dire need of infantry, the needs on other fronts proved even greater. So on 4 March the now combat-ready *1. SS–Romanische– Waffen–Grenadier Regiment*, some 3,000 strong, was transferred to the Oder front without the rest of its parent formation. The division's other regiment immediately intensified its efforts to become battle-worthy, while a 3rd Regiment was still in the initial stages of assembly.

SS–Hauptsturmführer Emilian, the Romanian officer who had defected with his cavalry troop from the Red Army back in January, was sent to a special school for battalion and detachment commanders at Kuertrow, in Mecklenburg. There he bunked and went to class with officers from the two Hungarian *SS* divisions, the *28. SS-Freiwilligen-Grenadier-Division Wallonien*, and others from both the *Kriegsmarine* and the *Luftwaffe*, since both the navy and the air force fielded ground units.

In response to Ferenc Szalasi stripping the men of *SS-Brigade Ney* of their Hungarian citizenship, the brigade was designated as a *Sondereinheit der SS*, a Special Unit of the *SS* to give them an official combat status. In addition, the unit was only allowed to be manned by volunteers, was forbidden to advertise or promote in any way, was granted permission to use the

[424] Trevor-Roper, *Final Entries*, pp. 48-57.

unique Hungarian 'Harc' when addressing one another[425] and was promised help being outfitted.

    With the launch of *Unternehmen Frühlingserwachen* less than 48 hours away, *6. SS–Panzerarmee* continued trying to get its formations into their attack positions on overcrowded roads that were churned into little more than strips of deep churned mud, with continuing rain flooding the landscape and generally hampering all travel. *Heeresgruppe Süd* began to realize that all of *6. SS–Panzerarmee*'s assault units were not going to be in position by 0430 on 6 March, the designation hour for the attack, and that because of the weather forward movement would be nearly impossible. Otto Weidinger states categorically that "Division *Das Reich* was certain that it would not be ready in its assembly area."[426]

---

[425] Taken from the KABSZ, this greeting meant 'Fight/Battle.'
[426] Weidinger, *Das Reich V*, p. 329.

5 March, Monday

In Berlin, as Hitler impatiently waited for the launch of *Unternehmen Frühlingserwachen* the following day, someone[427] either asked Hitler to sign a copy of Mein Kampf, or was given one by the *Führer* as a gift. Bound in bright blue leather, with the title stamped in gold on the front cover with a golden sword above it, the book was one of only 1,000 specially bound copies printed to celebrate Hitler's 50th birthday in 1939. In all likelihood the special book was owned by a high official or officer who was captured by the Americans or British, since it survived the war in nearly pristine condition, which seems highly improbable had the owner lived in the Soviet zone. It was put up for auction in February, 2013, in Shropshire, England, by an anonymous owner; it does not defy probability that a British Tommy might have picked it up and lugged it home to sit in an attic for nearly 70 years. The selling price in 2013 was a staggering £42,000.

Around the time that Hitler signed the book, American fighter bombers were dropping leaflets on Cologne urging the population not to resist the approaching Allied ground forces; the city fell to the American Third Armored Division the next day. During the brief but violent fight for the city, an intrepid cameraman caught the only tank battle filmed live on the western front, as an American M26 Pershing heavy tank caught a *Mark V Panther* looking the wrong way near Cologne Cathedral. A series of 90mm shells fired at close range completely destroyed the *panzer* as surviving crew members scrambled for safety.

---

[427] Whether Hitler presented the book or was asked to sign it by someone is unknown now and seems likely to forever remain a mystery.

As the situation worsened with each passing day, Goebbels was forced to confront the issue of German collaboration and open surrender first in the face of the Western Allies, then more and more in the east. Despite his interminable speeches and propaganda designed to stiffen the spines of the soldiers and civilians, the truth that so many Germans just wanted the war to end was a cold reality.

"The news that the town of Rheydt received the Americans with white flags made me blush. I can hardly realize it, especially not the fact that one of these white flags flew from the house where I was born. At the moment, however, I do not even know who is living in the house and I can only suppose that this deed of madness was done by evacuees or people who were bombed out...If we ever return to Rheydt, however, I shall clear the matter up."

This is a paragraph that perfectly illustrates the torn minds of every German standing at their post, wherever that post happened to be. Just as soldiers on the fighting fronts were wondering about the safety of their families back home, so, too, did Goebbels have to wonder exactly what was going on in his hometown. But beyond merely being indignant and outraged, we also see his own defeatism at work in this paragraph. "If we ever return to Rehydt." Not "when", but "if." This one word would have been enough to get the average person arrested and no doubt would have been changed if Goebbels had ever gotten the chance to edit the diary. Clearly, as one privy to the truth about the military situation, he knew that counter-offensives to regain lost territories were not coming anytime soon, except in Hungary.

Likewise, the strategic bombing campaign was taking its toll on the morale even of the *Reichsminister*, as he once again despaired of the endless bombing, and while this has no direct bearing on the course of the war in Hungary and Austria, it must have constantly weighed on the minds of the men doing the fighting.

"Limitless terror from the air! It is quite impossible to record the results in detail."

For Goebbels the true extent of the damage was well known and probably horrifying, although given his callous contempt for civilians as individuals it was probably more the damage to Germany's war potential that worried him. To the average mechanic or *panzergrenadier* in the slimy mud of Hungary the worry was far more specific: was their mother or sister buried under the rubble of what was once their home? Were the power and water cut off to their family home in Dusselldorf or Munich or Berlin? Were their children plodding along some snowbound road with Russian Yaks strafing them, or on a train being rocketed by American Jabos? Goebbels knew the larger details of the German people's suffering, but one never quite gets the sense that he understood the individual worry, or empathized with it in the least.[428]

The final day before the launch of *Unternehmen Frühlingserwachen* arrived with more wet and near-freezing weather. As German commanders of all ranks peered through the mist across the murky, flooded battlefield that their men were expected to cross under fire the next morning, they must have known just how unrealistic their orders were; Major General Michael Reynolds puts it this way, "Hitler's precise aims for *Unternehmen Frühlingserwachen* were as wildly ambitious as those in the Ardennes three months earlier."[429] There was even talk of regaining the Ploesti Oilfields in distant Rumania, a target even more remote and absurd than recapturing Antwerp had been during the Ardennes Offensive. For the *panzergrenadiers* who

[428] Trevor-Roper, *Final Entries*, pp. 62-63.
[429] Reynolds, Major General Michael, *Operation Spring Awakening, Hitler's Last World War II Offensive*, (World War Two magazine, May, 2012), p. 62.

would be doing the actual fighting, simply making it safely across the sodden fields must have seemed wildly ambitious.

The idea for *Unternehmen Frühlingserwachen* probably began in December with the defunct Operation Spätlese (Late Harvest), a thrust south from the so-called Margarethe position on the line Lake Balaton-Stuhlweissenburg-Lake Velence and built around a reinforced *III. Panzerkorps*. In mid-December the weather was no better than it was in early March and might have been worse. Flooded roads and fields would have doomed the attack to failure; it was called off because Russian attacks north of the Danube were too dangerous to ignore and units slated for use in Spätlese were transferred to hold the line of the Gran River. Nevertheless, the basic plan survived in Hitler's memory and would see fruition in both *Unternehmen Konrad III* and *Unternehmen Frühlingserwachen*[430].

The final plan for *Unternehmen Frühlingserwachen* involved three armies from *Heeresgruppe Süd*: *6. Armee*, *6. SS–Panzerarmee*, and the Hungarian Third Army, with *2. Panzerarmee*[431] and support elements from *Heeresgruppe E* attacking in the center and south. The assembly of so many *panzer* and *panzergrenadier* divisions, especially those of the *Waffen-SS*, containing such a huge percentage of the remaining German tank inventory, was supposed to confer so much firepower and mobility on the assault units that they could penetrate the Russian front lines and then drive quickly to the Danube, after which the northern and southern pincers would meet and crush the bulk of Third Ukrainian Front in the pocket south of Lake Balaton and west of the Danube. A quick but

---

[430] As previously discussed, Hans Ulrich-Rudel's suggestion that the first two Konrad operations were in the wrong place probably reinforced Hitler's already firm belief in the viability of Spätlese, coming as it did less than a month after the cancelled December operation. Three months later, however, the attack formations slated for Spätlese were drastically weaker than they had been before.

[431] This is another ironically named German Army, since *2. Panzerarmee* actually had no panzer units.

decisive victory was the objective, along the lines of the blitzkrieg battles of the early war. That the German Army no longer had the strength, talent or logistics for such an operation was never considered. Nor did the plan allow for the impact of ruinously wet weather or the launching of the Red Army's own offensive on the northern flank. Both of those variables were well known to Hitler and his advisors, they simply ignored them and hoped for the best, realizing that without some sort of war-changing victory the end was in sight.

Unternehmen Frühlingserwachen was essentially a replay of *Konrad III*, fought on the exact same battlefield, with columns of *panzers* driving for the exact same cities on the Danube while others drove south to secure the flank. Bridgeheads would be thrown across the Danube for future operations further east. As had happened in *Konrad III*, when the weather was dry or frozen and vehicles could get traction the terrain was well suited to mobile warfare, being mostly rolling hills and farmland. Hills and ridges often had excellent fields of fire and were crucial to controlling the lands beyond, and so were highly prized by both sides. Once on the Danube, however, the impetus would diverge from that of *Konrad III*. The spearheads were to swing south to meet the forces of Army Group E driving north from the Drau[432], and not north toward Budapest as they had in Konrad; instead of relieving a Budapest garrison that no longer existed, the objective was to trap the Red Army forces west of the Danube, and thereby eliminate the threat to the oilfields around Nagykanizsa. Those forces of *2. Panzerarmee* moving east from the Nagykanizsa area were supposed to pin down the Red Army units facing them so they could not withdraw eastward and would be caught in the trap. On the southern side, other forces from *Heeresgruppe E* would cross the Drau River and move north to link up with the *Waffen–SS* divisions of *6. SS–Panzerarmee*. On paper the

---

[432] In Hungarian, the Drava River.

operational plan was a classic pincer movement in the pattern of *Unternehmen Zitadelle*.[433] No part of the plan bore any relation to reality.

On the northern flank, the 3rd Hungarian Army was too weak to achieve any offensive goals and so its primary objective was to defend against an enemy counter-attack, namely the Vienna Offensive that German intelligence (and the mysterious *Leutnant* Kernmayr) warned was coming. There was already a bulge in the German lines north of Stuhlweissenburg that jutted to the west of that city, putting it and its defenders in grave danger of being outflanked and surrounded by a Soviet offensive. The 3rd Hungarian Army was being counted on to hold the line in such an event, a duty it was totally incapable of achieving. German intelligence had already noted the enormous buildup of Soviet armor and motorized forces opposing 3rd Hungarian Army, which was desperately short of anti-tank weapons. Imagining that it could hold off a major Soviet attack for anything more than a brief period was sheer fantasy.

6. Armee was on the right flank south of 3rd Hungarian Army and was tasked with defending Stuhlweissenburg north to the junction with the Hungarians, as well as shoring up the left flank of 6. *SS–Panzerarmee,* but *6. Armee's* chief offensive force, *IV. SS–Panzerkorps* , had not recovered from the disastrous losses it suffered during the three Konrad operations and therefore had no offensive capability left; indeed, even on defense *6. Armee's* weakened units were so stretched that it was unlikely they could hold off a concerted attack for long . "Serious concerns were expressed by Sepp Dietrich and his senior staff officers that as the *6. SS–Panzerarmee* and *III. Panzerkorps* moved southeast and east they would become increasingly vulnerable to a counteroffensive launched by the Soviet forces already located north of

---

[433] Also known as The Battle of Kursk. The *Waffen–SS* had also been the chief offensive force during Operation Citadel, which had aimed to destroy another large bulge into the German front lines.

Szekesfehervar (Stuhlweissenburg), and west of the Danube."[434]. As previously noted Hitler was deaf to such warnings and ordered *Unternehmen Frühlingserwachen* to proceed as planned.

Four corps had a role in the offensive. On the army's left flank was *III. Panzerkorps*, with the *1. Panzer Division* and *3. Panzer Division*). Then came *II. SS–Panzerkorps* with *2. SS–Panzer Division Das Reich* and *9. SS–Panzer Division Hohenstaufen*, with the mission of driving to the east and southeast of the Sàrviz Canal and following that waterway to the Danube between Dunafoldvar and Dunapentele, and then to establish bridgeheads on the east side of the river. In other words, to repeat the success of *Konrad III*, once again with no plan of what to do after crossing the Danube. The starting positions for *II. SS–Panzerkorps* were on a line running due west from Seregelyes.

Infantry support would be provided by the *44. Infanterie Division Hoch und Deutschmeister*, one of the most storied infantry formations in the *Heer*. The division's roots went back to the Austro-Prussian War, and even before. It fought with distinction in the First World War, and remained in the Austrian Army during the interwar period.

After the Anschluss, the Austrian regiment to which the traditions applied, *Infanterie-Regiment 134*, was uniquely honored with the right to carry two distinct colors, unlike any other unit in the German Army. It was named *"Hoch- und Deutschmeister,"* after the historic Austrian regiment it was based on. On special occasions, both before and during the war, the regiment could carry the battalion colors of the now-defunct *Infanterie-Regiment 4* from which *Infanterie Regiment 134* had evolved..

While stationed in Italy on 23 March, 1944, the *44. Infanterie Division* introduced a new tradition. Its members were permitted to wear a metal emblem on

[434] Reynolds, *Operation Spring Awakening*, p. 62.

their uniform shoulder boards, known as the *Deutschmeister-Kreuz*. This small, blue-enameled Maltese cross, edged in gold with a *Reichsadler* (*Reich* Eagle) and a "Stalingrad" banner in the center, was also called the *Stalingrad-Kreuz* by the soldiers. The design was inspired by the cross worn by knights of the *Deutschmeister* Order, dating back to the 12th century. Although regulations typically prohibited wearing it on the left side of their field caps, many in the division did so anyway, reflecting a broader trend of units adopting distinctive emblems towards the end of the Second World War. Since by that point officers had become lenient toward anything that might increase morale, more units copies them.

On 6 February, 1945, the *OKH* issued an order granting *Infanterie-Regiment 134* of the *44. Infanterie Division* the honor of wearing a cuff title with the name *"Hoch- und Deutschmeister."* This recognition was due to their "heroic performance" in combat. However, given the late date of the order, it is believed that these titles were not actually worn during the war. Post-war veterans' organizations issued three variations of the Hoch- und Deutschmeister cuff title, which are often mistaken for those used during the war, although no such versions are confirmed to have been worn. If any infantry formation participating in *Unternehmen Frühlingserwachen* could be considered as 'elite,' *44. Infanterie Division* would be the one.

1. SS–Panzerkorps would attack on the west side of the Sàrviz Canal and cross the Sio Canal near Simontornya before also turning east for the Danube. As usual it commanded *1. SS–Panzer Division Leibstandarte Adolf Hitler (LAH)* and *12. SS–Panzer Division Hitlerjugend*.

I Kavallerie Korps was to drive south and southwest from the eastern tip of Lake Balaton into the rear areas of those Russian forces opposing *2. Panzerarmee* in the region of Nagykanizsa. The two cavalry brigades had been renamed as division during February, although neither received reinforcements of was enlarged. The reasons for this were that the brigade commanders were too low in rank when dealing with units to which they might be attached, who were unfamiliar with the best ways in which to use cavalry formations. Being divisions allowed them to be promoted to a rank commensurate with command of a division.

Otherwise both *3. Kavallerie Division* and *4. Kavallerie Division* continued to field two *Reiter* regiments, along with associated support sub-units, to form a division of approximately 6, 600 men. As before, they still relied on horses to ride into battle. Most the men in *I Kavallerie Korps* were hardened veterans who knew their business, and in mobile warfare could be very dangerous. But in the attack against strong fortifications and fixed defenses they did not have the firepower to be successful. On the western flank of *Unternehmen Frühlingserwachen* they would struggle to keep up with *I. SS–Panzerkorps*.

But that was yet in the future.

Farther south, *Heeresgruppe Süd's* fourth army, *2. Panzerarmee*, would move due east toward Kaposvar, less to penetrated the Russian defenses than to pin them in place so they could not be shifted to stop *6. SS–Panzerarmee* driving from the north, or the units of *Heeresgruppe E* that would cross the Drau and pin down Russian forces in that area.

In line abreast, therefore, (verify this) the assault divisions from east to west were *1.Panzer* Division, *3. Panzer Division, 2. SS–Panzer Division Das Reich, 9. SS–Panzer Division Hohenstaufen, 1. SS–Panzer Division Leibstandarte Adolf Hitler, 12. SS–Panzer Division Hitlerjugend, 4. Kavallerie Division* and, on the western flank, *4. Kavallerie Division*. Theoretically such a force should have commanded close to 1,000 AFVs of all types, at least that many *SPWs*, thousands more trucks and miscellaneous vehicles, hundreds of towed and self-propelled artillery pieces and tens of thousands of *panzergrenadiers*, as well as specialist units such as *pioneers*. Actual totals were somewhat different.

Michael Reynolds puts the total number of German *panzers* and *sturmgeschütze* in *6. SS–Panzerarmee* and *III. Panzerkorps* combined at a mere 300, an anemic number considering that *1. SS–Panzer Division Leibstandarte Adolf Hitler* by itself had more than 200 such vehicles prior to the Normandy Invasion. On *Das Reich's* front, the plan called for only *3. SS–Panzergrenadier Regiment Deutschland* to be in the initial assault with most of the division held back to exploit a break-through.

German intelligence had a good picture of the Soviet defenses and the Russians had a good idea where the German point of emphasis would be, so the gathered strength of both sides was guaranteed to collide. To defend against *Unternehmen Frühlingserwachen*, Marshal Tolbukhin had been given a large force, although exact numbers are hard to pin down. Official Soviet figures are never to be trusted, so Reynolds puts it this way: "according to the Soviet official history, his forces totaled 407,000 men, 6,890 guns and mortars, 407 tanks[435] and self-propelled guns, and 965 aircraft, but it is likely that many of his formations were much weaker than these figures suggest." Stalin's propaganda machine invariably changed statistics to suit whatever message was considered important at the moment. There is no question that both 2nd and 3rd Ukrainian Fronts were under-strength by the time of *Unternehmen Frühlingserwachen*, but exactly how far under-strength is almost impossible to say. Reynolds says that while the official Soviet account of the war reports one particular rifle division, the 233rd Rifle Division, as being at only about 30 percent of its authorized

---

[435] Most sources agree on a number of Russian tanks of somewhere between 407-410.

strength, in fact it was probably closer to 40 percent, with strength of around 5,000 men.[436]

Tolbukhin's 3rd Ukrainian Front deployed 7 rifle divisions in front of *6. SS–Panzerarmee*, 2 each facing *I Kavallerie Korps*, I *SS Panzer* Division and II *SS Panzer* Division, and the equivalent of another division in front of *III. Panzerkorps*; in reserve near Sarosd was the XVIII Tank Corps with about 75 tanks and assault guns, very close to the initial assault objectives for *2. SS–Panzer Division Das Reich* Das *Reich*. Further to the east, but also in the path of *Das Reich* on the west bank of the Danube, were yet another four rifle divisions and a Guards Mechanized Corps. Tolbukhin could also call on yet another 12 rifle divisions close to the Danube on the east bank, and three rifle divisions on the west bank just east of Lake Velence.

The fortifications built by the Red Army were formidable. Aside from sheer numbers, the Russian defenses consisted of multiple lines that were up to 30 kilometers deep in places and very well placed to defend against the offensive they knew was coming. Once again using the 233rd Rifle Division as an example, Reynolds details the extensive defensive preparations that unit had made between 18 February and 3 March. In those 13 days the division had "dug 27 kilometers of trenches, 130 gun and mortar positions, 113 dugouts, 70 command posts and observation posts, and laid 4,249 antitank and 5,058 antipersonnel mines, all this on a frontage of 5 kilometers." There were no tanks in the area, but the division had 114 guns and mortars, more than 22 guns of all types and 17 anti-tank guns per kilometer of front, and at least 67 that could bear on the most important areas.[437] Reynolds is once again cited, but other sources agree with his estimates in the whole.

The 233rd Rifle Division held the sector facing *1. SS–Panzer Division Leibstandarte Adolf Hitler*, and part

---

[436] Reynolds, *Operation Spring Awakening*, pp. 63-65.
[437] Reynolds, *Operation Spring Awakening*, p. 64.

of that facing *12. SS–Panzer Division Hitlerjugend,* but the other German assault divisions were facing similar defensive works.

Toland relates more about *SS–Obersturmbannführer* Hagen, a commander in the van of the assault units, as he moved his *panzers* into their starting positions.

"By midnight (presumably the night of 5-6 March, as the battle began at dawn on the 6th) *Kampfgruppe Hagen* neared its point of departure. Its tanks, water up to the bellies, churned slowly ahead as the supporting infantry marched silently single file, hand in hand, through the pitch dark. Gray dawn dimly revealed plains covered by water. Suddenly German shells flew over their heads in a heavy barrage. The tankers looked at one another proudly-just as salvos from Russian guns and rocket launchers blanketed the area in a barrage that made their own seem puny...The infantrymen were trapped, unable to dig foxholes in the foot-deep water, and most of them were killed or wounded."

Hagen requested permission to start his attack early but when his men tried to crank their engines many of them would not start, the fuel having been diluted with water. At risk to their own lives the tankers crawled into the muddy water and under the tanks to drain the polluted fuel. Meanwhile, others were scouring the area for more fuel, finally taking it from an adjacent unit at gun point.[438]

Whether this story is true or not, it certainly fits the situation. Charles Winchester also repeats the quote about having tanks, not submarines, in *Hitler's War on Russia.*[439] He does not identify our mysterious

---

[438] Toland, *The Last 100 Days*, p. 207.

[439] Winchester, Charles D., *Hitler's War on Russia*, (London: Bloomsbury, 2011), p. 194.

SS–Obersturmbannführer either, unfortunately. And while Fritz Hagen is never identified, the pseudonym that Toland chose might give us a clue. Fritz could easily be taken from Fritz Witt, former member of *1. SS–Panzer Division LAH* who rose to take command of *12. SS–Panzer Division Hitlerjugend* and was killed in Normandy. Witt was born in the town of Hagen. Since both *1. SS–Panzer Division LAH* and *12. SS–Panzer Division Hitlerjugend* were assault divisions in *Unternehmen Frühlingserwachen* the *nom de guerre* seem indicative that this Fritz Hagen was in one of those two divisions, probably in the *Panzer* Regiment, describes as a *kampfgruppe*. Extrapolating further, Toland gives his rank as *SS–Obersturmbannführer*, or Lieutenant Colonel, a pretty high rank. Combining all of this results in the most likely candidate for 'Fritz Hagen' being Joachim Peiper. The majority of sources support Peiper being on hand for *Unternehmen Frühlingserwachen*, many list him once again leading a *Kampfgruppe Peiper*, the rank fits, and Peiper survived the war and was eligible for interviews during the period when Toland was writing his book.

As is seen frequently with former *Waffen–SS* men, and especially with former officers, name changes were frequent and interviews only given if identities were protected. In the story of the Battle of Vienna this phenomenon has brought a lot of confusion over the veracity and real name of *panzer* commander Arno Giesen of *SS–Panzer Regiment 2*.[440] So whoever 'Fritz Hagen' really was had good reason for his subterfuge and our confusion.

As the Germans tried to launch what they hoped was a war-turning offensive that would rock the Red Army, their target readied the counteroffensive that

[440] The convoluted story of Arno Giesen is discussed at length in *Killing Hitler's Reich, The Battle for Austria, 1945.*

Sepp Dietrich knew was coming. The Vienna Offensive was slated to begin on 15 March[441] and would involve all of Tolbukhin's 3rd Ukrainian Front and much of Malinovsky's 2nd Ukrainian Front, a total of four armies. Even in the face of *Unternehmen Frühlingserwachen*, STAVKA ordered that two armies slated for the Vienna Offensive continue attack preparations instead of intervening to stop the Germans. *Fremde Heeren Ost* had built up an impressive amount of evidence to illustrate the danger, evidence which Hitler ignored[442]. For the next ten days, even as *6. SS–Panzerarmee* and its attached units slogged their way south and east toward the mirage of a distant prize, the weight of the attack that would fall upon Third Hungarian Army and Hermann Balck's *6. Armee* continued to build.

The twin battalions from *11. SS–Panzergrenadier Division Nordland, I./SS–Panzergrenadier Regiment 23 Norge* and *I./SS–Panzergrenadier Regiment 24 Danmark,* still attached to *5. SS–Panzer Division Wiking,* had been redeployed to the Stuhlweissenburg area to help that division provide flank support for *Unternehmen Frühlingserwachen. IV. SS–Panzerkorps* was too weak for offensive operations and would have the responsibility for holding back the Russians and protecting *6. SS–Panzerarmee*'s northern-eastern flank in the case of a Soviet counter-offensive, with

---

[441] In fact it started on 16 March.

[442] As Hitler must have realized, even if he had cancelled Spring Awakening and used 6th SS Panzer Army against the Soviet's Vienna Offensive, he was merely delaying the inevitable collapse. In a defensive role the *Waffen–SS* divisions could have prevented the collapse of the front in Hungary, of that there can be no doubt, but to what end? Holding ground in the southeast was pointless if Germany continued to lose territory elsewhere. Only a crushing victory could have provided relief and a crushing defensive victory was simply no longer possible. Therefore, if the war had to continue, Spring Awakening had to be launched.

Stuhlweissenburg the anchor of that protection. The two battalions were both weak, short of officers and NCOs and fleshed out with men from other services who had little training in ground warfare.

Although the move to the final positions near the front commenced early it was not until midday that final orders for the assault were received, meaning the attack forces were nowhere near their jumping-off positions with less than 16 hours remaining before the preliminary artillery barrage would begin. Moving into position would mean multiple *panzerkorps'* using the same flooded road system while trying to maneuver quickly... it simply was not possible. Yet orders were orders and whatever the difficulties, they had to try.

So, in the muck and mire of western Hungary the assault units of *Unternehmen Frühlingserwachen* struggled to get where they were supposed to be before time ran out. The assembly areas for both *I. SS–Panzerkorps* and *II. SS–Panzerkorps* were positioned well back from the front for secrecy reasons, but when moving forward *SS–Obergruppenführer* Hermann Preiss' *I. SS–Panzerkorps* did not have to move through Stuhlweissenburg, instead turning off at Polgardi without having to share the road south. Despite the weather problems the corps was able to get into position in time for the attack. *II. SS–Panzerkorps* and *III. Panzerkorps*, however, both had to move through Stuhlweissenburg; this meant that both Corps had to use the same main road to gain their attack positions near the Russian front lines. Four *panzer* divisions, as well as the assorted miscellaneous units attached to the two corps headquarters, comprising many hundreds of vehicles[443] and tens of thousands of men,

---

[443] Even as under-strength as the panzer divisions were, the number of vehicles of all types trying to move south was still more than the road network could handle.

all trying to move down the same road at the same time. The resulting traffic congestion would have been a tangled mess under ideal conditions, but in the cold, gloomy conditions prevailing in early March the snarl was a nightmare. Vehicles and men struggled to arrive where they were supposed to be in time for the great offensive that would begin the next morning, burning up precious fuel and personal energy to move as fast as possible, and a lot of them did not make it.

Kampfgruppe Ameiser arrived in the Bicske area on 5 March, astride the main highway from Bratislava to Budapest, as part of the *96. Infanterie Division*, VIII Hungarian Corps, *6. Armee*. The cavalry regiment represented a small but highly mobile reserve.

2. SS–Panzer Division Das Reich left its assembly areas near Varpalota before sunrise at 0300 hours, moving through Stuhlweissenburg and then toward Aba and the desolate area near Bolondvari-Tania, but by 1700 hours it was obvious that *II. SS–Panzerkorps* would not have all of its heavy units in place when the time came to attack. The extreme measures taken for secrecy had kept the assault units well back from their jump-off positions, which in turn lead to those units having a lengthy road march once they were outfitted for battle. Too lengthy, as it turned out, in the atrocious 'razputitza' conditions prevailing in the region. Thus were the infantry marching on roads that were often no more than water-filled trenches covering deep, boot-sucking mud; carrying everything they would need for the assault, including combat loads of heavy ammunition, in terrible weather and with every footstep a chore, the *panzergrenadiers* staggered forward until they were barely able to walk, much less go into the attack. A *panzer* division was an enormous assemblage of men and machines, even an under-strength one, and it took some fifteen hours for all parts of such a division to pass a given point in good weather on paved highways; on roads as poor as those in Hungary, as crowded as they were with multiple *panzer* divisions using the same march routes, in

486

weather as bad as prevailed at the time, it took considerably longer, and the strain on men and machines was extreme.

The commander of *II. SS–Panzerkorps*, *SS–Obergruppenführer* Wilhelm Bittrich, told his chief of staff, *SS–Obersturmbannführer* Keller, to make it quite clear to Sepp Dietrich at *6. SS–Panzerarmee* that the corps would not be in position to attack at the appointed time. A delay was requested, but denied. Regardless of how sympathetic Dietrich may have been to Bittrich's plight, Hitler had ordered that the attack would be made at the appointed hour and regardless of circumstances, *II. SS–Panzerkorps* was ordered to follow the plan and the timetable.[444] Bittrich, however, refused to order his men to go straight into the attack directly from their long march.

Sepp Dietrich was painfully aware of how bad the weather conditions were, as well as how this would bog down his attack formations. His own *Chef des Stabs SS–Brigadeführer* Fritz Kraemer wrote the following on the eve of the attack:

> "In the constricted area between Lakes Balaton and Valencei (sic) the mud became alarming. The closer one came to the...assembly area, the more widespread the land that was under water - impassable for all kinds of vehicles. It looked the same...in the enemy area, as far as the terrain permitted observation...A *Panzer* attack in open terrain under these conditions is out of the question."[445]

Panzers and *SPWs* wallowing in such conditions would have been easy targets for the Russian anti-tank guns; the commander and staff of *6. SS–Panzerarmee* knew this and were sympathetic with the plight of the assault units, but they were powerless to alter the plan

[444] Weidinger, *Das Reich V*, p. 330.
[445] Reynolds, *Operation Spring Awakening*, p. 63.

in the face of a *Führerbefehl* (*Führer* order, i.e., a direct order from Hitler personally). *Unternehmen Frühlingserwachen* would go in on time and damn the consequences!

Then, if conditions were not bad enough, as night came on 5 March so did the snow, like Belgium nearly three months before. Throughout the coming battle there would be numerous parallels with the Ardennes Offensive, from the poor weather and road network that would cause traffic jams and slow the Germans down, to the town that would be bitterly defended and would derail the whole offensive.[446] There were achievable tactical objectives that might have made the offensive worthwhile, but strategic objectives that were not. And in the end there would be an enormous casualty list with nothing to show for the sacrifice. *Unternehmen Frühlingserwachen* would pass into history as a classic example of how <u>not</u> to conduct offensive warfare.

---

[446] One could even argue that the stubborn defense of the towns in question, Bastogne during the Ardennes Offensive and Sarosd during Spring Awakening, saved the Germans from total destruction by not allowing them to succeed. In both cases the further the Germans advanced the more vulnerable they were to a counter-attack. Had Bastogne fallen quickly and the Germans pushed on to the Meuse, their flanks would have been more thinly held and Patton's counterattacks might have cut off entire corps', if not armies. Had Sarosd been taken by *II. SS–Panzerkorps* there would have been no need to re-direct any units of *I. SS–Panzerkorps* to help take that town on 15 March, leaving them much further south when the Russian's Vienna Offensive opened the next day.

6 March, Tuesday

Goebbels would have written this later in the day, when the first reports from *Unternehmen Frühlingserwachen* had come into Hitler's headquarters. What is illustrative here is the perfunctory comment about a great offensive designed to literally change the course of the war in the south, the first time in the entire war when six of the seven *SS–Panzer Divisions* lined up next to each other and (theoretically) rolled into the attack side by side. That he has so little to say, even when the details would still have been sketchy, tells much about the gloomy atmosphere that must have surrounded the situation conference.

"Our great offensive with Sepp Dietrich's Army has begun in Hungary. No forecast can be made at the moment. First reports say more or less nothing, merely that our troops met very stiff resistance and have therefore made no great gains of ground on the first day. The enemy is already taking strong counter-measures, mainly putting very strong air forces into action."[447]

Goebbels spends more time and effort discussing the counterattack at Lauban than on the major offensive in the south. Although there is no evidence, it seems likely that Germans generals told Goebbels in private not to expect much from the offensive in Hungary.

In Vienna the gloomy outlook of the city was getting worse. A report from *Wehrkreis* (Military District) *XVII*, issued on 6 March, 1945 stated: "The mood here is very depressed. Everybody is tired of the

---

[447] Trevor-Roper, *Final Entries*, p. 78.

war. Outright destructive tendencies are noticeable. Only a very few still believe in victory."[448]

And so at last came the day of attack, the day when Germany's last hope for a decisive victory over the Red Army would be realized or crushed. As 5 March slipped into history and the minutes of 6 March ticked off until the launch of *Unternehmen Frühlingserwachen,* there were few German commanders who would disagree with the people of Vienna that the war was lost. At least, they might have agreed in private. Publicly, it was never more dangerous to say something that could be interpreted as defeatist than the last months of the war; saying openly that the war was lost could result in a quick court-martial and execution.

Of all the ill-advised operations Hitler imposed on the *Wehrmacht, Unternehmen Frühlingserwachen* might have been the worst. The acknowledged logic behind the attack was not without some merit, to protect the Hungarian oil fields, because without oil the war could not continue for long. And if almost every general on both sides knew that continuing the war at that stage was pointless, that was not relevant; only Hitler's opinion mattered and his opinion was to keep fighting, and for that he needed oil. But the final attack plan had all of the same flaws that had doomed previous attacks, such as the Ardennes offensive, and some new flaws as well. The Germans could no longer muster the forces necessary to not only break through enemy defenses, but then to follow that success with troops who could protect the flanks and allow the assault units to keep moving forward without having to guard their own flanks. In essence, then, the more success the Germans had in the attack, the more dangerous their situation became as their flanks became

[448] Weyr, *The Setting of the Pearl*, p. 272.

progressively longer and weaker. It was Kursk all over again.

How did the German soldiers feel about the war at this point? It is hard to imagine that any experienced German soldier, from the lowliest private to Sepp Dietrich himself, held any hope that *Unternehmen Frühlingserwachen* would change anything. Dietrich may not have been Germany's most talented commander, but by this time he was very experienced; he knew better than most just how improbable victory was. He would carry out his orders as best he could, however, regardless of whether or not he personally held out hope for victory. Hermann Balck *was* one of Germany's most talented commanders, albeit after his demotion from *Heeresgruppe* command he seems to have lost some of his edge, but where he stood is harder to understand. Like so many former *Wehrmacht* officers, his post-war writings are very much in the 'cover your reputation' class and must be read with a healthy skepticism. As for Otto Wöhler, he would not even finish out the war as commander of *Heeresgruppe Süd*.

Guderian, as previously noted, was dead set against the attack. At least, he states this in his memoirs and Goebbels' cryptic references in his diary seem to back up this claim. According to Goebbels, Guderian came around to Hitler's way of thinking and endorsed the offensive, but if this happened at all it was likely just Guderian's recognition that he could not get the attack cancelled so he might as well go along with it. In his memoirs he writes that he would have preferred that starting in late January 6. *SS–Panzerarmee* be grouped into two strikes forces east of the Oder River, one in the Glogau-Kottbus area, the other in Pomerania, thereby setting up a classic two-pronged pincer attack to cut off the Russian spearheads in Poland and East Prussia in very much the same fashion as *Unternehmen Zitadelle* had been designed two years before[449]. This was the conventional thinking among German officers, to defend the capital of the *Reich* above all other priorities. Grudgingly he admits that with the German synthetic oil industry bombed almost out of existence, the defense of the oil resources in Austria and Hungary had some importance. This fact partially explains Hitler's otherwise incomprehensible decision to send the mass of the forces freed in the West to Hungary; he wanted to keep control of the remaining oil wells and oil refineries which were of vital importance both to the armored force and the air force.[450]

Here, Guderian illustrates the problem with most German post-war memoirs. Not only does he want to white-wash any wrong-doing or poor decisions on his part, but to second guess strategy that did not work. In one sense, the sentence quoted is completely contradictory. Guderian questions the incomprehensible decision to send *6. SS–Panzerarmee* to Hungary, then admits that the oil resources located there were vital to each and every machine in the *Wehrmacht* order of battle, thus admitting that the decision was quite comprehensible, even if he disagreed with the priorities involved. In essence, without oil the war could not continue. And therein lay the unsolvable problem for Guderian's logic: to him, and to almost every German General still alive in March of 1945, the war was irretrievably lost. There was no point in fighting for oil because there was no point fighting at all. Defending Berlin and Germany against the Red Army was all that could possibly matter, keeping the Russians out while letting the Allies in. If it is taken in that respect the argument for using *6. SS–Panzerarmee* in Eastern Germany makes total sense.

But Hitler was not thinking in terms of which enemy he preferred to overrun Germany; he was still fighting to win, even if winning was no longer possible.

---

[449] And which *Unternehmen Frühlingserwachen* would also be designed to do.

[450] Guderian, *Panzer Leader*, pp. 345-346.

And to win, he needed oil. Whether *6. SS–Panzerarmee* was better used elsewhere or not, Adolf Hitler had ordered *Unternehmen Frühlingserwachen* to proceed, and proceed it would.

While *SS-Brigade Ney* was still re-forming behind the lines, accepting new recruits and training them, a *kampfgruppe* of battalion strength that was combat ready was assigned to *6. SS–Panzerarmee* for use during *Unternehmen Frühlingserwachen*. By 14 March, the *kampfgruppe* had lost 58 men.[451]

In the predawn darkness the men of *3. SS–Panzergrenadier Regiment Deutschland* straggled into the collection areas near their jump-off positions, their uniforms soaked, cold, hungry and completely exhausted from their torturous road march that began the day before and lasted throughout the night. The temperature was near freezing and the snow that had started at twilight the previous day was still falling. A thin, frozen crust covered the ground, which easily gave way to swamps of mud beneath. Deutschland was the lead assault element of *2. SS–Panzer Division Das Reich* and so was the first to arrive near the front, while the rest of the division was still strung out in its march forward. The artillery of *II. SS–Panzerkorps* was already in place at 0430[452] when the time arrived for the launch of *Unternehmen Frühlingserwachen*; the bombardment began on time and was short, half an hour, but violent.

---

[451] Pencz, *Siegrunen Volume 76*, p. 21.

[452] Here again there is disagreement on exactly when something happened. In the May, 2012 issue of World War II Magazine, Major General Michael Reynolds says, "…it is generally agreed that the 30-minute artillery barrage heralding the beginning of Spring Awakening began as planned at 4 am on March 6" (p.65). Yet Otto

Map 8

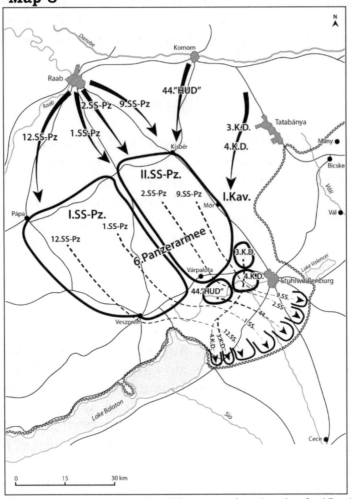

The plan for *Unternehmen Frühlingserwachen*. Russian fortifications and *pakfronts* stretched to Cece and beyond.

Das Reich's artillery regiment was tangled in the traffic mess leading to the front and had to pull off the road and unlimber quickly so that it could participate in the pre-attack bombardment, which was intended to shock the frontline Soviet defenses into temporary numbness. Led by *Deutschland*, the breakthrough was supposed to happen quickly so that the armored and tracked elements could rapidly move through the front lines on their way to the Danube, much as *IV. SS–Panzerkorps* had done during *Konrad III*, only with much more strength. Except *Deutschland* did not attack; the regiment was so late and so worn out when it finally gathered in the jump-off positions that the attack was postponed until the next morning.[453] Despite exhortations from *Heeresgruppe Süd* to get moving, and despite a direct *Führerbefehl* that *Das Reich* should attack without delay regardless of circumstances, Werner Ostendorff would not order his men to do the impossible. *Deutschland's* sister regiment, *SS–Panzergrenadier Regiment Der Führer* only made it as far as Urhida, still very short of the front, and none of the exploitation forces were ready for combat. So if the Russians were stunned or surprised by the opening bombardment, they were even more surprised when no attack followed the shelling. Precious ammunition that had been carefully hoarded had been fired off to soften up the Russian positions for an attack that never came. There could be no doubt that an attack was coming, however, so the Russians were alerted and ready; all of the elaborate efforts to maintain the element of surprise were wasted.[454]

As morning passed into afternoon it was clear that *Unternehmen Frühlingserwachen* was floundering in the mud. After small initial advances, Soviet counterattacks had driven *I Kavallerie Korps* back to its

---

[453] Sources differ on exactly when Das *Reich* finally went into the attack, with some saying late in the day on March 6th. The best sources say it was the morning of March 7th, however, and so that timing is used in the narrative.

[454] Weidinger, *Das Reich V*, p. 331. Weidinger definitively says that the artillery opened fire "exactly at 0430. This narrative has used the latter time because Weidinger is a primary source, he was actually there. It should be noted, though, that a counter-argument could be made that Reynolds' research is much the newer, as Weidinger's book is an English translation of a German work that was first published in the early 1980's.

start line; the corps was actually in danger of losing ground. *I. SS–Panzerkorps* had slugged its way forward up to four kilometers, a minimal gain made at great cost. Not only had *II. SS–Panzerkorps* not attacked yet, it was not close to being ready to attack. Finally, *III. Panzerkorps* was the only assault corps to have any real success, pushing forward into the outskirts of Seregelyes and threatening the rear of the Soviet XXX Corps, a potentially disastrous scenario for the Soviets. But the commander of Third Ukrainian Front, Marshal Tolbukhin, was not about to let his defenses be outflanked. XXX Corps was part of the 26th Army, commanded by Lt. General Gagyen. Tolbukhin gave the army two tank brigades as well as three anti-tank regiments from Third Ukrainian Front's reserves, and Gagyen sent them into the line facing both *II. SS–Panzerkorps* and *III. Panzerkorps*, along with a rifle division from 26th Army reserve. Tolbukhin was taking no chances, however, and he ordered even more forces forward from deep reserve, including another rifle division into the second line of defense facing *II. SS–Panzerkorps*, a rifle corps into the Simontornya area and two Guards Tank regiments to Sarbogard.

7 March, Wednesday

As more information came in from Hungary, Goebbels had more to record in his diary. The entry for 7 March leads off with news of *Unternehmen Frühlingserwachen*.

"In Hungary our local attacks between Lake Balaton and the Drava, made in greater strength, were very successful and in the Kaposvar area our forces pushed some 6-8 km towards Osien. At the same time, attacking from south to north across the Drava from Viroviticar, our forces also moved forward some 6-8 km. Satisfactory initial success was also achieved in attacks southwards and eastwards from the eastern top of Lake Balaton, in the area south of Stuhlweissenburg."

The objective observer might want to ask for the exact definition of 'satisfactory progress' and 'very successful', since it is doubtful that any soldier in Hungary would have used those terms to describe Day One of *Unternehmen Frühlingserwachen*. Goebbels must have been parroting what he had just heard in the daily military conference at the *Führer* conference, which makes this entry fascinating. A six or eight kilometer advance would be hard to justify as "very successful," although for the middle and southern arms of the attack it could have been enough had the following days brought more such. However, how the first day's fighting could have been interpreted as "satisfactory initial success" for *6. SS–Panzerarmee* and *III. Panzerkorps* of *6. Armee* is hard to imagine. The modern historian reading these words can almost sense the tension around the map table as Hitler bent forward from his chair, glasses perches on his long nose and holding a magnifying glass to inspect every farm on the battlefield, the atmosphere stuffy and stale and warm, Hitler's face flushed and his left arm twitching, and the Army and *Waffen–SS* liaison officers not wanting to give Hitler bad news and softening the disappointments of the first day's fighting.

Day by day Goebbels began to sense the end, though. As far as his diary reflects the realities facing the men of *Heeresgruppe Süd*, his comments on the state of morale ring very true.

"...on our side it must be stated that the morale of our men is slowly sinking. This, moreover, is explicable in the light of the fact that they have been fighting uninterruptedly for weeks and months. Somewhere the physical strength to resist runs out."

Once again we see defeatist words that would earn almost anyone else a ticket to the nearest concentration camp, or a noose on the closest light pole, true words that show the man who was arguably the second man of the *Reich*, and certainly one of the three most powerful at this point, knew quite well that the fighting forces had reached the end of their tether. That he continued exhorting resistance to the bitter end shows nothing if not the extent of his own narcissism and hypocrisy; the Wehrmacht was fighting to extend the reign of the Nazi government as long as possible, not to achieve some sort of military victory. As it relates to *Heeresgruppe Süd*, however, Goebbels knew very well the men were achieving everything possible, and this makes his defense of the *Waffen–SS* divisions following the cuff band order much more understandable.

Fairly late on 7 March he supplemented the earlier comments from Hungary. "A...It is reported from Hungary that our troops are meeting extraordinarily stiff resistance."

Further comments on the air war merely show what the men at the front must have felt as, day after day, week after week, bombs rained down on their homes and their families.

"There is no point saying much more about the air war. We are bombed uninterruptedly day and night..."[455]

The terrain over which the *Unternehmen Frühlingserwachen* assault divisions were supposed to rapidly drive to the Danube was mostly rolling farmland, but with prominent hills and ridges in strategic locations. During *Konrad III* the relatively small number of German *panzers* had broken through the weak Soviet defenses and moved quickly eastward on ground that was frozen solid, but neither of those conditions existed in early March. The Soviet defenses were very strong and very deep and the ground was a huge, sticky morass. During *Konrad III* the speed of the German advance made it difficult for the Soviet commanders to shift forces quickly enough to halt the offensive short of the Danube, but the razputitza slowed the Germans to a crawl, and Russian reinforcements kept pouring into the planned path of advance. In the conditions prevailing in early March, therefore, possession of the high ground gave the side that owned it distinct advantages in directing artillery fire, air support and discerning the future moves of the enemy, not to mention avoiding the worst effects of the torrential rainfall and melting snow on units caught in low ground. On top of the Soviet defenses, terrain and weather problems, the delay in attacking by *II. SS–Panzerkorps* meant that the pre-attack bombardment on 6 March had achieved nothing more than alerting the Russians of where an attack was coming, and also most likely when. Taking all of this into account, along with limiting factors on the German side such as fuel and ammunition shortages, the task given to *II. SS–Panzerkorps* was nearly impossible.

[455] Trevor-Roper, *Final Entries*, pp. 80-89.

Yet on 7 March *II. SS–Panzerkorps* finally went into the attack despite the difficulties, and immediately paid the price for attacking in such dreadful conditions. *9. SS–Panzer Division Hohenstaufen* started its drive on Sarosd as rain and snow fell and it was immediately obvious that *panzers* would be useless; they could only move on hard road surfaces, which were few in number. Moving cross-country was disastrous, leaving the infantry to slog on alone. "Two tanks disappeared in mud up to their turrets...the *SS Panzer*-Grenadiers, still struggling forward on their feet, were therefore without effective armored support."[456] Heavy caliber Russian artillery rounds fell all around the vehicles crossing the Sàrviz Canal, further disrupting movement. The division's infantry managed to close within three miles of the northwest side of Sarosd, but without tank support they did not have the firepower to blast through the well-constructed Soviet defenses; the clear fields of fire gave the advantage to whichever side could bring the most long-range heavy weapons to bear, and without German tanks or air support, that side was the Soviets. And if all of that were not enough, the Soviets had correctly discerned the most likely German attack routes and had placed their reserves perfectly to intercept the main thrust of the German attack.

Strictly by courage and professionalism *II. SS–Panzerkorps* did manage some small gains during the day, as the war diary entry for *Heeresgruppe Süd* makes clear. "*II. SS–Panzerkorps*, which did not get going yesterday because of a delayed arrival, today, primarily with infantry forces, drove a 6 km deep wedge into the enemy defenses as far as the hills west of Sarosd."[457] Gains of six kilometers, however, were not the war-turning results Hitler was counting on, and there was no breakthrough to exploit, even if the mobile forces could have done so.

[456] Reynolds, *Operation Spring Awakening*, p. 65.
[457] Ibid, p. 66.

In the second day of its attack *I. SS–Panzerkorps* was having some success. By the evening of 7 March, *1. SS–Panzer Division Leibstandarte Adolf Hitler* had blasted its way into through the second-line defenses of the 68th Rifle Division and this forced that division to retreat behind the Sarvis Canal or be destroyed. The *LAH* tried to disrupt this withdrawal but were unable to move fast enough and by early morning on 8 March the remnants of the 68th Rifle Division were safely across the canal and dug in. From the German point of view, the *LAH* was assigned an advance route west of the canal so this removed the 68th Rifle Division from its path, but this also meant that the Russians were sitting on their left flank with only the Sàrviz Canal as a barrier. Unless *II. SS–Panzerkorps* could get moving and clear the east bank, then the further the *LAH* moved toward its objectives in the south, the more exposed their flank became.

8 March, Thursday

War News

St. Malo, France- During the night of 8–9 a German commando raid, mounted from the occupied Channel Islands, successfully attacked the small French town of Granville, on the coast near St. Malo. A few US prisoners were taken, some German prisoners were released and the damage caused by such a small attacking force was extreme.

Switzerland- Acting under pressure from the Allies, Switzerland banned most transit traffic to Germany, and limited German imports to 1 million Swiss francs per month. While this might not seem to be a significant development, in truth the closer German came to defeat, the more people tried to escape there, or transfer funds into safe Swiss banks. For Swiss bankers and financiers this was a major blow. But it was now clear that soon enough there would no longer be an Axis Powers to deal with, and cozying up to the Western Allies was a good idea.

"In our offensive across the Drava two bridgeheads were formed despite stiff enemy resistance. Between the Drava and Lake Balaton our offensive continued despite violent enemy counterattacks. Considerable gains of ground were made between Lake Balaton and the Danube south-east and south of Stuhlweissenburg. Two Hungarian towns were recaptured."

Goebbels begins each day's entry with a succinct wrap-up of the military situation, gleaned from the daily conferences. This, therefore, would be pretty much a verbatim transliteration of what was said by the officers reporting to Hitler about the progress of *Unternehmen Frühlingserwachen*. What is significant is not that the information is not correct; it is, as far as it goes. What is significant is that no conclusions are drawn that the progress so far has been completely inadequate to the goals of the offensive.

The topic of troop morale was again on Goebbel's mind, as this was his department.

"The Party Chancellery is now planning a special operation to raise the troops' morale. Each *Gau* is to make available five selected political leaders of officer rank in an attempt to revive the sinking morale of the troops. Evidence of demoralization is to be seen primarily in the West..."

Troops facing the Western Allies were often glad to surrender and Goebbels by this time knew it. How to stiffen their spines? Although not directly relating to the Eastern Front, where horror stories of mass rape and murder by the Red Army were at least a partially effective antidote to defeatism, Goebbels must have known that eventually this would become a problem in the East anyway, as it did. During a visit to the newly re-captured city of Lauban he lauds *Generalfeldmarschall* Schörner for the measures he used to deal with men suspected of malingering or avoiding duty.

"His procedure with such types is fairly brutal; he hangs them on the nearest tree with a placard announcing: 'I am a deserter and have declined to defend German women and children.' The deterrent effect on other deserters and men who might have it in mind to follow them is obviously considerable."

And so the men at the fighting front found themselves continually fretting over the safety of families either in towns already captured, or cities bombed into oblivion, unable to stem the Allies tide of advance, short on food, fuel and ammunition, not allowed to retreat, hung or shot if caught behind the lines without authorization (and sometimes with authorization), hung or shot if a position was not held or an attack was not successful, knowing that the men on the Western Front were surrendering in large numbers and, as of the previous day, that the Allies were over the Rhine, and knowing that if the Red Army captured them they could expect no mercy, all the while awaiting a catastrophic bombardment or an overwhelming attack.

As Goebbels drove along behind the front east and southeast of Berlin, he first visited Lauban and then stopped at Gorlitz, where he met General Mader, commander of the Fuhrer Grenadier Division which would soon find itself assigned to *Heeresgruppe Süd* but had just finished helping liberate Lauban.

"The young General Mader, commanding the *Führer Grenadier Division* which played a part in the Lauban battle, is outstanding. He had his general's tabs at the age of 35. The mood of this circle is truly infectious. No trace of defeatism."[458]

Mader's division was essentially a Type 1945 *panzer* division. After re-capturing Lauban it would be refilled with armor and men, and in early April sent to the most critical danger point in Hitler's mind... Vienna.

As the German *4. Kavallerie Division* slogged south to secure the western flank of *Unternehmen Frühlingserwachen*, it was aided by several Hungarian units that were attached to it, namely the 20th Assault Gun Battalion with 15 *Hetzers* and the 25th Reconnaissance Battalion. In addition to flank protection, the mission of *I Kavallerie Korps* included clearing the southern bank of Lake Balaton. This

[458] Trevor-Roper, *Final Entries*, pp. 91-95.

meant the Corps was attacking to the south, southwest and west, all at the same time, against an entrenched enemy and in bad weather. Complicating matters, German cavalry did not have the heavy firepower of a regular infantry formation, so blasting through *pakfront* after *pakfront* without heavy armor or artillery support was not an option.

With the Russian 68th Rifle Division out of its way *I. SS–Panzerkorps* was able to start making some progress to the south. By nightfall the bank of the Sarvis Canal opposition the town of Nagy had been secured, and while at least one source lists Nagy itself as being captured, that cannot be unquestionably verified.

What is for certain is that despite the weather, and despite the lack of *panzer* support and all of the other hindrances, the *SS* men were fighting through. Once again the Germans moved forward only through the skill of the shrinking number of veterans still in the ranks, against a Russian enemy that loathed the *Waffen–SS* and was, by this point, at least as skilled at fighting as their German enemy.

The success of *I. SS–Panzerkorps* was meaningless unless *II. SS–Panzerkorps* could also make progress, but despite a maximum effort, one source says that *Das Reich* made nine separate attacks on 8 March,[459] the corps could not get much past the Aba-Sarosd road. As the distance opened between the two *SS* corps the danger to the left flank of *I. SS–Panzerkorps* increased; unless its flank could be protected by *II. SS–Panzerkorps*, as planned, then the *1. SS–Panzer Division Leibstandarte Adolf Hitler* would have to guard its own flank. This meant that it would have to cannibalize the combat units that were

---

[459] Michael Reynolds in the May issue of World War II Magazine, quoting a Russian study of the battle.

supposed to drive south to instead protect the left flank, so that the further the division moved south, the weaker its assault power became, even without factoring in casualties.

However, Marshal Malinovsky could read a map as well as the Germans, and understood the same battlefield dynamic. He made certain that Russian reinforcements deployed in the assault path of *II. SS–Panzerkorps* made the going even tougher than it had been on Day One. Recognizing this danger, during the early evening both Otto Wöhler and Sepp Dietrich agreed to the release of the *23. Panzer Division* from *Heeresgruppe Süd* reserve to help get *II. SS–Panzerkorps* moving.

The plan was for that division to follow the route of the Leibstandarte on the west side of the Sàrviz Canal, then cross the canal to the east bank, and finally to turn north to attack the Soviet defenses holding up *II. SS–Panzerkorps* from their rear, that is, from the south, forcing them to either withdraw or be destroyed. The resemblance to the American stand at Bastogne the previous December was clear.

Either result would allow *II. SS–Panzerkorps* to move forward and provide flank protection to *I. SS–Panzerkorps*. With some 50 *panzers*, *Jagdpanzers* and assault guns the *23. Panzer Division* was still fairly powerful by late-war standards and there was reason to believe that it could unhinge the Soviet defenses; but just like the Ardennes Offensive three months earlier, a stubborn defensive stand was holding up the German columns and would draw in more and more forces at time went on.

9 March, Friday

Like the Ardennes Offensive, the attention of all
Germans once again became hyper-focused on Sepp
Dietrich and *6. SS–Panzerarmee*. This was due to the
efforts of Joseph Goebbels, of course, who played up
every news bulletin as a major victory. And yet the
usually stoic *Reichsminister* himself seems to have been
caught up in the desperate hope.

"Our offensive made progress everywhere in
Hungary. Its success on the Malom Canal and southwest of Stuhlweissenburg is particularly noteworthy."
He expanded on this later. "Good news comes from
Hungary. The *6. SS–Panzerarmee* has succeeded in
penetrating deeply into the enemy defense positions.
An effort is now being made to reach the enemy rear
areas so as to annihilate his forces and it is thought
that a considerable portion of his front must collapse
as a result. The Soviets are naturally resisting tooth
and nail; it is to be hoped, however, that Sepp Dietrich
will succeed in implementing the *Führer's* plan." Is this
cleverly worded phrase the twisting of a propaganda
master shielding his idol? Or is there a resonance from
the daily military briefing in the implication here that,
if the offensive fails, it is Dietrich's fault for not
properly executing the plan?

By and large Goebbels doesn't mention *Luftwaffe*
operations much in his diary. Or, if he does, it is not
usually in a positive light. His animosity toward Göring
notwithstanding, by this point the *Luftwaffe* was
almost an after-thought because its impact on the
fighting was minimal. For this day, however, he does
mention air operations over the Eastern Front, which is
quite unusual.

"Enemy aircraft were very active in the East
yesterday. They attacked primarily localities near the
front and our supply lines. 1,400 sorties were noted in
the central sector alone. Our own air activity was also
very considerable. 365 German close support aircraft

were in action in the central sector. A total of 26 enemy aircraft were shot down."

It's almost impossible to know where these numbers came from, or how reliable they are. Presumably they were given at the daily military conference by the *Luftwaffe* liaison officer. Taken at face value, if the 1,400 Red Air Force sorties in the central sector represent 1/3 of the whole, that would put the sum over 4,200 sorties across the length of the Eastern Front, an enormous number that would have caused great harm behind the German lines, but a number that seems possible given the Red Air Force numbers at the time. But that would also imply that the German total was more than 1000 aircraft sorties, a figure that is very hard to believe. So as with much of the diary, the inference that 8 March, 1945, was a day of very heavy air activity by the Red Air Force, met with maximum efforts by the *Luftwaffe*, is probably correct. The numbers, however, should be taken with some skepticism.

On a completely different subject, Goebbels gives us a behind-the-scenes look at the madness afflicting the bureaucrats not just of Germany but also of Hungary. At this point in the war most of Hungary was occupied by the Soviets; there was not much of a Hungarian nation left outside of Soviet control, and the majority of the country that was occupied by the Soviets had a pro-Soviet puppet government in place that had already declared war on the Axis. And yet the Hungarian government of Ferenc Szalazi was apparently still pretending that it had a purpose in life.

"Measures now being taken in Hungary to set up a labor service on the German model come plenty late. Little help can now be given the Hungarians. They have missed their moment and can now only be regarded by the major belligerents as pawns in their game."

As always, his own area of responsibility, morale, was at the forefront of Goebbels' thoughts.

"Letters I am now receiving show that German fighting morale has reached its nadir. My correspondents bemoan the defeatist attitude to be seen on large sections of the front and also the considerable breakdown in morale among the civil population. Even the optimists are now beginning to waver…

But was this also true for Goebbels? Was defeatism beginning to sink even into his thought processes? His final entry for the day seems to sum up his innermost thoughts.

"We need a military victory now as much as our daily bread."[460]

Some eight kilometers south of Lake Balaton on the extreme western flank of *I. SS–Panzerkorps*, the Hungarian 25 Infantry Regiment, aided by the Hungarian 20th Assault Gun Battalion, began the fight for the town of Enying. Enying was vital as a defensive anchor for the western base of *Unternehmen Frühlingserwachen* as well as a springboard for further advances south. The road connecting Enying to Deg had already been cut by *I. SS–Panzerkorps*, but taking the town itself was vital. Without it, Soviet counterattacks would continually threaten to slice behind the assault divisions and cut them off.

I Kavallerie Korps itself was making some progress, thanks to a gap created by *12. SS–Panzer Division Hitlerjugend*; *3. Kavallerie Division* reached the road leading south from Enying to the small village of Mezökomarom, partially isolating Enying, while *4. Kavallerie Division* fought for Enying itself. The Hungarians showed determination in trying to liberate their countrymen from the Russian occupation.

On the 4th day of *Unternehmen Frühlingserwachen I. SS–Panzerkorps* began moving rapidly enough to give some hope that a breakthrough might yet be achieved; indeed, the Soviet CXXXV Corps

[460] Trevor-Roper, *Final* Entries, p. 103.

front was so badly broken by *I. SS–Panzerkorps* that the official Russian study of the battle notes the alarm the situation caused for Marshal Tolbukhin, and the danger it created for the XXX Rifle Corps opposing *II. SS–Panzerkorps* on the eastern side of the Sàrviz Canal. "From the morning of March 9, the operational situation on the XXX Rifle Corps front sharply deteriorated. The success of the enemy in breaking through the tactical defense zone of CXXXV Corps created a serious threat to the rear of 26th Army."[461] The situation was so alarming that Tolbukhin completely restructured Third Ukrainian Front to conform to the new tactical situation. 27th Army had been Tolbukhin's reserve army, but with *I. SS–Panzerkorps* beginning to overwhelm 26th Army, Tolbukhin assigned the defensive zone east of the Sàrviz Canal and north to Lake Velence to the former army, simultaneously transferring XXX Rifle Corps to that 27th Army and sending General Gagyen of 26th Army more reinforcements. He also ordered that the area between the Sàrviz Canal and Lake Balaton would receive priority in close air support.

The relief of finally seeing his forces make significant progress did not hide from Sepp Dietrich the fact that their very success was increasing their danger. With *II. SS–Panzerkorps* continuing to stall against the fierce Russian resistance near Sarosd, the left flank of *1. SS–Panzer Division Leibstandarte Adolf Hitler* became more and more exposed. Nor was Dietrich the only commander who noticed the danger; Marshal Tolbukhin saw it too, and was trying to find a way to strike the exposed Germans. Tolbukhin went so far as to request that STAVKA release forces being assembled for the Vienna Offensive to him, but in this he was denied. The only thing protecting *I. SS–Panzerkorps* was the Sàrviz Canal and River, and the swamps they flowed through; these were significant barriers, it was true. But the Red Army had forded

---

[461] Reynolds, *Operation Spring Awakening*, p. 67.

countless rivers and swamps in the past three years, some far more difficult than the ones in Hungary, and given enough time they would cross those, too.

Two separate kampfgruppen from *1. SS–Panzer Division Leibstandarte Adolf Hitler* gained important ground just north of Simontornya, one overcoming strong defenses to cut the road from Saregres to Nagy, the second taking some high ground north of Simontornya before being stopped by heavy defensive fire. Saregres was important because, being very close to Simontornya to the north-east, it served as a defensive anchor for the left flank of the attack. Just north of the town was a heavily flooded area known as the Retszilasi-tavak, a large area of shallow lakes which would have been difficult to ford, so taking Saregres allowed the offensive to have some measure of security from a direct flank attack.

Elsewhere, however, the danger to *Heeresgruppe Süd*, and *6. SS–Panzerarmee* in particular, was daily growing stronger. Marshal Tolbukhin's request for a reserve army to help his defense south of Lakes Balaton and Velence had been turned down, but he had, in fact, been given command of two those armies anyway. Not for defense and not in the south, but for offensive purposes north of Lake Velence during the coming Vienna Offensive. The Vienna Offensive was evolving into a larger and, from the German point of view, a far more dangerous situation. Just as Sepp Dietrich had feared all along, the Russians were adapting their offensive plans to take advantage of *6. SS–Panzerarmee*'s exposed position; this meant that not only was German movement to the south no longer relevant, the more success *Unternehmen Frühlingserwachen* achieved the greater the danger of being surrounded became. In effect, the Germans were fighting their way deeper and deeper into a trap, and both he and the Russians knew it. For the Germans, therefore, success meant failure, and while their progress on the west side of the Sàrviz Canal endangered those Russian troops directly engaged in the fighting, it did not overly concern STAVKA because "the fact that they were facing reverses in one area did not distract them from their long-term aim, and the albeit serious situation on the west side of the Sàrviz was seen as an opportunity rather than as a setback."[462] Dietrich knew this, and began looking for a way to finesse his men out of danger, no easy task when dealing with Hitler.

The offensive had already failed, but once again the last person to admit reality would be Adolf Hitler.

[462] Reynolds, *Operation Spring Awakening*, p. 67.

10 March, Saturday

"In Hungary German offensive operations achieved further local gains yesterday. Progress in the area between Lake Balaton and the Danube is especially satisfactory; there our attack is moving forward on a broad front along the Malom Canal."

Continuing to list enemy air operations in the East, Goebbels reports "...In the Central Sector alone 2100 sorties were counted."

This likely means Red Army tactical air strikes supporting Malinovsky's 2nd Ukrainian Front, which had been launching heavy attacks into Slovakia for some time against Schörner's *Heeresgruppe Mitte*. He gives no indication where the figures come from, or what they mean, but if pace of air operations could only be high if the weather permitted, and good weather in the air meant decent ground conditions for an attacking armored force.

The local Viennese SD sent Kaltenbrunner a report about deteriorating feelings toward the Party. Destruction from the air raids had left many people less afraid of retribution and more willing to speak their minds. There was even beginning to be criticism of the *Führer* himself, which was not only foolhardy but suicidal. This echoed what Goebbels had been hearing and mentions several times in his diary, but he does not mention his source, other than to say his correspondence, which very well may have been Kaltenbrunner forwarding intelligence reports. Goebbels was very well connected through his own sources, however, through the vast media network he had built throughout the *Reich*. The *Reichsminister* was very concerned about this defeatism, though, aiming as it did at the very heart of his ministry, so it becomes easy to see that things behind the lines were beginning to fall apart on the home front.

"The morale of our troops and our people in the West has suffered to an extraordinary degree. ..Nothing can be achieved in the West now except by brutal methods, otherwise we shall lose control of the situation...An iron hand is now the essential here..."

The battered and broken *Wehrmacht* and the bomb weary civilian population must be brought back into the fold by the bloodiest violence, concludes the man tasked with elevating the people's flagging spirits. Draconian measures will succeed in the place of arms and supplies. Beat them until they fight. It may seem to be beating a dead horse again to mention the methods of the government to keep the populace in check, except that these incidents are illustrative of just how desperate the troops and the civilian population were becoming. The Third *Reich* had zero tolerance for dissent even in the best of times, so for anyone, anywhere, to openly criticize the regime is itself incredible. The effect that all of this would have had on the troops at the front can be imagined. Some may have been indignant at being betrayed while they were risking their lives at the front, others would have sympathized and understood, differing opinions would have led to arguments and gnawed at unit cohesion. In the *Waffen–SS* and the better Wehrmacht units this effect would have been lessened, because by this point in the war veteran units were probably fighting for their comrades and not for the regime. In below average Wehrmacht units or Volkssturm units, however, where the men were not so well-trained and often-times hardly knew each other, it could have been like a rot.

By that evening the news from Hungary seemed even better. "In the East operations in Hungary are developing favorably at the moment. Our penetration was extended farther westwards.[463] One can already talk of a real break-through here. We have torn the enemy front apart to a breadth of 25 km. And also a depth of 25 km. The break-in at Lake Balaton has also

---

[463] Presumably Goebbels means either southwest or south, unless he is talking about I Cavalry Corps crawling west along the southern bank of Lake Balaton, but this seems unlikely.

been widened so that here too we have scored a considerable initial success."

Exactly what Goebbels means by this is hard to say.[464]

The weather in Hungary remained atrocious for offensive operations. *I. SS–Panzerkorps* was still struggling to close on the Sio Canal, with *1. SS–Panzer Division Leibstandarte Adolf Hitler* aiming for Simontornya and *12. SS–Panzer Division Hitlerjugend* making for Ozora, but despite maximum efforts neither division could move quickly enough to dislodge the Soviets from their defenses without having to dig them out. So they continued to struggle forward against stiff opposition. *Hitlerjugend* reported its strength on this day as five strong and one average *Panzergrenadier* Battalions, 12 75 mm anti-tank guns, six *Mark IVs*, nine *Mark V Panthers*, six *Jagdpanzer IVs*, 12 *Sturmgeschütze*, 16 105 mm howitzers, six 155 mm howitzers, three 100 mm field cannons and eight Nebelwerfers of unknown size. "In contrast to the 100 *Panzer* and *Sturmgeschütze* it had before the Ardennes Offensive, now only 33 were still operational."[465] Unlike most German divisions those of the *Waffen–SS* were kept up to numerical manpower strength as much as possible, at least in the premier formations, but while that might appear impressive in numbers their true fighting power was drastically diminished through lack of heavy weapons, fuel, supplies, trained replacements and officers of all ranks.

Nevertheless, in spite of everything working against them, the Germans slowly cut their way through the Russian defenses. Mesöszilas fell to the *Hitlerjugend*, and later they took Igar to close within a mile and a half of Simontornya on the northwest. The

[464] Trevor-Roper, *Final Entries*, p. 113.
[465] Michaelis, *Panzer Divisions of the Waffen–SS*, pp. 305-306.

LAH had lost much of its offensive punch through the necessity of protecting its flanks by leaving combat elements behind, but on 10 March the *23. Panzer Division* moved into the line and began to take over the flank in the Saregres area, so that the *SS* men could once again assemble the manpower at the point of attack to make progress. Firing across the canal from the eastern bank, the Russians tried to keep *23. Panzer Division* from getting into position but were unable to stop the division.

But although *I. SS–Panzerkorps'* progress was slow, it was still progress, while *II. SS–Panzerkorps* remained stuck in place despite desperate attempts to force the Soviets back, or to break through. Given the conditions under which the corps was fighting, and the strength of the Soviet defenses in the area, 6 admittedly depleted infantry divisions and significant armored forces[466], it probably would have been surprising if Bittrich's command had broken through. Reynolds quotes the official Soviet study of the battle about the fighting on 10 March: "Cruel Fighting took place around Hill 159 where artillery played a significant role in the destruction of the enemy. Unable to achieve success with frontal attacks, the enemy tried to outflank the objective; however, this maneuver was frustrated by tanks and SP guns in enfiladed positions. Fighting continued at night."[467] Try as they might, though, the men of *II. SS–Panzerkorps* could not drive the Soviets from their defenses. Consequently, this meant that the gap on *LAH's* left flank along the Sàrviz Canal grew to more than 15 miles, an invitation to disaster that was only held up by the weather and the difficulty of crossing the waterway, but a threat that was too dangerous to ignore for long. The

---

[466] A basic military rule of thumb was that the attacker should have a 3 to 1 advantage over the defender at the point of the attack. On paper, *II SS Panzer Corps* was actually outnumbered by the Russian defenders they were attacking, although the Soviet formations were so badly under-strength the actual numbers might have been even or slightly in the Germans' favor.

[467] Reynolds, *Operation Spring Awakening*, p. 67.

Russians had become quite adept at bridging such water obstacles and the canal itself was not very wide; danger could strike quickly and without warning.

I Kavallerie Korps was also having slow success. *3. Kavallerie Division* managed to throw a bridgehead across the Sio Canal west of Mesökomarom and *4. Kavallerie Division* finally surrounded Enying.

As if *Heeresgruppe Süd* did not already have its hands full trying to slog through the deep Russian defenses to fulfill an impossible mission, on 10 March it was ordered to create a brand new formation, *Panzerkorps Felldherrnhalle*, not only by organizing a corps staff and specialized units but also by recreating and/or refurbishing *Panzergrenadier Division Felldherrnhalle* and *13. Panzer Division*. The two divisions would subsequently be known as *Panzer* Division *Felldherrnhalle 1*, replacing *Panzergrenadier Division Felldherrnhalle*, and *Panzer Division Felldherrnhalle 2*, based on the remnants of *13. Panzer Division*. *Felldherrnhalle 1* was commanded by *Generalmajor* Günther Pape, lately commander of *Kampfgruppe Pape*, while *Felldherrnhalle 2* had *Generalmajor* Franz Bäke as its' commander.[468] The corps commander was by *General der Panzertruppen* Ulrich Kleemann, winner of the Knight's Cross with Oakleaves and the Wound Badge in Black, a very experienced soldier who once commanded the famous *90. Licht (Afrika) Division*.

There had been numerous formations with the appellate of Felldherrnhalle,[469] which was the name of the monument to Bavarian military leaders on the Odeonsplatz in Munich and the spiritual center of

---

[468] Bäke had won the Knight's Cross with Swords and was an experienced panzer commander; he ranked as one of the top scoring German tank aces of the war.

[469] In English, '*Generalfeldmarschall*s;' Hall.'

National Socialism; indeed, keeping all of the units called Felldherrnhalle straight virtually required a scorecard. With Hitler's rise to power those pedestrians passing by the Felldherrnhalle in Munich were required to give the Nazi salute and woe unto anyone who did not. *SS* guards kept vigilance there at all times. The idea of the *Felldherrnhalle* units was for them to be filled out with recruits from the *SA*, and the concept of a *Panzerkorps Felldherrnhalle* had been around for some months prior to its organization; the corps was to be based on the model of *Panzerkorps Grossdeutschland* and *Fallschirm-Panzerkorps Hermann Göring*. In other words, the purpose of the corps was political as much as it was military.

With every German armored formation under-strength in vehicles, and *SS* divisions such as *3. SS–Panzer Division Totenkopf* and *5. SS Panzer Division Wiking* having so few men and vehicles as to be relegated to defense only, it would have been a much better use of scarce resources to fill up such veteran formations rather than build new ones that had no time to train or build unit cohesion.[470] But Hitler's penchant for building new units rather than bringing existing ones back up to strength was well known by this point, an argument dating back to the early days in Russia and the debate about whether to use excess *Luftwaffe* men as replacements for *Heer* or *SS* units, or to build new *Luftwaffe Feld Divisions* around them. In the end Göring won that argument and the *Luftwaffe* built infantry divisions that proved largely ineffectual, while *Heer* divisions withered under constant attrition.

During this period of organizing the new *panzerkorps,* from March 9-12, some 19 *Mark V Panthers* and five *Mark IVs* were shipped from Army depots to *Panzer Division Felldherrnhalle 1,*[471] while *Panzer Division Felldherrnhalle 2* received 21 *Mark V*

---

[470] Although technically both divisions were refurbishments of the two divisions destroyed in Budapest, in reality neither had a substantial complement from their namesakes; virtually no one got out of Budapest alive.

[471] In other words, two weak or one strong company of tanks.

Panthers and 20 *Mark IVs*. In addition, *Panzer Abteilung 208* was incorporated into *Panzer Division Felldherrnhalle* as *I./Panzer Regiment Felldherrnhalle.*[472]

5. *SS Panzer Division Wiking* was still in defensive position around Stuhlweissenburg. On 10 March it reported itself as only 50 percent mobile, but the AFV situation was somewhat improved, with four *Mark IVs*, 13 *Mark V Panthers* and eight *Sturmgeschütze* on hand, for a total of 25, with six light and four heavy artillery batteries. The biggest concern was that there was no fuel for the vehicles, which within a fortnight would prove fatal for the *panzer* regiment.[473]

[472] Jentz, *Panzertruppen 2*, p. 235.
[473] Michael, *Panzer Divisions of the Waffen–SS*, p. 202.

11 March, Sunday

Reading Goebbel's entry for 11 March shows the fantasy bubble-world of the highest echelons of the German command. Losses to this point had been severe, and the situation was simply *Konrad III* without the breakthrough. Regardless how much ground might eventually be gained, the blood it cost to capture meant that it could never be held.

"In the East things are developing somewhat more favorably for us. Our offensive in Hungary has got off to a good start. Gains of ground, however, have not been so great that we are altogether over the hump. We must wait a few days before giving a final verdict on this offensive. "Our offensive in Hungary is making slow but sure progress. In general developments there may be called satisfactory. Our penetration has been considerably extended. We also have advanced near Lake Velencze, so that we can now talk of a real major offensive."

Goebbels visited Hitler that evening and discussed the flying courts martial roaming in the rear areas executing people they believed to be deserters, gleefully describing the vicious methods in use by then *Generaloberst* Schörner .

"Deserters get no mercy from him. They are hung from the nearest tree with a placard around their neck saying: I am a deserter. I have refused to defend German women and children and therefore I have been hung. Naturally such methods are effective. Every man in Schorner's area knows that he may die at the front but will inevitably die in the rear. That is a very good lesson which will assuredly strike home."

For the third time in this day's entry Goebbels returns to the subject of *Unternehmen Frühlingserwachen*. "Developments in Hungary, which the *Führer* considers very promising, show that if we really concentrate for an offensive, we succeed." Of course, after the 5th day of battle the offensive was far from being successful, but it must have been on Goebbels' mind because he keeps repeating essentially the same thing.

And morale was also on his mind, leading to one of the more humorous passages in the diary, although he meant it to be deadly serious.

"As far as morale in the West is concerned, we must try to revive it, if necessary by forceful methods."

This could almost be slapstick. *If the people are depressed and worried we will beat them until they are optimistic again!* Goebbels was usually a master of motivating the masses, yet he has been reduced, in the end, to threats and bellicosity to raise flagging spirits. Nothing better shows the desperate straits to which the leaders of the *Reich* had fallen, the frantic despair as knowledge that events were spinning out of their control became ever more obvious. Every tidbit of positive news brought unwarranted euphoria, not matter how trivial. It is this very attitude that would manifest itself in orders to the units fighting in Hungary in the coming weeks.[474]

Goebbels' enthusiasm was not entirely unfounded. For the 6th day in a row the men asked to carry out *Unternehmen Frühlingserwachen* struggled forward in deep, clinging mud, with limited heavy weapons support, while entrenched Soviet gunners fired at them with everything from rifles and machines guns to katyusha rockets, and overhead the Red Air Force strafed and bombed at will. Like most of the

[474] Trevor-Roper, *Final Entries*, p. 123.

terrain over which *Heeresgruppe Süd* was trying to advance the ground was either flat and virtually featureless, or low rolling hills with few paved roads. The mud made movement very difficult for vehicles of any sort, but especially for wheeled vehicles, while anti-tank guns had a clear field of fire. Yet in the face of these difficulties, *Unternehmen Frühlingserwachen* moved forward and gained ground.

Ominously, the weather had begun to clear. Hitler and his entourage might have viewed this as a good omen; Otto Wöhler, Hermann Balck and Sepp Dietrich all knew better.

On the western base of the offensive the Hungarian 25th Infantry Regiment, supported by the 20th Hungarian Assault Gun Battalion, finally took the small town of Enying, just south of Lake Balaton. The 20th had suffered heavily in the fighting and had only six working Hetzers left, with 32 more under repair. Although a vital objective had finally been taken, the slow pace of advance for *I Kavvallerie Korps* on the western flank, and *II. SS–Panzerkorps* on the eastern flank, still left *I. SS–Panzerkorps* in the center moving forward alone, having to guard its own flanks while also attacking due south. Nevertheless, the Corps continued fighting its way slowly forward and *1. SS–Panzer Division Leibstandarte Adolf Hitler* cleared the high ground north of Simontornya, while *12. SS–Panzer Division Hitlerjugend* captured a crucial road junction almost a mile south of Igar, putting both divisions in position to attack Simontornya itself the next day. *23. Panzer Division* fought its way into Saregres but could not capture the town, meaning not only that a Soviet bridgehead remained on the western bank of the Sàrviz Canal, but also that plans to cross the canal and attack in support of *II. SS–Panzerkorps* were not feasible, at least in time to speed up the offensive.

Despite all of the difficulties, the weather, the Russian defenses, constant attacks by the Red Air Force and the relative lack of heavy weapon's support, *II. SS–Panzerkorps* finally managed to stagger forward somewhat on 11 March. *2. SS–Panzer Division Das Reich* launched an attack that Otto Weidinger described as "right out of the textbook."[475] The momentum of the attack pushed the division some three and a half miles southeast of the small town of Sarkeresztur, to a tiny village called Heinrich Major. Given the huge gap between the left flank of *I. SS–Panzerkorps* and the right flank of *II. SS–Panzerkorps*, the progress was welcome news, even if the gap itself remained dangerously large. At the tactical level this push gave some hope that *II. SS–Panzerkorps* could outflank the Soviet defenses around Sarosd to the east. Even better from the German point of view was the capture of a vineyard northeast of Sarkeresztur that left the Soviet forces still holding Aba all but cut off; with the Sàrviz Canal on their west, and the west bank already cleared by *I. SS–Panzerkorps*, their escape route was dangerously thin. The Germans were encouraged by these successes and saw them as giving hope that some type of attack momentum could still be achieved, if not an outright breakthrough.

Of course, the situation was analogous to Bastogne during the Ardennes Offensive. Taking the objective no longer mattered, since the defense had already held long enough for the enemy to bring in reinforcements. Much worse for the Germans was the massive Russian offensive that was ready to cave in the front north of Stuhlweissenburg; the only thing holding them back was the weather, which now had ample sunshine to dry the sodden roads and fields. The tether holding the Sword of Damocles over the head of *6. SS–Panzerarmee* grew ever more thin.

[475] Reynolds, *Operation Spring Awakening*, p. 67.

12 March, Monday

"When the all-clear sounded on March 12, 1945, at 2:30 pm, Hella Kinn stepped out of her half-destroyed office building into another city. Bombs had sheared off a corner of the art museum and the statue in front had lost its head. Trees lay smashed and broken. When she looked down the other side of the Ring she screamed. The Opera was on fire...for Ernst Andreas, destruction of the Opera was the worst blow of a day that saw cultural landmarks fall like ninepins- Opera, art museum, the imperial stables, the Spanish riding school, the Academy of Fine Arts, the stock exchange on the Ring. A bomb had torn the balcony off the Hofburg where Hitler had harangued the multitudes in 1938."[476]

An enormous strike force comprising 747 Bombers escorted by 229 fighters were sent to hit the Floridsdorf oil refinery but mostly missed, the refinery taking no severe hits. Instead the massive strike hit the center of the city, the Altstadt, cultural heart of Vienna. When the fires subsided the only thing left of the Opera House was the facade, the outer walls and the world-famous staircase. All of the decorations, scores of musical instruments and the archives of vocal scores and instrumental parts, as well as 150,000 priceless costumes were destroyed. The Burgtheater was also hit and set on fire, with more damage to the Albertina, the Heinrichshof and the Messepalast, the Trade Fair Palace. A block of apartments near the Opera House, the Philipphof, just east of Heldenplatz and around the corner from the Burggarten, suffered multiple bomb hits and collapsed, burying more than 200 people who were using the cellars as air raid shelters. [477] The

---

[476] Weyr, *The Setting of the Pearl*, pp. 269-270.
[477] It was never rebuilt, instead having the Memorial Against War and Fascism erected on its site.

Volksoper, the Municipal Opera House, suffered only slight damage. Working class districts were also bombed.

The storied *1. Gebirgs Division*, formed from Bavarians and Austrians just days after the Anschluss in 1938, was renamed on 12 March as *1. Volks–Gebirgs Division*. The division had fought in every significant eastern campaign during the war; the invasion of Poland in 1939, France in 1940, then Yugoslavia, Crete and Russia in 1941, back to the Balkans in 1943 where it was rebuilt and stayed fighting partisans until finally joining the fight for Hungary and Austria in November of 1944.

Despite the urgency of moving forward, *II. SS–Panzerkorps* could not make headway on 12 March, although the veteran *44. Reichs–Grenadier Division Hoch und Deutschmeister* did manage to finally capture Aba. Further attacks south of Aba near the tiny hamlet of Heinrich Major were unsuccessful and triggered Soviet counterattacks, which were also repulsed, with both sides losing several armored vehicles.

I. SS–Panzerkorps was finally ready to start the battle for Simontornya, using the high ground north of the town as the anchor. The town was ancient, with Neolithic artifacts dating its settlement to at least the 4th Century B.C., and remained active throughout the Roman period. This had also been the home turf of Attila, with his people scattered throughout the area. Bisected by the Sio Canal, it had a thriving leather industry and was well-known for its 700 year old castle. House-to-house fighting lasted throughout the day until most of the town north of the canal was in German hands.

12. SS–Panzer Division Hitlerjugend also managed to get across the canal on *LAH's* right flank, forming a small bridgehead on the south side that withstood Russian counterattacks.

Even as the *SS* divisions were either stuck or plowing forward against fierce opposition, *I Kavallerie Korps* made unexpected progress. *3. Kavallerie Division* crossed the Sio Canal west of Mezökomarom and *4. Kavallerie Division* approached Balatonszabadi. These relatively minor successes could not hide the fact that *Unternehmen Frühlingserwachen* was running out of whatever small momentum it had as the German divisions were becoming worn down from losses and fatigue. A week of trudging and fighting in miserable conditions had taken its toll.

Although the Russian High Command was paying close attention to the progress of *Unternehmen Frühlingserwachen,* the buildup for their planned counter-stroke, the Vienna Offensive, continued without pause. Sixth Guards Tank Army was in place west of Budapest with more than 500 tanks. The crews of those 3,000 vehicles Fritz Hagen had been told did not exist were anxious to crush the Germans once and for all.

13 March, Tuesday

After taking Enying the day before, the extreme right flank unit of *I Kavallerie Korps* attacked along the southern shore of Lake Balaton when the Hungarian 26th Infantry Regiment, supported by 15 Hetzers of the 20th Assault Gun Battalion, battered their way through the defenses of the Russian 93rd Rifle Division at Siofok. From Siofok the Hungarians could look across the pale blue waters of Lake Balaton to the German-held northern shore and, in the distance, the Bakony Hills. Siofok had long been a popular resort. As early as 1861 the railroad linking Budapest to Nagykanizsa had been opened to the public, making the resort easily accessible to the wealthy and influential of the Austro-Hungarian Empire traveling either from Vienna or Budapest. Because of its extreme beauty the early villa owners were mostly painters and artists, and the cross-lake swimming competitions were held there.

None of that mattered in 1945. Even as the Hungarians retook the town, counterattacks lead to heavy fighting and the Hungarians were finally driven back with the loss of six Hetzers. Damage to the town was extensive; even the shipyard was destroyed.

Meanwhile, as the remainder of *SS–Brigade Ney* that was left behind prepared for combat, the five B-24 crewmen who were tried as spies were executed in Crow Forest near Sur. An eyewitness testified that the prisoners had been beaten for days, several had legs broken and the men were stripped naked before being cut down by a squad of four-six men using a machine gun. Four of the prisoners were reported to have crossed themselves before being shot, while the fifth was a Jew. They were buried in an unmarked grave.

Facing five infantry divisions and a cavalry corps, *II. SS–Panzerkorps* gave up trying to drive forward and went over to the defensive as Soviet counterattacks continued. The Soviet units had been worn down before the fighting ever started, but the overall lack of training for the new *SS* recruits, and the critical lack of heavy weapons support from the armored vehicles, had left Preiss' command unable to make significant headway. *9. SS–Panzer Division Hohenstaufen* was stalled outside of Sarosd while *2. SS–Panzer Division Das Reich* had partially surrounded Sarkerestur but could not get further; Das *Reich*'s armored elements were in the exposed salient at Heinrich Major, but their requests to be withdrawn were denied and the division continued suffering vehicle losses.

Having cleared the north bank of the Sio Canal at Simontornya and crossed to the southern bank, *I. SS–Panzerkorps* found the going increasingly tough, with the Soviets fiercely counter-attacking using both tanks and planes. By this point the German spearheads were a spent force.

14 March, Wednesday

The Hungarian 2nd Armored Division, with 16 *Panzer* Mark *IV*s, four batteries and four motorized battalions, was subordinated to *IV. SS–Panzerkorps* of *6. Armee*. The term 'division' is misleading, as this formation was really nothing more than a large *kampfgruppe*. Morale in the division wasn't terrible, the men were willing to stand and fight if there was a chance of victory, but against overwhelming force they would quickly lose motivation to risk death.

As *Unternehmen Frühlingserwachen* ran out of momentum the weather began to warm and the ground began to dry out, making armored operations in the coming days much easier. But the Germans had shot their bolt, whether Hitler was ready to admit it or not, and the improving weather could only help the Russians when it came time for their counter-offensive, a time that was rapidly drawing nigh.

But so counter-intuitive was the situation of *Heeresgruppe Süd* that fortune smiled on I *SS Panzer Division Leibstandarte Adolf Hitler* in the form of a setback. The division's pioneers had built a bridge across the Sio Canal strong enough for armor to cross, but on the 14th Soviet artillery damaged it too badly for that to happen. With the weather improving, the armor would have been used to try and force the Soviets out of Simontornya as Hitler insisted on *Unternehmen Frühlingserwachen* continuing, despite the looming Soviet counter-offensive and the impossibility of further attacks to achieve anything worth the price. Being in contact with the enemy would have made it difficult for the armor to disengage, so when the Soviet Vienna Offensive began 2 days later the *LAH* would have had a hard time reacting quickly and, if the bridge had been damaged with armor on the southern bank, there would have been no way to save the machines. By damaging it before the *LAH's* armor could cross the canal the Soviets actually did the Germans a favor. Even without armor support the *LAH's* *panzer*grenadiers kept fighting and expanded the bridgehead south of the canal.

The Soviet intention to launch a massive counter-offensive was becoming more and more obvious; what was first thought to be local reinforcements on the east bank of the Sàrviz Canal near Saregres was soon enough recognized as an ominous sign of something much more dangerous; the signs were clear that a Soviet attack was imminent. *23. Panzer Division* had cleared Saregres and tried to cross the Sàrviz Canal to help get *II. SS–Panzerkorps* moving by driving into the rear of the Russian forces holding it up, but the opposition to its attempt to cross the canal was fierce and the enemy numerous. Such strong Soviet forces opposing *Unternehmen Frühlingserwachen* combined with the best intelligence reports to make it quite clear to Wöhler, Dietrich and their subordinates that the Soviets were not content with merely defending the line of the Sàrviz Canal but intended to cross it with their own attack to cut off *I. SS–Panzerkorps*, or, failing that, to fix it in place so that it could be cut off by even stronger forces attacking to the north, from the Zámoly area. Reynolds extensively quotes the *Heeresgruppe Süd* War Diary in revealing the German commanders' awareness of the threat by 14 March:

"Today's movements leave no doubt of the enemy's intentions. Based on the results of aerial observation, motorized columns of at least 3,000 vehicles are moving out of the rear area from Budapest...to the southwest, most of them in the direction of Zámoly. His objective will be to cut the rear connections of the German forces [*6. SS–Panzerarmee* and *III. Panzerkorps*] which have advanced from the narrow passage of Szekesfehervar, by an attack in the direction of Lake Balaton."[478]

Such a huge gathering of force just north of Stuhlweissenburg at Zámoly was a mortal and obvious danger. But observing enemy troop movements and anticipating future attacks by good intelligence work was pointless, because Hitler ignored the mountain of intelligence spelling out the danger while insisting that *Unternehmen Frühlingserwachen* continue. All of the pieces seemed in place for another colossal disaster on the order of Falaise or Stalingrad.

Further south, in the area of *2. Panzerarmee*, the much weaker forces there found the going no better. The only significant armored force belonged to *16. SS–Panzergrenadier Division Reichsführer–SS*, which advanced from the area east of the oil fields at Nagykanizsa as far as Kaposvar. There it ran into strong Russian defenses, against which it didn't have the firepower, air or artillery support to penetrate. On 14 March, after reorganizing, the division turned north and attacked toward the village of Nikla, not far from Lake Balaton. The idea was to link up with *I Kavallerie Korps* driving from the north, but once again German plans did not match German capabilities, and *16 SS–Panzergrenadier Division Reichsführer–SS* lost heavily in the attempt, with nothing to show for its losses.

[478] Reynolds, *Operation Spring Awakening*, p. 69.

15 March, Thursday

Marshals Tolbukhin and Malinovsky issued their final orders for the Vienna Offensive scheduled to launch the next day. The massive Russian attack force would hit the weakest units along the fragile German front in the Pilis and Vértes Mountains. Nor should the term 'mountains' be construed to mean more than is true.

The Vértes in particular are little more than tall hills separated by broad valleys, with an average height of around 300 meters; the tallest peak is only 487 meters. There are few waterways of any kind, much less significant barriers. Thirty kilometers long from north to south, and in places no more than 10 kilometers wide, as a defensive position the Vértes offered defenders some excellent vantage points atop its 'mountains,' *if* they had guns to take advantage, but also exposed those positions to counter-battery fire and air attack.

Positioning the weakest forces in the Vértes Mountains was therefore illusory, giving the impression of it being strong defensive terrain when the reality was otherwise. Neither Hermann Balck or Otto Wöhler could do anything else, though; there wasn't any other units to position there except the Hungarians. Much like at Stalingrad, the Germans had to rely on unreliable allied units that would evaporate under Russian hammer blows.

What was coming was the last act of the Second World War in the area of Hungary and Austria. As such, it is worth pausing in the narrative to examine German strength on the eve of destruction.

The Ides of March is the last day for which reliable strength figures are available for the German armored units; from this point forward accurate record

537

keeping became more and more difficult as units were scattered, shattered and destroyed, were rapidly assigned and re-assigned to various headquarters and general chaos was the order of the day. On this last day before the Russians launched the Vienna Offensive the southern front was reasonably stable, repair and supply depots behind the front could function in an orderly manner and timetables for deliveries could at least be guessed at with some degree of accuracy. There was time to write and deliver the various reports without which an army group cannot function properly, including the strength of the units under *Heeresgruppe Süd's* command. The 15th of March, therefore, was the last day that Otto Wöhler had any sort of clear picture concerning the state of his command, or upon which he could exert any influence over events. After 15 March he could not act, he could only react, and usually after his orders were rendered moot by the course of events.

Source generally agree that on the final day before the Red Army launched the Vienna Operation, the German tank inventory totals for the entire *Wehrmacht* were: 793 *Mark IVs*, 434 *Jagdpanzer IV's* and 954 *Mark V Panthers*. This total does not include heavy *panzers* or heavy *Jagdpanzers*, such as the both *Tiger Is* and *Tiger IIs*, and the *Jagdpanther* and *Jagdtiger*, or *Sturmgeschütz* assault guns. On the Eastern Front by itself the totals were 603 *Mark IVs*, 357 *Jagdpanzer IV/70s* and 776 *Mark V Panthers*, but again, this is for the entire front and not just *Heeresgruppe Süd*. These would also seem to be total inventory on hand, including units in short or long-term repair. The vast majority of Germany's fast shrinking armored force was in the east and most of the best armored units were in *Heeresgruppe Süd*.

Overall, and with allowance for differences between sources, *Heeresgruppe Süd* had the following totals for all armored units on the eve of battle: 209 total *Mark IVs*, with only 103 operational; 423 *Mark V*

Panthers, but a mere 155 combat ready;[479] 102 *Tiger IIs*, 42 operational; 161 *Sturmgeschütz/40s*, with 96 in working order; 112 *Jagdpanzer IV/70s*, but with only 33 ready to fight; and, finally, a mere 42 *Flakpanzer IVs*, the excellent *'Wirbelwind'* air-defense vehicle that mounted a four-barreled 20 mm battery housed in a revolving turret, with only 17 of these vital *panzers* ready in the entire army group.

Wirbelwind

Flakpanzer IV (SdKfz. 161/4)

Wirbelwind

Mounting four 20mm *Flak 38* anti-aircraft cannon, the *Wirbelwind* and its rarely seen up-gunned cousin, the *Ostwind* with a single 37mm gun, were the culmination of a long series of mobile AA vehicles used by the Germans throughout the war. Heinz Guderian loved the *Wirbelwind*. Built on a *Panzer Mark IV* chassis, the 20mm guns proved extremely effective against aircraft and infantry. No more than 105 were built.

Thus, *Heeresgruppe Süd*'s combined AFV strength of all types was 446 combat-ready units to hold back the imminent Russian armored tsunami, with the huge number of 603 units under either short

---

[479] Although the *Mark V Panther* had undergone numerous revisions since first introduced in the summer of 1943, the model remained essentially fragile in terms of its mechanical reliability; a high percentage would require repair even after short commitments to battle.

or long-term repair.[480] The very high percentage of *Heeresgruppe Süd's* armored force that was undergoing repair would shortly lead to huge and rapid losses, since the speed of the Russian advance would mean that vehicles awaiting repair in German depots that were unable to be driven away from danger, or loaded onto freight cars, would have to be destroyed to keep them from being captured, repaired, and turned back on their former owners.

These figures meant that *Heeresgruppe Süd* had more than 40 percent of the total number of *Mark V Panthers* in the entire German inventory[481] and a massive 55 percent of those on the Eastern Front; for *Mark IVs* the percentages were much lower, representing 26 percent of the German total and 35 percent of those in the east, and finally in *Jagdpanzer IV/70s* the army group had 26 percent of the existing inventory and 31 percent of those units on the eastern front. Since there were three main Army Groups fighting in the east, *Süd, Mitte* and *Vistula,* it might be expected that each would have one-third of the inventory for a given weapon's system, and the figures for *Mark IVs* and *Jagdpanzer IV/70s* are very close to this percentage. But Otto Wöhler's command had a huge preponderance of the available *Mark V Panthers,* not just on the Eastern Front but for the entire *Wehrmacht.* This probably occurred because *6. SS– Panzerarmee* had priority of new vehicles after the Ardennes Offensive, and the subsequent *Unternehmen Frühlingserwachen* was one in which German armor played a much smaller role than envisaged in the

---

[480] The total number of AFVs in *Heeresgruppe Süd's* inventory was 1,049.

[481] It has often been stated that Waffen SS panzer divisions had priority for the best weapons, including tanks, but in the distribution of Panthers among the panzer divisions of *Heeresgruppe Süd* this is revealed as a fallacy. 4 of the top 5 panzer divisions with the highest total of Panthers on hand on March 15th are Army divisions, not Waffen-SS. Nor is this due to lack of recent combat, since all 4 Army divisions, 1st, 3rd, 6th and 23. *Panzer Division,* all had seen extensive fighting.

planning due to the weather. Therefore, losses were lower than expected as well.

For *6. SS–Panzerarmee* the numbers broke down this way;[482] *I. SS–Panzerkorps'* *1. SS–Panzer Division Leibstandarte Adolf Hitler* had 29 *Mark IVs* with 14 operational, 32 *Mark V Panthers* with 18 operational, 32 *Mark VI Tiger IIs* from the attached *Schwere–Panzer Abteilung501* with eight operational, seven *Sturmgeschütz* with only three operational, 20 *Jagdpanzer IV/70s* with a paltry two operational, and six *Flakpanzer IV Wirbelwinds*, with three operational, for a total *panzer* strength of all types of 126, of which only 48 were operational. *12. SS–Panzer Division Hitlerjugend* fielded 23 *Mark IVs* with 10 in running order, 24 *Mark V Panthers* with nine operational, 30 *Jagdpanzer IV/70s* with 10 operational and 5 *Flakpanzer IV Wirbelwinds* with three operational, giving *Hitlerjugend* a tank strength on paper of 82 AFVs, but only 32 combat ready. *I. SS–Panzerkorps*, therefore, had 208 total armored vehicles but only 80 *panzers* of all types ready to fight.

As one example of the difficulty in settling on final tank inventory totals for late-war German units, the below come from various sources and represent the best estimates for accuracy. Regarding *II. SS–Panzerkorps*, the totals for both *9. SS–Panzer Division Hohenstaufen* and *2. SS–Panzer Division Das Reich* as follows: Hohenstaufen had 35 *Mark V Panthers*, 20, 32 *Jagdpanzers* and 25 *Sturmgeschütze*, and 220 other self-propelled weapons and armored cars. One source has a similar total for Das *Reich*, but list 18 Jag*dpanzer* IV/70s instead of 28. This total seems

---

[482] Sources differ on exact totals of vehicles that were on hand and operational; sometimes the differences are not small. For purposes of this illustration, Thomas Jentz's Panzer Truppen 2 is used, quoting the chart on page 247, because the best sources agree with Jentz.

almost astronomical, until it is factored in that 42 percent of these vehicles were under repair, either short or long-term. What mattered to the armored units on a day-to-day basis was how many vehicles could fight that day, not how many were on hand in total. Indeed, vehicles under repair could even become a liability if prime movers or other transport were not immediately available in a fluid tactical situation, such as the one that was about to engulf *Heeresgruppe Süd*. AFVs that could not be evacuated for lack of fuel or transport could only be destroyed, depriving the Germans not only of the vehicle itself once it was repaired, but also of whatever parts could be scavenged if the vehicle itself were not repairable. For additional consideration, it is once again apparent that the high number of armored vehicles under repair reflected the critical lack of spare parts plaguing the Wehrmacht in the final months of the war, not only from production problems but also transport difficulties and the rapid loss of territories where parts were either made or stored. This illustrates once again why recovery of damaged vehicles was so crucial for the Germans; even destroyed vehicles could be cannibalized for parts.

Sources disagree more on the totals for *II. SS–Panzerkorps*. Jentz[483] puts *9. SS–Panzer Division Hohenstaufen*'s totals at 20 *Mark IVs* with 11 operational, 35 *Mark V Panthers* with 12 ready for combat, 11 *Sturmgeschütz 40/IVs* operational out of 25, 22 *Jagdpanzer IV/70s* with 10 ready and three out of five *Flakpanzer IV Wirbelwinds* in commission, for a total of 47 AFVs of all types in fighting condition, barely an average strength battalion. For *2. SS–Panzer Division Das Reich* he has 22 *Mark IVs* on hand with 14 in fighting condition, 27 *Mark V Panthers* with 17 ready, 26 *Sturmgeschütz 40/IVs* but only nine ready for battle, 18 *Jagdpanzer IV/70s* with seven operational

---

[483] Again, Jentz's numbers are those accepted here; others are given for comparison of the variations in totals among the various sources.

and eight *Flakpanzer IVs*, of which four were operational, totaling 51 AFVs.

The Corps' third armored division, *23. Panzer*, was in poor condition, even for an Army *panzer* division in 1945, and that had seen almost continuous action in the preceding months. The division had 16 *Mark IVs* with six operational, 33 *Mark V Panthers* with only seven ready for combat, 10 *Sturmgeschütz 40/IVs* but with seven operational, eight *Jagdpanzer IV/70s* with none of them fit to fight and one *Flakpanzer IV Wirbelwind* that was not in working condition. This totaled 20 *panzers* of all types combat-ready; less than two companies.

The fourth division attached to *II. SS–Panzerkorps, 44. Reichs–Grenadier Division Hoch und Deutschmeister*, lists no armored vehicles attached. *II. SS–Panzerkorps*, therefore, had a total combat-ready *panzer* force of 118 units of all types, and *6. SS–Panzerarmee* had 198.

It should be noted that the ubiquitous light tank destroyer, the *Jagdpanzer 38 Hetzer*, is not individually listed. Based on the chassis of the very successful Czech *Panzer 38(t)*, the *Hetzer* was produced in huge quantities during the last 13 months of the war. Although having minimal armor protection that would not hold up to Russian tank or antitank guns, it mounted the 75mm *Pak 39 (L/48)* gun. Penetration value were good for this gun against most tanks in 2nd and 3rd Ukrainian Fronts, not only the T-34/85 but also the Lend-Lease Allied tanks such as the Sherman and Valentine. When facing the JS-1 or JS-2, however, a *Hetzer* could only threaten the big Russian tanks from close distance, and from the side of back.

Infantry Tank Mark III Valentine

The Red Army loved the Valentine tank, although the British considered it something of a failed design. Regardless, the tank was small, fast, and most remarkable for a British design… reliable. Vastly under-gunned with only a 2-Pounder for a main battery, the equivalent of a 40mm gun, on the steppes of Russian the Valentine found its niche as a reconnaissance and exploitation vehicle. More than 8,600 units were built during the war, some 3,782 were sent to the Russians, and it saw extensive service in Hungary and Austria. Of note, the British also sent more than 1,000 Matilda IIAs.

Measured from authorized strength these figures show just how depleted the German divisions were by this point in the war. By itself the Leibstandarte should have had more tanks than all of *6. SS–Panzerarmee* did, but keeping in mind how low the army's tank inventory was before *Unternehmen Frühlingserwachen,* the figures reveal the nature of the fighting in the first 10 days of the German offensive, namely, that *Hohenstaufen* actually had more working *panzers* than it had when the attack began, and only a handful fewer *Jagdpanzers* and *Sturmgeschütze. Das Reich* had suffered higher casualties in comparison to her sister division, but still very few considering how many attacks the division had launched against dug-in defenses. Reynolds states that *Das Reich* had lost seven *Panthers*, two *Mark IVs*, one and 3 *Sturmgeschütze*, as well as 38 other assorted vehicles, self-propelled artillery and armored cars, and those mostly in the salient at Heinrich Major. All of these figures indicate just how little the heavy units of *II. SS–Panzerkorps* were able to factor into the battle up to 15 March, since their light attrition level is a direct result of the foul weather preventing their useful employment in battle.

The armored formations of *6. Armee* were in no better condition. *3. SS–Panzer Division Totenkopf* had 17 *Mark IVs* and 16 of them combat ready; 17 *Mark 5 Panthers* with eight operational, nine *Mark VI Tiger IIs* with seven operational, and 17 *Sturmgeschütz 40/IVs* with 13 operational, giving an anemic AFV total of 44 vehicles; this may have been nearly full strength for a Type 1945 *Panzer* Division, but for an *SS–Panzer* division it was very low. But *5. SS–Panzer Division Wiking* had only four *Mark IVs* with three ready to fight, 18 *Mark V Panthers* with 12 in running order, and 5 Stug 40/IVs with four operational, for a grand total of 19 combat-ready *panzers*. Thus, *IV. SS–Panzerkorps* had an armored strength of one under-strength battalion, 63 AFVs of all types; the corps had never recovered from the bitter fighting in January and February, and it never would.

III. Panzerkorps' three divisions, *1. Panzer Division*, *3. Panzer Division* and *6. Panzer Division* were all the worse for wear after more than two months of constant combat. *1. Panzer Division* fielded five *Mark IVs* with two operational, the enormous total of 59 *Mark V Panthers* of which a mere 10 were combat ready, and two *Sturmgeschütz 40/IVs*, one ready for combat, giving the division 18 AFVs in combat condition. *3. Panzer Division* was only slightly better, with 14 *Mark IVs* and four operational, 39 *Mark V Panthers* with 13 fit to fight, seven *Sturmgeschütz 40/IVs* but only two operational and 11 *Jagdpanzer IV/70s*, with two in operation, for a total of 21 vehicles in combat condition. Finally, *6. Panzer Division* had 22 *Mark IVs* with four operational, 68 *Mark V Panthers* (!) with 19 ready and five *Flakpanzer IVs* with three operational, for a total of 26 AFVs. *III. Panzerkorps* therefore had 65 combat-ready *panzers* of all types.

8. Armee had still-forming units under its command, as mentioned earlier the two divisions of *Panzerkorps Felldherrnhalle. Panzer Division Felldherrnhalle 1* was virtually at full strength in AFVs for a Type 1945 *Panzer* Division,[484] with 18 *Mark IVs* on hand and 16 combat ready, 19 *Mark V Panthers* total with 18 operational and three *Jagdpanzer IV/70s* and two operational, for a total of 40 vehicles and 36 ready to fight. About half a battalion in earlier numbers, but formidable by 1945 standards. *Panzer Division Felldherrnhalle 2* (aka, *13. Panzer Division*), however, was nothing more than a glorified *kampfgruppe*. The 'division' had 18 *Mark IVs*, none of which were operational, five *Mark V Panthers*, all of which were operational, and one *Flakpanzer IV*, which was ready for combat. Thus, Panzer Division Felldherrnhalle 2 nominally had 24 AFVs on its rolls, but as of mid-March only six were fit to fight; in other words, one *Panther* platoon with AA protection. All of its other components were comparably weak too.

However, *Panzerkorps Felldherrnhalle* had two Heavy *Panzer* Battalions attached to it, *Schwere–Panzer Abteilung 509* and *Schwere–Panzer Abteilung Felldherrnhalle* as well as the independent *I./Panzer Regiment 24. Schwere–Panzer Abteilung 509* had seen heavy combat during January and February during *Konrad III*, losing 40 of its 45 Mark VI King Tigers, but only 10 were total losses. Thus, on 15 March it had 8 *Mark V Panthers* on hand but only two operational,[485] and 35 King Tigers, only three of which were fit for

---

[484] This last re-organization of the *Panzer* branch was designed to take advantage of existing machines, with little thought given to replenishment. A Type 1945 *Panzer* Division was authorized to have 2 companies of 10 *panzers* each of both *Mark IVs* and *Mark V Panthers*, a total of 40 actual tanks; at this point in its history *Panzer Division Felldherrnhalle* 1 had 36 operational and 40 on hand.

[485] These vehicles are mentioned in several sources, but a *Schwere–Panzer Abteilung* did not have a *Mark V Panther* component, so where they came from is unknown.

combat. Given time, however, the battalion could once again be formidable. *Schwere–Panzer Abteilung Felldherrnhalle* was in better shape, fielding seven *Mark V Panthers* with two operational and 26 *Mark IV Tiger IIs*, with 19 combat ready.

It is instructive to look at those two *Schwere–Panzer Abteilungs* and their respective numbers of operational AFVs. Given that the *Felldherrnhalle* units had priority for replacements over regular *Heer* units may be illustrated so many of its machines were operational, 19 out of 26, when compared to *Schwere–Panzer Abteilung 509* with only three of 35 combat ready. Spare parts were in short supply, but the higher priority for the *Felldherrnhalle* might explain the vast difference in *Tiger IIs* fit for service.

Lastly, the *I./Panzer Regiment 24* had 32 Panthers but only three operational, once again bringing up the availability of spare parts. Also forming under *8. Armee* control, *232. Panzer Division* was a *panzer* division in name only, having a strength of one Mark IV and one *Sturmgeschütz 40/IVs*, both of which were combat ready; the 'division' had a *panzer* inventory equivalent to half a platoon; having been formed from *Panzer* Division *'Tatra'*, it actually had a respectable combat history, but most of the men who fought in the Slovak uprising the previous year were long gone. It's hard to imagine why it remained on the rolls.

Lastly, *2. Panzerarmee* had one significant mechanized force for its contribution to *Unternehmen Frühlingserwachen*, namely *16. SS–Panzergrenadier Division Reichsführer—SS* had a very strong *Panzerjäger Abteilung* of 62 vehicles on hand and 47 combat ready.[486] This gave *6. SS–Panzerarmee* and its associated assault elements an operational total vehicles of 103 *Mark IVs*, 155 *Mark V Panthers*, 42 *Mark IV Tiger IIs*,[487] 96 *Sturmgeschütz 40/IVs*, 33

---

[486] It is unknown if this total is only *Sturmgeschütz 40/IVs* or includes *Hetzers.*

[487] A few *Tiger Is* might be in this total.

Jagdpanzer IV/70s and 17 *Flakpanzer IVs*, for a sum of 446 AFVs. What *Heeresgruppe Süd* did not have was sufficient fuel for these vehicles to maneuver to best effect.

With the Soviet Vienna Offensive looming, the Hungarian Order of Battle in *Heeresgruppe Süd* was as follows:

Records are problematic, but the Hungarian Order of Battle stood roughly as follows: II Corps, situated between Lakes Balaton and Velence, had the 20th and 25th Infantry Divisions and the Svent Laszlo Parachute Division, by far the best Hungarian unit. In the Vértes Mountains was the Hussar Division, likely with part of the 25th Infantry Division. North of that, in the Gran bridgehead south of the Danube, 3rd Army had the 2nd Armored Division and the 23rd Reserve Division, although some sources have the Hungarian 2nd Armored Division attached to *IV. SS–Panzerkorps* further south. Even further north in Slovakia, north of the Danube, the Hungarian 1st Army had 16th and 24th Infantry Divisions, 3rd Replacement Division, 1st Mountain Brigade, as well as two divisions still forming, the 27th Infantry and the 9th Border Guard Division. On the surface these sounds like imposing formations, especially 2nd Armored Division. In reality its numbers were closer to a brigade and it was desperately short of vehicles, especially armored vehicles, and none of the Hungarian units was anywhere close to authorized strength, being particularly deficient in heavy weapons of all types. Their worst defect was their morale.

Nor does this order of battle does not include either of the two *SS* divisions still undergoing training, which technically were under Hungarian Army control. *SS–Brigade Ney* had already been disowned.

Sometime in mid-March, the combat ready pieces of *37. SS–Freiwilligen–Kavallerie Division Lützow* not already committed to combat were ordered to Znaim (Znojmo in Czech), north-northwest of Vienna near the Czech border, to prepare for battle. A small city on the banks of the picturesque Thaya River, it was one of those areas still undisturbed by total war. Founded in 1226, filled with ancient ruins and historical sites at every glance, it must have given a false sense of peace to the men getting ready to fight. Included in the elements transferred to Znaim were *SS–Reiter Regiment 92, SS–Artillerie Abteilung 37* and the Divisional Headquarters Staff. However, some part of *SS–Artillerie Abteilung 37* seems to have gone into action in the Gran Bridgehead area in early March, along with the division's other cavalry regiment. Under the command of *SS–Obersturmbannführer* Toni Ameiser, it was known as *SS-Kampfgruppe (SS-KG) Ameiser,* and fought alongside the *96. Infanterie Division* as part of *8. Armee,* in the defensive battles along the Gran River, and the subsequent withdrawals.[488] Late in the month the *kampfgruppe* would be reunited with its parent division.

Like newly forming units all over the *Reich,* it was no longer possible to allow units the full time necessary to complete their formation. As soon as a sizable portion of this or that unit became operational, or even close to operational, it was committed to battle. Nor were most of these units fully armed, with *Lützow* being no exception. Too much industry had been lost, too little transport was available. With motor transport

---

[488] This would make sense, as it puts both of the 37th SS regiments in the same basic area north of the Danube. However, the timeline does not make sense. If this were in support of Spring Awakening then the early March timeline works. However, if it=s after the start of the Soviet Vienna Offensive, March 16, then this would make much more sense, especially taking into account the transfer of the rest of the division to Znaim. Once again the lack of records and conflicting evidence make it virtually impossible to pin down an exact narrative.

in short supply, and fuel even more precious, horses and even oxen had to be used to haul everything from supplies to artillery. Soon enough the *SS–Reiter Regiment 92* would form the basis for *Kampfgruppe Keitel*.

Also around the middle of March, the newly expanded *SS-Brigade Ney* was given its official title of *1. Ungarishe–Hussars Brigade der SS*, for which its founder, Karoly Ney, was inordinately proud.[489] A reconnaissance detachment had been added by then, and a 4th battalion as well, although a second regiment was not formed. This fourth battalion was named 'Imredy' in honor of the President of the Eastern Front Comradeship Organization, Dr. Bela vitez Imredy de Omoravicza.

In Berlin, with all of the Ukraine back in Soviet hands, the Germans had run out of reasons not to allow a Ukrainian nationalist movement to exist with their blessing, since it was highly unlikely they would ever again control the Ukraine. Therefore, they announced that Pavlo Shandruk had been appointed to head the Ukrainian National Committee and to be commander of the Ukrainian National Army. Such an army did not yet exist, but was to be made up of Ukrainians currently serving in the German military and any other formations or personnel that could be scraped together. The main unit around which this

---

[489] Could this be the mysterious 'Hussars' that Fritz Hagen is told are holding the line when he expresses worry about the coming Soviet offensive? It seems unlikely, Ney's unit was not in the line at the time, but was still reforming in a rear area. Also, the timeline does not quite match up to that put forward by Toland.

army would be built was the *14. Waffen–Grenadier Division der SS (Galizien).*

As a veteran of the Czarist Imperial Army and the cauldron of the First World War, Shandruk had fought for Ukrainian independence as far back as the postwar period when the Ukrainians had temporarily driven the Reds from Kharkov. When Hitler finally gave permission for Shandruk to lead a Ukrainian Army, he immediately began amalgamating all Ukrainian forces then under German command, including the *Schutzmannschaft Bataillon der Sicherheitspolizei 31* commanded by *Oberst* Pytor Dyachenko; the *Reserve–Infanterie Regiment 281* Regiment, stationed in Denmark; two infantry regiments pulling garrison duty in Holland and Belgium; three battalions of military police and 400 men in the Brigade for Special Tasks commanded by T. Bulba-Borovets.[490] It all sounded quite grand.

Hitler kept dithering about allowing all of this to take place, not wanting the Ukrainians to ever think he would grant them independence. Not that it mattered, of course, but Hitler continued to pretend that it did. None of the plans for a Ukrainian National Army would actually happen until Berlin was surrounded.

Even then, however, nothing changed. The *14. Waffen-Grenadier Division der SS (Galizien 1)* remained under *Waffen–SS* command, the officers and noncoms were all the same, the uniforms were the same, even the shoulder patch was the same; the Halychyna Lion, despite Shandruk's order to replace it with a yellow trident on a blue background. There was, however, a new oath to be taken. The men swore to God, the Ukrainian National Army and the Ukrainian Homeland under the new blue and yellow standard. They would fight and die to free their homeland. The first unit to

---

[490] Borovets' history with the Germans deserves a book all to itself. His 'brigade' was part of the *SS* after Borovets himself was released from Sachsenhausen Concentration Camp. Having no other choice, he agreed to form a partisan unit to be dropped behind Russian lines, a plan which never came to fruition.

take the new oath was a 1,900 man regiment assigned to defend Berlin, a mission which had nothing to do with fighting and dying to free the Ukraine.

Meanwhile, after being virtually destroyed at Brody in the summer of 1944, the re-constituted *14. Waffen-Grenadier Division der SS (Galizien 1)* now contained men from a number of formations noted for their brutality, including the head-strong *Nachtigall* Battalion (aka, *Battalion Ukrainische Gruppe Nachtigall*) that had been disbanded for refusing to take a loyalty oath to Hitler, the Roland Battalion, (aka, *Battalion Ukrainische Gruppe Roland*) that had marched into the Soviet Union during *Unternehmen Barbarossa*, as well as the two police battalions, a punishment detachment, and, most ominous of all, parts of the most odious *SS* unit of them all, the *SS–Sturmbrigade Dirlewanger*.[491] The division's personnel roll was huge; on paper it was a formidable fighting force.

Hanging over 3rd Hungarian, *6. Armee* and *6. SS–Panzerarmee*'s heads like the aforementioned Sword of Damocles, Marshal Tolbukhin's long-awaited Vienna Offensive would be carried out by a massive force that was designed to pulverize and engulf whatever defenses the Germans could throw in their way. Nor was the initial target for the offensive particularly distant or difficult: Veszprem and its all-important railhead was only 22 miles from the area near the western tip of the Soviet bulge at Bodajk, and the northeastern tip of Lake Balaton was even closer, about 20 miles. And while there were no major highways that ran straight to their objective, the best roads went through Stuhlweissenburg before turning west, Tolbukhin's mobile forces would only have to move cross-country to Varpalota before picking up the main road leading to

---

[491] Dirlewanger's infamous unit was upgraded to division status, but some of its members instead were routed to join the Ukrainians.

Veszprem, an overland distance of less than 10 miles. From Veszprem to Balatonfuzfo at the tip of the lake was about 7 miles and commanders on both sides knew what would happen if the Red Army got there quickly and in strength: any German units to the east and south would be cut off, and that would probably be all of both 6th and 6th *SS Panzer* Armies. Such a catastrophe would leave Austria completely defenseless; there would be nothing to stop the Red Army from pouring into the Alps. The aim of the offensive was nothing less than the complete destruction of *Heeresgruppe Süd.*

    II. SS–Panzerkorps spent 15 March fighting back Soviet counterattacks. *I. SS–Panzerkorps* was faced with a serious dilemma on 15 March, one that should have been foreseen before *Unternehmen Frühlingserwachen* was ever launched. The ground lying before both *1. SS–Panzer Division Leibstandarte Adolf Hitler* and *12. SS–Panzer Division Hitlerjugend* was very broken and hilly, with dense woods and multiple waterways; poor ground for tank warfare, even in dry weather. Flat farmlands were behind them. Even if the *LAH* could seize all of Simontornya and get its armor across the Sio Canal, opportunities for exploitation were poor because of the terrain. Of greater concern was its open left flank. Although *23. Panzer Division* was deployed in the area around Saregres, there was still a huge gap along the Sàrviz Canal up to *II. SS–Panzerkorps*, and Soviet forces were known to be gathering along the canal's eastern bank. Disaster loomed.

    It is often remarked that Sepp Dietrich was a good division commander, a mediocre corps commander, and a poor army commander. Whether this is a fair evaluation or not, there is the possibility that on 15 March, 1945, he personally saved his army from total destruction because of his understanding of the mind of Adolf Hitler.

Dietrich and Hitler had a close bond, and Dietrich recognized the crisis of his army's situation. He had seen this moment coming and proposed a rational solution: withdraw to a more defensible line farther north. In other words, give up the hard-won ground captured in the previous 10 days because it was indefensible and should never have been seized in the first place. Otto Wöhler rejected this idea for the likely reason that he knew Hitler would never agree. What happened next is up for debate.

Around 1500 hours, Wöhler sent his estimation of the situation to Berlin and proposed a change in operations that Hitler might approve. Instead of giving up the ground held by *I. SS–Panzerkorps*, he suggested using *I Kavallerie Korps* to go on the defensive and take over the sector held by *I. SS–Panzerkorps* while also defending the ground where it stood. *23. Panzer Division* would also stay where it was around Saregres. Thus freed from its positions on the Sio Canal, *I. SS–Panzerkorps* would move north to the area west of Sarozd behind *II. SS–Panzerkorps* and *III. Panzerkorps* to help get their stalled attack moving east toward the Danube.

This is precisely the type of thinking which would appeal to Hitler. What is unclear is whether Dietrich proposed this to Wöhler, who passed it on as his own idea. Either way Hitler approved the scheme and the generous observer might credit Otto Wöhler for a brilliant slight-of-hand. According to Reynolds, "although this revised concept was considered impractical by most of the field commanders involved, the necessary orders were issued at 11 PM, and during the night the first units of *I. SS–Panzerkorps* were withdrawn from the battle area."[492] Mere hours before the Russians launched the Vienna Offensive, Dietrich's

---

[492] Reynolds, *Final Entries*, p. 69.

units were moving in the right direction to intercept them. The question now was whether would be in time.

The field commanders did not like the idea but they might not have given their commanders enough credit. Both Sepp Dietrich and Otto Wöhler had dealt with Hitler for years and would have had a good idea what the *Führer* would, and would not, approve. A withdrawal for defensive purposes was unlikely to be approved in accordance with Hitler's well-known penchant for standing fast, regardless of circumstances. But a withdrawal to continue attacking elsewhere might earn Hitler's favor if he believed the move was offensive in spirit, not defensive. In other words, did whoever thought of the idea, Dietrich or Wöhler, truly believe that an attack to the east by *I. SS–Panzerkorps* might succeed in re-starting *Unternehmen Frühlingserwachen,* or did one (or both) trick Hitler into allowing the *SS* divisions to pull back before it was too late?

Unfortunately, as much as one might wish to credit Wöhler for brilliantly tricking his *Führer* into saving his namesake formations, the evidence suggests otherwise. Late in the evening of the next day, after the Soviets had spent the day crushing his defenses north of Stuhlweissenburg, Wöhler seems to have thought his three-corps attack to the east might still work. It was only Guderian's recommendation early on 17 March to have *I. SS–Panzerkorps* attack north into Tolbukhin's flank, rather than east, that *Unternehmen Frühlingserwachen* finally sputtered out. Regardless of whether Wöhler (or Dietrich) tricked Hitler or not, pulling *I. SS–Panzerkorps* north was the salient point; the further north the Corps was, the faster it could respond to the Soviet counter-offensive that would come the next morning. Had Wöhler not made this proposal, or had it not been approved, there is a high probability that the Vienna Offensive would have trapped most of *6. SS–Panzerarmee* as well as *III. Panzerkorps.* Had that happened there were no other German forces available to seal what would have been a gaping hole in the front, allowing Stalin's plan to drive all the way to Munich to come to fruition, with untold consequences. In that respect, then, by that one request and in that single moment in time, Otto Wöhler's proposal had enormous impact on the post-war world. The best time for the Russians to launch their offensive was before *I. SS–Panzerkorps* began moving north, i.e. 15 March, not 16 March. That 24 hour delay changed everything.

As the moment approached for the launch of the Vienna Offensive the Russians had to consider the best use of their remaining manpower. If most German formations were badly under-strength from almost four years of the meat-grinder of the Eastern Front, the same was true of the Russians, at least in terms of manpower; between Soviet industry and the massive infusion of Lend Lease equipment, Red Army formations tended to be much closer to authorized strength in vehicles and guns, and thanks for massive numbers of American built trucks they were almost fully mobile, although their tank formations used a wide variety of models from the USSR, USA and even England. Manpower was another story. During 1944 instructions were issued to all Red Army front commands on how to organize 'short' infantry divisions, that is, divisions that were far below authorized manpower; the numbers of the supporting arms, such as artillery, were not reduced, although their crew complements often were.[493] Instead, the infantry units were reduced in size from platoon to regimental level to compensate for the dwindling manpower pool. By necessity this also reduced the volume of small-arms fire that such an infantry unit

---

[493] The Wehrmacht had done the same thing. For example, the organization of the Volksgrenadier divisions, or the 1945 Panzer Division.

could produce on the battlefield. This problem meant that fewer men had to put out the same firepower as the larger units of previous years had, so a solution had to be found for how to do this. Similar to the Germans, therefore, the Russians tried to maintain firepower standards among depleted formations by keeping mortars, machine guns and sub-machine guns manned while discarding rifles. This lessened long-range firepower on open ground at long ranges but increased it for urban combat, or combat in restricted areas, such as forests. The Germans tried the same approach by introducing the *Sturmgewehr 44* automatic rifle[494] but were never able to make enough of this revolutionary weapon to equip all of their units; indeed, by the time of this narrative equipping a given unit with any sort of weapon was difficult, much less with the latest technology.

Russian formations had always been smaller than their counterparts in the western armies, Germany's included. A Russian tank corps, for example, was roughly equivalent to a German *Panzer* Division.[495] A 1941 Russian rifle division had a nominal strength of about 11,800 men, although most never reached that strength, while their German counterpart numbered some 16,500. But in 1945 it was unusual for a Russian Rifle Division to top 8,000 men total, while many were below 2,000. This was a conscious decision made at the highest levels, not to rebuild shattered divisions to full strength, but the decision was necessary because of severe Russian casualties over the previous 4 years; the seemingly endless pool of manpower was not endless after all.

As an example of this trend, a strength return for 10 March shows how badly the 4th Guards Army of 3rd Ukrainian Front was depleted from the years of fighting, although in comparison to Russian divisions elsewhere along the front those of 4th Guards Army

---

[494] The design upon which the famous AK-47 was based.
[495] Meaning the authorized strength of such a formation, not its actual strength in 1945.

were quite strong. The 4th Guards Army had three Guards Rifle Corps (the 20th, 21st and 31st); 2 Guards Parachute Divisions (5th and 7th); seven Guards Rifle Divisions (4th, 34th, 40th, 41st, 62nd, 69th and 80th) and the 9th Artillery Division, which contained seven artillery brigades, one artillery regiment, one anti-tank artillery regiment, one mortar regiment, one anti-aircraft regiment and one anti-aircraft battalion,[496] a sizeable formation with an authorized strength that should have exceeded 100,000 men. In fact, however, the army's seven rifle divisions had total strength of between 5246 on the low end and 5833 on the high, with the two parachute divisions numbering 5253 and 5384 men. Thus, those nine divisions fielded just under 50,000 men total.

For the army as a whole the total manpower was 64,927, a not overly impressive number, but the army possessed massive firepower to back them up. 4th Guards Rifle Army had 163 45 mm anti-tank guns, 342 76 mm artillery pieces, as well as 83 122 mm guns, 141 152 mm ones and 8 of the enormous 203 mm guns, not to mention 605 mortars of either 82 mm or 120 mm size. The storm of steel such an arsenal could produce was devastating, as would shortly be felt by *IV. SS–Panzerkorps* when the Russians launched the Vienna Offensive and 4th Guards Army took direct aim at *3. SS–Panzer Division Totenkopf* and *5. SS Panzer Division Wiking* in the vicinity of Stuhlweissenburg.[497] Nor did the Russians suffer from the crippling ammunition shortages that hampered German artillery; they could and did fire off enormous quantities of

[496] A further example of how Soviet strengths could vary at this stage of the war is the comparison of the 257th Anti-Aircraft Artillery Regiment and the 22 Anti-Aircraft Artillery Battalion. A regiment is typically at least double the size of a battalion, yet in this case the 257th Anti-Artillery Regiment had 370 men and 23 37 mm anti-aircraft guns, while the 22nd Anti-Aircraft Artillery Battalion had 1691 men, 14 small 4.5 mm anti-tank rifles and only 12 37 mm guns.

[497] Domański, Jacek & Ledwoch, Janusz, *Wien 1945* (Warsaw: Militaria, 2006), p. 24.

ordnance, whereas German batteries were often rationed to only a few rounds per day.

Perhaps the most important factor of the coming battle was the realization by the Russians in the front lines that the end of the war lay directly ahead, within sight now, along with the loot that came with being the victor. When moving through their homeland the Russian soldier was liberating his homeland, therefore plunder and rape were crimes punishable by death. Hungary was enemy territory, where to the victor went the spoils, but Hungary was a poor country compared to that of the Germans, and Austria was their next objective...

16 March, Friday

Thunder in the east broke the pre-dawn quiet as the day long feared by Otto Wohler and Sepp Dietrich had finally arrived: the great Soviet Vienna Offensive had begun. 3rd Ukrainian Front deployed some 728 tanks and self-propelled guns, 320 more than it had 11 days earlier when the Germans launched *Unternehmen Frühlingserwachen*. According to Domanski and Ledwoch, part of the Russian AFV inventory broke down as follows: 99 T-34s, with 18th Armored Corps having 48 and 23rd Armored Corps another 34; 60 American M4A2 Shermans[498] in 1st Guards Armored Corps; 119 SU-76Ms, 142 SU-100s, 10 ISU-122s and 14 ISU-152s. There were even 12 captured German *Hummels* and *Wespes* in 1st Guards Heavy Self-Propelled Artillery Regiment and a smattering of other German vehicles, including at least one *Mark V Panther*.[499] There were also lend-lease British Valentine tanks in 5th Guards Cavalry Corps; the British considered the Valentine a failure, but the Russians liked it enough to ask the British to continue manufacturing them for Lend Lease.

Tolbukhin's 2nd Ukrainian and Malinovsky's 3rd Ukrainian Front were disposed from north to south as follows: north of the Danube and east of the Gran River was 7th Guards Army, still recovering from being driven back east over the river during *Unternehmen Südwind* and slated to remain inactive during the first stages of the Vienna Offensive.

---

[498] The M4A2 featured an upgraded main battery, the long-barreled 76 mm gun that had drastically improved penetrating power over the original short-barreled, lower velocity 75 mm gun. American and British crews disliked the Sherman for its relatively thin armor and propensity to catch on fire when hit; thus its nickname of 'the Ronson', after the famous American cigarette lighter. The Russians, however, loved the tank for its ease of maintenance and, above all, the radio that came in every tank.

[499] Domanski & Ledwoch, *Wien 1945*, p. 9.

Wespe

Leichte Feldhaubitze 18 auf Fahrgestell Panzerkampfwagen II (SdKfz. 124)

Wespe

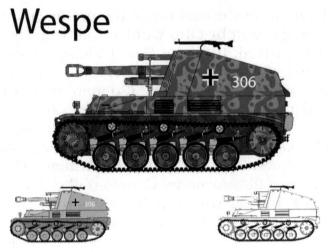

Mounting a 105mm howitzer , the *Wespe* used the very successful *Panzer Mark II* chassis in an open-topped configuration that was able keep up with *panzer* formations. Production ended in June, 1944, a 676 machines, but many were still in service with the *panzer* divisions in 1945.

Hummel

Panzerfeldhaubitze 18M auf Geschützwagen III/IV (Sf) (SdKfz. 165)

Hummel

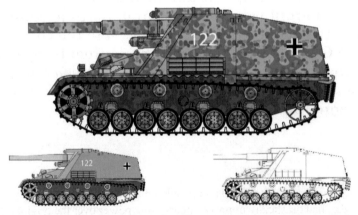

Like the *Wespe,* the *Hummel* allowed artillery support to accompany fast moving mobile troops. A vehicle equipped with an artillery field howitzer was referred to as a '*Geschützwagen,*' which translates directly to 'gun vehicle.' The abbreviation 'Sf' stands for '*Selbstfahrlafette,*' meaning self-propelled carriage. The term '*Panzerfeldhaubitze*' translates to 'armored field howitzer.'

South of the Danube was 46th Army and then 6th Guards Tank Army, with the latter being the breakthrough exploitation force north of Lake Velence . The 46th Army line of attack was through Tatabanya to Tata and then Komarom on the Danube, straight between the 1st Hungarian Hussar Division and the German *96. Infanterie Division*; this would cut off several divisions near Eztergom (Gran), including the *711. Infanterie Division*. The direction of attack was designed to drive through the valley separating the Vértes and the Gerecse Hills, a natural highway that bisected flat, wet ground that offered no natural defense barriers. With sufficient firepower the Germans and Hungarians could have fortified the hills on either side of the valley and fired down on the advancing Russians, but that firepower did not exist anymore; at best they could maintain a harassing fire that might slow, but would not stop, the onrushing Russians.

South of 46th Army was 9th Guards Army followed by 4th Guards Army; both were primarily rifle armies although 4th Guards Army did have the 23rd Mechanized Corps. 4th Guards Army's target was the northern flank of *IV. SS–Panzerkorps*, the very weak 2nd Hungarian Armored Division, while 9th Guards

Map 9

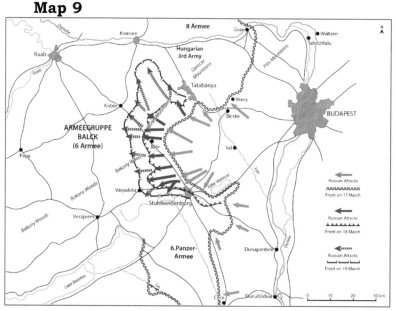

563

Army would attack the Stuhlweissenburg area.
On 9th Guards Army's left flank, south of Lake Velence,
was the weak 27th Army facing the brunt of *6. SS–
Panzerarmee*'s drive to the Danube; ideally this army
would have launched attacks to pin the two *SS–
Panzerkorps'* in place, but it was too weak for this and
consequently the German formations had freedom of
maneuver behind their own lines. To the west of 27th
Army facing *I Kavallerie Korps* was 26th Army, which
was also too weak to hold its opponents in place, thus
allowing *3. Kavallerie Division* to pull out of the line and
race north toward Mör and *4. Kavallerie Division* to
cover the entire defensive front formerly held by *3.
Kavallerie Division* and *I. SS–Panzerkorps*. The coming
weeks would therefore become a race to the west, with
the Germans desperately trying to move into Austria
before the Russians could cut them off; many Germans
would lose the race, but enough would escape to
change the complexion of the post-war world. Had the
Russian 26th and 27th Armies been strong enough to
also attack in conjunction with the rest of the Russian
armies it is unlikely this could have happened.

Lastly, on the southern flank, the Russian 57th
Army faced the German *2. Panzerarmee*, with 57th
Army commanding 3 rifle corps. *2. Panzerarmee* was
entrenched behind the Drava River screening the all-
important oilfields at Nagykanizsa, although it was also
weak. Elements had attacked east during *Unternehmen
Frühlingserwachen*, primarily *16. SS–Panzergrenadier
Division Reichsführer SS*. Nevertheless, far from the
main offensive, 57th Army was not strong enough to
breakthrough on its own and would only move forward
when *2. Panzerarmee*'s northern flank was in danger of
being turned.

The dispositions of *Heeresgruppe Süd* were, from north to south: *8. Armee* held the front west of the Gran River with *Panzerkorps Felldherrnhalle* commanding from north to south, with *357. Infanterie Division* Infantry, *46. Infanterie Division* and *271. Volksgrenadier Division* north of the Danube, and *Panzer Division Felldherrnhalle* in reserve near Komarom. *Panzer Division Felldherrnhalle 2/13. Panzer Division* and *232. Panzer Division* were not technically combat operative, although that status would shortly not matter.

South of the Danube stood *Armeegruppe Balck*, where 3rd Hungarian Army was holding the front from Eztergom (Gran) southwest almost to Bicske, with Hungarian VIII Corps commanding *711. Infanterie Division* near Eztergom, then moving southwest came the 23rd Hungarian Infantry Division and *96. Infanterie Division*; in reserve were *Kampfgruppe Reichert* and *Kampfgruppe Ameiser*. On 3rd Hungarian Army's right flank was *6. Armee*, holding a bulge in the front west of Bicske running south almost to Stuhlweissenburg. *III. Panzerkorps* was still trying to punch through the Russian defenses between Sarozd and Lake Velence, with *1. Panzer Division* nearest the lake, then 3rd *Panzer* and finally *6. Panzer Division*.

Finally, *6. SS–Panzerarmee* was on the southern end of the line between Lakes Balaton and Velence, with a bulge that stretched to Simontornya at the very limit of the German advance. *II. SS–Panzerkorps* was just west of Sarozd, with *44. Reichs Grenadier Division Hoch und Deutschmeister* on *6. Panzer Division* Division's right flank, followed by *9. SS–Panzer Division Hohenstaufen* and then *2. SS–Panzer Division Das Reich* Das *Reich*. *I. SS–Panzerkorps* was just to the south, with *23. Panzer Division* along the Sàrviz Canal, followed by *1. SS–Panzer Division Leibstandarte Adolf Hitler* with the attached *SS–Schwere–Panzer Abteilung 501*, then *12. SS–Panzer Division Hitlerjugend*. West of *I. SS–Panzerkorps* was *I Kavallerie Korps*. *3. Kavallerie Division* was on *Hitlerjugend*'s right flank, then *4.*

Kavallerie Division and finally 25th Hungarian Infantry Division, with the attached 20th Assault Gun Battalion. The last army on the southern end of *Heeresgruppe Süd's* front was *2. Panzerarmee,* screening the oil fields at Nagykanisza. XXII Corps had the *118. Jäger Division* near the southwestern tip of Lake Balaton, then *16. SS–Panzergrenadier Division Reichsführer–SS (RFSS).*[500] LXVIII Army Corps commanded *1. Volks–Gebirgs Division* on the right flank of *Reichsführer–SS,* followed by *71. Infanterie Division,* 2nd Hungarian Infantry Division and finally *13. Waffen–Gebirgs Division der SS Handschar (1. Kroatische). Handschar* was on the extreme right flank of *Heeresgruppe Süd* and defended up to the boundary with *Heeresgruppe E* and was not the most reliable of divisions; it had performed quite well when fighting partisans, but once transferred to front-line duties in Hungary it suffered heavily from desertions as men left German service to return home to protect their families from the incoming Russian tide.

The concentration of combat power between Lakes Balaton and Velence left *Heeresgruppe Süd* dangerously vulnerable to attacks elsewhere, but even worse was the complete lack of significant reserves; essentially every major combat formation was already at the front, with nothing left for the emergencies that would shortly arise other than *kampfgruppen* and formations such as *SS–Brigade Ney.*[501] In the coming days only the German expertise at mobile warfare would save *6. Armee* and *6. SS–Panzerarmee* from total destruction.

[500] This division was also very well led, being commanded by a stalwart SS veteran, winner of the Knight's Cross with Oak Leaves and Swords *SS–Brigadeführer* Otto Baum, who temporarily commanded 2nd SS Panzer Division Das *Reich* during the Battle of the Falaise Gap the previous summer.

[501] The official name of *1. Ungarische–Sturm Brigade der SS* seems not to have been commonly used, although information about this unit is scarce.

The key to the coming battle would be the road network of Western Hungary. Paved roads were few, highways even fewer; consequently, defense of the all-weather roads leading west was key to the survival of *Heeresgruppe Süd* and its defense of Austria. The key city was Raab (Gyor), some 8 kilometers south of the Danube. The two best highways leading into Austria both converged there, with one paralleling the river to the northwest leading first to Pressburg (Bratislava) and then into Vienna, and the second heading more or less due west and passing the southern tip of the *Neuseidler See* before turning northwest into Sopron, crossing the Austrian border at Klingenbach and then continuing into Vienna from the south. A third major road led from Weiner Neustadt due north into Vienna and a fourth entered the city from the west. Possession of these thoroughfares not only allowed rapid forward movement but also made resupply of the attack units much easier. In poor weather the German defense could center around the major roads because cross-country movement for motorized units were slow and difficult, but as the weather improved the Russians could outflank defensive positions on the main highways.

For the Germans on the southern end of the fighting survival would depend on withdrawal over secondary roads, as there were no major highways heading west from the Lake Balaton region; life and death would center on narrow paved roads or rutted dirt tracks under constant threat of air attack.

At last the moment came for which the Russians had prepared so carefully, the grand assault against the weakest points in the German front lines that was known as the Vienna Offensive. Preceded by a massive artillery barrage that almost obliterated the Hungarian

2nd Armored Division north of Stuhlweissenburg near Zámoly, Marshal Tolbukhin's Third Ukrainian Front and Marshal Malinovsky's Second Ukrainian Front attacked on a line from Lake Velence to the Danube, with three separate axes of attack: the first driving northwest from the vicinity of Biscke through the area of *96. Infanterie Division* and the 1st Hungarian Hussar Division, through Tatabanya and Tata to the Danube, then moving along the Danube valley to Komarom; a second thrust toward Weiner Neustadt on the Austrian border, and another heading southeast for Croatia. Between Stuhlweissenburg and the Vértes Mountains the main initial target was the Hungarian 3rd Army and the 'Hussars' that Fritz Hagen had been told he could rely on to hold the line. On a front of just over 18 kilometers two Soviet Armies struck the hapless Hungarians, with Sixth Guards Tank Army ready to exploit a breakthrough. Short of heavy weapons, manpower and morale, the Hungarians were smashed by the ferocious opening bombardment and would quickly crumple under the hammer blows.

The immediate targets were Tata and Raab in the north, and Varpalota and Veszprem in the south, with the southern thrust being the more dangerous of the two. During the coming weeks the Germans would find themselves fighting their way out of one trap after another, in constant danger of being surrounded, as there simply were not enough German units left to form a continuous line. As the situation developed, however, the slow pace of advance in *Unternehmen Frühlingserwachen,* and the need to drain away strength from the schwerpunkt of the attack of *I. SS– Panzerkorps* to guards its flanks and to help *II. SS– Panzerkorps,* may have kept the German units just close enough to their initial attack positions to avoid being surrounded by the Soviet steamroller that would come pouring from the Vértes Mountains within days. Otto Wohler's prescient request to pull *I. SS– Panzerkorps* back to renew the attack near *II. SS– Panzerkorps* had put that formation on the move mere hours before the Soviets unleashed their attack, giving them a chance to pull out of the trap *Unternehmen Frühlingserwachen* had fashioned for them. But it would be a close run thing.

In Vienna the apathy and, indeed, the torpor of the population-at-large could not be shaken even with the Russians on the way. Normal life, at least as normal as possible in the circumstances, was the order of the day, almost as if by sheer inertia the Viennese could push through the coming maelstrom with their city and cultural heritage intact.

Ralf Roland Ringler had tickets to a Wolfgang Schneiderhan concert. "Music and culture, those were things we believed worth fighting for. I look at the faces around me and begin to doubt. Nothing could arouse these people. They'd never lift a finger to help themselves. They just want to preserve the values of culture, with or without battle."[502]

As Tolbukhin and Malinovsky's troops drove into the left and rear flanks of *Unternehmen Frühlingserwachen,* General Wöhler at *Heeresgruppe Süd* was faced with the very real possibility of the complete and utter destruction of almost his entire command. *Heeresgruppe Süd* was not a formation built for defense, with its abundance of *panzer* divisions. The high proportion of armored formations improved mobility, but armored units were built for offense, not defense; dug in infantry supported by heavy anti-tank guns were the best choice for defending ground, even

[502] Ringler, Ralf Roland, *Illusion einer Jugend. Lieder, Fahnen und das bittere Ende. Hitler-Jugend in Österreich. Ein Erlebnisbericht* (St. Pölten: Niederösterreichisches Pressehaus, 1977), p. 33.

against tank attacks, and Wohler was woefully short of infantry. Nor could the *panzer* divisions take advantage of their greatest asset, mobility, since the shortage of fuel was both chronic and critical. Maneuvers had to be considered in the light of whether fuel was available to execute them, with prioritization the order of the day. The situation was bad in the extreme, but not hopeless, not if the armored divisions were handled with a sure touch.

Before the war no less a personage than George Patton had envisioned exactly the sort of battle that *Heeresgruppe Süd* was now facing,[503] a defensive battle of delay and movement fought primarily with mobile troops. In a 1936 treatise, selected for their book on military history by Chambers & Piehler on the future employment of armored units, Patton wrote: "So far as I know hardly any emphasis has been placed on the great value of A.F.V.'s in delaying actions, yet I believe that here their capacity is even greater than on the offensive while circumstances under which they can be employed will make their casualties negligible."[504] It is not hard to see that Patton's nimble mind envisioned a scenario where mobile forces would fight a fluid defense to hit and run without being drawn into a slug-it-out brawl with superior forces. What he could not foresee was Hitler's stubborn insistence on defending every foot of ground, nor the fuel shortage and weather conditions with which *Heeresgruppe Süd* had to contend, not to mention almost continuous air attacks. Nevertheless, in the end many of the German mobile forces fought precisely this sort of delaying defense, chiefly because there was no other choice.

As the Soviet offensive developed and drove further westward, Hitler's stand-fast orders were often ignored, even by the *Waffen–SS* formations; or, perhaps, especially by the *Waffen–SS* formations. The

[503] Without worrying about fuel shortages, it should be noted.
[504] Chambers, John Whiteclay II, & Piehler, G. Kurt, *Major Problems in American Military History: Documents and Essays* (New York: Simon & Schuster, 1998), p. 291.

veteran troops and their commanders knew the reality of their situation and were not eager to be destroyed for no reason. Historian Thiele notes that the commanders on the spot often requested freedom of movement but were denied. "Many times commanders requested permission for a tactical retreat. One of those was General Meyer of the *12. SS–Panzer Division*, but he, as others, were always referred to Hitler's order to defend every foot of territory. But many disobeyed the order as Meyer did..."[505] Some of this insubordination was no doubt because of the grimness of the overall situation, but some also has to have been caused by the dilution of the *Waffen–SS* recruiting standards and lack of training before being enrolled into a unit; where previously the unparalleled training and morale of the *SS* units allowed them to perform near-miracles on the battlefield, most of those veterans were gone and their replacements simply did not have their energy, experience or tactical expertise. Asking the impossible of the *SS* divisions had once been possible, but no longer, and their commanders knew it.

As the Germans retreated through first Hungary and then Austria, two things should be kept in mind: first, whenever units of *6. SS–Panzerarmee* are mentioned the question should be asked, 'what if they had gone to the Oder Front', as most German generals wanted, including Dietrich, the army commander. There were no other units of comparable strength to substitute, so the remaining German formations would have had to fight the Soviet offensive on their own. Second, few German mobile divisions fought as integral units anymore. There simply weren't enough divisions to go around, so they were constantly being broken up and used in danger spots. Thiele puts it this way: "In the final analysis, one should be aware that after 1942-43 it was a rare occasion when elite formations fought as closed units of divisional strength...Frequently

[505] Thiele, Karl H., *Beyond Monsters and Clowns, The Combat SS: De-Mythologizing Five Decades of German Elite Formations* (Lanham: University Press of America, 1997), p. 188.

regiments and even battalions fought as independent battle groups, and were not united with their divisions for months."[506] The saga of *1. SS–Panzer Division's Aufklärung Abteilung* in the coming days is but one example of this. Detached temporarily to Hermann Balck's command, Dietrich repeatedly requested its return to its parent division, Otto Wöhler repeatedly *ordered* Balck to return it, but Balck only did so many days later; he simply refused to give back such a valuable unit until he felt like doing so. Whatever disdain he felt for the *Waffen–SS* officers, Balck recognized their combat prowess.

In essence, the coming weeks would see numerous knots of armed men wandering westward in groups numbering from the hundreds to the thousands, stopping occasionally to fight back at the Soviets dogging their steps, sometimes being surrounded and having to fight their way out of the trap, sometimes dying where they stood, sometimes being captured, all the while being forced westward toward the relative safety of the Alps and their foothills, and the hope of surrendering to the Americans. In the process, those men held back the Red Army long enough for Austria to be overrun by the Western Allies enough so that Stalin did not attempt to swallow it, as he did Poland and Hungary and Czechoslovakia. Had they not done so, or had *6. SS–Panzerarmee* gone north to die on the banks of the Oder, the question that can never be answered is whether or not Stalin would have allowed Austria its freedom if the Red Army had penetrated all the way to the Swiss border. The topic was certainly on the mind of Winston Churchill, who considered it a real possibility.[507]

---

[506] Thiele, *Beyond Monsters and Clowns*, p. 273.
[507] Churchill's suspicion of Soviet intentions is dealt with at length in the next volume.

Under pressure of the Soviet offensive, the Hungarian 3rd Army was in danger of being annihilated. This should come as little surprise, as the Hungarian Army formations were weak in both manpower and firepower. Those Hungarians who were eager to continue fighting were largely already taken by the *Waffen–SS* and made a good showing in units such as Ney's. But in general the average Hungarian soldier had little appetite for continuing the fight on Germany's side. Pierik states that as early as the previous fall Hungary was unable to come anywhere close to filling its ranks with conscripts. "When a previous attempt had been made to recruit Hungarian armed soldiers only 29 men had turned up out of the 1,862 who had been called up to fight."[508] The Hungarians were still there when the Germans had expected them to quit, but not many of them were eager to fight.

There *were* enough Hungarians and *Volksdeutsch* willing to fight to keep a few special units up to strength, though, with *SS-Brigade Ney* being one of them. Maybe the men were devoted anti-communists fleeing the coming retribution once Hungary was occupied by Russians, maybe they were Hungarian nationalists, or maybe they were just hungry and thought the *SS* gave them the best chance of being fed; whatever their motives, some Hungarian formations would actually grow stronger in the coming weeks. *SS-Brigade Ney* was still getting itself reorganized when the Soviet offensive rolled over the Hungarian 3rd Army. Having anticipated such an attack, and knowing how vulnerable his command was to being outflanked, General Wöhler was desperate for reserves to throw into the path of the Red Army before it enveloped all of *Heeresgruppe Süd* and the brigade soon received orders to move the short distance from Sur to the area of Mor,

---

[508] Pierik, p. 132.

close by to the east. At this point the brigade was close to 5,000 strong, as large as some divisions of the time. Before long it would be fighting for its life.

In ten short days *2. SS–Panzer Division Das Reich* had lost half of its fighting strength, giving a rifle strength on 16 March of about 5,000 men and its mobility was only 60 percent. Although many men were wounded and would return to service, and others were stragglers, the loss of more than 500 men per day of combat was a staggering indictment of how poorly designed *Unternehmen Frühlingserwachen* had been. With too little firepower and virtually no armored support, the *Panzergrenadiers* had fought a dirty, brutal battle in the muddy Hungarian farmland, paying for each meter of advance either with their life, or the life of a comrade. Now the division was once again a burned-out wreck, and the vengeful Russians were coming for revenge.

17 March, Saturday

Around 0120 hours on 17 March, Heinz Guderian suggested to Otto Wöhler that he forget attacking eastward with *I. SS–Panzerkorps*, *II. SS–Panzerkorps* and *III. Panzerkorps*, and instead send *I. SS–Panzerkorps* north into the flank of the Soviet attack driving for Varpalota and Veszprem. Such a change to the basic plan for *Unternehmen Frühlingserwachen* that involved re-deployment of major units required Hitler's personal approval. The situation was critical, however, the danger obvious, and so at 0145 the Chief of Staff for *Heeresgruppe Süd*, *Generalleutnant* von Grolman, ordered such an attack without waiting for Hitler's permission. It was only later in the morning that *Heeresgruppe Süd* officially asked for approval of this plan, and it was not until the next day that Hitler reluctantly gave it. Thus did *Unternehmen Frühlingserwachen*, the final major German offensive of the Second World War, finally sputter to an end; yet the re-direction of *I. SS–Panzerkorps* to the north was accomplished in a surprisingly rapid fashion. The movement north that had begun late on the night of 15 March meant that Wöhler had the only force capable of slowing down the Russians already on the road hours before the Vienna Offensive even began. Moreover, the distance between the staging areas that *I. SS–Panzerkorps* had been driving toward between Seregèlyes and Aba, and its new destination north of Varpalota, was less than 30 miles. Since *Heeresgruppe Süd* had no reserves to bolster the already-collapsing front around Mör, the two *SS panzer* divisions were the only hope of slowing the Russians down enough to allow the rest of *6. SS–Panzerarmee* and most of *6. Armee* to escape complete destruction.

As the Soviet attack continued and began to pick up speed in the coming days and weeks, it was plainly obvious that the rampaging Red Army bore no similarities whatsoever to the poorly lead and tentative formations of the early war. The Soviet commanders, and the tank commanders in particular, had learned their lessons from the best teachers in the world: the Germans themselves.

The confidence of Russian commanders in their handling of armor was having a curious side-effect. Gone were the days of nervousness and hesitation, when sometimes it seemed that only Zhukov had the will-power and the demonic energy to take the right decisions. Now the Russian tanks were becoming the vehicle for private ambition as well as national victory...However, the writing of history in Soviet Russia was a very different thing from what it was farther west, and Russian commanders were well aware that they would have to fight for their places.[509]

As the Germans frantically tried to form a line in front of the Soviet advance, with thoughts of perhaps attacking the flanks as they had done so often in the past, they continually found that it was the hard-driving Russians who were flanking them. No defensive position was safe for long. Already by the 17th cohesion was being lost. The front north of Stuhlweissenburg was not broken because there was no front, just hedgehog positions. The next two days would be critical to whether or not *Heeresgruppe Süd* could save anything from the coming disaster, and, by extension, whether there would be anybody left to defend Austria.

As the Soviet attack developed, the small town of Mör became a key position. First, it was astride the main highway from Kisber to Stuhlweissenburg, making it possible for the Russians to rapidly outflank that crucial city from the northwest. Second, almost directly south-southeast of Mör was Veszprem, a strategic position whose possession would determine

[509] Orgill, Douglas, *T-34 Russian Armor* (New York: Ballantine, 1971), p. 47.

the fate of most of *Heeresgruppe Süd*. Close to Veszprem was the rail junction at Herend, through which all rail traffic heading south or east had to travel; its capture would leave only a narrow corridor separating Veszprem from Lake Balaton through which all of *6. Armee* and *6. SS–Panzerarmee* would have to flow in order to escape being encircled. If the Russians could capture Veszprem and Herend before the Germans could withdraw west of their position, then escape would be difficult at best. Therefore, slowing the Russian onslaught became imperative, with the only question being what forces could be found to help accomplish that; *I. SS–Panzerkorps* was a start but it was still moving into position. Somehow, somewhere, other forces had to be found.

To that end, *SS-Brigade Ney* hastily made its way to the front near Mör from the area of Sur, where it had been reorganizing, minus one battalion-strength *kampfgruppe* already committed elsewhere. The brigade went into action immediately. The Russians were already threatening Mör, but by nightfall they had been stopped short.

The *IV/SS-Brigade Ney* had been named for the President of the Eastern Front Comradeship Organization, the KABSZ, Dr. Bela vitez Imredy de Omoravicza. On 17 March, that parent organization was ordered out of existence. Somewhere, bureaucrats associated with Ferenc Szalasi with no real authority were still issuing edicts that were unenforceable and universally ignored.

After ten days of crawling through Russian defenses the *Panzer* regiment of the *1. SS–Panzer Division LAH* was worn down to less than 20 percent operational vehicles; Michaelis gives a strength total on 17 March as 14 *Mark IVs*, 14 *Mark V Panthers* and four attached *Sturmgeschütze*, along with nine *Tiger IIs*

operational.[510] This was roughly three companies, spread over two battalions, so the *II./SS Panzer Regiment 1* was essentially disbanded and re-organized to fight as infantry, and all of the *panzers* were collected into the *I./SS–Panzer Regiment 1*. This was done on the fly as the division was moving north to intercept the advancing Russians. Overall manpower losses during the push south had been comparatively as heavy: 23 officers and 1412 other ranks either killed, wounded or missing. The utter futility of what had been accomplished made such losses even more painful. The division was supposed to be 100 percent mobile but reported itself only 68 percent mobile.

Amid the chaos of the Russian offensive, *9. SS–Panzer Division Hohenstaufen* reported its strength on 17 March as 10,820 of all ranks, with a combat strength of 4,614 men, which means that the division had lost 9,000 men since the end of January. Such losses are hard to account for. Casualties had been heavy, it was true, but not half the division. Michaelis posits a theory for this baffling total: "One possibility is that it was reclassified as a *Panzer*-Division 45 (Type 1945)."[511] The problem with this theory is that the order for *Hohenstaufen* to reorganize was not issued until 25 March 25th, eight days after this puzzling report, and was never carried out. To cloud the picture even more, *Hohenstaufen* would end the war over-strength.

[510] Michaelis, *Panzer Divisions of the Waffen–SS*, p. 50.
[511] Michaelis, *Panzer Divisions of the Waffen–SS*, p. 236.

18 March, Sunday

At 0120, word arrived from Hitler's headquarters in Berlin endorsing *Heeresgruppe Süd*'s re-deployment of *I. SS–Panzerkorps* to the area north of Varpalota and the withdrawal of *II. SS–Panzerkorps* to a point behind and just north of its sister corps. Orders to that effect were issued by *Heeresgruppe Süd* at 0200 with *I. SS–Panzerkorps* detached from Dietrich's command and attached to Hermann Balck's *6. Armee*. Relief at *Heeresgruppe Süd* headquarters must have been palpable; at that state of the war, any unauthorized movements could result in summary execution, even of generals, and maybe even of Hitler's personal friends.[512]

As the momentum of the Red Army offensive increased, threatening to completely overwhelm the Hungarian 3rd Army defending the line north of *6. Armee* from Komarno to Kisper, the weak, demoralized Hungarian formations began to break up and dissolve. Many men deserted outright and disappeared into the surrounding countryside, and many more changed sides and went over to the Russians, apparently in hopes of avoiding the harsh realities of being a prisoner of the Red Army. The Hungarian 2nd Armored Division lost its last 15 tanks at Söred.[513] The most defensible territory in *Heeresgruppe Süd*'s sector was rapidly being lost and the Soviets were pouring through, heading for the key town of Veszprem at the northeast corner of Lake Balaton. If they could get there quickly

---

[512] During the fight for Berlin, for example, the commander of *LVI Panzerkorps*, *General der Artillerie* Helmut Weidling, was sentenced to death by Hitler based on a report that he had moved his headquarters without permission. In fact, Weidling's headquarters was on the front lines and when he answered Hitler's summons to report to the *Führerbunker* his execution was cancelled and he was given command of the entire defense of Berlin.

[513] These were likely 41M and 43M Turan II medium tanks; this is based on photos taken by the victorious Russians of Hungarian 41M and 43M tanks loaded onto railroad flatcars for transport to the Soviet Union sometime in March of 1945. 2nd Hungarian Armored Division is the only viable candidate for having still had such vehicles.

and take the town, virtually all of *Heeresgruppe Süd* would be cut off south of the land bridge connecting Lakes Balaton and Velence. With no sizeable forces outside the pocket to free them, there would be no hope for rescue and the way west would be open as the entire front south of *Heeresgruppe Mitte* would be laid bare. There would be no important German formations left in position to stop the Russians from overrunning Austria, very possibly all the way to the Swiss Alps. In the southern sector Tito's partisans would have had free rein in Graz, as well as outflanking the British in Trieste and making that sticky situation worse. With the long-range consequences of such Soviet successes impossible to predict the moment of history was at hand.

Otto Wöhler was desperately trying to redeploy *Heeresgruppe Süd* from south of Lakes Balaton and Velence to form a defensive position to prevent that very thing, as the main weight of Tolbukhin's thrust hit his now-open left flank, where the remnants of the Hungarian 3rd Army fled west in headlong rout. This allowed even heavier pressure to be brought on Mor, where *SS-Brigade Ney* was engaged in trying to hold the town along with elements of *3. SS–Panzer Division Totenkopf* and 2nd Hungarian Armored Division. Mor was crucial to the defense as the longer it was held, the more time the two *SS Panzerkorps* had to move into position to hold the critical flank. Each minute gained was precious to the survival of the army group. The fighting was heavy and the defense stout, almost fanatical, but the Russians were too strong to hold off indefinitely; in the end Mor fell, although a counterattack by those same units in the early evening retook the main defense lines just to the southwest. A makeshift bulwark had been thrown in the path of the Russians, but it could not hold for long. *SS-Brigade Ney* and the remnants of 2nd Hungarian Armored Division were then combined to make up *Kampfgruppe Schell*, commanded by *Oberst* Zoltan Schell, the former commander of the Hungarian 1st Hussar Division. On the shoulders of this relatively small formation fell a heavy defensive burden.

The badly damaged *Totenkopf* was in the line south of Kisber on the Hungarian 3rd Army's right flank. When that army began to crumble *Totenkopf* immediately had to begin bowing backwards to the west, to keep from being outflanked. Refusing its flank was a dangerous maneuver in the face of the enemy, but there was no choice. Directly south of *Totenkopf* was *Wiking*, also depleted from the Konrad operations, with its few remaining units heavily engaged and deployed forward against Russian thrusts designed to pin them in place.

With a hole being ripped in the front to its north, and pinned on their front, *IV. SS–Panzerkorps* faced the very real danger of being surrounded unless units could be found to stitch together a defense. *1. SS–Panzer Division LAH* was moving north but was targeted to patch the break in the line, with *12. SS–Panzer Division Hitlerjugend* holding back the Russians in the south. That left *Das Reich* as the only sizeable formation to throw into the breach created between Kisper and the Danube to the north, a gaping hole in the German defense. Since *II. SS–Panzerkorps* had not been able to drive nearly as far as *I. SS–Panzerkorps* had during *Unternehmen Frühlingserwachen,* and with that corps already earmarked for the area around Mör, *Das Reich* was much closer to the scene of crisis and had the only mobile units capable of interceding in time.

Both of the division's *panzergrenadier* regiments moved north, paralleling the front to race into the breach on *Totenkopf*'s left flank, with both *Totenkopf* and the next-division-in-line, *9. SS–Panzer Division Hohenstaufen,* extending their fronts to cover the ground uncovered by the withdrawal of Das *Reich*'s *panzer*-grenadiers. Like all of the assault formations of *Unternehmen Frühlingserwachen, Das Reich* was battered and exhausted after fighting for 12 days straight, in need of rest and replacements and maintenance. Her infantry regiments were badly depleted but, even at full strength, two *panzergrenadier* regiments were not a substitute for an entire army, regardless how weak of an army; they were simply the only men available for the mission, and they were expected to once again do the impossible. The Russian 18th Guards Rifle Corps and 68th Rifle Corps were driving for the Danube from the area near Biscke, wrenching open the front and driving a wedge between the German *96. Infanterie Division* on the east and the *356. Infanterie Division* on the west; *Das Reich* was heading for the right flank of the latter division to block the Russians. They would not be enough. When the Red Army spearheads reached the Danube it created a bridgehead near Eztergom on the south bank that contained the *96. Infanterie Division* and *711. Infanterie Division*, plus the 23rd Hungarian Infantry Division.

Das *Reich's* *panzer* regiment was withdrawn westward even as the *panzergrenadiers* headed north into the breach. The regiment was badly in need of repairs and headed for the railhead at Veszprem. Although not used extensively during *Unternehmen Frühlingserwachen* due to the weather, the regiment had nevertheless seen action and the watery weather had played havoc with the *panzers'* mechanical status. *Panzers* were not the ideal choice for defense anyway, unless infantry was there to support them, and with the breach in the line some 60 kilometers to the north this meant that using the *panzers* to support the *panzergrenadiers* would have required a long road march[514] putting unnecessary strain on machines already past due for maintenance. Tanks were powerful machines but also, in some respects, fragile. *2. SS–Panzer Regiment* was already weak in numbers and if the *panzers* were not operation then the division's combat power would have been further crippled. Once rested and repaired, the regiment could be a powerful

---

[514] There were no convenient railroads available to transport the panzers from the area near Seregelyes.

fire brigade to seal off breakthroughs, assuming a defensive line could be formed.

The German leadership had to consider all of this at once. It should also be remembered that modern armies are scattered behind the front lines covering a great area. Supply depots, parts depots, repair facilities, hospitals, rail junctions, collection points, veterinary clinics, administrative facilities, headquarters, airfields, an endless list of support services were needed to keep armies like *6. SS–Panzerarmee* in the field. These requirements needed time to set up, and time to move. Evacuation in the face of an onrushing enemy tank force was rarely calm and organized.

In trying to respond to the growing catastrophe, the first job of the various commanders, from Otto Wöhler down the chain of command, was to try and stop the Soviet onslaught. But the army, corps and division commanders also had to try and save their support services, with wounded being the top priority. Decisions had to be made on the spot that would affect more than the immediate battlefield considerations. Complicating all of this was the lack of fuel and rail transport. Outrunning the Russians would, in many cases, involve trying to outrun T-34s with horse-drawn carts.

I./SS–Panzergrenadier Regiment 23 Norge was ordered to the small town of Pakozd on the northern shore of Lake Velence, to block the main highway from Budapest. The Russians were less than seven miles to the northeast and approaching fast. How long such an under-strength battalion could block such a crucial road was problematic.

The deceptive measures prior to *6. SS–Panzerarmee*'s transfer to Hungary were no longer needed, so on 18 March formations such as *Hitlerjugend*, aka *'Ersatz-Staffel Wiking'*, were again referred to by their real designation in communications.

19 March, Monday

As the Soviet Vienna Offensive entered its fourth day the German defenses began to break up and completely give way, as the Red Army broke through between the Hungarian 1st Armored Division and the German *96. Infanterie Division.*

The Soviets had two immediate targets: Stuhlweissenburg and Veszprem. Seizing the former would be akin to dislodging a large stone that was holding back a flood, washing everything away as it tumbled downstream. Capturing the second would entrap every German unit still south or east of Lake Balaton. Either one would be catastrophic for the German defense of the Hungarian oilfields and Austria, but as the Russians rolled onward it became obvious that both were going to fall, and the only question was when. The battle was developing into a race to evacuate the endangered German forces before it was too late.

The Russians were moving on Stuhlweissenburg from the northwest, west, east and south. In response to the direct thrust from the east, *I./SS–Panzergrenadier Regiment 23 Norge* was ordered to take and hold hill 351, southwest of Nadap east of Stuhlweissenburg itself near Lake Velence. Despite air attacks the battalion managed to take the hill, albeit not without serious casualties, including the commander of *2. Kompanie*, a Norwegian *SS–Untersturmführer* named Oskar Stromness. Once there, however, the volume of Soviet fire increased, including both artillery and mortar barrages, as well as small arms fire from Nadap. Casualties mounted throughout the day. Finally, after nightfall, a strong Soviet infantry attack drove the depleted battalion back down the hill.

North of Stuhlweissenburg the offensive picked up speed as the fragmented defenders were forced to retreat time and again or be destroyed piecemeal. Neither the elements of *Totenkopf* fighting there, nor *Kampfgruppe Schell*, could prevent the Russians from capturing Csor, Bodajk and Isztimer, and in the process shoving the defenders into the area near Aka-Sur. There simply were not enough defenders to do more than fortify important positions] no cohesive defense was possible, and the road to Veszprem via Varpalota was open.

To help *IV. SS–Panzerkorps* , the elements of *9. SS–Panzer Division Hohenstaufen* that could move were ordered to Stuhlweissenburg and subordinated to that Corps, but much of the division was heavily engaged in defensive fighting between Aba and Sarosd. The German lines were cracking and chaos came on apace.

20 March, Tuesday

1. Panzer Division was encircled at Jeno, less than 10 miles southwest of Stuhlweissenburg. The division managed to fight its way out of the town while suffering very heavy casualties. Somehow, despite its losses, the division kept its cohesion and did not disintegrate under the continuing Soviet attacks, certainly due to the veterans remaining in its ranks, but it was not out of danger yet. At Stuhlweissenburg itself, however, much of *23. Panzer Division* was trapped.

From the German point of view the situation in northwest Hungary on 20 March was a disastrous mess. And not even an identifiable mess, since the crumbling of the Hungarian 3rd Army left a gap both in the defense and in the intelligence of where the enemy was and where he was heading, leading to a fluid re-deployment of units that changed almost hourly in reaction to new information. *Heeresgruppe Süd's* Commander, Otto Wöhler, was desperately trying to find a way to hold the line north of Stuhlweissenburg, counterattack into the void left by the destruction of the Hungarians all while pulling his endangered units south and east of the Lakes Line to safety before they could be cut off. And he was trying to do all of this while being micro-managed from the *Führerbunker*. Wöhler's only advantage for what seemed like an impossible situation was that his best units were veteran divisions that had been in dire straits many times before; desperation was nothing new to them. But they were all exhausted, depleted and low on fuel, and the fighting ahead promised to be bitter.

With a red flood coming from the east, before dawn the first elements of *SS–Panzer Regiment 2* pulled up to the railhead near Veszprem, in the small but ancient village of Herend. The regiment had been pulled back two days earlier when the division's *panzergrenadiers* raced north to try and plug the gap left by the dissolution of the Hungarian 3rd Army. Two weeks of offensive combat had left Das *Reich's* tanks in bad shape and they were withdrawn for repairs and reorganization.

Dating back to Roman times, Veszprem was already famous for its porcelain works when the German *Mark V Panthers* and *Mark IVs* clanked up to its railway complex. Herend Porcelain had been manufactured there since 1826 and had once been a supplier to the Hapsburgs, which made the company popular with European aristocracy of the 19th and early 20th century. In the 21st century it would become the world's largest porcelain factory. In most other respects, however, it was just a small Hungarian farming community on the outskirts of the Bakony Hills. Corn was a staple crop.

What happened to the *Das Reich panzers* that day may well have been the pivotal moment in the Soviet offensive, when the virtual destruction of *Heeresgruppe Süd* came very close to happening. The encounter perfectly illustrates the difference that experienced German troops still held over their Russian counterparts, even when outnumbered and caught off-guard. As told in a report from *I./Panzer Regiment 24*, even in 1945 "the Russian tank forces are inferior in mobile battles, apparently due to the lack of strict command. The enemy is not in a situation to hold his forces together during an attack of long duration. Instead, he leans toward scattering."[515] That is exactly what happened at Herend.

As told by historian Captain B.H. Friesen, U.S. Army, the *panzers* pulled into Herend piecemeal and by mid-morning some 40 were on hand.[516] The *Panthers*

---

[515] Jentz, *Panzertruppen 2*, p. 224.

[516] This is a big number compared to *panzers* listed as operational, but likely includes machines that could be driven but had other issues that kept them out of combat.

began to load onto the railcars as the Regimental Motor Officer, *SS–Sturmbannführer* Alois Ennsberger, supervised. At this late point in the war *panzers* in general were a precious commodity, but *Panthers* were even more valuable than the older *Mark IVs*. Although updated continuously for more than five years the basic *Mark IV* design was still the same one that had driven over the border into Poland in September of 1939. The *Panther,* on the other hand, was heavily influenced by experiences against the T-34 and is widely considered one of, if not the best, medium tank used by either side during the Second World War. And while the *Panther* and *Mark IV* both had 75 mm main guns, the Panther's higher velocity gun was much the better of the two for its designed purpose of destroying armored vehicles; although the final *Mark IVs* were up-gunned to the 75L/48 main battery which could be dangerous in the right situation, it was still inferior to the *Panthers'* high velocity 75L/70 gun. As a matter of course the *Panthers* were given priority for loading on the rail cars.

It was not long before vehicles from other German units began racing toward the railhead with the news that Russian tanks were just over a mile east of Herend and coming on fast. The tanks almost surely were from 23ʳᵈ Tank Corps. The Russians had pushed aside scattered defenders such as *Kampfgruppe Schell* and elements of *3. SS–Panzer Division Totenkopf,* and had made straight for Veszprem from the area of Csor, on the western side of Stuhlweissenburg.

This was the worst news possible. Not only had the German front completely collapsed north of Stuhlweissenburg, but an armored formation concentrated to board a train could not use it's best feature to defend itself, namely mobility. Nor did they have their attached infantry for defense, as the divisions' two *Panzergrenadier* regiments were somewhere to the northeast trying to plug the gap left by the Hungarians. *Das Reich* was a veteran formation, however, and even with the repeated influx of replacements it=s officers knew their jobs and did not panic easily. A fast defensive perimeter was thrown together, but the *panzers* already loaded could not be unloaded in time to deploy so they were left on their railcars, while the others took up firing positions near the edge of the village.

Friesen tells his story through the experiences of *SS–Unterscharführer* Peter Rauch, using them as illustrative of this engagement; Rauch's *Panther* had not yet been loaded when the Russians were spotted.

"Peter Rauch had been with the division (*Das Reich*) since 1943. Originally from München-Gladbach, in the Rhineland, his first position with *Das Reich* was as a loader on a *Tiger* tank. After several months he became a gunner and eventually rose to command a Panther tank in the Battle of the Bulge. His tank was part of the regimental headquarters section, which consisted of seven Panthers in March 1945. Rauch positioned his tank behind a slight rise between two barns. He could see other vehicles from his section occupy positions among the buildings to his left and right. Ahead of him were 2,000 meters of cornfields, followed by a wooded area. Several minutes after Rauch took position, T-34's crept from the wooded area to his direct front. Six Russian tanks probed towards the village, apparently unaware of the German presence. When they had closed to within 1,000 meters, a voice came over the radio (Rauch thought it sounded like one of the regiment=s company commanders) directing the company on the right flank to engage the T-34's. Several seconds later, the crack of 75-mm cannon erupted from the right, and all six T-34's received hits in their flanks. Some exploded violently, while the others just burned. None of the crew members emerged."[517]

Desultory Soviet artillery fire started hitting the area without effect, mostly mortar fire. German artillery was not in position to help, being too far behind and strung out. It was not long before 15 or 20 T-34's charged the German left flank at full speed, bouncing and throwing mud in all directions, racing over the fields with infantrymen hanging onto their sides for dear life. They were firing as they charged, which was designed more to keep the Germans' heads down than to actually hit anything. The Germans waited for orders to engage the Russian tanks, following well established routines as to who would fire at which target.

After they received their firing orders Rauch picked out a target that appeared to be a company commander's tank, because it had a radio antenna. Even at this late stage of the war the Red Army eschewed the widespread use of radios, preferring to use their manufacturing resources in other areas. Orders were relayed through the commander's tank, but if the commander was put out of action the rest of his command would be without orders. Rauch's first shell blew up the T-34, leaving the remainder of the Russian tanks with no choice but to follow the last order given, namely to attack. The infantry dropped from the T-34s and began to fan out but the Germans kept firing and soon no fewer than 19 T-34s were burning in the fields as close as 400 meters from the German positions. Russian infantry kept attacking the German center until hundreds of their dead were piled up in the cornfields, mowed down by the tank's machine guns, some as close as 100 meters. These were frontal assaults with little subtlety against the German center, where the Germans had a clear field of fire over flat farmland; the outcome was predictable.

[517] Friesen, Captain B. H. *Breakout from the Veszprem Railhead* (Armor Magazine, Jan-Feb 1988), pp. 21-22).

Before long T-34s were spotted moving along both the left and right flank in company strength of 14 and 17 tanks respectively, an obvious attempt to encircle the railhead. The German command and control training made sure that none of these tanks went unnoticed and the Germans opened fire on both groups, destroying about a third of the attackers before the Russian commander finally called things off and the T-34s retreated into the woods and out of sight. Just as the report from *I./Panzer Regiment 24* indicated, the Russians had launched their attacks piecemeal and without coordination, squandering the advantages of surprise and superior numbers when the veteran *SS* commanders kept their wits about them and coolly fought off their attackers.

With the attack beaten off the Germans went back to loading up the rail cars, as teams of landser roamed the perimeter with *panzerfäuste*.[518] An air raid from a flight of IL-2's did no damage as the trains' flak cars discouraged them from pressing home their attacks. Friesen says of this attack: The Russian Air Force was by no means as tenacious as the Red Army. A crusty old *SS–Hauptscharführer* (master sergeant) remarked "if those had been American planes, we would all be dead."[519] The German disdain for the Red Air Force was palpable, a common joke being that during a Soviet air raid the safest place to be was on the target, but in reality the Germans suffered terribly under Soviet air attacks.

The Russians kept trying to infiltrate the railhead even as the Germans loaded their tanks; some of the tanks already loaded were firing while on the cars, rocking them back and forth and threatening to topple them. It was only after the arrival of the 10 *Panthers* of the *4. Kompanie* that the position was finally secured

---

[518] Friesen does not identify what unit the German infantry was from; they could have been support troops from Das *Reich*, *panzer* crews without a *panzer*, or from one of the many broken German formations roaming the area who would have been more than happy to latch onto a *Waffen–SS* unit.

[519] Friesen, *Breakout*, p. 24.

enough for the already loaded *panzers* to leave. As for the *4. Kompanie*, eight days later most of its personnel rejoined the division at Esterhazy, without any of the 10 *Panthers*, all of which had been destroyed in action in the meantime. One of the men among the survivors was the legendary German tank ace *SS–Oberscharführer* Ernst Barkmann, commander of *4. Kompanie* in *Panther 401*. Barkmann still had plenty of fighting to do during the Battle of Vienna.

The 23rd Tank Corps' attempt to take Herend had failed. German experience and initiative had saved the day; the chance to trap *Heeresgruppe Süd* in a coup-de-main was gone. For the time being there were no follow-on forces capable of forcing their way through the thin German defenses. No one can say whether the individual Red Army riflemen knew the big picture he was fighting for, that if they had captured Herend it would have cut off virtually all of *Heeresgruppe Süd* still to the east and southeast, and left almost nothing with which the Germans could defend Austria. But the Germans were not safe yet; it would be days before the last of them withdrew through the narrow gap between Veszprem and Balatonfuzfo at the northeastern tip of the lake, a strip no more than 7 miles wide, with more Russians were pouring down from the northeast. All of *Heeresgruppe Süd* east of that point would have to funnel through that bottleneck before the Russians were strong enough to close the gap or the result would be total destruction. Indeed, the battlefield was so crowded that the Russians would be unable to fully deploy their own forces because of the narrowness of the front, leaving substantial forces out of the battle until the Germans had been pushed west of Lake Balaton.

If Sepp Dietrich felt déjà vu at the developing disaster, it is no wonder. The situation was a replay of the Battle of the Falaise Gap the previous summer in France, when another German Army was almost surrounded and destroyed. Dietrich had commanded *I. SS–Panzerkorps* at the time, and if the price the

Germans paid in Hungary was not quite as high as that paid in France, it was still ruinous.[520]

While fighting near Pakozd on the northern shore of Lake Velence, the commander of *I./SS–Panzergrenadier Regiment 23 Norge, SS–Sturmbannführer* Barth, was killed and replaced by *SS–Obersturmführer* Radtke, the battalion's third commanding officer in three weeks. Radtke would command what was left of the battalion for the duration of the war.

From his castle near Baden, *SS–Obergruppenführer* Jeno Ruszkay issued the proclamation that Hungarian soldiers serving in the *Waffen–SS* were not required to join the Nazi Party. Behind the front such proclamations may have seemed important; at the front they could not have been more irrelevant.

Scattered throughout the Protectorate of Bohemia and Moravia were schools for training *Waffen–SS* men in the various skills and duties necessary for service in a combat unit. South of Prague at Beneschau, the commandant of the *SS–Panzergrenadier/Junkerschule Beneschau 'Böhmen,'* *SS–Oberführer* Wilhelm Trabant, was ordered to speed up the formation of three regimental *kampfgruppen* of three battalions each, along with their associated

---

[520] One major difference was that, while the Red Air Force dominated the skies over Hungary, it was not nearly as deadly as the Allied ground-attack aircraft were in France.

specialist troops, such as engineers and artillery.[521] Individually, history would commonly refer to these formations as *Kampfgruppen Trabant I, Trabant II* and *Trabant III*; collectively they would be called *SS–Kampfgruppe Division Böhmen and Mähren*.[522] The *Kampfgruppe Division* would reach the size of a 1945 division, somewhere between 8,000 and 10,000 men, and while each regimental-sized component would have an artillery and engineer battalion attached, the larger unit would not have some of the components of a true division, such as a Signals Battalion or a Reconnaissance Battalion;[523] thus its designation as *SS–Kampfgruppe Division*. Nor was it counted among the 38 'true' *Waffen–SS* divisions, despite being larger in numbers than some of the very late war divisions that are listed among those 38 'real' ones.

If such a composite unit was to have any chance in battle it needed a proven commander. Wilhelm Trabandt was a veteran officer, having fought with the *LAH* during the Battle of France in 1940, then being assigned to the *1. SS–Infanterie Brigade (Mot.)*, which he commanded starting in October, 1943, and finally to command the *18. SS–Freiwilligen–Panzergrenadier Division Horst Wessel* when the brigade was upgraded to a full division in 1944. He was also a Knight's Cross winner, and is credited with having designed the *1. SS–Panzer Division Leibstandarte Adolf Hitler*'s divisional symbol of a picklock.[524]

---

[521] As part of the *Kampfgruppe Division* there was a 'Northern Force' and a 'Southern Force.' The 'Northern Force' remained in the area of Prague in the zone of *Heeresgruppe Mitte* and therefore falls outside the scope of this book.

[522] The three regimental-sized kampfgruppen were also known by their commander's name instead of Trabant's, making them SS Regiment Schulze, SS Regiment Siegmann and SS Regiment Konopacki.

[523] Richard Landwehr states that the division had a bicycle reconnaissance battalion as well as a signals battalion, and that both remained in Prague (Siegrunen #38, p. 18).

[524] This clever symbol had two meanings. First, the 1st SS division was the key, or picklock, that opened all doors during a battle, but second, the division's commander at the time was Sepp Dietrich, and Dietrich is German for picklock.

The Trabant *Kampfgruppen* were drawn from the various *Waffen–SS* training schools scattered around the *Reich*s Protectorate for Bohemia and Moravia. The enormous *SS–Panzergrenadier/Junkerschule Beneschau 'Böhmen,'* (SS-Troop Training Area Böhmen-Mähren) in the *Reich* Protectorate included the *SS-Panzergrenadier Schule Kienschlag, SS-Artillerie Schule II Beneschau, SS-Pioneer Schule Hradischko, SS-Panzerjäger Schule Janowitz, SS–Junkerschule Prag,* and a number of other establishments.[525] The artillery component seems to have consisted of two field artillery batteries, and two truck-mounted *nebelwerfers* of unknown size; the artillery commander was the veteran *SS–Obersturmbannführer* Dr. Arthur Curtius. [526] From January, 1945 through March, 1945, Curtius had been the commander of *SS–Schwere–Artillerie Abteilung 503,* attached to *III Germanisches SS–Panzerkorps*, before being ordered to form his new unit as part of *Böhmen und Mähren*.[527] The artillery *kampfgruppe* was fleshed out by both instructors and students from the *SS–Artillerie Schule II Beneschau*. In addition to men from the various *SS* schools and formations, there were also men from the Slovak Army and the Slovak Hlinka Guard Militia.

The three *SS–Regiments* were unofficially known by the name of their commanders: *Panzergrenadier Regiment Schulze* (*SS–Kampfgruppe Trabandt I*) and *Panzergrenadier Regiment Konopacki* (*SS–Kampfgruppe Trabandt II*), which together formed and were referred to by Army staff officers as *SS–Kampfgruppe Böhmen*, and *Panzergrenadier-Regiment Siegmann* (or *SS–*

---

[525] Richard Landwehr states that part of SS Grenadier and Training Replacement Battalion 10 from Brno was incorporated into Kampfgruppe Konopacki (Siegrunen #38, p. 17).

[526] Jordan, Franz, *April, 1945. Die Kampfe in nordostlichen Niederossterreich,* (Salzburg: Österr. Miliz-Verlag, 2003).

[527] III SS Panzer Corps was evacuated from the Courland Pocket only in late January, 1945, when it was attached to Felix Steiner's 11th SS Panzer Army on the Oder Front and participated in Operation Solstice; however, both Curtius and his battalion wound up in Austria, as the 503rd was added to SS Artillery Detachment Curtius in late April.

Kampfgruppe Trabandt III), referred to by Army staff officers as *SS–Kampfgruppe Mähren*; each Regiment had elements of the *SS* Artillery Battalion and *SS* Pioneer Battalion attached. A number of replacement and training schools also contributed personnel. In addition, the survivors of *Panzerjäger Ausbildungs und Ersatz Abteilung 1*, aka *Kampfgruppe Kiss*, were also added[528].

Since this division-sized *kampfgruppe* was known as *Böhmen und Mähren*, great confusion reigns over exactly which units this pertains to; it is often confused as being part of, attached to or in some fashion related to *31. Waffen–Grenadier Division der SS.*[529] However, there is no relation between the two units. 31st *SS* Division had the distinction of being the only *Waffen–SS* division without either an honorific title or an ethnic designation, and has sometimes been mislabeled with the honorific >Bohemia and Moravia=, which it was never given. 31st *Waffen–SS* Grenadier Division did not include the aforementioned units[530].

The new recruits and students at the various schools were almost all quite young, some no older than 15 or 16, and while all youth in the Third *Reich* had had some type of preliminary military training, there was no substitute for the maturity that came only with age and combat experience. Many of those young teenagers were issued ill-fitting tunics and helmets that slid around on their heads because they were too large.

The instructors, on the other hand, were mostly combat veterans, often disqualified from front-line

[528] Richard Landwehr states two that additional regimental-sized kampfgruppen, confusingly named Böhmen and Mähren, under the command of *SS–Brigadeführer* Pückler-Burghaus, were formed in April, 1945.

[529] To this day there is no agreement over the exact order of battle for this unit. Some sources cite up to 5 regiments, some have multiple regiments titled 'Böhmen' and 'Mähren'…the one used here accepts that the first two regiments, Trabandt I and II, were collectively known as 'Böhmen', while the third regiment, Trabandt III, was also known as 'Mähren.'

[530] For a definitive discussion of this still-debated point, the curious reader is referred to Rudolf Pencz's exhaustive study of 31st *Waffen–SS* Volunteer Grenadier Division, *For the Homeland.*

service because of wounds. Forming these mismatched elements into the various squads, companies, battalions and regiments that made up a division-sized unit would have been difficult enough under ordinary circumstances, but making them combat-ready in a matter of days before they were thrown into action against seasoned Russian troops was impossible. Almost as soon as the organizational tables were finalized and the personnel assignments finished, the various elements were committed to battle, usually assigned to existing Army commands, with the result that the unit never fought as a unified entity. There were simply too many holes in the defense; regardless of quality, the Germans needed bodies to throw in the path of the hard-charging Red Army.

21 March, Wednesday

The Hungarian 20th Assault Gun Battalion was withdrawn from the front line after two weeks of heavy fighting on the southern shores of Lake Balaton. It had 13 Hetzers left. Like the rest of *6. SS–Panzerarmee*, the race was on to pass the northeast corner of Lake Balaton before the Russians got there and cut them off. Whatever their morale status might have been during the previous fortnight, escaping capture by the Russians was all the motivation they needed to fight for their lives.

Elsewhere, Joszef Grassy was appointed commander of *26. SS–Grenadier Division Hungaria*.

Kampfgruppe Schell was still in the area near Sur but could do nothing to prevent the Russians from taking both that town and Bakonycsernye, forcing the German/Hungarians further backward. The area was hilly and there were no highways leading west, giving the defenders a slim advantage that was desperately needed against the superior forces of the Red Army.

Meanwhile, the situation in Stuhlweissenburg was desperate. With the Red Army pressing in from the east, south, north and northwest, the city was virtually surrounded with only one road southwest still open, and that one under heavy pressure. *5. SS Panzer Division Wiking* had been out of radio contact until around midday on 21 March, and once contact had been re-established *SS–Standartenführer* Karl Ullrich was given the *Führerbefehl* that every German commander had come to dread: "hold Stuhlweissenburg at all costs."[531] This was tantamount to a death sentence for both *Wiking* and the other units holding the city, such as *1. Panzer Division*, and Ullrich

---

[531] Strassner, p. 325.

elected not to commit mass suicide but to break out
instead. Most of the trek would have to be on foot,
since there was no fuel for the vehicles. This meant
losing not only the *panzers* but the artillery that could
not be drawn by horses, since the prime movers did not
have fuel, either. Nevertheless, Ulrich was not going to
sacrifice his men for no purpose, Hitler order or not;
even the *Waffen–SS* was beginning to ignore the
unrealistic orders coming from Berlin.

But it might already have been too late, as the
Red Army continued forcing their way to the west.
North of Stuhlweissenburg, the Russian 180th Rifle
Division[532] captured Felshyogalla, a section of
Tatabanya, after fierce fighting. Four days later in
Moscow, the division was awarded a 20 salvo salute
from more than 200 guns in recognition of its
accomplishments.

With the rest of *IV. SS–Panzerkorps* still fighting
near Stuhlweissenburg, on 21 March the *3. SS–Panzer
Division Totenkopf* was attached to *I. SS–Panzerkorps*.
In five days of fighting *Totenkopf* had gone from being
over-strength in infantry with a reasonably strong
armored battalion and adequate artillery, to a shattered
kampfgruppe with groups of men scattered over a wide
swath of Western Hungary. Most of the heavy weapons
were lost in the headlong retreat to the area of Csatka,
about 27 kilometers north of Veszprem; *panzers* were
abandoned due to lack of fuel, men lost radio contact
and straggled westward...in short, *Totenkopf* was in
danger of disintegrating. It was hoped that fleeing units
could rally at the so-called *Klara* Defense Line near
Zirc, about 16 kilometers north of Veszprem, but amid
the chaos the Russians arrived at the position before it
could be manned. Small *kampfgruppe* coalesced
around leaders and tried to fight back, but without a

---

[532] The division was part of 75th Rifle Corps of *46. Armee.*

cohesive front they were continually threatened with attacks from the flanks and rear; there was nothing for it but to continue retreating westward toward Papa, shedding blood with every kilometer, looking for a place to regroup.

22 March, Thursday

Kampfgruppe Schell, including *SS-Brigade Ney,* was ordered to fall back even further westward to the so-called *'Klara'* positions, between the small towns of Lokut and Veszpremvarsany. This was a huge area with a distance of more than 25 kilometers that, to be properly defended, would require far more forces than were available. Worse, there were no solid front lines on either side and the Russians were coming on strong.

Amid the general collapse of the front line, the mangled remnants of *SS–Ungarische–Sturm Regiment 1,* probably now fewer than 500 men in number, finally began to withdraw west after holding their positions near Stuhlweissenburg since early February. Shortages of food, fuel and supplies of all kind had become critically low, making holding on longer impossible and forcing a retreat, notwithstanding the general flood of the Red Army advance. Hitler had ordered the city held to the last man, but *5. SS–Panzer Division Wiking Divisions* commander, Karl Ullrich, had ignored the order and decided to save what could be saved, and that included the Hungarians.

Wiking concentrated in the area of Urhida, less than three miles southwest of Stuhlweissenburg and about 20 miles east of Veszprem. The small village was ancient, its first habitation being traced to at least 896 AD, and had seen many wars. The area had been shaped by the marshy nature of the land, with firms roads through the soft ground being crucial; one of the nearby roads dated back to Roman times. As the sun rose the Germans began moving west in two *kampfgruppen.* The first, built around *SS–Panzergrenadier Regiment 10 Westland,* moved slightly north to the area of Nadasdalany to act as a blocking force against the Soviet attacks that began almost immediately. The other *kampfgruppe*, essentially the rest of the division including all *panzers*, *SPWs*, *sturmgeschütze* and *artillerie*, led the charge to the west; before the division made it to safety, every one of those vehicles would be lost.

The situation was beyond chaotic as the front collapsed all around the fleeing Germans. Soviets attacks were coming in from every direction except west, with the front south of *Wiking's* march route in danger of collapse. Veszprem was already in Russian hands, but there was one very narrow corridor still open between that city and Lake Balaton's northeastern tip, about 10 kilometers. If anything was to be saved, somebody had to make a stand somewhere, and be willing to sacrifice themselves for the sake of their comrades.

The *SS* formations kept their discipline even amidst the chaos, which is probably what saved any of them. *9. SS–Panzer Division Hohenstauffen's* commander, *SS–Oberführer* Sylvester Stadler, disobeyed orders and not only stayed in position, but extended his division's front to keep the corridor open, defending the line Berhida-Ösi-Varpolata at enormous cost. This line ran north-south, west of Stuhlweissenburg on the direct line to the small town of Balatonfűzfő. Located at the northeast corner of Lake Balaton, the town had suddenly became the most critical place in Western Hungary, as any German or German-allied Hungarian still to the south after the Russians arrived, would be cut off and lost. The distance from Berhida at the southern end of *Hohenstaufen's* position, to the crucial town of Balatonfűzfő, was only 12 kilometers. Through that narrow gap had to pass all of *6. SS–Panzerarmee* not already north of Lake Balaton, along with the remnants of German forces in Stuhlweissenburg.

Only three days earlier *Hohenstaufen* had been detached from *II. SS–Panzerkorps* and attached to *IV. SS–Panzerkorps*, but in the maelstrom of ferocious fighting swirling through Western Hungary that situation was no longer feasible and it was re-assigned to *I Kavallerie Korps*. Enduring a tempest of artillery fire and air attacks, the strung out men of *Hohenstaufen* endured horrific punishment to save their *SS* comrades. Whether or not those men had committed war crimes as part of the division, or were new conscripts having no other choice than to serve or be shot, the stand they made on 22 March against vastly superior forces was remarkable. Largely forgotten now, their refusal to allow the Red Army to force them backward saved thousands of German lives. Early in the afternoon *Wiking's* leading elements met up with the headquarters of *Hohenstaufen* in the village of Papkezi, just short of the northeastern tip of Lake Balaton. By 1800 hours the whole division was there.

23 March, Friday

North of the Danube *8. Armee* had not yet been attacked from east of the Gran, but that day was coming. Nor had *2. Panzerarmee* seen much in the way of assaults... yet. Once the Russians reached the western end of Lake Balaton, however, *2. Panzerarmee* would be outflanked and its position would become untenable. Given that its primary mission was to protect the oil fields at Nagikanizsa, the army could neither stay in place nor retreat. The time for such a decision was fast approaching.

One week after the Russians launched the Vienna Offensive the dispositions of *Heeresgruppe Süd* were a jumble of intertwined units, fragments of units and hastily thrown together *kampfgruppen*. On a map the German positions seemed to have formed a defensive line but this was an illusion; *Heeresgruppe Süd* was in desperate straits by 23 March. There was no cohesive front between Lake Balaton and the Danube, with defense centered as much as possible around critical landmarks such as road junctions. North of Vezsprem the front had collapsed and the only defenses were isolated units and kampfgruppen moving toward Austria, often surrounded and out of contact with their higher headquarters. Into this void plunged fast-moving Soviet columns trying to beat them to the border of the *Reich*. Confusion reigned among the Germans.

The Germans found themselves trying to hold a long, narrow corridor of escape that stretched from Stuhlweissenburg past Veszprem in the direction of Tapolca, with the Red Army attacking all along the perimeter as German units withdrew past their comrades who were manning the bulwarks. At the eastern end the *44. Reichs Grenadier Division Hoch und*

Deutschmeister was still holding out in Stuhlweissenburg as a rear guard,[533] but in desperate fighting the division lost both its' commander, *Generalleutnant* Hans-Günther von Rost, and its *Ia* or Operations Officer. Rost was an experienced general with a long and distinguished career, as the rank of *Generalleutnant* indicates, and his loss was dearly felt.

Near Lake Balaton the units of *6. Armee* and *6. SS–Panzerarmee* had become jumbled together as the Germans tried to simultaneously form a defensive stance while retreating west. They were squeezed into a narrow strip on the lake's northern shore, with only two significant roads leading west, one following the shoreline and another from Veszprem heading southwest through Tapolca. *5. SS–Panzer Division Wiking* was once again detached from *III. Panzerkorps* and reassigned to *IV. SS–Panzerkorps* . The division was still trying to reorganize behind the lines of *9. SS–Panzer Division Hohenstaufen* after its narrow escape from Stuhlweissenburg the day before, but the chaos of the situation demanded they go back into the line. "The division was in position on both sides of the Vesprem-Tapolca road and had collected itself somewhat once again. Contact was established to the right. However, there were apparently no German forces to the left."[534] Southwest of Stuhlweissenburg, Tapolca was known for the recently discovered Cave Lake below its town square; in 1942 it had been declared a protected area by the Horthy Government. The Germans would have no time for sight-seeing, though; in essence, *Wiking*, *Hohenstaufen* and the other German units were surrounded, including *44. Reichs-Grenadier Division Hoch und Deutschmeister*, which endured heavy attacks near Jeno and was shattered, being reduced to *kampfgruppe* strength.[535] Jeno was a few miles

---

[533] One source puts the 44th *Reich*'s Grenadier Division west of Veszprem on the 23rd.

[534] Strassner, p. 326.

[535] Mitcham, Samuel W., *The German Order of Battle, 1st-290th Infantry Divisions* (Mechanicsburg: Stackpole, 2007), p. 88.

southwest of Stuhlweissenburg and the division was caught as it tried to withdraw to the west where seesaw fighting raged in Balatonfüzfö, at the northeast tip of Lake Balaton, with both sides knowing that if it was taken by the Russians the whole German position would be shattered; at the end of the day the smoking ruins were still in German hands. With Soviet forces driving hard to the west, though, the race was on for the Germans to withdraw before the Red Army could push south to Lake Balaton and cut them off completely.

24 March, Saturday

On 24 March anxious Germans who were worried about the Russian advance from the east heard on the Armed Forces radio broadcast that "north of the *Plattensee* [Lake Balaton], the Bolshevists' forward attack groups had been brought to a standstill on both sides of Veszprem and north of Zirez after heavy enemy losses."[536] What was not revealed was that the German withdrawal to Austria was more of a race than a battle, with the Russians constantly threatening to surround units that moved too slow, and often succeeding, leaving the trapped Germans no choice but to try and cut their way out of the trap; but with fuel, ammunition and supplies of every type in short supply, endangered units were often forced to leave behind anything that could not be towed or driven away, with orders that such abandoned equipment should be destroyed so that the Russians did not inherit a windfall to use against its former owners, orders that were not always followed. Only units sacrificing themselves to make a stand against enormous odds prevented the Russian tide from completely overwhelming the fleeing Germans.

Most of *Heeresgruppe Süd's* heavy weapons, supply depots, parts depots, and repair facilities were overrun and lost. The only things saved were easily portable items, or those near a convenient mode of transport not already in use. Otto Wöhler had no real control over the battle anymore, and could only try and salvage anything possible. Sepp Dietrich and Hermann Balck did everything possible to save their commands, but even now Balck's hatred of the *Waffen–SS* colored his actions. With a week there would be a huge hole ripped in *6. Armee's* front that he would blame on the *Waffen–SS* units not retreating where he instructed them to retreat, despite those areas already being occupied by the Red Army. He would claim they

---

[536] Heimer & Glantz, p. 1117.

disobeyed, and that only his (Balck's) actions closed the gap; neither was true.

In Berlin, the *Führer's* evening military conference for 23 March actually began after 0200 on Saturday, 24 March; discussions about fighting and positions referred to events that took place the previous day. After discussing such topics as Goebbels' request to cut down the lampposts on the East-West Axis to turn that roadway into an emergency landing strip, and whether or not some trees in the Tiergarten might also need to be felled, Hitler made an off-hand statement that led to the temporary disarming of the *14. Waffen–Grenadier Division der SS (Galizien 1)*.

The official transcript for the Evening Situation Report for 23-24 quotes Hitler as saying: "Now I hear for the first time, to my surprise, that a Ukrainian *SS* division has suddenly appeared." Were they reliable? How were they armed? It was sheer insanity, he said, to give weapons to a Ukrainian division that was not quite trustworthy, although he assumed that since they were an *SS* division they were well armed. "...I'd rather take the weapons away from them and draw up a German division."[537]

This is a strange comment. *14. Waffen–Grenadier Division der SS (Galizien 1)*.was not one of the best *SS* divisions but it had given good service so far and Hitler must have been aware of its existence. For a few crucial days in the summer of 1944 the division had stood its ground at Brody against overwhelming odds and allowed *XIII Armeekorps* to escape complete destruction near Lviv. Aside from its fairly lengthy combat history, therefore, being at ground zero for 1st Ukrainian Front's assault on Lviv where it was steam-rolled at Brody would forever remain the division's greatest contribution. Given how thoroughly Hitler was briefed

---

[537] Heimer & Glantz, p. 711. Later in the meeting an inventory of the division's weapons on hand listed 610 machine pistols and 9,000 rifles among the armaments, which clearly indicates that not every man in the unit had a weapon at this point. Likewise, it only listed four *SPWs* on hand. These were the numbers reported to higher command; the actual numbers may well have been larger.

daily it is almost beyond belief that he did not know a Ukrainian Division was fighting in the Waffen–SS, although he did admit that: "maybe it was reported to me a long, long time ago. I don't know."[538]

Regardless of why he made the comment, though, Hitler missed the point that there were not a lot of surplus Germans standing around waiting for weapons. And, for those formations that did need weapons, the issue of transport was always a problem. Whether weapons were available or not was secondary to whether they could be transported to the men who needed them. However, his comment led to *Galizien* being ordered to turn in its weapons, an order which was quickly countermanded.

Exactly why Hitler said this is unknown. Beside the fact that raising and arming a Ukrainian *SS* division would have required his approval, during the Battle of Brody Hitler would have discussed their situation repeatedly and known exactly who and what the *14. Waffen–Grenadier Division der SS (Galizien 1)* was. Who was the commander, what was its strength? He asked these questions frequently of many formations. After Brody, when *Galizien* lost anywhere from half to 90 percent of its strength, new recruits and various other Ukrainian formations were absorbed by the division to bring it back up to strength. Among these were an amalgam of police and even *Einsatzgruppen* personnel. The division had also seen extensive combat during the Slovak uprising the previous fall and had fought partisans in a number of places; if it is assumed that Hitler was not pretending to be unaware of the prior existence of the Ukrainian division, and it's hard to understand why he would have done that, the only possible explanation is the division's honorific name change, from *Galizien* to *Ukrainische*, yet according to most sources this had not happened yet, although perhaps it was those very discussions that prompted Hitler's outburst.

[538] Ibid.

Given the political implications of that change it would seem to have required Hitler's approval; regardless, it seems this exchange is what prompted the incident. Hitler himself even asks if the Ukrainian division is the same as the Galician division, but seems strangely ignorant of its personnel makeup. *SS–Sturmbannführer* Göhler, who tried to explain to him what the division was, actually confused the *14. Waffen–Grenadier Division der SS (Galizien 1)* with another unit he calls the *30. SS*, but then correctly identified it as having been encircled with *XIII* Corps the previous summer. The division's authorized strength is given as 11,000, but actual strength as 14,000. Other sources, however, project it as high as 22,000. Given that *OKW* couldn't even get the name right, then perhaps it is no surprise that Hitler was also confused. This does show the haphazard atmosphere now prevailing around Germany's supreme commander.

As the Red Army offensive gained momentum around Lake Balaton, German formations of all service branches and sizes found themselves either looking for a place to make a stand, or looking for a road to anywhere safe. The remnants of *SS–Ungarische Sturm Regiment 1*, now little more than an average strength battalion, split up into two *kampfgruppen*. *SS–Sturmbannführer* Rideph led three companies in one *kampfgruppe*, which was immediately attached to an unnamed Hungarian mountain brigade. The other group was commanded by *SS–Hauptsturmführer der Reserve* Dr. Lenk, also three companies. Lenk's group was attached to *1. Volksgebirgs Division of XXII Gebirgskorps*. Extrapolating numbers from this is difficult, but there were likely 300-400 means total in the two *kampfgruppen*.

In the same area was *16. SS–Panzergrenadier Division Reichsführer SS*. The previous September it had a ration strength of 14,683, and likely combat strength of around 9,000 men. By 24 March, 1945, it listed 9,389 men in total, with only 3,134 in condition to fight. The non-stop attacks of the previous fortnight had rendered it unable to attack, and weak in defense.

The Soviet offensive was making rapid gains everywhere as the German defense collapsed and the Germans were constantly faced with the threat of being outflanked. A few miles northwest of Veszprem, near the small town of Markö, there was a gap in the defense and nothing to plug it with; north of that gap was yet another hole in the front, but for the moment the defense was holding at the so-called *Klara* positions between Veszpremvarsany and Lokut, where *Kampfgruppe Schell* had been in position since the previous day. On 23 March they had held their ground but *Kampfgruppe Schell* and the other units trying to hold north of Lokut were simply too weak and too spread out to offer an effective defense. The Red Army broke through in numerous places and there was little the Hungarians and Germans could do except flee west and offer resistance whenever they could, always at the risk of being surrounded. "That afternoon the towns of Porva, Borzavar and Fenyoto all fell to the enemy."[539] Those three towns were north of Lokut and just east of the massive Bakony Woods forest, with no major roads leading west, but no significant German formations to put up a defense, either. By driving cross-country due west the Russians would threaten to split *Heeresgruppe Süd* in two; between Veszprem and Komarom there was no contiguous German defense line. The German situation was dire.

5. SS Panzer Division Wiking had formed a patchwork defensive line near Vesprem to incorporate more new replacements; the line would not hold for long. The replacements were virtually worthless, being

---

[539] Pencz, *Siegrunen Volume 76*, p. 21.

either young children who had been assigned to flak
units, or men of 50-60 who were deployed in cities after
air raids. None of them had combat training and the
only thing *Wiking* could do was assign them to the
supply service, thus freeing up able-bodied men to fight
as infantry.[540] This helped a little, but not much, and
the makeshift defenses were soon crushed.

Driving west from Veszprem, around 1600 hours
the Russians slammed into *Wiking's* defenses on the
Vesprem-Tapolca road in overwhelming strength. With
heavy fighting at the key town of Balatonfüzfö, and
with the Germans trying to hang onto an attachment to
Lake Balaton, the Russians drove southwest from
Vesprem in an attempt to outflank them on the west,
and *Wiking* stood in their way. The division had few
heavy weapons left and could not hold for long. It was
not that they could not hold their lines; there were no
lines left to hold. Even after an infusion of men from
the supply services *Wiking* was too weak to maintain a
contiguous defense. The infantry broke up into knots of
resistance centered on the few remaining *SPWs*, and
even the division commander's *SPW* became involved in
the fighting.

The 12 kilometer-wide corridor previously held by
9. SS–Panzer Division Hohenstaufen had now shrunk to
a handful of kilometers. The entire escape route was
under Russian artillery fire, and endured constant air
attacks. It was Falaise Gap all over again.

As the Russians fought their way west the
German units still east and south of Veszprem
desperately tried to escape through this ever-narrowing
corridor on the north side of Lake Balaton still held by
*Heeresgruppe Süd. I Kavallerie Korps, 3. Panzer
Division* and *9. SS–Panzer Division Hohenstaufen* stood
their ground against heavy attacks, but as *Wiking's*
defense of the Veszprem-Tapolca Road illustrates,
fighting as unified divisions was almost impossible in
the chaos of retreat; knots of soldiers coalesced around

---

[540] Michaelis, *Panzer Divisions of the Waffen–SS*, p. 202.

and defended strongpoints wherever they could be found be they a burned out *panzer*, a ruined farmhouse or even a big rock. For many if not most of the fleeing divisions, unit cohesion should have been lost, but was not; somehow, instead of disintegrating under the extreme Russian pressure, the German units stayed intact enough to continue functioning. But the price was enormous.

Despite the disorganization, however, Hitler insisted that a general withdrawal was out of the question. "The connection to the lake must not be lost under any circumstances. If it's lost, it's all over."[541]. Nevertheless, the true condition of *Heeresgruppe Süd*, and especially his faithful *SS* namesake, was painfully obvious. As had happened so many times in the past, however, the Leibstandarte had been bled white in battle and was to be rebuilt at all costs. Hitler made this quite clear. "I demand one thing now: that the last man, wherever he may be hidden, be sent immediately to the Leibstandarte, to the entire Sixth [SS] *Panzer* Army... The last man that 6th [SS] *Panzer* [Army] has must be sent in."[542] (Heimer & Glantz, p. 700-701).

In all likelihood this was the genesis of the Cuff Band Order. Hitler railed that every last man should be sent to *6. SS–Panzerarmee* and was told that Himmler had already sent Sepp Dietrich a telegram to the effect that troop strength must not be allowed to 'decrease', prompting Hitler to reiterate that "the last man that Sixth [SS] *Panzer* [Army] must be sent in" Apparently there were already suspicions that Dietrich had a secret cache of replacements, that he had not yet committed to battle. And once suspicion crept into Hitler's mind, however unfounded it might have been, it festered and grew like a fungus. Nor would Otto Wöhler

---

[541] Hitler probably meant that without Lake Balaton being a major barrier on its flank both *6. Armee* and *6. SS Panzerarmee* would be unable to protect the Nagykanisza oilfield on the north, which would inevitably lead to its capture by the Russians. Saving the oilfield had been the stated reason for launching *Unternehmen Frühlingserwachen*.

[542] Heimer & Glantz, p. 701.

or especially Hermann Balck and his *Chef der Stabs* have done anything to quell the *Führer's* paranoia.

     XXXXIII Armeekorps was assigned to protect the oil refineries on the Danube, east of Komárom (Komarom), and to take command of all German forces in the Gran Bridgehead. *Kampfgruppe Ameiser* was still attached to *96. Infanterie Division* and consequently tasked with holding off the Red Army while the Corps' heavy weapons were evacuated to the north bank of the Danube. Despite constant attacks they fought off at least six separate assaults on 24 March and allowed the weapons to be safely ferried across the river. To the Corps' north, however, the Soviets crossed the Gran River and threatened to encircle them. With no other recourse, the Gran bridgehead was ordered given up.

     A curious incident during this period was the fate of 2,800 *Kriegsmarine* men who were drafted into the *Waffen–SS* and sent to Hungary as replacements for *12. SS–Panzer Division Hitlerjugend*. Sources differ as to exactly when, where and how they came to be absorbed by *2. SS–Panzer Division Das Reich* instead of *Hitlerjugend*, but the basic facts are not in dispute.

     The former *Kriegsmarine* men arrived on a train at Raab, (Győr in Hungarian), where officers from *Das Reich* promptly pulled them off the train and announced they were now members of the premier division in the *Waffen–SS*. Untrained or not, a regimental-sized group of fit young men was an infusion of manpower the division sorely needed. They would soon be in desperate combat.

Map 10

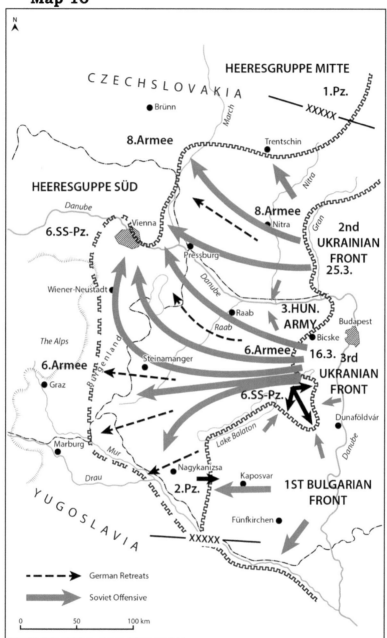

Once the Russian Vienna Offensive began rolling, the Germans had nothing to stop it. By 1 April they were over the Austrian border.

619

25 March, Sunday

Palm Sunday brought no respite from killing Hitler's *Reich*. Not just *Heeresgruppe Süd* was reeling backward, but the *Wehrmacht* was retreating on all fronts. As units became fragmented and scattered, the overall low quality of officers and non-coms compounded the problem as men of lower rank were promoted from necessity, not merit. Losses could not be made good and the organization of the German war machine began to disintegrate. In response, the High Command issued a desperate order for all *panzer* divisions to immediately re-organize according to the table of organization for a Type 1945 *panzer* division, an order titled *Grundgliederung der Panzer-Division 45*. Although this order had little practical effect, the authorized strength of a *panzer* division was officially down-graded to a level that left them too weak to affect the outcome of a battle on anything more than a local scale. The *panzer* regiment was reduced to one battalion of four companies, with a second battalion of *panzergrenadiers* replacing the second *panzer* regiment, allowing only 40 *panzers* and 22 *Jagdpanzers* in the one *panzer* battalion.[543].

Strength was authorized as 11,422 for all ranks. Instead of two infantry regiments that had one truck-mounted and one mounted in *SPWs*, both would be in trucks.

Those units that could not re-organize for one reason or another according to the new 1945 divisional tables were ordered to re-organize as set forth in the guidelines for '*Kampfgruppe Panzer Division 1945*', an even smaller formation than the new division, with only one infantry regiment mounted in trucks. The total strength of a *Kampfgruppe Panzer Division 1945* was set at 8,602 men of all ranks but with the same vehicle allotment as a *Panzer* Division, the savings in

---

[543] Any units that actually had 60 combat-ready panzers or jagdpanzers would have been the premier unit in its theater.

personnel coming from having only one *Panzergrenadier* regiment instead of two. In both cases the object would have been to free up forces for other units and spread the dwindling armor resources over a broader area, watering down their fighting ability and thus sapping armored units of their very reason for being, namely, concentrating a lot of firepower in a small area in a highly mobile unit. There was also the issue of the shortage of quality officers of all ranks, and the consequent shrinking of units to a more manageable size to match the more limited capabilities of many officers. All units were ordered to have this completed by 1 May.

Of course, with men, trucks, rail transport, *SPWs*, *panzers* and fuel in chronically short supply, this was more an exercise among staff officers than a meaningful directive. As an historical footnote, however, it is interesting to see the complete realignment of pre-war thinking by the adversaries, as the Allies and Soviets adopted the German principle of concentration of masses of armor, and the Germans spread their armor to support infantry forces.

Panzer units in *Heeresgruppe Süd* would have no chance of even beginning this process, as by 25 March most were constantly either moving or fighting, although both *Feldherrnhalle* divisions were rebuilt along the lines of a 1945 division.

The lesson for the reader is cautionary; there is a temptation when seeing the name of some famous armored division such as *6. Panzer Division* for the mind to instantly form an image of swarms of tanks and APCs pouring over some flatland in a show of power. When the eye sees the name *1. SS–Panzer Division Leibstandarte Adolf Hitler*, the mind may see a huge and powerful fighting force with lots of *Mark V Panthers* and hard-bitten *panzergrenadier* veterans, it makes no allowance for losses or replacements, as if

Jagdtiger

Jagdpanzer VI Ausf. B (SdKfz. 186)

Jagdtiger

At some point during the fighting in Hungary or after, *653. Schwere—Panzerjäger Abteilung* entered the fighting with the fearsome *Jagdtiger*. Slow, mechanically unreliable due to the strain its great weight put on the engine, the *Jagdtiger* nevertheless mounted a massive 128mm Pak 44 L/55 gun, which fire the equivalent round to the main battery of a naval destroyer. No enemy tank, Allied or Russian, could withstand being hit by such a weapon. At it's thickest the armor was 250mm, making the *Jagdtiger* virtually impervious to other tanks..

such a unit remained unchanged by combat, constant in strength and fighting power. But moreso than most organizations, military units are organic structures existing in extreme conditions. It is, therefore, recommended to the reader that he or she constantly keep in mind that military units, armored divisions in particular, varied greatly in strength from month to month, or even week to week. This narrative has made clear that while a *Waffen–SS panzer* division might be authorized to have 180 *panzers* and *Jagdpanzers*, for example, on any given day it might have only 10 such vehicles ready to fight, or it might have 100. At about this time, *5. SS Panzer Division Wiking* had less than 10 *panzers* in service; the previous year it had had more than 150. The name on the map could remain unchanged but the power it represented might vary wildly.

By the middle of March the Austrian resistance group *0-5* was convinced that Hitler was going to fight for Vienna, which would mean declaring it a fortress. That, in turn, would lead to the city's destruction. As fighting raged in Hungary and the splintered units of *Heeresgruppe Süd* danced and weaved to avoid being surrounded, *Major* Carl Szokoll informed a meeting of *0-5* that if Vienna were defended it would meet the same fate as Budapest, that it would be destroyed in the fighting, and that the only way to save it was to allow the Red Army to seize it without a fight. "If they accept our terms, we must offer to hand over the city to them," he said.[544]

Szokoll was assigned to *Wehrkreis XVII* headquarters and was tasked with building the defensive line around Vienna. In such a capacity he had quietly placed several battalions loyal to *0-5* in the Vienna Woods, south and west of the city.[545] At the right moment he could simply order those units withdrawn, he explained, in the area of Baden, 22 kilometers to the south. The Soviets could then march through the gap straight into the city. His plan was accepted with enthusiasm. Like so many others before and after them, the members of *0-5* seemed to believe the Soviets could be trusted.

Still training in the picturesque Seetaler Alps region near Judenberg, the *1. Ungarische SS–Ski Abteilung* was infused with 1,500 new men, leftovers from a Honved Mountain Brigade that was destroyed

---

[544] Toland, *the Last 100 Days*, p. 374.
[545] These were a collection of *Volkssturm* and miscellaneous personnel from various military and administrative services, none of whom had any great desire to die fighting the Russians.

near Raab (Gyor) The next day, 26 March, the new men were inducted into the *Waffen SS*, and were armed and clothed from *SS* depots at Dachau, although shortages left 300 of the men still wearing their Honved uniforms. Incredibly, even at this late point in the war the *SS* was able to arrange transport from the Munich area to eastern Austria, an indication not only of the power the *SS* still wielded inside the *Reich*, but also that areas free of Allied tactical air attacks could still efficiently move goods from one point to another.

Because of this influx the Ski Battalion fleshed out its II Battalion and formed a third, creating one of those strange units the Germans seemed to have a plethora of during the final months of the war, a Ski Battalion that was three battalions strong; it's third battalion would therefore be *III./1. Ungarische SS–Ski Abteilung*, which really put it at the size of a strong regiment. Ski training continued despite the crisis at the front.

South of the Danube *Kampfgruppe Schell*, still including *SS-Brigade Ney*, fought stubbornly to defend Papa, a key road junction of the highways leading north, south and west. Fifteen kilometers to the east was *3. SS–Panzer Division Totenkopf*, fighting on all sides and unable to help in the defense of the city. Despite their tenacity, however, the Hungarians were unable to prevent the city from falling to the Red Army, forcing the defenders to retreat once more, this time behind Raab. The loss of Papa meant that Raab itself was being outflanked to the south, thus putting the German position near the Danube in jeopardy and making holding onto Komarom, with its oil refineries and vital bridge over the Danube, very difficult. The Red Army was gobbling up what was left of Hungary in huge chunks, like a shark ripping meat off the carcass of a dead whale.

26 March, Monday

To understand how desperate the German situation was on that Monday of Easter Week, all of a sudden the *232. Reserve Panzer Division* had a crucial role to play in the salvation of *Heeresgruppe Süd*. No reliable ration strength total is available for this 'division,' but if it was larger than a weak regiment that would be surprising. It was stationed at the small town of Marcalto, southwest of Raab. Marcalto was on the eastern bank of the Raba, sandwiched between that river and the Marcel Canal, making it a good defensive position to protect the flank of *12. SS–Panzer Division Hitlerjugend*, which was defending the Raab area. Should the *232. Reserve Panzer Division* give way, *Hitlerjugend* would have no choice but to retreat or be outflanked. With no armor to speak of, and likely only a smattering of heavy weapons and artillery, the division was not the ideal choice for such a crucial defensive mission; such an *ad hoc* unit was not designed for active combat, but in the emergency situation then threatening to overwhelm *Heeresgruppe Süd* any cohesive unit was fair game for the front lines.

Ten days after launching their Vienna Offensive the Russians had broken the German defense and sped through the gaps headed for Austria. By late afternoon on 26 March the racing Russian spearheads were 30 kilometers west of Papa and had crossed the Marcel Canal near Celldomolk. Having captured Papa the day before the Soviets wasted no time driving straight down the main highway leading to the southwest, a highway that crossed the Marcel Canal at Celldomolk and headed straight for the crossings of the Raba River at Sarvar. Aside from the staggering speed of their advance, the Russians had found the boundary between *6. Armee* and *6. SS–Panzerarmee* and were threatening the entire German position in southwestern Hungary. The seam of two armies was always a weak spot, but with the Germans having no reserves to speak of the danger at Celldomolk was even greater than usual. Of course, the idea of the two German armies having delineated boundaries is overselling the concept; at best they had areas of concentration.

An immediate counterattack was needed to halt the Russian surge beyond Papa, and the only force available was *SS-Brigade Ney*. Celldomolk was the key to the area and both sides knew it. The old town had the ruins of a 12th century abbey on the western side and had been settled for more than seven centuries. Holding the line of the Raba was critical for the Germans to have any chance of stopping the Red Army short of the Austrian border, but time was needed to build up defenses behind that river. Celldomolk was the road junction necessary for the Russians to beat the Germans to the Raba River crossings and get to the western side before proper defenses could be erected. The Hungarian *Waffen–SS* men fought bitterly and stopped the Russian advance in its tracks, but only temporarily; they soon found themselves facing stronger and stronger attacks as the Russians brought more forces forward to capture the town. In response, *6. SS–Panzerarmee* rushed whatever reinforcements it could scrape together to support *SS-Brigade Ney*. As combat raged below, the Trianon Remembrance Cross towered on top of nearby Sag Mountain, as it had since 1934.[546]

Meanwhile, 50 kilometers *east* of the front lines at Celldomolk, *3. SS–Panzer Division Totenkopf* found itself still on the wrong side of Papa. With Russian forces in all directions the division headed for the Raba River crossings and found a gap in the enemy spearheads that would take them over the Raba to

---

[546] This Cross was a memorial in opposition to the Treaty of Trianon that redrew Hungary's boundaries after the First World War.

Sopron. If the Russians had turned around significant forces they could have utterly destroyed *Totenkopf,* but Malinovsky had his eyes fixed on bigger prizes. He wanted Vienna, and after that, maybe even Munich.

5. SS Panzer Division Wiking was still trying to hold back the Russian tide around Lake Balaton, but there was not much left with which to fight back. The only component of the division that had had any time to rest, reorganize, repair and maintain its equipment, the *SS–Aufklärung Abteilung 5* with its new commander Fritz Vogt,[547] was ordered 26 March to take over responsibility for the division's entire sector. The assignment shows how desperate things really were: for a battalion to hold the lines of an entire division was seemingly impossible, but somehow Vogt's command managed to do exactly that for the entire day, withdrawing only after dark to the division's new position further west.

In the ten days since the Red Army had launched the Vienna Offensive, German resistance had been far more effective than the Soviets had any reason to expect. On 16 March *6. SS–Panzerarmee,* and large elements of *6. Armee,* were virtually in a pocket already. Outflanked to the north when Hungarian resistance in the Vértes Mountains collapsed, with no German reserves to fill the void, Malinovsky forces were in the perfect position to drive quickly to the northeastern tip of Lake Balaton and trap all of *Heeresgruppe Süd*'s most powerful units. Such a disaster would have left Austria virtually defenseless; both Malinovsky and Tolbukhin would have had more than a month to drive as far westward as they could against little opposition.

---

[547] Former commander of Norge's I Battalion that had been bled white in both Konrad I and III.

This did not happen because time and again heavily outnumbered and outgunned German forces made defensive stands at key landmarks, and were usually able to withdraw to fight again. Strassner quotes Alexander Werth[548] to good effect in illustrating how the Soviets viewed this: "as there had been in the past there were excellent German soldiers-above all in the *Waffen-SS*-who were ready to fight to the end and who would sooner commit suicide than surrender."[549] Most remarkable is how effective the *Waffen–SS* formations were considering their overall steep decline in training, experience and leadership from the earlier years of the war, particularly leadership from officers.

No amount of determination could make up for a lack of numbers, however. As things began to deteriorate on 26 March, for a short period *Wiking's* commanding officer, *SS–Oberführer* Karl Ullrich, was cut off and out of contact. According to Strassner, some of *Wiking's* men believed their officers were all dead, but the units were held together by the non-coms and corporals, in fact, giving life to the German concept of the Strategic Corporal. In the absence of officers they took charge and maintained discipline; the division could have dissolved under the pressure, and the Assistant Operations Officer apparently thought that it had, but because of the veterans who led their squads and platoons back to the division assembly point *Wiking* held together.[550] The following days would be a race to avoid being surrounded, a race the Germans would often lose.

---

[548] The German born Werth was an emigrant who experienced the war in the Soviet Union and later wrote one of the earliest accounts of the conflict, which proved to be a cornerstone for many later works.

[549] Strassner, p. 327.

[550] Ibid.

Wehrmacht Kommandant of Vienna *Generalleutnant* Werner Merker received terrible news on 26 Match: he was appointed *Kampfkommandant Wien*, a post he would hold for a week. 50 years old, Merker had combat command experience, he had commanded *35. Infanterie Division* in Russia during the brutal winter of 1942-43 among other assignments, but at that stage of the unfolding drama there was little he or anybody else could do to stem the Russian tide. Being *Kampfkommandant* was a virtual death sentence, as Hitler expected you to either save the city of die trying.

27 March, Tuesday

The Cuff Band Order

Aside from the fighting itself, the major event of the day was the infamous 'Cuff Band Order.' This self-defeating episode is almost surely the result of Otto Wöhler and Hermann Balck hatred for the *Waffen–SS*, combined with Hitler's pathological need to blame someone else for his mistakes. Two sources are best for a discussion of this perplexing and paranoid episode.

In response to the failure of *Unternehmen Frühlingserwachen* Hitler reacted to information that Sepp Dietrich had not taken all of his troops to Hungary, and had not fought with the necessary ferocity because he did not believe in the offensive. Neither was true, but this smacks of malicious rumors spread by *Heer* officers against the *Waffen–SS*, which probably lead back to Wöhler and Balck. In response, Hitler ordered the two divisions bearing his name to remove their cuff bands as a punishment.

The first source on this incident is Joseph Goebbels, who was told of the decision and the rationale behind it by Hitler himself, so it is necessary to explore his extensive writings about it in depth. Clearly, the incident both confused and depressed him. According to the Goebbels Diary, "In Hungary the severe defensive fighting south of the Danube moved to the Marczal Canal, south-west of Papa and to the lower Raab. All attacks on the Komárom area and on our bridgeheads on the Danube were repulsed. The enemy was able to form two small bridgeheads north of the mouth of the Gran."

Later, summoned to Hitler's side for a conference, Goebbels learns of the Cuff Band Order and his initial reaction is highly informative. In essence he says that the *SS* units are burned out, the experienced and reliable men are too few to offset the lower quality of the replacements, and the shortage of

633

quality officers is too severe to properly lead the formations.

"The situation is critical...in Hungary. There we are running the risk of possibly losing our vital oilfield. Our *SS* formations have put up a wretched show in this area. Even the Leibstandarte is no longer the old Leibstandarte since its officer material and men have been killed off. The *Leibstandarte* bears its honorary title in name only. The *Führer* has nevertheless decided to make an example of the *SS* formations. He has commissioned Himmler to fly to Hungary to remove their armbands. This will, of course, be the greatest imaginable disgrace for Sepp Dietrich. The army generals are rubbing their hands at this blow to their rivals. The *SS* formations in Hungary not only failed to carry their offensive but withdrew and in some cases pulled out. Inferior human material left its mark in most unpleasant fashion. Sepp Dietrich is to be pitied, Himmler too however, since he, the head of the *SS* with no war decorations, now has to carry out this severe punishment in face of Sepp Dietrich who wears the Diamonds. What is far worse, of course, is that our oilfield is now in most serious danger."

There is one sentence in the above paragraph which seems highly illustrative. "The army generals are rubbing their hands at this blow to their rivals." Where did Hitler's sudden suspicion of the *SS* come from? No doubt the reports from Balck about *Waffen–SS* incompetence and intransigence, with the tacit or open agreement of Wöhler, combined with whatever rumors the generals in Berlin might have heard, were fed to Hitler on a daily basis to smear the SS. That would certainly explain his rationale for ordering Himmler to berate Dietrich and his troops.

During a long walk in the bomb-gouged Chancellery garden, Hitler kept coming back to the subject of events in Hungary.

"...the *Führer* is pleased with developments except in Hungary...the situation in Hungary is terrible. Here we are faced with a serious crisis which - as already mentioned - raises the spectre of the loss of the Hungarian oilfields. The *Führer* is very angry that Sepp Dietrich should have hoodwinked him. He left major units of his Sixth Army[551] (*6. SS–Panzerarmee*) at home in order to have them available as replacement units on his return and so went into action with 40,000 men instead of 70,000. ..The *Führer* proposes to call Dietrich to account most severely. According to the *Führer* Sepp Dietrich has quickly acquired the *Wehrmacht's* habit of juggling with figures. The *Führer* has despatched Himmler to Hungary to put things right there and institute the necessary punitive measures. Nevertheless it is established that the offensive by our *SS* formations met an enemy offensive and, had it not been made, we should have lost the oilfields long ago. In Hungary too everything now hangs by a thread."

It is to be assumed that Goebbels is honestly paraphrasing Hitler's remarks, which are almost entirely fantasy, shifting the blame for his own decisions by claiming he was failed by his subordinates. These delusions make it quite clear what prompted the cuff band order, but what is not clear is where the delusions originated, so that he lashed out at loyal troops who were asked to do the impossible one too many times. But Hitler was not finished. Goebbels laments that Hitler has no competent staff officers surrounding him and that he must do everything himself, including micro-managing even down to the smallest level.

"Nevertheless it must be added that the *Führer* is taking action on material matters rather than personnel. The result is that he is increasingly in conflict with his staff. For instance Himmler and Sepp Dietrich are now in high disfavor. Where will all this lead? What will be left at the end of it all? When I picture to myself Himmler tearing the armbands off the *SS* formations, I feel weak at the knees. It will give the

---

[551] *6. SS–Panzerarmee*. Goebbels consistently mixes up Balck's command with Dietrich's.

SS a real shock. I am seriously worried at Sepp Dietrich for he is not the sort of man to take such a humiliation lying down."

Of all the background material and insights Goebbels gives us on the fighting in Hungary, and of *6. SS–Panzerarmee* in particular, this is easily the most extraordinary. In so many words the Propaganda Minister openly worries that Sepp Dietrich and the *Waffen–SS* could revolt; certainly he understands that their close bond to Hitler has been severed forever. Perhaps the most ruthless man in the Third *Reich* pales with fright at something he knows is not only wrong, but dangerous. But even here Goebbels is not finished wringing his hands over *6. SS–Panzerarmee* and the collapse in morale he senses coming.

"Nevertheless it is established that the offensive by our *SS* formations met an enemy offensive and, had it not been made, we should have lost the oilfields long ago. In Hungary too everything now hangs by a thread. The *Führer* thinks that we must stand firm here if we are not to have the ground cut from under our feet. But military developments are such that today's hopes frequently turn into tomorrow's theories. As I have already discussed the *Führer* perceives everything correctly but draws no conclusions...I am determined not to admit that it is too late and I am firmly convinced that a way out will be found at the most critical moment."

This last sentence achieves two things: to himself Goebbels admits that all is lost, telling himself "I am determined not to admit that it is too late..." He knows it but refuses to admit it. But he also covers himself because, in the Third *Reich*, nobody, not even the *Reich* Minister of Propaganda and Enlightenment, was exempt from paranoia. "I am firmly convinced that a way out will be found at the most critical moment." This rings false but would make an ideal defense should it come to that. Whether or not this was his intention is unknown. It is instructive, however, in trying to determine the mood of those around Hitler during this period of severe trial for *6. SS–Panzerarmee*, to look at Goebbel's last paragraph entry for the day.

"In the evening...I thumb through various papers...from the time of our struggle period...Their effect is almost that of a salute from the good old days which will never return." Meanwhile, the fragments of *Heeresgruppe Süd* were desperately trying to stem the Red flood in the hills and fields of Hungary.[552]

The second source for a full understanding is Georg Maier, Deputy Ia of *6. SS–Panzerarmee*, who was on hand when the order arrived at headquarters and who then discussed it with Sepp Dietrich. If Goebbels gives us the closest thing we have to a transcript of Hitler's reaction, Maier tells us Dietrich's response as an eye witness.

In essence, Dietrich was thoroughly disgusted at the order. More to the point he was personally disappointed; after everything he had done for Adolf Hitler, after all of the trials and suffering, to have his loyalty called into question during the war's final actions was too much to stomach. Dietrich did not pass on the order to his troops, although it got out anyway. Making the whole thing worse, the men of *I. SS–Panzerkorps* had removed their cuff bands for security reasons during the transfer to Hungary.

Postwar stories about this grew in the telling. One of the most common is that Dietrich and his officers threw their medals into a spittoon and sent it to Hitler, but this story is apocryphal; it never happened.

At Marcalto, the Soviet juggernaut slammed into *232. Reserve Panzer Division* in the morning, but was

---

[552] Trevor-Roper, *Final Entries*, pp. 292-314.

repulsed in heavy fighting. The Russians were not so easily driven off, though, and by the afternoon they had broken through and cut off an entire battalion. Unlike the *SS* divisions who still had enough veterans to retain some cohesion in desperate situations, second-rate formations like the *232. Reserve Panzer Division* could only face so much adversity before they fell apart, which is exactly what happened next. The division retreated, and some elements simply ran away. *Generalmajor* Hans-Ulrich Back was severely wounded, so there was no one to rally the troops and stop the disintegration.

Seeing their right flank collapsing, the men of *Hitlerjugend* tried to blow up the bridges over the Raba but failed, leaving them for the Soviets to use. The *Heeresgruppe Süd* War Diary notes: "Among the very young age groups (Div. Hitlerjugend) there is fear of artillery fire because of the experience in the West. With lack of energetic *Führer* [leaders], the soldiers halt ready when artillery fire starts."[553] *Hitlerjugend* then withdrew westward in the direction of Sopron, only to find the Russians there ahead of them. Intense fighting resulted and the division moved north toward Baden and would keep moving northwest until it reached the area near St. Corona am Schöpfl, due west of Mödling.

All over northwestern Hungary the situation was fluid, changing by the hour. At Celldomolk, *SS-Brigade Ney* once again led the counterattack to try and hold the town, along with elements of *2. SS–Panzer Division Das Reich* and *6. Panzer Division* that had been rushed into the battle. They successfully drove the Russians back, but it was already too late. The Russians had crossed the Marcel Canal elsewhere and raced west, so that by afternoon the Russians had entered Sarvar, 20 kilometers to the west and in the rear of the German formations. There was imminent danger of them being cut off, until a battalion from *99. Gebirgsjäger Regiment* retook the position, allowing *SS-Brigade Ney* and the

---

[553] Michaelis, *Panzer Divisions of the Waffen–SS*, p. 306.

other German units to withdraw west yet again, this time behind the Raba River, even though that river had already been crossed by the Russians on their left flank. The brigade's *III. Batallion* was retreating in the vicinity of Papa when it was attached to *3. SS–Panzer Division Totenkopf*, which had been almost shattered by this point. The battalion would stay with *Totenkopf* for the duration of the war. *Totenkopf* was, in turn, assigned to *II. SS–Panzerkorps*.[554]

On 27 March, *6. SS–Panzerarmee* reported that the combat ready elements of *37. SS–Kavallerie Division Lützow* were being readied in the vicinity of Pressburg (Bratislava), per orders. *SS-Kampfgruppe Keitel* and *SS-Kampfgruppe Ameiser* were already in combat, but the rest of the division kept forming, including a small assortment of artillery and supply troops, as well as veterinary and medical services.

Meanwhile, the parts of the division that were already fighting in *Kampfgruppe Ameiser* were being shoved across the Neutra (Nitra) River into the area north of Bratislava, in company with the *96. Infanterie Division*, as the Red Army launched new attacks from their bridgehead over the Gran River.

[554] Pencz, *Siegrunen Volume 76*, p. 21.

28 March, Wednesday

"In Hungary the Soviets, attacking on a broad front, reached the Raab Valley. Farther south they reached the railway line to Lake Balaton. Apart from a minor break-in all attacks on the Komárom bridgehead were contained. Our own strong bridgehead farther east was withdrawn to the north bank of the Danube. Soviet attacks on the lower Gran were repulsed."

As Goebbels expounded on the daily situation Goebbels comes to the main problem of the moment, *Heeresgruppe Süd*. It is illustrative that during all of the discussions about the failures in the south it is never *Heeresgruppe Süd* that is blamed, nor is Balck's *6. Armee* called to task, it is always Dietrich's *6. SS–Panzerarmee*, even though Balck had *IV. SS–Panzerkorps* attached to his army and could point to no more success than Dietrich, and possibly even less. Granted, the two *SS* divisions of *IV. SS–Panzerkorps* were ghosts of their former selves with a mere handful of tanks, but the point remains valid that only *6. SS–Panzerarmee* was singled out for criticism. Goebbels has previously admitted that the Army generals were happy about the discomfiture of the *Waffen–SS*. The blame for the failures was consistently laid at the feet of Dietrich's formations.

"The only news from the east is that the crisis in Hungary has become even more acute. Our *SS* divisions fighting there seem unable to regain their foothold. The oilfield is now seriously threatened-something the *Führer* wished to avoid in all circumstances."

Heeresgruppe Süd was not an *SS* formation. Most of its units were not *Waffen–SS*. Yet, there is no mention here of any *Heer* formations, not *6. Armee*, not *8. Armee*, not *I Kavallerie Korps* fighting in *6. SS–Panzerarmee*, or *Luftwaffe* divisions, or even Hungarian divisions, only those of the *Waffen–SS*. Goebbels is only repeating what he has heard in the military briefings given to Hitler, a receptive audience for anything detrimental to the *Waffen–SS*, with no thought given to the nearly impossible tasks asked of every German formation, *WaffenSS*, *Luftwaffe* and *Heer* alike.

During his tenure as Chief of the General Staff, Heinz Guderian had stood up to Hitler in ways few men could have done and still survived. He had often had shouting matches with the *Führer* and had harped on what he considered crucial questions to the point of angering the already volatile Hitler, a very dangerous course of action. He had tried to direct the German Army to best use its dwindling resources, almost always in direct opposition to Hitler's ideas, and had won the occasional victory. The *Generaloberst* had continually confronted Hitler about this poor decisions, and with the front collapsing in the south he once again launched into the need for an armistice with the west and commitment of the *SS* formations at Berlin.

The situation then grew more heated. The two men shouted at each other over the failure of *General der Infanterie* Busse's *9. Armee* to break through to the surrounded city of Küstrin on the Oder River, until others present worried that Hitler might have a stroke, or order Guderian's execution. Guderian was semi-dragged from the room by the excuse of a phone call. When he returned to the conference room, Guderian was sacked by Hitler ostensibly for health reasons. Guderian *did* need a rest; he had already suffered two heart attacks. promised to recall him in six weeks. Never one to hold his tongue, Guderian quipped that he would try to find some place that would not be overrun by the enemy within the next six weeks.

And so the Father of the so-called *Blitzkrieg*, one of the greatest German generals of the war and a first-class military mind, would sit out the final battles of the Third *Reich* patiently waiting to be captured by the

Americans. *General der Infanterie* Hans Krebs replaced him.

SS-*Brigade Ney* was parceled out among several units to try and form some semblance of a defense, somewhere. The Regiment's *I., II.* and *IV. Abteilung* were attached to the *SS–Panzergrenadier Ausbildungs und Reserve Abteilung 18* commanded by *SS–Obersturmbannführer der Reserve* Heinrich Kremer.[555] These formed the basis of *Kampfgruppe Schweitzer,* along with the 504th Engineer Construction Battalion and the I Battalion of *Panzer* Regiment 24[556].

Although SS–*Brigade Ney* fought hard to hold the Russians east of the Raba, it was hopeless. The Soviets broke through on a broad front, and there was nothing the brigade could do to stop them. By this point, the Soviets were almost on the Austrian border; the Hungarians were running out of Hungary to defend. Indeed, advance spearheads of the *46. Armee* reached the Austrian border.

The *232. Reserve Panzer Division* was unable to reorganize itself after being routed the day before, and the remaining units scattered away from the oncoming Russians. It officially ceased to exist.

Further south, in the small town of Keszthely at the northwest corner of Lake Balaton, *23. Panzer Division* briefly turned and tried to make a stand, but it was hopeless. With German formations streaming west

---

[555] One small component was assigned to a Hungarian fortress battalion.

[556] Sources do not agree on what day this kampfgruppe was created, with some saying the 28th and others the 29th. Nor do sources all agree on which battalion was attached where.

and Russians in close pursuit, anyone who stopped for long became either a prisoner or a casualty.

Nor had the *SS* divisions fared any better. *2. SS–Panzer Division Das Reich* found itself near Kapuvar, attempting to regroup; the respite would only be momentary. The *Panzer* regiment had only five *Panzer Mark IVs*, two *Mark V Panthers*, two *Jagdpanzer IVs*, five *Jagdpanzer Vs* and three *Sturmgeschütze*; even counting the fixed barrel vehicles as tanks, the regiment had only 17 *panzers* ready to fight. The artillery regiment had 43 barrels, 19 105 mm and 21 150 mm howitzers and three 105 mm field cannon.[557] Considering how many *panzers* loaded up at the railhead at Veszprem a week earlier, losses in the flight across Western Hungary had been extraordinarily heavy. Scattered in the wake of their retreat were armored vehicles that either ran out of fuel, or were damaged and could not be salvaged in the chaos of the moment.

The tactical imagination once indicative of the Germans was now a trait of the Russians. After the fall of Budapest the Russians had organized the Danube Flotilla (Rear-Admiral G.N. Kholostyakov) and, in one of the more impressive tactical innovations of the campaign, these river craft ferried the 83rd Marine Brigade from the south bank of the Danube west of Sutto, to the north bank at Moca. The marines seized the village and suddenly the Germans had a sizeable Russian force in their rear, with no reserves to seal it off.

[557] Michaelis, *Panzer Division of the Waffen–SS*, p. 112.

29 March, Thursday

Goebbels began the day with a recap of the unfolding disaster in the south.

"In Hungary the Bolshevists continued their attack westwards in strength. They crossed the Raab at several points and penetrated into the southern quarter of the town of that name. Leading enemy troops are at Csorna and Sarvar. Enemy attacks between the Raab Valley and Lake Balaton were held on a stop-line running southeast to the western tip of Lake Balaton. Continuing his attacks all along the Gran sector the enemy drove German troops back to a line running northwards to the northwest of Neuhausel. Further attacks on this line were in some cases repulsed and in others achieved local penetrations. The enemy penetrated somewhat deeper into our Komárom bridgehead. In addition he extended the front of his offensive into Slovakia."

Maintaining German morale was one of Goebbels' prime duties as Propaganda minister and throughout March he had been forced to admit that, by and large, morale in the West had collapsed. Most of all he had to face the fact of public protests, something heretofore unknown in the draconian Third *Reich*, and so he did again. Open discontent had broken out in various places, with Vienna soon to follow.

"In Siegburg, for instance, a woman=s demonstration took place outside the Town Hall demanding the laying down of arms and capitulation. In a radio message Grohe denies that this women=s demonstration was of any great size and maintains that it has been artificially exaggerated by Commander-in-Chief West. Nevertheless the fact remains that, even though they may be on a smaller scale than described, such incidents did take place."

His only further comments on *Heeresgruppe Süd* were brief and blunt: "In the East developments in Hungary are extraordinarily critical and disagreeable."[558]

Near the frontier town of Deutsch Schuetzen, in Burgenland in the Oberwart District, 57 Hungarian Jewish forced laborers were reportedly killed by members of *5. SS–Panzer Division Wiking Division*, after digging defensive fortifications and trenches. The next day, 30 March, a 58th victim was said to have been shot during a forced march from Deutsch Schuetzen to Hartberg when he could not keep up. The little town is in the heart of Austria's wine growing region, very near the Hungarian border. In 2009 a 90 year old survivor of *Wiking*, Adolf Storms, was charged with the last killing and implicated in the massacre of the other 57 when his name turned up in some documents, although no witnesses to the killings were found and Storms denied knowing anything about the shootings. Storms died in late June of 2010 without ever going to trial. The mass grave was said to have been dug by a detachment of *Hitlerjugend.*

The reason *Wiking* was in the general vicinity of Deutsch Schuetzen, in the area of Vasvar, was that it had been pushed northwest in the past few days as time and again it withdrew to a position only to find the Red Army there ahead of them. Indeed, units of 3rd Ukrainian Front were preparing to cross the Austrian border near Guns, a village northwest of Steinmanger (Szombathely) in the vicinity of Rechnitz, cutting off *Wiking's* path to the west and northwest, in the general direction of Wiener Neustadt. If the division was going

[558] Trevor-Roper, *Final Entries*, p. 319.

to escape it would have to change direction to the southwest.

Less than a mile from the border with Austria, Russian forces seized the 800 year-old Hungarian town of Köszeg. The town's coat-of-arms depicted a castle with a red-topped turret and crenelated walls on a blue background, depicting its traditional role of being a front line defensive fortification against Austrian aggression coming from the west. None of that helped it avoid Soviet capture from the east, however. With no cohesive front and the field forces in disarray, an anti-tank battalion from the Cadet Academy at Weiner Neustadt was ordered forward to block the roads and passes leading west from Köszeg to Gloggnitz, Neunkirchen and Weiner Neustadt.

The Russians drove hard for the oil fields at Nagykanizsa, with only remnants of units in their way. The best division in *2. Panzerarmee, 16. SS–Panzergrenadier Division Reichsführer SS*, was by this point virtually without combat power. The division was split by the rapidity of the Russian advance, with the bulk being shoved toward Nagykanizsa. They were the only serious defense force left in the area.

30 March, Friday

Goebbels continued his narrative about *Heeresgruppe Süd*:

"In Hungary the Soviets attack our forward positions west of Kapsovar and penetrated in some places. At the north-west corner of Lake Balaton the enemy was held at Keszthely. Between Keszthely and Steinamanger the Bolshevists broke through our stop-line and reached Zalaegerszeg. These coordinated attacks are directed on the Nagykanisza oilfield. On the German-Hungarian frontier the enemy penetrated into Steinamanger and Guns and reached Kaposvar, moving along the Raab-Weiner Neustadt railway. His attacks on Raab failed. North-east of Raab the enemy succeeded in crossing the river and moving some kilometers up the Danube. The enemy also made violent attacks on our positions on the Neutra between Komárom, Neuhausel and Neutra...This is the most horrible Good Friday I have ever had in my life."

It would also be the last.

"Developments in Hungary are an equal source of anxiety. We shall soon be faced with the question whether we can hold the oilfield. The Soviets are anyway already over the German frontier. Sepp Dietrich's Sixth Army (*6. SS–Panzerarmee*-author) has simply allowed itself to be swept away by them."[559]

---

[559] Throughout his diary Goebbels continually refers to 'Sixth Army', often blaming them for failures on the battlefield, but as this quote makes clear he confused Dietrich's *6. SS–Panzerarmee* with Balck's Sixth Army, making it hard to decipher precisely who he meant unless, as in this case, he made clear the commander of the army in question. He did not usually do this, however.

Goebbels once again mistakes Dietrich's *6. SS–Panzerarmee* with Balcks *6. Armee.* Unless Goebbels was actually blaming Balck's Army but he, like so many Army officers appeared to have done, laid all failures in the south at Dietrich's feet.

Then, building on the idea of why Goebbels was so attentive of civilian morale, it appears this subject was a frequent topic of conversation between he and Hitler.

"The *Führer* stresses yet again that the morale of the troops and the civil population are interdependent. He is firmly convinced, he says, that the troops have infected the civilians with their bad morale, not the civilians the troops."

Whether or not Hitler actually said this, which laid the blame for the morale problem on the military, not on the *Reichsminister*, it served his purpose to deflect responsibility. Still, whether this was true or not it shows the level of worry at the highest levels about the morale of both the troops and the populace.

Goebbels finally comes to the big lie behind the Cuff band Order, the story that condemned *6. SS–Panzerarmee* as the culprit for the failures in Hungary. Somewhere, the story made the rounds that Dietrich had intentionally not used all of the manpower allotted to him, starving his front line units to keep reserves behind for later use elsewhere. That Hitler, with a month to live and crises on every front, should take time to discuss this specious story, indicates how badly the information at *Führer* Headquarters had been distorted, and how eager Hitler was to place blame on anyone but himself.

"A real tragedy is now being staged in Hungary. As I emphasized last time, Sepp Dietrich only put a portion of his troops into action in Hungary and told the *Führer* a direct lie about his manpower.[560] He wanted to leave reserves behind in the *Reich* for his next operation on the Oder Front. As A result he was short of replacements in Hungary. The *Führer* is most hurt by Sepp Dietrich's behavior. He has also reproached Himmler severely on the subject. The result is, as I have said, that Himmler has taken away their armbands from the *SS* formations in Hungary."

Goebbels was not done with his subject yet, continuing to repeat what Hitler had said about his *Waffen–SS* commanders. This is as close to first hand of Hitler's thinking as we have, as Goebbels discussed this with Hitler at the time, and alone, and is, therefore, the closest we will ever get to a primary source.

"In general the *Führer* is of the opinion that no high-class commander has emerged from the *SS*. Neither Sepp Dietrich nor Hausser have great operational talent."

Goebbels' comments smack of second guessing and fixing blame, as Dietrich was unable to deliver the offensive miracle that Hitler had come to expect from the Waffen SS, although defensive miracles were another matter. Even with this, though, Goebbels was not finished with the subject yet of his talk with Hitler. After lamenting the loss of Huber and Dietl, Hitler kept going on about the commanders and Goebbels paraphrases him.

"Who is then left? Schörner who has great talent and is outstanding...He is a devil of a fellow and can

---

[560] The source of this rumor may harken back to something said at the midday situation conference on January 27, 1945. Himmler's representative at the meeting, Gruppenführer Hermann Fegelein, brought up the matter of 6,000 men then stationed at the barracks of the 1. SS–Panzer Division Liebstandarte Adolf Hitler Adolf Hitler and intended as replacements for I SS Panzer Corps. Fegelein wanted the men sent to the commander of *Heeresgruppe Mitte*, Colonel General Ferdinand Schörner, but Hitler refused. He wanted the men trained and then sent to I SS Panzer Corps but Fegelein said they were already trained.

always be relied on. Above all he tells the *Führer* the truth." This last sentence ignores that fact that for most commanders, telling Hitler a truth he did not want to hear was often a fatal mistake.

"The fact that in the case of Hungary Sepp Dietrich did not do so has greatly embittered the *Führer*. He even talks of guilt before history that must be laid at Dietrich's door. In any case we must now reckon that we may lose the Hungarian oilfield...Taking into account the debacle in Pomerania the *SS* has a good deal to account for recently."

Finally, working late into the night in his study, Goebbels records the inevitable news that Soviet troops had entered Austria. "...pressure on the German frontier in Hungary has become heavier. The enemy has crossed the frontier at one point and captured two Austrian villages. We are still holding on south of Lake Balaton in an effort to retain the oilfield."[561]

Throughout the controversy it did not help Dietrich's case that his reputation was one of misleading superiors. He could also have contempt for those above him, including Himmler, so that such grossly false reports as those that sparked the cuff band order seemed within his character. Karl Thiele puts it this way: "Dietrich did have a reputation for making false reports to higher commands...he also showed contempt for absolute authority even if it endangered himself." Dietrich had opposed *Unternehmen Frühlingserwachen* from the beginning, so perhaps Hitler could sense that his heart was not in the attack, or perhaps he was just heaping blame on his latest scapegoat. Regardless, the failure of *Unternehmen Frühlingserwachen* had nothing to do with Dietrich and everything to do with Hitler. "Their

[561] Trevor-Roper, *Final Entries*, pp. 335-338.

targets, timing and location were wrong, over which he (Dietrich) had no control."[562]

As the Viennese tried to maintain a semblance of normalcy that Good Friday, on the streets of Vienna there could be heard deep booms, distant but insistent, like a severe thunderstorm growing slowly closer. It was the first reports of Soviet artillery as the Red Army crossed into Austria.

The *Gauleiter* of Vienna, Baldur von Schirach, declared martial law in Vienna. At that point it really was not necessary, the government had all the power it needed to do whatever it wanted. Executions, restrictions, regulations...whatever power Schirach needed to govern, he had. Indeed, Hitler expected his Gauleiters to use draconian measures to keep the population in line and fighting the enemy. Schirach could have slaughtered civilians under whatever pretext he wished to invent, as long as it was to further the war effort, and Hitler would have applauded his courage. The only real effect of declaring martial law was to increase the anxiety of the population. Considering that when night fell and the sky to the southeast turned purple, increasing the anxiety levels was not really necessary to make people aware of the gravity of the situation. Party officials suddenly disappeared from the streets; those who did venture out no longer wore their uniforms. Despite the rubble the streets were jammed as those with enough influence to merit travel permits fled the city, even with the various injunctions to stay off the streets. The Red Flood was coming and like rats on a sinking ship those with the clout to do so were pouring out of Vienna before it engulfed them all.

"Most of the people could not flee but, being Viennese, they had not lost their sense of humor and

[562] Thiele, *Beyond Monsters and Clowns*, pp. 263-264.

the latest joke was: 'On Easter you'll be able to take a street car to the front lines.' By Easter it was no longer a joke..."[563]

Schirach did what was expected of him, he made speeches and said all the right things. He declared Vienna a *Festung* and called up the *Volkssturm*. With the Red Army nearly in the suburbs he belatedly started fortifying the city, putting old men and children to work building barricades in the streets or digging trenches, and generally making a good show of doing what a *Gauleiter* should do. Meanwhile his family was packing to leave.

Broken units wandered all over the battle area. Somewhere near the town of Steinamanger (Szombathely), just inside the Hungarian border with Austria south of Sopron, 100 kilometers from Vienna and 117 kilometers from Graz, *Kampfgruppe Lenk*, one of the two remnants of *SS–Ungarische–Sturm Regiment 1*, found itself once again attached to *IV. SS–Panzerkorps* . Happily, the Hungarian ski troops actually found themselves subordinated to their countrymen in *SS– Brigade Ney*, which was also attached to *IV. SS–Panzerkorps. SS-Brigade Ney* had moved with as much speed as possible down the main highway heading west, and had wound up near the Austrian border in the area of Rechnitz, under the direct command of the 2nd Hungarian Armored Division. Later, however, the brigade was parceled out to *III. Panzerkorps*, then *6. Armee* and finally *I. SS–Panzerkorps* of *6. SS–Panzerarmee*. As confusing as the command structure may have been, it was not the chief concern for any of them: in essence, they were all surrounded, a large *kessel* staggering toward Austria, while the *IV. SS–Panzerkorps* was trying to fight its way

[563] Toland, *The Last 100 Days*, pp. 374-375.

654

west and south before the Red Army could block it with too many troops to defeat.

In the same trap, the headquarters of *5. SS Panzer Division Wiking* moved to the southernmost part of the 'bridgehead', close to the last remaining bridge over the Raba. The division was ordered to assemble at Furstenfeld, southwest of Steinamanger, and then to take up positions in the so-called *Reich* Defensive Position. The exodus immediately caused a massive traffic-jam as vehicles of all types jammed the roads leading to Furstenfeld, over the Austrian border. Strassner indicates the stoic attitude with which the men of *Wiking* received these orders: "even the streaming sunshine could not change the serious expressions on the hardened faces of the men."[564]

Supposedly they were heading to a line of reinforced bunkers and fortifications. The *Reichstellung*, the *Reich* Defensive Position was intended to be something of a Westwall for the Eastern Front, but under the complacent Balder von Shirach very little work had actually been done. In some places there were some trenches and tank traps, in others... nothing. That was nowe irrelevant, however; in many places the Red Army had overrun the positions before the Germans were able to man them.

With Sopron in Russian hands, the alarm units ordered into the frontier fortifications by *Wehrkreis XVII* were rolled over by Russian tanks before they could even reach them, depriving the defenders the use not only of the rudimentary fixed defenses prepared for them but also of the Rosalien Mountains. This small mountain range was an eastern outcropping of the Alps, the very beginnings of the Alpine foothills that ringed the valley where Sopron was situated. That same valley ran from Sopron west to Mattersburg,

[564] Strassner, p. 328.

turned north and then west again before reaching Weiner Neustadt, a veritable highway through the high terrain. Despite losing the fortifications of the *Reich* Defense Line, the German blocking forces defending the valley near Mattersburg put up a stiff resistance and the Russians were repulsed; without reinforcements, however, they could not hold on for long. It was only a matter of time until Mattersburg was captured by the Red Army.

31 March, Saturday

In one of the last entries extant, Goebbel's tone has undergone a subtle shift from one of emotional hope and a desperate feeling, to one better described as resigned objectivity. Had the *Reichsminister* ever had the chance to edit his diary, it seems likely he would have wrung the sometimes overwrought emotions from his previous posts.

"The main fighting on the Eastern Front was in Hungary. Between the Drau and the Western end of Lake Balaton the enemy attacked frontally towards Nagykanizsa and made a deep penetration bringing him to within 20 kilometers of the oilfield. Simultaneously the Soviets advanced south and south-west from Zalaegerszeg with the intention of encircling the oilfield. The enemy swung north-west from Steinamanger and Guns, reached the German frontier west of Steinamanger and crossed it north-west of Guns. Leading enemy tanks reached Kirchschlag. At the same time the enemy advanced farther along the Raab-Odenburg-Weiner Neustadt Railway; here he is some 20 km east of Odenburg. Advancing through Raab, which fell into enemy hands, the Soviets gained some 10 km of ground towards Bratislava. The enemy succeeded in breaking into our rear-guard positions on the Neutra at several points and advancing as far as the Waag where he formed bridgeheads on the west bank... Some 500 American four-engined bombers from Italy raided Vienna, Weiner Neustadt, Klagenfurt and Graz. Our Sturmvogel shot down 8 enemy aircraft."

Returning again to the topic of morale, Goebbels seems almost matter-of-fact about it. "*Gauleiter* Wagner...complains bitterly that the morale both of the civilian population and the troops has sunk extraordinarily low. People no longer shrink from sharp criticism of the *Führer*."

Mere weeks before this would have led to a swift and grisly end to the malcontents, but no longer. Goebbels does not even waste time boasting about what would happen to the defeatists; even he realizes the hollowness of such threats.

"In the East the course of events in Hungary and on the Austro-Hungarian frontier gives rise to the greatest anxiety at the moment. Cerff, (a functionary in the Ministry) who has just returned from the Hungarian Front, gives me an account of events there. He says that the offensive bogged down because the weather was unbelievably bad, the offensive necessarily took place in very marshy ground so that our tanks simply could not move. Sepp Dietrich did his utmost to keep the offensive going but he is no army commander. He is capable of commanding no more than a division. In any case our casualties were extraordinarily high and Sixth Army (sic. Once again Goebbels confuses Balck's army with Deitrich's) can hardly be scheduled for future operations. This is a fearful thing for Sepp Dietrich of course. One can imagine how unhappy he is over this development."[565]

The Russian 46. Army, after reaching the Austrian border near Guns on 28 March, finally crossed the *Reich* frontier into Austria on 31 March. The *Reichsstellung*, touted by von Schirach but scoffed at by Austrian native *SS–Obergruppenführer* Dr. Ernst Kaltenbrunner, Head of the *Reichssicherheitshauptamt* (*Reich* Security Main Office), and hampered by *Major* Szokoll of *O–5*, was no deterrent; in numerous places the Red Army reached its locations even before the Germans assigned to man the rudimentary defenses.

[565] Trevor-Roper, *Final Entries*, pp. 349-351.

One Soviet thrust headed south for Semmering and the current position of Balck's *6. Armee,* while a second skirted the northern shore of Lake Neuseidler and headed for Vienna, which was being screened by Sepp Dietrich and what was left of the *6. SS–Panzerarmee.*

On Holy Saturday morning Allied air attacks had hit the Vienna railroad marshaling yards, as well as the Danube bridges and important intersections. Wreckage blocked streets, fires and smoke hampered movement. The fire brigades did what they could but there were too many fires and too much confusion for them to be truly effective. The availability of gas and electricity was sporadic at best. In some districts there was no water. The railroads no longer ran and the streetcars were mostly immobilized. Simply moving through the damaged city was difficult.

In addition, four battalions of motorized *Volkssturm* were ordered to the front. They were mostly teenage boys. This mobilization did not sit well with the mothers of Vienna.

"That triggered one of the few demonstrations of the war, and the only one by women. The mothers and sisters wanted more than merely to keep their boys at home. They took to the streets to protest fighting for Vienna at all."[566]

Viewed from a distance in time this may not seem so remarkable, but the Third *Reich* did not tolerate dissent, ever, from anyone. Soldiers and Generals had been shot for less. And yet as Goebbels has noted repeatedly in his diary, morale in both the military and the home front had been collapsing for some time. Previously overt demonstrations had been mostly confined to the West, where capture by American of British troops did not seem so bad, despite Goebbels best efforts to demonize them. In the East the Red Army's reputation preceded it and the people were terrified of being overrun. At least, they had been. But the demonstration against sending those Hitler Youth

566 Weyr, *The Setting of the Pearl,* p.275.

to the front shows just how far morale had sunk as the women folk did everything they could to save their children and siblings, even if it meant leaving their own fate in the hands of the Red Army.

The hope was that Vienna would be declared an open city, much as Rome had been. At this point, however, that was impossible; Hitler's fortress mentality was almost a part of his persona. No inch of German ground would be given up uncontested. Cities such as Konigsberg and Breslau could fight to the death, why not Vienna? Not only was it the capital of the old Austro-Hungarian Empire, but it was the capital of the country where the *Führer* was born. Giving it up without a fight just would not do. Von Schirach claimed to have wanted to give up the city but was forbidden by Bormann. Whether von Schirach actually wanted to save Vienna or not, it is certainly credible that Bormann would have ordered it held to the last, and with Hitler's full blessing. As to *0-5* and its plan to surrender Vienna without a fight, this was known only to a select few; the average citizen would have known nothing of the plan.

The situation around Sopron grew more critical by the hour. Unable to successfully storm the city by direct assault, the Russians maintained pressure on the German flanks. Near Mattersburg the Russians kept attacking the forces blocking their way through the valley that lead first to Mattersburg and then to Wiener Neustadt, using infantry and tanks, but fanatical resistance kept them at bay for one more day. Likewise, southeast of Sopron the Russians were trying to force another defile leading south in the direction of Nagycenk, but once again were repulsed with heavy losses. The Germans had blocked the way to the Nagykanizsa oilfields but were unable to form a coherent front, so the Russians veered southwest in the direction of Deutschenkreuz and Neckenmarkt, outflanking the Germans yet again.

Just west of Mattersdorf two other battalions from the Wiener Neustadt *Kadettenakademie* made a stand against Russian forces debouching from the Rosalien Mountains, momentarily halting them and inflicting severe losses; the fighting continued throughout the day and into 1 April.[567] The desperation of the situation is shown by the German commitment of those future officers, who were of much greater value as junior officers than as infantry. Armed with nothing more than personal weapons and some *panzerfäuste* they reportedly destroyed some 30 tanks. Whether this figure is accurate or exaggerated there is no doubt that the fighting was fierce, an indication of just how violent the war remained; with Hitler less than a month from pointing a pistol at his head the Germans could still muster fanatical resistance that took a terrible toll on the Red Army, a toll that was not forgotten when the Russians inevitably broke through.

Also near Sopron, *3. SS–Panzer Division Totenkopf* was detached from *I. SS–Panzerkorps* and given to *II. SS–Panzerkorps*, then immediately marched due north through the Leitha Mountains some 48 kilometers to Schwechat.

Like every other German unit, *1. SS–Panzer Division Leibstandarte Adolf Hitler* was a shattered shadow of what it had been a month before, which in turn was only a ghost of what it once had been. Sometime near the end of March it moved into the vaunted *Reichstellung* near Deutschkreuz, where for once they arrived before the Russians, only to discover that the fortifications were nothing more than a very long trench. Most of the division's armor was gone and

---

[567] A full accounting of this action is given in the second half of this history, *Killing Hitler's Reich, The Battle for Austria, 1945.*

what remained was worn out and in urgent need of repair. In particular, the treads on all tracked vehicles were either worn out or missing altogether, along with the rubber blocks, limiting mobility even more than the shortage in transport vehicles and fuel already had; on sharp turns the treads tended to work loose, usually leaving the vehicle disabled on the side of the road.

The saga of the *Ukrainishe Division Galizien*, aka *14. Waffen–Grenadier Division der SS (Galizien 1)*, shows just far the German command situation had deteriorated. On 31 March the Division was attached to *2. Panzerarmee*, finally giving it a home from which to draw not only supplies, but orders; until that happened it had been in a perilous limbo.

With Germany collapsing on all fronts, running out of supplies, weapons, territory and manpower, the Division was not only a fully armed infantry division, completely battle ready and flush with new and highly motivated recruits, it was also over-strength, even in comparison with a full-strength *Wehrmacht* or *SS* division. At least 20,000 strong in late March, some sources say 22,000, it was arguably one of the most powerful formations on paper left in *Heeresgruppe Süd*'s order of battle; and yet it was not part of *Heeresgruppe Süd*, or any other German command. It was just there, on its own, without orders or a regular supply chain until finally attached to *2. Panzerarmee*.

Their limbo status was referred to earlier in the narrative when the topic came up during one of Hitler's daily conference. Situated in southwest Austria during late winter, mostly training and fighting partisans, starting on 20 March the Ukrainians were variously ordered to give up all of their weapons (an order signed by Himmler himself, probably from Hitler's off-hand comment about disarming the Ukrainian Division); then to disband; next, to reform and retrain as a

Luftwaffe fallschirmjäger division (as if there were enough transports left in the entire *Luftwaffe* for such an absurd idea); then to give up part of their weapons; to give up all of their supplies, and final to keep 20 percent of their supplies. About the only thing they were not ordered to do was fight the Russians.

It seems almost sure that the order to give up their weapons was based on Hitler's passing comment about them, questioning why they were ever given weapons in the first place. Perhaps he was confusing the Ukrainians with Vlasov's Russian Volunteers, two divisions of which were organized but not yet armed.

Indeed, there were so many strange and contradictory orders that the Division became frantic. With partisans all around and the front drawing closer daily, the Ukrainians needed to know something definitive and know it fast.

"In response to its queries the Division soon received many replies containing new orders from the following authorities: the *Reichsführer–SS*, Field Command Post of the *Reichsführer–SS*, Operations Department of the German High Command, Chief Quartermaster of the German High Command, *Heeresgruppe Süd*, *Heeresgruppe Südost*, 18th Military District Headquarters, 2nd Army Headquarters [meaning *2. Panzerarmee*- author], *6. Armee* Headquarters. In this flurry of messages some orders grossly contravened others."[568]

Nothing more illustrates the panic and pandemonium rife in the German chain in command than the experience of *Galizien.* Hitler and his toady court, men like Keitel, Jodl and Goebbels, allowed his micro-management of the war to pass without challenge. No matter how much they agreed with men like Heinz Guderian, they never had the courage to put their own lives and careers on the line to stand up for what they knew to be correct. Even in a military sense

---

[568] Heike, Wolf-Dietrich, *The Ukrainian Division 'Galicia' 1943-1945* (Shevchenko Scientific Society, 1988), p. 111.

they nodded 'yes' to Hitler's wildest orders, and the result was Germany's rush to destruction in disasters like the Ardennes Offensive and *Unternehmen Frühlingserwachen.*

Epilogue

Catholicism has long been the largest religion in Austria, with other branches of Christianity also popular. Even as the Nazis tried to stamp out any creed beyond their own ill-defined version of Paganism, people throughout the *Reich* stuck to their beliefs. So as the clock ticked over from Holy Saturday to Easter Sunday, it is probable that hundreds of thousands of Austrians put their hands together in prayers of deliverance from the onrushing tide of atheistic Communism.

On a more Earthly level, their potential salvation lay with the broken *Heeresgruppe Süd* and its pantheon of paladins; Otto Wöhler, Hermann Balck, and Sepp Dietrich. No doubt some took heart from all of the famous division names standing between them and the Red Army which, it must be admitted, looks impressive even now. That these shattered formations had no hope of doing more than delaying the Red Army for a few days was unknown outside of the higher German headquarters. After all, wasn't the *Waffen–SS* the elite of the *Wehrmacht*? And wasn't most of the *Waffen–SS* defending Austria?

They were. Two had already been destroyed in Budapest. In order:

    1. SS–Panzer Division Leibstandarte Adolf Hitler
    2. SS–Panzer Division Das Reich
    3. SS–Panzer Division Totenkopf
    5. SS–Panzer Division Wiking
    9. SS–Panzer Division Hohenstaufen
    12. SS–Panzer Division Hitlerjugend
    13. Waffen–Gebirgs Division der SS Handschar
    14. Waffen–Grenadier Division der SS (now Ukrainische 1)
    16. SS–Panzergrenadier Division Reichsführer SS and
    37. SS–Freiwilligen–Kavallerie Division Lützow.

665

Surely such a powerful force could hold back the Russians, couldn't they? At least until the *Wunder Waffe* promised by Goebbels could be deployed to change the course of the war?

The final month of fighting would not wind down from the tempo set in Hungary, if anything it would accelerate as *Heeresgruppe Süd* fell back into the mountains of Central Austria where the rough terrain negated much of the Russian advantage in armor. The Battle for Vienna would fierce, and those men pulled off their trains in Raab to be incorporated into *Das Reich* would find out at first hand the terrible reality of urban warfare.

Reliable Axis casualty figures for the fighting in Hungary are not available. Thanks to post-Soviet Union records-access, however, we *do* know what the fighting cost the Soviet Armed Forces, not including allied forces such as Rumanians, Bulgarians and Hungarians. Malinovsky's 2nd Ukrainian suffered fewer casualties than Tolbukhin's 3rd Ukrainian Front. The period covered starts on 13 October, 1944, and ends 13 February, 1945.

During that time, Malinovsky's command suffered 35,027 men killed and 130,156 wounded or sick, an average of 1,529 per day. Tolbukhin's 3rd Ukrainian Front had more men killed, 44,887, and fewer wounded at 109,900.

In the end, and for reasons covered in the second volume of this two-volume history of *Heeresgruppe Süd* in 1945, all of the suffering and death in both Hungary and Austria would have a profound effect on the postwar world. Had Heinz Guderian won his argument with Hitler to transfer 6. *SS–Panzerarmee* to the Berlin Front, the world might be a very different place now. The Warsaw Pact might very well have included Austria, or parts of Austria, with ramifications that cannot be judged today.

Some might say the Austrians who were on their knees that distant midnight as the calendar flipped over to Easter Sunday, had their prayers answered, just not in the manner they envisioned. The Russians did, in fact, overrun must of their country... but not enough to keep what they had conquered.

Das Ende

About the Author

William Alan Webb grew up in a family of Second World War veterans. Like so many men who saw combat, they did not often speak of their experiences, but what little they said had a powerful influences on him. From a very young age he grew up watching TV shows and movies about the war, and later devoured books on esoteric topics long before the age of ten. Wargames followed, and models, and miniatures, pretty much any way he could immerse himself in the conflict. His decision to focus on chronicling the Eastern Front came about because Americans have so few choices to learn more than Stalingrad, the Invasion of Russia or the Battle of Berlin.

For those interested in following him, Webb maintains a Patreon page at https://www.patreon.com/WilliamAlanWebb. He may be reached at webbwritingservices@gmail.com. Signed copies of his books may be ordered at www.thelastbrigade.com.

669

Select Bibliography

This is a representative sample of sources used, but by no means is it *all* of the sources used. That would comprise a volume to itself.

The reader is reminded that many official German records for this period were destroyed in the chaotic final days of the war.

Websites

https://core.ac.uk/download/pdf/62685762.pdf

https://panzerworld.com/

Government and research sources

Translation of Taped Conversation with German Hermann Balck, 13 April, 1979, Performed Under Contract No. DAAK40-78-C-0004 (Battelle Columbus Tactical Technology Center, July, 1979),

Books and Periodicals

Ailsby, Christopher, *SS Hell on the Eastern Front: The Waffen–SS War in Russia 1941-1945* (Osceola: MBI, 1998).

Altner, Helmut, *Berlin Dance of Death* (Havertown: Casemate , 2002).

Angolia, J.R., *The HJ Volume 1* (San Jose: R. James Bender, 1991).
        The HJ Volume 2 (San Jose: R. James Bender, 1991).

Axell, Albert, *Stalin's War Through the Eyes of His Commanders* (London: Arms and Armour Press, 1997).

Balck, Hermann, Edited and Translated by Major General David T. Zabecki, USA (Ret.), and *Oberstleutnant* Dieter J. Biedekarken, USA (Ret.), *Order in Chaos, The Memoirs of General of Panzer–Troops Hermann Balck*, (Lexington: The University Press of Kentucky, 2015).

Barea, Ilsa, *Vienna* (New York: Knopf, 1966).

Barnett, Correlli, editor, *Hitler's Generals* (New York: Grove Wiedenfeld, 1989).
Baryatinskiy, Mikhail, *The IS Tanks IS-1, IS-2, IS-3* (Hersham: Ian Allan Publishing, 2006).

Battistelli, Pier Paolo, *Panzer Divisions 1944-45* (Oxford: Osprey, 2009).
Bender, Roger James & Taylor, Hugh Page, *Uniforms, Organization and History of the Waffen–SS Volume 1* (Mountain View: Bender, 1971).
     Uniforms, Organization and History of the Waffen–SS Volume 2 (Mountain View: Bender, 1971).

     Uniforms, Organization and History of the Waffen–SS Volume 3 (San Jose: R. James Bender Publishing, 1986).

     Uniforms, Organization and History of the Waffen–SS Volume 4 (San Jose: R. James Bender Publishing, 1986).

     Uniforms, Organization and History of the Waffen–SS Volume 5 (San Jose: R. James Bender Publishing, 1986).

Benz-Casson, Lotte, *Wien 1945* (Wien: Paul Kaltschmid, 1945).

Bessonov, Evgeni, *Tank Rider: Into the Reich With the Red Army* (London: Greenhill Books, 2003).

Bishop, Chris, *Hitler's Foreign Divisions: Foreign Volunteers in the Waffen–SS 1940-1945* (London: Amber Books, 2005).

Panzergrenadier Divisions 1939-1945 (London: Amber, 2007).

Waffen–SS Divisions 1939-1945 (London: Amber, 2011).

Bonn, Keith E. /editor, *Slaughterhouse The Handbook of the Eastern Front* (Bedford: Aberjona, 2005).

Bradley, General of the Army Omar N. and Blair, Clay *A General's Life, An Autobiography* (New York: Simon & Schuster, 1983).

Brettner, Friedrich, *Die Letzten Kämpfe des II. Weltkrieges, Fotoband I* (Berndof: Kral, 2014).

Die Letzten Kämpfe des II. Weltkrieges, Fotoband II (Berndorf: Kral, 2014).
Geflüchtet Vertrieben Besetzt, Niederösterrecih, Burgenland, Steiermark und Kärnten Kriegsende–Nachkriegzeit (Kral: Berndorf, 2014).

Die Letzten Kämpfe des II Weltkrieges, Pinka–Lafnitz–Hochwechsel–1743 m: 1 Gebirgsdivision – 1 Panzerdivision – Divisionsgruppe Krause – 117. Jägerdivision – Kampfgruppe Arko 3, (Eigenverlag Friedrich Brettner: Gloggnitz, 1999).
Die Letzten Kämpfe des II. Weltkrieges um das Semmeringgebiet (Wiener Neustadt: Brettner, 2003).

Brett–Smith, Richard *Hitler's Generals* (San Rafael: Presidio Press, 1977).
Bukey, Evan Burr, *Hitler's Austria: Popular Sentiment in the Nazi Era 1938-1945* (Chapel Hill: The University of North Carolina Press, 2002).

Chambers, John Whiteclay II & Piehler, G. Kurt
/editors, *Major Problems in American Military History*
(Knoxville: The University of Tennessee Press, 1999).
Churchill, Winston S., *Triumph and Tragedy* (Boston:
Houghton Mifflin, 1953).

Citino, Robert M. *The Werhmacht's Last Stand, The
German Campaigns of 1944-1945* (Lawrence: University
Press of Kansas, 2017).

Clemens, Diane Shaver *Yalta* (London: Oxford
University Press, 1972).

Cornish, Nik *Armageddon Ost: The German Defeat on
the Eastern Front 1944-45* (Hersham: Ian Allan, 2006).

Davis, Brian L., *Waffen–SS* (Blandford Press, 1987).

Degrelle, Leon, *The Waffen–SS On the Eastern Front*
(Torrance: Institute For Historical Review, 1986).

Detre, Gyula László *History First Hand* (Lakitelek:
Antológia, 2007).

Doilea, In Al & Mondial, Razboi, *Romanian Army in
World War II* (Bucharest: Editura Meridiane, 1995).

Domanski, Jazek & Ledwoch, Janusz, *Wien, 1945*
(Warsaw: Wydawnictwo Militaria, 2006).

Duffy, Christopher, *Red Storm on the Reich* (New York:
Atheneum, 1991).

Dulles, Allen, *The Secret Surrender* (New York: Popular
Library, 1966).

Dunn, Walter S., Jr., *Hitler's Nemesis The Red Army,
1940–1945* (Westport: Praeger, 1994).

Eby, Cecil D. *Hungary at War: Civilians and Soldiers in World War II* (University Park: Pennsylvania State University Press, 1998).

Eisenhower, Dwight D., *Crusade in Europe* (New York: Doubleday & Co., 1948).

Ertel, Heinz & Schulze-Kossens, Richard, *Europaische Freiwilligen im Bild*
(Coburg: Nation Europa Verlag, 1997).

Fey, Will, translated by Henschler, Henri, *Armor Battles of the Waffen–SS 1943–1945* (Mechanicsburg: Stackpole Books, 2003).

Fischer, Thomas, *The SS Panzer–Artillery–Regiment 1: Leibstandarte Adolf Hitler (LAH) 194—1945* (Atglen: Schiffer, 2004).

Foedrowitz, Michael, *The Flak Towers in Berlin, Hamburg and Vienna 1940-1950* (Atglen: Schiffer, 1998).

Foley, Charles *Commando Extraordinary, The Remarkable Exploits of Otto Skorzeny* (New York: Berkley Medallion, 1969).

Fritz, Stephen G., *Frontsoldaten, The German Soldier in World War II* (Lexington: The University Press of Kentucky, 1995).

Galland, Adolf, *The First and the Last* (New York: Ballantine, 1963).

Glantz, David M., *The Role of Intelligence in Soviet Military Strategy in World War II* (Novato: Presidio Press, 1991).

Gilbert, Martin, *Churchill A Life* (New York: Henry Holt & Co., 1991).

Goldsworthy, Terry, *Valhalla's Warriors A History of the Waffen–SS on the Eastern Front 1941-1945* (Indianapolis: Dog Ear Publishing, 2007).

Guderian, Heinz, *Panzer Leader* (New York: Ballantine, 1968).

Guillemot, Philippe, *Hungary 1944-45 The Panzers' Last Stand* (Paris: Histoire & Collections, 2011).

Hargreaves, Richard, *The Germans in Normandy* (South Yorkshire: Pen & Sword, 2006).

Hart, B. H. Liddell, *Strategy Second Revised Edition* (New York: Meridian, 1991).

       The German Generals Talk (New York: William Morrow, 1975).

       The Red Army (New York: Harcourt, Brace & Company, 1956).

Heiber, Helmut & Glantz, David M., *Hitler and His Generals: Military Conferences 1942-1945* (New York: Enigma, 2004).

Heike, Wolf-Dietrich, *The Ukrainian Division 'Galicia' 1943-45* (Toronto: Shevchenko Scientific Society, 1988).

Hogg, Ian V., *The Guns 1939-1945* (New York: Ballantine, 1971).

Holzträger, Hans, *In A Raging Inferno, Combat Units of the Hitler Youth 1944–45* (Solihull: Helion, 2008).

Hughes, Dr. Matthew & Mann, Dr. Chris, *Fighting Techniques of a Panzergrenadier 1941-1945* (Osceola: MBI Books, 2000).

Huxley-Blythe, Peter J., *Under the St. Andrew's Cross: Russian & Cossack Volunteers in World War II 1941-1945* (Bayside: Europa Books, 2003).
Infield, Glenn B., *Skorzeny, Hitler's Commando* (New York: St. Martin's Press, 1962).

Isaev, Aleksei & Kolomiets, Maksim, translated and edited by Britton, Stuart *Tomb of the Panzerwaffe, The Defeat of the 6. SS–Panzerarmee in Hungary 1945* (Solihull: Helion Books, 2014).

Janjetovic, Zoran, *Between Hitler and Tito: Disappearance of the Ethnic Germans From the Vojvodina, 2nd Revised Edition* (Belgrade: University of Mary, 2005).

Jentz, Thomas L. /editor, *Panzer Truppen 2: The Complete Guide to the Creation & Combat Employment of Germany's Tank Force 1943-1945* (Atglen: Schiffer, 1996).

Jordan, Franz, *April 1945 – Die Kämpfe im nordöstlichen Niederösterreich, Österreichischer* (Militärverlag: Salzburg, 2003).

Jurado, Carlos Caballero, *Breaking the Chains: 14 Waffen-Grenadier Division der SS and Other Ukrainian Volunteer Formations, Eastern Front, 1942-1945* (Halifax: Shelf Books, 1998).

Keegan, John, *Waffen SS: The Asphalt Soldiers* (New York: Ballantine, 1970).

Kern, Ernst, *War Diary 1941-1945 A Report* (New York: Vantage Press, 1993).

Kershaw, Ian, *The End: the Defiance and Destruction of Hitler's Germany, 1944-1945* (New York: The Penguin Press, 2011).

Kissel, Hans *Hitler's Last Levy: The Volkssturm 1944–1945* (Solihull: Helion, 2005).

Klapdor, Ewald, *Viking Panzers* (Mechanicsburg: Stackpole, 2011).

Krivosheev, Colonel–General G.F., editor *Soviet Casualties and Combat Losses in the Twentieth Century* (London: Greenhill Books, 1997).

Kurowski, Franz, *Hitler's Last Bastion: The Final Battles for the Reich 1944-1945* (Atglen: Schiffer, 1998).

    Panzer Aces (New York: Ballantine, 2002).

    Panzer Aces III (Mechanicsburg: Stackpole, 2010).

    Infantry Aces (New York: Ballantine, 2002).

Kursietis, Andris J., with Munoz, Antonio J., *The Hungarian Army and Its Military Leadership in World War II 3rd Revised Edition* (Bayside: Axis Europa, 1999).

Landwehr, Richard, *Estonian Vikings: Estnisches SS-Freiwillingen Battalion Narwa and Subsequent Units, Eastern Front, 1943-1944* (Halifax: Shelf Books, 2000).

    Fighting For Freedom: The Ukrainian Volunteer Division of the Waffen–SS (Silver Spring: Bibliophile Legion Books, 1993).

    Romanian Volunteers of the Waffen-SS, 1944-45 (Brookings: Siegrunen, 1991).

    Siegrunen Vol. XIV No. 2 – Whole Number 82 – Fall, 2013 (Bennington: Merriam Press, 2014).

Steadfast Hussars, The Last Cavalry Divisions of the Waffen–SS (Bennington: Merriam Press, 1006).

Linderman, Gerald F., *Embattled Courage, the experience of combat in the American Civil War* (New York: Free Press, 1989).

Littlejohn, David, *Foreign Legions of the Third Reich Vol. 1: Norway, Denmark, France* (San Jose: R. James Bender Publishing, 1979).

Foreign Legions of the Third Reich Vol. 2: Belgium, Great Britain, Holland, Italy and Spain (San Jose: R. James Bender Publishing, 1979).

Littman, Sol, *Pure Soldiers or Sinister Legion, the Ukrainian 14th Waffen–SS Division* (Montreal: BlackRose Books, 2003).
Lochmann, Dr. Franz-Wilhelm; Rosen, Richard Freiherr von & Rubbel, Alfred, *The Combat History of German Tiger Tank Battalion 503 in World War II* (Mechanicsburg: Stackpole, 2000).

Lochner, Louis B., *The Goebbels Diaries,* (New York: Popular Library, 1948).

Logusz, Michael O. *Galicia Division, The Waffen–SS 14th Grenadier Division 1943-1945* (Atglen: Schiffer, 1997).

Loewenheim, Francis L.; Langley, Harold D. and Jonas, Manfred, editors, *Roosevelt and Churchill Their Secret Wartime Correspondence* (New York: Saturday Review Press, 1975).

Loza, Dmitriy, translated & Edited by Gebhardt, James F., *Commanding the Red Army's Sherman Tanks: The World War II Memoirs of Hero of the Soviet Union Dmitriy Loza* (Lincoln: University of Nebraska Press, 1996).

Lucas, James, *Battle Group: The Story of Germany's Fearsome Shock Troops* (London: Rigel, 2004).

Last Days of the Third Reich, The Collapse of Nazi Germany, May, 1945 (New York: William Morrow and Co., 1986).

Das Reich, The Military Role of the 2nd SS Division (London: Arms & Armour Press, 1993).

Maclean, Major French L., *The Unknown Generals – German Corps Commanders of World War II* (West Point: The US Military Academy, 1974).

Maeger, Herbert *Lost Honour, Betrayed Loyalty, The Memoir of a Waffen–SS Soldier on the Eastern Front* (London: Frontline Books, 2015).

Maier, Goerg, *Drama Between Budapest and Vienna, The Final Battles of the 6. Panzer-Armee in the East– 1945* (Winnipeg: J.J. Fedorowicz, 2004).

Manvell, Roger, *SS and Gestapo* (New York: Ballantine, 1973).

Manvell, Roger and Fraenkel, Heinrich, *Himmler* (New York: Paperback Library, 1968).

Mawdsley, Evan, *Thunder in the East: The Nazi-Soviet War 1941-1945* (London: Hodder Arnold, 2007).

Maslov, Alexander A. *Fallen Soviet Generals: Soviet General Officers Killed in Battle, 1941–1945* (Abingdon: Routledge Press, 1998).

Megargee, Geoffrey P. *Inside Hitler's High Command* (Lawrence: University Press of Kansas, 2000.

Melnyk, Michael James, *To Battle: The Formation and History of the 14th Galician Waffen–SS Division* (Solihul: Helion, 2002).

Merridale, Catherine, *Ivan's War, Life and Death in the Red Army, 1939-1945* (New York: Metropolitan Books, 2006).

Messenger, Charles, *Hitler's Gladiator, The Life and Wars of Panzer Army Commander Sepp Dietrich* (New York: Skyhorse Publishing, 2011).

Meyer, Hubert, *The 12th SS, The History of the Hitler Youth Panzer Division: Volume Two* (Mechanicsburg: Stackpole, 2005).

Michaelis, Rolf, *Cavalry Divisions of the Waffen–SS* (Atglen: Schiffer, 2010).

Panzer Divisions of the Waffen–SS (Atglen: Schiffer, 2013).

Miklós, Szabó *Establishment of the Hungarian Air Force and the Activity of the Hungarian Royal "Honvéd" Air Force in World War II Respectively, N.º 110 - 3* (The Institute of National Defense: Primavera, 2005).

Mitcham, Samuel W. Jr. *Hitler's Legions, German Army Order of Battle World War II* (London: Leo Cooper, 1985).

The Panzer Legions: A Guide to the German Army Tank Divisions of WWII and Their Commanders (Mechanicsburg: Stackpole Books, 2007).

The German Defeat in the East 1944–45 (Mechanicsburg: Stackpole, 2007).
The German Order of Battle: 1st–290th Infantry Divisions in World War II (Mechanisburg: Stackpole, 2007).

Military Intelligence Division, War Department *The German Replacement Army (Ersatzheer) February, 1945* (Washington D.C.: US Army, 1945)

Order of Battle of the German Army March, 1945 (Washington D.C.: US Army, 1945).

Mooney, Peter, *Dietrich's Warriors, The History of the 3. Kompanie/1st Panzergrenadier Regiment, 1. SS–Panzer Division Leibstandarte Adolf Hitler* (Atglen: Schiffer, 2004).
Mosier, John, *Deathride: Hilter vs. Stalin, The Eastern Front 1941-1945* (New York: Simon & Schuster, 2010).

Mosley, Leonard, *The Reich Marshal A Biography of Hermann Goering* (New York: Dell, 1974).

Mujzer, Dr. Peter, *The Royal Hungarian Army 1920-1945 Volume II Hungarian Mobile Forces* (Bayside: Axis Europa, 2000).

Munoz, Antonio J., *For Croatia & Christ: The Croatian Army in World War II 1941-1945* (Bayside: Axis Europa Books, 2003).

Hitler's Eastern Legions: Volume II The Osttruppen, 1941-1945 (Bayside: Axis Europa Books, 2004).

Göring's Grenadiers, The Luftwaffe Field Divisions 1942–1945 (Bayside: Axis Europa Books, 2002).

Munoz, Antonio J./editor, *The East Came West: Muslim, Hindu, and Buddhist Volunteers in the German Armed Forces 1941-1945* (Bayside: Axis Europa Books, 2001).

Nafziger, George F., *German Order of Battle World War II, Volume I Panzer, Panzer Grenadier, Light and Cavalry Divisions* (Nafziger: West Chester, 1994).

The German Order of Battle Panzers and Artillery in World War II (London: Greenhill Books, 1999).

Nasil, Douglas E., Sr. *From the Realm of a Dying Sun, Volume III: IV. SS–Panzerkorps from Budapest to Vienna, February–May 1945* (Philadelphia: Casemate, 2021)

Neumann, Peter, *The Black March: The Personal Story of an SS Man* (New York: Bantam, 1967).

Nevenkin, Kamen, *Fire Brigades: The Panzer Divisions 1943-1945* (Winnipeg: JJ Fedorowicz, 2008).

Newton, Steven H., *German Battle Tactics on the Russian Front 1941–1945* (Atglen: Schiffer, 1994).

Niehorster, Leo W.G. *The Royal Hungarian Army 1920-1945* (Bayside: Axis Europa Books, 1998).

Novak, Josip & Spencer, David, *Hrvatski Orlovi: Paratroopers of the Independent State of Croatia 1942-1945* (Bayside: Axis Europa, 1998).

Orgill, Douglas, *T-34 Russian Armor* (New York: Ballantine, 1971).

Pencz, Rudolf, *For the Homeland: the 31st Waffen–SS Volunteer Grenadier Division in WWII* (Mechanicsburg: Stackpole, 2010).

Perrett, Bryan, *Knights of the Black Cross* (New York: St. Martin's Press, 1988).
Piekalkiewicz, Janusz, translated by Heurck, Jan van, *Tank War 1939–1945* (New York: Historical Times, 1986).

Pierik, Perry, *Hungary 1944-1945 The Forgotten Tragedy 2nd Edition* (Nieuwegein: Aspekt, 1998).

Poirier, Robert G. and Conner, Albert Z. *The Red Army Order of Battle in the Great Patriotic War, including date from 1919 to postwar years* (Novato: Presidio Press, 1985).

Porter, David, *Order of Battle The Red Army in WWII* (London: Amber Books, 2009).

Rauchenstiener, Manfred, *Schriften des Heeresgeschichtlichen Museums in Wien Band 5 Krieg in Össterreich 1945* (Wien: OsterReichischer Bundesverlag Fur Unterricht, Wissenschaft und Kunst, 1970).

Ravenscroft, Trevor, *The Spear of Destiny* (York Beach: Samuel Weiser, 1982).
Rebentisch, Dr. Ernst, *To the Caucusus and the Austrian Alps: The History of the 23. Panzer Division in World War II* (Winipeg: J.J. Fedorowicz, 2009).

Reimer, Hans, *This Pearl Vienna* (Vienna: Publisher's Jugend und Volk, 1946).

Reynolds, Michael, *Men of Steel, I. SS–Panzerkorps, The Ardennes and Eastern Front 1944–45* (New York: Sarpdeon, 1999).

Sons of the Reich, II. SS–Panzerkorps, Normandy, Arnhem, Ardennes, Eastern Front (Havertown: Casemate, 2002).

The Devil's Adjutant Jochen Peiper, Panzer Leader (New York: Sarpedon, 1995).

Richter, Klaus Christian, *Cavalry of the Wehrmacht 1941-1945* (Atglen: Schiffer, 1995).

Rikmenspoel, Marc, *Soldiers of the Waffen-SS: Many Nations, One Motto* (Winnipeg: J.J. Fedorowicz, 1999).

Ringler, Ralf Roland, *Illusion einer Jugend, Hitler–Jugend in Österrech* (St. Pölten: Verlag Niederöster*Reich*isches Pressehaus, 1977).

Ripley, Tim, *The Waffen–SS at War: Hitler's Praetorians 1923-1945* (St. Paul: Zenith Press, 2004).

Rosado, Jorge & Bishop, Chris, *Wehrmacht Panzer Divsions 1939-1945 The Essential Tank Identification Guide* (London: Amber, 2006).

Rottman, Gordon L., *Soviet Rifleman 1941–1945* (Oxford: Osprey, 2007).

Ryan, Cornelius, *The Last Battle* (New York: Simon & Schuster, 1967).

Sanchez, Alfonso Escuadra, *Feldherrnhalle: Forgotten Elite, The Panzerkorps Feldherrnhalle and Antecedent Formations, Eastern and Other Front, 1942-1945* (Bradford: Shelf Books, 1996).

Scheibert, Horst, *Bildband der 6. Panzer Division* (Bad Nauheim: Hans-Henning Podzun, 1958).

Schirach, Henriette von, *Der Preis der Herrlichkeit, Erlebte Zeitgeschichte* (München: Herbig, 1975).

Schmidt, Hans *SS Panzergrenadier, a true story of World War II Second Edition* (Pensacola: H. Schmidt Productions, 2002).

Schneider, Wolfgang, *Tigers in Combat II* (Mechanicsburg: Stackpole, 2005).

Totenkopf Tigers (Winnipeg: J.J. Fedorowicz, 2001).

Shukman, Harold, editor, *Stalin's Generals* (New York: Grove Press, 1983).

Sklar, D. *The Nazis and the Occult* (New York: Dorset Press, 1989).
Skorzeny, Otto *My Commando Operations, The Memoirs of Hitler's Most Daring Commando* (Atglen: Schiffer, 1995).

Snyder, Timothy, *Bloodlands Europe between Hitler and Stalin* (New York: Basic Books, 2010).

Stewart, Emilie Caldwell, *Signatures of the Third Reich* (New Jersey: Private, 1996).

Stone, David R., editor, *The Soviet Union at War 1941–1945* (Barnsley: Pen & Sword Military, 2010).

Strassner, Peter, *European Volunteers: The 5. SS Panzer Division Wiking* (Winnipeg: J.J. Fedorowicz, 2006).

Sundin, Claes & Bergstrom, Christer, *Luftwaffe Fighter Aircraft in Profile* (Atglen: Schiffer, 1997).

Sydnor, Charles W., Jr., *Soldiers of Destruction, The SS Death's Head Division, 1933-1945* (Princeton: Princeton University Press, 1977).

Számvéber, Norbert, *Days of Battle, Armoured operations north of the River Danube, Hungary 1944–45* (Solihull: Helion Books, 2013).

Taylor, Hugh Page & Bender, Roger James *Uniforms, organization and history of the Waffen–SS volume 5* (San Jose: R. James Bender Publishing, 1986).

Tessin, Georg: *Verbände und Truppen der deutschen Wehrmacht und Waffen–SS im Zweiten Weltkrieg* 1939-1945 (Osnabrück: Biblio, 1972).

Thiele, Karl H., *Beyond Monsters and Clowns, The Combat SS: De-Mythologizing Five Decades of German Elite Formations* (Lanham: University Press of America, 1997).

Thorwald, Juergen, *Defeat in the East, 1945: The Collapse of Hitler's Germany and the Russian Drive on Berlin* (New York: Ballantine, 1967).

Tieke, Wilhelm, translated by Steinhardt, Frederick, *In The Firestorm Of The Last Years Of The War, II. SS–Panzerkorps with the 9. And 10. SS–Divisions "Hohenstaufen" and "Frundsberg"* (Winnipeg: J.J. Fedorowicz, 1999).

Tiemann, Ralf, *The Leibstandarte IV/2* (Winnipeg: J.J. Fedorowicz, 1998).

Chronicle of the 7. Panzer–Kompanie 1. SS–Panzerdivision "Leibstandarte" (Atglen: Schiffer, 1998).

Toland, John, *The Last 100 Days* (New York: Bantam, 1967).

Toliver, *Oberst* Raymond F. & Constable, Trevor J., *The Blond Knight of Germany: The True Story of Erich Hartmann, the Greatest Fighter Pilot of all Time* (New York: Ballantine, 1971).

Tooze, Adam, *The Wages of Destruction: The Making and Breaking of the Nazi Economy* (New York: Viking, 2007).

Trang, Charles, *Totenkopf* (Bayeux: Heimdal, 2006).

Trevor-Roper, Professor Hugh, Translator and Editor, *Final Entries 1945 The Diaries of Joseph Goebbels* (New York: Avon, 1978).

Tsouras, Peter G., editor, *Panzers on the Eastern Front, General Erhard Raus and his Panzer Divisions in Russia 1941–1945* (London: Greenhill Books, 2002).
Ullrich, Karl *Like a Cliff in the Ocean: The History of the 3. SS–Panzer Division Totenkopf* (Altona: J.J. Fedorowicz, 2002).

Ungvary, Krisztián, *The Siege of Budapest* (New Haven: Yale University Press, 2005).

Vassiltchikov, Marie, *Berlin Diaries, 1940–1945* (New York: Alfred A. Knopf, 1987).

Veterans of the *3. Panzer Division, Armored Bears, The German 3. Panzer Division in World War II* (Mechanicsburg: Stackpole Books, 2013).

Walther, Herbert, *The 12. SS–Panzer Division HJ A Pictorial History* (Atglen: Schiffer, 1989).

Warlimont, Gen. Walter, translated from the German by Barry, R.H., *Inside Hitler's Headquarters 1939–1945* (Navato: Presidio Press, 1990).

Weidinger, Otto, *Comrades to the End, The 4th SS Panzergrenadier Regiment "Der Fürher" 1938-1945, The History of a German–Austrian Fighting Unit* (Atglen: Schiffer, 1998).

        Das Reich, Volume V: 1943-1945 (Manitoba: J.J. Fedorowicz, 2012).

Weingartner, James J., *Hitler's Guard, Inside the Führer's Personal SS Force* (New York: Berkley Books, 1990).

Weiss, Wilhelm, translated by Prof. Dr. phil. Percy Ernst Schramm Major d. Reserve ehmaals Führer des Kriegstagebuches *Die Aufzeichnungen Vol. 1 Januar 1945 bis zur Kapitulation; Das Kriegstagebuch des Wehrmachtführungsstabes*, (Monee: Weiss, 2013).

Welch, David, *The Third Reich Politics and Propaganda* (London: Routledge, 1995).

Werth, Alexander *Russia At War 1941–1945* (New York: Avon, 1970).

Weyr, Thomas, *The Setting of the Pearl: Vienna Under Hitler 1938-1945* (Oxford: Oxford University Press, 2005).

Wilbeck, Christopher W., *Sledgehammers: Strengths and Flaws of Tiger Tank Battalions in World War II* (Bedford: Aberjona Press, 2004).

Winninger, Michael, *The OKH Toy Factor The Nibelungenwerke: Tank Production in St. Valentin* (Havertown: Casemate, 2013).

Wood, Ian Michael, *Tigers of the Death's Head, SS Totenkopf Division's Tiger Company* (Mechanicsburg: Stackpole, 2013).

History of the Totenkopf's Panther–Abteilung (Bessenyei György: PeKo Books, 2015).

Yeltin, David K., *Hitler's Volkssturm The Nazi Militia and the Fall of Germany, 1944-1945* (Lawrence: University Press of Kansas, 2002).

Yerger, Mark C., *Knights of Steel: Das Reich Volume 2 The Structure, Development and Personalities of the 2. SS–Panzer Division* (Lancaster: Yerger, 1994).

SS-Sturmbannführer Ernst August Krag
(Atglen: Schiffer, 1996).

SS-SS–Obersturmbannführer Otto Weidinger
(Atglen: Schiffer, 2000).

Waffen–SS Commanders, The Army, Corps and Divisional Leaders of a Legend, Ausberger to Kreutz (v. 1), (Atglen: Schiffer, 1997).

Waffen–SS Commanders, The Army, Corps and Divisional Leaders of a Legend, Krüger to Zimmermann (v. 2), (Atglen: Schiffer, 1999).

Zaloga, Steven J. and Ness, Leland S., *Red Army Handbook 1939–1945* (Sutton Publishing, 1998).

Zaloga, Stephen J. and Grandsen, James, *The Eastern Front Amor Camouflage and Markings, 1941–1945* (Carrollton: Squadron/Signal Publications, 1983).

Zaloga, Steven J. and Volstad, Ron, *The Red Army of the Great Patriotic War 1941–1945, Osprey Military Men–at–Arms Series 216* (Oxford: Osprey, 1984).

Zirk, Georg, *Red Griffins Over Russia* (Mesa: Champlin Museum Press, 1987).

Made in the USA
Columbia, SC
25 September 2024

42400647R00383